The Java™ Programming Language

Third Edition

The Java™ Series

Lisa Friendly, Series Editor
Tim Lindholm, Technical Editor
Ken Arnold, Technical Editor of The Jini™ Technology Series
Jim Inscore, Technical Editor of The Java™ Series, Enterprise Edition

---

Ken Arnold, James Gosling, David Holmes
The Java™ Programming Language, Third Edition

Greg Bollella, James Gosling, Ben Brosgol, Peter Dibble,
Steve Furr, David Hardin, Mark Turnbull
The Real-Time Specification for Java™

Mary Campione, Kathy Walrath, Alison Huml
The Java™ Tutorial, Third Edition:
A Short Course on the Basics

Mary Campione, Kathy Walrath, Alison Huml,
Tutorial Team
The Java™ Tutorial Continued: The Rest of the JDK™

Patrick Chan
The Java™ Developers Almanac 2000

Patrick Chan, Rosanna Lee
The Java™ Class Libraries, Second Edition, Volume 2:
java.applet, java.awt, java.beans

Patrick Chan, Rosanna Lee
The Java™ Class Libraries Poster, Fifth Edition: Covering
the Java™ 2 Platform, Standard Edition, v1.3

Patrick Chan, Rosanna Lee, Douglas Kramer
The Java™ Class Libraries, Second Edition, Volume 1:
java.io, java.lang, java.math, java.net, java.text, java.util

Patrick Chan, Rosanna Lee, Douglas Kramer
The Java™ Class Libraries, Second Edition, Volume 1:
Supplement for the Java™ 2 Platform,
Standard Edition, v1.2

Zhiqun Chen
Java Card™ Technology for Smart Cards:
Architecture and Programmer's Guide

Li Gong
Inside Java™ 2 Platform Security:
Architecture, API Design, and Implementation

James Gosling, Bill Joy, Guy Steele, Gilad Bracha
The Java™ Language Specification, Second Edition

Jonni Kanerva
The Java™ FAQ

Doug Lea
Concurrent Programming in Java™, Second Edition:
Design Principles and Patterns

Rosanna Lee, Scott Seligman
JNDI API Tutorial and Reference:
Building Directory-Enabled Java™ Applications

Sheng Liang
The Java™ Native Interface:
Programmer's Guide and Specification

Tim Lindholm, Frank Yellin
The Java™ Virtual Machine Specification, Second Edition

Henry Sowizral, Kevin Rushforth, Michael Deering
The Java 3D™ API Specification, Second Edition

Kathy Walrath, Mary Campione
The JFC Swing Tutorial: A Guide to Constructing GUIs

Seth White, Maydene Fisher, Rick Cattell,
Graham Hamilton, Mark Hapner
JDBC™ API Tutorial and Reference, Second Edition:
Universal Data Access for the Java™ 2 Platform

Steve Wilson, Jeff Kesselman
Java™ Platform Performance: Strategies and Tactics

The Jini™ Technology Series

Ken Arnold, Bryan O'Sullivan, Robert W. Scheifler,
Jim Waldo, Ann Wollrath
The Jini™ Specification

Eric Freeman, Susanne Hupfer, Ken Arnold
JavaSpaces™ Principles, Patterns, and Practice

The Java™ Series, Enterprise Edition

Patrick Chan, Rosanna Lee
The Java™ Class Libraries Poster, Enterprise Edition,
version 1.2

Nicholas Kassem, Enterprise Team
Designing Enterprise Applications with the Java™ 2
Platform, Enterprise Edition

Bill Shannon, Mark Hapner, Vlada Matena, James
Davidson, Eduardo Pelegri-Llopart, Larry Cable,
Enterprise Team
Java™ 2 Platform, Enterprise Edition:
Platform and Component Specifications

http://www.javaseries.com

The Java™ Programming Language
Third Edition

Ken Arnold
James Gosling
David Holmes

ADDISON-WESLEY

Boston • San Francisco • New York • Toronto • Montreal
London • Munich • Paris • Madrid
petown • Sydney • Tokyo • Singapore • Mexico City

The publisher offers discounts on this book when ordered in quantity for special sales. For more information, please contact:

Pearson Education Corporate Sales Division
One Lake Street
Upper Saddle River, NJ 07458
(800) 382-3419
corpsales@pearsontechgroup.com

Text printed on recycled and acid-free paper.

ISBN 0201704331

3 4 5 6 7 8   CRS   03 02 01 00

3rd Printing   November 2000

This book is dedicated to the Java team
From whose hard work and vision
A mighty oak has grown

To Susan—*K.A.*

To Judy and Kate—*J.A.G.*

To Lee, Taylor and Caitlin —*D.H.*

Contents

Preface

Beautiful buildings are more than scientific. They are true organisms,
spiritually conceived; works of art, using the best technology by inspiration
rather than the idiosyncrasies of mere taste or any averaging by the committee mind.
—Frank Lloyd Wright

THE Java™ programming language has been warmly received by the world community of software developers and Internet content providers. Users of the Internet and World Wide Web benefit from access to secure, platform-independent applications that can come from anywhere on the Internet. Software developers who create applications in the Java programming language benefit by developing code only once, with no need to "port" their applications to every software and hardware platform.

For many, the language was known first as a tool to create applets for the World Wide Web. An *applet* is a mini-application that runs inside a Web page. An applet can perform tasks and interact with users on their browser pages without using resources from the Web server after being downloaded. Some applets may, of course, talk with the server to do their job, but that's their business.

The Java programming language is indeed valuable for distributed network environments like the Web. However, it goes well beyond this domain to provide a powerful general-purpose programming language suitable for building a variety of applications that either do not depend on network features, or want them for different reasons. The ability to execute downloaded code on remote hosts in a secure manner is a critical requirement for many organizations.

Other groups use it as a general-purpose programming language for projects in which machine independence is less important. Ease of programming and safety features help you quickly produce working code. Some common programming errors never occur because of features like garbage collection and type-safe references. Support for multithreading caters to modern network-based and graphical user interface–based applications that must attend to multiple tasks simultaneously, and the mechanisms of exception handling ease the task of dealing with error conditions. While the built-in tools are powerful, it is a simple language in which programmers can quickly become proficient.

The Java programming language is designed for maximum portability with as few implementation dependencies as possible. An `int`, for example, is a 32-bit signed two's-complement integer in all implementations, irrespective of the CPU architecture on which the program executes. Defining everything possible about the language and its runtime environment enables users to run compiled code anywhere and share code with anyone who has a Java runtime environment.

ABOUT THIS BOOK

This book teaches the Java programming language to people who are familiar with basic programming concepts. It explains the language without being arduously formal or complete. This book is not an introduction to object-oriented programming, although some issues are covered to establish a common terminology. Other books in this series, and much online documentation, focus on applets, graphical interfaces, databases, components, and other specific kinds of programming tasks. For other references, see "Further Reading" on page 563.

This third edition includes the changes introduced in the Java 2 Platform, such as the new `strictfp` keyword, collection classes, and reference objects, as implemented in the Java 2 SDK, Standard Edition Version 1.3 (sometimes colloquially referred to as JDK 1.3 or simply 1.3). You will also find brief coverage of the other main packages. If you have already read the second edition, you will find that much of the information in this edition has been restructured to improve the presentation of language features—such as nested classes and interfaces—and class API's. This edition will give you a lot of new information, but since most of the language is unchanged, and almost all main package types are still usable, you will want to pay most attention to the newer areas.

The Java programming language shares many features common to most programming languages in use today. The language should look familiar to C and C++ programmers because it was designed with C and C++ constructs where the languages are similar. That said, this book is neither a comparative analysis nor a "bridge" tutorial—no knowledge of C or C++ is assumed. C++ programmers, especially, may be as hindered by what they must unlearn as they are helped by their knowledge.

Chapter 1—*A Quick Tour*—gives a quick overview of the language. Programmers who are unfamiliar with object-oriented programming notions should read the quick tour, while programmers who are already familiar with object-oriented programming paradigms will find the quick tour a useful introduction to the object-oriented features of the language.

Chapters 2, 3, 4, and 5 cover the object-oriented core features of the language, namely, class declarations that define components of a program, and objects manufactured according to class definitions. Chapter 2—*Classes and Objects*—describes the basis of the language: classes. Chapter 3—*Extending Classes*—describes how an existing class can be *extended*, or *subclassed*, to create a new class with additional data and behavior. Chapter 4—*Interfaces*—describes how to declare interface types which are abstract descriptions of behavior that provide maximum flexibility for class designers and implementors. Chapter 5—*Nested Classes and Interfaces*—describes how classes and interfaces can be declared inside other classes and interfaces, and the benefits that provides.

Chapters 6 and 7 cover standard constructs common to most languages. Chapter 6—*Tokens, Operators, and Expressions*—describes the tokens of the language from which statements are constructed, how the tokens and operators are used to build expressions, and how expressions are evaluated. Chapter 7—*Control Flow*—describes how control statements direct the order of statement execution.

Chapter 8—*Exceptions*—describes the language's powerful error-handling capabilities. Chapter 9—*Strings*—describes the built-in language and runtime support for `String` objects.

Chapter 10—*Threads*—explains the language's view of multithreading. Many applications, such as graphical interface–based software, must attend to multiple tasks simultaneously. These tasks must cooperate to behave correctly, and threads meet the needs of cooperative multitasking.

Chapter 11—*Programming with Types*—describes the type-related classes: individual objects that describe each class and interface, and classes that wrap primitive data types such as integers and floating-point values into their own object types.

Chapter 12—*Garbage Collection and Memory*—talks about garbage collection, finalization, and lower-strength reference objects.

Chapter 13—*Packages*—describes how you can group collections of classes and interfaces into separate packages.

Chapter 14—*Documentation Comments*—shows how to write reference documentation in comments.

Chapters 15 through 19 cover the main packages. Chapter 15—*The I/O Package*—describes the input/output system, which is based on *streams*. Chapter 16—*Collections*—covers the *collection* or *container classes* such as sets and lists. Chapter 17—*Miscellaneous Utilities*—covers the rest of the *utility classes* such as bit sets and random number generation. Chapter 18—*System Programming*—leads you through the *system classes* that provide access to features of the underlying platform. Chapter 19—*Internationalization and Localization*—covers some of the tools used to create programs that can run in many linguistic and cultural environments.

Chapter 20—*Standard Packages*—briefly explores the packages that are part of the standard platform, giving overviews of those packages not covered in more detail in this book.

Appendix A—*Runtime Exceptions*—lists all the runtime exceptions and errors that the runtime system itself can throw.

Appendix B—*Useful Tables*—has tables of information that you may find useful for quick reference.

Finally, *Further Reading* lists works that may be interesting for further reading on complete details, object orientation, programming with threads, software design, and other topics.

EXAMPLES AND DOCUMENTATION

All the code examples in the text have been compiled and run on the latest version of the language available at the time the book was written, which was the Java 2 SDK, Standard Edition, Version 1.3. Only supported features are covered—deprecated types, methods, and fields are ignored except where unavoidable. We have also covered issues beyond writing programs that simply compile. Part of learning a language is to learn to use it well. For this reason, we have tried to show principles of good programming style and design.

In a few places we refer to online documentation. Development environments provide a way to automatically generate documentation (usually HTML documents) from a compiled class using the documentation comments. This documentation is normally viewed using a Web browser.

ACKNOWLEDGMENTS (FIRST EDITION)

No technical book-writing endeavor is an island unto itself, and ours was more like a continent. Many people contributed technical help, excellent reviews, useful information, and book-writing advice.

Contributing editor Henry McGilton of Trilithon Software played the role of "chief editorial firefighter" to help make this book possible. Series editor Lisa Friendly contributed dogged perseverance and support.

A veritable multitude of reviewers took time out of their otherwise busy lives to read, edit, advise, revise, and delete material, all in the name of making this a better book. Kevin Coyle performed one of the most detailed editorial reviews at all levels. Karen Bennet, Mike Burati, Patricia Giencke, Steve Gilliard, Bill Joy, Rosanna Lee, Jon Madison, Brian O'Neill, Sue Palmer, Stephen Perelgut, R. Anders Schneiderman, Susan Sim, Bob Sproull, Guy Steele, Arthur van Hoff, Jim Waldo, Greg Wilson, and Ann Wollrath provided in-depth review. Geoff Arnold, Tom Cargill, Chris Darke, Pat Finnegan, Mick Jordan, Doug Lea, Randall Murray,

Roger Riggs, Jimmy Torres, Arthur van Hoff, and Frank Yellin contributed useful comments and technical information at critical junctures.

Alka Deshpande, Sharon Flank, Nassim Fotouhi, Betsy Halstead, Kee Hinckley, Dr. K. Kalyanasundaram, Patrick Martin, Paul Romagna, Susan Snyder, and Nicole Yankelovich collaborated to make possible the five words of non-ISO-Latin-1 text on pages 140 and 406. Jim Arnold provided research help on the proper spelling, usage, and etymology of "smoog" and "moorge." Ed Mooney helped with the document preparation. Herb and Joy Kaiser were our Croatian language consultants. Cookie Callahan, Robert E. Pierce, and Rita Tavilla provided the support necessary to keep this project going at many moments when it would otherwise have stalled with a sputtering whimper.

Thanks to Kim Polese for supplying us the capsule summary of why the Java programming language is important to computer users as well as programmers.

Support and advice were provided at critical moments by Susan Jones, Bob Sproull, Jim Waldo, and Ann Wollrath. And we thank our families, who, besides their loving support, would at times drag us out to play when we should have been working, for which we are deeply grateful.

And thanks to the folks at Peet's Coffee and Tea, who kept us buzzed on the best Java on the planet.

ACKNOWLEDGMENTS (SECOND EDITION)

The cast of characters for this second edition is much like the first.

Series Editor Lisa Friendly continued to be doggedly supportive and attentive. The set of reviewers was smaller, overlapping, and certainly as helpful and thorough. Overall reviews by Steve Byrne, Tom Cargill, Mary Dageforde, Tim Lindholm, and Rob Murray were critical to clarity. Brian Beck, Peter Jones, Doug Lea, Bryan O'Sullivan, Sue Palmer, Rosanna Lee, Lori Park, Mark Reinhold, Roger Riggs, Ann Wollrath, and Ken Zadek contributed focused reviews of important parts. Guy Steele's support was ongoing and warm. Rosemary Simpson's extensive and intensive efforts to make a useful index are deeply appreciated. Carla Carlson and Helen Leary gave logistic support that kept all the wheels on the tracks instead of in the ditch. Gerry Wiener provided the Tibetan word on page 406, and we also had help on this from Craig Preston and Takao Miyatani. All who submitted errata and suggestions from the first edition were helpful.

For some inexplicable reason we left the friendly folks of Addison-Wesley off the original acknowledgments—luckily, most of them were present again for this edition. A merged list for both editions includes Kate Duffy, Rosa Gonzales, Mike Hendrickson, Marina Lang, Shannon Patti, Marty Rabinowitz, Sarah Weaver, and Pamela Yee. Others did much that we are blissfully unaware of, but for which we are nonetheless abidingly grateful.

The revision was additionally aided by Josh Bloch, Joe Fialli, Jimmy Torres, Benjamin Renaud, Mark Reinhold, Jen Volpe, and Ann Wollrath.

And Peet's Coffee and Tea continued its supporting role as purveyor to the caffeine-consuming connoisseur.

ACKNOWLEDGMENTS (THIRD EDITION)

The third edition required yet more reviews and work, and the helper list is equally critical. Lisa Friendly continued her attempts to keep the project in line; someday we will cooperate better. The set of reviewers included new faces and old friends, all helpful: Joshua Bloch, Joseph Bowbeer, Gilad Bracha, Keith Edwards, Joshua Engel, Rich Gillam, Peter Haggar, Cay Horstmann, Alexander Kuzmin, Doug Lea, Keith Lea, Tim Lindholm, David Mendenhall, Andrew M. Morgan, Ray Ortigas, Brian Preston, Mark Schuldenfrei, Peter Sparago, Guy Steele, Antoine Trux, and our Russian compatriots Leonid Arbouzov, Valery Shakurov, Viatcheslav Rybalov, Eugene Latkin, Dmitri Khukhro, Konstantin Anisimov, Alexei Kaigorodov, Oleg Oleinik, and Maxim Sokolnikov. Several people let us bend their ears to figure out how to approach things better: Peter Jones, Robert W. Scheifler, Susan Snyder, Guy Steele, Jimmy Torres, and Ann Wollrath. Helen Leary made the logistics work smoothly, as always.

Material support is always provided by the Addison-Wesley team: Julie DiNicola, Mike Hendrickson, and Tracy Russ.

And since the last edition, Peet's Coffee and Tea has opened up on the East Coast, so the eastern part of this writing team can enjoy it regularly. The world continues to improve apace.

Any errors or shortcomings that remain in this book—despite the combined efforts of these myriads—are completely the responsibility of the authors.

> *Results! Why, man, I have gotten a lot of results.*
> *I know several thousand things that won't work.*
> *—Thomas Edison*

CHAPTER 1

A Quick Tour

See Europe! Ten Countries in Seventeen Days!
—Sign in a travel agent's window

THIS chapter is a whirlwind tour of the Java™ programming language that gets you started writing code quickly. We briefly cover the main points of the language, without slowing you down with full-blown detail. Subsequent chapters contain detailed discussions of specific features.

1.1 Getting Started

In the Java programming language, programs are built from *classes*. From a class definition, you can create any number of *objects* that are known as *instances* of that class. Think of a class as a factory with blueprints and instructions to build gadgets—objects are the gadgets the factory makes.

A class contains *members,* the primary kinds being *fields* and *methods.* Fields are data variables belonging either to the class itself or to objects of the class; they make up the *state* of the object or class. Methods are collections of *statements* that operate on the fields to manipulate the state. Statements define the behavior of the classes: they can assign values to fields and other variables, evaluate arithmetic expressions, invoke methods and control the flow of execution.

Long tradition holds that the first sample program for any language should print "Hello, world":

```
class HelloWorld {
    public static void main(String[] args) {
        System.out.println("Hello, world");
    }
}
```

Use your favorite text editor to type this program source code into a file. Then run the compiler to compile the source of this program into *bytecodes*, the "machine language" for the Java virtual machine (more on this later). Details of editing and compiling source vary from system to system—consult your system manuals for specific information. On the system we use most often—the Java 2 Software Development Kit (Java 2 SDK) provided free of charge by Sun Microsystems—you put the source for `HelloWorld` into a file named `HelloWorld.java`. To compile it you type the command

```
javac HelloWorld.java
```

To run the program you type the command

```
java HelloWorld
```

This executes the `main` method of `HelloWorld`. When you run the program, it displays

```
Hello, world
```

Now you have a small program that does something, but what does it mean?

The program declares a class called `HelloWorld` with a single member: a method called `main`. Class members appear between curly braces { and } following the class name.

The `main` method is a special method: the `main` method of a class, if declared exactly as shown, is executed when you run the class as an application. When run, a `main` method can create objects, evaluate expressions, invoke other methods, and do anything else needed to define an application's behavior.

The `main` method is declared `public`—so that anyone can invoke it (in this case the Java virtual machine)—and `static`, meaning that the method belongs to the class and is not associated with a particular instance of the class.

Preceding the method name is the return type of the method. The `main` method is declared `void` because it doesn't return a value and so has no return type.

Following the method name is the *parameter* list for the method—a sequence of zero or more pairs of types and names, separated by commas and enclosed in parentheses (and). The `main` method's only parameter is an array of `String` objects, referred to by the name `args`. Arrays of objects are denoted by the square brackets [] that follow the type name. In this case `args` will contain the program's arguments from the command line with which it was invoked. Arrays and strings are covered later in this chapter. The meaning of `args` for the `main` method is described in Chapter 2 on page 62.

The name of a method together with its parameter list constitute the *signature* of the method. The signature together with any modifiers (such as `public` and static) and exception throws list (covered later in this chapter) forms the method *header*. A method *declaration* consists of the method header followed by the method *body*—a block of statements appearing between curly braces.

In this example, the body of main contains a single statement that invokes the println method—the semicolon ends the statement. A method is invoked by supplying an object reference (in this case System.out—the out field of the System class) and a method name (println) separated by a dot (.).

HelloWorld uses the out object's println method to print a newline-terminated string on the standard·output stream. The string printed is the *string literal* "Hello, world", which is passed as an argument to println. A string literal is a sequence of characters contained within double-quotes " and ".

Exercise 1.1: Enter, compile, and run HelloWorld on your system.

Exercise 1.2: Try changing parts of HelloWorld and see what errors you get.

1.2 Variables

The next example prints a part of the *Fibonacci sequence,* an infinite sequence whose first few terms are

```
1
1
2
3
5
8
13
21
34
```

The Fibonacci sequence starts with the terms 1 and 1, and each successive term is the sum of the previous two terms. A Fibonacci printing program is simple, and it demonstrates how to declare *variables*, write a simple loop, and perform basic arithmetic. Here is the Fibonacci program:

```
class Fibonacci {
    /** Print out the Fibonacci sequence for values < 50 */
    public static void main(String[] args) {
        int lo = 1;
        int hi = 1;
```

```
System.out.println(lo);
while (hi < 50) {
    System.out.println(hi);
    hi = lo + hi;          // new hi
    lo = hi - lo;          /* new lo is (sum - old lo)
                              that is, the old hi */
    }
}
}
```

This example declares a `Fibonacci` class that, like `HelloWorld`, has a `main` method. The first two lines of `main` are statements declaring two *local* variables: `lo` and `hi`. In this program `hi` is the last term in the series and `lo` is the previous term. Local variables are declared within a block of code, such as a method body, in contrast to fields that are declared as members of a class. Every variable must have a *type* that precedes its name when the variable is declared. The variables `lo` and `hi` are of type `int`, 32-bit signed integers with values in the range -2^{31} through $2^{31}-1$.

The Java programming language has built-in "primitive" data types to support integer, floating-point, boolean, and character values. These primitive types hold data that is understood directly, as opposed to object types defined by programmers. The type of every variable must be defined explicitly. The primitive data types are:

`boolean`	either `true` or `false`
`char`	16-bit Unicode 2.1 character
`byte`	8-bit integer (signed)
`short`	16-bit integer (signed)
`int`	32-bit integer (signed)
`long`	64-bit integer (signed)
`float`	32-bit floating-point (IEEE 754-1985)
`double`	64-bit floating-point (IEEE 754-1985)

In the Fibonacci program, we declared `hi` and `lo` with initial values of 1. The initial values are set by initialization expressions, using the = operator, when the variables are declared. The = operator (also called the *assignment* operator), sets the variable named on the left-hand side to the value of the expression on the right-hand side.

Local variables are *undefined* prior to initialization. You don't have to initialize them at the point at which you declare them, but if you try to use local variables before assigning a value, the compiler will refuse to compile your program until you fix the problem.

As both `lo` and `hi` are of the same type, we could have used a short-hand form for declaring them. We can declare more than one variable of a given type by separating the variable names (with their initialization expressions) by commas. We could replace the first two lines of main with the single equivalent line:

```
int lo = 1, hi = 1;
```

Or the much more readable

```
int lo = 1,
    hi = 1;
```

Notice that the presence of line-breaks makes no difference to the meaning of the statement—line-breaks, spaces, tabs and other *white space* are purely for the programmer's convenience.

The `while` statement in the example demonstrates one way of looping. The expression inside the `while` is evaluated—if the expression is true, the body of the loop is executed and the expression tested again. The `while` is repeated until the expression becomes false. If it never becomes false, the loop will run forever unless something intervenes to break out of the loop, such as a `break` statement or an exception.

The body of the `while` consists of a single statement. That could be a simple statement (such as a method invocation), another control-flow statement, or a *block*—zero or more individual statements enclosed in curly braces.

The expression that `while` tests is a *boolean* expression that has the value `true` or `false`. Boolean expressions can be formed by using the *comparison* operators (`<`, `<=`, `>`, `>=`) to compare the relative magnitudes of two values, or the `==` operator or `!=` operator to test for equality or inequality respectively. The boolean expression `hi < 50` in the example tests whether the current high value of the sequence is less than 50. If the high value is less than 50, its value is printed and the next value is calculated. If the high value equals or exceeds 50, control passes to the first line of code following the body of the `while` loop. That is the end of the `main` method in this example, so the program is finished.

To calculate the next value in the sequence we perform some simple arithmetic and again use the `=` operator to assign the value of the arithmetic expression on the right to the variable on the left. As you would expect, the `+` operator calculates the sum of its operands, while the `-` operator calculates the difference. The language defines a number of arithmetic operators for the primitive integer and floating point types including addition(`+`), subtraction(`-`), multiplication(`*`) and division(`/`), as well as some other operators we will talk about later.

Notice that the `println` method accepts an integer argument in the `Fibonacci` example, whereas it accepted a string argument in the `HelloWorld` example. The `println` method is one of many methods that are *overloaded* so that they can accept arguments of different types. The runtime system decides which method to actually invoke based on the number and types of arguments you pass to it. This is a very powerful tool.

Exercise 1.3: Add a title to the printed list.

Exercise 1.4: Write a program that generates a different sequence, such as a table of squares.

1.3   Comments in Code

The English text scattered through the code is in *comments*. There are three styles of comments, all illustrated in the `Fibonacci` example. Comments enable you to write descriptive text alongside your code, annotating it for programmers who may read your code in the future. That programmer may well be *you* months or years later. You save yourself effort by commenting your own code. Also, you often find bugs when you write comments, because explaining what the code is supposed to do forces you to think about it.

Text that occurs between /* and */ is ignored by the compiler. This style of comment can be used on part of a line, a whole line, or more commonly (as in the example) to define a multi-line comment. For single line and part line comments you can use // which tells the compiler to ignore everything after it on that line.

The third kind of comment appears at the very top, between /** and */. A comment starting with two asterisks is a *documentation comment* ("doc comment" for short). Documentation comments are intended to describe declarations that follow them. The comment in the previous example is for the `main` method. These comments can be extracted by a tool that uses them to generate reference documentation for your classes. By convention, lines within a documentation comment or a /*...*/ comment have a leading asterisk (which is ignored by documentation tools) which gives a visual clue to readers of the extent of the comment.

1.4   Named Constants

Constants are values like 12, 17.9, and "Strings Like This". Constants, or literals as they are also known, are the way you specify values that are not computed and recomputed but remain, well, constant for the life of a program.

The `Fibonnaci` example printed all Fibonacci numbers with a value less than 50. The constant 50 was used within the expression of the `while` loop and within the documentation comment describing `main`. Suppose now that you want to modify the example to print the Fibonacci numbers with values less than 100. You have to go through the source code and locate and modify all occurrences of the constant 50. Though this is trivial in our example, in general it is a tedious and error-prone process. Further, if people reading the code see an expression like `hi < 50` they may have no idea what the constant 50 actually represents. Such "magic numbers" hinder program understandability and maintainability.

A *named constant* is a constant value that is referred to by a name. For example, we may choose the name MAX to refer to the constant 50 in the Fibonacci example. You define named constants by declaring fields of the appropriate type, initialized to the appropriate value. That itself does not define a constant, but a field whose value could be changed by an assignment statement. To make the value a constant we declare the field as `final`. A `final` field or variable is one which once initialized can never have its value changed—it is *immutable*. Further, because we don't want the named constant field to be associated with instances of the class, we also declare it as `static`.

We would rewrite the Fibonacci example as follows:

```
class Fibonacci2 {
    static final int MAX = 50;
    /** Print the Fibonacci sequence for values < MAX */
    public static void main(String[] args) {
        int lo = 1;
        int hi = 1;
        System.out.println(lo);
        while (hi < MAX) {
            System.out.println(hi);
            hi = lo + hi;
            lo = hi - lo;
        }
    }
}
```

You can group related constants within a class. For example, a card game might use these constants:

```
class Suit {
    final static int CLUBS    = 1;
    final static int DIAMONDS = 2;
```

```
        final static int HEARTS   = 3;
        final static int SPADES   = 4;
    }
```

To refer to a `static` member of a class we use the name of the class followed by dot and the name of the member. With the above declaration, suits in a program would be accessed as `Suit.HEARTS`, `Suit.SPADES`, and so on, thus grouping all the suit names within the single name `Suit`. Notice that the order of the modifiers `final` and `static` makes no difference—though you should use a consistent order. We have already accessed static fields in all of the preceding examples, as you may have realized—`out` is a `static` field of class `System`.

Exercise 1.5: Change the `HelloWorld` application to use a named string constant as the string to print.

Exercise 1.6: Change your program from Exercise 1.3 to use a named string constant for the title.

1.5   Unicode Characters

Suppose we were defining a class that dealt with circles and we wanted a named constant that represented the value π. In most programming languages we would name the constant "pi" because in most languages identifiers (the technical term for names) are limited to the letters and digits available in the ASCII character set. In the Java programming language, however, we can do this:

```
class CircleStuff {
    static final double π = 3.14159265358979323846;
}
```

The Java programming language moves you toward the world of internationalized software: you write code in *Unicode,* an international character set standard. Unicode characters are 16 bits and provide a character range large enough to write the major languages used in the world, and that is why we can use π for the name of the constant in the example. π is a valid letter from the Greek section of Unicode and is therefore valid in source. Most existing code is typed in ASCII, a 7-bit character standard, or ISO Latin-1, an 8-bit character standard commonly called Latin-1. But these characters are translated into Unicode before processing, so the character set is always Unicode.

1.6   Flow of Control

"Flow of control" is the term for deciding which statements in a program are executed and in what order. The while loop in the Fibonacci program is one control flow statement, as are blocks, which define a sequential execution of the statements they group. Other control flow statements include for, if–else, switch and do–while. We change the Fibonacci sequence program by numbering the elements of the sequence and marking even numbers with an asterisk:

```
class ImprovedFibonacci {
    /** Print out the first few Fibonacci
     * numbers, marking evens with a '*' */
    static final int MAX_INDEX = 9;

    public static void main(String[] args) {
        int lo = 1;
        int hi = 1;
        String mark;

        System.out.println("1: " + lo);
        for (int i = 2; i <= MAX_INDEX; i++) {
            if (hi % 2 == 0)
                mark = " *";
            else
                mark = "";
            System.out.println(i + ": " + hi + mark);
            hi = lo + hi;
            lo = hi - lo;
        }
    }
}
```

Here is the new output:

```
1: 1
2: 1
3: 2 *
4: 3
5: 5
6: 8 *
```

```
7: 13
8: 21
9: 34 *
```

To number the elements of the sequence, we used a `for` loop instead of a `while` loop. A `for` loop is shorthand for a `while` loop, with an initialization and increment section added. The `for` loop in `ImprovedFibonacci` is equivalent to this `while` loop:

```
int i = 2;   // define and initialize loop index
while (i <= MAX_INDEX) {
    // ...generate the next Fibonacci number and print it...
    i++;   // increment loop index
}
```

The use of the `for` loop introduces a new variable declaration mechanism: the declaration of the loop variable in the initialization section. This is a convenient way of defining loop variables that need exist only while the loop is executing, but it applies only to `for` loops—none of the other control-flow statements allow variables to be declared within the statement itself. The loop variable `i` is available only within the body of the `for` statement. A loop variable declared in this manner disappears when the loop terminates, which means you can reuse that variable name in subsequent `for` statements.

The ++ operator in this code fragment may be unfamiliar if you're new to C-derived programming languages. The plus-plus operator increments by one the value of any variable it abuts—the contents of variable `i` in this case. The ++ operator is a *prefix* operator when it comes before its operand, and *postfix* when it comes after. The two forms have slightly different semantics but we defer that discussion until Chapter 6. Similarly, minus-minus (--) decrements by one the value of any variable it abuts and can also be prefix or postfix. In the context of the previous example, a statement like

```
i++;
```

is equivalent to

```
i = i + 1;
```

Expressions where the value assigned to a variable is calculated from the original value of the variable, are common enough that there is a short-hand for writing them. For example, another way to write `i = i + 1` is to write

```
i += 1;
```

which adds the value on the right-hand side of the += operator (namely 1) to the variable on the left-hand side (namely i). Most of the binary operators (operators that take two operands) can be joined with = in a similar way (such as +=, -=, *=, and /=).

Inside the for loop body we use an if-else statement to see whether the current hi value is even. The if statement tests the boolean expression between the parentheses. If the expression is true, the statement (which can be a block) in the body of the if is executed. If the expression is false, the statement following the else clause is executed. The else part is optional: if the else is not present, nothing is done when the expression is false. After figuring out which (if any) clause to execute, and then actually executing it, control passes to the code following the body of the if statement.

The example tests whether hi is even using the %, or *remainder,* operator. It produces the remainder after dividing the value on the left side by the value on the right. In this example, if the left-side value is even, the remainder is zero, and the ensuing statement assigns a string containing the even-number indicator to mark. The else clause is executed for odd numbers, setting mark to an empty string.

The println invocations appear more complex in this example because the arguments to println are themselves expressions which have to be evaluated before println is invoked. In the first case we have the expression "1: " + lo, which concatenates a string representation of lo (initially 1) to the string literal "1: "—giving a string with the value "1: 1". The + operator is a concatenation operator when at least one of its operands is a string and an addition operator otherwise. Having the concatenation operation appear within the method argument list is a common short-hand for the more verbose and tedious:

```
String temp = "1: " + lo;
System.out.println(temp);
```

The println invocation within the for loop body constructs a string containing a string representation of the current loop count i, a separator string, a string representing the current value of hi and the marker string.

Exercise 1.7: Change the loop so that i counts backward instead of forward.

1.7 Classes and Objects

The Java programming language, like many object-oriented programming languages, provides a tool to solve programming problems using the notions of classes and objects. Every object has a class that defines its data and behavior. Each class has three kinds of members:

◆ Fields are data variables associated with a class and its objects. Fields store results of computations performed by the class.

◆ Methods contain the executable code of a class. Methods are built from statements. The way in which methods are invoked, and the statements contained within those methods, is what ultimately directs program execution.

◆ Classes and interfaces can be members of other classes or interfaces (you will learn about interfaces soon).

Here is the declaration of a simple class that might represent a point on a two-dimensional plane:

```
class Point {
    public double x, y;
}
```

This `Point` class has two fields representing the *x* and *y* coordinates of a point and has (as yet) no methods. A class declaration like this one is, conceptually, a plan that defines what objects manufactured from that class look like, plus sets of instructions that define the behavior of those objects.

Members of a class can have various levels of *visibility* or *accessibility*. The `public` declaration of x and y in the `Point` class means that any code with access to a `Point` object can read and modify those fields. Other levels of accessibility limit member access to code in the class itself or to other related classes.

1.7.1   Creating Objects

Objects are created using an expression containing the new keyword. Creating an object from a class definition is also known as *instantiation*; thus, objects are often called *instances*.

Newly created objects are allocated within an area of system memory known as the *heap*. All objects are accessed via *object references*—any variable that may appear to hold an object actually contains a reference to that object. The types of such variables are known as *reference types*, in contrast to the primitive types where variables hold values of that type. Object references are `null` when they do not reference any object.

Most of the time, you can be imprecise in the distinction between actual objects and references to objects. You can say, "Pass the object to the method" when you really mean "Pass an object reference to the method." We are careful about this distinction only when it makes a difference. Most of the time, you can use "object" and "object reference" interchangeably.

In the `Point` class, suppose you are building a graphics application in which you need to track lots of points. You represent each point by its own concrete `Point` object. Here is how you might create and initialize `Point` objects:

```
Point lowerLeft = new Point();
Point upperRight = new Point();
Point middlePoint = new Point();

lowerLeft.x = 0.0;
lowerLeft.y = 0.0;

upperRight.x = 1280.0;
upperRight.y = 1024.0;

middlePoint.x = 640.0;
middlePoint.y = 512.0;
```

Each `Point` object is unique and has its own copy of the x and y fields. Changing x in the object `lowerLeft`, for example, does not affect the value of x in the object `upperRight`. The fields in objects are known as *instance variables*, because there is a unique copy of the field in each object (instance) of the class.

1.7.2   Static or Class Fields

Per-object fields are usually what you need. You usually want a field in one object to be distinct from the field of the same name in every other object instantiated from that class.

Sometimes, though, you want fields that are shared among all objects of that class. These shared variables are known as *class variables*—variables specific to the class as opposed to objects of the class.

Why would you want to use class variables? Consider, for example, the Sony Walkman factory. Each Walkman has a unique serial number. In object terms, each Walkman object has its own unique serial number field. However, the factory needs to keep a record of the next serial number to be assigned. You don't want to keep that number with every Walkman object. You'd keep only one copy of that number in the factory, or, in object terms, as a class variable.

You obtain class-specific fields by declaring them `static`, and they are therefore commonly called *static fields*. For example, a `Point` object to represent the origin might be common enough that you should provide it as a static field in the `Point` class:

```
public static Point origin = new Point();
```

If this declaration appears inside the declaration of the `Point` class, there will be exactly one piece of data called `Point.origin` that always refers to an object at (0,0). This static field is there no matter how many `Point` objects are created, even if none is created. The values of x and y are zero because that is the default for numeric fields that are not explicitly initialized to a different value.

You can probably see now why named constants are declared `static`.

When you see *field* in this book, it generally means a per-object field, although the term *non-static field* is sometimes used for clarity.

1.7.3   The Garbage Collector

After creating an object using `new`, how do you get rid of the object when you no longer want it? The answer is simple—stop referring to it. Unreferenced objects are automatically reclaimed by a *garbage collector,* which runs in the background and tracks object references. When an object is no longer referenced, the garbage collector can remove it from the storage allocation heap, although it may defer actually doing so until a propitious time.

1.8   Methods and Parameters

Objects of the previously defined `Point` class are exposed to manipulation by any code that has a reference to a `Point` object, because its fields are declared `public`. The `Point` class is an example of the simplest kind of class. Indeed, some classes *are* this simple. They are designed to fit purely internal needs for a package (a group of cooperating classes) or when simple data containers are all you need.

The real benefits of object orientation, however, come from hiding the implementation of a class behind operations performed on its internal data. Operations of a class are declared via its *methods*—instructions that operate on an object's data to obtain results. Methods access internal implementation details that are otherwise hidden from other objects. Hiding data behind methods so that it is inaccessible to other objects is the fundamental basis of *data encapsulation*.

If we enhance the `Point` class with a simple `clear` method, it might look like this:

```
public void clear() {
    x = 0;
    y = 0;
}
```

The `clear` method has no parameters, hence the empty (and) after its name; `clear` is declared `void` because it does not return any value. Inside a method, fields and other methods of the class can be named directly—we can simply say x and y without an explicit object reference.

1.8.1 Invoking a Method

Objects in general do not operate directly on the data of other objects, although, as you saw in the `Point` class, a class can make its fields publicly accessible. Well-designed classes usually hide their data so that it can be changed only by methods of that class.

To *invoke* a method, you provide an object reference to the *target* object and the method name, separated by a dot. *Arguments* are passed to the method as a comma-separated list of values enclosed in parentheses. Methods that take no arguments still require the parentheses, with nothing between them.

A method can return only a single value as a result. To return more than one value from a method, you must create an object whose purpose is to hold return values in a single unit and then return that object.

When a method is invoked, the flow of execution leaves the current method and starts executing the body of the invoked method. When the invoked method has completed, the current method continues execution with the code after the method invocation. When we start executing the body of the method, the object that was the target of the method invocation is now the *current* or *receiver* object, from the perspective of that method. The arguments passed to the method are accessed via the parameters the method declared.

Here is a method called `distance` that's part of the `Point` class shown in previous examples. The `distance` method accepts another `Point` object as a parameter, computes the Euclidean distance between itself and the other point, and returns a double-precision floating-point result:

```
public double distance(Point that) {
    double xdiff = x - that.x;
    double ydiff = y - that.y;
    return Math.sqrt(xdiff * xdiff + ydiff * ydiff);
}
```

The `return` statement causes a method to stop executing its body and return execution to the invoking method. If an expression is part of the `return` statement then the value of that expression is returned as the value of the method invocation. The type of the expression must be compatible with the return type defined for the method. In the example we use the `sqrt` method of the `Math` library class to calculate the square root of the sum of the squares of the differences between the two *x* and *y* coordinates.

Based on the `lowerLeft` and `upperRight` objects created previously, you could invoke `distance` this way:

```
double d = lowerLeft.distance(upperRight);
```

Here `upperRight` is passed as an argument to `distance`, which sees it as the parameter `that`. After this statement executes, the variable d contains the Euclidean distance between `lowerLeft` and `upperRight`.

1.8.2   The `this` Reference

Occasionally, the receiving object needs to know its own reference. For example, the receiving object might want to add itself to a list of objects somewhere. An implicit reference named `this` is available to methods, and `this` is a reference to the current (receiving) object. The following definition of `clear` is equivalent to the one just presented:

```
public void clear() {
    this.x = 0;
    this.y = 0;
}
```

You usually use `this` as an argument to other methods that need an object reference. The `this` reference can also be used to explicitly name the members of the current object. Here's another method of `Point` named `move`, which sets the x and y fields to specified values:

```
public void move(double x, double y) {
    this.x = x;
    this.y = y;
}
```

This `move` method uses `this` to clarify which x and y are being referred to. Naming the parameters of `move` x and y is reasonable, because you pass *x* and *y* coordinates to the method. But then those parameters have the same names as the fields, and therefore the parameter names *hide* the field names. If we simply wrote x = x we would assign the value of the x parameter to itself, not to the x field as required. The expression `this.x` refers to the object's x field, not the x parameter of `move`.

Exercise 1.8: Add a method to the `Point` class that sets the current object's coordinates to those of a passed in `Point` object.

1.8.3   Static or Class Methods

Just as you can have per-class static fields, you can also have per-class static methods, often known as *class methods*. Class methods are usually intended to do class-like operations specific to the class itself, usually on static fields and not on specific instances of that class. Class methods are declared using the `static` keyword and are therefore also known as *static methods*.

As with the term *field,* when you see *method,* it generally means a per-object method, although the term *non-static method* is sometimes used for clarity.

Why would you need static methods? Consider the Sony Walkman factory again. The record of the next serial number to be assigned is held in the factory, not in every Walkman. A method that returned the factory's copy of the next available serial number would be a static method, not a method to operate on specific Walkman objects.

The implementation of `distance` in the previous example uses the static method `Math.sqrt` to calculate a square root. The `Math` class supports many methods that are useful for general mathematical manipulation. These methods are declared as static methods because they do not act on any particular instance of the `Math` class, but instead group a related set of functionality in the class itself.

A static method cannot directly access non-static members. When a static method is invoked, there's no specific object for the method to operate on, and so no `this` reference. You could work around this by passing an explicit object reference as an argument to the static method. In general, however, static methods perform class-related tasks and non-static methods perform object-related tasks. Asking a static method to work on object fields is like asking the Walkman factory to change the serial number of a Walkman hanging on the belt of a jogger in Golden Gate Park.

1.9   Arrays

Simple variables that hold one value are useful but are not sufficient for many applications. A program that plays a game of cards would want a number of `Card` objects it could manipulate as a whole. To meet this need, you use *arrays*.

An array is a collection of variables all of the same type. The components of an array are accessed by simple integer indexes. In a card game, a `Deck` object might look like this:

```
public class Deck {
    public static final int DECK_SIZE = 52;

    private Card[] cards = new Card[DECK_SIZE];
```

```
        public void print() {
            for (int i = 0; i < cards.length; i++)
                System.out.println(cards[i]);
        }
        // ...
    }
```

First we declare a constant called DECK_SIZE to define the number of cards in a deck. This constant is public so that anyone can find out how many cards are in a deck. Next we declare a cards field for referring to all the cards. This field is declared private, which means that only the methods in the current class can access it—this prevents anyone from manipulating our cards directly. The modifiers public and private are *access modifiers* because they control who can access a class, interface, field, or method.

We declare the cards field as an array of type Card by following the type name in the declaration with square brackets [and]. We initialize cards to a new array with DECK_SIZE variables of type Card. Each Card element in the array is implicitly initialized to null. An array's length is fixed when it is created and can never change.

The println method invocation shows how array components are accessed by enclosing the index of the desired element within square brackets following the array name.

You can probably tell from reading the code that array objects have a length field that says how many elements the array contains. The *bounds* of an array are integers between 0 and length-1, inclusive. It is a common programming error, especially when looping through array elements, to try to access elements that are outside the bounds of the array. To catch this sort of error, all array accesses are *bounds checked*, to ensure that the index is in bounds. If you try to use an index that is out of bounds, the runtime system reports this by throwing an exception in your program—an IndexOutOfBoundsException. You'll learn about exceptions a bit later in the chapter.

An array with length zero is an *empty array*. Methods that take arrays as arguments may require that the array they receive is non-empty and so will need to check the length. However, before you can check the length of an array you need to ensure that the array reference is not null. If either of these checks fail, the method may report the problem by throwing an IllegalArgumentException. For example, here is a method that averages the values in an integer array:

```
static double average(int[] values) {
    if (values == null)
        throw new IllegalArgumentException();
```

```
    else
        if (values.length == 0)
            throw new IllegalArgumentException();
        else {
            double sum = 0.0;
            for (int i = 0; i < values.length; i++)
                sum += values[i];
            return sum / values.length;
        }
}
```

This code works but the logic of the method is almost completely lost in the nested if-else statements ensuring the array is non-empty. To avoid the need for two if statements, we could try to test if the argument is null *or* if it has a zero length, using the boolean inclusive-OR operator (|):

```
if (values == null | values.length == 0)
    throw new IllegalArgumentException();
```

Unfortunately this code is not correct. Even if values is null, this code will still attempt to access its length field because the normal boolean operators always evaluate both operands. This situation is so common when performing logical operations that special operators are defined to solve it. The conditional boolean operators evaluate their right-hand operand only if the value of the expression has not already been determined by the left-hand operand. We can correct the example code by using the conditional-OR (||) operator:

```
if (values == null || values.length == 0)
    throw new IllegalArgumentException();
```

Now if values is null the value of the conditional-OR expression is known to be true and so no attempt is made to access the length field.

The binary boolean operators—AND (&), inclusive-OR (|), and exclusive-OR (^)—are logical operators when their operands are boolean values and bitwise operators when their operands are integer values. The conditional-OR (||) and conditional-AND (&&) operators are logical operators and can only be used with boolean operands.

Exercise 1.9: Modify the Fibonacci application to store the sequence into an array and print the list of values at the end.

Exercise 1.10: Modify the ImprovedFibonacci application to store its sequence in an array. Do this by creating a new class to hold both the value and a boolean value that says whether the value is even, and then having an array of object references to objects of that class.

1.10   String Objects

A `String` class type deals specifically with sequences of character data and provides language-level support for initializing them. The `String` class provides a variety of methods to operate on `String` objects.

You've already seen string literals in examples like the `HelloWorld` program. When you write a statement such as

```
System.out.println("Hello, world");
```

the compiler actually creates a `String` object initialized to the value of the specified string literal and passes that `String` object as the argument to the `println` method.

You don't need to specify the length of a `String` object when you create it. You can create a new `String` object and initialize it all in one statement, as shown in this example:

```
class StringsDemo {
    public static void main(String[] args) {
        String myName = "Petronius";

        myName = myName + " Arbiter";
        System.out.println("Name = " + myName);
    }
}
```

Here we declare a `String` variable called `myName` and initialize it with an object reference to a string literal. Following initialization, we use the `String` concatenation operator (+) to make a new `String` object with new contents and store a reference to this new string object into the variable. Finally, we print the value of `myName` on the standard output stream. The output when you run this program is

```
Name = Petronius Arbiter
```

The concatenation operator can also be used in the short-hand += form, to assign the concatenation of the original string and the given string, back to the original string reference. Here's an upgraded program:

```
class BetterStringsDemo {
    public static void main(String[] args) {
        String myName = "Petronius";
        String occupation = "Reorganization Specialist";

        myName += " Arbiter";
        myName += " ";
        myName += "(" + occupation + ")";
        System.out.println("Name = " + myName);
    }
}
```

Now when you run the program, you get this output:

```
Name = Petronius Arbiter (Reorganization Specialist)
```

String objects have a length method that returns the number of characters in the string. Characters are indexed from 0 through length() - 1, and can be accessed using the charAt method, which takes an integer index and returns the character at that index. In this regard a string is similar to an array of characters, but String objects are not arrays of characters and you cannot assign an array of characters to a String reference. You can, however, construct a new String object from an array of characters by passing the array as an argument to a String constructor. You can also obtain an array of characters with the same contents as a string using the toCharArray method.

String objects are *read-only,* or *immutable:* the contents of a String never change. When you see statements like

```
str = "redwood";
// ... do something with str ..
str = "oak";
```

the second assignment gives a new value to the variable str which is an object reference to a different string object with the contents "oak". Every time you perform operations that seem to modify a String object, such as the += operation in BetterStringsDemo, you actually get a new read-only String object, while the original String object remains unchanged. The StringBuffer class provides for mutable strings and is described in Chapter 9, where String is also described in detail.

The `equals` method is the simplest way to compare two `String` objects to see whether they have the same contents:

```
if (oneStr.equals(twoStr))
    foundDuplicate(oneStr, twoStr);
```

Other methods for comparing subparts of strings or ignoring case differences are also covered in Chapter 9. If you use `==` to compare the string objects, you are actually comparing `oneStr` and `twoStr` to see if they refer to the same object, not testing if the strings have the same contents.

Exercise 1.11: Modify the `StringsDemo` application to use different strings.

Exercise 1.12: Modify `ImprovedFibonacci` to store the `String` objects it creates into an array instead of invoking `println` with them directly.

1.11 Extending a Class

One of the major benefits of object orientation is the ability to *extend*, or *subclass*, the behavior of an existing class and continue to use code written for the original class when acting upon an instance of the subclass. The original class is known as the *superclass*. When you extend a class to create a new class, the new extended class *inherits* fields and methods of the superclass.

If the subclass does not specifically *override* the behavior of the superclass, the subclass inherits all the behavior of its superclass because it inherits the fields and methods of its superclass. In addition, the subclass can add new fields and methods and so add new behavior.

Consider the Walkman example. The original model had a single jack for one person to listen to the tape. Later models incorporated two jacks so two people could listen to the same tape. In the object-oriented world, the two-jack model extends, or is a subclass of, the basic one-jack model. The two-jack model inherits the characteristics and behavior of the basic model and adds new behavior of its own.

Customers told Sony they wanted to talk to each other while sharing a tape in the two-jack model. Sony enhanced the two-jack model to include two-way communications so people could chat while listening to music. The two-way communications model is a subclass of the two-jack model, inherits all of its behavior, and again adds new behavior.

Sony created many other Walkman models. Later models extend the capabilities of the basic model—they subclass the basic model and inherit features and behavior from it.

Let's look at an example of extending a class. Here we extend our former `Point` class to represent a pixel that might be shown on a screen. The new `Pixel` class requires a color in addition to *x* and *y* coordinates:

```
class Pixel extends Point {
    Color color;

    public void clear() {
        super.clear();
        color = null;
    }
}
```

`Pixel` extends both the *data* and *behavior* of its `Point` superclass. `Pixel` extends the data by adding a field named `color`. `Pixel` also extends the behavior of `Point` by overriding `Point`'s `clear` method.

Pixel objects can be used by any code designed to work with `Point` objects. If a method expects a parameter of type `Point`, you can hand it a `Pixel` object and it just works. All the `Point` code can be used by anyone with a `Pixel` in hand. This feature is known as *polymorphism*—a single object like `Pixel` can have many (*poly-*) forms (*-morph*) and can be used as both a `Pixel` object and a `Point` object.

Pixel's behavior extends `Point`'s behavior. Extended behavior can be entirely new (adding color in this example) or can be a restriction on old behavior that follows all the original requirements. An example of restricted behavior might be `Pixel` objects that live inside some kind of `Screen` object, restricting x and y to the dimensions of the screen. If the original `Point` class did not forbid restrictions for coordinates, a class with restricted range would not violate the original class's behavior.

An extended class often *overrides* the behavior of its superclass by providing new implementations of one or more of the inherited methods. To do this the extended class defines a method with the same signature and return type as a method in the superclass. In the `Pixel` example, we override `clear` to obtain the proper behavior that `Pixel` requires. The `clear` that `Pixel` inherited from `Point` knows only about `Point`'s fields but obviously can't know about the new `color` field declared in the `Pixel` subclass.

1.11.1 Invoking Methods from the Superclass

To make `Pixel` do the correct "clear" behavior, we provide a new implementation of `clear` that first invokes its superclass's `clear` using the `super` reference. The `super` reference is a lot like the `this` reference described previously except that `super` references things from the superclass, whereas `this` references things from the current object.

The invocation `super.clear()` looks to the superclass to execute `clear` as it would for an object of the superclass—namely, `Point`. After invoking `super.clear()` to clear out the `Point` part of the object, we add new functionality to set `color` to a reasonable empty value. We choose `null`, a reference to no object.

What would happen had we not invoked `super.clear()` in the previous example? `Pixel`'s `clear` method would set `color` to its `null` value, but the `x` and `y` variables that `Pixel` inherited from `Point` would not be set to any "cleared" values. Not clearing all the values of a `Pixel` object, including its `Point` parts, is probably a bug.

When you invoke `super.`*`method`*`()`, the runtime system looks back up the inheritance hierarchy to the first superclass that contains the required *method*. If `Point` didn't have a `clear` method, for example, the runtime system would look at `Point`'s superclass for such a method and invoke that, and so on.

For all other references, invoking a method uses the actual class of the *object*, not the type of the object *reference*. Here is an example:

```
Point point = new Pixel();
point.clear();  // uses Pixel's clear()
```

In this example, `Pixel`'s version of `clear` is invoked even though the variable that holds the `Pixel` is declared as a `Point` reference. But if we invoke `super.clear()` inside one of `Pixel`'s methods, that invocation will use the `Point` class's implementation of the `clear` method.

1.11.2 The `Object` Class

Classes that do not explicitly extend any other class implicitly extend the `Object` class. All objects are polymorphically of class `Object`, so `Object` is the generic type for references that can refer to objects of any class:

```
Object oref = new Pixel();
oref = "Some String";
```

In this example, `oref` is correctly assigned references to `Pixel` and `String` objects even though those classes have no relationship except that both have `Object` as a superclass. The `Object` class also defines several important methods that you'll learn about in Chapter 3.

1.11.3 Type Casting

The following code fragment seems quite reasonable (if not particularly useful) but results in a compile-time error:

```
String name = "Petronius";
Object obj = name;
name = obj;      // INVALID: won't compile
```

We declare and initialize a `String` reference which we then assign to a generic `Object` reference and then we try to assign the reference to a `String` back to the `String` reference. Why doesn't this work? The problem is that while a `String` is always an `Object`, an `Object` is not necessarily a `String`, and even though you can see that in this case it really is a `String`, the compiler is not so clever. To help the compiler you have to tell it that the object referred to by `obj` is actually a `String` and so can be assigned to `name`:

```
name = (String)obj;     // That's better!
```

Telling the compiler that the type of an expression is really a different type is known as *type casting* or *type conversion*. You perform a type cast by prefixing the expression with the new type in parentheses. The compiler doesn't automatically trust you when you do this and so it checks you are telling the truth. A smart compiler may be able to tell at compile time that you are telling the truth; otherwise it will insert a run time check to verify that the cast really is allowed. If you lie to the compiler and the run time check fails, the runtime system reports this by throwing a `ClassCastException`. As the Java programming language is *strongly typed* there are very strict rules concerning assignments between types.

Exercise 1.13: Sketch out a set of classes that reflects the class structure of the Sony Walkman product family we have described. Use methods to hide the data, making all the data `private` and the methods `public`. What methods would belong in the `Walkman` class? Which methods would be added for which extended classes?

1.12 Interfaces

Sometimes you want only to *declare* methods an object must support but not to supply the *implementation* of those methods. As long as their behavior meets specific criteria—called the *contract*—implementation details of the methods are irrelevant. These declarations define a *type,* and any class that implements those methods can be said to have that type, regardless of how the methods are implemented. For example, to ask whether a particular value is contained in a set of values, details of how those values are stored are irrelevant. You want the methods to work equally well with a linked list of values, a hashtable of values, or any other data structure.

To support this, you can define an *interface*. An interface is like a class but has only declarations of its methods. The designer of the interface declares the methods that must be supported by classes that *implement* the interface and declares what those methods should do. Here is a `Lookup` interface for finding a value in a set of values:

```
interface Lookup {
    /** Return the value associated with the name, or
     *  null if there is no such value */
    Object find(String name);
}
```

The `Lookup` interface declares one method, `find`, that takes a `String` and returns the value associated with that name, or `null` if there is no associated value. In the interface no implementation can be given for the method—a class that implements the interface is responsible for providing a specific implementation—so instead of a method body we simply have a semicolon. Code that uses references of type `Lookup` (references to objects that implement the `Lookup` interface) can invoke the `find` method and get the expected results, no matter what the actual type of the object is:

```
void processValues(String[] names, Lookup table) {
    for (int i = 0; i < names.length; i++) {
        Object value = table.find(names[i]);
        if (value != null)
            processValue(names[i], value);
    }
}
```

A class can implement as many interfaces as you choose. This example implements `Lookup` using a simple array (methods to set or remove values are left out for simplicity):

```
class SimpleLookup implements Lookup {
    private String[] names;
    private Object[] values;

    public Object find(String name) {
        for (int i = 0; i < names.length; i++) {
```

```
            if (names[i].equals(name))
                return values[i];
        }
        return null;      // not found
    }

    // ...
}
```

An interface can also declare named constants that are `static` and `final`. Additionally an interface can declare other *nested* interfaces and even classes. These nested types are discussed in detail in Chapter 5. All the members of an interface are implicitly, or explicitly, `public`—so they can be accessed anywhere the interface itself is accessible.

Interfaces can be extended using the `extends` keyword. An interface can extend one or more other interfaces, adding new constants or new methods that must be implemented by any class that implements the extended interface.

A class's *supertypes* are the class it extends and the interfaces it implements, including all the supertypes of those classes and interfaces. So an object is not only an instance of its particular class but also of any of its supertypes, including interfaces. An object can be used polymorphically with both its superclass and any superinterfaces, including any of their supertypes.

Exercise 1.14: Write an interface that extends Lookup to declare add and remove methods. Implement the extended interface in a new class.

1.13 Exceptions

What do you do when an error occurs in a program? In many languages, error conditions are signaled by unusual return values like –1. Programmers often don't check for exceptional values because they may assume that errors "can't happen." On the other hand, adding error detection and recovery to what should be a straightforward flow of logic can complicate that logic to the point where the normal flow is completely obscured. An ostensibly simple task such as reading a file into memory might require about seven lines of code. Error checking and reporting expands this to 40 or more lines. Making normal operation the needle in your code haystack is undesirable.

Checked exceptions manage error handling. Checked exceptions force you to consider what to do with errors where they may occur in the code. If a checked exception is not handled, this is noticed at compile time, not at run time when problems have compounded because of the unchecked error.

A method that detects an unusual error condition *throws* an exception. Exceptions can be *caught* by code farther back on the calling stack—this invoking code can handle the exception as needed and then continue executing. Uncaught exceptions result in the termination of the thread of execution, but before it terminates the thread's `ThreadGroup` is given the opportunity to handle the exception as best it can—perhaps doing nothing more than reporting that the exception occurred. `Threads` and `Threadgroups` are discussed in detail in Chapter 10.

An exception is an object, with type, methods, and data. Representing exceptions as objects is useful, because an exception object can include data, methods, or both to report on or recover from specific kinds of exceptions. Exception objects are generally derived from the `Exception` class, which provides a string field to describe the error. All exceptions must be subclasses of the class `Throwable`, which is the superclass of `Exception`.

The paradigm for using exceptions is the *try–catch–finally* sequence: you *try* something; if that something throws an exception, you *catch* the exception; and *finally* you clean up from either the normal code path or the exception code path, whichever actually happened.

Here is a `getDataSet` method that returns a set of data read from a file. If the file for the data set cannot be found or if any other I/O exception occurs, this method throws an exception describing the error. First, we define a new exception type `BadDataSetException` to describe such an error. Then we declare that the method `getDataSet` throws that exception using a `throws` clause in the method header:

```java
class BadDataSetException extends Exception { }

class MyUtilities {
    public double[] getDataSet(String setName)
        throws BadDataSetException
    {
        String file = setName + ".dset";
        FileInputStream in = null;
        try {
            in = new FileInputStream(file);
            return readDataSet(in);
        } catch (IOException e) {
            throw new BadDataSetException();
        } finally {
            try {
```

```
            if (in != null)
                in.close();
        } catch (IOException e) {
            ;      // ignore: we successfully read the data
        }
    }
}
    // … definition of readDataSet …
}
```

First we turn the data set name into a file name. Then we try to open the file and read the data using the method `readDataSet`. If all goes well, `readDataSet` will return an array of doubles, which we will return to the invoking code. If opening or reading the file causes an I/O exception, the `catch` clause is executed. The `catch` clause creates a new `BadDataSetException` object and throws it, in effect translating the I/O exception into an exception specific to `getDataSet`. Methods that invoke `getDataSet` can catch the new exception and react to it appropriately. In either case—returning successfully with the data set or catching and then throwing an exception—the code in the `finally` clause is executed to close the file if it was opened successfully. If an exception occurs during `close`, we catch it but ignore it—the semicolon by itself forms an *empty statement*, which does nothing. Ignoring exceptions is not a good idea in general, but in this case it occurs after successfully reading the data set and so the method has fulfilled its contract. If a problem with the file persists, it will be reported as an exception the next time we try to use it and can be more appropriately dealt with at that time.

You will use `finally` clauses for cleanup code that must always be executed. You can even have a `try-finally` statement with no `catch` clauses to ensure that cleanup code will be executed even if uncaught exceptions are thrown.

If a method's execution can result in checked exceptions being thrown, it must declare the types of these exceptions in a `throws` clause, as shown for the `getDataSet` method. A method can throw only those checked exceptions it declares—this is why they are called *checked exceptions*. It may throw those exceptions directly with `throw` or indirectly by invoking a method that throws exceptions. Exceptions of type `RuntimeException`, `Error`, or subclasses of these exception types, are *unchecked exceptions* and can be thrown anywhere, without being declared.

Checked exceptions represent conditions that, although exceptional, can reasonably be expected to occur, and if they do occur must be dealt with in some way—such as the `IOException` that may occur reading a file. Declaring the checked exceptions that a method throws allows the compiler to ensure that the method throws only those checked exceptions it declared and no others. This check prevents errors in cases when your method should handle another method's exceptions but does not. In addition, the method that invokes your method is assured that your method will not result in unexpected checked exceptions.

Unchecked exceptions represent conditions that, generally speaking, reflect errors in your program's logic and cannot be reasonably recovered from at run time. For example, the `IndexOutOfBoundsException` thrown when you access outside the bounds of an array, tells you that your program calculated an index incorrectly, or failed to verify a value to be used as an index. These are errors that should be corrected in the program code. Given that you can make errors writing any statement it would be totally impractical to have to declare or catch all the exceptions that could arise from those errors—hence they are unchecked.

Exercise 1.15: Add fields to `BadDataSetException` to hold the set name and the I/O exception that signaled the problem so that whoever catches the exception will know details about the error.

1.14 Packages

Name conflicts are a major problem when you're developing reusable code. No matter how carefully you pick names for classes, someone else is likely to use that name for a different purpose. If you use simple, descriptive names, the problem gets worse since such names are more likely to be used by someone else who was also trying to use simple, descriptive names. Words like "list," "event," "component," and so on are used often and are almost certain to clash with other people's uses.

The standard solution for name collision in many programming languages is to use a *package prefix* at the front of every class, type, global function, and so on. Prefix conventions create *naming contexts* to ensure that names in one context do not conflict with names in other contexts. These prefixes are usually a few characters long and are usually an abbreviation of the product name, such as `Xt` for the X-Windows Toolkit.

When code uses only a few packages, the likelihood of prefix conflict is small. However, since prefixes are abbreviations, the probability of a name conflict increases with the number of packages used.

The Java programming language has a formal notion of package that has a set of types and subpackages as members. Packages are named and can be imported. Package names are hierarchical, with components separated by dots. When you use part of a package, either you use its *fully qualified name*—the type name prefixed by the package name, separated by a dot—or you *import* all or part of the package. Importing all, or part, of a package, simply instructs the compiler to look in the package for types that it can't find defined locally. Package names also give you control over name conflicts. If two packages contain classes with the same name, you can use the fully qualified class name for one or both of them.

Here is an example of a method that uses fully qualified names to print the current day and time using the utility class Date (documented in Chapter 17), which, as with all time-based methods, considers time to be in milliseconds since the epoch (00:00:00 GMT, January 1, 1970):

```java
class Date1 {
    public static void main(String[] args) {
        java.util.Date now = new java.util.Date();
        System.out.println(now);
    }
}
```

And here is a version that uses import to declare the type Date:

```java
import java.util.Date;

class Date2 {
    public static void main(String[] args) {
        Date now = new Date();
        System.out.println(now);
    }
}
```

When the compiler comes to the declaration of now it determines that the Date type is actually the java.util.Date type, because that is the only Date type it knows about. Import statements simply provide information to the compiler; they don't cause files to be "included" into the current file.

The name collision problem is not completely solved by the package mechanism. Two projects can still give their packages the same name. This problem can be solved only by convention. The standard convention is to use the reversed Internet domain name of the organization to prefix the package name. For example, if the Acme Corporation had the Internet domain acme.com, it would use package names starting with com.acme, as in com.acme.tools.

Having dots separate package components may occasionally cause confusion, because the dot is also used to invoke methods and access fields through object references. This syntax may lead to confusion as to what can be imported. Novices often try to import System.out so they don't have to type it in front of every println. This does not work because System is a class in which out is a static field whose type supports the println method.

On the other hand, `java.util.Date` is a class, so you can import it (or `java.util.*` if you want everything from the package). If you are having problems importing something, check to make sure that you are importing a type.

Classes are always in a package. A package is named by providing a package declaration at the top of the source file:

```
package com.sun.games;

class Card {
    // ...
}
```

If a package is not specified via a `package` declaration, the class is made part of an *unnamed package*. An unnamed package is adequate for an application (or applet) that is not loaded with any other code. Classes destined for a library should be written in named packages.

1.15 The Java Platform

The Java programming language is designed to maximize portability. Many details are specifically defined for all implementations. For example, a `double` is a 64-bit IEEE 754-1985 floating-point number. Many languages leave precise definitions to particular implementations, making only general guarantees such as minimum range, or they provide a way to ask the system what the range is on the current platform.

These portable definitions for the Java programming language are specific all the way down to the machine language into which code is translated. Source code is compiled into Java *bytecodes*, which are designed to be run on a Java *virtual machine*. Bytecodes are a machine language for an abstract machine, executed by the virtual machine on each system that supports the Java programming language.[1] Other languages can also be compiled into Java bytecodes.

The virtual machine provides a *runtime* system, which provides access to the virtual machine itself (for example, a way to start the garbage collector) and to the outside world (such as the output stream `System.out`). The runtime system checks security-sensitive operations with a *security manager* or *access controller*. The security manager could, for example, forbid the application to read or write the local disk, or could allow network connections only to particular machines.

---

[1] A system can, of course, implement the Java virtual machine in silicon—that is, using a special-purpose chip. This does not affect the portability of the bytecodes; it is just another virtual machine implementation.

Exactly what an application is allowed to do, is determined by the *security policy* in force when the application runs.

When classes are loaded into a virtual machine, they will first be checked by a *verifier* that ensures the bytecodes are properly formed and meet security and safety guarantees (for example, that the bytecodes never attempt to use an integer as a reference to gain access to parts of memory).

These features combined give platform independence to provide a security model suitable for executing code downloaded across the network at varying levels of trust. Source code compiled into Java bytecodes can be run on any machine that has a Java virtual machine. The code can be executed with an appropriate level of protection to prevent careless or malicious class writers from harming the system. The level of trust can be adjusted depending on the source of the bytecodes—bytecodes on the local disk or protected network can be trusted more than bytecodes fetched from arbitrary machines elsewhere in the world.

1.16 Other Topics Briefly Noted

There are several other features that we mention briefly here and cover later in more detail:

- *Threads:* The language has built-in support for creating multithreaded applications. It uses per-object and per-class monitor-style locks to synchronize concurrent access to object and class data. See Chapter 10 for more details.

- *Type classes:* There are classes to represent the primitive types (such as `Integer`, `Double`, and `Boolean`) and a reflection mechanism to allow browsing class types and their members. See Chapter 11 for more information about programming with types.

- *I/O:* The `java.io` package provides many different kinds of input and output operations. See Chapter 15 for specifics of the I/O capabilities.

- *Collections:* You will find many useful collection classes, such as `List` and `HashMap` in the `java.util` package. See Chapter 16 for more information about collections.

- *Utility interfaces and classes:* The `java.util` package has many other useful classes, such as `BitSet` and `Date`. See Chapter 17 for more information about these utility classes.

Careful—we don't want to learn from this!
—Calvin and Hobbes

CHAPTER 2

Classes and Objects

First things first, but not necessarily in that order.
—Dr. Who, *Meglos*

THE fundamental programming unit of the Java programming language is the *class*. Classes provide the structure for *objects* and the mechanisms to manufacture objects from a class definition. Classes define *methods*: collections of executable code that are the focus of computation and which manipulate the data stored in objects. Methods provide the behavior of the objects of a class. Although you can compute using only primitive types—integer, floating-point, and so on—almost any interesting program will create and manipulate objects.

Object-oriented programming strictly separates the notion of *what* is to be done from *how* it is done. "What" is described as a set of methods (and sometimes publicly available data) and their associated semantics. This combination—methods, data, and semantics—is often described as a *contract* between the designer of the class and the programmer who uses it, because it says what happens when certain methods are invoked on an object. This contract defines a *type* such that all objects that are instances of that type are known to honor that contract.

A common assumption is that the methods declared in a class are its entire contract. The semantics of those operations are also part of the contract, even though they may be described only in documentation. Two methods may have the same name and parameters and throw the same exceptions, but they are not equivalent if they have different semantics. For example, not every method called `print` can be assumed to print a copy of the object. Someone might define a `print` method with the semantics "process interval" or "prioritize nonterminals." The contract of the method, both signature and semantics together, defines what it means.

The "how" of an object is defined by its class, which defines the implementation of the methods the object supports. Each object is an *instance* of a class. When a method is invoked on an object, the class is examined to find the code to

35

be run. An object can use other objects to do its job, but we start with simple classes that implement all their own methods directly.

2.1   A Simple Class

Here is a simple class, called Body that could be used to store data about celestial bodies such as comets, asteroids, planets and stars:

```
class Body {
    public long idNum;
    public String name;
    public Body orbits;

    public static long nextID = 0;
}
```

A class is declared using the keyword class, giving the class a name and listing the class members between curly braces. A class declaration creates a *type name*, so references to objects of that type can be declared with a simple

```
Body mercury;
```

This declaration states that mercury is a variable that can hold a reference to an object of type Body. The declaration does *not* create an object—it declares only a *reference* that is allowed to refer to a Body object. During its existence, the reference mercury may refer to any number of Body objects. These objects must be explicitly created. In this respect, the Java programming language is different from languages in which objects are created when you declare variables.

This first version of Body is poorly designed. This is intentional: we will demonstrate the value of certain language features as we improve the class in this chapter.

2.1.1   Class Members

A class can have three kinds of members:

- ◆ *Fields* are the data variables associated with a class and its objects, and hold the state of the class or object.
- ◆ *Methods* contain the executable code of a class and define the behavior of objects.

◆ *Nested classes* and *nested interfaces* are declarations of classes or interfaces that occur nested within the declaration of another class or interface.

In this chapter we concentrate on the basic members: fields and methods. Nested members are discussed in Chapter 5.

2.1.2   Class Modifiers

A class declaration can be preceded by class *modifiers* that give the class certain properties:

◆ *public*—a `public` class is publicly accessible—anyone can declare references to objects of the class or access its public members. Without this modifier a class is only accessible within its own *package*. You'll learn about general access control in Section 2.3 on page 41. Packages and related accessibility issues of classes and members are discussed in Chapter 13.

◆ *abstract*—an `abstract` class is considered incomplete and no instances of the class may be created. Usually this is because the class contains `abstract` methods that must be implemented by a subclass. You'll learn about this in "Abstract Classes and Methods" on page 85.

◆ *final*—a `final` class cannot be subclassed. Subclassing is discussed in Chapter 3.

◆ *strict floating point*—a class declared `strictfp` has all floating point arithmetic, defined within the class, evaluated strictly. See "Strict and non-Strict Floating-Point Arithmetic" on page 158 for details.

A class cannot be both `final` and `abstract`.

A class declaration can be preceded by several modifiers. Modifiers are allowed in any order, but we recommend that you adopt a consistent order to improve the readability of your code. We always use, and recommend, the order listed.

While we won't be concerned about class modifiers in this chapter you need to know a little about `public` classes. Most Java development tools require that a `public` class be declared in a file with the same name as the class and consequently, there can only be one `public` class declared per file.

Exercise 2.1: Write a simple `Vehicle` class that has fields for (at least) current speed, current direction in degrees, and owner name.

Exercise 2.2: Write a `LinkedList` class that has a field of type `Object` and a reference to the next `LinkedList` element in the list.

2.2   Fields

A class's variables are called *fields;* the `Body` class's `name` and `orbits` variables are examples. A field declaration consists of a type name followed by the field name and optionally an *initialization clause* to give the field an initial value. Every `Body` object has its own specific instances of three fields: a `long` that uniquely identifies the body from all others, a `String` that is its name, and a reference to another `Body` around which it orbits. Giving each separate object a different instance of the fields means that each object has its own unique state—such fields are known as *instance variables*. Changing the `orbits` field in one `Body` object does not affect the `orbits` field in any other `Body` object.

Field declarations can also be preceded by modifiers that control certain properties of the field. These modifiers consist of:

- *access modifiers*—discussed in Section 2.3 on page 41.
- *static*—discussed below
- *final*—discussed below
- *transient*—relates to object serialization and is discussed in "Object Serialization" on page 404.
- *volatile*—relates to synchronization and memory model issues and is discussed in "`volatile`" on page 260.

A field cannot be both `final` and `volatile`.

When multiple modifiers are applied to the same field declaration, we recommend using the order listed.

2.2.1   Field Initialization

When a field is declared it can be initialized by assigning it a value of the corresponding type. In the `Body` example, the `nextID` field is initialized to the value zero. The initialization expression, or more simply the *initializer*, need not be a constant however, it could be another field, a method invocation or an expression involving all of these. The only requirement is that the initializer be of the right type and, if invoking a method, no checked exceptions may be thrown as there is no surrounding code to catch the exception. For example, the following are all valid initializers:

```
double zero = 0.0;             // constant
double sum = 4.5 + 3.7;        // constant expression
double zeroCopy = zero;        // field
double rootTwo = Math.sqrt(2); // method invocation
double someVal = sum + 2*Math.sqrt(rootTwo); // mixed
```

Although initializers provide a great deal of flexibility in the way fields can be initialized, they are only suitable for simple initialization schemes. For more complex schemes we need additional tools—as we shall soon see.

If a field is not initialized a default initial value is assigned to it depending on its type:

Type	Initial Value
boolean	false
char	'\u0000'
byte, short, int, long	0
float	+0.0f
double	+0.0
object reference	null

2.2.2 Static Fields

Sometimes you want only one instance of a field shared by all objects of a class. You create such fields by declaring them static, so they are called *static fields* or *class variables*. When you declare a static field in a class only one copy of the field exists, no matter how many instances of the class are created.

In our case, Body has one static field, nextID, which contains the next body identifier to use. The nextID field is initialized to zero when the class is initialized after it is loaded—see "Loading Classes" on page 303. You will see that each newly created Body object will be assigned the current value of nextID as its identifier, and the value of nextID will be incremented. Hence we only want one copy of the nextID field, to be used when creating all Body instances.

Within its own class a static field can be referred to directly, but when accessed externally it must be accessed via the class name. For example, we could print the value of nextID as follows:

```
System.out.println(Body.nextID);
```

The use of System.out itself illustrates accessing a static field.

A static member may also be accessed via a reference to an object of that class, for example:

```
System.out.println(mercury.nextID);
```

but this form should be avoided as it gives the false impression that `nextID` is a member of the object `mercury`, not a member of the class `Body`. It is the type of the reference, not the type of the object it refers to, that determines the class to look in for the static variable. The reference can even be `null`.

In this book when we use the term *field,* we usually mean the non-static kind. When the context makes it ambiguous, we will use the term *non-static field* to be clear.

Exercise 2.3: Add a static field to your `Vehicle` class to hold the next vehicle identification number, and a non-static field to the `Vehicle` class to hold each car's ID number.

2.2.3   `final` Fields

A `final` variable is one whose value cannot be changed after it has been initialized—any attempt to assign to such a field will produce a compile-time error. We have seen `final` fields used to define named constants because constants don't change value. In general, a `final` field is used to define an *immutable* property of a class or object—a property that doesn't change for the lifetime of the class or object.

If a `final` field does not have an initializer it is termed a *blank final*. This is useful when simple initialization is not appropriate for the field. Such fields must be initialized once the class has been initialized (in the case of static `final` fields), or once an object of the class has been fully constructed (for non-static `final` fields). The compiler will ensure that this is done and refuse to compile a class if it determines that a `final` field does not get initialized.

Whether a property is immutable is determined by the semantics of the application for which the class was designed. When you decide whether a field should be `final`, consider three things:

- ◆ Does the field represent an immutable property of the object?
- ◆ Is the value of the field always known at the time the object is created?
- ◆ Is it always practical and appropriate to set the value of the field when the object is created?

If the property is merely infrequently changed rather than truly immutable then a `final` field is not appropriate. If the value of the field is not known when the object is created then it can't be made `final`, even if it is logically immutable once known. For example, in a simulation of celestial bodies a comet may become trapped by the gravitational pull of a star and commence to orbit that star. Once trapped the comet orbits the star forever or until it is destroyed. In this situation the `orbits` field will hold an immutable value once set, but that value is not known when the comet object is created and so the field cannot be `final`. Finally, if initialization of the field is expensive and the field's value is infrequently needed, then it may be more practical to defer the initialization of the field until its value is needed—this is generally termed *lazy initialization*—which cannot be done to a `final` field.

There are additional considerations concerning `final` fields if your object must be clonable—these are discussed in "Cloning Objects" on page 89.

Exercise 2.4: Consider your solution to Exercise 2.3. Do you think the identification number field should be `final`?

2.3 Access Control

If every member of every class and object was accessible to every other class and object then understanding, debugging and maintaining programs would be an almost impossible task. The contracts presented by classes could not be relied upon because any piece of code could directly access a field and change it in such a way as to violate the contract. One of the strengths of object-oriented programming is its support for *encapsulation* and *data-hiding*. To achieve this we need a way to control who has access to what members of a class or interface, and even access to the class or interface itself. This control is specified by using *access modifiers* on class, interface and member declarations.

All members of a class are always available to code in the class itself. To control access from other classes, class members have four possible access modifiers:

- *private*—members declared `private` are accessible only in the class itself.
- *package*—members declared with no access modifier are accessible in classes in the same package, as well as in the class itself. We discuss packages and related accessibility issues in Chapter 13.
- *protected*—members declared `protected` are accessible in subclasses of the class, in classes in the same package, and in the class itself. Extending classes is covered in Chapter 3.

♦ *public*—members declared `public` are accessible anywhere the class is accessible.

The `private` and `protected` access modifiers apply only to members not to the classes or interfaces themselves (unless nested). For a member to be accessible from a section of code in some class, the member's class must first be accessible from that code.

It is important to realize that access control is performed on a per-class (or interface) level not a per-object level. This means that members of a class are always accessible from all code written in that class regardless of which instance the code is being applied to. We'll illustrate this with an example later when we look at how methods can also be used to control access—Section 2.6.5 on page 57.

You should view public and protected members as contractual, because they can be relied upon by code you do not control. Changing them can be impossible after that code relies upon public or protected functionality. Package and private access are part of your implementation, hidden from outsiders (classes in the same package should be related).

We declared the Body class's fields `public` because programmers need access to them to do the work the class is designed for. In a later version of the Body class, you will see that such a design is not usually a good idea.

2.4   Creating Objects

In this first version of Body, objects that represent particular celestial bodies are created and initialized like this:

```
Body sun = new Body();
sun.idNum = Body.nextID++;
sun.name = "Sol";
sun.orbits = null; // in solar system, sun is middle

Body earth = new Body();
earth.idNum = Body.nextID++;
earth.name = "Earth";
earth.orbits = sun;
```

First we declare a reference variable (sun) that can refer to objects of type Body. As mentioned before, such a declaration does *not* create an object; it only defines a variable that *references* objects. The object it refers to must be created explicitly.

We create the object `sun` refers to using `new`. The `new` construct is by far the most common way to create objects (we cover the other ways in Chapter 11). When you create an object with `new`, you specify the type of object you want to create and any arguments for its construction. The runtime system allocates enough space to store the fields of the object and initializes it in ways you will soon see. When initialization is complete, the runtime system returns a reference to the new object.

If the system cannot find enough free space to create the object, it may have to run the garbage collector to try to reclaim space. If the system still cannot find enough free space, `new` throws an `OutOfMemoryError` exception.

Having created a new `Body` object, we initialize its variables. Each `Body` object needs a unique identifier, which it gets from the static `nextID` field of `Body`. The code must increment `nextID` so that the next `Body` object created will get a unique identifier.

We then make an `earth` object in a similar fashion. This example builds a solar system model. In this model, the Sun is in the center, and `sun`'s `orbits` field is `null` because it doesn't orbit anything. When we create and initialize `earth`, we set its `orbits` field to `sun`. A `moon` object would have its `orbits` field set to `earth`. In a model of the galaxy, the `sun` would orbit around the black hole presumed to be at the middle of the Milky Way.

You create objects using `new`, but you never delete them explicitly. The virtual machine manages memory for you using *garbage collection,* which means that objects that you cannot possibly use any longer can have their space reclaimed automatically by the virtual machine without your intervention. If you no longer need an object you should cease referring to it. With local variables in methods this can be as simple as returning from the method—when the method is no longer executing none of its variables can possibly be used. For more durable references, such as fields of objects, you can set them to `null`. Memory management is discussed in more detail in Chapter 12.

Exercise 2.5: Write a `main` method for your `Vehicle` class that creates a few vehicles and prints their field values.

Exercise 2.6: Write a `main` method for your `LinkedList` class that creates a few objects of type `Vehicle` and places them into successive nodes in the list.

2.5 Construction and Initialization

A newly created object is given an initial state. Fields can be initialized with a value when they are declared, or can accept their default value, which is sometimes sufficient to ensure a correct initial state. But often you need more than simple initialization to create the initial state; the creating code may need to supply initial data or perform operations that cannot be expressed as simple assignment.

2.5.1   Constructors

For purposes other than simple initialization, classes can have *constructors*. Constructors are blocks of statements that can be used to initialize an object before the reference to the object is returned by new. Constructors have the same name as the class they initialize. Like methods, they take zero or more arguments, but constructors are not methods and thus have no return type. Arguments, if any, are provided between the parentheses that follow the type name when the object is created with new. Constructors are invoked after the instance variables of a newly created object of the class have been assigned their default initial values and after their explicit initializers are executed.

This improved version of the Body class uses both constructors and initializers to set up each new object's initial state:

```
class Body {
    public long idNum;
    public String name = "<unnamed>";
    public Body orbits = null;

    private static long nextID = 0;

    Body() {
        idNum = nextID++;
    }
}
```

A constructor declaration consists of the class name followed by a (possibly empty) list of parameters within parentheses and a body of statements enclosed in curly braces. Constructors can have any of the same access modifiers as class members, but constructors are *not* members of a class—a distinction you can usually ignore, except when it comes to inheritance.

The constructor for Body takes no arguments, but it performs an important function—assigning a proper idNum to the newly created object. In the original code, a simple programmer error—forgetting to assign the idNum or not incrementing nextID after use—could result in different Body objects with the same idNum. That would create bugs in code that relies on the part of the contract that says "All idNum values are different."

By moving responsibility for idNum generation inside the Body class, we have prevented errors of this kind. The Body constructor is now the only entity that assigns idNum and is therefore the only entity that needs access to nextID. We can and should make nextID private so that only the Body class can access it. By doing so, we remove a source of error for programmers using the Body class.

We also are now free to change the way idNum values are assigned to Body objects. A future implementation of this class might, for example, look up the name in a database of known astronomical entities and assign a new idNum only if an idNum had not previously been assigned. This change would not affect any existing code, because existing code is not involved at all in the mechanism for idNum allocation.

The initializers for name and orbits set them to reasonable values. Therefore, when the constructor returns from the following invocations, all data fields in the new Body object have been set to some reasonable initial state. You can then set state in the object to the values you want:

```
Body sun = new Body();    // idNum is 0
sun.name = "Sol";

Body earth = new Body(); // idNum is 1
earth.name = "Earth";
earth.orbits = sun;
```

The Body constructor is invoked when new creates the object but *after* name and orbits have been set to their default initial values.

The case shown here—in which you know the name of the body and what it orbits when you create it—is likely to be fairly common. You can provide another constructor that takes both the name and the orbited body as arguments:

```
Body(String bodyName, Body orbitsAround) {
    this();
    name = bodyName;
    orbits = orbitsAround;
}
```

As shown here, one constructor can invoke another constructor from the same class using the this() invocation as its first executable statement. This is called an *explicit constructor invocation*. If the constructor you want to invoke has arguments, they can be passed to the constructor invocation—the type and number of arguments used determines which constructor gets invoked. Here we use it to invoke the constructor that has no arguments in order to set up the idNum. This means that we don't have to duplicate the idNum initialization code. Now the allocation code is much simpler:

```
Body sun = new Body("Sol", null);
Body earth = new Body("Earth", sun);
```

The argument list determines which version of the constructor is invoked as part of the new expression.

If provided, an explicit constructor invocation must be the first statement in the constructor body. Any expressions that are used as arguments for the explicit constructor invocation must not refer to any fields or methods of the current object—to all intents and purposes there is no current object at this stage of construction.

For completeness, you could also provide a one-argument constructor for constructing a Body object that doesn't orbit anything. This constructor would be used instead of invoking the two-argument Body constructor with a second argument of null:

```
Body(String bodyName) {
    this(bodyName, null);
}
```

and that is exactly what this constructor does, using another explicit constructor invocation.

Some classes always require that the creator supply certain kinds of data. For example, your application might require that all Body objects have a name. To ensure that all statements creating Body objects supply a name, you would define all Body constructors with a name parameter and you wouldn't bother initializing the name field.

Here are some common reasons for providing specialized constructors:

◆ Some classes have no reasonable initial state without parameters.

◆ Providing an initial state is convenient and reasonable when you're constructing some kinds of objects (the two-argument constructor of Body is an example).

◆ Constructing an object can be a potentially expensive operation, so you want objects to have a correct initial state when they're created. For example, if each object of a class had a table, a constructor to specify the initial size would enable the object to create the table with the right size from the beginning instead of creating a table of a default size which would later be discarded when the method that set the actual size was invoked.

◆ A constructor that isn't `public` restricts who can create objects using it. You could, for example, prevent programmers using your package from creating instances of a class by making all its constructors accessible only inside the package.

Constructors without arguments are so common that there is a term for them: they are called *no-arg* (for "no arguments") constructors. If you don't provide any constructors of any kind in a class, the language provides a default no-arg constructor that does nothing. This constructor—called the *default constructor*—is provided automatically only if no other constructors exist because there are classes for which a no-arg constructor would be incorrect (like the `Attr` class you will see in the next chapter). If you want both a no-arg constructor and one or more constructors with arguments, you must explicitly provide a no-arg constructor. The default constructor has the same accessibility as the class for which it was defined—if the class is `public` then the default constructor is `public`.

Another form of constructor is a *copy constructor*—this constructor takes an argument of the current object type and constructs the new object to be a copy of the passed in object. Usually this is simply a matter of assigning the same values to all fields, but sometimes the semantics of a class dictate more sophisticated actions. Here is a simple copy constructor for Body:

```
Body(Body other) {
    idNum = other.idNum;
    name = other.name;
    orbits = other.orbits;
}
```

This idiom is not used much within the Java class libraries, because the preferred way to make a copy of an object is by using the `clone` method—see "Cloning Objects" on page 89. However, the `String` class supports a copy constructor and the collections classes (described in Chapter 16) support more generalized copy constructors that allow one collection to be initialized with the same contents as another collection (which need not be of exactly the same type). Writing a correct copy constructor requires the same consideration as writing a correct `clone` method.

Constructors can also be declared to throw checked exceptions. The `throws` clause comes after the parameter list and before the opening curly brace of the constructor body. If a `throws` clause exists then any method that invokes this constructor as part of a `new` expression must either catch the declared exception or itself declare that it throws that exception. Exceptions and `throws` clauses are discussed in detail in Chapter 8.

Exercise 2.7: Add two constructors to `Vehicle`: a no-arg constructor and one that takes an initial owner's name. Modify the `main` program so that it generates the same output it did before.

Exercise 2.8: What constructors should you add to `LinkedList`?

2.5.2   Initialization Blocks

Another way to perform more complex initialization of fields is to use an *initialization block*. An initialization block is a block of statements that appears within the class declaration, outside of any member, or constructor, declaration and which initializes the fields of the object. It is executed as if it were placed at the beginning of every constructor in the class—with multiple blocks being executed in the order they appear in the class. An initialization block can throw a checked exception only if all of the classes constructors are declared to throw that exception.

For illustration, this variant of the `Body` class replaces the no-arg constructor with an equivalent initialization block:

```
class Body {
    public long idNum;
    public String name = "<unnamed>";
    public Body orbits = null;

    private static long nextID = 0;

    {
        idNum = nextID++;
    }

    public Body(String bodyName, Body orbitsAround) {
        name = bodyName;
        orbits = orbitsAround;
    }
}
```

Now the two-argument constructor doesn't need to perform the explicit invocation of the no-arg constructor, but we no longer have a no-arg constructor and so everyone is forced to use the two-argument constructor.

This wasn't a particularly interesting use of an initialization block but it did illustrate the syntax. In practice, initialization blocks tend to be used for non-trivial initialization, when construction arguments are not needed and there is a reason not to provide a no-arg constructor. Initialization is the purpose of having initialization blocks, but in practice you can make it do anything—the compiler won't check what it does.

2.5.3 Static Initialization

The static fields of a class can have initializers as we have already seen. But in addition we can perform more complex static initialization in a *static initialization block*. A static initialization block is much like a non-static initialization block except it is declared `static`, can only refer to static members of the class and cannot throw any checked exceptions. For example, creating a static array and initializing its elements sometimes must be done with executable statements. Here is example code to initialize a small array of prime numbers:

```
class Primes {
    static int[] knownPrimes = new int[4];

    static {
        knownPrimes[0] = 2;
        for (int i = 1; i < knownPrimes.length; i++)
            knownPrimes[i] = nextPrime();
    }
    // declaration of nextPrime ...
}
```

The order of initialization within a class is first-to-last—each field initializer or initialization block is executed before the next one, from the beginning of the source to the end. The static initializers are executed when the class is loaded. With this guarantee, our static block in the example is assured that the `knownPrimes` array is already created before the initialization code block executes. Similarly, anyone accessing a static field is guaranteed that the field has been initialized.

What if a static initializer in class X invokes a method in Y, but Y's static initializers invoke a method in X to set up *its* static values? This cyclic static initialization cannot be reliably detected during compilation because the code for Y may not be written when X is compiled. If cycles happen, X's static initializers will have been executed only to the point where Y's method was invoked. When Y, in turn, invokes the X method, that method runs with the rest of the static initializers yet to be executed. Any static fields in X that haven't had their initializers executed will still have their default values (`false`, `'\u0000'`, zero, or `null` depending on their type).

2.6   Methods

A class's *methods* typically contain the code that understands and manipulates an object's state. Some classes have `public` or `protected` fields for programmers to manipulate directly, but in most cases this isn't a very good idea (see "Designing a Class to Be Extended" on page 96). Many objects have tasks that cannot be represented as a simple value to be read or modified but require computation.

We have already seen a number of examples of methods in Chapter 1—all of our demonstration programs had a `main` method that was executed by the Java virtual machine. Here is another `main` method that creates a `Body` object and prints out the values of its fields.

```
class BodyPrint {
    public static void main(String[] args) {
        Body sun = new Body("Sol", null);
        Body earth = new Body("Earth", sun);
        System.out.println("Body " + earth.name +
                            " orbits " + earth.orbits.name +
                            " and has ID " + earth.idNum);
    }
}
```

A method declaration consists of two parts: the *method header* and the *method body*. The *method header* consists of a set of modifiers, the method return type, signature and a `throws` clause listing the exceptions thrown by the method. The method *signature* consists of the method name and the (possibly empty) parameter type list enclosed in parentheses. All methods must have a return type and signature, but modifiers and a `throws` clause are optional. Exceptions and `throws` clauses are discussed in detail in Chapter 8. The *method body* consists of statements enclosed between curly braces.

The method modifiers consist of the following:

- ◆ *access modifiers*— these were discussed on page 41.

- ◆ *abstract*—an `abstract` method is one whose body has not been defined in this class—the body is specified as a semicolon after the parameter list. A subclass is then responsible for providing a body for this method. This is discussed in "Abstract Classes and Methods" on page 85.

- ◆ *static*—discussed below

- ◆ *final*—a `final` method cannot be overridden in a subclass. This is discussed in "Marking Methods and Classes `final`" on page 84.

- *synchronized*—a `synchronized` method has additional semantics related to the control of concurrent threads within a program. This is discussed in "Synchronization" on page 235.

- *native*—discussed in Section 2.10 on page 63.

- *strict floating point*—a method declared `strictfp` has all floating point arithmetic evaluated strictly. If a method is declared within a class declared `strictfp`, then that method is implicitly declared `strictfp`. See "Strict and non-Strict Floating-Point Arithmetic" on page 158 for details.

An abstract method cannot be static, final, synchronized, native, or strict.

When multiple modifiers are applied to the same method declaration, we recommend using the order listed.

2.6.1 Static Methods

A `static` method is invoked on behalf of an entire class, not on a specific object instantiated from that class. Such methods are also known as *class methods*. A `static` method might perform a general task for all objects of the class, such as returning the next available serial number or something of that nature.

A `static` method can access only `static` fields and other `static` methods of the class. This is because non-`static` members have to be accessed via an object reference, and there is no object reference available within a static method—there is no `this` reference.

In this book when we use the term *method,* we usually mean the non-static kind. When the context makes it ambiguous, we will use the term *non-static method* to be clear.

Exercise 2.9: Add a static method to `Vehicle` that returns the highest identification number used thus far.

2.6.2 Method Invocations

Methods are *invoked* as operations on objects via references using the dot (`.`) operator:

reference.method(arguments)

In the `BodyPrint` example we invoke the `println` method on the object referred to by the static reference `System.out` and passing a single `String` argument formed by concatenating a number of other strings.

Each method is declared to have a specific number of parameters, each of a specific type: either a primitive type or a reference type. You cannot declare methods with a variable number of parameters—though you can declare a method with an array of objects as a parameter. When a method is invoked the caller must provide an argument of the appropriate type for each of the parameters declared by the method.

Methods also have a return type, either a primitive type or a reference type. If a method does not return any value, the place where a return type would go is filled with a `void`.

The `BodyPrint` example illustrates a common situation where you would like to examine the state of an object. Rather than having access to, and querying, all of the fields of the object, a class can define a method that returns a string representation of the state of the object. For example, here is a method of the `Body` class to return a `String` that describes the particular `Body` object it is invoked upon:

```
public String toString() {
    String desc = idNum + " (" + name + ")";
    if (orbits != null)
        desc += " orbits " + orbits.toString();
    return desc;
}
```

This method uses + and += to concatenate `String` objects. It first builds a string that describes the identifier and name. If the body orbits another body, we append the string that describes *that* body by invoking its `toString` method. This recursion builds a string of bodies orbiting other bodies until the chain ends with an object that doesn't orbit anything. The resulting string is then returned to the caller via the `return` statement.

The `toString` method of an object is special—it is invoked to get a `String` when an object is used in a string concatenation expression using the + operator. Consider these expressions:

```
System.out.println("Body " + sun);
System.out.println("Body " + earth);
```

The `toString` methods of `sun` and `earth` are invoked implicitly and produce the following output:

```
Body 0 (Sol)
Body 1 (Earth) orbits 0 (Sol)
```

All objects have a `toString` method whether their class explicitly defines one or not—this is because all classes extend the class `Object` and it defines the toString method. Class extension and the Object class are discussed in Chapter 3.

2.6.3 Method Execution and Return

When a method is invoked, the flow of control passes from the calling method into the invoked method and the statements of that method are executed in sequence according to the semantics of those statements. A method completes execution and returns to the caller when one of three things happens: a return statement is executed, the end of the method is reached or an uncaught exception is thrown.

If a method returns any result, it can only return a single result—either a primitive value or a reference to an object. Methods that need to return more than one result can achieve this effect in several ways: return references to objects that store the results as fields, take one or more parameters that reference objects in which to store the results, or return an array that contains the results. Suppose, for instance, that you want to write a method to return what a particular person can do with a given bank account. Multiple actions are possible (deposit, withdraw, and so on), so you must return multiple permissions. You could create a Permissions class whose objects store boolean values to say whether a particular action is allowed:

```java
public class Permissions {
    public boolean canDeposit,
                   canWithdraw,
                   canClose;
}
```

Here is a method that fills in the fields to return multiple values:

```java
public class BankAccount {
    private long number;     // account number
    private long balance;    // current balance

    public Permissions permissionsFor(Person who) {
        Permissions perm = new Permissions();
        perm.canDeposit = canDeposit(who);
        perm.canWithdraw = canWithdraw(who);
        perm.canClose = canClose(who);
        return perm;
    }

    // ... define canDeposit et al ...
}
```

In methods that return a value, every path through the method must either return a value that is *assignable* to a variable of the declared return type, or else throw an exception. The permissionsFor method could not return, say, a String, because you cannot assign a String object to a variable of type Permissions. But you could declare the return type of permissionsFor as Object without changing the return statement, because you can assign a Permissions object reference to a variable of type Object, as all classes extend Object as we have previously mentioned. The notion of being assignable is discussed in detail in Chapter 3.

Exercise 2.10: Add a toString method to Vehicle.

Exercise 2.11: Add a toString method to LinkedList.

2.6.4 Parameter Values

All parameters to methods are passed "by value." In other words, values of parameter variables in a method are copies of the values the invoker specified as arguments. If you pass a double to a method, its parameter is a copy of whatever value was being passed as an argument, and the method can change its parameter's value without affecting values in the code that invoked the method. For example:

```
class PassByValue {
    public static void main(String[] args) {
        double one = 1.0;

        System.out.println("before: one = " + one);
        halveIt(one);
        System.out.println("after:  one = " + one);
    }

    public static void halveIt(double arg) {
        arg /= 2.0;     // divide arg by two
        System.out.println("halved: arg = " + arg);
    }
}
```

The following output illustrates that the value of arg inside halveIt is divided by two without affecting the value of the variable one in main:

```
before: one = 1.0
halved: arg = 0.5
after:  one = 1.0
```

You should note that when the parameter is an object reference, the object *reference*—not the object itself—is what is passed "by value." Thus, you can change which object a parameter refers to inside the method without affecting the reference that was passed. But if you change any fields of the object or invoke methods that change the object's state, the object is changed for every part of the program that holds a reference to it. Here is an example to show this distinction:

```
class PassRef {
    public static void main(String[] args) {
        Body sirius = new Body("Sirius", null);

        System.out.println("before: " + sirius);
        commonName(sirius);
        System.out.println("after:  " + sirius);
    }

    public static void commonName(Body bodyRef) {
        bodyRef.name = "Dog Star";
        bodyRef = null;
    }
}
```

This program produces the following output:

```
before: 0 (Sirius)
after:  0 (Dog Star)
```

Notice that the contents of the object have been modified with a name change, while the variable sirius still refers to the Body object even though the method commonName changed the value of its bodyRef parameter variable to null. This requires some explanation.

The following diagram shows the state of the variables just after `main` invokes `commonName`:

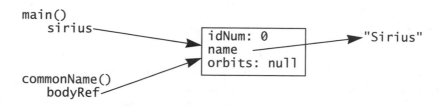

At this point, the two variables `sirius` (in `main`) and `bodyRef` (in `commonName`) both refer to the same underlying object. When `commonName` changes the field `bodyRef.name`, the name is changed in the underlying object that the two variables share. When `commonName` changes the value of `bodyRef` to `null`, only the value of the `bodyRef` variable is changed; the value of `sirius` remains unchanged because the parameter `bodyRef` is a pass-by-value copy of `sirius`. Inside the method `commonName`, all you are changing is the value in the parameter variable `bodyRef`, just as all you changed in `halveIt` was the value in the parameter variable `arg`. If changing `bodyRef` affected the value of `sirius` in `main`, the "after" line would say "null". However, the variable `bodyRef` in `commonName` and the variable `sirius` in `main` both refer to the same underlying object, so the change made inside `commonName` is visible through the reference `sirius`.

Some people will say incorrectly that objects are passed "by reference." In programming language design, the term *pass by reference* properly means that when an argument is passed to a function, the invoked function gets a reference to the original value, not a copy of its value. If the function modifies its parameter, the value in the calling code will be changed because the argument and parameter use the same slot in memory. If the Java programming language actually had pass-by-reference parameters, there would be a way to declare `halveIt` so that the preceding code would modify the value of `one`, or so that `commonName` could change the variable `sirius` to `null`. This is not possible. The Java programming language does not pass objects by reference; it passes object references by value. Because two copies of the same reference refer to the same actual object, changes made through one reference variable are visible through the other. There is exactly one parameter passing mode—pass by value—and that helps keep things simple.

You can declare method parameters to be `final`, meaning that the value of the parameter will not change while the method is executing. Had `bodyRef` been declared `final`, the compiler would not have allowed you to change its value to `null`. When you do not intend to change a parameter's value, you can declare it `final` so the compiler can enforce this expectation. The declaration can also help the compiler or virtual machine optimize some expressions using the parameter, because it is known to remain the same. A `final` modifier on a parameter is an implementation detail that affects only the method's code, not the invoking code, so you can change whether a parameter is `final` without affecting any invoking code.

2.6.5 Using Methods to Control Access

The Body class with its various constructors is considerably easier to use than its simple data-only form, and we have ensured that the `idNum` is set both automatically and correctly. But a programmer could still mess up the object by setting its `idNum` field after construction, because the `idNum` field is `public` and therefore exposed to change. The `idNum` should be read-only data. Read-only data in objects is common, but there is no keyword to apply to a field that allows read-only access outside the class while letting the class itself modify the field.

To enforce read-only access, you must either make the field `final`, which makes it read-only for the lifetime of the object, or you must hide it. You hide the field by making the `idNum` field `private` and providing a new method so that code outside the class can read its value using that method:

```
class Body {
    private long idNum;     // now "private"

    public String name = "<unnamed>";
    public Body orbits = null;

    private static long nextID = 0;

    Body() {
        idNum = nextID++;
    }

    public long getID() {
        return idNum;
    }

    //...
}
```

Now programmers who want to use the body's identifier will invoke the `getID` method, which returns the value. There is no longer any way for programmers to modify the identifier—it has effectively become a read-only value outside the class. It can be modified only by the internal methods of the Body class.

Methods that regulate access to internal data are sometimes called *accessor methods*.

Even if an application doesn't require fields to be read-only, making fields private and adding methods to set and fetch them enables you to add actions that may be needed in the future. If programmers can access a class's fields directly, you have no control over the values they will use or what happens when values are changed. Additionally, making a field part of the contract of a class locks in the implementation of that class—you can't change the implementation without forcing all clients to be recompiled. For example, a future version of Body may want to look-up the ID number in a database indexed by the body's name and not actually store the ID number in the object at all. Such a change cannot be made if idNum is accessible to clients. For these reasons, you will see very few public or protected fields in subsequent examples in this book.

Methods to get or set a value in an object's state are sometimes said to define a *property* of that object. For example, the Body class's getID can be said to define an ID property for Body objects that is retrieved by the getID method, and implemented by the idNum field. Some automatic systems, including those for the JavaBeans™ component architecture, use these conventions to provide automatic property manipulation systems; see "java.beans—Components" on page 533. We can and should define the name and orbits fields to be properties by making them private and providing set and get methods for them:

```
class Body {
    private long idNum;
    private String name = "<unnamed>";
    private Body orbits = null;

    private static long nextID = 0;

    // constructors omitted ...

    public long getID() { return idNum; }
    public String getName() { return name; }
    public void setName(String newName) {
        name = newName;
    }
    public Body getOrbits() { return orbits; }
    public void setOrbits(Body orbitsAround) {
        orbits = orbitsAround;
    }
}
```

Marking a field as `final` is sometimes an alternative that prevents unwanted modifications to a field but immutability and accessibility should not be confused. If a field is immutable then it should be declared `final` regardless of accessibility. Conversely, if you don't want a field to form part of the contract of a class you should hide it behind a method, regardless of whether the field is read-only or modifiable.

Now that we have made all the fields of `Body` private, we can return to an earlier comment that access control is per-class not per-object. Suppose a body could be captured by another body and forced to orbit around it, we could define the following method in `Body`:

```
public void capture(Body victim) {
    victim.orbits = this;
}
```

If access control were per-object, then the `capture` method when invoked on one object would not be able to access the private `orbits` field of the `victim` body object to modify it. But because access control is per-class, the code of a method in a class has access to all the fields of all objects of that class—it simply needs a reference to the object, such as via a parameter as above. Some object-oriented languages advocate per-object access control, but the Java programming language is not one of them.

Exercise 2.12: Make the fields in your `Vehicle` class `private`, and add accessor methods for the fields. Which fields should have methods to change them, and which should not?

Exercise 2.13: Make the fields in your `LinkedList` class `private`, and add accessor methods for the fields. Which fields should have methods to change them, and which should not?

Exercise 2.14: Add a `changeSpeed` method that changes the current speed of the vehicle to a passed-in value and add a `stop` method that sets the speed to zero.

Exercise 2.15: Add a method to `LinkedList` to return the number of elements in a list.

2.7 `this`

You have already seen (on page 45) how you can use an explicit constructor invocation to invoke another one of your class's constructors at the beginning of a constructor. You can also use the special object reference `this` inside a non-static method, where it refers to the current object on which the method was invoked. There is no `this` reference in a `static` method because there is no specific object being operated on.

The `this` reference is most commonly used as a way to pass a reference to the current object as an argument to other methods. Suppose a method requires adding the current object to a list of objects awaiting some service. It might look something like this:

```
service.add(this);
```

The `capture` method in class Body also used `this` to set the value of the victim's `orbits` field to the current object.

An explicit `this` can be added to the beginning of any field access or method invocation in the current object. For example, the assignment to `name` in the Body class two-argument constructor:

```
name = bodyName;
```

is equivalent to the following:

```
this.name = bodyName;
```

Conventionally, you use `this` only when it is needed: when the name of the field you need to access is hidden by a local variable or parameter declaration. For example, we could have written the two-argument Body constructor as:

```
public Body(String name, Body orbits) {
    this();
    this.name = name;
    this.orbits = orbits;
}
```

The `name` and `orbits` fields are hidden from the constructor by the parameters of the same name. To access, for example, the `name` field instead of the `name` parameter, we prefix it with `this` to specify that the name is for the field belonging to "this" object. Deliberately hiding identifiers in this manner is considered acceptable programming practice only in this idiomatic use in constructors and "set" methods. The way in which names are resolved is discussed in "The Meanings of Names" on page 152.

2.8 Overloading Methods

Each method has a *signature*, which is its name together with the number and types of its parameters. Two methods can have the same name if they have different numbers or types of parameters and thus different signatures. This feature is called *overloading*, because the simple name of the method has an overloaded (more than one) meaning. When you invoke a method, the compiler compares the number and type of arguments to find the method that best matches the available signatures. Here are some orbitsAround methods for our Body class that return true if the current body orbits around the specified body, or a body with the specified identifier:

```
public boolean orbitsAround(Body other) {
    return (orbits == other);
}

public boolean orbitsAround(long id) {
    return (orbits != null && orbits.idNum == id);
}
```

Both methods declare one parameter, but the type of the parameter differs. If the method orbitsAround is invoked with a Body reference as an argument, the version of the method that declares a Body parameter is invoked—that version compares the passed in reference to the body's own orbits reference. If orbitsAround is invoked with a long argument, the version of the method that declares a long parameter is invoked—that version of the method compares the passed in identification number with the idNum field of the object it orbits. If the invocation matches neither of these signatures, the code will not compile.

The signature does not include the return type or the list of thrown exceptions, and you cannot overload methods based on these factors. A full discussion of how the language chooses which available overloaded method to invoke for a given invocation can be found in "Member Access" on page 173.

As you may have realized, constructors can also be overloaded in the same way that methods are.

Exercise 2.16: Add two turn methods to Vehicle: one that takes a number of degrees to turn, and one that takes either of the constants Vehicle.TURN_LEFT or Vehicle.TURN_RIGHT.

2.9   The `main` Method

Details of invoking an application vary from system to system, but whatever the details, you must always provide the name of a class that drives the application. When you run a program, the system locates and runs the `main` method for that class. The `main` method must be `public`, `static`, and `void` (it returns nothing), and it must accept a single argument of type `String[]`. Here is an example that prints its arguments:

```
class Echo {
    public static void main(String[] args) {
        for (int i = 0; i < args.length; i++)
            System.out.print(args[i] + " ");
        System.out.println();
    }
}
```

The arguments in the string array passed to `main` are the *program arguments*. They are usually typed by users when they run the program. For example, on a command-line system such as UNIX or a DOS shell, you might invoke the `Echo` application this way:

```
java Echo in here
```

In this command, `java` is the Java bytecode interpreter, `Echo` is the name of the class, and the rest of the words are the program arguments. The `java` command finds the compiled bytecodes for the class `Echo`, loads them into a Java virtual machine, and invokes `Echo.main` with the program arguments contained in strings in the `String` array. The result is the following output:

```
in here
```

The name of the class is not included in the strings passed to `main`. You already know the name because it is the name of the class in which `main` is declared.

An application can have any number of `main` methods because each class in the application can have one. Only one `main` is used any given time you run a program. The `main` that's actually used is specified when the program is run, as `Echo` was.

Exercise 2.17: Change `Vehicle.main` to create cars with owners whose names are specified on the command line, and then print them.

2.10 Native Methods

If you need to write a program that will use some existing code that isn't written in the Java programming language, or if you need to manipulate some hardware directly, you can write *native methods*. A native method lets you implement a method that can be invoked from the Java programming language but is written in a "native" language, usually C or C++. Native methods are declared using the `native` modifier. Because the method is implemented in another language, the method body is specified as a semicolon. For example, here is a declaration of a native method that queries the operating system for the CPU identifier of the host machine:

```
public native int getCPUID();
```

Other than being implemented in native code, native methods are like all other methods: they can be overloaded, overridden, `final`, `static`, `synchronized`, `public`, `protected` or `private`. A native method cannot, however, be declared `abstract`, nor `strictfp`.

If you use a native method, all portability and safety of the code are lost. You cannot, for instance, use a native method in almost any code you expect to download and run from across a network connection (an applet, for example). The downloading system may or may not be of the same architecture, and even if it is, it might not trust your system well enough to run arbitrary native code.

Native methods are implemented using an API provided by the people who wrote the virtual machine on which the code executes. The standard one for C programmers is called JNI—Java Native Interface. Others are being defined for other native languages. A description of these APIs is beyond the scope of this book.

> *The significant problems we face cannot be solved*
> *by the same level of thinking that created them.*
> —Albert Einstein

CHAPTER 3

Extending Classes

You will understand this when I tell you that I can trace
my ancestry back to a protoplasmal primordial atomic globule.
—Gilbert and Sullivan, *The Mikado*

THE quick tour (Chapter 1) described briefly how a class can be *extended*, or *subclassed*, and how an object of an extended class can be used wherever the original class is required. The term for this capability is *polymorphism*, meaning that an object of a given class can have multiple forms, either as its own class or as any class it extends. The new class is a *subclass* or *extended class* of the class it extends; the class that is extended is its *superclass*.

The collection of methods and fields that are accessible from outside a class, together with the description of how those members are expected to behave, is often referred to as the class's *contract*. The contract is what the class designer has promised that the class will do. Class extension provides two forms of inheritance:

♦ inheritance of *contract* or *type*, whereby the subclass acquires the type of the superclass and thus can be used polymorphically wherever the superclass could be used; and

♦ inheritance of *implementation*, whereby the subclass acquires the implementation of the superclass in terms of its accessible fields and methods.

Class extension can be used for a number of purposes. Most commonly class extension is used for *specialization*—where the extended class defines new behavior and so becomes a specialized version of its superclass. Class extension may involve changing only the implementation of an inherited method, perhaps to make it more efficient. Whenever you extend a class, you create a new class with an expanded contract. You do not, however, change the part of the contract you inherit from the class you extended. Changing the way that the superclass's contract is implemented is reasonable, but you should never change the implementation in a way that violates that contract.

The ability to extend classes interacts with the access control mechanisms to expand the notion of contract that a class presents. Each class can present two different contracts—one for users of the class and one for extenders of the class. Both of these contracts must be carefully designed.

With class extension, inheritance of contract and inheritance of implementation always occur together. However, you can define new types independent of implementation using *interfaces*. You can also re-use existing implementations, without affecting type, by manually using *composition* and *forwarding*. Interfaces and composition are discussed in Chapter 4.

3.1   An Extended Class

To demonstrate subclassing, we start with a basic attribute class designed to store name–value pairs. Attribute names are human-readable strings, such as "color" or "location." Attribute values are determined by the kind of attribute; for example, a "location" may have a string value representing a street address, or it may be a set of integer values representing latitude and longitude.

```
class Attr {
    private final String name;
    private Object value = null;

    public Attr(String name) {
        this.name = name;
    }

    public Attr(String name, Object value) {
        this.name = name;
        this.value = value;
    }

    public String getName() {
        return name;
    }

    public Object getValue() {
        return value;
    }

    public Object setValue(Object newValue) {
```

```
            Object oldVal = value;
            value = newValue;
            return oldVal;
        }

        public String toString() {
            return name + "='" + value + "'";
        }
    }
```

An attribute must have a name, so each `Attr` constructor requires a name parameter. The name must be immutable (and so is marked `final`) because it may be used, for example, as a key into a hashtable or sorted list. In such a case, if the `name` field were modified, the attribute object would become "lost" because it would be filed under the old name, not the modified one. Attributes can have any type of value, so the value is stored in a variable of type `Object`. The value can be changed at any time. Both `name` and `value` are `private` members so that they can be accessed only via the appropriate methods. This ensures that the contract of `Attr` is always honored and allows the designer of `Attr` the freedom to change implementation details in the future without affecting clients of the class.

Every class you have seen so far is an extended class, whether or not it is declared as such. A class such as `Attr` that does not explicitly extend another class implicitly extends the `Object` class. `Object` is at the root of the class hierarchy. The `Object` class declares methods that are implemented by all objects—such as the `toString` method you saw in Chapter 2. Variables of type `Object` can refer to any object, whether it is a class instance or an array. The `Object` class itself is described in more detail on page 85.

The next class extends the notion of attribute to store color attributes, which might be strings that name or describe colors. Color descriptions might be color names like "red" or "ecru" that must be looked up in a table, or numeric values that can be decoded to produce a standard, more efficient color representation we call `ScreenColor` (assumed to be defined elsewhere). Decoding a description into a `ScreenColor` object is expensive enough that you would like to do it only once. So we extend the `Attr` class to create a `ColorAttr` class to support a method to retrieve a decoded `ScreenColor` object. We implement it so the decoding is done only once:

```
    class ColorAttr extends Attr {
        private ScreenColor myColor; // the decoded color

        public ColorAttr(String name, Object value) {
            super(name, value);
```

```java
            decodeColor();
        }

        public ColorAttr(String name) {
            this(name, "transparent");
        }

        public ColorAttr(String name, ScreenColor value) {
            super(name, value.toString());
            myColor = value;
        }

        public Object setValue(Object newValue) {
            // do the superclass's setValue work first
            Object retval = super.setValue(newValue);
            decodeColor();
            return retval;
        }

        /** Set value to ScreenColor, not description */
        public ScreenColor setValue(ScreenColor newValue) {
            // do the superclass's setValue work first
            super.setValue(newValue.toString());
            ScreenColor oldValue = myColor;
            myColor = newValue;
            return oldValue;
        }

        /** Return decoded ScreenColor object */
        public ScreenColor getColor() {
            return myColor;
        }

        /** set ScreenColor from description in getValue */
        protected void decodeColor() {
            if (getValue() == null)
                myColor = null;
            else
                myColor = new ScreenColor(getValue());
        }
    }
```

First we create a new `ColorAttr` class that extends the `Attr` class. The `ColorAttr` class does everything the `Attr` class does and adds new behavior. Therefore, the `Attr` class is the superclass of `ColorAttr`, and `ColorAttr` is a subclass of `Attr`. The *class hierarchy* for these classes looks like this, going bottom-up from subclass to superclass:

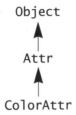

The extended `ColorAttr` class does three primary things:

- ◆ It provides three constructors: two to mirror its superclass and one to directly accept a `ScreenColor` object.
- ◆ It both overrides and overloads the `setValue` method of its superclass so that it can set the color object when the value is changed.
- ◆ It provides a new `getColor` method to return a value that is the color description decoded into a `ScreenColor` object.

We'll look at the intricacies of the construction process and the effect of inheritance on the different class members over the next few sections.

Note the use of the `protected` access modifier on the `decodeColor` method. By making this method `protected` it can be accessed in the current class or in a subclass but is not externally visible. We look in detail at what `protected` access really means on page 81.

Exercise 3.1: Starting with the `Vehicle` class from Chapter 2, create an extended class called `PassengerVehicle` to add a capability for counting the number of seats available in the car and the number currently occupied. Provide a new `main` method in `PassengerVehicle` to create a few of these objects and print them out.

3.2 Constructors in Extended Classes

An object of an extended class contains state variables (fields) that are inherited from the superclass and state variables defined locally within the class. To construct an object of the extended class you must correctly initialize both sets of state variables. The extended class's constructor can deal with local state variables but only the superclass knows how to correctly initialize its state such that its contract is honored. The extended class's constructors must delegate construction of the inherited state by either implicitly or explicitly invoking a superclass constructor.

A constructor in the extended class can directly invoke one of the superclass's constructors using another kind of explicit constructor invocation: the *superclass constructor invocation*, which uses the `super` construct. This is shown in the first constructor of the `ColorAttr` class. It passes the name and value up to the corresponding two-argument superclass constructor. Then it invokes its own `decodeColor` method to make `myColor` hold a reference to the correct `ScreenColor` object.

You can defer the choice of which superclass constructor to use by explicitly invoking one of your class's own constructors using `this` instead of `super`, as shown in the second constructor of `ColorAttr`. We chose to ensure that every color attribute has a color. If a color value is not supplied we provide a default of `"transparent"`, hence the one-argument constructor invokes the two-argument constructor using a *default argument*.

If you do not invoke a superclass constructor or one of your own constructors as your constructor's first executable statement, the superclass's no-arg constructor is automatically invoked before any statements of the new constructor are executed. That is, your constructor is treated as if

```
super();
```

were its first statement. If the superclass doesn't have a no-arg constructor, you must explicitly invoke another constructor.

The third constructor of `ColorAttr` enables the programmer creating a new `ColorAttr` object to specify the `ScreenColor` object itself. The first two constructors must convert their parameters to `ScreenColor` objects using the `decodeColor` method, and that presumably has some overhead. When the programmer already has a `ScreenColor` object to provide as a value, you want to avoid the overhead of that conversion. This is an example of providing a constructor that adds efficiency, not capability.

In this example, `ColorAttr` has constructors with the same signatures as its superclass's constructors. This arrangement is by no means required. Sometimes part of an extended class's benefit is to provide useful parameters to the superclass constructors based on few or no parameters of its own. It is common to have an extended class that has no constructor signatures in common with its superclass.

Constructors are not methods and are not inherited. If the superclass defines a number of constructors and an extended class wishes to have constructors of the same form, then the extended class must explicitly declare each constructor, even if all that constructor does is invoke the superclass constructor of the same form.

3.2.1 Constructor Order Dependencies

When an object is created, memory is allocated for all its fields, including those inherited from superclasses, and those fields are set to default initial values for their respective types (zero for all numeric types, `false` for `boolean`, `'\u0000'` for `char`, and `null` for object references). After this, construction has three phases:

1. Invoke a superclass's constructor.
2. Initialize the fields using their initializers and any initialization blocks.
3. Execute the body of the constructor.

First the implicit or explicit superclass constructor invocation is executed. If an explicit `this` constructor invocation is used then the chain of such invocations is followed until an implicit or explicit superclass constructor invocation is found. That superclass constructor is then invoked. The superclass constructor is executed using the same three phases—this is applied recursively, terminating when the constructor for `Object` is reached because there is no superclass constructor at that point. Any expressions evaluated as part of an explicit constructor invocation are not permitted to refer to any of the members of the current object.

In the second stage all of the field initializers and initialization blocks are executed in the order that they are declared. At this stage references to other members of the current object are permitted, provided they have already been declared.

Finally, the actual statements of the constructor body are executed. If that constructor was invoked explicitly then upon completion, control returns to the constructor that invoked it and executes the rest of its body. This process repeats until the body of the constructor specified as part of the `new` construct has been executed.

If an exception is thrown during the construction process, the `new` expression terminates by throwing that exception—no reference to the new object is returned. As an explicit constructor invocation must be the first statement in a constructor body, it is impossible to catch an exception thrown by another constructor. (If you were allowed to catch such exceptions it would be possible to construct objects with invalid initial states.)

Here is an example you can trace to illustrate the different stages of construction:

```
class X {
    protected int xMask = 0x00ff;
    protected int fullMask;
```

```
        public X() {
            fullMask = xMask;
        }

        public int mask(int orig) {
            return (orig & fullMask);
        }
    }

    class Y extends X {
        protected int yMask = 0xff00;

        public Y() {
            fullMask |= yMask;
        }
    }
```

If you create an object of type Y and follow the construction step by step, here are the values of the fields after each step:

Step	What Happens	xMask	yMask	fullMask
0	Fields set to default values	0	0	0
1	Y constructor invoked	0	0	0
2	X constructor invoked (super)	0	0	0
3	Object constructor invoked	0	0	0
4	X field initialization	0x00ff	0	0
5	X constructor executed	0x00ff	0	0x00ff
6	Y field initialization	0x00ff	0xff00	0x00ff
7	Y constructor executed	0x00ff	0xff00	0xffff

Understanding this ordering is important when you invoke methods during construction. When you invoke a method, you always get the implementation of that method for the actual type of the object. If the method uses fields of the actual type, they may not have been initialized yet. During step 5, if the constructor X invoked mask, it would use a fullMask value of 0x00ff, not 0xffff. This is true even though a later invocation of mask—after the object was completely constructed—would use 0xffff.

Also, imagine that class Y overrides mask with an implementation that explicitly uses the yMask field in its calculations. If the constructor for X used the mask method, it would actually invoke Y's mask method, and at that point yMask would be 0 instead of the expected 0xff00.

Methods you invoke during the construction phase of an object must be designed with these factors in mind. Your constructors should avoid invoking overridable methods—methods that are neither `private`, `static`, nor `final`. If you do invoke such methods, clearly list them in your documentation to alert anyone wanting to override these methods of their potential unusual use.

Exercise 3.2: Type in the classes X and Y as shown previously, and add print statements to trace the values of the masks. Add a `main` method and run it to see the results.

Exercise 3.3: If it were critical to set up these masks using the values from the extended class during construction, how could you work around these problems?

3.3   Inheriting and Redefining Members

When you extend a class you can both add new members to a class and redefine existing members. Exactly what effect redefining an inherited member has depends on the kind of member. You'll learn about field and method members here, but we defer discussion of nested members until Chapter 5.

3.3.1   Overriding

In our new `ColorAttr` class we have both *overridden* and *overloaded* the instance method `setValue`:

- ◆ *Overloading* a method is what you have already learned: providing more than one method with the same name but with different signatures to distinguish them.

- ◆ *Overriding* a method means replacing the superclass's implementation of a method with one of your own. The signatures must be identical.

Overloading an inherited method simply means that you have added a new method, with the same name as, but a different signature from, an inherited method. In `ColorAttr` we have gone from having one `setValue` method to having two overloaded forms of the method. This is no different from having overloaded forms of a method declared in the same class.

Overriding a method means that you have replaced its implementation so that when the method is invoked upon an object of the subclass, it is the subclass's version of the method that gets invoked. In the `ColorAttr` class, we overrode the

`Attr` class's `setValue(Object)` by providing a new `setValue(Object)` method in the `ColorAttr` class that uses the `super` keyword to invoke the super-class's implementation and then invokes `decodeColor`. The `super` reference can be used in method invocations to access methods from the superclass that are overridden in this class. You'll learn about `super` in detail on page 78.

When you're overriding methods, both the signature and return type must be the same as in the superclass. If two methods differ only in return type it is an error and the compiler will reject your class.

The overriding methods have their own access specifiers. A subclass can change the access of a superclass's methods, but only to provide more access. A method declared `protected` in the superclass can be redeclared `protected` (the usual thing to do) or declared `public`, but it cannot be declared `private` or have package access. Making a method less accessible than it was in a superclass would violate the contract of the superclass, as an instance of the subclass would not be usable in place of a superclass instance.

The overriding method is also allowed to change other method modifiers. The `synchronized`, `native` and `strictfp` modifiers can be freely varied because they are implementation concerns. The overriding method can be `final` but obvi-ously the method it is overriding cannot—see "Marking Methods and Classes `final`" on page 84 for a discussion on the implications of `final` methods. An instance method cannot have the same signature as an inherited static method, nor vice versa. The overridden method can, however, be made `abstract`, even though the superclass method was not—see "Abstract Classes and Methods" on page 85.

A subclass can change whether a parameter in an overridden method is `final`; a `final` modifier for a parameter is not part of the method signature, it is an implementation detail. Also, the overriding method's `throws` clause can be dif-ferent from that of the superclass method's as long as every exception type listed in the overriding method is the same or a subtype of the exceptions listed in the superclass's method. That is, each type in the overriding method's `throws` clause must be polymorphically compatible with at least one of the types listed in the `throws` clause of the supertype's method. This means that the `throws` clause of an overriding method can have fewer types listed than the method in the super-class, or more specific types, or both. The overriding method can even have no `throws` clause, which means that it results in no checked exceptions. Exceptions and `throws` clauses are described in detail in Chapter 8.

3.3.2 Hiding Fields

Fields cannot be overridden; they can only be *hidden*. If you declare a field in your class with the same name as one in your superclass, that other field still exists, but it can no longer be accessed directly by its simple name. You must use `super` or another reference of your superclass's type to access it. We'll show you an example in the next section.

3.3.3 Accessing Inherited Members

When a method accesses an object's member that has been redefined in a subclass, to which member will the method refer—the superclass member or the subclass member? The answer to that depends on the kind of member, its accessibility and how you refer to it.

When you invoke a method through an object reference, the *actual class of the object* governs which implementation is used. When you access a field, the *declared type of the reference* is used. The following example will help to explain:

```java
class SuperShow {
    public String str = "SuperStr";

    public void show() {
        System.out.println("Super.show: " + str);
    }
}

class ExtendShow extends SuperShow {
    public String str = "ExtendStr";

    public void show() {
        System.out.println("Extend.show: " + str);
    }

    public static void main(String[] args) {
        ExtendShow ext = new ExtendShow();
        SuperShow sup = ext;
        sup.show();
        ext.show();
        System.out.println("sup.str = " + sup.str);
        System.out.println("ext.str = " + ext.str);
    }
}
```

There is only one object, but we have two variables containing references to it: one variable has type SuperShow (the superclass) and the other variable has type ExtendedShow (the actual class). Here is the output of the example when run:

```
Extend.show: ExtendStr
Extend.show: ExtendStr
sup.str = SuperStr
ext.str = ExtendStr
```

For the show method, the behavior is as you expect: the actual class of the object, not the type of the reference, governs which version of the method is called. When you have an ExtendShow object, invoking show always calls ExtendShow's show even if you access it via a reference declared with the type SuperShow. This occurs whether show is invoked externally (as in the example), or internally within another method of either ExtendShow or SuperShow.

For the str field, the type of the *reference,* not the actual class of the *object,* determines which class's field is accessed. In fact, each ExtendShow object has *two* String fields, both called str, one of which is hidden by ExtendShow's own, different field called str:

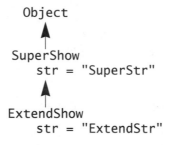

```
              Object
                ▲
                |
           SuperShow
              str = "SuperStr"
                ▲
                |
          ExtendShow
              str = "ExtendStr"
```

The field that gets accessed is determined at compile time based on the type of the reference used to access it.

Inside a method, such as show, a reference to a field always refers to the field declared in the class in which the method is declared, or else an inherited field if there is no declaration in that class. So in SuperShow.show the reference to str is to SuperShow.str, while in ExtendShow.show the reference to str is to ExtendShow.str.

You've already seen that method overriding enables you to extend existing code by reusing it with objects of expanded, specialized functionality not foreseen by the inventor of the original code. But where fields are concerned, it is hard to think of cases in which hiding them is a useful feature.

If an existing method had a parameter of type SuperShow and accessed str with that object's reference, it would always get SuperShow.str even if the method were actually handed an object of type `ExtendShow`. If the classes were designed to use a method instead of a field to access the string, the overridden method would be invoked in such a case and the `ExtendShow.str` could be returned. This hiding behavior is often another reason to prefer defining classes with private data accessed only by methods, which are overridden, not hidden.

Hiding fields is allowed because implementors of existing superclasses must be free to add new `public` or `protected` fields without breaking subclasses. If the language forbade using the same field name in a superclass and a subclass, adding a new field to an existing superclass could potentially break any subclasses already using those names.

If adding new fields to existing superclasses would break some unknown number of subclasses, you'd be effectively immobilized, unable to add `public` or `protected` fields to a superclass. Purists might well argue that classes should have only `private` data, but you get to decide on your style.

3.3.4 Accessibility and Overriding

A method can be overridden only if it is *accessible*. If the method is not accessible then it is not inherited, and if it is not inherited it can't be overridden. For example, a `private` method is not accessible outside its own class. If a subclass defines a method that coincidentally has the same signature and return type as the super-class's private method, they are completely unrelated—the subclass method does *not* override the superclass's private method.

What does this mean in practice? An external invocation of the subclass method (assuming it is accessible outside its class) results in the subclass implementation being invoked. This is normal behavior. But notice that in the super-class, any invocations of the private method result in the superclass's implementation of the method being invoked, not any like-named method in a subclass. In short, invocations of private methods always invoke the implementation of the method declared in the current class.

When a method is inaccessible due to the superclass and subclass being in different packages, things are more complicated. We defer a discussion of this until Chapter 13.

3.3.5 Hiding Static Members

Static members within a class cannot be overridden, they are always hidden— whether a field or a method. The fact that they are hidden has little effect how-ever—each static field or method should always be accessed via the name of its declaring class, hence the fact that it gets hidden by a declaration in a subclass is of little consequence. If a reference is used to access a static member then, as with instance fields, static members are always accessed based on the declared type of the reference, not the type of the object referred to.

3.3.6 The super Keyword

The super keyword is available in all non-static methods of a class. In field access and method invocation, super acts as a reference to the current object as an instance of its superclass. Using super is the only case where the type of the reference governs selection of the method implementation to be used. An invocation of super.*method* always uses the implementation of *method* the superclass would use. It does not use any overridden implementation of that method farther down the class hierarchy. Here is an example that shows super in action:

```
class That {
    /** return the class name */
    protected String nm() {
        return "That";
    }
}

class More extends That {
    protected String nm() {
        return "More";
    }

    protected void printNM() {
        That sref = (That)this;

        System.out.println("this.nm()  = " + this.nm());
        System.out.println("sref.nm()  = " + sref.nm());
        System.out.println("super.nm() = " + super.nm());
    }
}
```

Although sref and super both refer to the same object using the type That, only super will ignore the real class of the object to use the superclass's implementation of nm. The reference sref will act the same way this acts, selecting an implementation of nm based on the actual class of the object. Here is the output of printNM:

```
this.nm()  = More
sref.nm()  = More
super.nm() = That
```

3.4   Type Compatibility and Conversion

The Java programming language is *strongly typed*, which means that it checks for type compatibility at compile time in most cases—preventing incompatible assignments by forbidding anything questionable. Now that you understand the basic type relationship defined by subclasses and superclasses, we can revisit a few details regarding the compatibility of reference types within assignments (implicit or explicit) and how to convert between types. Type compatibility and conversions for primitive types are discussed in "Expressions" on page 168.

3.4.1   Compatibility

When you assign the value of an expression to a variable, either as part of an initializer, assignment statement, or implicitly when an argument value is assigned to a method parameter, the type of the expression must be compatible with the type of the variable. For reference types this means that the type of the expression must be the same type as, or a subtype of, the declared type of the variable. For example, any method that expects an Attr object as a parameter will accept a ColorAttr object because ColorAttr is a subtype of Attr. This is called *assignment compatibility*. But the converse is not true—you cannot assign an Attr object to a variable of type ColorAttr, nor pass an Attr object as an argument when a ColorAttr is expected.

The same rule applies for the expression used on a return statement within a method. The type of the expression must be assignment compatible with the declared return type of the method.

The null object reference is a special case in that it is assignment compatible with all reference types, including array types—a reference variable of any type can be assigned null.

The types higher up the type hierarchy are said to be *wider*, or *less specific*, than the types lower down the hierarchy. The lower types are said to be *narrower*, or *more specific*, than their supertypes. When you are expecting a supertype and get given a subtype, a *widening conversion* takes place. Such a conversion causes the subtype object to be treated as an instance of the supertype and can be checked at compile time. No action is needed by the programmer in a widening conversion. Going the other way—taking a reference to a supertype and converting it to a reference to a subtype—is known as a *narrowing conversion*. Narrowing conversions must be explicitly requested using the *cast* operator.

3.4.2   Explicit Type Casting

A cast can be used to tell the compiler that an expression should be treated as having the type specified by the cast. This can either be a wider or a narrower type, but usually casts are only used for narrowing conversions. A cast consists of a type name within parentheses, applied to an expression. In the previous example we used a widening cast in `printNM` to convert the type of `this` to its superclass type:

```
That sref = (That)this;
```

This cast was unnecessary but emphasized that we really wanted the current object to treated as an instance of its superclass. If we then try to assign `sref` back to a reference of the narrower `More` type, an explicit cast is essential:

```
More mref = (More)sref;
```

Even though we know the object referred to is of the right type, the compiler still requires an explicit cast.

A widening conversion is also known as an *upcast* because it casts from one type to another further up the type hierarchy—it is also a *safe cast* because it is always valid. A narrowing conversion is also known as a *downcast* because it casts from one type to another, further down the inheritance hierarchy—it is also an *unsafe cast* because it may not be valid.

When a narrowing conversion is requested via a cast, the compiler does not assume that the cast is correct. If the compiler can tell that a cast is incorrect then a compile time error can occur. If the compiler cannot ascertain that the cast is correct at compile time, then a run time check will be performed. If the run time check fails because the cast is incorrect, then a `ClassCastException` is thrown.

3.4.3   Testing for Type

You can test the class of an object using the `instanceof` operator, which evaluates to `true` if the expression on its left is assignment compatible with the type name on its right, and `false` otherwise, although `null` is not an instance of any type, and so `instanceof` for `null` always returns `false`. Using `instanceof` you can safely downcast a reference, knowing that no exception will be thrown. For example:

```
if (sref instanceof More)
    mref = (More)sref;
```

Note that we still have to apply the cast—that's to convince the compiler that we really meant to use the object as a subclass instance.

Type testing with `instanceof` is particularly useful when a method doesn't require an object of a more extended type, but if passed such an object it can make use of the extended functionality. For example, a `sort` method may accept a generic `List` type as an argument, but if it actually receives a `SortedList` then it doesn't have to do anything:

```
public static void sort(List list) {
    if (list instanceof SortedList)
        return;
    // else sort the list ...
}
```

3.5   What protected Really Means

We noted briefly that making a class member `protected` means it can be accessed by classes that extend that class, but that is loose language. More precisely, beyond being accessible within the class itself and to code within the same package (see Chapter 13), a protected member can also be accessed from a class through object references that are of at least the same type as the class—that is, references of the class's type or one its subtypes. An example will make this easier to understand.

Consider a linked-list implementation of a queue, class `SingleLinkQueue`, with methods `add` and `remove` for storing an object at the tail of the queue and removing the object from the head of the queue, respectively. The nodes of the queue are made up of `Cell`s which have a reference to the next cell in the queue, and a reference to the object stored in the current cell.

```
class Cell {
    private Cell next;
    private Object element;
    public Cell(Object element) {
        this.element = element;
    }
    public Cell(Object element, Cell next) {
```

```
            this.element = element;
            this.next = next;
        }
        public Object getElement() {
            return element;
        }
        public void setElement(Object element) {
            this.element = element;
        }
        public Cell getNext() {
            return next;
        }
        public void setNext(Cell next) {
            this.next = next;
        }
    }
```

A queue then consists of a reference to the head and tail cells and the implementation of add and remove.

```
    public class SingleLinkQueue {
        protected Cell head;
        protected Cell tail;

        public void add(Object item) {/* ... */}
        public Object remove() {/* ... */}
    }
```

We make the head and tail references protected so that extended classes can manipulate the linked-list cells directly, rather than having to use add and remove—which would involve wrapping and unwrapping the elements each time.

One group decides that it needs a priority queue, where items are stored in the queue in a specific order rather than always being inserted at the tail. So it defines a PriorityQueue class in another package that extends SingleLinkQueue and overrides add to insert the object in the right place. The PriorityQueue class's implementation of add can access the head and tail fields inherited from SingleLinkQueue—the code is in a subclass of SingleLinkQueue and the type of the object reference used (this) is the same as that subclass, namely PriorityQueue, so access to the protected members is allowed. This is what you would expect.

The group designing the priority queue needs an additional feature—it wants to be able to merge two priority queues together. In a merge operation the target queue ends up with the elements of both queues, while the queue with which it was merged becomes empty. The merge operation starts like this:

```
public void merge(PriorityQueue q) {
    Cell first = q.head;
    // ...
}
```

We are not accessing the protected member of the current object, but the protected member of an object passed as an argument. This is allowed because the class attempting the access is PriorityQueue and the type of the reference q is also PriorityQueue. If q were a subclass of PriorityQueue this would still be valid.

Later the group determines that there is a new requirement: it wants to be able to merge a SingleLinkQueue with a PriorityQueue. So it defines an overloaded version of merge that starts like this:

```
public void merge(SingleLinkQueue q) {
    Cell first = q.head;
    // ...
}
```

But this code won't compile.

The problem is that the class attempting to access the protected member is PriorityQueue while the type of the reference to the object being accessed is SingleLinkQueue. SingleLinkQueue is not the same as, nor a subclass of, PriorityQueue, so the access is not allowed. Although each PriorityQueue is a SingleLinkQueue, not every SingleLinkQueue is a PriorityQueue.

The reasoning behind the restrictions this: Each subclass inherits the contract of the superclass and expands that contract in some way. Suppose that one subclass, as part of its expanded contract, places constraints on the values of protected members of the superclass. If a different subclass could access the protected members of objects of the first subclass then it could manipulate them in a way that would break the first subclass's contract—and this should not be permissible.

Protected static members can be accessed in any extended class. If head were a static field, any method (static or not) in PriorityQueue could access it. This is allowed because a subclass can't modify the contract of its static members as it can only hide them, not override them—hence there is no danger of another class violating that contract.

Members declared protected are also available to any code within the package of the class. If these different queue classes were in the same package, they could access one another's head and tail fields, as could any unrelated type in that package. Classes in the same package are assumed to be fairly trustworthy and not to violate each other's contracts—see Chapter 13. In the list "private, package, protected, public," each access level adds to the kinds of code to which a member is accessible.

3.6   Marking Methods and Classes `final`

Marking a method `final` means that no extended class can override the method to change its behavior. In other words, this is the *final* version of that method. Entire classes can also be marked `final`:

```
final class NoExtending {
    // ...
}
```

A class marked `final` cannot be extended by any other class, and all the methods of a final class are themselves effectively `final`.

Final classes and methods can improve security. If a class is `final`, nobody can declare a class that extends it, and therefore nobody can violate its contract. If a method is `final`, you can rely on its implementation details (unless it invokes non-`final` methods, of course). You could use `final`, for example, on a `validatePassword` method to ensure that it does what it is advertised to do instead of being overridden to always return `true`. Or you can mark as `final` the class that contains the method so that it can never be extended to confuse the implementation of `validatePassword`.

Marking a method or class `final` is a serious restriction on the use of the class. If you make a method `final`, you should really intend that its behavior be completely fixed. You restrict the flexibility of your class for other programmers who might want to use it as a basis to add functionality to their code. Marking an entire class `final` prevents anyone else from extending your class, limiting its usefulness to others. If you make anything `final`, be sure that you want to create these restrictions.

In many cases, you can achieve the security of marking a whole class `final` by leaving the class extensible and instead marking each method in the class as `final`. In this way, you can rely on the behavior of those methods while still allowing extensions that can add functionality without overriding methods. Of course, fields that the `final` methods rely on should be `final` or `private`, or else an extended class could change behavior by changing those fields.

Another ramification of `final` is that it simplifies optimizations. When a non-`final` method is invoked, the runtime system determines the actual class of the object, binds the method invocation to the correct implementation of the method for that type, and then invokes that implementation. But if, for example, the getName method was `final` in the `Attr` class and you have a reference to an object of type `Attr` or any extended type, it may be possible to simplify the steps needed to invoke the method. In the simplest case, such as `getName`, an invocation can be replaced with the actual body of the method. This mechanism is known as *inlining*. The inlined method makes the following two statements perform equivalently:

```
System.out.println("id = " + rose.name);
System.out.println("id = " + rose.getName());
```

Although the two statements are equally efficient, a `getName` method allows the `name` field to be read-only and gives you the benefits of abstraction, allowing you to change the implementation.

The same optimizations can be applied to private and static methods, because they too cannot be overridden.

Some type checks become faster with `final` classes. In fact, many type checks become compile time checks, and errors can be caught earlier. If the compiler encounters a reference to a `final` class, it knows that the object referred to is exactly that type. The entire class hierarchy for that class is known, so the compiler can check whether any use is valid or invalid. With a non-`final` reference, some checks can happen only at run time.

Exercise 3.4: Which methods (if any) of `Vehicle` and `PassengerVehicle` might reasonably be made `final`?

3.7 Abstract Classes and Methods

An extremely useful feature of object-oriented programming is the concept of the *abstract class*. Using abstract classes, you can declare classes that define only part of an implementation, leaving extended classes to provide specific implementation of some or all of the methods. The opposite of *abstract* is *concrete*—a class that has only concrete methods, including implementations of any abstract methods inherited from superclasses, is a concrete class.

Abstract classes are helpful when some of the behavior is defined for most or all objects of a given type, but some behavior makes sense only for particular classes and not a general superclass. Such a class is declared `abstract`, and each method not implemented in the class is also marked `abstract`. (If you need to define some methods, but you don't need to provide any implementation, you probably want to use interfaces instead, which are described in Chapter 4.)

For example, suppose you want to create a benchmarking harness to provide an infrastructure for writing benchmarked code. The class implementation could understand how to drive and measure a benchmark, but it couldn't know in advance which benchmark would be run. Most `abstract` classes fit a pattern in which a class's particular area of expertise requires someone else to provide a missing piece—this is commonly known as the "Template Method" pattern. In many cases the expertise methods are good candidates for being `final` so that the expertise cannot be compromised in any way. In this benchmarking example, the missing piece is code that needs to be benchmarked. Here is what such a class might look like:

```
abstract class Benchmark {
    abstract void benchmark();

    public final long repeat(int count) {
        long start = System.currentTimeMillis();
        for (int i = 0; i < count; i++)
            benchmark();
        return (System.currentTimeMillis() - start);
    }
}
```

Any class with any `abstract` methods must be declared `abstract`. This redundancy helps the reader quickly see that the class is `abstract` without scanning to see whether any method in the class is declared `abstract`.

The `repeat` method provides the benchmarking expertise. It can time a run of `count` repetitions of the benchmark. The method `System.currentTimeMillis` returns the current time in milliseconds. By subtracting the starting time from the finishing time you get an approximation of the time spent executing the benchmark. If the timing needs become more complex (perhaps measuring the time of each run and computing statistics about the variations), this method can be enhanced without affecting any extended class's implementation of its specialized benchmark code.

The `abstract` method `benchmark` must be implemented by each subclass that is not `abstract` itself. This is why it has no implementation in this class, just a declaration. Here is an example of a simple Benchmark extension:

```
class MethodBenchmark extends Benchmark {
    /** Do nothing, just return. */
    void benchmark() {
    }

    public static void main(String[] args) {
        int count = Integer.parseInt(args[0]);
```

```
        long time = new MethodBenchmark().repeat(count);
        System.out.println(count + " methods in " +
                                time + " milliseconds");
    }
}
```

This class times how long it takes to invoke an empty method benchmark, plus the loop overhead. You can now time method invocations by running the application `MethodBenchmark` with the number of times to repeat the test. The count is taken from the program arguments and decoded using the `Integer` class's `parseInt` method on the argument string, as described in "String Conversions" on page 217.

Any class can override methods from its superclass to declare them `abstract`, turning a concrete method into an `abstract` one at that point in the type tree. This technique is useful, for example, when a class's default implementation is invalid for a part of the class hierarchy.

You cannot create an object of an `abstract` class because there would be no valid implementation for some methods that might well be invoked.

Exercise 3.5: Write a new extended class that benchmarks something else, such as how long it takes to run a loop from zero to some passed-in parameter.

Exercise 3.6: Change `Vehicle` so that it has an `EnergySource` object reference, which is associated with the `Vehicle` in its constructor. `EnergySource` must be an `abstract` class, because a `GasTank` object's measure of fullness will differ from that of a `Battery` object. Put an `abstract` empty method in `EnergySource` and implement it in `GasTank` and `Battery` classes. Add a `start` method to `Vehicle` that ensures that the energy source isn't `empty`.

3.8   The `Object` Class

The `Object` class is the root of the class hierarchy. Every class directly or indirectly extends `Object` and so a variable of type `Object` can refer to any object, whether a class instance or an array. For example, the `Attr` class can hold an attribute of any type, so its `value` field was declared to be of type `Object`. Such a class cannot hold primitive types (`int`, `boolean`, and so on), but you can make objects that contain values of these types if you need to, using the *wrapper classes* (`Integer`, `Boolean`, and so on) described in Chapter 11.

The `Object` class defines a number of methods that are inherited by all objects. These methods fall into two categories: general utility methods and methods that support threads. Thread support is covered in Chapter 10. This section describes the utility methods and how they affect classes. The utility methods are:

public boolean **equals(Object obj)**

Compares the receiving object and the object referenced by obj for equality, returning true if they have the same value and false if they don't. If you want to determine whether two references refer to the same object, you can compare them using == and !=. The equals method is concerned with value equality. The default implementation of equals in Object assumes that an object is equal only to itself, by testing if this == obj.

public int **hashCode()**

Returns a hash code for this object. Each object has a hash code for use in hashtables. The default implementation returns a value that is usually different for different objects. It is used when storing objects in hashed collections, as described in Chapter 16.

protected Object **clone()** throws CloneNotSupportedException

Returns a clone of this object. A *clone* is a new object that is a copy of the object on which clone was invoked. Cloning is discussed in the next section.

public final Class **getClass()**

Returns the particular object of type Class that represents the class of this object. Objects of class Class are the run time expression of a class. The class Class is described in "The Class class" on page 282.

protected void **finalize()** throws Throwable

Finalizes the object during garbage collection. This method is discussed in detail in "Finalization" on page 316.

public String **toString()**

Returns a string representation of the object. The toString method is implicitly invoked whenever an object reference is used within a string concatenation expression as an operand of the + operator. The Object version of toString constructs a string containing the object's class's name, an @ character, and a hexadecimal representation of the instance's hash code.

Both the hashCode and equals methods should be overridden if you want to provide a notion of equality different from the default implementation provided in the Object class. The default is that any two different objects are not equal and their hash codes are usually distinct.

If your class has a notion of equality in which two different objects can be equal, those two objects should return the same value from hashCode. This is because the Hashtable mechanism relies on equals returning true when it finds a key of the same value in the table. For example, the String class overrides equals to return `true` if the two `String` objects have the same contents. It also overrides `hashCode` to return a hash based on the contents of the `String` so that two strings with the same contents have the same `hashCode`.

The term *identity* is used for reference equality: if two references are identical, then `==` between the two will be `true`. The term *equivalence* is used to describe value equality—objects that may or may not be identical, but for which `equals` will return `true`. So one can say that the default implementation of `equals` is that equivalence is the same as identity. A class that defines a broader notion of equality can have objects that are not identical be equivalent by overriding `equals` to return `true` based on the states of the objects instead of their identities.

Some hashtables are concerned with identity of objects, not equivalence. If you need to write such a hashtable, you want hash codes corresponding to the identify of objects, not their states. The method `System.identityHashCode` returns the same value that the `Object` class's implementation of `hashCode` would return for an object if it were not overridden. If you simply use `hashCode` on the objects you are storing, you might get a hash code based on equivalence, not on identity, which could be far less efficient.

Exercise 3.7: Override `equals` and `hashCode` for `Vehicle`.

3.9   Cloning Objects

The `Object.clone` method helps you write *clone* methods for your own classes. A clone method returns a new object whose initial state is a copy of the current state of the object on which `clone` was invoked. Subsequent changes to the new clone object should not affect the state of the original object.

3.9.1   Strategies for Cloning

There are three important factors in writing a `clone` method:

- The empty `Cloneable` interface, which you must implement to provide a `clone` method that can be used to clone an object.[1]
- The `clone` method implemented by the `Object` class, which performs a simple clone by copying all fields of the original object to the new object.

---

[1]   `Cloneable` should have been spelled `Clonable`, and the current, incorrect spelling may be deprecated in a future release.

This method works for many classes but may need to be supplemented by an overriding method.

◆ The `CloneNotSupportedException`, which can be used to signal that a class's `clone` method shouldn't have been invoked.

A given class can have one of four different attitudes toward `clone`:

◆ Support `clone`. Such a class implements `Cloneable` and declares its `clone` method to throw no exceptions.

◆ Conditionally support `clone`. Such a class might be a collection class that can be cloned in principle but cannot successfully be cloned unless its contents can be cloned. This kind of class will implement `Cloneable`, but will let its `clone` method pass through any `CloneNotSupportedException` it may receive from other objects it tries to clone. Or a class may have the ability to be cloned itself but not require that all subclasses also have the ability to be cloned.

◆ Allow subclasses to support `clone` but don't publicly support it. Such a class doesn't implement `Cloneable`, but if the default implementation of `clone` isn't correct, the class provides a protected `clone` implementation that clones its fields correctly.

◆ Forbid `clone`. Such a class does not implement `Cloneable` and provides a `clone` method that always throws `CloneNotSupportedException`.

`Object.clone` checks whether the object on which it was invoked implements the `Cloneable` interface and throws `CloneNotSupportedException` if it does not. Otherwise, `Object.clone` creates a new object of exactly the same type as the original object on which `clone` is invoked and initializes the fields of the new, cloned object to have the same values as the fields of the original object. When `Object.clone` is finished, it returns a reference to the new object.

The simplest way to make a class that can be cloned is to declare that it implements the `Cloneable` interface, and redeclare the `clone` method to be public:

```java
public class MyClass extends HerClass implements Cloneable {
    public Object clone() throws CloneNotSupportedException {
        return super.clone();
    }
    // ...
}
```

Now, any other code can make a clone of a MyClass object. In this simple case, all fields of MyClass will be assigned by Object.clone into the new object that is returned.

The clone method in Object has a throws CloneNotSupportedException declaration. This means a class can declare that it can be cloned, but a subclass can decide that it can't be cloned. Such a subclass would implement the Cloneable interface because it extends a class that does so, but the subclass could not, in fact, be cloned. The extended class would make this known by overriding clone to always throw CloneNotSupportedException and documenting that it does so. Be careful—this means that you cannot determine whether a class can be cloned by a run time check to see whether the class implements Cloneable. Some classes that can't be cloned will be forced to signal this condition by throwing an exception.

3.9.2   Correct Cloning

Objects of most classes can be cloned in principle. Even if your class does not support the Cloneable interface, you should ensure that its clone method is correct. In many classes, the default implementation of clone will be wrong because it duplicates a reference to an object that shouldn't be shared. In such cases, clone should be overridden to behave correctly. The default implementation assigns each field from the source to the same field in the destination object.

If, for example, an object has a reference to an array, a clone of one of the objects will refer to the same array. If the array holds read-only data, such a shared reference is probably fine. But if it is a list of objects that should be distinct for each of your objects, you probably don't want the clone's manipulation of its own list to affect the list of the original source object, or vice versa.

Here is an example of the problem. Suppose you have a simple integer stack class:

```
public class IntegerStack implements Cloneable { // dangerous
    private int[] buffer;
    private int top;

    public IntegerStack(int maxContents) {
        buffer = new int[maxContents];
        top = -1;
    }

    public void push(int val) {
        buffer[++top] = val;
```

```
        }

        public int pop() {
            return buffer[top--];
        }
    }
```

Now let's look at some code that creates an `IntegerStack` object, puts some data onto the stack, and then clones it:

```
IntegerStack first = new IntegerStack(2);
first.push(2);
first.push(9);
IntegerStack second = (IntegerStack) first.clone();
```

With the default `clone` method, the data in memory will look something like this:

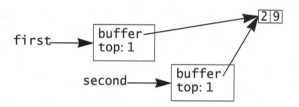

Now consider what happens when future code invokes `first.pop()`, followed by `first.push(17)`. The top element in the stack `first` will change from 9 to 17, which is expected. The programmer will probably be surprised, however, to see that the top element of `second` will *also* change to 17 because there is only one array that is shared by the two stacks.

The solution is to override `clone` to make a copy of the array:

```
public Object clone() {
    try {
        IntegerStack nObj = (IntegerStack) super.clone();
        nObj.buffer = (int[]) buffer.clone();
        return nObj;
    } catch (CloneNotSupportedException e) {
        // Cannot happen -- we support
        // clone, and so do arrays
        throw new InternalError(e.toString());
    }
}
```

First the `clone` method invokes `super.clone`. This invocation is very important because the superclass may be working around its own problem of shared objects. If you do not invoke the superclass's method, you solve your own cloning problem but may create another one. Furthermore, `super.clone` will eventually invoke the method `Object.clone`, which creates an object of the correct type. If the `IntegerStack` implementation of `clone` used `new` to create an `IntegerStack` object, it would be incorrect for any object that extended `IntegerStack`. The extended class's invocation of `super.clone` would give it an `IntegerStack` object, not an object of the correct, extended type. The return value of `super.clone` is then cast to an `IntegerStack` reference.

`Object.clone` initializes each field in the new clone object by assigning it the value from the same field of the object being cloned. You then need write special code only to deal with fields for which copying the value is incorrect. `IntegerStack.clone` doesn't need to copy the `top` field, because it is already correct from the "copy values" default. It does, however, need to make a copy of the `buffer` array, which is done by cloning the array—all arrays can be cloned.

With the specialized `clone` method in place, the example code now creates memory that looks like this:

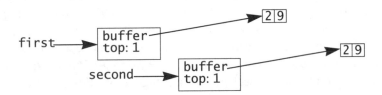

Cloning is an alternative form of construction but is not recognized as construction by the system. This means that you have to be wary of using *blank finals* (see page 40) that can be set only in constructors. If the value of the final field should be a copy of the value in the object being cloned, then there is no problem as `Object.clone` will achieve this. If copying is not appropriate for the field then it cannot be declared `final`. In this example, the `buffer` array is immutable for the life of the object, but it can't be declared `final` because its value needs to be explicitly set in `clone`.

If the object that should not be shared between the clone and the original, is not an array, that object should support copying in some way. That may mean that the object itself supports `clone`, or that it has a *copy constructor* that allows a duplicate object to be created. For example, the `String` class does not support `clone` but it does have a copy constructor that creates a new `String` with the same contents as the `String` passed to the constructor. The issues when writing copy constructors are the same as those for writing `clone`—you must decide when a simple field copy is sufficient and when more specific action is required. One advantage the copy constructor has is that it can deal with `final` fields in situations where `clone` cannot.

Sometimes making `clone` work correctly is not worth the trouble, and some classes should not support `clone`. In such cases, you should define a `clone` method that throws `CloneNotSupportedException` so that objects with bad state will never be created by an unsuspecting subclass that uses `clone`.

You can declare that all subclasses of a class must support `clone` properly by overriding your class's `clone` method with one that drops the declaration of `CloneNotSupportedException`. Subclasses implementing the `clone` method cannot throw `CloneNotSupportedException`, because methods in a subclass cannot add an exception to a method. In the same way, if your class makes `clone` public, all extended classes must also have `public clone` methods, because a subclass cannot make a method less visible than it was in its superclass.

3.9.3   Shallow versus Deep Cloning

The default implementation of clone provides what is known as a *shallow* clone or copy—it simply performs a field by field copy. A *deep* clone would clone each object referred to by a field and each entry in an array. This would apply recursively and so deep cloning an object would clone all of the objects reachable from that object. In general, `clone` is overridden to perform a deeper clone, whenever a shallow clone is not appropriate—such as in the `IntegerStack` example.

The object serialization mechanism (see page 405) allows you to write entire object graphs to a stream of bytes and, using that generated stream of bytes, create an equivalent copy of the original object graphs. Serialization can provide a way to make deeper copies than those provided by `Object.clone`.

Exercise 3.8: Make `Vehicle` and `PassengerVehicle` into `Cloneable` types. Which of the four described attitudes should each class take toward cloning? Is the simple copying done by `Object.clone` correct for the clone methods of these classes?

Exercise 3.9: Write a `Garage` class whose objects can hold up to some number of `Vehicle` objects in an array. Make `Garage` a `Cloneable` type, and write a proper `clone` method for it. Write a `Garage.main` method to test it.

Exercise 3.10: Make your `LinkedList` class `Cloneable`, with `clone` returning a new list that refers to the same values as the original list, not clones of the values. In other words, changes to one list should not affect the other list, but changes to the objects referenced by the list would be visible in both lists.

3.10 Extending Classes: How and When

The ability to write extended classes is a large part of the benefits of object-oriented programming. When you extend a class to add new functionality, you create what is commonly termed an *IsA* relationship—the extension creates a new kind of object that "is a" kind of the original class. The IsA relationship is quite different from a *HasA* relationship, in which one object uses another object to store state or do work—it "has a" reference to that other object.

Let's look at an example. Consider a `Point` class that represents a point in two-dimensional space by an (*x, y*) pair. You might extend `Point` to create, say, a `Pixel` class to represent a colored point on a screen. A `Pixel` IsA `Point`: anything that is true of a simple `Point` would also be true of a `Pixel`. The `Pixel` class might add mechanisms to represent the color of the pixel or a reference to an object that represents the screen on which the pixel is drawn. As a point in a two-dimensional space (the plane of a display) with an extension to the contract (it has color and a screen), a `Pixel` IsA `Point`.

On the other hand, a circle is not a point. Although a circle can be described by a point and a radius, a point has uses that no circle would have. For example, if you had a method to place the center of a rectangle at a particular point, would it really make sense to pass in a circle? A circle HasA center that IsA point, but a circle Is*Not*A point with a radius, and therefore should not be a subclass of `Point`.

There are times when the correct choice is not obvious and for which different choices will be correct depending on the application. In the end, applications must run and make sense.

Getting IsA versus HasA relationships correct is both subtle and potentially critical. For example, one obvious and common way to design an employee database using object-oriented tools is to use an `Employee` class that has the properties all persons share (such as name and employee number) and extend it to classes for particular kinds of employees, such as `Manager`, `Engineer`, and `FileClerk`.

This design fails in real-world situations, in which one person operates simultaneously in more than one role. For example, an engineer might be an acting manager in a group and must now appear in two guises. As another example, a teaching assistant is often both a student and a staff member at a university.

A more flexible design would create a `Role` class and extend it to create classes for roles such as `Manager`. Then you would change the design of the `Employee` class to have a set of `Role` objects. Now a person could be associated with an ever-changing set of roles in the organization. We have changed from saying that a manager IsAn employee to saying that manager IsA role, and that an employee can HaveA manager's role as well as other roles.

If the wrong initial choice is made, changing deployed systems will be hard, because changes could require major alterations in code. For example, methods in the first employee database design would no doubt rely on the fact that a `Manager` object could be used as an `Employee`. This would no longer be true if we had to change to the role-based design, and all the original code would break.

3.11 Designing a Class to Be Extended

The `Attr` class is an example of a well designed class—it follows the design principles that you learned in Chapter 2. The fields of the class are `private` and accessible only via accessor methods, which protects them from being modified contrary to the class's contract. The `Attr` class presents a clean interface to users of the class and at the same time decouples itself from those classes to allow for its own implementation to change in the future.

Given that `ColorAttr` extends `Attr`, should we have designed `Attr` differently to make it more suitable for extension? Should the `name` and `value` fields have been `protected`, instead of `private`, so that a subclass could access them directly? Such decisions require careful thought and consideration of both the benefits and consequences of making that decision. Making the `Attr` fields protected would not provide any benefit to a subclass as all of the actions that can be performed on those fields are accessible via the `public` methods that `Attr` provides. On the other hand, making the fields `protected` would prevent any future modifications to the implementation of `Attr` because subclasses could depend on the existence and type of those fields, as well as direct access to them. So in this case, `Attr`'s current design is suited for extension as well as general use.

In our linked-list queue class, `SingleLinkQueue`, we did make the `head` and `tail` fields `protected`. In that case there was a great performance benefit in having the subclass being able to access the cells of the linked list directly—it would be impractical to implement the override of `add` in `PriorityQueue` if the only tools available to use were the original `add` and `remove` methods. The low-level nature of the `SingleLinkQueue` class also means that we are not concerned about locking in implementation details—it is after all a linked-list implementation of a queue and that doesn't really leave much scope for change. If we had written a more general queue class that just happened to be using a linked-list implementation, then it would be a different story.

A non-final class has two interfaces. The *public* interface is for programmers *using* your class. The *protected* interface is for programmers *extending* your class. Do not casually make fields of your classes protected: both interfaces are real contracts, and both should be designed carefully.

3.11.1 Designing an Extensible Framework

Suppose you want to provide a benchmarking harness for comparing varieties of sorting algorithms. Some things can be said of all sorting algorithm benchmarks: they all have data on which they must operate; that data must support an ordering mechanism; and the number of comparisons and swaps they require to do their work is an important factor in the benchmark.

You can write an abstract class that helps you with these features, but you cannot write a generic sort method—the actual operations of sorting are determined by each extended class. Here is a SortDouble class that sorts arrays of double values, tracking the number of swaps, comparisons, and tests required in a SortMetrics class we will define later:

```
abstract class SortDouble {
    private double[] values;
    private final SortMetrics curMetrics = new SortMetrics();

    /** Invoked to do the full sort */
    public final SortMetrics sort(double[] data) {
        values = data;
        curMetrics.init();
        doSort();
        return getMetrics();
    }

    public final SortMetrics getMetrics() {
        return (SortMetrics)curMetrics.clone();
    }

    /** For extended classes to know the number of elements*/
    protected final int getDataLength() {
        return values.length;
    }

    /** For extended classes to probe elements */
    protected final double probe(int i) {
        curMetrics.probeCnt++;
        return values[i];
    }

    /** For extended classes to compare elements */
    protected final int compare(int i, int j) {
```

```
        curMetrics.compareCnt++;
        double d1 = values[i];
        double d2 = values[j];
        if (d1 == d2)
            return 0;
        else
            return (d1 < d2 ? -1 : 1);
    }

    /** For extended classes to swap elements */
    protected final void swap(int i, int j) {
        curMetrics.swapCnt++;
        double tmp = values[i];
        values[i] = values[j];
        values[j] = tmp;
    }

    /** Extended classes implement this -- used by sort */
    protected abstract void doSort();
}
```

This class defines fields to hold the array being sorted (`values`) and a reference to a metrics object (`curMetrics`) to track the measured operations. To ensure that these counts are correct, `SortDouble` provides routines to be used by extended sorting classes when they need to examine data or perform comparisons and swaps.

When you design a class, you can decide whether to trust its extended classes. The `SortDouble` class is designed not to trust them, and that is generally the best way to design classes for others to extend. A guarded design not only prevents malicious use, it also prevents bugs.

`SortDouble` carefully restricts access to each member to the appropriate level. It uses `final` on all its non-`abstract` methods. These factors are all part of the contract of the `SortDouble` class, which includes protecting the measurement of the sort algorithm from tampering. Making the methods `final` ensures that no extended class overrides these methods to change behavior, and also allows the compiler and runtime system to make them as efficient as possible.

`SortMetrics` objects describe the cost of a particular sorting run. The class has three public fields. Its only task is to communicate data, so there is no need to hide that data behind accessor methods. `SortDouble.metrics` returns a copy of the data so that it doesn't give out a reference to its internal data. This prevents both the code that creates SortDouble objects and the code in the extended classes from changing the data. Here is the SortMetrics class:

```java
final class SortMetrics implements Cloneable {
    public long probeCnt,        // simple data probes
                compareCnt,      // comparing two elements
                swapCnt;         // swapping two elements

    public void init() {
        probeCnt = swapCnt = compareCnt = 0;
    }

    public String toString() {
        return probeCnt + " probes " +
               compareCnt + " compares " +
               swapCnt + " swaps";
    }

    /** This class supports clone */
    public Object clone() {
        try {
            return super.clone(); // default mechanism works
        } catch (CloneNotSupportedException e) {
            // can't happen: this and Object both clone
            throw new InternalError(e.toString());
        }
    }
}
```

The following class extends SortDouble. The SimpleSortDouble class implements doSort with a very slow but simple sort algorithm (a "selection sort") whose primary advantage is that it is easy to code and easy to understand:

```java
class SimpleSortDouble extends SortDouble {
    protected void doSort() {
        for (int i = 0; i < getDataLength(); i++) {
            for (int j = i + 1; j < getDataLength(); j++) {
                if (compare(i, j) > 0)
                    swap(i, j);
            }
```

```
            }
        }
    }
```

Now we can write a test harness for sort algorithms that must be changed only slightly to test a new sort algorithm. Here it is shown as a driver for testing the class `SimpleSortDouble`:

```java
public class TestSort {
    static double[] testData = {
                    0.3, 1.3e-2, 7.9, 3.17,
            };

    public static void main(String[] args) {
        SortDouble bsort = new SimpleSortDouble();
        SortMetrics metrics = bsort.sort(testData);
        System.out.println("Metrics: " + metrics);
        for (int i = 0; i < testData.length; i++)
            System.out.println("\t" + testData[i]);
    }
}
```

The `main` method shows how code that drives a test works: it creates an object of a class extended from `SortDouble`, provides it with the data to be sorted, and invokes `sort`. The `sort` method stores the data, initializes the metrics and then invokes the abstract method `doSort`. Each extended class implements `doSort` to do its sorting, invoking `getDataLength`, `compare`, and `swap` when it needs to. When `doSort` returns, the counts reflect the number of each operation performed. To test a different algorithm, you can simply change the class name after the `new`. Here is what one run of `TestSort` looks like:

```
Metrics: 0 probes 6 compares 2 swaps
        0.013
        0.3
        3.17
        7.9
```

Now let us return to the issue of designing a class to be extended, with these classes as examples. We carefully designed the protected interface of `SortDouble` to allow extended classes more intimate access to the data in the object but only to things we *want* them to manipulate. The access for each part of the class design has been carefully chosen:

- *public:* The `public` part of the class is designed for use by the code that tests how expensive the sorting algorithm is. An example of testing code is in `TestSort.main`. This code provides the data to be sorted and gets the results of the test. For the test code, the metrics are read-only. The public `sort` method we provide for the test code ensures that the metrics are initialized before they are used.

  Making the actual `doSort` method `protected` forces the test code to invoke it indirectly via the public `sort` method; thus, we guarantee that the metrics are always initialized and avoid another possible error.

  To the test code, the only available functionality of the class is to drive a test of a particular sorting algorithm and provide the results. We used methods and access protection to hide the rest of the class, which should not be exposed to the testing code.

- *protected:* The `protected` part of the class is designed for use by the sorting code to produce a properly metered sort. The `protected` contract lets the sorting algorithm examine and modify the data to produce a sorted list by whatever means the sort desires. It also gives the sorting algorithm a context in which it will be properly driven so it can be measured. This context is the `doSort` method.

  The extended class is not considered trustworthy, and that is why it can access the data only indirectly, through methods that have access to the data. For example, to hide a comparison by avoiding `compare`, the sort would have to use `probe` to find out what is in the array. Because calls to `probe` are also metered, this would, in the end, hide nothing.

  In addition, `getMetrics` returns a clone of the actual metrics, so a sorting implementation cannot modify the values.

- *private:* The class keeps private to itself data that should be hidden from the outside—namely, the data being sorted and the metrics. Outside code cannot access these fields, directly or indirectly.

As we said earlier, in order to prevent intentional cheating and accidental misuse, `SortDouble` is designed not to trust its extended classes. For example, if `SortDouble.values` (the array being sorted) were `protected` instead of `private`, we could eliminate the `probe` method, because sort algorithms normally count only comparisons and swaps. But if we had, the programmer writing an extended class could avoid using `swap` to swap data. The results would be invalid in ways that might be hard to notice. Counting probes and declaring the array `private` preclude some bugs as well as intentionally devious programming.

If a class is not designed to be extended, it often will be misused by sub-classes. If your class will have subclasses, you should design its `protected` parts carefully. The end result may be to have no `protected` members if extended classes need no special access. If you do not design the `protected` part of your class, the class should have no `protected` members, making subclasses rely on its public contract.

Exercise 3.11: Find at least one security hole in `SortDouble` that would let a sorting algorithm cheat on its metrics without getting caught. Fix the security hole. Assume that the sorting algorithm author doesn't get to write `main`.

Exercise 3.12: Write a generic `SortHarness` class that can sort any object type. How would you provide a way to represent ordering for the objects in a generic way, given that you cannot use < to compare them?

3.12   Single Inheritance versus Multiple Inheritance

A new class can extend exactly one superclass, a model known as *single inherit-ance*. Extending a class means that the new class inherits not only its superclass's contract but also its superclass's implementation. Some object-oriented languages employ *multiple inheritance,* in which a new class can have two or more super-classes.

Multiple inheritance is useful when a new class wants to combine multiple contracts and inherit some, or all, of the implementation of those contracts. But when there is more than one superclass, problems arise when a superclass's behavior is inherited in two ways. Assume, for a moment, the following type tree:

This is commonly called *diamond inheritance,* and there is nothing wrong with it. Many legitimate designs show this structure. The problems exist in the inheritance of implementation, when W's implementation stores some state. If class W had, for example, a public field named `goggin`, and if you had a reference to an object of type Z called `zref`, what would `zref.goggin` refer to? It might refer to X's copy of `goggin`, or it might refer to Y's copy, or X and Y might share a single copy of `goggin` because Z is really only a W once even though it is both an X and a Y.

Resolving such issues is non-trivial and complicates the design and use of class hierarchies. To avoid such issues, the Java programming language uses the single-inheritance model of object-oriented programming.

Single inheritance precludes some useful and correct designs. The problems of multiple inheritance arise from multiple inheritance of implementation, but in many cases multiple inheritance is used to inherit a number of abstract contracts and perhaps one concrete implementation. Providing a means to inherit an abstract contract without inheriting an implementation allows the typing benefits of multiple inheritance without the problems of multiple implementation inheritance. The inheritance of an abstract contract is termed *interface inheritance*. The Java programming language supports interface inheritance by allowing you to declare an `interface` type—the subject of the next chapter.

> *Insanity is hereditary. You can catch it from your kids.*
> —Erma Bombeck

CHAPTER 4

Interfaces

"Conducting" is when you draw "designs" in the nowhere—with your stick,
or with your hands—which are interpreted as "instructional messages"
by guys wearing bow ties who wish they were fishing.
—Frank Zappa

THE fundamental unit of programming in the Java programming language is the *class*, but the fundamental unit of object-oriented design is the *type*. While classes define types, it is very useful and powerful to be able to define a type without defining a class. *Interfaces* define types in an abstract form as a collection of methods or other types that form the contract for that type. Interfaces contain no implementation and you cannot create instances of an interface. Rather, classes can expand their own types by *implementing* one or more interfaces. An interface is an expression of pure design, whereas a class is a mix of design and implementation.

A class can implement the methods of an interface in any way that the designer of the class chooses. An interface thus has many more possible implementations than a class. Every major class in an application should be an implementation of some interface that captures the contract of that class.

Classes can implement more than one interface. The Java programming language allows multiple inheritance of interface but only single inheritance of implementation—a class can extend only one other class. Classes can use inheritance of interfaces to expand their type and then use, for example, composition to provide an implementation for those interfaces. This design allows the typing flexibility of multiple inheritance, while avoiding the pitfalls of multiple implementation inheritance, at the cost of some additional work for the programmer.

In a given class, the classes that are extended and the interfaces that are implemented are collectively called the *supertypes,* and from the viewpoint of the supertypes, the new class is a *subtype.* The new class includes all its supertypes, so a reference to an object of the subtype can be used polymorphically anywhere a reference to an object of any of its supertypes (class or interface) is required. Interface declarations create type names just as class declarations do; you can use the name of an interface as the type name of a variable, and any object whose class implements that interface can be assigned to that variable.

4.1   A Simple Interface Example

Many simple interfaces define a property that is ascribable to a variety of different objects from different classes. These properties are often defined in terms of an object being "able" to do something. For example, in the standard packages there are a number of "ability" interfaces, such as:

- ◆ Cloneable: objects of this type support cloning, as you learned in detail on page 89.
- ◆ Comparable: objects of this type have an ordering that allows them to be compared.
- ◆ Runnable: objects of this type have behavior that can execute in an independent thread of control (see Chapter 10).
- ◆ Serializable: objects of this type can be written to an object byte stream, for shipping to a new virtual machine, or storing persistently, and then reconstituted into a live object (see "Object Serialization" on page 404).

Let's look at the Comparable interface in more detail. This interface can be implemented by any class whose objects can be compared to each other based on the class's "natural ordering." The interface contains a single method and is declared as follows:

```
public interface Comparable {
    int compareTo(Object o);
}
```

An interface declaration is very similar to a class declaration, except the keyword interface is used instead of class. There are also special rules concerning the members of an interface, as you will soon learn.

The compareTo method takes a single object argument and compares it to the current object, returning a negative, zero, or positive integer if the current object is less than, equal to, or greater than the argument, respectively. If the two objects are not *mutually comparable* (which usually means they have incompatible types) a ClassCastException is thrown.

Consider the celestial body class we introduced in Chapter 2. The natural ordering for celestial bodies that orbit the same body could be defined as their orbital distance from that body. We could then make Body objects Comparable as follows:

```
class Body implements Comparable {
    // body fields omitted ...
    int orbitalDistance = ...; // set during construction

    public int compareTo(Object o) {
        Body other = (Body)o;
        if (orbits == other.orbits)
            return orbitalDistance - other.orbitalDistance;
        else
            throw new IllegalArgumentException("bad orbit");
    }
}
```

First we declare that Body is a Comparable class. A class identifies the interface types that it implements by listing them after the keyword implements, before the class body is defined (and after any extends clause). All such interfaces are the *superinterfaces* of the class. The class must provide an implementation for all of the methods defined in its superinterfaces, or else the class must be declared abstract, thereby requiring that any non-abstract subclass implement them.

In our Body example, as with most compareTo implementations, we have to use a type cast to convert the generic Object reference into a specific Body reference before making the actual comparison. If the argument passed in was not in fact a Body object, the cast will result in a ClassCastException. We can then compare the orbital distances of the two bodies and return an appropriate value. If the two bodies don't orbit the same body they can't be meaningfully compared, so we throw an IllegalArgumentException. Exceptions are discussed in detail in Chapter 8.

Interfaces introduce type names just as classes do, so you can declare variables of those types. For example:

```
Comparable obj;
```

In fact much of the power of interfaces comes from declaring and using only variables of interface type rather than of some specific class type. For example, you can define a generic sort routine that can sort any array of Comparable objects (assuming the objects are compatible) without regard for what the class of those objects actually is.

```
class Sorter {
    public static Comparable[] sort(Comparable[] list) {
        // implementation details ...
        return list;
    }
}
```

References of interface type, however, can be used only to access members of that interface. For example, the following will produce a compile-time error:

```
Comparable obj = new Body();
String name = obj.getName(); // INVALID: Comparable has
                            //                no getName method
```

If you want to treat `obj` as a `Body` object you must explicitly cast it to that type. The exception to this rule is that you can treat any interface reference as a reference to `Object` because the object referred to must be of some class and all classes extend `Object`. Hence the following is legal:

```
String desc = obj.toString();
```

as is assigning an interface reference to an `Object` reference.

4.2   Interface Declarations

An interface is declared using the keyword `interface`, giving the interface a name and listing the interface members between curly braces.

An interface can declare three kinds of members:

- ◆ constants (fields)
- ◆ methods
- ◆ nested classes and interfaces

All interface members are implicitly public, but, by convention, the `public` modifier is omitted. Having non-public members in an interface would make little sense, and where it does make sense you can use the accessibility of the interface itself to control access to the interface members.

We defer a discussion of nested classes and interfaces until Chapter 5.

4.2.1 Interface Constants

An interface can declare named constants. These constants are defined as fields but are implicitly `public`, `static`, and `final`—again, by convention, the modifiers are omitted from the field declarations. These fields must also have initializers—*blank finals* are not permitted.

Because interfaces contain no implementation details, they cannot define normal fields—such a definition would be dictating implementation policy to the classes that choose to implement the interface. Interfaces can define named constants because these are useful in the design of types. For example, an interface that had differing levels of verbosity in its contract might have the following:

```
interface Verbose {
    int SILENT  = 0;
    int TERSE   = 1;
    int NORMAL  = 2;
    int VERBOSE = 3;

    void setVerbosity(int level);
    int getVerbosity();
}
```

`SILENT`, `TERSE`, `NORMAL`, and `VERBOSE` can be passed to the `setVerbosity` method, giving names to constant values that represent specific meanings.

If you need shared, modifiable data in your interface, you can achieve this effect using a named constant that refers to an object that holds the data. A nested class is good for defining that object, so we'll defer an example until Chapter 5.

4.2.2 Interface Methods

The methods declared in an interface are implicitly `abstract` because no implementation is, or can be, given for them. For this reason the method body is specified as a semicolon after the method header. By convention, the `abstract` modifier on the method declaration is omitted.

No other method modifiers are permitted on an interface method declaration. They are implicitly `public` and so can have no other access modifier; they cannot have modifiers that define implementation characteristics—such as `native`, `synchronized`, or `strictfp`—because an interface does not dictate implementation; they cannot be `final` because they haven't been implemented yet, nor can they be `static` because `static` methods can't be `abstract`. Of course the implementation of these methods within a specific class can have whichever modifiers are appropriate.

4.2.3   Interface Modifiers

An interface declaration can be preceded by interface modifiers:

- *public*—a `public` interface is publicly accessible. Without this modifier an interface is only accessible within its own package.

- *abstract*—all interfaces are implicitly `abstract` because their methods are all abstract—they have no implementation. Again, by convention, the `abstract` modifier is always omitted.

- *strict floating point*—an interface declared `strictfp` has all floating point arithmetic, defined within the interface, evaluated strictly. In contrast to classes, this does not imply that each method in the interface is implicitly `strictfp`, as that is an implementation detail. See "Strict and non-Strict Floating-Point Arithmetic" on page 158 for details.

When multiple modifiers are applied to the same interface declaration, we recommend using the order listed above.

4.3   Extending Interfaces

Interfaces can be extended using the `extends` keyword. Interfaces, unlike classes, can extend more than one other interface:

```
public interface SerializableRunnable
                extends java.io.Serializable, Runnable
{
    // ...
}
```

The `SerializableRunnable` interface extends both `java.io.Serializable` and `Runnable`, which means that all methods and constants defined by those interfaces are now part of the `SerializableRunnable` contract, together with any new methods and constants it defines. The interfaces that are extended are the *superinterfaces* of the new interface and the new interface is a *subinterface* of its superinterfaces.

Because interfaces support multiple inheritance, the inheritance graph can contain multiple paths to the same superinterface. This means that constants and methods can be accessed in different ways. However, because interfaces define no implementation of methods, and provide no per-object fields, there are no issues regarding the semantics of this form of multiple inheritance.

4.3.1   Inheriting and Hiding Constants

An extended interface inherits all of the constants declared in its superinterfaces. If an interface declares a constant of the same name as an inherited constant, regardless of their types, then the new constant hides the inherited one; this is the same hiding of fields described in "Hiding Fields" on page 74. In the subinterface, and in any object implementing the subinterface, any reference to the constant using its simple name will refer to the constant defined in the subinterface. The inherited constant can still be accessed by using the qualified name of the constant—that is, the interface name followed by dot and then the constant name— the usual way of referring to static members.

```
interface X {
    int val = 1;
}
interface Y extends X {
    int val = 2;
    int sum = val + X.val;
}
```

Interface Y has two constants: val and sum. From inside Y, to refer to the hidden val in its superinterface you must qualify it as X.val. Externally you can access the constants of Y using the normal static forms of Y.val and Y.sum, and of course you can access X's val constant using X.val.

These rules are, of course, identical to those concerning the inheritance of static fields in classes.

When a class implements Y you can access the constants in Y as though they were constants declared in the class. For example, given

```
class Z implements Y { }
```

you can do

```
System.out.println("Z.val=" + Z.val + ", Z.sum=" + Z.sum);
```

but there is no way to refer to X.val via Z. However, given an instance of Z you can use an explicit cast to access X.val:

```
Z z = new Z();
System.out.println("z.val=" + z.val +
                ", ((Y)z).val=" + ((Y)z).val +
                ", ((X)z).val=" + ((X)z).val);
```

which prints out

```
z.val=2, ((Y)z).val=2, ((X)z).val=1
```

as you would expect. Again these are the same rules that apply to static fields in extended classes—it doesn't matter whether a class inherits a static field from a superclass or a superinterface.

While all these rules are necessary from a language perspective, they have little practical consequence—there are few reasons to hide existing fields and all accesses to static fields, whether class or interface, should be via the type name for where that field is declared.

If an interface inherits two or more constants with the same name, then any simple reference to the constant is ambiguous and results in a compile-time error. For example, given the previous interface declarations and the following

```
interface C {
    String val = "Interface C";
}
interface D extends X, C { }
```

then the expression `D.val` is ambiguous—does it mean the integer `val` or the `String` reference `val`? Inside `D` you would have to explicitly use `X.val` or `C.val`.

A class that implements more than one interface, or which extends a class and implements one or more interfaces, can experience the same hiding and ambiguity issues as an interface that extends more than one interface—the class's own static fields can hide the inherited fields of the interfaces it implements or the class it extends, and simple references to multiply-inherited non-hidden fields will be ambiguous.

4.3.2   Inheriting, Overriding, and Overloading Methods

A subinterface inherits all of the methods declared in its superinterfaces. If a declared method in a subinterface has the same signature (name and parameter list) as an inherited method and the same return type, then the new declaration *overrides* any and all existing declarations. Overriding in interfaces, unlike overriding in classes, has no semantic effect—the interface effectively contains multiple declarations of the same method, but in any one implementing class there can only be one implementation of that method.

Similarly, if an interface inherits more than one method with the same signature, or a class implements different interfaces containing a method with the same signature, there is only one such method—whose implementation is ultimately defined by the class implementing the interfaces. There is no question of ambiguity in this case.

The real issue is whether a single implementation of the method can honor all the contracts implied by that method being part of the different interfaces. This may be an impossible requirement to satisfy in some circumstances. For example:

```
interface CardDealer {
    void draw();          // flip top card
    void deal();          // distribute cards
    void shuffle();
}
interface GraphicalComponent {
    void draw();             // render on default device
    void draw(Device d);  // render on 'd'
    void rotate(int degrees);
    void fill(Color c);
}
interface GraphicalCardDealer
          extends CardDealer, GraphicalComponent { }
```

Here it is difficult to write an implementation of draw() that can satisfy the two different contracts independently. If you try to satisfy them simultaneously, you are unlikely to achieve the desired results: flipping a card each time the screen gets repainted.

As with overriding in class extension, the overriding method is not permitted to throw more checked exceptions than the method it overrides. If two or more method declarations are inherited, without overriding, and differ in the exceptions they throw, then the implementation of that method must satisfy all of the throws clauses of those declarations. Again the main issue is whether such distinct methods can have a single implementation that honors all contracts. We will look further at the issues of overriding and exception throwing in Chapter 8.

If a declared method has the same name but different parameters from an inherited method, then the declared method is an *overloaded* form of the inherited method. The eventual class implementation will provide a method body for each of the overloaded forms.

If a declared method differs only in return type from an inherited method, or if two inherited methods differ only in return type, then an error occurs.

4.4 Working with Interfaces

The previous chapter introduced the Attr class and showed how to extend it to make specialized types of attribute objects. Now all you need is the ability to associate attributes with objects.

The first decision to make is whether having attributes is reflected in the type of the object. An object could, if you chose, contain a set of attributes and allow programmers access to that set. Or you could say that being able to store attributes on an object is a part of its type and so should be part of the type hierarchy. Both positions are legitimate. We believe that representing the ability to hold attributes in the type hierarchy is most useful. We will create an `Attributed` type to be used for objects that can be attributed by attaching `Attr` objects to them.

To create an `Attributed` type you could define a class that would form the superclass for all attributed objects. But then programmers must decide whether to inherit from `Attributed` or from some other useful class. Instead we make `Attributed` into an interface:

```
public interface Attributed {
    void add(Attr newAttr);
    Attr find(String attrName);
    Attr remove(String attrName);
    java.util.Iterator attrs();
}
```

This interface declares four methods: one for adding a new attribute to an `Attributed` object; one for finding whether an attribute of a given name has been added to that object; one for removing an attribute from an object; and one for returning a list of the attributes currently attached to the object. This list is returned using the `Iterator` interface defined for the collection classes. `java.util.Iterator` is covered in detail in Chapter 17.

4.4.1 Implementing Interfaces

Interfaces describe contracts in a pure, abstract form, but an interface is interesting only if a class implements it.

Some interfaces are purely abstract—they do not have any useful general implementation but must be implemented afresh for each new class. Most interfaces, however, may have several useful implementations. In the case of our `Attributed` interface, we can imagine several possible implementations that use various strategies to store a set of attributes.

One strategy might be simple and fast when only a few attributes are in a set; another one might be optimized for attribute sets that are queried more often than they are changed; yet another design might be optimized for sets that change frequently. If there were a package of various implementations for the `Attributed` interface, a class might choose to implement the `Attributed` interface through any one of them or through its own implementation.

As an example, here is a simple implementation of `Attributed` that uses the utility `java.util.HashMap` class. The class `AttributedImpl` declares that it `implements` the interface `Attributed`, so the class must implement all the interface's methods. `AttributedImpl` implements the methods using a `HashMap`, described in "HashMap" on page 440. Later, this implementation is used to implement the `Attributed` interface for a specific set of objects to which you would want to add attributes. First, here is the `AttributedImpl` class:

```
import java.util.*;

class AttributedImpl implements Attributed {
    protected HashMap attrTable = new HashMap();

    public void add(Attr newAttr) {
        attrTable.put(newAttr.getName(), newAttr);
    }

    public Attr find(String name) {
        return (Attr)attrTable.get(name);
    }

    public Attr remove(String name) {
        return (Attr)attrTable.remove(name);
    }

    public Iterator attrs() {
        return attrTable.values().iterator();
    }
}
```

The initializer for `attrTable` creates a `HashMap` object to hold attributes. This `HashMap` object does most of the actual work. The `HashMap` class uses the key object's `hashCode` method to hash any object it is given as a key. No explicit hash method is needed since `String` already provides a good `hashCode` implementation.

When a new attribute is added, the `Attr` object is stored in the hash map under its name, and then you can easily use the hash map to find and remove attributes by name.

The `attrs` method returns an `Iterator` that lists all the attributes in the set. `Iterator` is an interface defined in `java.util` for *collection classes* like `HashMap` to use when returning lists (see "Iteration" on page 425). The same type is used here because it is a standard way for classes to represent a list. In effect, the `Attributed` interface defines a collection type, so we use the normal mechanism for returning the contents of a collection, namely, the `Iterator` class. Using `Iterator` has another benefit: it is easy to implement `Attributed` using a standard collection class that uses `Iterator`, such as `HashMap`, because the standard collection's methods return `Iterator` objects.

4.4.2 Using an Implementation

You can use an implementing class like `AttributedImpl` by simply extending the class. This is the simplest tool when it is available because all the methods and their implementations are inherited. But if you need to support more than one interface or extend a different class, you must use a different approach. The most common approach is to create an object of an implementing class and *forward* all the methods of the interface to that object, returning any values—this is often called *composition*.

In composition and forwarding, each method in the class that is inherited from the interface invokes the implementation from another object and returns the result. Here is an implementation of the `Attributed` interface that uses an `AttributedImpl` object to build an attributed version of our previously-defined celestial body class `Body`:

```
import java.util.Iterator;

class AttributedBody extends Body
    implements Attributed
{
    private AttributedImpl attrImpl = new AttributedImpl();

    public AttributedBody() {
        super();
    }

    public AttributedBody(String name, Body orbits) {
        super(name, orbits);
    }

    // Forward all Attributed methods to the attrImpl object

    public void add(Attr newAttr)
        { attrImpl.add(newAttr); }
    public Attr find(String name)
```

```
            { return attrImpl.find(name); }
        public Attr remove(String name)
            { return attrImpl.remove(name); }
        public Iterator attrs()
            { return attrImpl.attrs(); }
    }
```

The declaration that `AttributedBody` extends Body and implements `Attributed` defines the contract of `AttributedBody`. The implementations of all Body's methods are inherited from the Body class itself. Each method of `Attributed` is implemented by forwarding the invocation to the `AttributedImpl` object's equivalent method, returning its value (if any). This also means that you must add a field of type `AttributedImpl` to use in the forwarding methods and initialize that field to refer to an `AttributedImpl` object.

Forwarding is both straightforward and much less work than implementing `Attributed` from scratch. Forwarding also enables you to quickly change the implementation you use, should a better implementation of `Attributed` become available at some future date. However, forwarding must be set up manually and that can be tedious and sometimes error prone.

4.5   Marker Interfaces

Some interfaces do not declare any methods but simply mark a class as having some general property. The `Cloneable` interface is such a *marker* interface—it has neither methods nor constants, but marks a class as partaking in the cloning mechanism (see page 89).

Marker interfaces are the degenerate case of contract because they define no language-level behavior—no methods or values. All their contract is in the documentation that describes the expectations you must satisfy if your class implements that interface. The interfaces `Serializable` and `Externalizable` (described in "Object Serialization" on page 404) are marker interfaces, as are both `java.rmi.Remote` (see "java.rmi—Remote Method Invocation" on page 538) and `java.util.EventListener` (see "java.awt—The Abstract Window Toolkit" on page 529).

Marker interfaces can have a profound impact on the behavior of the classes that implement them—consider `Cloneable`. Do not be fooled into thinking that they are unimportant merely because they have no methods.

4.6   When to Use Interfaces

An interface defines a type with an abstract contract. An abstract class also defines a type with an abstract contract. Which should you use and when?

There are two major differences between interfaces and abstract classes:

♦ Interfaces provide a form of multiple inheritance, because you can implement multiple interfaces. A class can extend only one other class, even if that class has only `abstract` methods.

♦ An `abstract` class can have a partial implementation, protected parts, static methods, and so on, whereas interfaces are limited to public constants and public methods with no implementation.

These differences usually direct the choice of which tool is best to use in a particular implementation. If multiple inheritance is important or even useful, interfaces are used. However, an abstract class enables you to provide some or all of the implementation so that it can be inherited easily, rather than by explicit forwarding. Additionally, an abstract class can control the implementation of certain methods by making them `final`—for example, our `SortDouble` class in Chapter 3, ensures that sorting is done using the appropriate metrics. However, if you find yourself writing an abstract class with all abstract methods, you're really writing an interface.

Any major class you expect to be extended, whether abstract or not, should be an implementation of an interface. Although this approach requires a little more work on your part, it enables a whole category of use that is otherwise precluded. For example, suppose we had created an `Attributed` class instead of an `Attributed` interface with an `AttributedImpl` implementation class. In that case, programmers who wanted to create new classes that extended other existing classes could never use `Attributed`, since you can extend only one class—the class `AttributedBody` could never have been created. Because `Attributed` is an interface, programmers have a choice: they can extend `AttributedImpl` directly and avoid the forwarding, or, if they cannot extend, they can at least use composition and forwarding to implement the interface. And if the general implementation provided is incorrect, they can write their own implementation. You can even provide multiple possible implementations of the interface to prospective users. Whatever implementation strategy programmers prefer, the objects they create are `Attributed`.

Exercise 4.1: Rewrite your solution to Exercise 3.6 on page 87 using an interface if you didn't write it that way in the first place.

Exercise 4.2: Rewrite your solution to Exercise 3.12 on page 102 using an interface if you didn't write it that way in the first place.

Exercise 4.3: Should the LinkedList class from previous exercises be an interface? Rewrite it that way with an implementation class before you decide.

Exercise 4.4: Design a collection class hierarchy using only interfaces.

Exercise 4.5: Think about whether the following types should be represented as interfaces, abstract classes, or concrete classes: (a) TreeNode to represent nodes in an N-ary tree; (b) TreeWalker to walk the tree in a particular order (such as depth-first or breadth-first); (c) Drawable for objects that can be drawn by a graphics system; (d) Application for programs that can be run from a graphical desktop.

Exercise 4.6: What changes in your assumptions about each of the problems in Exercise 4.5 would make you change your answers?

> *There are two ways of constructing a software design:*
> *one way is to make it so simple that there are obviously no deficiencies;*
> *the other is to make it so complicated that there are no obvious deficiencies.*
> —C.A.R. Hoare

CHAPTER 5

Nested Classes and Interfaces

Every nonzero finite-dimensional inner product space has an orthonormal basis.
It makes sense, when you don't think about it.
—Math Professor, U.C. Berkeley

CLASSES and interfaces can be declared inside other classes and interfaces, either as members or within blocks of code. These *nested classes* and *nested interfaces* can take a number of different forms, each with their own properties.

The ability to define nested types serves two main purposes. Firstly, nested classes and nested interfaces allow types to be structured and scoped into logically related groups. Secondly, and more importantly, nested classes can be used to connect logically related objects in a simple and effective manner. This latter capability is used extensively of event frameworks, such as that used in AWT (see "java.awt—The Abstract Window Toolkit" on page 529) and the JavaBeans™ component architecture (see "java.beans—Components" on page 533).

A nested type is considered a part of its enclosing type and they share a trust relationship where each can access all members of the other. Differences between nested types arise depending on whether the nested type is a class or interface, and whether the enclosing type is a class or interface. Nested types are declared either static or not: the former allows simple structuring of types, while the latter defines a special relationship between a nested object and an object of the enclosing class. Static nested types are more basic, so you will learn about them first.

5.1 Static Nested Types

A nested class or interface that is declared as a static member of its enclosing class or interface acts just like any non-nested, or top-level, class or interface, except that its name and accessibility are defined by its *enclosing type*. The name

121

of a nested type is expressed as *EnclosingName.NestedName* and it is accessible only if the enclosing type is accessible.

Static nested types serve as a structuring and scoping mechanism for logically related types. However, static nested types are members of their enclosing type and as such can access all other members of the enclosing type including private ones. This gives the nested type a special, privileged relationship with the enclosing type.

As static nested types are members of their enclosing type, the same accessibility rules apply to them as for other members. For classes this means that a static nested class or interface can have private, package, protected or public access, while for interfaces all members are implicitly public, including nested types.

5.1.1   Static Nested Classes

The static nested class is the simplest form of nested class and is declared by preceding the class declaration with the `static` modifier. When nested in an interface, a class declaration is always static and the modifier is omitted. A static nested class acts just like any top-level class. It can extend any other class, implement any interface and itself be used for further extension by any class to which it is accessible. It can be declared `final` or `abstract`, just as a top-level class can.

Static nested classes serve as a mechanism for defining logically related types within a context where that type makes sense. For example, on page 53 we showed a `Permissions` class that bears information about a `BankAccount` object. Because the `Permissions` class is related to the contract of the `BankAccount` class—it is how a `BankAccount` object communicates a set of permissions—it is a good candidate to be a nested class:

```
public class BankAccount {
    private long number;          // account number
    private long balance;         // current balance

    public static class Permissions {
        public boolean canDeposit,
                       canWithdraw,
                       canClose;
    }
    // ...
}
```

The `Permissions` class is defined inside the `BankAccount` class, making it a member of that class. When `permissionsFor` returns a `Permissions` object, it can call the class simply `Permissions` in the same way it can refer to `balance` without qualification: `Permissions` is a member of the class. The full name of the class is `BankAccount.Permissions`. This is a clear indication that this class exists as part of the `BankAccount` class, not as a stand-alone type. Code outside the `BankAccount` class must use the full name, for example:

```
BankAccount.Permissions perm = acct.permissionsFor(owner);
```

If `BankAccount` were in a package named `bank`, the full name of the class would be `bank.BankAccount.Permissions`—packages are discussed in Chapter 13. In your own code, you could import the class `BankAccount.Permissions` and then use the simple name `Permissions`, but you would lose the important information about the subsidiary nature of the class.

Static nested classes, within a class, are class members, and you can declare them to be accessible in any way you like. You can, for example, declare a class that is an implementation detail to be `private`. We declare `Permissions` to be `public` because programmers using `BankAccount` need to use the class.

As `Permissions` is a member of `BankAccount`, the `Permissions` class can access all other members of `BankAccount`, including all inherited members. For example, if `Permissions` declared a method that took a `BankAccount` object as an argument, that method would be able to directly access both the `number` and `balance` fields of that account. In this sense the nested class is seen as part of the implementation of the enclosing class and so is completely trusted.

There is no restriction on how a static nested class can be extended—it can be extended by any class to which it is accessible. Of course, the extended class does not inherit the privileged access that the nested class has to the enclosing class.

5.1.2   Nested Interfaces

Nested interfaces are always static though, by convention, the `static` modifier is omitted from the interface declaration. They serve simply as a structuring mechanism for related types. When we look at non-static nested classes you will see that they are inherently concerned with implementation issues. Since interfaces do not dictate implementation they cannot be non-static.

5.2   Inner Classes

Non-static nested classes are called *inner classes*. Non-static class members are associated with instances of the class—non-static fields are instance variables and non-static methods operate on an instance. Similarly an inner class is also associated with an instance of the class, or more specifically an object of an inner class is always associated with an object of its enclosing class—the *enclosing object*.

You often need to closely tie a nested class object to a particular object of the enclosing class. Consider, for example, a method for the BankAccount class that lets you see the last action performed on the account, such as a deposit or withdrawal:

```
public class BankAccount {
    private long number;        // account number
    private long balance;       // current balance
    private Action lastAct;     // last action performed

    public class Action {
        private String act;
        private long amount;
        Action(String act, long amount) {
            this.act = act;
            this.amount = amount;
        }
        public String toString() {
            // identify our enclosing account
            return number + ": " + act + " " + amount;
        }
    }

    public void deposit(long amount) {
        balance += amount;
        lastAct = new Action("deposit", amount);
    }

    public void withdraw(long amount) {
        balance -= amount;
        lastAct = new Action("withdraw", amount);
    }
    // ...
}
```

The class Action records a single action on the account. It is not declared static, and that means its objects exist relative to an object of the enclosing class.

The relationship between an Action object and its BankAccount object is established when the Action object is created, as shown in the deposit and withdraw methods. When an inner class object is created, it must be associated with an object of its enclosing class. Usually, inner class objects are created inside instance methods of the enclosing class, as in deposit and withdraw. When that occurs the current object this is associated with the inner object by default. The creation code in deposit is the same as the more explicit

```
lastAct = this.new Action("deposit", amount);
```

Any BankAccount object could be substituted for this. For example, suppose we add a transfer operation that takes a specified amount from one account and places it in the current account—such an action needs to update the lastAct field of both account objects:

```
public void transfer(BankAccount other, long amount){
    other.withdraw(amount);
    deposit(amount);
    lastAct = this.new Action("transfer", amount);
    other.lastAct = other.new Action("transfer", amount);
}
```

In this case we bind the second Action object to the other BankAccount object.

An inner class declaration is just like a top-level class declaration except for one restriction—inner classes cannot have static members, except for final static fields that are initialized to constants or expressions built up from constants. The rationale for allowing constants to be declared in an inner class is the same as that for allowing them in interfaces—it can be convenient to define constants within the type that uses them.

As with top-level classes, inner classes can extend any other class, implement any interface and be extended by any other class. An inner class can be declared final or abstract.

5.2.1 Accessing Enclosing Objects

The toString method of Action uses the number field of its enclosing BankAccount object directly. A nested class can access all members of its enclosing class—including private fields and methods—without qualification, because it is part of the enclosing class's implementation. An inner class can simply name the members of its enclosing object to use them. The names in the enclosing class are all said to be *in scope*. The enclosing class can also access the private members of the inner class, but only via an explicit reference to an inner class object— such as lastAct. While an object of the inner class is always associated with an object of the enclosing class, the converse is not true. An object of the enclosing class need not have any inner class objects associated with it, or it could have many.

When `deposit` creates an `Action` object, a reference to the enclosing `BankAccount` object is automatically stored in the new `Action` object. Using this saved reference, the `Action` object can always refer to the enclosing `BankAccount` object's `number` field by the simple name `number`, as shown in `toString`. The name of the reference to the enclosing object is `this` preceded by the enclosing class name. For example, `toString` could reference the `number` field of the enclosing `BankAccount` object explicitly:

```
return BankAccount.this.number + ": " + act + " " + amount;
```

The `this` nomenclature reinforces the idea that the enclosing object and the inner object are tightly bound as part of the same implementation of the enclosing class.

A nested class can have its own nested classes and interfaces. References to enclosing objects can be obtained for any level of nesting in the same way: the name of the class and `this`. If class X encloses class Y which encloses class Z, code in Z can explicitly access fields of X by using `X.this`.

The language does not prevent you from deeply nesting classes, but good taste should. A doubly-nested class such as Z has three name scopes: itself, its immediate enclosing class Y, and outermost class X. Someone reading the code for Z must understand each class thoroughly to know in which context an identifier is bound and which enclosing object was bound to which nested object. We recommend nesting only one level under most circumstances. Nesting more than two levels invites a readability disaster and should probably never be attempted.

5.2.2   Extending Inner Classes

An inner class can be extended just as any static nested class or top-level class can. The only requirement is that objects of the extended class must still be associated with objects of the original enclosing class or a subclass. Usually this is not a problem as the extended inner class is often declared within an extension of the outer class:

```
class Outer {
    class Inner { }
}

class ExtendedOuter extends Outer {
    class ExtendedInner extends Inner { }
    Inner ref = new ExtendedInner();
}
```

The `ref` field is initialized when an `ExtendedOuter` object is created. The creation of the `ExtendedInner` instance uses the default no-arg constructor of

ExtendedInner, which in turn implicitly invokes the default no-arg constructor of Inner using super. The constructor for Inner requires an object of Outer to bind to, which in this case is implicitly the current object of ExtendedOuter.

If the enclosing class of the inner subclass is not a subclass of Outer, or if the inner subclass is not itself an inner class, then an explicit reference to an object of Outer must be supplied when the Inner constructor is invoked via super. For example:

```
class Unrelated extends Outer.Inner {
    Unrelated(Outer ref) {
        ref.super();
    }
}
```

When the construction of an Unrelated object gets to the point where the superclass constructor is invoked, there must be an object of class Outer to which the superclass object can be bound. As Unrelated is not itself an inner class of Outer, there is no implicit enclosing object. Similarly, because Unrelated is not a subclass of Outer, the current object of Unrelated is not a valid enclosing object. We must provide an explicit reference to an Outer object for the superclass object to bind to. We chose to supply that reference using an argument to the Unrelated constructor. That constructor uses it as an explicit binding reference in the invocation of the superclass constructor.

Note that you cannot use the inner class creation syntax to externally provide an Outer object, as in

```
Outer ref = new Outer();
Unrelated u = ref.new Unrelated(); // INVALID
```

because this syntax supplies an enclosing object for the Unrelated class, and Unrelated is *not* an inner class.

An inner class can extend another, unrelated, inner class provided an appropriate enclosing instance is supplied to the superclass, as just described. The resulting inner class then has two enclosing instances—one for the extended class and one for the superclass. Such designs are convoluted, however, and are best avoided.

5.2.3   Inheritance, Scoping, and Hiding

Within an inner class, all names declared within the enclosing class are said to be *in scope*—they can be used as if the inner class code were declared in the outer class. An inner class's own fields and methods (and nested types) can *hide* those of the enclosing object. There are two ways in which this can occur:

◆ a field or method is declared in the inner class

◆ a field or method is inherited by the inner class

In the first case any use of the simple name refers to the declaration within the inner class. The enclosing object's field or method must then be accessed explicitly using the `this` nomenclature.

In the second case the use of the simple name is not allowed. Instead the name must be explicitly qualified using `this` or `super`, if it should refer to the inner class name, or using *OuterName*.`this` if it should refer to a member of the enclosing class. The reason for this is to avoid code that looks like it is doing one thing when really it is doing something else. Consider the following:

```
class Host {
    int x;

    class Helper extends Unknown {
        void increment() { x++; }    // INVALID
    }
}
```

The `increment` method appears to increment the `x` field of the enclosing `Host` instance. In fact, `Unknown` declares a field `x` and that field is inherited by `Helper`. The inherited `x` field hides the `x` field from the enclosing scope, so if the above were allowed, it would be the inherited field that was incremented and people reading the code would get the wrong impression about what is happening. Instead, the reference to `x` must be explicitly qualified to indicate which `x` it is meant to refer to: `this.x` or `Host.this.x`.

An inner method with the same name as an enclosing method hides all overloaded forms of the enclosing method, even if the inner class itself does not declare those overloaded forms. For example:

```
class Outer {
    void print() { }
    void print(int val) { }

    class Inner {
        void print() { }
        void show() {
            print();
            Outer.this.print();
            print(1);    // INVALID: no Inner.print(int)
```

```
                    }
                }
            }
```

Here the declaration of `Inner.print` hides all forms of `Outer.print`. When `Inner.show` invokes `print(1)`, the compiler reports that `Inner` has no method `print` that takes an integer argument. The `show` method must explicitly qualify the method invocation with `Outer.this`. As usual, there are few reasons to hide fields or methods in this way.

Exercise 5.1: Create a version of `BankAccount` that records the last ten actions on the account. Add a `history` method that returns a `History` object that will return `Action` objects one at a time via a `next` method, returning `null` at the end of the list. Should `History` be a nested class? If so, should it be static or not?

5.3   Local Inner Classes

You can define inner classes in code blocks, such as a method body, constructor or initialization block. These *local inner classes* are not members of the class of which the code is a part but are local to that block, just as a local variable is. Such classes are completely inaccessible outside of the block in which they are defined—there is simply no way to refer to them—but instances of such classes are normal objects that can be passed as arguments, returned from methods, and which exist until they are no longer referenced. The only modifier which can be applied to local class declarations is `final`—which, as usual, prevents the class from being extended.

A local inner class can access all of the variables that are in scope where the class is defined—local variables, method parameters, instance variables (assuming it is a non-static block) and static variables. The only restriction is that a local variable or method parameter can be accessed only if it is declared `final`. The reason for this restriction relates mainly to multithreading issues (see Chapter 10) and ensures that all such variables have well-defined values when accessed from the inner class. Given that the method accessing the local variable or parameter could be invoked after the completion of the method in which the local class was defined—and hence the local variables and parameters no longer exist—the value of those variables must be frozen before the local class object is created. If needed, you can copy a non-final variable into a `final` one which is subsequently accessed by the local inner class.

Consider the standard interface `Iterator` defined in the `java.util` package. This interface defines a way to iterate through a group of objects. It is commonly used to provide a sequence of elements in a container object but can be used for any generic iteration:

```
package java.util;

public interface Iterator {
    boolean hasNext();
    Object next() throws NoSuchElementException;
    void remove() throws NoSuchElementException;
}
```

The hasNext method returns true if there are more elements to return via next. The remove method deletes the last element returned by next. The exception NoSuchElementException—also part of the java.util package—is thrown if next is invoked when there are no more elements, or if remove is invoked before the first next. See Exercise 16.1 on page 437 for more details.

Here is a simple method that returns an Iterator to walk through an array of objects:

```
public static Iterator walkThrough(final Object[] objs) {
    class Iter implements Iterator {
        private int pos = 0;
        public boolean hasNext() {
            return (pos < objs.length);
        }
        public Object next() throws NoSuchElementException {
            if (pos >= objs.length)
                throw new NoSuchElementException();
            return objs[pos++];
        }
        public void remove() {
            throw new UnsupportedOperationException();
        }
    }

    return new Iter();
}
```

The Iter class is local to the walkThrough method; it is not a member of the enclosing class. Because Iter is local to the method, it has access to all the final variables of the method—in particular the parameter objs. It defines a pos field to keep track of where it is in the objs array. (This code assumes that Iterator and

NoSuchElementException are imported from `java.util` in the source that contains walkThrough.)

Members of local inner classes can hide the local variables and parameters of the block they are declared in, just as they can hide instance fields and methods. The rules discussed on page 127 apply in all cases. The only difference is that once a local variable or parameter has been hidden it is impossible to refer to it.

5.4 Anonymous Inner Classes

When a local inner class seems too much for your needs, you can declare *anonymous classes* that extend a class or implement an interface. These classes are defined at the same time they are instantiated with new. For example, consider the walkThrough method. The class Iter is fairly lightweight and is not needed outside the method. The name Iter doesn't add much value to the code—what is important is that it is an Iterator object. The walkThrough method could use an anonymous class instead:

```
public static Iterator walkThrough(final Object[] objs) {
    return new Iterator() {
        private int pos = 0;
        public boolean hasNext() {
            return (pos < objs.length);
        }
        public Object next() throws NoSuchElementException {
            if (pos >= objs.length)
                throw new NoSuchElementException();
            return objs[pos++];
        }
        public void remove() {
            throw new UnsupportedOperationException();
        }
    };
}
```

Anonymous classes are defined in the new expression itself, as part of a statement. The type specified to new is the supertype of the anonymous class. Because Iterator is an interface, the anonymous class in walkThrough implicitly extends Object and implements Iterator. An anonymous class cannot have an explicit extends or implements clause.

Anonymous inner classes cannot have explicit constructors declared because they have no name to give the constructor. If an anonymous inner class is complex enough that it needs explicit constructors then it should probably be a local inner class. In practice, many anonymous inner classes need little or no initialization. In either case, an anonymous inner class can have initializers and initialization blocks which can access the values that would logically have been passed as a constructor argument. The only construction problem that remains is the need to invoke an explicit superclass constructor. To solve this problem the `new` expression actually invokes the superclass constructor. For example, the following anonymous subclass of `Attr` (see page 66) invokes the single-argument `Attr` constructor and overrides `setValue` to print out the new value each time it is changed:

```
Attr name = new Attr("Name") {
    public Object setValue(Object nv) {
        System.out.println("Name set to " + nv);
        return super.setValue(nv);
    }
};
```

In the `Iterator` example we invoked the no-arg superclass constructor for `Object`—the only constructor that can ever be used when an anonymous class has an interface type.

Anonymous classes are simple and direct but can easily become very hard to read. The further they nest, the harder they are to understand. The nesting of the anonymous class code that will execute in the future inside the method code that is executing now adds to the potential for confusion. You should probably avoid anonymous classes that are longer than about six lines, and use them in only the simplest of expressions. We stretch this rule in the `walkThrough` example because the sole purpose of the method is to return that object, but when a method does more, anonymous classes must be kept quite small to keep the code legible. When anonymous classes are used properly, they are a good tool for keeping simple classes simple. When misused, they create impenetrable inscrutability.

5.5   Inheriting Nested Types

Nested types, whether static classes or interfaces, or inner classes, are inherited in the same manner that fields are inherited. A declaration of a nested type with the same name as that of an inherited nested type *hides* the definition of the inherited type. The actual type referred to is determined by the type of the reference used. Within a given class, the actual nested type referred to is the one defined in the current class or inherited in the current class.

Consider a framework that models devices that can be connected together via different ports. The class `Device` is an abstract class that captures some common behavior of all devices. A port also has some common generic behavior so it is also modelled as an abstract class and, because ports exist only within devices, the `Port` class is made an inner class of `Device`. A concrete device class defines the state for the device and the concrete inner port classes for that device. During construction of a concrete device class, references to the concrete ports of that class are initialized:

```
abstract class Device {
    abstract class Port {
        // ...
    }
    // ...
}
class Printer extends Device {
    class SerialPort extends Port {
        // ...
    }
    Port serial = new SerialPort();
}
```

A concrete device may itself be extended and also the concrete inner port classes, to specialize their behavior.

```
class HighSpeedPrinter extends Printer {
    class SerialPort extends Printer.SerialPort {
        // ...
    }
}
```

The intent is that the class `HighSpeedPrinter.SerialPort` overrides the class `Printer.SerialPort` so that `serial` is set to refer to the correct type of object. But the class `Printer` is not affected by the new subclass of `SerialPort` defined inside `HighSpeedPrinter`, even though the new subclass seems to have the same name.

One solution to this design problem is to abstract construction of the inner class objects into a *factory method* which can then be overridden in a subclass to construct the right kind of inner class. For example:

```
class Printer extends Device {
    class SerialPort extends Port {
        // ...
```

```
        }
        Port serial = createSerialPort();
        protected Port createSerialPort(){
            return new SerialPort();
        }
    }
```

The `HighSpeedPrinter` class now defines its specialized inner class and overrides the factory method to construct an instance of that class. Now that we realize that nested type definitions hide and don't override, we aren't tempted to use the same name for the inner class, as we know that hiding is usually a bad thing.

```
class HighSpeedPrinter extends Printer {
    class EnhancedSerialPort extends SerialPort {
        // ...
    }
    protected Port createSerialPort(){
        return new EnhancedSerialPort();
    }
}
```

Now when a `HighSpeedPrinter` is constructed and the initializers in `Printer` execute, we invoke the overridden `createSerialPort` method that returns an instance of `EnhancedSerialPort`.

This is one example of a situation where a method of the subclass is invoked before the subclass object has been fully constructed and so care must be taken to ensure that things work correctly. For example, if `EnhancedSerialPort` initializes a field using a field from the enclosing `HighSpeedPrinter` instance, then at the time the `EnhancedSerialPort` object is constructed, the fields of the enclosing object will have the default "zero" values for their type.

An alternative design would have the constructor for `HighSpeedPrinter` simply reassign `serial` to refer to an `EnhancedSerialPort` object. However, that causes the unnecessary construction of the original `SerialPort` object, and that construction may be non-trivial and undesirable—in this example it may involve configuring hardware.

5.6   Nesting in Interfaces

You declare nested classes and interfaces in an interface for the same reason that you declare nested classes and interfaces in a class: nested classes and interfaces allow you to associate types that are strongly related to an interface inside that interface. For example, a class that was used only to return multiple values from an interface's method could be represented as a nested class in that interface:

```
interface Changeable {
    class Record {
        public Object changer;
        public String changeDesc;
    }

    Record getLastChange();
    // ...
}
```

The method `getLastChange` returns a `Changeable.Record` object that contains which object made the change and a string describing the change. This class has meaning relative only to the `Changeable` interface, so making a top-level class not only is unnecessary, but would also separate it from the context of its use. As a nested class it is tightly bound to its origin and context.

Another use for a nested class within an interface, is to define a (partial or complete) default implementation for that interface. A class that implements the interface could then choose to extend the default implementation class, or to forward method invocations to an instance of that class.

As with all interface members, any class or interface nested inside an interface is public and static.

5.6.1 Modifiable Variables in Interfaces

We mentioned on page 109 that if you need shared, modifiable, data in an interface, then an inner class is a simple way of achieving this. Declare an inner class whose fields hold the shared data, and whose methods provide access to that data, then maintain a reference to an instance of that class. For example:

```
interface SharedData {
    class Data {
        private int x = 0;
        public int getX() { return x; }
        public void setX(int newX) { x = newX; }
    }
    Data data = new Data();
}
```

Now all implementors and users of `SharedData` can share common state via the `data` reference.

5.7   Implementation of Nested Types

How the compiler and runtime system deal with nested types would ideally be transparent to the programmer. Unfortunately this is not quite the case. Nested types were added as a language extension and that extension had to maintain compatibility with older Java virtual machines. Consequently, nested types were implemented in terms of a source code transformation that the compiler applies.

As a programmer the only thing you should need to know about this process is the naming conventions that are used. Consider a static, or non-local, nested type defined as `Outer.Inner`. This is the source name for the class. At the virtual machine level the class is renamed as `Outer$Inner`—in essence, dots in a nested name are converted to dollar signs. For local inner classes, the transformation is less specific because these classes are inaccessible, hence their name is less important—such classes may be named, for example as `Outer$1`, `Outer$2` and so on.

These issues have to be dealt with in two main cases. First, when bundling up the class files for your applications you have to recognize what all the strange files are with $ in their name. Second, if you use the reflection mechanism discussed in Chapter 11 to create nested class instances, you'll need to know the transformed name. But in most programming this is something you can blissfully ignore.

Conscience is the inner voice that warns us somebody is looking.
—H.L. Mencken

CHAPTER 6

Tokens, Operators, and Expressions

There's nothing remarkable about it.
All one has to do is hit the right keys at the right time
and the instrument plays itself.
—Johann Sebastian Bach

THIS chapter teaches you about the fundamental building blocks of the programming language—namely, its tokens, operators, and expressions. You have already seen a lot of code and have gained familiarity with its components. This chapter describes the basic elements in detail.

6.1 Lexical Elements

A program starts as a sequence of characters contained in a file—the source code. Interpreting those characters, according to the rules of a given language, is the job of the compiler, or interpreter. Some characters will represent the names of variables, others will be special keywords used by the language, still others will be operators or "punctuation" characters used to separate the other elements. All of these textual constructs form the *lexical elements* of the program. One of the first phases of compilation is the *scanning* of the lexical elements into *tokens*. This phase ignores *whitespace* and *comments* that appear in the text. Tokens must then be identified as keywords, literals, variables, operators, or whatever else is appropriate for the given language. In this section we look at the basic lexical elements of a Java program. The following sections look in more detail at literals, variables and the various operators.

6.1.1   Character Set

Most programmers are familiar with source code that is prepared using one of two major families of character representations: ASCII and its variants (including Latin-1) and EBCDIC. Both character sets contain characters used in English and several other Western European languages.

The Java programming language, on the other hand, is written in *Unicode*, a 16-bit character set. The first 256 characters of Unicode are the Latin-1 character set, and most of the first 128 characters of Latin-1 are equivalent to the 7-bit ASCII character set. Current environments read ASCII or Latin-1 files, converting them to Unicode on the fly.[1]

Few existing text editors support Unicode characters, so you can use the *escape sequence* \u*xxxx* to encode Unicode characters, where each *x* is a hexadecimal digit (0–9, and a–f or A–F to represent decimal values 10–15). This sequence can appear anywhere in code—not only in character and string constants but also in identifiers. More than one u may appear at the beginning; thus, the character ஒ can be written as \u0b87 or \uuu0b87.[2]

6.1.2   Comments

Comments within source code exist for the convenience of human programmers. They play no part in the generation of code and so are ignored during scanning. There are three kinds of comments:

`// comment`	Characters from // to the end of the line are ignored.
`/* comment */`	All characters between /* and the next */ are ignored.
`/** comment */`	All characters between /** and the next */ are ignored. These documentation comments come immediately before identifier declarations and are included in automatically generated documentation. These comments are described in Chapter 14.

---

[1]   The Java programming language uses Unicode 2.1 (with bug fixes). See "Further Reading" on page 563 for reference information.

[2]   There is a good reason to allow multiple u's. When translating a Unicode file into an ASCII file, you must translate Unicode characters that are outside the ASCII range into an escape sequence. Thus, you would translate ஒ into \u0b87. When translating back, you make the reverse substitution. But what if the original Unicode source had not contained ஒ but had used \u0b87 instead? Then the reverse translation would not result in the original source (to the parser, it would be equivalent, but possibly not to the reader of the code). The solution is to have the translator add an extra u when it encounters an existing \u*xxxx*, and have the reverse translator remove a u and, if there aren't any left, replace the escape sequence with its equivalent Unicode character.

Comments can include any valid Unicode character, such as yin-yang (\u262f), asterism (\u2042), interrobang (\u203d), won (\u20a9), scruple (\u2108), or a snowman (\u2603).[3]

Comments do not nest. This following tempting code does not compile:

```
/* Comment this out for now: not implemented
    /* Do some really neat stuff */
    universe.neatStuff();
*/
```

The first /* starts a comment; the very next */ ends it, leaving the code that follows to be parsed; and the invalid, stand-alone */ is a syntax error. The best way to remove blocks of code from programs is either to put a // at the beginning of each line or use if (false) like this:

```
if (false) {
    // invoke this method when it works
    dwim();
}
```

This technique requires that the code to be removed is complete enough to compile without error. In this case we assume that the dwim method is defined somewhere.

6.1.3 Tokens

The *tokens* of a language are its basic words. A parser breaks source code into tokens and then tries to figure out which statements, identifiers, and so forth make up the code. *White space* (spaces, tabs, newlines, and form feeds) is not significant except to separate tokens or as the contents of character or string literals. You can take any valid code and replace any amount of intertoken white space (white space outside strings and characters) with a different amount of white space (but not none) without changing the meaning of the program.

White space must be used to separate tokens that would otherwise constitute a single token. For example, in the statement

```
return 0;
```

you cannot drop the space between return and 0 because that would create

```
return0;
```

---

[3] These characters are ☯, ⁂, ‽, ₩, ⸘, and ☃, respectively.

consisting of the single identifier `return0`. Use extra white space appropriately to make your code human-readable, even though the parser ignores it. Note that the parser treats comments as white space.

The tokenizer is a "greedy" tokenizer. It grabs as many characters as it can to build up the next token, not caring if this creates an invalid sequence of tokens. So because ++ is longer than +, the expression

```
j = i+++++i;      // INVALID
```

is interpreted as the invalid expression

```
j = i++ ++ +i;   // INVALID
```

instead of the valid

```
j = i++ + ++i;
```

6.1.4   Identifiers

Identifiers, used for names of declared entities such as variables, constants and labels, must start with a letter, followed by letters, digits, or both. The terms *letter* and *digit* are broad in Unicode: if something is considered a letter or digit in a human language, you can probably use it in identifiers. "Letters" can come from Armenian, Korean, Gurmukhi, Georgian, Devanagari, and almost any other script written in the world today. Thus, not only is `kitty` a valid identifier, but mačka, кошка, پیشی, புனைக்குட்டி, and 猫 are, too.[4] Letters also include any currency symbol (such as $, ¥, and £) and connecting punctuation (such as _). For a complete definition, see the tables "Unicode Digits" on page 558 and "Unicode Letters and Digits" on page 559.

Any difference in characters within an identifier makes that identifier unique. Case is significant: A, a, á, À, Å, and so on, are different identifiers. Characters that look the same, or nearly the same, can be confused. For example, the Latin capital letter n "N" and the Greek capital ν "N" look alike but are different characters (`\u004e` and `\u039d`, respectively). The only way to avoid confusion is to write each identifier in one language—and thus in one known set of characters—so that programmers trying to type the identifier will know whether you meant E or E.[5]

Identifiers can be as long as you like, but use some taste. Identifiers that are too long are hard to use correctly and actually obscure your code.

---

[4]   These are the word "cat" or "kitty" in English, Serbo-Croatian, Russian, Persian, Tamil, and Japanese, respectively.

[5]   One is a Cyrillic letter, the other is ASCII. Determine which is which and win a prize.

6.1.5 Keywords

Language keywords cannot be used as identifiers because they have special meaning within the language. The following table lists the keywords (keywords marked with a [†] are reserved but currently unused):

abstract	default	if	private	this
boolean	do	implements	protected	throw
break	double	import	public	throws
byte	else	instanceof	return	transient
case	extends	int	short	try
catch	final	interface	static	void
char	finally	long	strictfp	volatile
class	float	native	super	while
const[†]	for	new	switch	
continue	goto[†]	package	synchronized	

Although they appear to be keywords, `null`, `true`, and `false` are formally literals, just like the number 12, so they do not appear in the above table. However, you cannot use `null`, `true`, or `false` as identifiers, just as you cannot use 12 as an identifier. These words can be used as parts of identifiers, as in `annulled`, `construe`, and `falsehood`.

6.2 Types and Literals

Every expression has a type that determines what values the expression can produce. The type of an expression is determined by the types of values and variables used within that expression. Types are divided into the primitive types and the reference types.

The primitive data types are:

boolean	either `true` or `false`
char	16-bit Unicode character
byte	8-bit signed two's-complement integer
short	16-bit signed two's-complement integer
int	32-bit signed two's-complement integer
long	64-bit signed two's-complement integer
float	32-bit IEEE 754-1985 floating-point number
double	64-bit IEEE 754-1985 floating-point number

Each primitive data type has a corresponding class type in the `java.lang` package. These *wrapper classes*—`Boolean`, `Character`, `Byte`, `Short`, `Integer`,

Long, Float, and Double—also define useful constants and methods. For example, most of these types declare constants MIN_VALUE and MAX_VALUE in their corresponding language classes.

The Float and Double classes also have NaN, NEGATIVE_INFINITY, and POSITIVE_INFINITY constants. Both also provide an isNaN method that tests whether a floating-point value is "Not a Number"—that is, whether it is the result of a floating-point expression that has no valid result, such as dividing zero by zero. The NaN value can be used to indicate an invalid floating-point value; this is similar to the use of null for object references that do not refer to anything. The wrapper classes are covered in more detail in Chapter 11.

There is no unsigned integer type. If you need to work with unsigned values originating outside of your program, they must be stored in a larger signed type. For example, unsigned bytes produced by an analogue-to-digital converter, can be read into variables of type short.

The reference types are class types, interface types and array types. Variables of these types can refer to objects of the corresponding type.

Each type has *literals*, which are the way that constant values of that type are written. The next few subsections describe how literal (unnamed) constants for each type are specified.

6.2.1   Reference Literals

The only literal object reference is null. It can be used anywhere a reference is expected. Conventionally, null represents an invalid or uncreated object. It has no class, not even Object, but null can be assigned to any reference variable.

6.2.2   Boolean Literals

The boolean literals are true and false.

6.2.3   Character Literals

Character literals appear with single quotes: 'Q'. Any valid Unicode character can appear between the quotes. You can use \uxxxx for Unicode characters inside character literals just as you can elsewhere. Certain special characters can be represented by an *escape sequence*. These are:

\n	newline (\u000A)
\t	tab (\u0009)
\b	backspace (\u0008)
\r	return (\u000D)

\f	form feed (\u000C)
\\	backslash itself (\u005C)
\'	single quote (\u0027)
\"	double quote (\u0022)
\ddd	a char by octal value, where each d is one of 0–7

Octal character constants can have three or fewer digits and cannot exceed \377 (\u00ff).

6.2.4 Integer Literals

Integer constants are strings of octal, decimal, or hexadecimal digits. The start of the constant declares the base of the number: a leading 0 (zero) denotes an octal number (base 8); a leading 0x or 0X denotes a hexadecimal number (base 16); any other set of digits is assumed to be a decimal number (base 10). All the following numbers have the same value:

```
29 035 0x1D 0X1d
```

Integer constants are long if they end in L or l, such as 29L; L is preferred over l because l (lowercase L) can easily be confused with 1 (the digit one). Otherwise, integer constants are assumed to be of type int. If an int literal is directly assigned to a short, and its value is within the valid range for a short, the integer literal is treated as if it were a short literal. A similar allowance is made for integer literals assigned to byte variables. In all other cases you must explicitly cast when assigning int to short or byte—see "Explicit Type Casts" on page 171.

6.2.5 Floating-Point Literals

Floating-point numbers are expressed as decimal numbers with an optional decimal point, optionally followed by an exponent. At least one digit must be present. The number can be followed by f or F to denote a single-precision constant, or by d or D to denote a double-precision constant. All these literals denote the same floating-point number:

```
18. 1.8e1 .18E2
```

Floating-point constants are of type double unless they are specified with a trailing f or F, which makes them float constants, such as 18.0f. A trailing d or D specifies a double constant. There are two zeros: positive 0.0 and negative -0.0. Positive and negative zero are considered equal when you use == but produce different results when used in some calculations. For example, the expression 1d/0d is +∞, whereas 1d/-0d is -∞.

A `double` constant cannot be assigned directly to a `float` variable, even if the value of the `double` is within the valid `float` range. The only constants you may directly assign to `float` variables and fields are `float` constants.

6.2.6   String Literals

String literals appear with double quotes: `"along"`. Any character can be included in string literals, with the exception of newline. Newlines are not allowed in the middle of strings. If you want to embed a newline character in the string, use the escape sequence `\n`. A string literal references an object of type `String`. To learn more about strings, see Chapter 9.

Characters in strings can be specified using the octal digit mechanism, but all three octal digits should be used to prevent accidents when an octal value is specified next to a valid octal digit in the string. For example, the string `"\0116"` is equivalent to `"\t6"`, whereas the string `"\116"` is equivalent to `"N"`.

6.2.7   Class Literals

For every type there is an associated `Class` object. You can name the `Class` object for a type directly by following the type name with `".class"`, as in

```
String.class
java.lang.String.class
java.util.Iterator.class
boolean.class
```

The first two of these class literals refer to the same `Class` object because `String` and `java.lang.String` are two different names for the same class. The third class literal is a reference to the `Class` object for the `Iterator` interface mentioned on page 115. The last is a `Class` object that represents the primitive type `boolean`. For more on `Class` objects, see Chapter 11.

6.3   Variables

A *variable* is a storage location—something that can hold a value—to which a value can be assigned. Variables include fields, local variables in a block of code, and parameters. A variable *declaration* states the identifier (name), type, and other attributes of a variable. The type part of a declaration specifies which kinds of values and behavior are supported by the declared entity.

6.3.1   Field and Local Variable Declarations

Fields and local variables are declared in the same way. A declaration is broken into three parts: *modifiers*, followed by a *type*, followed by a list of *identifiers*. Each identifier can optionally have an *initializer* associated with it to give it an initial value.

There is no difference between variables declared in one declaration or in multiple declarations of the same type. For example:

```
float x, y;
```

is the same as

```
float x;
float y;
```

Any initializer is expressed as an assignment (using the = operator) of an expression of the appropriate type. For example:

```
float x = 3.14f, y = 2.81f;
```

is the same as the more readable

```
float x = 3.14f,
      y = 2.81f;
```

is the same as the preferred

```
float x = 3.14f;
float y = 2.81f;
```

Field variables are members of classes, or interfaces, and are declared within the body of that class or interface. Fields can he initialized using an initializer, within an initialization block, or within a constructor, but need not be initialized at all as they have default initial values, as discussed on page 38. Details of field initialization and the modifiers that can be applied to fields were discussed in Chapter 2.

Local variables can be declared anywhere within a block of statements, not just at the start of the block, and can be of primitive or reference type. As a special case, a local variable declaration is also permitted within the initialization section of a for loop—see "for" on page 186. A local variable must be assigned to before it is used. There is no default initialization value for them, because failure to provide an initial value for a local variable is usually a bug. The compiler will refuse to compile code that doesn't ensure that assignment takes place before a variable is used:

```
int x;      // uninitialized, can't use
int y = 2;
x = y * y; // okay now it has a value
```

Local variables cease to exist when the flow of control reaches the end of the block in which they were declared—though any referenced object is subject to normal garbage collection rules.

The only modifier that can be applied to a local variable is `final`, which is usually done only when the local variable will be accessed by a local or anonymous inner class.

6.3.2   Parameter Variables

Parameter variables are the parameters declared in methods, constructors, or `catch` blocks—see "try, catch, and `finally`" on page 202. A parameter declaration consists of an optional modifier, a type name, and a single identifier.

Parameters cannot have explicit initializers because they are implicitly initialized with the value of the argument passed when the method or constructor is invoked, or a reference to the exception object caught in the `catch` block. Parameter variables cease to exist when the block in which they appear completes. As with local variables, the only modifier that can be applied to a parameter is `final`.

6.3.3   `final` Variables

The `final` modifier declares that the value of the variable is set exactly once and will thereafter always have the same value—it is *immutable*. Any variable—fields, local variables, or parameters—can be declared `final`. Variables that are `final` must be initialized before they are used. Typically this is done directly in the declaration:

```
final int id = nextID++;
```

You can defer the initialization of a final field or local variable. Such a final variable is called a *blank final*. A blank final field must be initialized within an initialization block or constructor (if it's an instance field) while a blank final local variable, like any local variable, must be initialized before it is used.

Blank final fields are useful when the value of the field is determined by a constructor argument:

```
class NamedObj {
    final String name;

    NamedObj(String name) {
        this.name = name;
    }
}
```

or when you must calculate the value in something more sophisticated than an initializer expression:

```
static final int[] numbers = numberList();
static final int maxNumber; // max value in numbers

static {
    int max = numbers[0];
    for (int i = 1; i < numbers.length; i++)
        if (numbers[i] > max)
            max = numbers[i];
    maxNumber = max;
}
```

The compiler will verify that all static final fields are initialized by the end of any static initializer blocks, and that non-static final fields are initialized by the end of all construction paths for an object. A compile-time error will occur if the compiler cannot determine that this happens.

Blank final, local variables are useful when the value to be assigned to the variable is conditional on the value of other variables. As with all local variables, the compiler will ensure that a final local variable is initialized before it is used.

Local variables and parameters are usually declared final only when they will be accessed by a local, or anonymous inner, class—though some people advocate always making parameters final, as a matter of style. Issues regarding when you should, and should not, use `final` on fields, were discussed on page 40.

6.4   Array Variables

Arrays provide ordered collections of elements. Components of an array can be primitive types or references to objects, including references to other arrays. Arrays themselves are objects and extend `Object`. The declaration

```
int[] ia = new int[3];
```

declares an array named `ia` that initially refers to an array of three `int` values.

Array dimensions are omitted in the type declaration of an array variable. The number of components in an array is determined when it is *created* using `new`, not when an array variable is declared. An array object's length is fixed at its creation and cannot be changed. Note that it is the length of the array *object* that is fixed. In the example, a new array of a different size could be assigned to the array variable `ia` at any time.

You access array elements by their position in the array. The first element of an array has index 0 (zero), and the last element has index *length*–1. An element is accessed using the name of the array and the index enclosed between [and]. In our example, the first element of the array is `ia[0]` and last element of the array is `ia[2]`. Every index use is checked to ensure that it is within the proper range for that array, throwing an `ArrayIndexOutOfBoundsException` if the index is out of bounds.[6] The index expression must be of type `int`—this limits the maximum size of an array.

The length of an array is available via its `length` field (which is implicitly `public` and `final`). In our example, the following code would loop over the array, printing each value:

```
for (int i = 0; i < ia.length; i++)
    System.out.println(i + ": " + ia[i]);
```

An array with length zero is said to be an *empty* array. There is a big difference between a `null` array reference and a reference to an empty array—an empty array is a real object, it simply has no elements. Empty arrays are useful for returning from methods instead of returning `null`. If a method can return `null`, then users of the method must explicitly check the return value for `null` before using it. On the other hand, if the method returns an array which may be empty, no special checking is needed provided the user always uses the array length to check valid indexes.

---

[6]   The range check can often be optimized away when, for example, it can be proven that a loop index variable is always within range, but you are guaranteed that an index will never be used if it is out of range.

If you prefer, you can put the array brackets after the variable name instead of after the type:

```
int ia[] = new int[3];
```

This code is equivalent to the original definition of ia. However, the first style is preferable because it places the type declaration entirely in one place.

6.4.1   Array Modifiers

The normal modifiers can be applied to array variables, depending on whether the array is a field or local variable. The important thing to remember is that the modifiers apply to the array variable *not* to the elements of the array the variable references. An array variable that is declared final means that the array reference cannot be changed after initialization. It does not mean that array elements cannot be changed. There is no way to apply any modifiers (specifically final and volatile) to the elements of an array.

6.4.2   Arrays of Arrays

You can have arrays of arrays. The code to declare and print a two-dimensional matrix, for example, might look like this:

```
float[][] mat = new float[4][4];
setupMatrix(mat);
for (int y = 0; y < mat.length; y++) {
    for (int x = 0; x < mat[y].length; x++)
        System.out.print(mat[y][x] + " ");
    System.out.println();
}
```

The first (left-most) dimension of an array must be specified when the array is created. Other dimensions can be left unspecified, to be filled in later. Specifying more than the first dimension is a shorthand for a nested set of new statements. Our new creation could have been written more explicitly as:

```
float[][] mat = new float[4][];
for (int y = 0; y < mat.length; y++)
    mat[y] = new float[4];
```

One advantage of arrays of arrays is that each nested array can have a different size. You can emulate a 4×4 matrix, but you can also create an array of four int arrays, each of which has a different length sufficient to hold its own data.

6.4.3   Array Initialization

When an array is created, each element of the array is set to the default initial value for its type—zero for the numeric types, `'\u0000'` for `char`, `false` for `boolean`, and `null` for reference types. When you declare an array of a reference type, you are really declaring an array of variables of that type. Consider the following code:

```
Attr[] attrs = new Attr[12];

for (int i = 0; i < attrs.length; i++)
    attrs[i] = new Attr(names[i], values[i]);
```

After the initial `new` of the array, `attrs` has a reference to an array of 12 variables that are initialized to `null`. The `Attr` objects themselves are created only when the loop is executed.

Arrays can be initialized by providing values inside braces following their declaration. The following array declaration creates and initializes an array object:

```
String[] dangers = { "Lions", "Tigers", "Bears" };
```

The following code gives the same result:

```
String[] dangers = new String[3];

dangers[0] = "Lions";
dangers[1] = "Tigers";
dangers[2] = "Bears" ;
```

When you initialize an array within its declaration, you don't have to explicitly create the array using `new`—it is done implicitly for you by the system. The length of the array to create is determined by the number of initialization values given. You can use `new` explicitly if you prefer, but in that case you have to omit the array length, as again it is determined from the initializer list.

```
String[] dangers = new String[] {"Lions", "Tigers", "Bears"};
```

This form of array creation expression allows you to create and initialize an array anywhere. For example, you can create and initialize an array when you invoke a method:

```
printStrings(new String[] { "one", "two", "many" });
```

An unnamed array created with `new` in this way is called an *anonymous array*.

Arrays of arrays can be initialized by nesting array initializers. Here is a declaration that initializes an array to the top few rows of Pascal's triangle, with each row represented by its own array:

```
int[][] pascalsTriangle = {
            { 1 },
            { 1, 1 },
            { 1, 2, 1 },
            { 1, 3, 3, 1 },
            { 1, 4, 6, 4, 1 },
    };
```

Indexes in an array of arrays work from the outermost inward. For example, in the preceding array, `pascalsTriangle[0]` refers to the `int` array that has one element, `pascalsTriangle[1]` refers to the `int` array that has two elements, and so forth.

For convenience, the `System` class provides an `arraycopy` method that allows you to assign the values from one array into another, instead of looping through each of the array elements—this is described in more detail in "Utility Methods" on page 483.

6.4.4 Arrays and Types

Arrays are implicit extensions of `Object`. Given a class `X`, classes `Y` and `Z` that extend `X`, and arrays of each, the class hierarchy looks something like this:

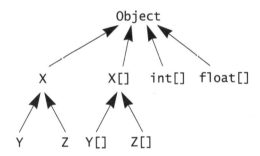

This class relationship allows polymorphism for arrays. You can assign an array to a variable of type `Object` and cast it back. An array of objects of type `Y` is usable wherever an array of objects of its supertype `X` is required. This seems natural but can require a run time check that is sometimes unexpected. An array of `X` can contain either `Y` or `Z` references, but an array of `Y` cannot contain references to `X` or `Z`

objects. The following code would generate an `ArrayStoreException` at run time on either of its final two lines, which violate this rule:

```
Y[] yArray = new Y[3];      // a Y array
X[] xArray = yArray;        // valid: Y is assignable to X
xArray[0] = new Y();
xArray[2] = new X();        // INVALID: can't store X in Y[]
xArray[1] = new Z();        // INVALID: can't store Z in Y[]
```

If `xArray` were a reference to a real `X[]` object, it would be valid to store both an X and a Z object into it. But `xArray` actually refers to a `Y[]` object so it is not valid to store either an X reference or a Z reference in it. Such assignments are checked at run time if needed to ensure that no improper reference is stored into an array.

Like any other object, arrays are created and are subject to normal garbage collection mechanisms. They inherit all of the methods of `Object` and additionally they implement the `Cloneable` interface—see page 89.

The major limitation on the "object-ness" of arrays is that they cannot be extended to add new methods. The following construct is not valid:

```
class ScaleVector extends double[] { // INVALID
    // ...
}
```

In a sense, arrays behave like final classes.

Exercise 6.1: Write a program that calculates Pascal's triangle to a depth of 12, storing each row of the triangle in an array of the appropriate length and putting each of the row arrays into an array of 12 `int` arrays. Design your solution so that the results are printed by a method that prints the array of arrays using the lengths of each array, not a constant 12. Now change the code to use a constant other than 12 without modifying your printing method.

6.5 The Meanings of Names

Identifiers are used to give names to a range of things within our programs—types, variables, fields, methods, and so forth. When you use a particular name in your program, the compiler has to determine what that name refers to, so that it can decide if you are using it correctly and so it can generate the appropriate code. The rules for determining the meaning of a name trade off convenience with complexity. At one extreme the language could require that every name in a program be unique—this makes things simple for the compiler but makes life very inconvenient for the programmer. If names are allowed to be interpreted based on the context that they are used, the programmer gets the convenience of reusing names (such as always using i for a for loop counter), but the compiler has to be able to determine what the name means—and so does anyone reading the code.

Name management is achieved using two mechanisms. First, the *namespace* is partitioned to give different namespaces for different kinds of names. Second, scoping is used to control the visibility of names declared in one part of a program to other parts. Different namespaces allow you to give the same name to a method and a field (not that we recommend doing this), while scoping allows you to use the same name for all your for loop counters.

There are six different namespaces:

- ◆ package names,
- ◆ type names,
- ◆ field names,
- ◆ method names,
- ◆ local variable names (including parameters), and
- ◆ labels

When a name is used in a program, its context helps determine what kind of name it is. For example, in the expression x.f = 3, we know that f must be a field—it can't be a package, type, method, or label because we are assigning a value to it, and it can't be a local variable because we are accessing it as a member of x. We know that x must be a typename, or a field, or a local variable that is an object reference—exactly which is determined by searching the enclosing scope for an appropriate declaration, as you will see.

The use of separate namespaces gives you greater flexibility when writing code (especially when combining code from different sources) but can be abused. Consider this pathological, but perfectly valid, piece of code:

```
package Reuse;
class Reuse {
    Reuse Reuse(Reuse Reuse) {
      Reuse:
        for (;;) {
            if (Reuse.Reuse(Reuse) == Reuse)
                break Reuse;
        }
        return Reuse;
    }
}
```

Every declaration of a name has a scope in which that name can be used. The exact rules differ depending on the kind of name—type name, member name, local variable, and so on. For example, the scope of a parameter in a method is the entire body of that method; the scope of a local variable is the block in which the local variable is declared; the scope of a loop variable declared in the initialization section of a `for` loop is the rest of that `for` loop.

A name cannot be used outside of its scope—for example, one method in a class cannot refer to the parameter of another method. However, scopes also nest and an inner scope has access to all names declared in the outer scope before the inner scope is entered. For example, the body of a `for` loop can access the local variables of the method in which it was declared.

When a name is used that could be a variable or field, the meaning of the name is determined by searching the current and enclosing scopes for declarations of that name in the different namespaces. The search process is as follows:

1. Local variables declared in the code block, `for` loop, or as parameters to the `catch` clause of a `try` statement. Then local variables declared in any enclosing code block. This applies recursively up to the method containing the block, or until there is no enclosing block (as in the case of an initialization block).

2. If the code is in a method or constructor, the parameters to the method or constructor.

3. A member of the class or interface. These are the fields and methods of the type, including any accessible inherited members.

4. If the type is a nested type, the enclosing block or class. If the type is a static nested type, only static members of an enclosing block or class are searched. Reapply this search rule to any blocks and classes enclosing the enclosing type recursively.

There are special rules for determining how members of a class are accessed, as you'll see in "Member Access" on page 173.

The order of searching determines which declaration will be found. This implies that names declared in outer scopes can be hidden by names declared in inner scopes. This means, for example, that local variable names can hide class member names, that nested class members can hide enclosing instance members and that locally declared class members can hide inherited class members—as you have already seen.

Hiding is generally bad style because a human reading the code must check all levels of the hierarchy to determine which variable is being used. Hiding is permitted to make local code robust. If hiding outer variables were not allowed, adding a new field to a class or interface could break existing code in subtypes that used variables of the same name. Scoping is meant as protection for the system as a whole rather than support for reusing identifier names.

To avoid confusion, hiding is not permitted in nested scopes within a code block. This means that a local variable in a method cannot have the same name as a parameter of that method; that a `for` loop variable cannot have the same name as a local variable or parameter; and that once there is a local variable called, say, über, you cannot create a new, different variable with the name über in a nested block.

```
{
    int über = 0;
    {
        int über = 2; // INVALID: already defined
        // ...
    }
}
```

However, you can have different (non-nested) `for` loops in the same block, or different (non-nested) blocks in the same method, that do declare variables with the same name.

If a name appears in a place where a type name is expected, then the different type scopes must be searched for that name. Type scopes are defined by packages. The search order is as follows:

1. The current type including inherited types.

2. A nested type of the current type.

3. Explicitly named imported types.

4. Other types declared in the same package.

5. Implicitly named imported types.

Again, hiding of type names is possible, but a type can always be explicitly referred to using its fully qualified name, which includes package information, such as `java.lang.String`. Packages and type imports are discussed in detail in Chapter 13.

6.6   Arithmetic Operations

There are several binary arithmetic operators that operate on any of the primitive numerical types:

+	addition
–	subtraction
*	multiplication
/	division
%	remainder

You can also use unary - for negation. The sign of a number can be inverted with code like this:

```
val = -val;
```

For completeness there is also a unary +, as in +2.0.

The exact actions of the binary arithmetic operators depend on the types of operands involved. The following sections look at the different rules for integer and floating-point arithmetic.

6.6.1   Integer Arithmetic

Integer arithmetic is modular two's-complement arithmetic—that is, if a value exceeds the range of its type (int or long), it is reduced modulo the range. So integer arithmetic never overflows or underflows but only wraps.

Integer division truncates toward zero (7/2 is 3, and –7/2 is –3). For integer types, division and remainder obey the rule

```
(x/y)*y + x%y == x
```

So 7%2 is 1, and –7%2 is –1. Dividing by zero or remainder by zero is invalid for integer arithmetic and throws ArithmeticException.

Character arithmetic is integer arithmetic after the char is implicitly converted to int—see "Expression Type" on page 169.

6.6.2   Floating-Point Arithmetic

Floating-point arithmetic can overflow to infinity (become too large for a double or float) or underflow to zero (become too small for a double or float). The result of an invalid expression, such as dividing infinity by infinity, is a NaN value—for "Not a Number."

Arithmetic with finite operands performs as expected, within the limits of precision of `double` or `float`. Signs of floating-point arithmetic results are also as expected. Multiplying two numbers having the same sign results in a positive value; multiplying two numbers having opposite signs results in a negative value.

Adding two infinities results in the same infinity if their signs are the same, and NaN if their signs differ. Subtracting infinities of the same sign produces NaN; subtracting infinities of opposite signs produces an infinity of the same sign as the left operand. For example, $(\infty - (-\infty))$ is ∞. Arithmetic operations involving any value that is NaN have a result that is also NaN. Overflows result in a value that is an infinity of the proper sign. Underflows result in a zero of the proper sign. Floating-point arithmetic has a negative zero `-0.0`, which compares equal to `+0.0`. Although they compare equal, the two zeros can produce different results. For example, the expression `1f/0f` yields positive infinity and `1f/-0f` yields negative infinity.

If the result of an underflow is `-0.0` and if `-0.0 == 0.0`, how do you test for a negative zero? You must use the zero in an expression where sign matters and then test the result. For example, if `x` has a zero value, the expression `1/x` will yield negative infinity if `x` is negative zero, or positive infinity if `x` is positive zero.

The rules for operations on infinities match normal mathematical expectations. Adding or subtracting any number to or from either infinity results in that infinity. For example, $(-\infty + x)$ is $-\infty$ for any finite number x.

You can get an infinity value from the constants `POSITIVE_INFINITY` and `NEGATIVE_INFINITY` in the wrapper classes `Float` and `Double`. For example, `Double.NEGATIVE_INFINITY` is the `double` value of minus infinity.

Multiplying infinity by zero yields NaN. Multiplying infinity by a non-zero finite number produces an infinity of the appropriate sign.

Floating-point division and remainder can produce infinities or NaN but never raise an exception. This table shows the results of the various combinations:

x	y	x/y	x%y
Finite	±0.0	±∞	NaN
Finite	±∞	±0.0	x
±0.0	±0.0	NaN	NaN
±∞	Finite	±∞	NaN
±∞	±∞	NaN	NaN

Otherwise, floating-point remainder (%) acts analogously to integer remainder as described earlier. See the `IEEEremainder` method in "`Math` and `StrictMath`" on page 477 for a different remainder calculation.

6.6.3   Strict and non-Strict Floating-Point Arithmetic

Floating point arithmetic can be executed in one of two modes: *FP-strict* or *not FP-strict*. For simplicity, we refer to these as strict and non-strict, respectively. *Strict* floating point evaluation follows constrained rules about exact floating point operations: when you execute strict floating point code you will always get exactly equivalent results on all Java virtual machine implementations. Floating point arithmetic that is *non-strict* can be executed with somewhat relaxed rules if the virtual machine implementation chooses: when you execute such code on different virtual machines you may not always get precisely the same results, but you allow each virtual machine implementation to choose evaluation rules that are faster.

The strictness of floating point arithmetic is determined by the presence of the modifier `strictfp`, which can be applied to a class, interface, or method. When you declare a method `strictfp`, all the code in the method will be executed according to strict constraints. When you use `strictfp` on a class or interface, all code in the class, including initializers and code in nested types, will be evaluated strictly. When determining whether an expression is strict, all methods, classes, and interfaces, within in which the expression is contained, are examined; if any of them is declared `strictfp` then the expression is strict. However, strictness is not inherited—the presence of `strictfp` on a class or interface declaration does not cause extended classes or interfaces to be strict.

Constant expressions that require floating point are always evaluated strictly. Otherwise, any code that is not marked as `strictfp` can be executed using rules which do not require repeatable results. If you want to guarantee bit-for-bit exact results across all Java virtual machine implementations, you should use `strictfp` on relevant methods, classes and interfaces. You should also note that a virtual machine can satisfy the rules for non-strict floating-point by always acting strictly: Non-strict floating-point does not *require* the virtual machine to act differently, it offers the virtual machine a degree of freedom to optimize code where repeatable results are not required.

Non-strict floating point execution allows intermediate results from calculations to be stored in an extended format different from either the IEEE-754-1985 32-bit (`float`) or 64-bit (`double`) formats. These extended formats can also be used for parameters, local variables and return values within non-strict code. However, fields and array elements are always stored in the standard formats, as are all values (parameters and return values) passed between strict and non-strict code. When an extended format value must be converted to a standard format, the closest representable value is used.

Non-strict floating point evaluation may give you slightly less precision than `strictfp` code. This distinction will affect some, but not most, applications.

If you need a complete understanding of these issues, you should consult *The Java*[TM] *Language Specification.*

6.7 General Operators

In addition to the main arithmetic operators, there are a range of other useful operators for comparing and manipulating values. Member access operators, method invocation and type conversion operators are discussed in following sections.

6.7.1 Increment and Decrement Operators

The `++` and `--` operators are the increment and decrement operators, respectively, and can only be applied to numeric variables or numeric array elements. The expression `i++` is equivalent to `i = i + 1` except that `i` is evaluated only once. For example, the statement

```
++arr[where()];
```

invokes `where` only once and uses the result as an index into the array only once. On the other hand, in the statement

```
arr[where()] = arr[where()] + 1;
```

the `where` method is called twice: once to determine the index on the right-hand side, and a second time to determine the index on the left-hand side. If `where` returns a different value each time it is invoked, the results will be quite different from those of the `++` expression. To avoid the second invocation of `where` you would have to store its result in a temporary—hence the increment (and decrement) operator allows a simpler, succinct expression of what you want to do.

The increment and decrement operators can be either *prefix* or *postfix* operators—they can appear either before or after what they operate on. If the operator comes before (prefix), the operation is applied before the value of the expression is returned. If the operator comes after (postfix), the operation is applied after the original value is used. For example:

```
class IncOrder {
    public static void main(String[] args) {
        int i = 16;
        System.out.println(++i + " " + i++ + " " + i);
    }
}
```

The output is

```
17 17 18
```

The expression ++i preincrements the value of i to 17 and evaluates to that value (17); the expression i++ evaluates to the current value of i (17) and postincrements i to have the value 18; finally the expression i is the value of i after the postincrement from the middle term. Modifying a variable more than once in an expression makes code hard to understand, and should be avoided.

The increment and decrement operators ++ and -- can also be applied to char variables to get to the next or previous Unicode character.

6.7.2   Relational and Equality Operators

The language provides a standard set of relational and equality operators, all of which yield boolean values:

>	greater than
>=	greater than or equal to
<	less than
<=	less than or equal to
==	equal to
!=	not equal to

Both the relational and equality operators can be applied to the primitive numeric types, with the usual mathematical interpretation applying.

Floating-point values follow normal ordering (-1.0 is less than 0.0 is less than positive infinity) except that NaN is an anomaly. All relational and equality operators that test a number against NaN return false, except !=, which always returns true. This is true even if both values are NaN. For example,

```
Double.NaN == Double.NaN
```

is always false. To test whether a value is NaN, use the type-specific NaN testers: the static methods Float.isNaN(float) and Double.isNaN(Double).

Only the equality operators == and != are allowed to operate on boolean values, because the question of whether true is greater than or less than false is meaningless. These operators can be used to create a "logical XOR" test. The following code invokes `sameSign` only if both x and y have the same sign (or zero); otherwise it invokes `differentSign`:

```
if ((x < 0) == (y < 0))
    sameSign();
else
    differentSign();
```

The equality operators can also be applied to reference types. The expression `ref1==ref2` is `true` if the two references refer to the same object or if both are `null`, even if the two references are of different declared types. Otherwise, it is `false`.

The equality operators test for reference *identity,* not object *equivalence.* Two references are identical if they refer to the same object; two objects are equivalent if they logically have the same value. Equivalence is tested using the `equals` method defined by `Object`, which should be overridden by classes for which equivalence and identity are different. `Object.equals` assumes an object is equal only to itself. For example, the `String` class overrides `equals` to test whether two `String` objects have the same contents—see Chapter 9.

6.7.3   Logical Operators

The logical operators combine boolean expressions to yield boolean values and provide the common operations of boolean algebra:

&	logical AND
|	logical inclusive OR
^	logical exclusive or (XOR)
!	logical negation
&&	conditional AND
||	conditional OR

A "logical AND" is true if and only if both its operands are true, while a "logical OR" is true if and only if either of its operands are true. The "exclusive OR" operator yields true if either, but not both, of its operands are true—which is the same as testing the equality of the two operands, so we can rewrite our earlier example as:

```
if ((x < 0) ^ (y < 0))
    differentSign();
else
    sameSign();
```

The unary operator ! negates, or inverts, a boolean, so !true is the same as false and !false is the same as true.

Boolean values are normally tested directly—if x and y are booleans, the code

```
if (x || !y) {
    // ...
}
```

is considered cleaner than the equivalent, but more verbose

```
if (x == true || y == false) {
    // ...
}
```

The && ("conditional AND") and || ("conditional OR") operators perform the same logical function as the simple & and | operators, but they avoid evaluating their right operand if the truth of the expression is determined by the left operand. For example, consider:

```
if (w && x) {        // outer "if"
    if (y || z) {   // inner "if"
        // ...        inner "if" body
    }
}
```

The inner if is executed only if both w *and* x are true. If w is false then x will not be evaluated because the expression is already guaranteed to be false. The body of the inner if is executed if either y or z is true. If y is true, then z will not be evaluated because the expression is already guaranteed to be true.

A lot of code relies on this rule for program correctness or efficiency. For example, the evaluation shortcuts make the following code safe:

```
if (0 <= ix && ix < array.length && array[ix] != 0) {
    // ...
}
```

The range checks are done first. The value array[ix] will be accessed only if ix is within bounds. There is no "conditional XOR" because the truth of XOR always depends on the value of both operands.

6.7.4   instanceof

The instanceof operator evaluates if a reference refers to an object that is an instance of a particular class or interface. The left hand side is a reference to an object, and the right hand side is a class or interface name. You learned about `instanceof` on page 80.

6.7.5 Bit Manipulation Operators

The binary bitwise operators are:

     `&`   bitwise AND
     `|`   bitwise inclusive OR
     `^`   bitwise exclusive or (XOR)

The bitwise operators apply only to integer types (which includes `char`) and perform their operation on each pair of bits in the two operands. The AND of two bits yields a 1 if both bits are 1, the OR of two bits yields a 1 if either bit is 1 and the XOR of two bits yields a 1 only if the two bits have different values. For example:

```
0xF00F & 0x0FF0 yields 0x0000
0xF00F | 0x0FF0 yields 0xFFFF
0xAAAA ^ 0xFFFF yields 0x5555
```

There is also a unary bitwise complement operator ~, which toggles each bit in its operand. An `int` with value `0x00003333` has a complemented value of `0xFFFFCCCC`.

Although the same characters are used for the bitwise operators and the logical operators, they are quite distinct. The types of the operands determine whether, for example, `&` is a logical or a bitwise AND. As logical operators only apply to booleans and bitwise operators only apply to integer types, any expression involving operands of the different types, such as `true & 0xAAAA`, is a compile-time error.

There are other bit manipulation operators to shift bits within an integer value:

     `<<`   Shift bits left, filling with zero bits on the right-hand side
     `>>`   Shift bits right, filling with the highest (sign) bit on the left-hand side
     `>>>`   Shift bits right, filling with zero bits on the left-hand side

The left-hand side of a shift expression is what is shifted, and the right-hand side is how much to shift. For example, `var >>> 2` will shift the bits in `var` two places to the right, dropping the bottom two bits from the end and filling the top two bits with zero.

The two right shift operators provide for an arithmetic shift (`>>`) and a logical shift (`>>>`). The arithmetic shift preserves the sign of the value by filling in the highest bit positions with the original sign bit (the bit in the highest position). The logical shift inserts zeroes into the high order bits. It is often used when extracting subsets of bits from a value. For example, in binary coded decimal (BCD) each decimal digit is represented by four bits (0x00 to 0x09—the remaining bit patterns are invalid) and so every byte can encode two decimal digits. To extract the low order digit you AND the byte with a mask of 0x0F to zero out the high order digit. To extract the high order digit you logically shift right the value by four positions, moving the valid bits down to the least significant positions and filling the new high-order bits with zero:

```
class BCD {
    static int getBCDLowDigit(byte val) {
        return (val & 0x0F);
    }
    static int getBCDHighDigit(byte val) {
        return val >>> 4 ;
    }
}
```

Shift operators have a slightly different type rule from most other binary integer operations. For shift operators, the resulting type is the type of the left-hand operand—that is, the value that is shifted. If the left-hand side of the shift is an int, the result of the shift is an int, even if the shift count is provided as a long.

If the shift count is larger than the number of bits in the word, or if it is negative, the actual count will be different from the provided count. The actual count used in a shift is the count you provide, masked by the size of the type minus one. For a 32-bit int, for example, the mask used is 0x1f (31), so both (n << 35) and (n << -29) are equivalent to (n << 3).

Shift operators can be used only on integer types. In the rare circumstance when you actually need to manipulate the bits in a floating-point value, you can use the conversion methods on the classes Float and Double, discussed in "The Floating-Point Wrapper Classes" on page 280.

6.7.6   The Conditional Operator ?:

The *conditional operator* provides a single expression that yields one of two values based on a boolean expression. The statement

```
value = (userSetIt ? usersValue : defaultValue);
```

is equivalent to

```
if (userSetIt)
    value = usersValue;
else
    value = defaultValue;
```

The primary difference between the `if` statement and the `?:` operator is that the latter has a value and so can be used as part of an expression. The conditional operator results in a more compact expression, but programmers disagree about whether it is more clear. We use whichever seems clearer at the time. When to use parentheses around a conditional operator expression is a matter of personal style, and practice varies widely. Parentheses are not required by the language.

The result expressions (the second and third ones) must have assignment-compatible types. The type of one result expression must be assignable to the type of the other one without an explicit cast, no matter which one is assignable to the other. The type of the result of the conditional operator is the more general of the two types. For example, in

```
double scale = (halveIt ? 1 : 0.5);
```

the two sides are `int` (1) and `double` (0.5). An `int` is assignable to a `double`, so the `1` is cast to `1.0` and the result of the conditional operator is `double`. This rule also holds for reference types—if one type is assignable to the other, the least-extended type is the type of the operation. If neither type is assignable to the other, the operation is invalid.

This operator is also called the *question/colon operator* because of its form, and the *ternary operator* because it is the only ternary (three-operand) operator in the language.

6.7.7 Assignment Operators

The assignment operator = assigns the value of its right operand expression to its left operand, which must be a variable (either a variable name or an array element). The type of the expression must be assignment compatible with the type of the variable—an explicit cast may be needed. For reference types assignment compatibility means the expression must be same type as, or a subtype of, the variable's type. For primitive types, the numeric types are compatible with each other, while only a boolean value can be assigned to a boolean variable.

An assignment operation is itself an expression and evaluates to the value being assigned. For example, the assignment

```
z = 3;
```

has the value 3. This value can be assigned to another variable, which also evaluates to 3 and so that can be assigned to another variable and so forth. Hence assignments can be chained together to give a set of variables the same value:

```
x = y = z = 3;
```

This also means that assignment can be performed as a side-effect of evaluating another expression—though utilizing side-effects in expressions is often considered poor style. An acceptable, and common, example of this is to assign and test a value within a loop expression. For example:

```
while ((v = stream.next()) != null)
    processValue(v);
```

Here the next value is read from a stream and stored in the variable v. Provided the value read was not null, it is processed and the next value read. Note that as assignment has a lower precedence than the inequality test (see "Operator Precedence and Associativity" on page 176), you have to place the assignment expression within parentheses.

The simple = is the most basic form of assignment operator. There are many other assignment forms. Any binary arithmetic, logical, or bit manipulation operator can be concatenated with = to form another assignment operator—a *compound assignment operator.* For example,

```
arr[where()] += 12;
```

is the same as

```
arr[where()] = arr[where()] + 12;
```

except that the expression on the left-hand side of the assignment is evaluated only once. In the example, arr[where()] is evaluated only once in the first expression, but twice in the second expression—as you learnt earlier with the ++ operator.

Given the variable var of type T, the value expr, and the binary operator *op*, the expression

```
var op= expr
```

is equivalent to

```
var = (T)((var) op (expr))
```

except that var is evaluated only once. This means that *op=* is valid only if *op* is valid for the types involved. You cannot, for example, use <<= on a double variable because you cannot use << on a double value.

Note the parentheses used in the expanded form you just saw. The expression

```
a *= b + 1
```

is analogous to

```
a = a * (b + 1)
```

and not to

```
a = a * b + 1
```

Although a += 1 is the same as ++a, ++ is considered idiomatic and is preferred.

6.7.8   String Concatenation Operator

You can use + to concatenate two strings. Here is an example:

```
String boo = "boo";
String cry = boo + "hoo";
cry += "!";
System.out.println(cry);
```

And here is its output:

```
boohoo!
```

The + operator is interpreted as the string concatenation operator whenever at least one of its operands is a String. If only one of the operands is a String then the other is implicitly converted to a String as discussed in "String Conversions" on page 172.

6.7.9   new

The new operator is a unary prefix operator—it has one operand that follows the operator. Technically the use of new is known as an *instance creation expression*—because it creates an instance of a class or array. The value of the expression is a reference to the object created. The use of new and the associated issue of constructors was discussed in detail from page 43.

6.8   Expressions

An *expression* consists of operators and their operands, which are evaluated to yield a result. This result may be a variable or a value, or even nothing if the expression was the invocation of a method declared void. An expression may be as simple as a single variable name or a complex sequence of method invocations, variable accesses, object creations and the combination of the results of those sub-expressions using other operators, further method invocations and variable accesses.

6.8.1   Order of Evaluation

Regardless of their complexity, the meanings of expressions are always well-defined. Operands to operators will be evaluated left-to-right. For example, given x+y+z, the compiler evaluates x, evaluates y, adds the values together, evaluates z, and adds that to the previous result. The compiler does not evaluate, say, y before x, or z before either y or x. Similarly, argument expressions for method, or constructor, invocations are evaluated from left to right, as are array index expressions for multi-dimensional arrays.

Order of evaluation matters if x, y, or z has side-effects of any kind. If they are, for instance, invocations of methods that affect the state of the object or print something, you would notice if they were evaluated in any other order. The language guarantees that this will not happen.

Except for the operators &&, || and ?:, every operand of an operator will be evaluated before the operation is performed. This is true even for operations that raise exceptions. For example, an integer division by zero results in an ArithmeticException, but it will do so only after both operands have been fully evaluated. Similarly all arguments for a method or constructor invocation are evaluated before the invocation occurs.

If evaluation of the left operand of a binary operator causes an exception, no part of the right-hand operand is evaluated. Similarly if an expression being evaluated for a method, or constructor, argument causes an exception, no argument expressions to the right of it will be evaluated—and likewise for array index expressions. The order of evaluation is very specific and evaluation stops as soon as an exception is encountered.

One further detail concerns object creation using new. If insufficient memory is available for the new object, an OutOfMemoryError exception is thrown. This occurs before evaluation of the constructor arguments occurs—because the value of those arguments is not needed to allocate memory for the object—in which case those arguments won't be evaluated. In contrast, when creating an array, the array dimension expressions must be evaluated first to find out how much memory to allocate—consequently, array creation throws the `OutOfMemoryError` after the dimension expressions are evaluated.

6.8.2   Expression Type

Every expression has a type. The type of an expression is determined by the types of its component parts and the semantics of operators.

If an arithmetic or bit manipulation operator is applied to integer values, the result of the expression is of type `int` unless one or both sides are `long`, in which case the result is `long`. The exception to this rule is that the type of shift operator expressions are not affected by the type of the right hand side. All integer operations are performed in either `int` or `long` precision, so the smaller `byte` and `short` integer types are always promoted to `int` before evaluation.

If either operand of an arithmetic operator is floating-point, the operation is performed in floating-point arithmetic. Such operations are done in `float` unless at least one operand is a `double`, in which case `double` is used for the calculation and result.

A + operator is a `String` concatenation when either operand to + is of type `String` or if the left-hand side of a += is a `String`.

When used in an expression, a `char` value is converted to an `int` by setting the top 16 bits to zero. For example, the Unicode character \uffff would be treated as equivalent to the integer `0x0000ffff`. This treatment is different from the way a `short` with the value `0xffff` would be treated—sign extension makes the `short` equivalent to –1, and its `int` equivalent would be `0xffffffff`.

The Java programming language is a *strongly typed* language, which means that it checks for type compatibility at compile time in almost all cases. Incompatible assignments are prevented by forbidding anything questionable. It also provides *cast* operations for when the compatibility of a type can be determined only at run time, or when you want to explicitly force a type conversion for primitive types that would otherwise lose range, such as assigning a `double` to a `float`. You learned about type compatibility and conversion for reference types on page 79. In this section you learn about the primitive types. We discuss these conversions in terms of assignment, but the rules are the same for conversions within expressions and when using values as method parameters.

6.8.3   Implicit Type Conversions

Some kinds of conversions happen automatically, without any work on your part—these are *implicit* conversions.

Any numeric value can be assigned to any numeric variable whose type supports a larger range of values—a *widening* conversion. A `char` can be used wherever an `int` is valid. A floating-point value can be assigned to any floating-point variable of equal or greater precision.

You can also use implicit conversion of integer types to floating-point, but not vice versa. There is no loss of range going from integer to floating-point, because the range of any floating-point type is larger than the range of any integer.

Preserving magnitude is not the same as preserving the precision of a value. You can lose precision in some implicit conversions. Consider, for example, assigning a `long` to a `float`. The `float` has 32 bits of data and the `long` has 64 bits of data. A `float` stores fewer significant digits than a `long`, even though a `float` stores numbers of a larger range. You can lose data in an assignment of a `long` to a `float`. Consider the following:

```
long orig = 0x7efffff00000000L;
float fval = orig;
long lose = (long) fval;

System.out.println("orig = " + orig);
System.out.println("fval = " + fval);
System.out.println("lose = " + lose);
```

The first two statements create a `long` value and assign it to a `float` value. To show that this loses precision, we explicitly cast `fval` to a `long` and assign it to another variable (explicit casts are covered next). If you examine the output, you can see that the `float` value lost some precision: the `long` variable `orig` that was assigned to the `float` variable `fval` has a different value from the one generated by the explicit cast back into the `long` variable `lose`:

```
orig = 9151314438521880576
fval = 9.1513144E18
lose = 9151314442816847872
```

As a convenience, compile-time constants of integer type can be assigned to smaller integer types, without a cast, provided the value of the constant can actually fit in the smaller type and the integer type is not `long`. For example, the first two assignments are legal while the last is not:

```
short s1 = 27;    // implicit int to short
byte  b1 = 27;    // implicit int to byte
short s3 = 0x1FFFF; // INVALID: int value too big for short
```

Such a conversion, from a larger type to a smaller type, is a *narrowing* conversion.

6.8.4   Explicit Type Casts

When one type cannot be assigned to another type with implicit conversion, often it can be explicitly *cast* to the other type—usually to perform a narrowing conversion. A cast requests a new value of a new type that is the best available representation of the old value in the old type. Some casts are not allowed—for example, a `boolean` cannot be cast to an `int`—but explicit casting can be used to assign a `double` to a `long`, as in this code:

```
double d = 7.99;
long l = (long) d;
```

When a floating-point value is cast to an integer, the fractional part is lost by rounding toward zero; for instance, `(int)-72.3` is `-72`. Methods are available in the `Math` and `StrictMath` classes that round floating-point values to integers in other ways. See "`Math` and `StrictMath`" on page 477 for details.

A `double` can also be explicitly cast to a `float`, or an integer type can be explicitly cast to a smaller integer type. When casting from a `double` to a `float`, three things can happen: you can lose precision, you can get a zero, or you can get an infinity where you originally had a finite value outside the range of a `float`.

Integer types are converted by chopping off the upper bits. If the value in the larger integer fits in the smaller type to which it is cast, no harm is done. But if the larger integer has a value outside the range of the smaller type, dropping the upper bits changes the value, including possibly changing sign. The code

```
short s = -134;
byte b = (byte) s;

System.out.println("s = " + s + ", b = " + b);
```

produces the following output because the upper bits of s are lost when storing the value in b:

```
s = -134, b = 122
```

A `char` can be cast to any integer type and vice versa. When an integer is cast to a `char`, only the bottom 16 bits of data are used; the rest are discarded. When a `char` is cast to an integer type, any additional upper bits are filled with zeros. Once those bits are assigned, they are treated as they would be in any other value. Here is some code that casts the highest Unicode character to both an `int` (implicitly) and a `short` (explicitly). The `int` is a positive value equal to `0x0000ffff`, because the upper bits of the character were set to zero. But the same bits in the short are a negative value, because the top bit of the short is the sign bit:

```java
class CharCast {
    public static void main(String[] args) {
        int i = '\uffff';
        short s = (short) '\uffff';

        System.out.println("i = " + i);
        System.out.println("s = " + s);
    }
}
```

And here is the program's output:

```
i = 65535
s = -1
```

6.8.5   String Conversions

There is one special type of implicit conversion that involves both the primitive and reference types—string conversion. Whenever a + operator has at least one String operand, it is interpreted as the string concatenation operator and the other operand, if not a String, is implicitly converted into a String. Such conversions are defined for all primitive types and are accomplished for any object by invoking its toString method—which is either inherited from Object, or overridden to provide a meaningful string representation for the class. For example, the following method brackets a string with the guillemet characters used for quotation marks in many European languages:

```java
public static String guillemete(String quote) {
    return '«' + quote + '»';
}
```

This implicit conversion of primitive types and objects to strings happens only when you're using + or += in expressions involving strings. It does not happen anywhere else. A method, for example, that takes a String parameter must be passed a String. You cannot pass it an object or primitive type and have it converted implicitly.

When a null reference is converted to a String, the result is the string "null", hence a null reference can be used freely within any string concatenation expression.

6.9   Member Access

You access members of types using the dot (`.`) operator, as in `ref.method()`. This is used to access instance members or static members. Because types can inherit members from their supertypes, there are rules regarding which member is accessed in any given situation. Most of these rules were covered in detail in Chapter 2 and Chapter 3, but we'll briefly recap them.

Static members are accessed using either the type name or an object reference. When a type name is used, the member referred to is the member declared in that type (or inherited by it if there was no declaration in that type). When you use an object reference, the declared type of the reference determines which member is accessed, not the type of the object being referred to. Within a class, reference to a static member always refers to the member declared in, or inherited by, that class.

Non-static members are accessed via an object reference—either an explicit reference, or implicitly `this` (or one of the enclosing objects) if the non-static member is a member of the current object (or enclosing object). Fields and nested types are accessed based on the declared type of the object reference—similarly, within a method, reference to a field or nested type always refers to the declaration within that class, or else the inherited declaration. In contrast, methods are accessed based on the class of the object being referred to. Further, the existence of method overloading means that the system has to determine which method to invoke based on the compile-time type of the arguments used in the invocation—this process is described in detail in the next section. The only operator that can be applied to a method member is the method invocation operator (`)`.

You will get a `NullPointerException` if you use `.` on a reference with the value `null`, unless you are accessing a static member, in which case the value of the reference is never considered, because it is the type of the reference that determines the class in which to locate the member.

6.9.1   Finding the Right Method

For an invocation of a method to be correct, arguments of the proper number and type must be provided so that exactly one matching method can be found in the class. If a method is not overloaded, determining the correct method is simple, because only one parameter count is associated with the method name. Matching is also simple if only one method is declared with the name and number of arguments provided.

If two or more methods of the same name have the same number of parameters, choosing the correct method is more complex. The compiler uses a "most specific" algorithm to do the match:

1. Find all the methods that could possibly apply to the invocation—namely, all the overloaded methods that have the correct name and whose parameters are of types that can be assigned the values of all the arguments. If one method matches exactly for all arguments, invoke that method.

2. If any method in the set has parameter types that are all assignable to any other method in the set, the other method is removed from the set because it is less specific. Repeat until no eliminations can be made.

3. If exactly one method remains, that method is the most specific and will be invoked. If more than one method remains, the invocation is ambiguous because there is no most specific method, so the invoking code is invalid.

For instance, suppose you had the following type hierarchy:

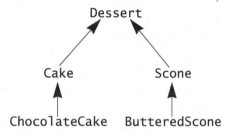

Also suppose you had several overloaded methods that took particular combinations of `Dessert` parameters:

```
void moorge(Dessert d, Scone s)       { /* first form  */ }
void moorge(Cake c, Dessert d)        { /* second form */ }
void moorge(ChocolateCake cc, Scone s) { /* third form  */ }
```

Now consider the following invocations of `moorge`:

```
moorge(dessertRef, sconeRef);
moorge(chocolateCakeRef, dessertRef);
moorge(chocolateCakeRef, butteredSconeRef);
moorge(cakeRef, sconeRef);       // INVALID
```

The first invocation uses the first form of `moorge` because the parameter and argument types match exactly. The second invocation uses the second form because it is the only form for which the provided arguments can be assigned to the parameter types. In both cases, the method to invoke is clear after step 1 in the method-matching algorithm.

The third invocation requires more thought. The list of potential overloads includes all three forms, because a ChocolateCakeRef is assignable to any of the first parameter types, a ButteredScone reference is assignable to either of the second parameter types, and none of the signatures matches exactly. So after step 1, you have a set of three candidate methods.

Step 2 requires you to eliminate less specific methods from the set. In this case, the first form is removed from the set because the third form is more specific—a ChocolateCake reference can be assigned to the first form's Dessert parameter and a Scone reference can be assigned to the first form's Scone parameter, so the first form is less specific. The second form is removed from the set in a similar manner. After this, the set of possible methods has been reduced to one—the third form of moorge—and that method form will be invoked.

The final invocation is invalid. After step 1, the set of possible matches includes the first and second forms. Because neither form's parameters are assignable to the other, neither form can be removed from the set in step 2. Therefore, you have an ambiguous invocation that cannot be resolved by the compiler, and so it is an invalid invocation of moorge. You can resolve the ambiguity by explicitly casting one of the arguments to the Dessert type: if you cast cakeRef, then the first form is invoked; if you cast sconeRef, then the second form is invoked.

These rules also apply to the primitive types. An int, for example, can be assigned to a float, and resolving an overloaded invocation will take that into account just as it considered that a ButteredScone reference was assignable to a Scone reference. However, implicit integer conversions to smaller types are not applied—if a method takes a short argument and you supply an int you will have to cast the int to short explicitly; it won't match the short parameter, regardless of its value.

The method resolution process takes place at compile time based on the declared types of the object reference and the argument values. This process determine which form of a method should be invoked, but not which implementation of that method. At run time the actual type of the object the method is invoked upon is used to find an implementation of the method that was determined at compile time.

Methods may not differ only in return type or in the list of exceptions they throw, because there are too many ambiguities to determine which overloaded method is wanted. If, for example, there were two doppelgänger methods that differed only in that one returned an int and the other returned a short, both methods would make equal sense in the following statement:

```
double d = doppelgänger();
```

A similar problem exists with exceptions, because you can catch any, all, or none of the exceptions a method might throw in the code where you invoke the overloaded method. There would be no way to determine which of two methods to use when they differed only in thrown exceptions.

Such ambiguities are not always detectable at compile time. For example, a superclass may be modified to add a new method that differs only in return type from a method in an extended class. If the extended class is not recompiled, then the error will not be detected. At run time there is no problem because the exact form of the method to be invoked was determined at compile time, hence that is the method that will be looked for in the extended class. In a similar way, if a class is modified to add a new overloaded form of a method, but the class invoking that method is not recompiled, then the new method will never be invoked by that class—the form of method to invoke was already determined at compile time and that form is different from that of the new method.

6.10   Operator Precedence and Associativity

Operator *precedence* is the "stickiness" of operators relative to each other. Operators have different precedences. For example, relational operators have a higher precedence than boolean logic operators, so you can say

```
if (min <= i && i <= max)
    process(i);
```

without any confusion. Because * (multiply) has a higher precedence than - (minus), the expression

```
3 - 3 * 5
```

has the value –12, not zero. Precedence can be overridden using parentheses; if zero were the desired value, for example, the following would do the trick:

```
(3 - 3) * 5
```

When two operators with the same precedence appear next to each other, the *associativity* of the operators determines which is evaluated first. Because + (add) is left-associative, the expression

```
a + b + c
```

is equivalent to

```
(a + b) + c
```

The following table lists all the operators in order of precedence from highest to lowest. All the operators are binary, except those shown as unary with *expr*, the creation and cast operators (which are also unary), and the conditional operator (which is ternary). Operators with the same precedence appear on the same line of the table:

postfix operators	`[]` `.` `(params)` `expr++` `expr--`
unary operators	`++expr` `--expr` `+expr` `-expr` `~` `!`
creation or cast	`new` `(type)expr`
multiplicative	`*` `/` `%`
additive	`+` `-`
shift	`<<` `>>` `>>>`
relational	`<` `>` `>=` `<=` `instanceof`
equality	`==` `!=`
AND	`&`
exclusive OR	`^`
inclusive OR	`|`
conditional AND	`&&`
conditional OR	`||`
conditional	`?:`
assignment	`=` `+=` `-=` `*=` `/=` `%=` `>>=` `<<=` `>>>=` `&=` `^=` `|=`

All binary operators except assignment operators are left-associative. Assignment is right-associative. In other words, a=b=c is equivalent to a=(b=c), which allows assignments to be chained together. The conditional operator ?: is right-associative.

Parentheses are often needed in expressions in which assignment is embedded in a boolean expression, or in which bitwise operations are used. For an example of the former, examine the following code:

```
while ((v = stream.next()) != null)
    processValue(v);
```

Assignment operators have lower precedence than equality operators; without the parentheses, it would be equivalent to

```
while (v = (stream.next() != null)) // INVALID
    processValue(v);
```

and probably not what you want. It is also likely to be invalid code since it would be valid only in the unusual case in which v is boolean.

Many people find the precedence of the bitwise and logical operators &, ^, and | hard to remember. In complex expressions these operators should be parenthesized for readability and to ensure correct precedence.

Our use of parentheses is sparse—we use them only when code seems otherwise unclear. Operator precedence is part of the language and should be generally understood. Others inject parentheses liberally. Try not to use parentheses everywhere—code becomes illegible, looking like LISP with none of LISP's saving graces.

Exercise 6.2: Using what you've learned in this chapter but without writing code, figure out which of the following expressions are invalid and what the type and values are of the valid expressions:

```
3 << 2L - 1
(3L << 2) - 1
10 < 12 == 6 > 17
10 << 12 == 6 >> 17
13.5e-1 % Float.POSITIVE_INFINITY
Float.POSITIVE_INFINITY + Double.NEGATIVE_INFINITY
Double.POSITIVE_INFINITY - Float.NEGATIVE_INFINITY
0.0 / -0.0 == -0.0 / 0.0
Integer.MAX_VALUE + Integer.MIN_VALUE
Long.MAX_VALUE + 5
(short) 5 * (byte) 10
(i < 15 ? 1.72e3f : 0)
i++ + i++ + --i       // i = 3 at start
```

Math was always my bad subject.
I couldn't convince my teachers that many of my answers were meant ironically.
—Calvin Trillin

CHAPTER 7

Control Flow

> *"Would you tell me, please, which way I ought to go from here?"*
> *"That depends a good deal on where you want to get to."*
> —Lewis Carroll, *Alice in Wonderland*

A program consisting only of a list of consecutive statements is immediately useful because the statements are executed in the order in which they're written. But the ability to control the order in which statements are executed—that is, to test conditions and execute different statements based on the results of the tests— adds enormous value to our programming toolkit. This chapter covers almost all the *control flow statements* that direct the order of execution. Exceptions are covered separately in Chapter 8.

7.1   Statements and Blocks

The two basic statements are *expression statements* and *declaration statements*, of which you've seen a plethora. Expression statements, such as i++ or method invocations, are expressions that have a semicolon at the end. The semicolon terminates the statement.[1] In fact, a semicolon by itself is a statement that does nothing—the *empty statement*. Not all expressions can become statements, since it would be almost always meaningless to have, for example, an expression such as x <= y stand alone as a statement. Only the following types of expressions can be made into statements by adding a terminating semicolon:

---

[1] There is a distinction between *terminator* and *separator*. The comma between identifiers in declarations is a separator because it comes between elements in the list. The semicolon is a terminator because it ends each statement. If the semicolon were a statement separator, the last semicolon in a code block would be unnecessary and (depending on the choice of the language designer) possibly invalid.

- ◆ Assignment expressions—those that contain = or one of the *op=* operators
- ◆ Prefix or postfix forms of ++ and --
- ◆ Method calls (whether or not they return a value)
- ◆ Object creation expressions—those that use new to create an object

Declaration statements (formally called *local variable declaration statements*) declare a variable and initialize it to a value. They can appear anywhere inside a block, not just at the beginning. Local variables exist only as long as the block containing their declaration is executing. Local variables must be initialized before use, either by initialization when declared or by assignment. If any local variable is used before it is initialized, the code will not compile.

Local class declaration statements declare a local inner class that can be used within the block in which it was declared. Local classes were discussed in detail on page 129.

In addition to the expression statements listed, several other kinds of statements, such as if and for statements, affect flow of control through the program. This chapter covers each type of statement in detail.

Curly braces, { and }, group zero or more statements into a *block*. A block can be used where any single statement is allowed because a block *is* a statement, albeit a compound one.

7.2 if–else

The most basic form of conditional control flow is the if statement, which chooses whether to execute statements that follow it. Its syntax is:

```
if (boolean-expression)
    statement1
else
    statement2
```

First, the boolean expression is evaluated. If its value is true, then *statement1* is executed; otherwise, if there is an else clause, *statement2* is executed. The else clause is optional.

A series of tests can be built by joining another if to the else clause of a previous if. Here is a method that maps a string—expected to be one of a particular set of words—into an action to be performed with a value:

```
public void setProperty(String keyword, double value)
    throws UnknownProperty
{
    if (keyword.equals("charm"))
        charm(value);
    else if (keyword.equals("strange"))
        strange(value);
    else
        throw new UnknownProperty(keyword);
}
```

What if there is more than one preceding if without an else? For example:

```
public double sumPositive(double[] values) {
    double sum = 0.0;

    if (values.length > 1)
        for (int i = 0; i < values.length; i++)
            if (values[i] > 0)
                sum += values[i];
    else    // oops!
        sum = values[0];
    return sum;
}
```

The else clause *looks* as if it is bound to the array length check, but that is a mirage of indentation, and indentation is ignored. Instead, an else clause is bound to the most recent if that does not have one. Thus, the previous block of code is equivalent to

```
public double sumPositive(double[] values) {
    double sum = 0.0;

    if (values.length > 1)
        for (int i = 0; i < values.length; i++)
            if (values[i] > 0)
                sum += values[i];
            else    // oops!
                sum = values[0];
    return sum;
}
```

This is probably not what was intended. To bind the else clause to the first if, you can use braces to create blocks:

```
public double sumPositive(double[] values) {
    double sum = 0.0;

    if (values.length > 1) {
        for (int i = 0; i < values.length; i++)
            if (values[i] > 0)
                sum += values[i];
    } else {
        sum = values[0];
    }
    return sum;
}
```

Exercise 7.1: Using if-else in a loop, write a method that takes a string parameter and returns a string with all the special characters in the original string replaced by their language equivalents. For example, a string with a " in the middle of it should create a return value with that " replaced by \". (Section 6.2.3 on page 142 lists all special characters).

7.3   switch

A switch statement allows you to transfer control to a labeled entry point in a block of statements, based on the value of an integer expression. The general form of a switch statement is:

```
switch (expression) {
    case n: statements
    case m: statements
    . . .
    default: statements
}
```

The body of the switch statement is known as the *switch block* and it can contain statements that are prefixed with case labels. A case label is an integer constant. If the value of the switch expression matches the value of a case label then control is transferred to the first statement following that label. If a matching case label is not found, control is transferred to the first statement following a default label. If there is no default label, the entire switch statement is skipped.

For example, consider our `Verbose` interface from page 109:

```
interface Verbose {
    int SILENT  = 0;
    int TERSE   = 1;
    int NORMAL  = 2;
    int VERBOSE = 3;

    void setVerbosity(int level);
    int getVerbosity();
}
```

Depending on the verbosity level, the state of the object is dumped, adding new output at greater verbosity levels and then printing the output of the next lower level of verbosity:

```
Verbose v = ... ; // initialized as appropriate
public void dumpState() {
    int verbosity = v.getVerbosity();
    switch (verbosity) {
      case Verbose.SILENT:
        break; // do nothing

      case Verbose.VERBOSE:
        System.out.println(stateDetails);
        // FALLTHROUGH

      case Verbose.NORMAL:
        System.out.println(basicState);
        // FALLTHROUGH

      case Verbose.TERSE:
        System.out.println(summaryState);
        break;

      default:
        throw new IllegalStateException(
                    "verbosity=" + verbosity);
    }
}
```

Once control has transferred to a statement following a `case` label, the following statements are executed in turn, according to the semantics of those statements, even if those statements have their own different case labels. The FALLTHROUGH comments, in the example, document where control *falls through* the next case label to the code below. Thus, if the verbosity level is VERBOSE, all three output parts are printed; if verbosity is NORMAL, two parts are printed; and if verbosity is TERSE, only one part is printed.

A case or default label does *not* force a break out of the switch. Nor does it imply an end to execution of statements. If you want to stop executing statements in the switch block you must explicitly transfer control out of the switch block. This can be achieved using the break statement. Within a switch block, a break statement transfers control to the first statement after the switch. This is why we have a break statement after the TERSE output is finished. Without the break, execution would continue through into the code for the default label and throw the exception every time. Similarly, in the SILENT case, all that is executed is the break because there is nothing to print.

Falling through to the next case can be useful in some circumstances. But in most cases a break should come after the code that a case label selects. Good coding style suggests that you always use some form of FALLTHROUGH comment to document an intentional fall-through.

A single statement can have more than one case label, allowing a singular action in multiple cases. For example, here we use a switch statement to decide how to translate a hexadecimal digit into an int:

```java
public int hexValue(char ch) throws NonHexDigitException {
    switch (ch) {
    case '0': case '1': case '2': case '3': case '4':
    case '5': case '6': case '7': case '8': case '9':
      return (ch - '0');

    case 'a': case 'b': case 'c':
    case 'd': case 'e': case 'f':
      return (ch - 'a') + 10;

    case 'A': case 'B': case 'C':
    case 'D': case 'E': case 'F':
      return (ch - 'A') + 10;

    default:
      throw new NonHexDigitException(ch);
    }
}
```

There are no `break` statements because the `return` statements exit the switch block (and the whole method) before control can fall through.

You should terminate the last group of statements in a switch with a `break`, `return`, or `throw`, as you would a group of statements in an earlier case. Doing so reduces the likelihood of accidentally falling through the bottom of what *used* to be the last part of the switch when a new `case` is added.

The `switch` expression must be of type `char`, `byte`, `short` or `int`. All `case` labels must be constant expressions—the expressions must contain only literals or named constants initialized with constant expressions—and must be assignable to the type of the `switch` expression. In any single `switch` statement, each `case` value must be unique, and there can be at most one `default` label.

Only statements directly within the switch block can have `case` labels. This means that you cannot, for example, transfer control to a statement within the switch block that is in the middle of a loop, or a statement within a nested block of code. You can, however, skip the declaration and initialization of a local variable within the switch block (not that we recommend it). The effect of this is that the local variable is still considered to be declared, but the initializer has not been executed. As local variables must be initialized, any attempt to read the value of that local variable will result in a compile-time error—the first use of that variable must be an assignment.

The first statement in a switch block must be labeled, otherwise it is unreachable (all cases will jump over it) and your code will not compile.

Exercise 7.2: Rewrite your method from Exercise 7.1 to use a `switch`.

7.4   `while` and `do-while`

The `while` loop looks like this:

```
while (boolean-expression)
    statement
```

The boolean expression is evaluated and, if it is `true`, the statement (which may be a block) is executed. Once the statement completes, the expression is re-evaluated and, if still `true`, the statement is executed again. This repeats until the expression evaluates to `false`, at which point control transfers after the `while`.

We introduced the `while` loop with our second program in Chapter 1, the `Fibonacci` program:

```
while (hi < MAX) {
    System.out.println(hi);
    hi = lo + hi;
    lo = hi - lo;
}
```

This loops around printing and calculating new Fibonacci values until the highest value computed exceeds the maximum limit.

A `while` loop executes zero or more times since the boolean expression might be `false` the first time it is evaluated. Sometimes you want to execute a loop body at least once, which is why you also have a do–`while` loop:

```
do
    statement
while (boolean-expression);
```

Here, the boolean expression is evaluated *after* the statement is executed. While the expression is `true`, the statement is executed repeatedly. The statement in a do–`while` loop is almost always a block.

7.5   for

The `for` statement is used to loop over a range of values from beginning to end. It looks like this:

```
for (init-expr; boolean-expr; incr-expr)
    statement
```

The *init-expr* allows you to declare and/or initialize loop variables, and is executed only once. Next the boolean loop expression is evaluated and if it is `true` the statement in the body of the loop is executed. After executing the loop body, the *incr-expr* is evaluated, usually to update the values of the loop variables, and then the loop expression is re-evaluated. This cycle repeats until the loop expression is found to be `false`. This is roughly equivalent to

```
{
    init-expr;
    while (boolean-expr) {
        statement
```

```
        incr-expr;
    }
}
```

with the exception that *incr-expr* is always executed if a `continue` is encountered in the loop body (see "`continue`" on page 192).

The initialization and iteration parts of a `for` loop can be comma-separated lists of expressions. The expressions separated by the commas are, like most operators, evaluated left-to-right. For example, to march two indexes through an array in opposite directions, the following code would be appropriate:

```
for (i = 0, j = arr.length - 1; j >= 0; i++, j--) {
    // ...
}
```

The initialization section of a `for` loop can also be a local variable declaration statement. For example, if i and j are not used outside of the `for` loop, you could rewrite the previous example as:

```
for (int i = 0, j = arr.length - 1; j >= 0; i++, j--) {
    // ...
}
```

If you have a local variable declaration, however, each part of the expression after a comma is expected to be a part of that local variable declaration. For example, if you want to print out the first MAX members of a linked list you need to maintain a count as well as iterate through the list members. You might be tempted to try the following:

```
for (int i = 0, Cell node = head;           // INVALID
    i < MAX && node != null;
    i++, node = node.next)
{
    System.out.println(node.getElement());
}
```

This will not compile: in a variable declaration the comma separates the different variables being declared, and `Cell` is a type, not a variable. Declarations of different types of variables are distinct statements terminated by semicolons. If you change the comma to a semicolon, however, you get a `for` loop with four sections, not three—still an error. If you need to initialize two different types of variables then neither of them can be declared within the `for` loop:

```
int i;
Cell node;
for (i = 0, node = head;
        i < MAX && node != null;
        i++, node = node.next)
{
        System.out.println(node.getElement());
}
```

Typically, the `for` loop is used to iterate a variable over a range of values until some logical end to that range is reached. You can define what an iteration range is. A `for` loop is often used, for example, to iterate through the elements of a linked list or to follow a mathematical sequence of values. This capability makes the `for` construct more powerful than equivalent constructs in many other languages, which restrict `for`-style constructs to incrementing a variable over a range of values.

Here is an example of such a loop, designed to calculate the smallest value of *exp* such that 10^{exp} is greater than or equal to a value:

```
public static int tenPower(int value) {
        int exp, v;
        for (exp = 0, v = value - 1; v > 0; exp++, v /= 10)
            continue;
        return exp;
}
```

In this case, two variables step through different ranges. As long as the loop variable `v` is greater than zero, the exponent value is incremented and `v` is divided by ten. When the loop completes, the value 10^{exp} is the smallest power of ten that is greater than or equal to `value`. Both the test value and the exponent are updated on each loop iteration. In such cases, a comma-separated list of expressions is a good technique to ensure that they are always in lockstep.

The body of this loop is simply a `continue` statement, which starts the next iteration of the loop. The body of the loop has nothing to do—all the work of the loop is in the test and iteration clauses of the `for` statement itself. The `continue` style shown here is one way to show an empty loop body; another way is to put a simple semicolon on a line by itself or to use an empty block with braces. Simply putting a semicolon at the end of the `for` line is dangerous—if the semicolon is accidentally deleted or forgotten, the statement that follows the `for` can silently become the body of the `for`.

All the expressions in the for construct are optional. If either *init-expr* or *incr-expr* is left out, its part in the loop is simply omitted. If *boolean-expr* is left out, it is assumed to be true. Thus, the idiomatic way to write an infinite loop is as a "for ever" loop:

```
for (;;)
    statement
```

Presumably, the loop is terminated by some other means, such as a break statement (described later) or by throwing an exception.

Conventionally, the for loop is used only when you are looping through a range of related values. It is bad style to violate this convention by using initialization or increment expressions that are unrelated to the boolean loop test.

Exercise 7.3: Write a method that takes two char parameters and prints the characters between those two values, including the end points.

7.6 Labels

Statements can be labeled to give them a name by which they can be referred. A label precedes the statement it names:

```
label: statement
```

Labels can be referred to only by the break and continue statements (discussed next).

7.7 break

A break statement can be used to exit from any block, not just from a switch. There are two forms of break statement. The *unlabeled break*:

```
break;
```

and the *labeled break*:

```
break label;
```

An unlabeled break terminates the innermost switch, for, while, or do statement—and so can appear only within one of those statements. A labeled break can terminate any labeled statement.

A break is most often used to break out of a loop. In this example, we are looking for the first empty slot in an array of references to Contained objects:

```
class Container {
    private Contained[] Objs;

    // ...

    public void addIn(Contained obj)
        throws NoEmptySlotException
    {
        int i;
        for (i = 0; i < Objs.length; i++)
            if (Objs[i] == null)
                break;
        if (i >= Objs.length)
            throw new NoEmptySlotException();
        Objs[i] = obj;     // put it inside me
        obj.inside(this); // let it know it's inside me
    }
}
```

To terminate an outer loop or block, you label the outer statement and use its label name in the break statement:

```
private float[][] Matrix;

public boolean workOnFlag(float flag) {
    int y, x;
    boolean found = false;

  search:
    for (y = 0; y < Matrix.length; y++) {
        for (x = 0; x < Matrix[y].length; x++) {
            if (Matrix[y][x] == flag) {
                found = true;
                break search;
            }
        }
    }
    if (!found)
        return false;
```

```
    // do some stuff with flagged value at Matrix[y][x]
    return true;
}
```

Here we label the outer `for` loop and if we find the value we are looking for, we terminate both inner and outer loops by using a labeled `break`. This simplifies the logic of the loops because we do not need a `!found` clause in the loop expressions.

Whether to always use labels is a matter of individual preference. It is a good defensive measure against a later maintainer of the code enclosing your code with a switch statement or a loop.

Note that a labeled `break` is not a `goto`. The `goto` statement would enable indiscriminate jumping around in code, obfuscating the flow of control. A `break` or `continue` that references a label, on the other hand, exits from or repeats only that specific labeled block, and the flow of control is obvious by inspection. For example, here is a modified version of `workOnFlag` that labels a block instead of a loop, allowing you to dispense with the `found` flag altogether:

```
public boolean workOnFlag(float flag) {
    int y, x;

  search:
    {
        for (y = 0; y < Matrix.length; y++) {
            for (x = 0; x < Matrix[y].length; x++) {
                if (Matrix[y][x] == flag)
                    break search;
            }
        }

        // if we get here we didn't find it
        return false;
    }
    // do some stuff with flagged value at Matrix[y][x]
    return true;
}
```

7.8   `continue`

A `continue` statement can be used only within a loop (`for`, `while`, or `do`) and transfers control to the end of the loop's body. In the case of `while` and `do` loops, this causes the loop expression to be evaluated next. In a `for` loop it causes the *incr-expr* to be evaluated before the loop expression.

Like the `break` statement, the `continue` statement comes in an unlabeled:

```
continue;
```

and labeled form:

```
continue label;
```

In the unlabeled form, `continue` transfers control to the end of the innermost loop's body. The labeled form transfers control to the end of the loop with that label. The label must belong to a loop statement.

A `continue` is often used to skip over an element of a loop range that can be ignored or treated with trivial code. For example, a token stream that included a simple "skip" token might be handled this way:

```
while (!stream.eof()) {
    token = stream.next();
    if (token.equals("skip"))
        continue;
    // ... process token ...
}
```

A labeled `continue` will break out of any inner loops on its way to the next iteration of the named loop. No label is required on the `continue` in the preceding example since there is only one enclosing loop. Consider, however, nested loops that iterate over the values of a two-dimensional matrix. Suppose that the matrix is symmetric (`matrix[i][j]` == `matrix[j][i]`). In that case, you need only iterate through one half of the matrix. For example, here is a method that doubles each value in a symmetric matrix:

```
static void doubleUp(int[][] matrix) {
    int order = matrix.length;
column:
    for (int i = 0; i < order; i++) {
        for (int j = 0; j < order; j++) {
            matrix[i][j] = matrix[j][i] = matrix[i][j]*2;
            if (i == j)
                continue column;
```

```
         }
      }
   }
```

Each time a diagonal element of the matrix is reached, the rest of that row is skipped by continuing with the outer loop that iterates over the columns.

7.9   return

A `return` statement terminates execution of a method and returns to the invoker. If the method returns no value, a simple return statement will do:

```
return;
```

If the method has a return type, the `return` must include an expression of a type that could be assigned to the return type. For example, if a method returns `double`, a `return` could have an expression that was a `double`, `float`, or integer:

```
protected double nonNegative(double val) {
    if (val < 0)
        return 0;    // an int constant
    else
        return val; // a double
}
```

A `return` can also be used to exit constructors and static initializer code. Neither construct has a return type, so `return` is used without specifying a return value. Constructors are invoked as part of the new process that in the end returns a reference to an object, but each constructor plays only a part of that role; no constructor "returns" the final reference.

7.10   What, No goto?

The Java programming language has no `goto` construct to transfer control to an arbitrary statement in a method, although `goto` is common in languages to which the language is related. The primary uses for `goto` in these other languages are:

◆ Controlling outer loops from within nested loops. Use labeled `break` and `continue` statements to meet this need.

◆ Skipping the rest of a block of code that is not in a loop when an answer or error is found. Use a labeled `break`.

◆ Executing cleanup code before a method or block of code exits. Use either a labeled break or, more cleanly, the `finally` construct of the `try` statement covered in the next chapter.

Labeled `break` and `continue` have the advantage that they transfer control to a strictly limited place. A `finally` block is even stricter as to where it transfers control, and it works in all circumstances, including exceptions. With these constructs you can write clean code without a `goto`.

Furious activity is no substitute for understanding.
—H.H. Williams

CHAPTER 8

Exceptions

A slipping gear could let your M203 grenade launcher fire when you least expect it.
That would make you quite unpopular in what's left of your unit.
—The U.S. Army's *PS* magazine, August 1993

DURING execution, applications can run into many kinds of errors of varying degrees of severity. When methods are invoked on an object, the object can discover internal state problems (inconsistent values of variables), detect errors with objects or data it manipulates (such as a file or network address), determine that it is violating its basic contract (such as reading data from an already closed stream), and so on.

Many programmers do not test for all possible error conditions, and for good reason: code becomes unintelligible if each method invocation checks for all possible errors before the next statement is executed. This trade-off creates a tension between correctness (checking for all errors) and clarity (not cluttering the basic flow of code with many error checks).

Exceptions provide a clean way to check for errors without cluttering code. Exceptions also provide a mechanism to signal errors directly rather than use flags or side effects such as fields that must be checked. Exceptions make the error conditions that a method can signal an explicit part of the method's contract. The list of exceptions can be seen by the programmer, checked by the compiler, and preserved (if needed) by extended classes that override the method.

An exception is *thrown* when an unexpected error condition is encountered. The exception is then *caught* by an encompassing clause further up the method invocation stack. Uncaught exceptions result in the termination of the thread of execution, but before it terminates, the thread's ThreadGroup is given the opportunity to handle the exception as best it can, usually printing useful information about where the exception was thrown (such as a call stack)—see "Threads and Exceptions" on page 266.

8.1 Creating Exception Types

Exceptions are objects. All exception types—that is, any class designed for throwable objects—must extend the class `Throwable` or one of its subclasses. The `Throwable` class contains a string that can be used to describe the exception. By convention, new exception types extend `Exception`, a subclass of `Throwable`.

Exceptions are primarily *checked exceptions,* meaning that the compiler checks that your methods throw only exceptions they have declared themselves to throw. The standard runtime exceptions and errors extend one of the classes `RuntimeException` and `Error`, making them *unchecked exceptions.* All exceptions you create should extend `Exception`, making them checked exceptions.

Checked exceptions represent conditions that, although exceptional, can reavsonably be expected to occur, and if they do occur must be dealt with in some way. Making these exceptions checked, documents the existence of the exception and ensures that the caller of a method deals with the exception in some way. Unchecked exceptions represent conditions that, generally speaking, reflect errors in your program's logic and cannot be reasonably recovered from at run time. For example, the `IndexOutOfBoundsException` thrown when you access outside the bounds of an array, tells you that your program calculated an index incorrectly, or failed to verify a value to be used as an index. These are errors that should be corrected in the program code. Given that you can make errors writing any statement it would be totally impractical to have to declare or catch all the exceptions that could arise from those errors—hence they are unchecked.

Sometimes it is useful to have more data to describe the exceptional condition than just the string that `Exception` provides. In such cases, `Exception` can be extended to create a class that contains the added data (usually set in the constructor).

For example, suppose a `replaceValue` method is added to the `Attributed` interface discussed in Chapter 4. This method replaces the current value of a named attribute with a new value. If the named attribute doesn't exist, an exception should be thrown, because it is reasonable to assume that one should replace only existing attributes. That exception should contain the name of the attribute. To represent the exception, we create the `NoSuchAttributeException` class:

```
public class NoSuchAttributeException extends Exception {
    public String attrName;

    public NoSuchAttributeException(String name) {
        super("No attribute named \"" + name + "\" found");
```

```
                attrName = name;
        }
}
```

NoSuchAttributeException extends Exception to add a constructor that takes the name of the attribute; it also adds a public field to store the data. The constructor invokes the superclass's constructor with a string description of what happened. This exception type is useful to code that catches the exception, because it holds both a human-usable description of the error and the data that created the error. Adding useful data is one reason to create a new exception type.

Another reason to create a new exception type is that the type of the exception is an important part of the exception data, because exceptions are caught according to their type. For this reason, you would invent NoSuchAttributeException even if you did not want to add data. In this way, a programmer who cared only about such an exception could catch it exclusive of other exceptions that might be generated either by the methods of the Attributed interface, or by other methods used on other objects in the same area of code.

In general, new exception types should be created when programmers will want to handle one kind of error and not another kind. Programmers can then use the exception type to execute the correct code rather than examine the contents of the exception to determine whether they really care about the exception, or catch an irrelevant exception by accident.

8.2   throw

Exceptions are thrown using the throw statement:

```
throw expression;
```

where the expression must evaluate to a value or variable that is assignable to Throwable—or in simple terms, a reference to a Throwable object. For example, here is an addition to AttributedImpl from Chapter 4 that implements replaceValue:

```
public void replaceValue(String name, Object newValue)
    throws NoSuchAttributeException
{
    Attr attr = find(name);          // look up the attr
    if (attr == null)                // it isn't found
        throw new NoSuchAttributeException(name);
    attr.setValue(newValue);
}
```

The `replaceValue` method first looks up the current `Attr` object for the name. If there isn't one, it throws a new object of type `NoSuchAttributeException`, providing the constructor with the attribute name. Exceptions are objects, so they must be created before being thrown. If the attribute does exist, its value is replaced with the new value. An exception can also be generated by invoking a method that itself throws an exception.

8.2.1 Transfer of Control

When an exception is thrown, the statement or expression that caused the exception is said to *complete abruptly*. This abrupt completion of statements causes the call chain to gradually unwind, as each block, or method invocation, completes abruptly, until the exception is caught. If the exception is not caught, the thread of execution terminates. Before it terminates, the thread's `ThreadGroup` is given the opportunity to handle the exception—see "Threads and Exceptions" on page 266.

Once an exception occurs, actions after the point at which the exception occurred do not take place. If evaluation of a left-operand causes an exception then no part of the right-operand is evaluated; if evaluation of a left argument expression results in an exception, then no argument to the right is evaluated. The next action to occur will be in either a `finally` block, or a `catch` block that catches the exception.

8.2.2 Asynchronous Exceptions

A `throw` statement results in a *synchronous* exception, as does, say, a divide-by-zero arithmetic exception—the exception occurs directly as a result of executing a particular instruction; either the `throw` or performing the division. In contrast an *asynchronous* exception is one that can occur at any time, regardless of the instructions being executed.

Asynchronous exceptions can occur in only two specific ways. The first is an internal error in the Java virtual machine—such exceptions are considered asynchronous because they are caused by the execution of instructions in the virtual machine, not the instructions of the program. Needless to say, there is little that you can do about an internal error.

The second mechanism is the use of the deprecated `Thread.stop` methods, or the related, and not deprecated, `stopThread` methods of the Java™ Virtual Machine Debug Interface (JVMDI)—a native code interface to the virtual machine which allows for the inspection, and control of, a running application. These methods allow an asynchronous exception of any kind (checked or unchecked) to be thrown at any point during the execution of the target thread. Such a mechanism is inherently dangerous, which is why it has been deprecated in the `Thread` class—we discuss this further in Chapter 10.

8.3 The `throws` Clause

The definition of the `replaceValue` method declares which checked exceptions it throws. The language requires such a declaration because programmers invoking a method need to know the exceptions it can throw just as much as they need to know its normal behavior. The checked exceptions that a method throws are as important as the type of value it returns. Both must be declared.

The checked exceptions a method can throw are declared with a `throws` clause, which declares a comma-separated list of exception types. Only those exceptions which are not caught within the method must be listed.

You can throw checked exceptions that are extensions of the type of exception in the `throws` clause because you can use a class polymorphically anywhere its superclass is expected. A method can throw several different classes of checked exceptions—all of them extensions of a particular exception class—and declare only the superclass in the `throws` clause. By doing so, however, you hide potentially useful information from programmers invoking the method, because they don't know which of the possible extended exception types could be thrown. For documentation purposes, the `throws` clause should be as complete and specific as possible.

The contract defined by the `throws` clause is strictly enforced—you can throw only a type of checked exception that has been declared in the `throws` clause. Throwing any other type of checked exception is invalid, whether you use `throw` directly or use it indirectly by invoking another method. If a method has no `throws` clause, it does not mean that *any* exceptions can be thrown: it means *no* checked exceptions can be thrown.

All the standard runtime exceptions (such as `ClassCastException` and `ArithmeticException`) are extensions of the `RuntimeException` class. The more serious errors are signaled by exceptions that are extensions of `Error`, and these exceptions can occur at any time in any code. `RuntimeException` and `Error` are the only exceptions you do not need to list in your `throws` clauses. They are ubiquitous, and every method can potentially throw them. This is why they are unchecked by the compiler. The complete list of standard unchecked exception classes is in Appendix A.

Because checked exceptions must be declared in a `throws` clause, it follows that any code fragment outside of a method with a `throws` clause cannot throw a checked exception. This means that initializers and static initialization blocks cannot throw checked exceptions, either directly or by invoking a method that throws such an exception. Constructors can declare and throw checked exceptions, and non-static initialization blocks can throw checked exceptions provided all the constructors of the class declare those checked exceptions.

Checked exception handling is strictly enforced because doing so helps avoid bugs that come from not dealing with errors. Experience has shown that programmers forget to handle errors or defer writing code to handle them until some future time that never arrives. The throws clause states clearly which exceptions are being thrown by methods and makes sure they are dealt with in some way by the invoker.

If you invoke a method that lists a checked exception in its throws clause, you have three choices:

◆ Catch the exception and handle it.

◆ Catch the exception and map it into one of your exceptions by throwing an exception of a type declared in your own throws clause.

◆ Declare the exception in your throws clause and let the exception pass through your method (although you might have a finally clause that cleans up first; see the next section for details).

To do any of these things, you need to catch exceptions thrown by other methods, and that is the subject of the next section.

You should be explicit in your throws clause, listing all the exceptions you know that you throw, even when you could encompass several exceptions under some superclass they all share. This is good self-documentation. Deciding how explicit you should be requires some thought. If you are designing a general interface or superclass you have to think about how restrictive you want to be to the implementing classes. It may be quite reasonable to define a general exception you use in the interface's throws clause, and expect that the implementing classes will be more specific where possible. This tactic is used by the java.io package, which defines a general IOException type for its methods to throw. This lets implementing classes throw exceptions specific to whatever kind of I/O is being done. For example the classes that do I/O across network channels can throw various network-related subclasses of IOException, while those dealing with files throw file-related subclasses.

8.3.1   throws Clauses and Method Overriding

When you override an inherited method, or implement an inherited abstract method, the throws clause of the overriding method must be compatible with the throws clause of the inherited method (whether abstract or not).

The simple rule is that an overriding or implementing method is not allowed to declare more checked exceptions in the throws clause than the inherited method does. The reason for this rule is quite simple—code written to deal with the original method declaration will not be prepared to catch any additional checked exceptions and so no such exceptions are allowed to be thrown. Subtypes of the declared exceptions can be thrown as they will be caught in a catch block for their supertype. If the overriding or implementing method does not throw a checked exception then it need not declare it—for example, as you saw in "Strategies for Cloning" on page 89, a class that implements the Cloneable interface need not declare that clone may throw a CloneNotSupportedException. Whether to declare it or not is a matter of design—if you declare it in the overriding method then subclasses of your class will be allowed to throw the exception in that method, otherwise they will not.

If a method declaration is multiply inherited—as it exists in more than one inherited interface, or both an inherited interface and a superclass—then the throws clause of that method must satisfy all of the inherited throws clauses. As we discussed in "Inheriting, Overriding, and Overloading Methods" on page 112, the real issue in such multiple inheritance situations, is whether a single implementation of a method can honor all of the inherited contracts.

8.3.2   throws Clauses and Native Methods

A native method declaration (see page 63) can provide a throws clause which forces all users of that method to catch or redeclare the specified checked exceptions. However, the implementation of native methods is beyond the control of the Java compiler and so they cannot be checked to ensure that only the declared exceptions are thrown. Well written native methods, however, will throw only those checked exceptions that they declare.

Exercise 8.1: Create an ObjectNotFoundException class for the LinkedList class we've built in previous exercises. Add a find method that looks for an object in the list and either returns the LinkedList object that contains the desired object or throws the exception if the object isn't found in the list. Why is this preferable to returning null if the object isn't found? What additional data if any should ObjectNotFoundException contain?

8.4   try, catch, and finally

Exceptions are caught by enclosing code in `try` blocks. The basic syntax for a
try block is:

```
try {
    statements
} catch (exception_type1 identifier1) {
    statements
} catch (exception_type2 identifier2) {
    statements
...
} finally {
    statements
}
```

The body of the `try` statement is executed until either an exception is thrown or it
finishes successfully. If an exception is thrown, each `catch` clause is examined in
turn, from first to last, to see whether the type of the exception object is assignable
to the type declared in the `catch`. When an assignable `catch` clause is found, its
block is executed with its identifier set to reference the exception object. No other
`catch` clause will be executed. Any number of `catch` clauses can be associated
with a particular `try`, including zero, as long as each clause catches a different
type of exception. If no appropriate `catch` is found, the exception percolates out
of the `try` statement into any outer `try` that might have a `catch` clause to handle
it.

If a `finally` clause is present with a `try`, its code is executed after all other
processing in the `try` is complete. This happens no matter how completion was
achieved, whether normally, through an exception, or through a control flow statement such as `return` or `break`.

This example code is prepared to handle one of the exceptions `replaceValue`
throws:

```
Object value = new Integer(8);
try {
    attributedObj.replaceValue("Age", value);
} catch (NoSuchAttributeException e) {
    // shouldn't happen, but recover if it does
    Attr attr = new Attr(e.attrName, value);
    attributedObj.add(attr);
}
```

The `try` sets up a statement (which must be a block) that does something that is normally expected to succeed. If everything succeeds, the block is finished. If any exception is thrown during execution of the code in the `try` block, either directly via a `throw` or indirectly by a method invoked inside it, execution of the code inside the `try` stops, and the attached `catch` clause is examined to see whether it wants to catch the exception that was thrown.

A `catch` clause is somewhat like an embedded method that has one parameter—namely, the exception to be caught. Inside a `catch` clause, you can attempt to recover from the exception, or you can clean up and rethrow the exception so that any code calling yours also has a chance to catch it. Or a `catch` can do what it needs to and then fall out the bottom, in which case control flows to the statement after the `try` statement (after executing the `finally` clause, if there is one).

A general `catch` clause—one that catches exceptions of type `Exception`, for example—is usually a poor implementation choice since it will catch *any* exception, not just the specific one you are interested in. Had we used such a clause in our code, it could have ended up handling, for example, a `ClassCastException` as if it were a missing attribute problem.

You cannot put a superclass `catch` clause before a `catch` of one of its subclasses. The `catch` clauses are examined in order, so a `catch` that picked up one exception type before a `catch` for an extended type of exception would be a mistake. The first clause would always catch the exception, and the second clause would never be reached. The compiler will not accept the following code:

```
class SuperException extends Exception { }
class SubException extends SuperException { }

class BadCatch {
    public void goodTry() {
        /* This is an INVALID catch ordering */
        try {
            throw new SubException();
        } catch (SuperException superRef) {
            // Catches both SuperException and SubException
        } catch (SubException subRef) {
            // This would never be reached
        }
    }
}
```

Only one exception is handled by any single encounter with a `try` clause. If a `catch` or `finally` clause throws another exception, the `catch` clauses of the `try` are not reexamined. The `catch` and `finally` clauses are outside the protection of the `try` clause itself. Such exceptions can, of course, be handled by any encompassing `try` block in which the inner `catch` or `finally` clauses were nested.

8.4.1 `finally`

The `finally` clause of a `try` statement provides a mechanism for executing a section of code whether or not an exception is thrown. Usually the `finally` clause is used to clean up internal state or to release non-object resources, such as open files stored in local variables. Here is a method that closes a file when its work is done, even if an error occurs:

```
public boolean searchFor(String file, String word)
    throws StreamException
{
    Stream input = null;

    try {
        input = new Stream(file);
        while (!input.eof())
            if (input.next().equals(word))
                return true;
        return false;        // not found
    } finally {
        if (input != null)
            input.close();
    }
}
```

If the new fails, `input` will never be changed from its initial `null` value. If the new succeeds, `input` will reference the object that represents the open file. When the `finally` clause is executed, the `input` stream is closed only if it has been open. Whether or not the operations on the stream generate an exception, the contents of the `finally` clause ensure that the file is closed, thus conserving the limited resource of simultaneous open files. The `searchFor` method declares that it throws `StreamException` so that any exceptions generated are passed through to the invoking code after cleanup, including any `StreamException` thrown by the invocation of `close`.

There are two main coding idioms for using `finally` correctly. The general situation is that we have two actions, call them `pre` and `post`, such that if `pre` occurs then `post` must occur—regardless of what other actions occur between pre and post and regardless of whether those actions complete successfully or throw exceptions. One idiom for ensuring this is:

```
pre();
try {
    // other actions
} finally {
    post();
}
```

If pre succeeds then we enter the try block and no matter what occurs we are guaranteed that post gets executed. Conversely, if pre itself fails for some reason and throws an exception, then post does not get executed—it is important that pre occurs outside the try block in this situation, as post must not execute if pre fails.

The second form of the idiom is what we used in the stream searching example. In that case pre returns a value which can be used to determine whether or not it completed successfully. Only if pre completed successfully is post invoked in the finally clause:

```
Object val = null;
try {
    val = pre();
    // other actions
} finally {
    if (val != null)
        post();
}
```

In this case, we could still invoke pre outside the try block, and then we would not need the if statement in the finally clause. The advantage of placing pre inside the try block comes when we want to catch both the exceptions that may be thrown by pre and those that may be thrown by the other actions—with pre inside the try block we can have one set of catch blocks, but if pre were outside the try block we would need to use an outer try-catch block to catch the exceptions from pre. Having nested try blocks can be further complicated if both pre and the other actions can throw the same exceptions—quite common with I/O operations—and we wish to propagate the exception after using it in some way; an exception thrown by the other actions would get caught twice and we would have to code our catch blocks to watch for and deal with that situation.

A finally clause can also be used to clean up for break, continue, and return, which is one reason you will sometimes see a try clause with no catch clauses. When any control transfer statement is executed, all relevant finally clauses are executed. There is no way to leave a `try` block without executing its `finally` clause.

The preceding example relies on `finally` in this way to clean up even with a normal `return`. One of the most common reasons `goto` is used in other languages is to ensure that certain things are cleaned up when a block of code is complete, whether or not it was successful. In our example, the `finally` clause ensures that the file is closed when either the `return` statement is executed or the stream throws an exception.

A `finally` clause is always entered with a reason. That reason may be that the `try` code finished normally, that it executed a control flow statement such as `return`, or that an exception was thrown in code executed in the `try` block. The reason is remembered when the `finally` clause exits by falling out the bottom. However, if the `finally` block creates its own reason to leave by executing a control flow statement (such as `break` or `return`) or by throwing an exception, that reason supersedes the original one, and the original reason is forgotten. For example, consider the following code:

```
try {
    // ... do something ...
    return 1;
} finally {
    return 2;
}
```

When the `try` block executes its return, the `finally` block is entered with the "reason" of returning the value 1. However, inside the `finally` block the value 2 is returned, so the initial intention is forgotten. In fact, if any of the other code in the `try` block had thrown an exception, the result would still be to return 2. If the `finally` block did not return a value but simply fell out the bottom, the "return the value 1" reason would be remembered and carried out.

8.5   When to Use Exceptions

We used the phrase "unexpected error condition" at the beginning of this chapter when describing when to throw exceptions. Exceptions are not meant for simple, expected situations. For example, reaching the end of a stream of input is expected, so the method that returns the next input from the stream has "hit the end" as part of its expected behavior. A return code indicating end-of-input is reasonable, as it is for callers to check the return value, and such a convention is also easier to understand. Consider the following typical loop using a return flag:

```
while ((token = stream.next()) != Stream.END)
    process(token);
stream.close();
```

Compare that to this loop, which relies on an exception to signal the end of input:

```
try {
    for (;;) {
        process(stream.next());
    }
} catch (StreamEndException e) {
    stream.close();
}
```

In the first case, the flow of control is direct and clear. The code loops until it reaches the end of the stream, and then it closes the stream. In the second case, the code seems to loop forever. Unless you know that end of input is signaled with a StreamEndException, you don't know the loop's natural range. Even when you know about StreamEndException, this construction can be confusing since it moves the loop termination from inside the for loop into the surrounding try block.

In some situations no reasonable flag value exists. For example, a class for a stream of double values can contain any valid double, and there is no possible end-of-stream marker. The most reasonable design is to add an explicit eof test method that should be called before any read from the stream:

```
while (!stream.eof())
    process(stream.nextDouble());
stream.close();
```

On the other hand, continuing to read *past* the end of input is not expected. It means that the program didn't notice the end and is trying to do something it should never attempt. This is an excellent case for a ReadPastEndException. Such behavior is outside the expected use of your stream class, and throwing an exception is the right way to handle it.

Deciding which situations are expected and which are not is a fuzzy area. The point is not to abuse exceptions as a way to report expected situations.

Exercise 8.2: Decide which way the following conditions should be communicated to the programmer:

- Someone tries to set the capacity of a `PassengerVehicle` object to a negative value.

- A syntax error is found in a configuration file that an object uses to set its initial state.

- A method that searches for a programmer-specified word in a string array cannot find any occurrence of the word.

- A file provided to an "open" method does not exist.

- A file provided to an "open" method exists, but security prevents the user from using it.

- During an attempt to open a network connection to a remote server process, the remote machine cannot be contacted.

- In the middle of a conversation with a remote server process, the network connection stops operating.

There is something to be said for every error;
but whatever may be said for it,
the most important thing to be said about it is that it is erroneous.
—G.K. Chesterton

CHAPTER 9

Strings

What's the use of a good quotation if you can't change it?
—Dr. Who, *The Two Doctors*

Sᴛʀɪɴɢꜱ are standard objects with built-in language support. You have already seen many examples of using string literals to create string objects. You've also seen the + and += operators that concatenate strings to create new strings. The String class, however, has much more functionality to offer. String objects are immutable (read-only), so you also have a StringBuffer class for mutable strings. This chapter describes the String and StringBuffer classes, including conversion of strings to other types such as integers and booleans.

9.1 Basic String Operations

The String class provides read-only strings and supports operations on them. Strings can be created implicitly either by using a string literal (such as "Größe") or by using + or += on two String objects to create a new one.

You can also construct String objects explicitly using the new mechanism. The String class supports the following simple constructors (other constructors are shown in later sections):

public **String()**

Constructs a new String with the value ""—an empty string.

public **String(String value)**

Constructs a new String that is a copy of the specified String object value—this is a copy constructor. Because String objects are immutable, this is rarely used.

The most basic methods of String objects are length and charAt. The length method returns the number of characters in the string, and charAt returns the `char` at the specified position, as if the string were an array of characters. This loop counts the number of each kind of character in a string:

```
for (int i = 0; i < str.length(); i++)
    counts[str.charAt(i)]++;
```

Note that `length` is a method for `String`, in contrast to arrays, in which it is a field—it's common for beginners to confuse the two.

In most `String` methods, using a string position less than zero or greater than `length() - 1` throws an `IndexOutOfBoundsException`—some implementations throw the more specific `StringIndexOutOfBoundsException`, which can take the illegal index as a constructor argument and then include it in a detailed message. Methods, or constructors that copy values to or from an array will also throw `IndexOutOfBoundsException` if any attempt is made to access outside the bounds of that array.

There are also simple methods to find the first or last occurrence of a particular character or substring in a string. The following method returns the number of characters between the first and last occurrences of a given character in a string:

```
static int countBetween(String str, char ch) {
    int begPos = str.indexOf(ch);
    if (begPos < 0)           // not there
        return -1;
    int endPos = str.lastIndexOf(ch);
    return endPos - begPos - 1;
}
```

The `countBetween` method finds the first and last positions of the character `ch` in the string `str`. If the character does not occur twice in the string, the method returns –1. The difference between the two character positions is one more than the number of characters in between (if the two positions were 2 and 3, the number of characters in between is zero).

Several overloads of the method `indexOf` search forward in a string, and several overloads of `lastIndexOf` search backward. Each method returns the index of what it found, or returns –1 if the search was unsuccessful:

Method	Returns Index Of...
`indexOf(char ch)`	first position of ch
`indexOf(char ch, int start)`	first position of ch $\geq$ start
`indexOf(String str)`	first position of str
`indexOf(String str, int start)`	first position of str $\geq$ start
`lastIndexOf(char ch)`	last position of ch

Method	Returns Index Of...
`lastIndexOf(char ch, int start)`	last position of `ch` $\leq$ `start`
`lastIndexOf(String str)`	last position of `str`
`lastIndexOf(String str, int start)`	last position of `str` $\leq$ `start`

Exercise 9.1: Write a method that counts the number of occurrences of a given character in a string.

Exercise 9.2: Write a method that counts the number of occurrences of a particular string in another string.

9.2   String Comparisons

The `String` class supports several methods to compare strings and parts of strings. Before we describe the methods, though, you should be aware that internationalization and localization issues of full Unicode strings are not addressed with these methods. For example, when you're comparing two strings to determine which is "greater," characters in strings are compared numerically by their Unicode values, not by their localized notion of order. To a French speaker, c and ç are the same letter, differing only by a small diacritical mark. Sorting a set of strings in French should ignore the difference between them, placing "açb" before "acz" because b comes before z. But the Unicode characters are different—c (\u0063) comes before ç (\u00e7) in the Unicode character set—so these strings will actually sort the other way around. Internationalization and localization are discussed in Chapter 19.

The first compare operation is `equals`, which returns `true` if it is passed a reference to a `String` object having the same contents—that is, the two strings have the same length and exactly the same Unicode characters. If the other object isn't a `String` or if the contents are different, `String.equals` returns `false`. As you learned on page 88, this overrides `Object.equals` to define equivalence instead of identity.

To compare strings while ignoring case, use the `equalsIgnoreCase` method. By "ignore case," we mean that Ë and ë are considered the same but are different from E and e. Characters with no case distinctions, such as punctuation, compare equal only to themselves. Unicode has many interesting case issues, including a notion of "titlecase." Case issues in `String` are handled in terms of the case-related methods of the `Character` class, described in "`Character`" on page 275.

To sort strings, you need a way to compare them. The `compareTo` method returns an `int` that is less than, equal to, or greater than zero when the string on which it is invoked is less than, equal to, or greater than the other string. The ordering used is Unicode character ordering. The String class declares two over-loads of compareTo—one which takes a String argument and one which takes an Object argument, and so implements the Comparable interface (see page 106), by casting the Object to String and invoking the other compareTo. There is also a compareToIgnoreCase method.

The compareTo method is useful for creating an internal canonical ordering of strings. A binary search, for example, requires a sorted list of elements, but it is unimportant that the sorted order be local language order. Here is a binary search lookup method for a class that has a sorted array of strings:

```
private String[] table;

public int position(String key) {
    int lo = 0;
    int hi = table.length - 1;
    while (lo <= hi) {
        int mid = lo + (hi - lo) / 2;
        int cmp = key.compareTo(table[mid]);
        if (cmp == 0)          // found it!
            return mid;
        else if (cmp < 0)   // search the lower part
            hi = mid - 1;
        else                   // search the upper part
            lo = mid + 1;
    }
    return -1;                 // not found
}
```

This is the basic binary search algorithm. It first checks the midpoint of the search range to determine whether the key is greater than, equal to, or less than the element at that position. If they are the same, the element has been found and the search is over. If the key is less than the element at the position, the lower half of the range is searched; otherwise, the upper half is searched. Eventually, either the element is found or the lower end of the range becomes greater than the higher end, in which case the key is not in the list.

In addition to entire strings, regions of strings can also be compared for equality. The method for this is regionMatches, and it has two forms:

public boolean **regionMatches(int start, String other, int ostart, int count)**

> Returns true if the given region of this String has the same Unicode characters as the given region of the string other. Checking starts in this string at the position start, and in the other string at position ostart. Only the first count characters are compared.

public boolean **regionMatches(boolean ignoreCase, int start, String other, int ostart, int count)**

> This version of regionMatches behaves exactly like the previous one, but the boolean ignoreCase controls whether case is significant.

For example:

```
class RegionMatch {
    public static void main(String[] args) {
        String str = "Look, look!";
        boolean b1, b2, b3;

        b1 = str.regionMatches(6, "Look", 0, 4);
        b2 = str.regionMatches(true, 6, "Look", 0, 4);
        b3 = str.regionMatches(true, 6, "Look", 0, 5);

        System.out.println("b1 = " + b1);
        System.out.println("b2 = " + b2);
        System.out.println("b3 = " + b3);
    }
}
```

Here is its output:

```
b1 = false
b2 = true
b3 = false
```

The first comparison yields false because the character at position 6 of the main string is 'l', and the character at position 0 of the other string is 'L'. The second comparison yields true because case is not significant. The third comparison yields false because the comparison length is now 5, and the two strings are not the same over five characters, even ignoring case.

In querying methods, such as regionMatches, and those we mention next, any invalid indexes simply cause false to be returned rather than throwing exceptions. Passing a null argument when an object is expected generates a NullPointerException.

You can do simple tests for the beginnings and ends of strings using `startsWith` and `endsWith`:

public boolean **startsWith(String prefix, int start)**
>   Returns `true` if this `String` starts (at `start`) with the given `prefix`.

public boolean **startsWith(String prefix)**
>   Equivalent to `startsWith(prefix, 0)`.

public boolean **endsWith(String suffix)**
>   Returns `true` if this `String` ends with the given `suffix`.

9.2.1   String Literal Equivalence

In general, using `==` to compare strings will give you the wrong results. Consider the following code:

```
if (str == "¿Peña?")
    answer(str);
```

This does not compare the contents of the two strings. It compares one object reference (`str`) to another (the string object representing the literal `"¿Peña?"`). Even if `str` contains the string `"¿Peña?"` this `==` expression will almost always yield `false` because the two strings will be held in different objects. Using `==` on objects only tests whether the two references refer to the same object, not whether they are equivalent objects.

However, any two string literals with the same contents will refer to the same `String` object. For example, `==` works correctly in the following code:

```
String str = "¿Peña?";
// ...
if (str == "¿Peña?")
    answer(str);
```

Because `str` is initially set to a string literal, comparing against another string literal is equivalent to comparing the strings for equal contents. But be careful—this works only if you are sure that all string references involved are references to string literals. If `str` is changed to refer to a manufactured `String` object, such as the result of a user typing some input, the `==` operator will return `false` even if the user types ¿Peña? as the string.

9.3   Utility Methods

The String class provides two methods that are useful in special applications. One is hashCode, which returns a hash based on the contents of the string. Any two strings with the same contents will have the same hash code, although two different strings might also have the same hash. Hash codes are useful for hash-tables, such as the HashMap class in java.util—see "HashMap" on page 440.

The other utility method is intern, which returns a String that has the same contents as the one it is invoked on. However, any two strings with the same contents return the same String object from intern, which enables you to compare string *references* to test equality, instead of the slower test of string *contents*. For example:

```
int putIn(String key) {
    String unique = key.intern();
    int i;
    // see if it's in the table already
    for (i = 0; i < tableSize; i++)
        if (table[i] == unique)
            return i;
    // it's not there--add it in
    table[i] = unique;
    tableSize++;
    return i;
}
```

All the strings stored in the table array are the result of an intern invocation. The table is searched for a string that was the result of an intern invocation on another string that had the same contents as the key. If this string is found, the search is finished. If not, we add the unique representative of the key at the end. Dealing with the results of intern makes comparing object references equivalent to comparing string contents, but much faster.

9.4   Making Related Strings

Several String methods return new strings that are like the old one but with a specified modification. New strings are returned because String objects are immutable. You could extract delimited substrings from another string using a method like this one:

```
public static String delimitedString(
    String from, char start, char end)
{
    int startPos = from.indexOf(start);
    int endPos = from.lastIndexOf(end);
    if (startPos > endPos)     // start after end
        return null;
    else if (startPos == -1)  // no start found
        return null;
    else if (endPos == -1)     // no end found
        return from.substring(startPos);
    else                               // both start and end found
        return from.substring(startPos, endPos + 1);
}
```

The method `delimitedString` returns a new `String` object containing the string inside `from` that is delimited by `start` and `end`—that is, it starts with the character `start` and ends with the character `end`. If `start` is found but not `end`, the method returns a new `String` object containing everything from the start position to the end of the string. The method `delimitedString` works by using the two overloaded forms of `substring`. The first form takes only an initial start position and returns a new string containing everything in the original string from that point on. The second form takes both a start and an end position and returns a new string that contains all the characters in the original string from the start to the endpoint, including the character at the start but *not* the one at the end. This "up to but not including the end" behavior is the reason that the method adds one to `end-Pos` to include the delimiter characters in the returned string. For example, the string returned by

```
delimitedString("Il a dit «Bonjour!»", '«', '»');
```

is

«Bonjour!»

Here are the rest of the "related string" methods:

public String **replace(char oldChar, char newChar)**
    Returns a new `String` with all instances of `oldChar` replaced with the character `newChar`.

```
public String trim()
```
> Returns a new `String` with any leading and trailing white space removed.

Case issues are *locale sensitive*—that is, they vary from place to place and from culture to culture. The platform allows users to specify a locale, which includes language and character case issues. Locales are represented by `Locale` objects, which you'll learn about in more detail in Chapter 19. The methods `toLowerCase` and `toUpperCase` use the current default locale, or you can pass a specific locale as an argument:

```
public String toLowerCase()
```
> Returns a new `String` with each character converted to its lowercase equivalent if it has one according to the default locale.

```
public String toUpperCase()
```
> Returns a new `String` with each character converted to its uppercase equivalent if it has one according to the default locale.

```
public String toLowerCase(Locale loc)
```
> Returns a new `String` with each character converted to its lowercase equivalent if it has one according to the specified locale.

```
public String toUpperCase(Locale loc)
```
> Returns a new `String` with each character converted to its uppercase equivalent if it has one according to the specified locale.

The `concat` method returns a new string that is equivalent to the string returned when you use + on two strings. The following two statements are equivalent:

```
newStr = oldStr.concat(" not");
newStr = oldStr + " not";
```

Exercise 9.3: As shown, the `delimitedString` method assumes only one such string per input string. Write a version that will pull out all the delimited strings and return an array.

9.5 String Conversions

You often need to convert strings to and from something else, such as integers or booleans. The convention is that the type being converted *to* has the method that does the conversion. For example, converting from a `String` to an `integer` requires a static method in class `Integer`. This table shows all the types that you can convert, and how to convert each to and from a `String`:

Type	To String	From String
boolean	String.valueOf(boolean)	new Boolean(String).booleanValue()
byte	String.valueOf(int)	Byte.parseByte(String, int base)
short	String.valueOf(int)	Short.parseShort(String, int base)
int	String.valueOf(int)	Integer.parseInt(String, int base)
long	String.valueOf(long)	Long.parseLong(String, int base)
float	String.valueOf(float)	Float.parseFloat(String)
double	String.valueOf(double)	Double.parseDouble(String)

For `Boolean`, the technique is to create an actual object and then ask for its value. For the other types there are methods that directly parse a value. The integer parsing methods have two overloaded forms: one which takes a numeric base, between 2 and 32, in addition to the string to parse, and one which takes only the string and assumes base 10. In all cases, except for `Boolean`, if the string does not represent a valid value of that type, a `NumberFormatException` is thrown. The `Boolean` class adopts the convention that any string not equal to `true` (ignoring case) results in the creation of a `Boolean` object representing `false`.

There is no method that converts characters of the recognizable language forms (\b, \u*xxxx*, and so on) into `char` variables or vice versa. You can invoke `String.valueOf` with a single `char` to obtain a `String` containing that one character.

Neither are there ways to create number strings in the language's format, with a leading `0` meaning an octal number or a leading `0x` meaning a hexadecimal number. The integer wrapper classes do support `decode` methods that decode strings into the appropriate types, understanding a leading `0` to mean an octal number and a leading `0x` to mean a hexadecimal number.

Your classes can support string encoding and decoding by having an appropriate `toString` method and a constructor that creates a new object given the string description. The method `String.valueOf(Object obj)` is defined to return either `"null"` (if `obj` is `null`) or the result of `obj.toString`. The `String` class provides enough overloads of `valueOf` that you can convert any value of any type to a `String` by invoking `valueOf`.

9.6   Strings and char Arrays

A `String` maps to an array of `char` and vice versa. You often want to build a string in a `char` array and then create a `String` object from the contents. Assuming that the writable `StringBuffer` class (described later) isn't adequate, several `String` methods and constructors help convert a `String` to an array of `char`, or convert an array of `char` to a `String`.

There are two constructors for creating a `String` from a `char` array:

public **String(char[] chars, int start, int count)**
> Constructs a new `String` whose contents are the same as the `chars` array, from index `start` up to a maximum of `count` characters.

public **String(char[] chars)**
> Equivalent to `String(chars, 0, chars.length)`.

Both of these constructors make copies of the array, so you can change the array contents after you have created a `String` from it without affecting the contents of the `String`.

For example, the following simple algorithm squeezes out all occurrences of a character from a string:

```
public static String squeezeOut(String from, char toss) {
    char[] chars = from.toCharArray();
    int len = chars.length;
    int put = 0;
    for (int i = 0; i < len; i++)
        if (chars[i] != toss)
            chars[put++] = chars[i];
    return new String(chars, 0, put);
}
```

The method `squeezeOut` first converts its input string `from` into a character array using the method `toCharArray`. It then sets up `put`, which will be the next position into which to put a character. After that it loops, copying any character that isn't a `toss` character into the array. When the method is finished looping over the array, it returns a new `String` object that contains the squeezed string.

You can use the two static `String.copyValueOf` methods instead of the constructors if you prefer. For instance, `squeezeOut` could have been ended with

```
return String.copyValueOf(chars, 0, put);
```

There is also a single-argument form of `copyValueOf` that copies the entire array. For completeness, two static `valueOf` methods are also equivalent to the two `String` constructors.

The `toCharArray` method is simple and sufficient for most needs. When more control is required over copying pieces of a string into a character array, you can use the `getChars` method:

public void **getChars(int srcBegin, int srcEnd, char[] dst,**
  int dstBegin)

> Copies characters from this `String` into the specified array. The characters of the specified substring are copied into the character array, starting at `dst[dstBegin]`. The specified substring is the part of the string starting at `srcBegin`, up to but *not* including `srcEnd`.

9.7 Strings and byte Arrays

There are methods to convert arrays of raw 8-bit characters to and from 16-bit Unicode `String` objects. This conversion must be done under some encoding, which will be different depending on the source of the 8-bit characters. For example, an array of ASCII or Latin-1 bytes would be converted to Unicode characters simply by setting the high bits to zero, but that would not work for other 8-bit encodings, such as those for Hebrew. In the following constructors and methods, you can name an encoding or use the user or platform's default encoding:

public **String(byte[] bytes, int start, int count)**

> Constructs a new `String` by converting the bytes, from index `start` up to a maximum of `count` bytes, into characters using the default encoding for the default locale.

public **String(byte[] bytes)**

> Equivalent to `String(bytes, 0, bytes.length)`.

public **String(byte[] bytes, int start, int count, String enc)**
  throws UnsupportedEncodingException

> Constructs a new `String` by converting the bytes, from index `start` up to a maximum of `count` bytes, into characters using the encoding named in `enc`.

public **String(byte[] bytes, String enc)**
  throws UnsupportedEncodingException

> Equivalent to `String(bytes, 0, bytes.length, enc)`.

public byte[] **getBytes()**

> Returns a byte array that encodes the contents of the string using the default encoding for the default locale.

```
public byte[] getBytes(String enc)
    throws UnsupportedEncodingException
```
> Returns a byte array that encodes the contents of the string using the encoding named in enc.

The String constructors for building from byte arrays make copies of the data, so further modifications to the arrays will not affect the contents of the String.

9.7.1 Character Encodings

A character encoding specifies how to convert between raw 8-bit characters and their 16-bit Unicode equivalents. Encodings are named using their standard and common names. The local platform defines which character encodings are understood, but every implementation is required to support the following:

US-ASCII	Seven-bit ASCII, also known as ISO646-US, and as the Basic Latin block of the Unicode character set
ISO-8859-1	ISO Latin Alphabet No. 1, also known as ISO-LATIN-1
UTF-8	Eight-bit Unicode Transformation Format
UTF-16BE	Sixteen-bit Unicode Transformation Format, big-endian byte order
UTF-16LE	Sixteen-bit Unicode Transformation Format, little-endian byte order
UTF-16	Sixteen-bit Unicode Transformation Format, byte order specified by a mandatory initial byte-order mark (either order accepted on input, big-endian used on output)

Consult the release documentation for your implementation to see if any other encodings are supported.

To test whether an encoding is supported, create a string from an empty byte array using the encoding name: if you get an UnsupportedEncodingException, the encoding is not supported.

Every instance of the Java virtual machine has a default character encoding. The default encoding is determined during virtual-machine startup and typically depends upon the locale and encoding being used by the underlying operating system.

9.8   The StringBuffer Class

If immutable strings were the only kind available, you would have to create a new String object for each intermediate result in a sequence of String manipulations. Consider, for example, how the compiler would evaluate the following expression:

```
public static String guillemete(String quote) {
    return '«' + quote + '»';
}
```

If the compiler were restricted to String expressions, it would have to do the following:

```
quoted = String.valueOf('«').concat(quote)
              .concat(String.valueOf('»'));
```

Each valueOf and concat invocation creates another String object, so this operation would construct four String objects, of which only one would be used afterward. The others strings would have incurred overhead to create, to set to proper values, and to garbage collect.

The compiler is more efficient than this. It uses a StringBuffer object to build strings from expressions, creating the final String only when necessary. StringBuffer objects can be modified, so new objects are not needed to hold intermediate results. Using StringBuffer, the previous string expression would be represented as:

```
quoted = new StringBuffer().append('«')
              .append(quote).append('»').toString();
```

This code creates just one StringBuffer object to hold the construction, appends stuff to it, and then uses toString to create a String from the result.

To build and modify a string, you probably want to use the StringBuffer class. StringBuffer provides the following constructors:

public **StringBuffer()**

Constructs a StringBuffer with an initial value of ""—an empty string.

public **StringBuffer(String str)**

Constructs a StringBuffer with an initial value the same as str.

StringBuffer is similar to String, and it supports methods that have the same names and contracts as some String methods. However, StringBuffer does not extend String or vice versa. They are independent classes—both of them extend Object.

9.8.1 Modifying the Buffer

There are several ways to modify the buffer of a `StringBuffer` object, including appending to the end and inserting in the middle. The simplest method is `setCharAt`, which changes the character at a specific position. The following `replace` method does what `String.replace` does, except that it uses a `StringBuffer` object. The `replace` method doesn't need to create a new object to hold the results, so successive `replace` calls can operate on one buffer:

```
public static void
    replace(StringBuffer str, char oldChar, char newChar)
{
    for (int i = 0; i < str.length(); i++)
        if (str.charAt(i) == oldChar)
            str.setCharAt(i, newChar);
}
```

The `setLength` method truncates or extends the string in the buffer. If you invoke `setLength` with a length smaller than the length of the current string, the string is truncated to the specified length. If the length is longer than the current string, the string is extended by filling with null characters (`'\u0000'`).

There are also `append` and `insert` methods to convert any data type to a `String` and then append the result to the end or insert the result at a specified position. The `insert` methods shift characters over to make room for inserted characters as needed. The following types are converted by these `append` and `insert` methods:

Object	String	char[]
boolean	char	int
long	float	double

There are also `append` and `insert` methods that take part of a `char` array as an argument. Here is some code that uses various `append` invocations to create a `StringBuffer` that describes the square root of an integer:

```
String sqrtInt(int i) {
    StringBuffer buf = new StringBuffer();

    buf.append("sqrt(").append(i).append(')');
    buf.append(" = ").append(Math.sqrt(i));
    return buf.toString();
}
```

The append and insert methods return the StringBuffer object itself, enabling you to append to the result of a previous append.

The insert methods take two parameters. The first is the index at which to insert characters into the StringBuffer. The second is the value to insert, after conversion to a String if necessary. Here is a method to put the current date at the beginning of a buffer:

```
public static StringBuffer addDate(StringBuffer buf) {
    String now = new java.util.Date().toString();
    buf.insert(0, now).insert(now.length(), ": ");
    return buf;
}
```

The addDate method first creates a string with the current time using java.util.Date, whose default constructor creates an object that represents the time it was created. Then it inserts the string that represents the current date, followed by a simple separator string. Finally, it returns the buffer it was passed so that invoking code can use the same kind of method concatenation that proved useful in StringBuffer's own methods.

The reverse method reverses the order of characters in the StringBuffer. For example, if the contents of the buffer are "good", the contents after invoking reverse are "doog".

You can remove part of the buffer using delete, which takes a starting and ending index. The segment of the string up to but *not* including the ending index is removed from the buffer, and the buffer is shortened. You can remove a single character using deleteCharAt.

You can also replace and insert characters in the buffer using more complex invocations:

public StringBuffer **replace(int start, int end, String str)**
> Replace the characters starting at start up through but *not* including end with the contents of str. The buffer is grown or shrunk as the length of str is greater than or less than the range of characters replaced.

public StringBuffer **insert(int pos, char[] chars, int start,**
> **int count)**
> Inserts characters from the array chars into the string so that the first inserted character is at position pos, shifting other characters in the buffer down to make room. Only count characters are copied from chars, starting from chars[start].

9.8.2 Getting Data Out

To get a String object from a StringBuffer object, you simply invoke the toString method. If you need a substring of the buffer, the substring methods works analogously to those of String. If you want some or all of the contents as a character array, you can use getChars, which is analogous to String.getChars.

public void **getChars(int srcBegin, int srcEnd, char[] dst,**
   int dstBegin)

> Copies characters from this StringBuffer into the specified array. The characters of the specified substring are copied into the character array, starting at dst[dstBegin]. The specified substring is the part of the string buffer starting at srcBegin, up to but *not* including srcEnd.

Here is a method that uses getChars to remove part of a buffer:

```
public static StringBuffer
    remove(StringBuffer buf, int pos, int cnt)
{
    if (pos < 0 || cnt < 0 || pos + cnt > buf.length())
        throw new IndexOutOfBoundsException();

    int leftover = buf.length() - (pos + cnt);
    if (leftover == 0) {      // a simple truncation
        buf.setLength(pos);
        return buf;
    }

    char[] chrs = new char[leftover];
    buf.getChars(pos + cnt, buf.length(), chrs, 0);
    buf.setLength(pos);
    buf.append(chrs);
    return buf;
}
```

First, remove ensures that the array references will stay in bounds. You could handle the actual exception later, but checking now gives you more control. Then remove calculates how many characters follow the removed portion. If there are none, it truncates and returns. Otherwise, remove retrieves them using getChars and then truncates the buffer and appends the leftover characters before returning.

9.8.3   Capacity Management

The buffer of a `StringBuffer` object has a capacity, which is the length of the string it can store before it must allocate more space. The buffer grows automatically as characters are added, but it is more efficient to specify the size of the buffer only once.

The initial size of a `StringBuffer` object can be set by using the constructor that takes a single `int`:

public **StringBuffer(int capacity)**
> Constructs a `StringBuffer` with the given initial `capacity` and an initial value of "".

public void **ensureCapacity(int minimum)**
> Ensures that the capacity of the buffer is at least the specified `minimum`.

public int **capacity()**
> Returns the current capacity of the buffer.

You can use these methods to avoid repeatedly growing the buffer. Here, for example, is a rewrite of the `sqrtInt` method from page 223 that ensures you allocate new space for the buffer at most once:

```
String sqrtIntFaster(int i) {
    StringBuffer buf = new StringBuffer(50);
    buf.append("sqrt(").append(i).append(')');
    buf.append(" = ").append(Math.sqrt(i));
    return buf.toString();
}
```

The only change is to use a constructor that creates a `StringBuffer` object large enough to contain the result string. The value `50` is somewhat larger than required; therefore, the buffer will never have to grow.

Exercise 9.4: Write a method to convert strings containing decimal numbers into comma-punctuated numbers, with a comma every third digit from the right. For example, given the string "1543729", the method should return the string "1,543,729".

Exercise 9.5: Modify the method to accept parameters specifying the separator character to use and the number of digits between separator characters.

> *When ideas fail, words come in very handy.*
> —Johann Wolfgang von Goethe

CHAPTER 10

Threads

How can you be in two places at once when you're not anywhere at all?
—Firesign Theater

WE usually write programs that operate one step at a time, in a sequence. In the following picture, the value of a bank balance is fetched, it is increased by the value of the deposit, and then it is copied back into the account record:

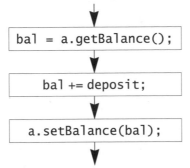

Real bank tellers and computer programs go through similar sequences. In a computer, a sequence of steps executed one at a time is called a *thread*. This *single-threaded* programming model is the one most programmers use.

In a real bank, more than one thing happens at a time:

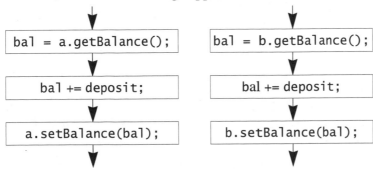

Inside a computer, the analogue to having multiple real-world bank tellers is called *multithreading*. A thread, like a bank teller, can perform a task independent of other threads. And just as two bank tellers can use the same filing cabinets, threads can share access to objects.

This shared access is simultaneously one of the most useful features of multithreading and one of its greatest pitfalls. This kind of get–modify–set sequence has what is known as a *race hazard* or *race condition*. A race hazard exists when two threads can potentially modify the same piece of data in an interleaved way that can corrupt data. In the bank example, imagine that someone walks up to a bank teller to deposit money into an account. At almost the same time, a second customer asks another teller to handle a deposit into the same account. Each teller

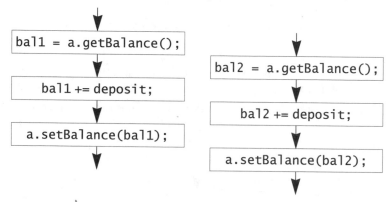

goes to the filing cabinet to get the current account balance (assuming this is an old-fashioned bank that still uses paper files) and gets the same information. Then the tellers go back to their stations, add in the deposit, and return to the filing cabinet to record their separately calculated results. Using this procedure, only the last deposit recorded actually affects the balance. The first modification is lost.

In a real bank this problem can be handled by having the first teller put a note into the file that says, "I'm working on this one, wait until I'm finished." Essentially the same thing is done inside the computer: a *lock* is associated with an object to tell when the object is or is not being used.

Many real-world software problems can best be solved by using multiple threads of control. For example, an interactive program that displays data graphically often needs to let users change display parameters in real time. Interactive programs often obtain their best dynamic behavior using threads. Single-threaded systems usually provide an illusion of multiple threads either by using interrupts or by *polling*. Polling mixes the display and user input parts of an application. In particular, the display code must be written so it will poll often enough to respond to user input in fractions of a second. Display code either must ensure that display operations take minimal time or must interrupt its own operations to poll. The resulting mixture of two unrelated functional aspects of a program leads to complex and often unmaintainable code.

These kinds of problems are more easily solved in a multithreaded system. One thread of control updates the display with current data, and another thread responds to user input. If user input is complex—for example, filling out a form—display code can run independently until it receives new data. In a polling model, either display updates must pause for complex input or complicated handshaking must be used so that display updates can continue while the user types data into the form. Such a model of shared control within a process can be directly supported in a multithreaded system instead of being handcrafted for each new polling case.

This chapter describes the constructs, classes, and methods that control multithreading in the Java programming language, but it cannot teach you effective multithreaded program design. You can read *Concurrent Programming in Java*™, a book in this series, to get advice on how to create well-designed multithreaded programs. "Further Reading" on page 563 has other useful references to give you a background in thread and synchronization design.

10.1 Creating Threads

To create a thread of control, you start by creating a `Thread` object:

```
Thread worker = new Thread();
```

After a `Thread` object is created, you can configure it and then run it. Configuring a thread involves setting its initial priority, name, and so on. When the thread is ready to run, you invoke its `start` method. The `start` method spawns a new thread of control based on the data in the `Thread` object, then returns. Now the virtual machine invokes the new thread's `run` method, making the thread active. You can invoke `start` only once for each thread—invoking it again results in an `IllegalThreadStateException`.

When a thread's `run` method returns, the thread has exited. You can request that a thread cease running by invoking its `interrupt` method—a request a well-written thread will always respond to. While a thread is running you can interact with it in other ways, as you shall soon see.

The standard implementation of `Thread.run` does nothing. To get a thread that does something you must either extend `Thread` to provide a new `run` method or create a `Runnable` object and pass it to the thread's constructor. We first discuss how to create new kinds of threads by extending `Thread`. We'll describe how to use `Runnable` in the next section.

Here is a simple two-threaded program that prints the words "ping" and "PONG" at different rates:

```
public class PingPong extends Thread {
    private String word;   // what word to print
    private int delay;     // how long to pause

    public PingPong(String whatToSay, int delayTime) {
        word = whatToSay;
        delay = delayTime;
    }

    public void run() {
        try {
            for (;;) {
                System.out.print(word + " ");
                Thread.sleep(delay); // wait until next time
            }
        } catch (InterruptedException e) {
            return;                  // end this thread
        }
    }
    public static void main(String[] args) {
        new PingPong("ping",  33).start(); // 1/30 second
        new PingPong("PONG", 100).start(); // 1/10 second
    }
}
```

We define a type of thread called PingPong. Its run method loops forever, printing its word field and sleeping for delay milliseconds. PingPong.run cannot throw exceptions because Thread.run, which it overrides, doesn't throw any exceptions. Accordingly, we must catch the InterruptedException that sleep can throw (more on InterruptedException later).

Now we can create some working threads, and PingPong.main does just that. It creates two PingPong objects, each with its own word and delay cycle, and invokes each thread object's start method. Now the threads are off and running. Here is some example output:

```
ping PONG ping ping PONG ping ping ping PONG ping
ping PONG ping ping ping PONG ping ping PONG ping
ping ping PONG ping ping PONG ping ping ping PONG
```

```
ping ping PONG ping ping ping PONG ping ping PONG
ping ping ping PONG ping ping PONG ping ping ping
PONG ping ping PONG ping ping ping PONG ping ping ...
```

You can give a thread a name, either as a `String` parameter to the constructor or as the parameter of a `setName` invocation. You can get the current name of a thread by invoking `getName`. Thread names are strictly for programmer convenience—they are not used by the runtime system—but a thread must have a name and so if none is specified, the runtime system will give it one, usually using a simple numbering scheme like `thread@1`, `thread@2` and so on.

You can obtain the `Thread` object for the currently running thread by invoking the static method `Thread.currentThread`. There is always a currently running thread, even if you did not create one explicitly—`main` itself is executed by a thread created by the runtime system.

Exercise 10.1: Write a program that displays the name of the thread that executes `main`.

10.2 Using `Runnable`

Threads abstract the concept of a worker—an entity that gets something done. The work done by a thread is packaged up in its `run` method. When you need to get some work done, you need both a worker and the work—the `Runnable` interface abstracts the concept of work and allows that work to be associated with a worker—the thread. The `Runnable` interface declares a single method:

```
public void run();
```

The `Thread` class itself implements the `Runnable` interface because a thread can also define a unit of work.

You have seen that `Thread` can be extended to provide specific computation for a thread, but this approach is awkward in many cases. First, class extension is single inheritance—if you extend a class to make it runnable in a thread, you cannot extend any other class, even if you need to. Also, if your class needs only to be runnable, inheriting all the overhead of `Thread` is more than you need.

Implementing `Runnable` is easier in many cases. You can execute a `Runnable` object in its own thread by passing it to a `Thread` constructor. If a `Thread` object is constructed with a `Runnable` object, the implementation of `Thread.run` will invoke the runnable object's `run` method.

Here is a `Runnable` version of the `PingPong` class. If you compare the versions, you will see that they look almost identical. The major differences are in the supertype (implementing `Runnable` versus extending `Thread`) and in `main`.

```
class RunPingPong implements Runnable {
    private String word;      // what word to print
    private int delay;        // how long to pause

    RunPingPong(String whatToSay, int delayTime) {
        word = whatToSay;
        delay = delayTime;
    }

    public void run() {
        try {
            for (;;) {
                System.out.print(word + " ");
                Thread.sleep(delay); // wait until next time
            }
        } catch (InterruptedException e) {
            return;                  // end this thread
        }
    }

    public static void main(String[] args) {
        Runnable ping = new RunPingPong("ping",  33);
        Runnable pong = new RunPingPong("PONG", 100);
        new Thread(ping).start();
        new Thread(pong).start();
    }
}
```

First, a new class is defined that implements `Runnable`. Its implementation of the run method is the same as `PingPong`'s. In `main`, two `RunPingPong` objects with different timings are created; a new `Thread` object is then created for each object and is started immediately.

Four `Thread` constructors enable you to specify a `Runnable` object:

public **Thread(Runnable target)**

Constructs a new `Thread` that uses the run method of the specified `target`.

public **Thread(Runnable target, String name)**
> Constructs a new Thread with the specified name and uses the run method of the specified target.

public **Thread(ThreadGroup group, Runnable target)**
> Constructs a new Thread in the specified ThreadGroup and uses the run method of the specified target. You will learn about ThreadGroup later.

public **Thread(ThreadGroup group, Runnable target, String name)**
> Constructs a new Thread in the specified ThreadGroup with the specified name and uses the run method of the specified target.

Classes that have only a run method are not very interesting. Real classes define complete state and behavior, where having something execute in a separate thread is only a part of their functionality. For example, consider a print server that spools print requests to a printer. Clients invoke the print method to submit print jobs. But all the print method actually does is place the job in a queue and a separate thread then pulls jobs from the queue and sends them to the printer. This allows clients to submit print jobs without waiting for the actual printing to take place.

```
class PrintServer implements Runnable {
    private Queue requests = new Queue();
    public PrintServer() {
        new Thread(this).start();
    }
    public void print(PrintJob job) {
        requests.add(job);
    }
    public void run() {
        for(;;)
            realPrint((PrintJob)requests.take());
    }
    private void realPrint(PrintJob job) {
        // do the real work of printing
    }
}
```

When a PrintServer is created it creates a new Thread to do the actual printing and passes itself as the Runnable instance. Starting a thread in a constructor in this way can be risky in the general case if a class may be extended. If that happened, the thread could access fields of the object before the extended class constructor had been executed.

The `requests` queue takes care of synchronizing the different threads that access it—those calling `print` and our own internal thread—we'll look at such synchronization in later sections and define the `Queue` class on page 245.

You may be wondering about the fact that we don't have a reference to the thread we created—doesn't that mean that the thread can be garbage collected? The answer is no. While we didn't keep a reference to the thread, the thread itself, when it was created, stored a reference to itself in its `ThreadGroup`—we'll talk more about thread groups later.

The work that you define within a `run` method is normally of a fairly private nature—it should be performed only by the worker to whom the work was assigned. However, as part of an interface, `run` is public and so can be invoked indiscriminately by anyone with access to your object—something you usually don't desire. For example, we definitely don't want clients to invoke the `run` method of `PrintServer`. One solution is to use `Thread.currentThread` to establish the identity of the thread that invokes `run` and to compare it with the intended worker thread. But a simpler solution is not to implement `Runnable`, but to define an inner `Runnable` object. For example, we can rewrite `PrintServer` as follows:

```
class PrintServer2 {
    private Queue requests = new Queue();
    public PrintServer2() {
        Runnable service = new Runnable() {
            public void run() {
                for(;;)
                    realPrint((PrintJob)requests.take());
            }
        };
        new Thread(service).start();
    }
    public void print(PrintJob job) {
        requests.add(job);
    }
    private void realPrint(PrintJob job) {
        // do the real work of printing
    }
}
```

The `run` method is exactly the same as before, but now it is part of an anonymous inner class that implements `Runnable`. When the thread is created we pass `service` as the `Runnable` to execute. Now the work to be performed by the thread is completely private and can't be misused.

Using `Runnable` objects you can create very flexible multithreaded designs. Each `Runnable` becomes a unit of work and each can be passed around from one part of the system to another. We can store `Runnable` objects in a queue and have a pool of worker threads servicing the work requests in the queue—a very common design used in multithreaded server applications.

Exercise 10.2: Modify the first version of `PrintServer` so that only the thread created in the constructor can successfully execute `run`, using the identity of the thread as suggested.

10.3 Synchronization

Recall the bank teller example from the beginning of this chapter. When two tellers (threads) need to use the same file (object), there is a possibility of interleaved operations that can corrupt the data. Such potentially interfering actions are termed *critical sections* or *critical regions*, and you prevent *interference* by *synchronizing* access to those critical regions. In the bank, tellers synchronize their actions by putting notes in the files and agreeing to the protocol that a note in the file means that the file can't be used. The equivalent action in multithreading is to acquire a *lock* on an object. Threads cooperate by agreeing to the protocol that before certain actions can occur on an object, the lock of the object must be acquired. Acquiring the lock on an object prevents any other thread from acquiring that lock, until the holder of the lock releases it. If done correctly, multiple threads won't simultaneously perform actions that could interfere with each other.

Every object has a lock associated with it, and that lock can be acquired and released through the use of `synchronized` methods and statements. The term *synchronized code* describes any code that is inside a `synchronized` method or statement.

10.3.1 `synchronized` Methods

A class whose objects must be protected from interference in a multithreaded environment usually has appropriate methods declared `synchronized` ("appropriate" is defined later). If one thread invokes a `synchronized` method on an object, the lock of that object is first acquired, the method body executed, and then the lock released. Another thread invoking a `synchronized` method on that same object will block until the lock is released:

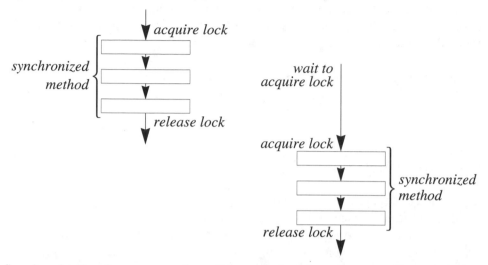

Synchronization forces execution of the two threads to be *mutually exclusive* in time. Unsynchronized access does not wait for any locks but proceeds regardless of locks that may be held on the object.

Locks are owned *per thread,* so invoking a synchronized method from within another method synchronized on the same object will proceed without blocking, releasing the lock only when the outermost synchronized method returns. This per-thread behavior prevents a thread from blocking on a lock it already has, and permits recursive method invocations and invocations of inherited methods, which themselves may be synchronized.

The lock is released as soon as the synchronized method terminates—whether normally, via a `return` statement or reaching the end of the method body, or abnormally by throwing an exception. In contrast to systems where locks must be explicitly acquired and released, this synchronization scheme makes it impossible to forget to release a lock.

Synchronization makes the interleaved execution example work: if the code is in a synchronized method, then when the second thread attempts to access the object while the first thread is using it, the second thread is blocked until the first one finishes.

For example, if the `Account` class were written to live in a multithreaded environment, it would look like this:

```
class Account {
    private double balance;
```

```
        public Account(double initialDeposit) {
            balance = initialDeposit;
        }
        public synchronized double getBalance() {
            return balance;
        }
        public synchronized void deposit(double amount) {
            balance += amount;
        }
    }
```

Now we can explain what is "appropriate" in synchronizing methods.

The constructor does not need to be synchronized because it is executed only when creating an object, and that can happen in only one thread for any given new object. Constructors, in fact, cannot be declared synchronized.

The balance field is defended from unsynchronized modification by the synchronized accessor methods. If the value of a field can change, its value should never be read at the same time another thread is writing it. If one thread were reading the value while another was setting it, the read might return an invalid value. Even if the value were valid, a get-modify-set sequence requires that the value not change between being read and being set, otherwise the set value will be wrong. Access to the field must be synchronized. This is yet another reason to prefer accessor methods to public or protected fields: using methods, you can synchronize access to the data, but you have no way to do so if the fields can be accessed directly outside your class.

With the synchronized declaration, two or more running threads are guaranteed not to interfere with each other. Each of the methods will execute in mutual exclusion—once one invocation of a method starts execution, no other invocations of any of the methods can commence until the original has completed. However, there is no guarantee as to the order of operations. If the balance is queried about the same time as a deposit occurs, one of them will complete first but you can't tell which. If you want actions to happen in a guaranteed order, threads must coordinate their activities in some application-specific way.

When an extended class overrides a synchronized method, the new method can be synchronized or not. The superclass's method will still be synchronized when it is invoked. If the unsynchronized method uses super to invoke the superclass's method, the object's lock will be acquired at that time, and will be released when the superclass's method returns. Synchronization requirements are a part of the implementation of a class. An extended class may be able to modify a data structure such that concurrent invocations of a method do not interfere and so the method need not be synchronized; conversely the extended class may enhance the behavior of the method in such a way that interference becomes possible and so it must be synchronized.

10.3.2 Static Synchronized Methods

Static methods can also be declared `synchronized`. Associated with every class is a `Class` object—see "The `Class` class" on page 282. Static synchronized methods acquire the lock of the `Class` object for their class. Two threads cannot execute static synchronized methods of the same class at the same time, just as two threads cannot execute synchronized methods on the same object at the same time. If static data is shared between threads then access to it must be protected using static synchronized methods.

Acquiring the `Class` object lock in a static synchronized method has no affect on any objects of that class. You can still invoke synchronized methods on an object while another thread holds the `Class` object lock in a static synchronized method. Only other static synchronized methods are blocked.

10.3.3 synchronized Statements

The `synchronized` statement enables you to execute synchronized code that acquires the lock of any object, not just the current object, or for durations less than the entire invocation of a method. The `synchronized` statement has two parts: an object whose lock is to be acquired and a statement to execute when the lock is obtained. The general form of the `synchronized` statement is:

```
synchronized (expr) {
    statements
}
```

The expression *expr* must evaluate to an object reference. When the lock is obtained, the *statements* in the block are executed. At the end of the block the lock is released—if an uncaught exception occurs within the block, the lock is still released. A `synchronized` method is simply a syntactic shorthand for a method whose body is wrapped in a `synchronized` statement with a reference to `this`.

Here is a method to replace each element in an array with its absolute value, relying on a `synchronized` statement to control access to the array:

```
/** make all elements in the array non-negative */
public static void abs(int[] values) {
    synchronized (values) {
        for (int i = 0; i < values.length; i++) {
            if (values[i] < 0)
```

```
                     values[i] = -values[i];
            }
        }
    }
```

The `values` array contains the elements to be modified. We synchronize `values` by naming it as the object of the `synchronized` statement. Now the loop can proceed, guaranteed that the array is not changed during execution by any other code that is similarly synchronized on the `values` array. This is an example of what is generally termed *client-side* synchronization—all of the clients using the shared object (in this case the array) agree to synchronize on that object before manipulating it. For objects such as arrays, this is the only way to protect them when they can be shared directly, as they have no methods that can be synchronized.

The `synchronized` statement has a number of uses and advantages over a synchronized method. First, it can define a synchronized region of code that is smaller than a method. Synchronization affects performance—while one thread has a lock another thread can't get it—and a general rule of concurrent programming is to hold locks for as short a period as possible. Using a `synchronized` statement, you can choose to hold a lock only when it is absolutely needed—for example, a method that performs a complex calculation and then assigns the result to a field often needs to protect only the actual field assignment not the calculation process.

Second, `synchronized` statements allow you to synchronize on objects other than `this`, allowing a number of different synchronization designs to be implemented. One situation is where you want to increase the concurrency level of a class by using a finer granularity of locking. It may be that different groups of methods within a class act on different data within that class and that, while mutual exclusion is needed within a group, it is not needed between groups. Instead of making all the methods synchronized, you can define separate objects to be used as locks for each such group and have the methods use `synchronized` statements with the appropriate lock object. For example:

```java
class SeparateGroups {
    private double aVal = 0.0;
    private double bVal = 1.1;
    protected Object lockA = new Object();
    protected Object lockB = new Object();

    public double getA() {
        synchronized (lockA) {
            return aVal;
        }
```

```
        }
        public void setA(double val) {
            synchronized (lockA) {
                aVal = val;
            }
        }
        public double getB() {
            synchronized (lockB) {
                return bVal;
            }
        }
        public void setB(double val) {
            synchronized (lockB) {
                bVal = val;
            }
        }
        public void reset() {
            synchronized (lockA) {
                synchronized (lockB) {
                    aVal = bVal = 0.0;
                }
            }
        }
    }
```

The two lock references are protected so that an extended class can correctly synchronize its own methods—such as a method to set aVal and bVal to the same value. Also notice how reset acquires both locks before modifying both values.

Another common use of the synchronized statement is for an inner object to synchronize on its enclosing object:

```
public class Outer {
    private int data;
    // ...

    private class Inner {
        void setOuterData() {
            synchronized (Outer.this) {
                data = 12;
            }
```

```
            }
        }
    }
```

Like any other object, an inner object is independently synchronized—acquiring the lock of an inner object has no affect on its enclosing object's lock, nor does acquiring the lock of an enclosing object affect any enclosed inner objects. An inner class that needs to synchronize with its enclosing object must do so explicitly and a synchronized statement is the perfect tool—the alternative would be to declare a synchronized method in the enclosing class just for the inner class to use.

If you need a synchronized statement to use the same lock used by static synchronized methods, you can use the class literal for your class. This also applies if you need to protect access to static data from within non-static code. For example, consider the Body class. It maintains a static field, nextID, to hold the next identifier for a new Body object. That field is accessed in the Body class's no-arg constructor. If Body objects were created concurrently, interference could occur when updating the nextID field. To prevent that from happening you can use a synchronized statement within the Body constructor that uses the lock of the Body.class object:

```
Body() {
    synchronized (Body.class) {
        idNum = nextID++;
    }
}
```

The synchronized statement in the constructor acquires the lock of the Class object for Body in the same way a synchronized static method of the class would. It would be wrong to synchronize on this because that would use a different object for each invocation and so would not prevent threads from accessing nextID concurrently. It would also be wrong to use the Object method getClass to retrieve the Class object for the current instance: in an extended class, such as AttributedBody, that would return the Class object for AttributedBody not Body, and so again, different locks would be used and interference would not be prevented. The simplest rule is to always protect access to static data using the lock of the Class object for the class in which the static data was declared.

In many cases, instead of using a synchronized statement you can factor the code to be protected into a synchronized method of its own. You'll need to use your own experience and judgment to decide when this is preferable. For example, in the Body class we could encapsulate access to nextID in a static synchronized method getNextID.

Finally, the ability to acquire locks of arbitrary objects using `synchronized` statements makes it possible to perform the client-side synchronization that you saw in the array example. This capability is important, not only for protecting access to objects that don't have synchronized methods, but also for synchronizing a series of accesses to an object. We'll look more at this in the next section.

10.3.4 Synchronization Designs

Designing the appropriate synchronization for a class can be a complex matter and it is beyond the scope of this book to delve too deeply into these design issues. We can take a brief look at some of the issues involved.

Client-side synchronization involves all the clients of a shared object to use `synchronized` statements to acquire the lock of the shared object before accessing it. Such a protocol is fragile, as it relies on all of the clients doing the right thing. It is generally better to have shared objects protect access to themselves by making their methods `synchronized` (or using appropriate `synchronized` statements inside those methods). This makes it impossible for a client to use the object in a way that is not synchronized. This approach is sometimes termed *server-side* synchronization, but is just an extension of the object-oriented perspective that objects encapsulate their own behavior, including synchronization.

Sometimes a designer hasn't considered a multithreaded environment when designing a class, and none of its methods are synchronized. To use such a class in a multithreaded environment, you have to decide whether to use client-side synchronization via `synchronized` statements, or to create an extended class to override the appropriate methods, declare them `synchronized`, and forward method calls through the `super` reference.

If you are working with an interface instead of a class, you can provide an alternate implementation that wraps the methods of the interface in synchronized methods that forward the calls on to another unsynchronized object that implements the same interface. This will work with any implementation of the interface, and is therefore a better solution than extending each class to use `super` in a synchronized method. This flexibility is another reason to design your system using interfaces. You can see an example of this synchronized wrapper technique in the collections classes; see "Wrapped Collections and the `Collections` Class" on page 442.

The synchronization you have learned about so far is the simplest notion of "thread safety"—the idea that methods on objects can be invoked by multiple threads concurrently and each thread will have the method perform its expected job. Synchronization, however, has to extend to more complex situations involving multiple method invocations on an object, or even method invocations on multiple objects. If these series of invocations must appear as an atomic action you will need synchronization. In the case of multiple method invocations, you can encapsulate the series of invocations within another method and synchronize that method, but generally this is impractical—you can't define all combinations of the basic methods as methods themselves, nor are you likely to know at the time the class is designed which method combinations may be needed. In the case of operations on multiple objects, where could you put a synchronized method? In these situations, the ability to use client-side synchronization via synchronized statements, is often the only practical approach. An object can have its lock acquired, thus preventing any of its synchronized methods from being invoked, except by the lock holder performing the series of invocations. Similarly, you can acquire the locks of each of the objects involved and then invoke the series of methods on those objects—but watch out for deadlock (see Section 10.7 on page 252). As long as the object's methods are already synchronized on the current object's lock, then other clients of the object need not use client-side synchronization.

The way that synchronization is enforced in a class is an implementation detail. The fact that it is enforced is an important part of the contract of the class and must be clearly documented—the presence of the synchronized modifier on a method might only be an implementation detail of the class, not part of a binding contract. Additionally, the synchronization mechanism used within a class may need to be documented and made accessible to users of the class and/or to extended classes. An extended class needs to adhere to the synchronization policy enforced by its superclass and it can do that only if the programmer knows what that policy is and has access to the mechanisms that enforce it. For example, a class that uses a private field as a lock object prevents an extended class from using the same synchronization mechanism—the extended class would have to define its own lock object (perhaps this) and override every method of the superclass to use this new synchronization mechanism. Users of a class may need to know what synchronization mechanism is used so that they can safely apply client-side synchronization to invoke multiple methods on an object, without needing all users of that object to apply client-side synchronization.

Exercise 10.3: Write a class whose objects hold a current value and have a method that will add to that value, printing the new value. Write a program that creates such an object, creates multiple threads, and invokes the adding method repeatedly from each thread. Write the class so that no addition can be lost.

Exercise 10.4: Modify your code from Exercise 10.3 to use static data and methods.

Exercise 10.5: Modify your code from Exercise 10.4 so that threads can safely decrement the value without using a static synchronized method.

10.4 `wait`, `notifyAll`, and `notify`

The `synchronized` locking mechanism suffices for keeping threads from inter-fering with each other, but you also need a way to communicate between threads. For this purpose, the `wait` method lets one thread wait until some condition occurs, and the notification methods `notifyAll` and `notify` tell waiting threads that something has occurred that might satisfy that condition. The `wait` and notifi-cation methods are defined in class `Object` and are inherited by all classes. They apply to particular objects, just as locks do.

There is a standard pattern that is important to use with `wait` and notification. The thread waiting for a condition should always do something like this:

```
synchronized void doWhenCondition() {
    while (!condition)
        wait();
    … Do what must be done when the condition is true …
}
```

A number of things are going on here:

◆ Everything is executed within synchronized code. If it were not, the state of the object would not be stable. For example, if the method were not declared `synchronized`, then after the `while` statement, there would be no guarantee that the condition remained `true` because another thread may have changed the situation that the condition tests.

◆ One of the important aspects of the definition of `wait` is that when it pauses the thread, it *atomically* releases the lock on the object. Saying that the thread suspension and lock release are atomic means that they happen together, indivisibly. Otherwise, there would be a race hazard: a notification could happen after the lock is released but before the thread is suspended. The notification would have no affect on the thread, effectively getting lost. When a thread is restarted after being notified, the lock is atomically reac-quired.

◆ The condition test should *always* be in a loop. Never assume that being awakened means that the condition has been satisfied—it may have changed again since being satisfied. In other words, don't change the `while` to an `if`.

On the other side, the notification methods are invoked by synchronized code that changes one or more conditions on which some other thread may be waiting. Notification code typically looks something like this:

```
synchronized void changeCondition() {
    … change some value used in a condition test …
    notifyAll(); // or notify()
}
```

Using `notifyAll` wakes up all waiting threads, while `notify` picks only one thread to wake up.

Multiple threads may be waiting on the same object, possibly for different conditions. If they are waiting for different conditions, you should always use `notifyAll` to wake up all waiting threads instead of using `notify`. Otherwise you may wake up a thread that is waiting for a different condition from the one you satisfied. That thread will discover that its condition has not been satisfied and go back to waiting, while some thread waiting on the condition you *did* satisfy will never get awakened. Using `notify` is an optimization that can be applied only when:

- All threads are waiting for the same condition;
- At most one thread can benefit from the condition being met; and
- This is contractually true for *all* possible subclasses

Otherwise you must use `notifyAll`. If a subclass violates either of the first two conditions, code in the superclass that uses `notify` may well be broken. To that end it is important that waiting and notification strategies, which includes identifying the reference used (`this` or some other field), are documented for use by extended classes.

The following example implements the `Queue` class that we used with the `PrintServer` on page 233. The class has methods to insert and remove elements from the queue.

```
class Queue {
        // The first and last elements in the queue
    private Cell head, tail;

    public synchronized void add(Object o) {
        Cell p = new Cell(o); // Wrap o in a cell
        if (tail == null)
            head = p;
        else
            tail.next = p;
        p.next = null;
        tail = p;
        notifyAll();              // Tell waiters: object added
```

```
    }

    public synchronized Object take()
        throws InterruptedException
    {
        while (head == null)
            wait();                 // Wait for an object

        Cell p = head;              // Remember first object
        head = head.next;           // Remove it from the queue
        if (head == null)           // Check for an empty queue
            tail = null;
        return p.item;
    }
}
```

This implementation of a queue looks very much like a queue used in single-threaded systems—such as the SingleLinkQueue we outlined in Chapter 3 on page 82. It differs in a few aspects: the methods are synchronized to avoid interference; when an item is added to the queue, waiters are notified; and instead of returning null when the queue is empty, the take method waits for some other thread to insert something so that take will block until an item is available. Many threads (not just one) may be adding items to the queue, and many threads (again, not just one) may be taking items from the queue. Because wait can throw InterruptedException, we declare that in the throws clause—you'll learn about InterruptedException a little later.

Looking back at the PrintServer example, you can now see that although the internal thread appears to sit in an infinite loop, continually trying to take jobs from the queue, the use of wait means that the thread is suspended whenever there is no work for it to do. In contrast, if we used a queue that returned null when empty, the printing thread would continually invoke take, using the CPU the whole time—a situation known as *busy-waiting*. In a multithreaded system you very rarely want to busy-wait. You should always suspend until told that what you are waiting for may have happened. This is the essence of thread communication using the wait and notifyAll/notify mechanism.

10.5 Details of Waiting and Notification

There are three forms of wait and two forms of notification. All of them are methods in the Object class, and all final so that their behavior cannot be changed:

`public final void` **`wait(long timeout)`** `throws InterruptedException`
>   The current thread waits until one of four things happens: `notify` is invoked on this object and this thread is selected to be runnable; `notifyAll` is invoked on this object; the specified `timeout` expires; or the thread has its `interrupt` method invoked. `timeout` is in milliseconds. If `timeout` is zero, the wait will not time out but will wait indefinitely for notification. During the wait the lock of the object is released and is automatically reacquired before `wait` completes—regardless of how, or why, `wait` completes. An `InterruptedException` is thrown if the wait completes because the thread is interrupted.

`public final void` **`wait(long timeout, int nanos)`**
>   `throws InterruptedException`
>   A finer-grained `wait`, with the time-out interval as the sum of the two parameters: `timeout` in milliseconds and `nanos` in nanoseconds, in the range 0–999999).

`public final void` **`wait()`** `throws InterruptedException`
>   Equivalent to `wait(0)`.

`public final void` **`notifyAll()`**
>   Notifies *all* the threads waiting for a condition to change. Threads will return from the `wait` invocation once they can reacquire the object's lock.

`public final void` **`notify()`**
>   Notifies *at most one* thread waiting for a condition to change. You cannot choose which thread will be notified, so use this form of `notify` only when you are sure you know which threads are waiting for what at which times. If you are not sure of any of these factors, you should use `notifyAll`.

If no threads are waiting when either `notifyAll` or `notify` is invoked, the notification is not remembered. If a thread subsequently decides to `wait`, an earlier notification will have no affect on it. Only notifications that occur after the `wait` commences will affect a waiting thread.

These methods can be invoked only from within synchronized code, using the lock for the object on which they are invoked. The invocation can be directly made from the synchronized code, or can be made indirectly from a method invoked in such code. You will get an `IllegalMonitorStateException` if you attempt to invoke these methods on an object when you don't hold its lock.

When a `wait` completes due to the expiration of the time-out period, there is no indication that this occurred rather than the thread being notified. If a thread needs to know whether or not it timed out, it has to track elapsed time itself. The use of a time-out is a defensive programming measure that allows you to recover from situations where some condition should have been met, but for some reason (probably a failure in another thread) has not. Because the lock of the object must be reacquired, the use of a time-out cannot guarantee that `wait` will return in a finite amount of time.

It is also possible that some implementations will allow so-called "spurious wakeups" to occur—when a thread returns from `wait` without being the recipient of a notification, interruption, or time-out. This is another reason that `wait` should always be performed in a loop that tests the condition being waited upon.

Exercise 10.6: Write a program that prints out the elapsed time from the start of execution with a thread that prints a message every fifteen seconds. Have the message-printing thread be notified by the time-printing thread. Add another thread that prints a different message every seven seconds without modifying the time-printing thread.

10.6 Thread Scheduling

Threads perform different tasks within your programs and those tasks can have different importance levels attached to them. To reflect the importance of the tasks they are performing, each thread has a *priority* which is used by the runtime system to help determine which thread should be running at any given time. Programs can be run on both single- and multiprocessor machines and you can run with multiple threads or a single thread, so the thread scheduling guarantees are very general. On a system with N available processors, you will usually see N of the highest-priority runnable threads executing. Lower-priority threads generally run only when higher-priority threads are blocked (not runnable). But lower-priority threads might, in fact, run at other times to prevent starvation—a feature generally known as *priority aging*—though you cannot rely on it.

A running thread continues to run until it performs a blocking operation (such as `wait`, `sleep` or performing some types of I/O), or it is preempted. A thread can be preempted by a higher priority thread becoming runnable, or because the thread scheduler decides it's another thread's turn to get some cycles—for example, *time slicing* limits the amount of time a single thread can run before being preempted.

Exactly when preemption can occur depends on the virtual machine you have. There are no guarantees, only a general expectation that preference is typically given to running higher priority threads. Use priority only to affect scheduling policy for efficiency purposes. Do not rely on thread priority for algorithm correctness. To write correct, cross-platform multithreaded code you must assume that a thread could be preempted at any time, and so you always protect access to shared resources. If you require that preemption occurs at some specific time, you must use explicit thread communication mechanisms such as `wait` and `notify`. You also can make no assumptions about the order in which locks are granted to threads, nor the order in which waiting threads will received notifications—these are all system dependent.

A thread's priority is initially the same as the priority of the thread that created it. The priority can be changed using `setPriority` with a value between `Thread`'s constants `MIN_PRIORITY` and `MAX_PRIORITY`. The standard priority for the default thread is `NORM_PRIORITY`. The priority of a running thread can be changed at any time. If you assign a thread a priority lower than its current one, the system may let another thread run, because the original thread may no longer be among those with the highest priority. The `getPriority` method returns the priority of a thread.

Generally, the continuously running part of your application should run in a lower-priority thread than the thread dealing with rarer events such as user input. When users push a "Cancel" button, for example, they expect the application to cancel what it's doing. If display update and user input are at the same priority and the display is updating, considerable time may pass before the user input thread reacts to the button. If you put the display thread at a lower priority, it will still run most of the time because the user interface thread will be blocked waiting for user input. When user input is available, the user interface thread will typically pre-empt the display thread to act on the user's request. For this reason, a thread that does continual updates is often set to `NORM_PRIORITY-1` to avoid hogging all available cycles, while a user interface thread is often set to `NORM_PRIORITY+1`.

Using small "delta" values around the normal priority level is usually preferable to using `MIN_PRIORITY` or `MAX_PRIORITY` directly. Exactly what effect priorities have depends on the system you are running on and in some systems your thread priorities not only assign an importance relative to your program, they assign an importance relative to other applications running on the system. The extreme priority settings may result in undesirable behavior and so should be avoided unless their effects are known and needed.

10.6.1 Voluntary Rescheduling

There are several methods of the `Thread` class that allow a thread to relinquish its use of the CPU. By convention, static methods of the `Thread` class always apply to the currently executing thread, and as you can never take the CPU from another thread, these voluntary rescheduling methods are all static:

public static void **sleep(long millis)** throws InterruptedException
      Puts the currently executing thread to sleep for at least the specified number of milliseconds. "At least" means there is no guarantee the thread will wake

up in exactly the specified time. Other thread scheduling can interfere, as can the granularity and accuracy of the system clock, among other factors. If the thread is interrupted while it is sleeping, then an `InterruptedException` is thrown.

public static void **sleep(long millis, int nanos)**
throws InterruptedException
> Puts the currently executing thread to sleep for at least the specified number of milliseconds and nanoseconds. Nanoseconds are in the range 0–999999.

public static void **yield()**
> Provides a hint to the scheduler that the current thread need not run at the present time, so the scheduler may choose another thread to run. The scheduler may follow or ignore this suggestion as it sees fit—you can generally rely on the scheduler to "do the right thing" even though there is no specification of exactly what that is.

The following program illustrates how `yield` can affect thread scheduling. The application takes a list of words and creates a thread that is responsible for printing each word. The first parameter to the application says whether each thread will yield after each `println`; the second parameter is the number of times each thread should repeat its word. The remaining parameters are the words to be repeated:

```java
class Babble extends Thread {
    static boolean doYield;  // yield to other threads?
    static int howOften;     // how many times to print

    private String word;     // my word

    Babble(String whatToSay) {
        word = whatToSay;
    }

    public void run() {
        for (int i = 0; i < howOften; i++) {
            System.out.println(word);
            if (doYield)
                Thread.yield(); // let other threads run
        }
    }

    public static void main(String[] args) {
```

```
        doYield = new Boolean(args[0]).booleanValue();
        howOften = Integer.parseInt(args[1]);

        // create a thread for each word
        for (int i = 2; i < args.length; i++)
            new Babble(args[i]).start();
    }
}
```

When the threads do not yield, each thread gets large chunks of time, usually enough to finish all the prints without any other thread getting cycles. For example, suppose the program is run with doYield set to false in the following way:

```
Babble false 2 Did DidNot
```

The output may well look like this:

```
Did
Did
DidNot
DidNot
```

If each thread yields after each println, other printing threads will have a chance to run. Suppose we set doYield to true with an invocation such as this:

```
Babble true 2 Did DidNot
```

The yields give the other threads a chance to run, and the other threads will yield in turn, producing an output more like this:

```
Did
DidNot
DidNot
Did
```

The output shown is only approximate—perhaps you expected the words to alternate? A different thread implementation could give different results, or the same implementation might give different results on different runs of the application. But under all implementations, invoking yield can give other threads a more equitable chance at getting cycles.

There are two other factors that affect the behavior of this program (and many like it that try to demonstrate scheduling behavior). The first is that println uses synchronization and so the different threads must all contend for the same lock.

The second factor is that there are three threads in the program, not two. The main thread has to create and start the two Babble threads and that means that it

contends with them for scheduling as well. It is entirely possible that the first
Babble thread will run to completion before the main thread even gets the chance
to create a second Babble thread.

Exercise 10.7: Run Babble multiple times and examine the output: is it always the
same? If possible, run it on different systems and compare.

10.7 Deadlocks

Whenever you have two threads and two objects with locks, you can have a *dead-lock*, in which each thread has the lock on one of the objects and is waiting for
the lock on the other object. If object *X* has a synchronized method that invokes
a synchronized method on object *Y*, which in turn has a synchronized method
invoking a synchronized method on object *X*, two threads may wait for each
other to complete in order to get a lock, and neither thread will be able to run. This
situation is also called a *deadly embrace*. Here's a Friendly class in which one
friend, upon being hugged, insists on hugging back his partner:

```java
class Friendly {
    private Friendly partner;
    private String name;

    public Friendly(String name) {
        this.name = name;
    }

    public synchronized void hug() {
        System.out.println(Thread.currentThread().getName()+
            " in " + name + ".hug() trying to invoke " +
             partner.name + ".hugBack()");
        partner.hugBack();
    }

    private synchronized void hugBack() {
        System.out.println(Thread.currentThread().getName()+
            " in " + name + ".hugBack()");
    }

    public void becomeFriend(Friendly partner) {
```

```
            this.partner = partner;
    }
}
```

Now consider this scenario, in which `jareth` and `cory` are two `Friendly` objects that have become friends:

1. Thread number 1 invokes synchronized method `jareth.hug`. Thread number 1 now has the lock on `jareth`.

2. Thread number 2 invokes synchronized method `cory.hug`. Thread number 2 now has the lock on `cory`.

3. Now `jareth.hug` invokes synchronized method `cory.hugBack`. Thread number 1 is now blocked waiting for the lock on `cory` (currently held by thread number 2) to become available.

4. Finally, `cory.hug` invokes synchronized method `jareth.hugBack`. Thread number 2 is now blocked waiting for the lock on `jareth` (currently held by thread number 1) to become available.

We have now achieved deadlock: `cory` won't proceed until the lock on `jareth` is released and vice versa, so the two threads are stuck in a permanent embrace.

We can try to set this scenario up as follows:

```
public static void main(String[] args) {
    final Friendly jareth = new Friendly("jareth");
    final Friendly cory = new Friendly("cory");
    jareth.becomeFriend(cory);
    cory.becomeFriend(jareth);

    new Thread(new Runnable() {
        public void run(){ jareth.hug(); }
    }, "Thread1").start();

    new Thread(new Runnable() {
        public void run(){ cory.hug(); }
    }, "Thread2").start();
}
```

And when you run the program, you might get the following output before the program "hangs":

```
Thread1 in jareth.hug() trying to invoke cory.hugBack()
Thread2 in cory.hug() trying to invoke jareth.hugBack()
```

You could get lucky, of course, and have one thread complete the entire `hug` without the other one starting. If steps 2 and 3 happened to occur in the opposite order, `jareth` would complete both `hug` and `hugBack` before `cory` needed the lock on `jareth`. But a future run of the same application might deadlock because of a different choice of the thread scheduler. Several design changes would fix this problem. The simplest would be to make `hug` and `hugBack` not `synchronized` but have both methods synchronize on a single object shared by all `Friendly` objects. This technique would mean that only one hug could happen at a time in all the threads of a single application, but it would eliminate the possibility of deadlock. Other, more complicated techniques would enable multiple simultaneous hugs without deadlock.

You are responsible for avoiding deadlock. The runtime system neither detects nor prevents deadlocks. It can be frustrating to debug deadlock problems, so you should solve them by avoiding the possibility in your design. One common technique is to use *resource ordering*. With resource ordering you assign an order on all objects whose locks must be acquired, you then ensure that you always acquire locks in that order. By doing this it is impossible for two threads to hold one lock each and be trying to acquire the lock held by the other—they must both request the locks in the same order so once one thread has the first lock, the second thread will block trying to acquire that lock, and then the first thread can safely acquire the second lock.

Exercise 10.8: Experiment with the `Friendly` program. How often does the deadlock actually happen on your system? If you add `yield` calls, can you change the likelihood of deadlock? If you can, try this exercise on more than one kind of system. Remove the deadlock potential without getting rid of the synchronization.

10.8 Ending Thread Execution

A thread that has been started becomes *alive* and the `isAlive` method will return `true` for that thread. A thread continues to be alive until it terminates, which can occur in one of three ways:

- the `run` method returns normally
- the `run` method completes abruptly
- the `destroy` method is invoked on that thread

Having `run` return is the normal way for a thread to terminate. Every thread performs a task and when that task is over the thread should go away. If something goes wrong, however, and an exception occurs which is not caught, then that will also terminate the thread—we'll look at this further in Section 10.12 on page 266. By the time a thread terminates it will not hold any locks, as all synchronized code must have been exited by the time `run` has completed.

Invoking a thread's `destroy` method is drastic. It stops the thread dead in its tracks, whatever it was doing, without releasing any held locks, so using `destroy` could leave other threads blocked forever. The `destroy` method is a method of last resort, when the cooperative cancellation techniques we discuss next don't work. In practice, many systems have never implemented the `destroy` method, other than to throw `NoSuchMethodError`—which may terminate the invoking thread instead of the target one.

A thread can also be terminated when its program terminates, which you'll learn about in "Ending Application Execution" on page 259.

10.8.1 Cancelling a Thread

There are often occasions when you create a thread to perform some work and then need to cancel that work before it is complete—the most obvious example being a user clicking a cancel button in a user interface. To make a thread *cancellable* takes a bit of work on the programmer's part, but it is a clean and safe mechanism for getting a thread to terminate. Cancellation is requested by *interrupting* the thread and by writing the thread such that it watches for, and responds to, being interrupted. For example:

Thread 1
```
thread2.interrupt();
```

Thread 2
```
while (!interrupted()) {
    // do a little work
}
```

Interrupting the thread advises it that you want it to pay attention, usually to get it to halt execution. An interrupt does *not* force the thread to halt, although it will interrupt the slumber of a sleeping or waiting thread.

Interruption is also useful when you want to give the running thread some control over when it will handle an event. For example, a display update loop might need to access some database information using a transaction and would prefer to handle a user's "cancel" after waiting until a transaction completes normally. The user interface thread might implement a "Cancel" button by interrupting the display thread to give the display thread that control. This approach will work well as long as the display thread is well behaved and checks at the end of every transaction to see whether it has been interrupted, halting if it has.

The methods that relate to interrupting a thread are: `interrupt`, which sends an interrupt to a thread; `isInterrupted`, which tests whether a thread has been interrupted; and `interrupted`, a `static` method that tests whether the current thread has been interrupted and then clears the "interrupted" state of the thread. The interrupted state of a thread can be cleared only by that thread—there is no way to "un-interrupt" another thread. There is generally little point in querying the interrupted state of another thread, so these methods tend to be used by the current thread on itself. When a thread detects that it has been interrupted, it often needs to perform some cleanup before actually responding to the interrupt. That cleanup may involve actions that could be affected if the thread is left in the interrupted state, so the thread will test and clear its interrupted state using `interrupted`.

Interrupting a thread will normally not affect what it is doing, but a few methods, such as `sleep` and `wait`, throw `InterruptedException`. If your thread is executing one of these methods when it is interrupted, the method will throw the `InterruptedException`. Such a thrown interruption clears the interrupted state of the thread, so handling code for `InterruptedException` commonly looks like this:

```
void tick(int count, long pauseTime) {
    try {
        for (int i = 0; i < count; i++) {
            System.out.println('.');
            System.out.flush();
            Thread.sleep(pauseTime);
        }
    } catch (InterruptedException e) {
        Thread.currentThread().interrupt();
    }
}
```

The `tick` method prints a dot every `pauseTime` milliseconds up to a maximum of `count` times—see "Timer and TimerTask" on page 473 for a better way to do this. If something interrupts the thread in which `tick` is running, `sleep` will throw `InterruptedException`. The ticking will then cease, and the `catch` clause will re-interrupt the thread. You could instead declare that `tick` itself throws `InterruptedException` and simply let the exception percolate upward, but then every invoker of `tick` would have to handle the same possibility. Reinterrupting the thread allows `tick` to clean up its own behavior and then let other code handle the interrupt as it normally would.

In general any method that performs a blocking operation (either directly or indirectly) should allow that blocking operation to be cancelled with `interrupt` and should throw an appropriate exception if that occurs. This is what `sleep` and wait do. In some systems, blocking I/O operations will respond to interruption by throwing `InterruptedIOException` (which is a subclass of the general `IOException` that most I/O methods can throw—see Chapter 15 for more details on I/O). Even if the interruption cannot be responded to during the I/O operation, systems may check for interruption at the start of the operation and throw the exception—hence the need for an interrupted thread to clear its interrupted state if it needs to perform I/O as part of its cleanup. In general, however, you cannot assume that `interrupt` will unblock a thread that is performing I/O.

Every method of every class executes in some thread, but the behavior defined by those methods generally concerns the state of the object involved, not the state of the thread executing the method. Given that, how do you write methods that will allow threads to respond to interrupts and be cancellable? If your method can block, then it should respond to interruption as just discussed. Otherwise you must decide what interruption, or cancellation, would mean for your method and make that behavior part of the methods contract—in the majority of cases methods need not concern themselves with interruption at all. The golden rule, however, is to never hide an interrupt by clearing it explicitly, or by catching an `InterruptedException` and continuing normally—that prevents any thread from being cancellable when executing your code.

The interruption mechanism is a tool for cooperating code to use to make multithreading effective. Neither it, nor any other mechanism, can deal with hostile or malicious code.

10.8.2 Waiting for a Thread to Complete

One thread can wait for another thread to terminate by using one of the `join` methods. The simple form waits forever for a particular thread to complete:

```
class CalcThread extends Thread {
    private double result;

    public void run() {
        result = calculate();
    }

    public double getResult() {
        return result;
    }

    public double calculate() {
        // ... calculate a value for "result"
```

```
        }
    }

class ShowJoin {
    public static void main(String[] args) {
        CalcThread calc = new CalcThread();
        calc.start();
        doSomethingElse();
        try {
            calc.join();
            System.out.println("result is "
                + calc.getResult());
        } catch (InterruptedException e) {
            System.out.println("No answer: interrupted");
        }
    }

}
```

First, a new thread type, CalcThread, is defined to calculate a result. We start a CalcThread, do something else for a while, and then join that thread. When join returns, CalcThread.run is guaranteed to have finished, and result will be set. If CalcThread is already finished when doSomethingElse has completed, join returns immediately. When a thread dies, its Thread object doesn't go away, so you can still access its state. You are not required to join a thread before it can terminate.

Two other forms of join take time-out values analogous to wait. Here are the three forms of join:

public final void **join(long millis)**
  throws InterruptedException
> Waits for this thread to finish or the specified number of milliseconds to elapse, whichever comes first. A time-out of zero milliseconds means to wait forever. If the thread is interrupted while it is waiting an InterruptedException is thrown.

public final void **join(long millis, int nanos)**
  throws InterruptedException
> Waits for this thread to finish, with more precise timing. Again, a total time-out of zero nanoseconds means to wait forever. Nanoseconds are in the range 0–999999.

```
public final void join() throws InterruptedException
```
Equivalent to join(0).

Internally, join is defined in terms of isAlive and can be logically considered to act as if written as

```
while (isAlive())
    wait();
```

with the understanding that the runtime system will invoke notifyAll when the thread actually terminates.

10.9 Ending Application Execution

Each application starts with one thread—the one that executes main. If your application creates no other threads, the application will finish when main returns. But if you create other threads, what happens to them when main returns?

There are two kinds of threads: *user* and *daemon*. The presence of a user thread keeps the application running, whereas a daemon thread is expendable. When the last user thread is finished, any daemon threads are terminated and the application is finished. This termination is like that of invoking destroy—abrupt and with no chance for any cleanup—so daemon threads are limited in what they can do. You use the method setDaemon(true) to mark a thread as a daemon thread, and you use getDaemon to test that flag. By default, daemon status is inherited from the thread that creates the new thread and cannot be changed after a thread is started; an IllegalThreadStateException is thrown if you try.

If your main method spawns a thread, that thread inherits the user-thread status of the original thread. When main finishes, the application will continue to run until the other thread finishes, too. There is nothing special about the original thread—it just happened to be the first one to get started for a particular run of an application, and it is treated just like any other user thread. An application will run until all user threads have completed. For all the runtime system knows, the original thread was designed to spawn another thread and die, letting the spawned thread do the real work. If you want your application to exit when the original thread dies, you can mark all the threads you create as daemon threads.

We can force an application to end by invoking either the System or Runtime method exit. This method terminates the current execution of the Java virtual machine and again, is like invoking destroy on each thread. However, an application can install special threads to be run prior to the application shutting down—the methods for doing this are described in "Shutdown" on page 488.

Many classes implicitly create threads within an application. For example, the Abstract Window Toolkit (AWT), described briefly in Chapter 20, provides an event-based graphical user interface, and creates a special thread for dealing with all events associated with the user interface. Similarly Remote Method Invocation, also mentioned in Chapter 20, creates threads for responding to remote method invocations. Some of these threads may be daemons and others may not, and so use of these classes can keep your application running longer than you may intend. In these circumstances the use of the `exit` method becomes essential, if there is no other way to terminate the threads.

10.10 `volatile`

Any mutable (that is, changeable) value shared between different threads should always be accessed under synchronization to prevent interference from occurring. Synchronization comes at a cost however, and may not always be necessary to prevent interference. The language guarantees that reading or writing any variables, other than those of type `long` or `double`, is atomic—the variable will only ever hold a value that was written by some thread, never a partial value intermixing two different writes. This means, for example, that an atomic variable that is only written by one thread and read by many threads, need not have access to it synchronized to prevent corruption as there is no possibility of interference. This does not help with get-modify-set sequences, which always require synchronization.

Atomic access does not ensure that a thread will always read the most recently written value of a variable. In fact, without synchronization, a value written by one thread may *never* become visible to another thread. There are a number of factors that affect when a variable written by one thread becomes visible to another thread. Modern multi-processing hardware can do very strange things when it comes to the way in which shared memory values get updated. To the programmer these things are not only strange, they often seem completely unreasonable and invariably not what the programmer wanted. These factors are allowed for by letting threads have a working memory from which values are read and written. Unless told otherwise, the compiler may work completely from working memory and never read or update a main memory variable. For example, if you had a value that was continuously displayed by a graphics thread and that could be changed by non-synchronized methods, the display code might look something like this:

```
currentValue = 5;
for (;;) {
    display.showValue(currentValue);
    Thread.sleep(1000); // wait 1 second
}
```

If there is no way for `showValue` to change the value of `currentValue`, the compiler might assume that it can treat `currentValue` as unchanged inside the loop and simply use the constant 5 each time it invokes `showValue`. But if `currentValue` is a field that is updated by other threads while the loop is running, the compiler's assumption would be wrong.

Proper use of synchronization avoids this problem—a compiler isn't allowed to make assumptions about fields accessed in synchronized code and must read or write main memory as needed.

In the absence of synchronization, there is a second mechanism for dealing with this problem—you can declare a field as `volatile`. This tells the compiler that the value of the field could change at any time, unknown to the compiler, and prevents the compiler from making assumptions about the field. Declaring the field `currentValue` to be `volatile` forces the compiler to reread the value on every iteration of the loop. Thus a read of a volatile variable always returns the most recently written value. However, just because you have the most recent value of an object reference, does *not* mean that you will see the most recent values of that object's fields—it is the reference that is volatile, not the object. Finally, the guarantee about atomic accesses is extended to `long` and `double` values if they are declared `volatile`.

10.11 Thread Management, Security and `ThreadGroup`

When you're programming multiple threads—some of them created by library classes—it can be useful to organize them into related groups, manage the threads in a group as a unit and, if necessary, place limitations on what threads in different groups can do.

Threads are organized into *thread groups* for management and security reasons. A thread group can be contained within another thread group, providing a hierarchy—originating with the top-level or system thread group. Threads within a group can be managed as a unit, for example, by interrupting all threads in the group at once, or placing a limit on the maximum priority of threads in a group. The thread group can also be used to define a security domain. Threads within a thread group can generally modify other threads in that group, including any threads farther down the hierarchy. In this context "modifying" means invoking any method that could affect a thread's behavior—such as changing its priority, or interrupting it. However, an application can define a security policy that prevents a thread from modifying threads outside of its group. Threads within different thread groups can also be granted different permissions for performing actions within the application, such as performing I/O.

Generally speaking, security-sensitive methods always check with any installed security manager before proceeding. If the security policy in force forbids the action, the method throws a `SecurityException`. By default there is no security manager installed when an application starts. If your code is executed in the context of another application, however, such as an applet within a browser, you can be fairly certain that a security manager has been installed. Actions such as creating threads, controlling threads, performing I/O, or terminating an application, are all security sensitive. For further details on these issues see "Security" on page 493.

Every thread belongs to a thread group. Each thread group is represented by a `ThreadGroup` object that describes the limits on threads in that group and allows the threads in the group to be interacted with as a group. You can specify the thread group for a new thread by passing it to the thread constructor. By default each new thread is placed in the same thread group as that of the thread that created it, unless a security manager specifies differently. For example, if some event-handling code in an applet creates a new thread, the security manager can make the new thread part of the applet thread group rather than the system thread group of the event-processing thread. When a thread terminates, the `Thread` object is removed from its group and so may be garbage collected if no other references to it remain.

There are three `Thread` constructors that allow you to specify the `ThreadGroup` of the thread. You saw two of them on page 233 when looking at `Runnable`. The third is:

public **Thread(ThreadGroup group, String name)**
    Constructs a new thread in the specified thread group with the given name.

To prevent threads from being created in arbitrary thread groups (which would defeat the security mechanism), these constructors can themselves throw `SecurityException` if the current thread is not permitted to place a thread in the specified thread group.

The `ThreadGroup` object associated with a thread cannot be changed after the thread is created. You can get a thread's group by invoking its `getThreadGroup` method. You can also check whether you are allowed to modify a `Thread` by invoking its checkAccess method, which throws SecurityException if you cannot modify the thread and simply returns if you can (it is a void method).

A thread group can be a *daemon group*—which is totally unrelated to the concept of daemon threads. A daemon ThreadGroup is automatically destroyed when it becomes empty. Setting a ThreadGroup to be a daemon group does not affect whether any thread or group contained in that group is a daemon. It affects only what happens when the group becomes empty.

Thread groups can also be used to set an upper limit on the priority of the threads they contain. After you invoke setMaxPriority with a maximum priority, any attempt to set a thread priority higher than the thread group's maximum is silently reduced to that maximum. Existing threads are not affected by this invocation. To ensure that no other thread in the group will ever have a higher priority than that of a particular thread, you can set that thread's priority and then set the group's maximum priority to be less than that. The limit also applies to the thread group itself. Any attempt to set a new maximum priority for the group that is higher than the current maximum will be silently reduced.

```
static synchronized void
    maxThread(Thread thr, int priority)
{
    ThreadGroup grp = thr.getThreadGroup();
    thr.setPriority(priority);
    grp.setMaxPriority(thr.getPriority() - 1);
}
```

This method works by setting the thread's priority to the desired value and then setting the group's maximum allowable priority to less than the thread's priority. The new group maximum is set to one less than the thread's actual priority—not to priority - 1 because an existing group maximum might limit your ability to set the thread to that priority. Of course, this method assumes that no thread in the group already has a higher priority.

ThreadGroup supports the following constructors and methods:

public **ThreadGroup(String name)**
> Creates a new ThreadGroup. Its parent will be the ThreadGroup of the current thread. Like Thread names, the name of a group is not used by the runtime system—but it can be null.

public **ThreadGroup(ThreadGroup parent, String name)**
> Creates a new ThreadGroup with a specified name in the ThreadGroup parent. A NullPointerException is thrown if parent is null.

public final String **getName()**
> Returns the name of this ThreadGroup.

`public final ThreadGroup` **`getParent()`**
> Returns the parent `ThreadGroup`, or `null` if it has none (which can only occur for the top-level thread group).

`public final void` **`setDaemon(boolean daemon)`**
> Sets the daemon status of this thread group.

`public final boolean` **`isDaemon()`**
> Returns the daemon status of this thread group.

`public final void` **`setMaxPriority(int maxPri)`**
> Sets the maximum priority of this thread group.

`public final int` **`getMaxPriority()`**
> Gets the current maximum priority of this thread group.

`public final boolean` **`parentOf(ThreadGroup g)`**
> Checks whether this thread group is a parent of the group g, or is the group g. This might be better thought of as "part of," since a group is part of itself.

`public final void` **`checkAccess()`**
> Throws `SecurityException` if the current thread is not allowed to modify this group. Otherwise, this method simply returns.

`public final void` **`destroy()`**
> Destroys this thread group. The thread group must contain no threads or this method throws `IllegalThreadStateException`. If the group contains other groups, they must also be empty of threads. This does *not* destroy the threads in the group.

You can examine the contents of a thread group using two parallel sets of methods: one gets the threads contained in the group, and the other gets the thread groups contained in the group.

`public int` **`activeCount()`**
> Returns an estimate of the number of active threads in this group, including threads contained in all subgroups. This is an estimate because by the time you get the number it may be out of date. Threads may have died, or new ones may have been created, during or after the invocation of `activeCount`. An active thread is one for which `isAlive` returns true.

`public int` **`enumerate(Thread[] threadsInGroup, boolean recurse)`**
> Fills the `threadsInGroup` array with a reference to every active thread in the group, up to the size of the array, and returns the number of threads stored. If `recurse` is `false`, only threads directly in the group are included; if it is `true`, all threads in the group's hierarchy will be included. `ThreadGroup.enumerate` gives you control over whether you recurse, but `ThreadGroup.activeCount` does not. You can get a reasonable estimate of

the size of an array needed to hold the results of a recursive enumeration, but you will overestimate the size needed for a non-recursive `enumerate`.

`public int` **`enumerate(Thread[] threadsInGroup)`**
Equivalent to enumerate(threadsInGroup, true).

`public int` **`activeGroupCount()`**
Like `activeCount`, but counts groups, instead of threads, in all subgroups. "Active" means "existing." There is no concept of an inactive group; the term "active" is used for consistency with `activeCount`.

`public int` **`enumerate(ThreadGroup[] groupsInGroup,`**
  `boolean recurse)`
Like the similar `enumerate` method for threads, but fills an array of `ThreadGroup` references instead of `Thread` references.

`public int` **`enumerate(ThreadGroup[] groupsInGroup)`**
Equivalent to enumerate(groupsInGroup, true).

You can also use a `ThreadGroup` to manage threads in the group. Invoking `interrupt` on a group invokes the `interrupt` method on each thread in the group, including threads in all subgroups. This method is the only way to use a `ThreadGroup` to directly affect threads—there used to be others but they have been deprecated.

There are also two static methods in the `Thread` class to act on the current thread's group. They are shorthands for invoking `currentThread`, invoking `getThreadGroup` on that thread, and then invoking the method on that group.

`public static int` **`activeCount()`**
Returns the number of active threads in the current thread's `ThreadGroup`.

`public static int` **`enumerate(Thread[] threadsInGroup)`**
Equivalent to invoking enumerate(threadsInGroup) on the `ThreadGroup` of the current thread.

The `ThreadGroup` class also supports a method that is invoked when a thread dies because of an uncaught exception:

`public void` **`uncaughtException(Thread thr, Throwable exc)`**
Invoked when thread `thr` in this group dies because of the uncaught exception `exc`.

We'll look at this in more detail in the next section.

Exercise 10.9: Write a method that takes a thread group and starts a thread that periodically print the hierarchy of threads and thread groups within that group. Test it with a program that creates several short-lived threads in various groups.

10.12 Threads and Exceptions

Exceptions always occur in a specific thread, due to the actions of that thread—for example, trying to perform division by zero, or explicitly throwing an exception. Such exceptions are synchronous exceptions and always remain within the thread.

When an exception is thrown it causes statements to complete abruptly and propagates up the call stack as each method invocation completes abruptly. If the exception is not caught by the time the `run` method completes abruptly then it is, by definition, an *uncaught exception*. At that point the thread that experienced the exception has terminated and the exception no longer exists. Because uncaught exceptions are usually a sign of a serious error, their occurrence needs to be tracked in some way. To enable this, the runtime system invokes the method `uncaughtException` in the dying thread's thread group.

The default implementation of the `uncaughtException` method invokes `uncaughtException` on the group's parent group if there is one, or invokes the exception's `printStackTrace` method if there is no parent group, so that information about the exception is displayed. You can override the method `uncaughtException` to handle uncaught exceptions in your own way. If you were writing a graphical environment, you might want to display the stack trace in a window rather than simply print it to `System.err`, which is where the method `printStackTrace` puts its output. You could override `uncaughtException` in your group to create the window you need and redirect the stack trace into the window.

If a "parent" thread wants to know why a "child" terminated, the child will have to store that information somewhere the "parent" can get it. Placing a thread `start` invocation in a `try-catch` block does *not* catch exceptions that may be thrown by the new thread—it simply catches any exception thrown by `start`.

10.12.1 Don't `stop`

We mentioned in Chapter 8 that two forms of asynchronous exceptions are defined—internal errors in the Java virtual machine, and exceptions caused by the invocation of the deprecated `Thread.stop` method.

As a general rule we don't discuss deprecated methods in this book, but `stop` is special—partly because of what it does, but mostly because it is, as they say, "out there" and you may well come across code that uses it (or tries to).

The `stop` method causes an asynchronous `ThreadDeath` exception to be thrown in the thread upon which it is invoked. There is nothing special about this exception—just like any other exception it can be caught, and if it is not caught it will propagate until eventually the thread terminates. The exception can occur at almost any point during the execution of a thread, but not while trying to acquire a lock.

The intent of `stop` was to force a thread to terminate in a controlled manner. By throwing an exception that was unlikely to be caught, it allowed the normal cleanup procedure of using `finally` clauses to tidy up as the thread's call stack unwound. But `stop` failed to achieve this in two ways. First, it couldn't *force* any thread to terminate because a thread could catch the exception that was thrown and ignore it—hence it was ineffective against malicious code. Second, rather than allowing a controlled cleanup, it actually allowed the corruption of objects. If `stop` was invoked while a thread was in a critical section, the synchronization lock would be released as the exception propagated, but the object could have been left in a corrupt state due to the partial completion of the critical section. Because of these serious flaws `stop` was deprecated. Instead, `interrupt` should be used for cooperative cancellation of a thread's actions.

A second form of `stop` took any `Throwable` object as an argument and caused that to be the exception thrown in the target thread—this is even more insidious because it allows "impossible" checked exceptions to be thrown from code that doesn't declare them.

10.13 ThreadLocal Variables

The `ThreadLocal` class allows you to have a single logical variable that has independent values in each separate thread. Each `ThreadLocal` object has a `set` method that lets you set the value of the variable in the current thread, and a `get` method that returns the value. This is a feature you may well never need, but if you do need it this class may simplify your work.

For example, you might want to have a user object associated with all operations, set on a per-thread basis. You could create a `ThreadLocal` object to hold each thread's current user object:

```
public class Operations {
    private static ThreadLocal users = new ThreadLocal() {
        /** Initially start as the "unknown user". */
        protected Object initialValue() {
            return User.UNKNOWN_USER;
        }
    };

    private static User currentUser() {
        return (User) users.get();
```

```
        }

        public static void setUser(User newUser) {
            users.set(newUser);
        }

        public void setValue(int newValue) {
            User user = currentUser();
            if (!canChange(user))
                throw new SecurityException();
            // ... modify the value ...
        }

        // ...
    }
```

The static field `users` holds a `ThreadLocal` variable whose initial value in each thread will be `User.UNKNOWN_USER`. This initial value is defined by overriding the method `initialValue`, whose default behavior is to return `null`. The programmer can set the user for a given thread by invoking `setUser`. Once set, the method `currentUser` will return that value when invoked in that thread. As shown in the method `setValue`, the current user might be used to determine privileges.

When a thread dies, the values set in `ThreadLocal` variables for that thread are not reachable, and so can be collected as garbage if not otherwise referenced.

When you spawn a new thread, the values of `ThreadLocal` variables for that thread will be the value returned by its `initialValue` method. If you want the value in a new thread to be inherited from the spawning thread, you can use the class `InheritableThreadLocal`, a subclass of `ThreadLocal`. It has a protected method `childValue` that is invoked to get the child's (spawned thread's) initial value. The method is passed the parent's value for the variable and returns the value for the child. The default implementation of `childValue` returns the parent's value, but you can subclass to do something different, such as cloning the parent's value for the child.

Thread local variables present an inherently risky tool. You should use them only where you thoroughly understand the thread model that will be used. The problems arise with *thread pooling,* a technique that is sometimes used to reuse threads instead of creating new ones for each task. In a thread pooling system a thread might be used several times. Any `ThreadLocal` variable used in such an environment would contain the state set by the last code that happened to use the same thread, instead of an uninitialized state expected at the beginning of a new thread of execution. If you write a general class that uses thread local variables and someone uses your class in a thread pool the behavior might be dangerously wrong.

For example, the users variable in the Operations example above could have just this problem—if an Operations object was used in multiple threads, or different Operations objects were used in the same thread, the "current user" notion could easily be wrong. Programmers who use Operations objects must understand this and only use the objects in threading situations that match the assumptions of the class's code.

10.14 Debugging Threads

A few Thread methods are designed to help you debug a multithreaded application. These print-style debugging aids can be used to print the state of an application. You can invoke the following methods on a Thread object to help you debug your threads:

public String **toString()**
> Returns a string representation of the thread, including its name, its priority, and the name of its thread group.

public static void **dumpStack()**
> Prints a stack trace for the current thread on System.out.

There are also debugging aids to track the state of a thread group. You can invoke the following methods on ThreadGroup objects to print their state:

public String **toString()**
> Returns a string representation of the ThreadGroup, including its name and priority.

public void **list()**
> Lists this ThreadGroup recursively to System.out. This prints the toString value for each of the threads and thread groups within this group.

I'll play it first and tell you what it is later.
—Miles Davis

CHAPTER 11

Programming with Types

I'm gonna wrap myself in paper,
I'm gonna dab myself with glue—
Stick some stamps on top of my head!
I'm gonna mail myself to you.
—Woody Guthrie, *Mail Myself to You*

TYPES are represented by classes and interfaces. There are classes for all primitive types (byte, float, and so on) and a general Class class to represent types of classes and interfaces. These classes provide three advantages:

- ◆ Useful methods for a type have a logical home. For example, the methods to convert a string to a float are static methods of the Float class.
- ◆ Descriptive methods and fields also have a logical home. MIN_VALUE and MAX_VALUE constants are available in the classes for each numeric primitive type, and a host of methods of the Class class and related objects let you examine, modify, and use objects and their types.
- ◆ For primitive types, wrapper objects can be created to hold their values. Then those objects can be used in any context where an Object reference is required. That's why classes for primitive types are called *wrapper classes*.

The type hierarchy for these classes looks like this:

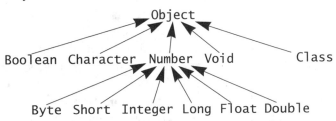

This chapter describes how to use these type-related classes. The first part of the chapter covers wrapper classes for primitive types. The second part of the chapter looks at how to use the *reflection* classes and interfaces, including class `Class`, to query the type details of an object and to dynamically create objects, access their members and invoke methods upon them. The final part of the chapter looks at the mechanism by which classes are loaded into the Java virtual machine and how you can increase your program's flexibility by providing your own specialized class loaders.

11.1 Wrapper Classes

All primitive language types have wrapper classes to represent them. These classes have two primary functions. The first is to provide a home for methods and variables related to the type (such as string conversions and value range constants). Here, for example, is how you might check whether you could use a faster `float` calculation on a particular value or whether the value requires a larger range than a `float` provides and so must be performed as a `double` calculation:

```
double aval = Math.abs(value);
if (Float.MAX_VALUE >= aval && aval >= Float.MIN_VALUE)
    return fasterFloatCalc((float) value);
else
    return slowerDoubleCalc(value);
```

The second purpose of wrappers is to create objects to hold values of a primitive type for generically written classes that know only how to handle `Object` references. The `HashMap` class, for example, stores only `Object` references, not primitive types—see "HashMap" on page 440. To use an `int` as a key or value in a `HashMap` object, you must create an `Integer` object to hold the value:

```
int key = ... ;
Integer keyObj = new Integer(key);
map.put(keyObj, value);
```

The reflection classes you will see later in this chapter also have to deal with generic objects and so require the wrapper classes for handling primitive values.

The following sections cover methods and constants available to each particular wrapper class, but first let's look at some things that are common to all the wrapper classes.

Each wrapper class defines an immutable object for the primitive value that it is wrapping. This means that once a wrapper object has been created, the value represented by that object can never be changed. So, for example, the object created by `new Integer(1)` will always have the value 1 and there are no methods of class `Integer` that allow you to modify this value.

Each wrapper class has the following constructors:

◆ A constructor that takes a value of the primitive type and creates an object of the corresponding wrapper class. The constructors `Character(char)` and `Integer(int)` are examples.

◆ A constructor that converts a single `String` parameter into the object's initial value (except `Character`, which has no such constructor)—for example, `new Float("6.02e23")`. For numeric types the string is assumed to be a base 10 representation and if it cannot be decoded into an appropriate value a `NumberFormatException` is thrown.

The term *radix,* used in several places in the wrapper classes, is another word for numeric base. For example, decoding a `long` in radix 8 means the same as decoding it in base 8.

Each wrapper class also has the following methods:

`public static` *Type* **valueOf(String str)**

Returns a new object of the specified *Type* with the value decoded from `str`. For numeric types, a radix of 10 is assumed. `Float.valueOf("6.02e23")` and `Integer.valueOf("16")` are examples. This is equivalent to invoking `new` with the string-converting constructor. If `str` cannot be decoded, a `NumberFormatException` is thrown. `Character` does not have this method as it does not have the string-converting constructor. Again, `Boolean` has its own interpretation of the format of `str`.

`public String` **toString()**

Overrides `Object.toString()` to provide a string representation of the wrapper object's value.

`public` *type* **typeValue()**

Returns the primitive value corresponding to the current wrapper object. For example, `new Integer(6).intValue()` returns 6.

`public int` **compareTo(*Type* other)**

Returns a value less than, equal to, or greater than zero as the object on which it is invoked is less than, equal to, or greater than the object (of the same type *Type*) passed as a parameter. This method does not exist in class `Boolean`.

`public int` **compareTo(Object obj)**

If `obj` is of the same type as this object, this is just like `compareTo(*Type*)`. Otherwise a `ClassCastException` is thrown. This method implements the method in the `Comparable` interface; see "Ordering using `Comparable` and `Comparator`" on page 427. This method does not exist in class `Boolean`.

public boolean `equals(Object obj)`

Returns `true` if the two objects are the same type and wrap the same value. For example, for two `Integer` objects x and y, `x.equals(y)` is true if and only if, `x.intValue()` == `y.intValue()`. If obj is not of the same type as the current object, or is `null`, `false` is returned.

public int `hashCode()`

Returns a value-based hash code for use in hashtables.

All wrapper classes have these methods as described, so we do not list them in each class's description. The system property fetch-and-decode methods described in "System Properties" on page 481 are not discussed in this chapter.

Each wrapper class has a static TYPE field, which is the `Class` object for that primitive type. These fields are equivalent to the `Class` objects you can obtain from `.class` class literal expressions as described in "Reflection" on page 282. For example, `Integer.TYPE` is the same `Class` object you will get from the expression `int.class`.

11.1.1 Void

The `Void` class is the exception to all the preceding rules because it has no values to wrap, provides no methods, and cannot be instantiated. It has only a static TYPE field containing a reference to the `Class` object obtained using `void.class`. The language has no `void` type—`void` is a placeholder indicating no return type. The `Void` class represents that lack of an actual return type and is only used in reflection—see Section 11.3 on page 303.

11.1.2 Boolean

The `Boolean` class represents the `boolean` type as a class. Both the constructor that decodes a string and the `valueOf` method understand `"true"`, with any mixture of uppercase and lowercase characters, to be `true`. Any other string is interpreted as `false`.

The `Boolean` class has two static references to objects corresponding to each of the primitive boolean values: `Boolean.TRUE` and `Boolean.FALSE`.

`Boolean` objects are not `Comparable` as the relational operators make no sense on boolean values.

11.1.3 Character

The Character class represents the char type as a class. It provides methods for determining the type of a character and for converting between uppercase and lowercase. Many of the methods of class Character are defined in terms of a "Unicode Attribute Table" which defines a name for every Unicode character and the attributes for those characters, such as a decimal value, an uppercase equivalent, or a lowercase equivalent.

In addition to MIN_VALUE and MAX_VALUE constants, Character provides the constants MIN_RADIX and MAX_RADIX, which are the minimum and maximum radices understood by methods that translate between digit characters and integer values or vice versa,. The radix must be in the range 2–36; digits for values greater than 9 are the letters A through Z or their lowercase equivalents. There are three methods for converting between characters and integer values:

public static int **digit(char ch, int radix)**

Returns the numeric value of ch considered as a digit in the given radix. If the radix is not valid or if ch is not a digit in the radix, −1 is returned. For example, digit('A', 16) returns 10, while digit('9', 10) returns 9 and digit('a', 10) returns −1.

public static int **getNumericValue(char ch)**

Returns the numeric value of the digit ch as specified by the Unicode Attribute Table. For example, the character \u217F is the Roman Numeral *M,* representing the number 1000, so getNumericValue('\u217F') returns 1000. These numeric values are non-negative. If ch has no numeric value, −1 is returned; if it has a value that is not a non-negative integer (such as a fractional value), −2 is returned. For example, for the fractional character ¼ (\u00bc), getNumericValue returns −2.

public static char **forDigit(int digit, int radix)**

Returns the character value for the specified digit in the specified radix. If the digit is not valid in the radix, returns the character '\u0000'. For example, forDigit(10, 16) returns 'a' while forDigit(16, 16) returns '\u0000'.

There are three character cases in Unicode: upper, lower, and title. Uppercase and lowercase are familiar to most people. Titlecase is used to distinguish characters that are made up of multiple components and are written differently when used in titles, where the first letter in a word is traditionally capitalized. For example, in the string "ljepotica",[1] the first letter is the lowercase letter lj (\u01C9,

---

[1] "Ljepotica" is a Croatian diminutive of "beauty," often used as a term of endearment and admiration.

a letter in the Extended Latin character set that is used in writing Croatian digraphs). If the word appeared in a book title, and you wanted the first letter of each word to be in uppercase, the correct process would be to use `toTitleCase` on the first letter of each word, giving you "`Ljepotica`" (using `Lj`, which is `\u01C8`). If you incorrectly use `toUpperCase`, you would get the erroneous string "`LJepotica`" (using `LJ`, which is `\u01C7`).

All case issues are handled as defined in Unicode. For example, in Georgian, uppercase letters are considered archaic, and translation into uppercase is usually avoided. Therefore, `toUpperCase` will not change lowercase Georgian letters to their uppercase equivalents, although `toLowerCase` will translate uppercase Georgian letters to lowercase. Because of such details, you cannot assume that all characters that are equivalent ignoring case will be the same if you invoke either `toLowerCase` or `toUpperCase`. However, the expression

```
Character.toUpperCase(Character.toLowerCase(ch));
```

leaves you with a character that you can compare with another similarly constructed character to test for equality ignoring case distinctions. If the two resulting characters are the same, then the original characters were the same except for possible differences in case. The case conversion methods are:

public static char toLowerCase(char ch)
> Returns the lowercase character equivalent of ch. If there is no lowercase equivalent, ch is returned.

public static char toUpperCase(char ch)
> Returns the uppercase character equivalent of ch. If there is no uppercase equivalent, ch is returned.

public static char toTitleCase(char ch)
> Returns the titlecase character equivalent of ch. If there is no titlecase equivalent, the result of `toUpperCase(ch)` is returned.

The `Character` class has many methods to test whether a given character is of a particular type. The methods are passed a `char` as a parameter and return a `boolean` that answers the question asked. These methods are:

Method	Is the Character...
isDefined	a defined Unicode character
isDigit	a digit in any Unicode character set
isIdentifierIgnorable	can be in a code or Unicode identifier without effect (such as a direction control directive)
isISOControl	a Latin-1 control character
isJavaIdentifierPart	valid after first character of an identifier

Method	Is the Character...
`isJavaIdentifierStart`	valid as first character of an identifier
`isLetter`	a letter in any Unicode character set
`isLetterOrDigit`	a letter or digit in any Unicode character set
`isLowerCase`	a lowercase letter
`isSpaceChar`	a space in any Unicode character set
`isTitleCase`	a titlecase letter
`isUnicodeIdentifierPart`	valid after first character of a Unicode identifier
`isUnicodeIdentiferStart`	valid as first character of a Unicode identifier
`isUpperCase`	an uppercase letter
`isWhitespace`	a language whitespace character

Unicode identifiers are defined by the Unicode standard. Unicode identifiers must start with a letter (connecting punctuation such as _ and currency symbols such as ¥ are not letters in Unicode, although they are in the Java programming language) and must contain only letters, connecting punctuation (such as _), digits, numeric letters (such as Roman numerals), combining marks, nonspacing marks, or ignorable control characters (such as text direction markers).

All these types of characters, and several others, are defined by the Unicode standard. The static method `getType` returns an `int` that defines a character's Unicode type. The return value is one of the following constants:

```
COMBINING_SPACING_MARK      MODIFIER_SYMBOL
CONNECTOR_PUNCTUATION       NON_SPACING_MARK
CONTROL                     OTHER_LETTER
CURRENCY_SYMBOL             OTHER_NUMBER
DASH_PUNCTUATION            OTHER_PUNCTUATION
DECIMAL_DIGIT_NUMBER        OTHER_SYMBOL
ENCLOSING_MARK              PARAGRAPH_SEPARATOR
END_PUNCTUATION             PRIVATE_USE
FORMAT                      SPACE_SEPARATOR
LETTER_NUMBER               START_PUNCTUATION
LINE_SEPARATOR              SURROGATE
LOWERCASE_LETTER            TITLECASE_LETTER
MATH_SYMBOL                 UNASSIGNED
MODIFIER_LETTER             UPPERCASE_LETTER
```

Unicode is divided into blocks of related characters. The static nested class `Character.Subset` is used to define subsets of the Unicode character set. The static nested class `Character.UnicodeBlock` extends `Subset` to define a set of standard Unicode character blocks, which are available as static fields of

UnicodeBlock. The static method UnicodeBlock.of returns the UnicodeBlock object representing the Unicode character block for a particular character. The UnicodeBlock class also defines constants for all the blocks, such as GREEK, KATAKANA, TELUGU, and COMBINING_MARKS_FOR_SYMBOLS. The of method will return one of these values, or null if the character is not in any block. For example, the code

```
boolean isShape =
    (Character.UnicodeBlock.of(ch) ==
     Character.UnicodeBlock.GEOMETRIC_SHAPES);
```

tests to see if a character is in the GEOMETRIC_SHAPES block. The list of block name constants is shown in "Unicode Character Blocks" on page 561.

Two Subset objects define the same Unicode subset if they are the same object, a semantic enforced in Subset by declaring equals and hashCode to be final, and defining them to have the default Object behavior for these methods. If you define your own subsets for some reason, you should give people a way analogous to of to get a single Subset object for each different kind of Subset you define.

11.1.4 Number

The Number class is an abstract class extended by all wrapper classes that represent primitive numeric types: Byte, Short, Integer, Long, Float, and Double.

The abstract methods of Number return the value of the object converted to any of the numeric types:

```
public byte byteValue()
public short shortValue()
public int intValue()
public long longValue()
public float floatValue()
public double doubleValue()
```

Each extended Number class overrides these methods to convert its own type to any of the others under the same rules used for an explicit cast. For example, given a Float object with the value 32.87, the return value of intValue on the object would be 32, just as (int)32.87 would be 32.

11.1.5 The Integer Wrappers

The classes `Byte`, `Short`, `Integer`, and `Long` extend `Number` to represent the corresponding integer types as classes. In addition to the standard `Number` methods, each of the integer wrapper classes support the following methods:

`public static` *type* **parse***Type***(String str, int radix)**

Converts the string `str` into a numeric value of the specified *type*, using the given radix. For example, `Integer.parseInt("1010", 2)` returns the value 10, while `Integer.parseInt("-1010", 2)` returns the value −10. A `NumberFormatException` is thrown if `str` cannot be decoded or `radix` is out of range.

`public static` *type* **parse***Type***(String str)**

Equivalent to parse*Type*(str, 10).

`public static` *type* **valueOf(String str, int radix)**

Returns a wrapper object of class *type* with the value obtained by decoding `str` using the specified radix. Note that there are no equivalent constructors with this form. This is equivalent to the two-step process of parsing the string and using that value to construct a new wrapper object. For example, `Integer.valueOf("1010", 2)` is equivalent to the more verbose expression `new Integer(Integer.parseInt("1010", 2))`. If `str` cannot be decoded or `radix` is out of range, a `NumberFormatException` is thrown.

`public static String` **toString(***type* **val)**

Returns a string representation of the given primitive value of type *type*. For example, `Integer.toString(66)` returns the string `"66"`. It is these conversion functions that are used when converting primitive argument types used as string concatenation operands, such as `("i=" + 66)`.

In addition, the `Integer` and `Long` classes each have the following methods, where *type* is either `int` or `long`, respectively:

`public static String` **toString(***type* **val, int radix)**

Returns a string representation of the given value in the given radix. If radix is out of range, a radix of 10 is used.

`public static String` **toBinaryString(***type* **val)**

Returns a string representation of the two's complement bit pattern of the given value. For positive values this is the same as `toString(value, 2)`. For negative values the sign of the value is encoded in the bit pattern, not as a leading minus character. For example, `Integer.toBinaryString(-10)` returns `"11111111111111111111111111110110"`. These string representations for negative values cannot be used with corresponding parse*Type* methods because the magnitude represented by the string will always be greater than MAX_VALUE for the given type.

`public static String `**`toOctalString(`***`type`* **`val)`**

Returns a string representation of the given value in an unsigned base 8 format. For example, `Integer.toOctalString(10)` returns `"12"`. Negative values are treated as described in `toBinaryString`.

`public static String `**`toHexString(`***`type`* **`val)`**

Returns a string representation of the given value in an unsigned base 16 format. For example, `Integer.toHexString(10)` returns `"a"`. Negative values are treated as described in `toBinaryString`.

Note that none of the string formats include information regarding the radix in that format—there is no leading `0` for octal, or `0x` for hexadecimal. If radix information is needed then you must construct it yourself.

11.1.6 The Floating-Point Wrapper Classes

The `Float` and `Double` classes extend `Number` to represent the `float` and `double` types as classes. With only a few exceptions, the names of the methods and constants are the same for both types. In the following list, the types for the `Float` class are shown, but `Float` and `float` can be changed to `Double` and `double`, respectively, to get equivalent fields and methods for the `Double` class. In addition to the standard `Number` methods, `Float` and `Double` have the following constants and methods:

`public final static float `**`POSITIVE_INFINITY`**

The value for $+\infty$.

`public final static float `**`NEGATIVE_INFINITY`**

The value for $-\infty$.

`public final static float `**`NaN`**

Not-a-Number. This constant provides a tool to get a NaN value, not to test one. To test whether a number is NaN, use the `isNaN` method—don't compare it to this constant. as the result will always be false.

`public static boolean `**`isNaN(float val)`**

Returns `true` if `val` is a Not-a-Number (NaN) value.

`public static boolean `**`isInfinite(float val)`**

Returns `true` if `val` is either positive or negative infinity.

`public boolean `**`isNaN()`**

Returns `true` if this object's value is a Not-a-Number (NaN) value.

`public boolean` **`isInfinite()`**

> Returns `true` if this object's value is either positive or negative infinity.

In addition to the usual constructor forms, `Float` has a constructor that takes a `double` argument to use as its initial value after conversion to `float`.

To manipulate the bits inside a floating-point value's representation, `Float` provides methods to get the bit pattern as an `int`, as well as a way to convert a bit pattern in an `int` into a `float` value. The `Double` class provides equivalent methods to turn a `double` value into a `long` bit pattern or vice versa:

`public static int` **`floatToIntBits(float val)`**

> Returns the bit representation of the `float` value as an `int`, according to the IEEE-754 floating point "single precision" bit layout. NaN is always represented by the same bit pattern.

`public static int` **`floatToRawIntBits(float val)`**

> Equivalent to `floatToIntBits` except that the actual bit pattern for a NaN is returned, rather than collapsing all NaNs into a single value.

`public static float` **`intBitsToFloat(int bits)`**

> Returns the `float` corresponding to the given bit representation, according to the IEEE-754 floating point "single precision" bit layout.

We can parse strings into the floating-point primitive types, and convert floating-point types to strings, similar to the way integer types are parsed and converted:

`public static` *`type`* **`parse`*`Type`*`(String str)`**

> Converts the string `str` into a numeric value of the primitive *type*. If `str` cannot be decoded a `NumberFormatException` is thrown. For example, `Float.parseFloat("3.14")` gives the value `3.14`. Equivalent to using `valueOf(str)` and then extracting the primitive value from the created wrapper object, as in `Float.valueOf("3.14").floatValue()`.

`public static String` **`toString(`*`Type`*` val)`**

> Returns a string representation of the given primitive value of type *type*. For example, `Double.toString(0.3e2)` returns the string `"30.0"`. It is these conversion functions that are used when converting primitive argument types used as string concatenation operands. NaN values return the string `"NaN"`.

Exercise 11.1: Write a program to read a file with lines of the form "*type value*", where `type` is one of the type class names (`Boolean`, `Character`, and so on) and `value` is a string that the type's constructor can decode. For each such entry, create an object of that type with that value and add it to an `ArrayList`—see

"ArrayList" on page 435. Display the final result when all the lines have been read.

11.2   Reflection

The package `java.lang.reflect` contains the *reflection* package, the classes you can use to examine a type in detail. You can write a complete type browser using these classes, or write an application that interprets code that a user writes, turning that code into actual uses of classes, creation of objects, invocations of methods, and so on. All the types mentioned in this discussion on reflection are contained in the package `java.lang.reflect`, except for the classes `Class` and `Package`, which are part of the package `java.lang`.

Reflection starts with a `Class` object. From the `Class` object you can obtain a complete list of members of the class, find out all the types of the class (the interfaces it implements, the classes it extends) and find out information about the class itself, such as the modifiers applied to it (`public`, `abstract`, `final` and so on) or the package it is contained in. Reflection is also sometimes called *introspection*; both terms use the metaphor of asking the type to look at itself and tell you something. These capabilities can be used by type browsers to show the structure of an application and also form the first step for you to dynamically create and manipulate objects.

Reflection allows you to write code that performs actions that you can more simply execute directly in code if you know what you are doing. Given the name of a class (which may not have existed when the program was written) you can obtain a `Class` object and use that `Class` object to create new instances of that class. You can interact with those objects just as you would an object created via `new`. You can, for example, invoke a method using reflection, as you will soon see, but it is much harder to understand than a direct method invocation. You should use reflection only when you have exhausted all other object-oriented design mechanisms. For example, you should not use a `Method` object as a "method pointer," because interfaces and abstract classes are better tools. There are times when reflection is necessary—usually when you're interpreting or displaying some other code—but use more-direct means whenever possible.

11.2.1   The `Class` class

There is a `Class` object for every type. This includes each class, interface, array, and the primitive types. There is also a special `Class` object representing the keyword `void`. These objects can be used for basic queries about the type and, for the reference types, create new objects of that type.

The Class class is the starting point for reflection. It also provides a tool to manipulate classes, primarily for creating objects of types whose names are specified by strings, and for loading classes using specialized techniques, such as across the network. We'll look in more detail at class loading in Section 11.3 on page 303.

There are four ways to get a Class object: ask an object for its class object using its getClass method; use a class literal (the name of the class followed by .class, as in String.class); look it up by its fully qualified name (all packages included) using the static method Class.forName; or get it from one of the reflection methods that return Class objects for nested classes and interfaces (such as Class.getClasses).

The Class class provides a number of methods for obtaining information about a particular class. Some of these provide information on the type of the class—which interfaces it implements, which class it extends—and others return information on the members of the class, including nested classes and interfaces. You can ask if a class represents an interface or an array, or whether a particular object is an instance of that class. We'll look at these different methods over the next few pages.

The most basic Class methods are those that walk the type hierarchy, displaying information about the interfaces implemented and the classes extended. As an example, this program prints the type hierarchy of the type represented by a string passed as an argument:

```java
public class TypeDesc {
    public static void main(String[] args) {
        TypeDesc desc = new TypeDesc();
        for (int i = 0; i < args.length; i++) {
            try {
                Class startClass = Class.forName(args[i]);
                desc.printType(startClass, 0, basic);
            } catch (ClassNotFoundException e) {
                System.err.println(e);  // report the error
            }
        }
    }

    // by default print on standard output
    private java.io.PrintStream out = System.out;

    // used in printType() for labeling type names
```

```
    private static String[]
        basic  = { "class",    "interface"  },
        supercl = { "extends", "implements" },
        iFace  = { null,        "extends"  };

    private void printType(
        Class type, int depth, String[] labels)
    {
        if (type == null) // stop recursion -- no supertype
            return;

        // print this type
        for (int i = 0; i < depth; i++)
            out.print("  ");
        out.print(labels[type.isInterface() ? 1 : 0] + " ");
        out.println(type.getName());

        // print out all interfaces this class implements
        Class[] interfaces = type.getInterfaces();
        for (int i = 0; i < interfaces.length; i++)
            printType(interfaces[i], depth + 1,
                        type.isInterface() ? iFace : supercl);

        // recurse on the superclass
        printType(type.getSuperclass(), depth + 1, supercl);
    }
}
```

This program loops through the names provided on the command line, obtains a
Class object for each named type and invokes printType on each of them. It
must do this inside a try block in case there is no class of the specified name.
Here is its output when invoked on the utility class java.util.HashMap:

```
class java.util.HashMap
    implements java.util.Map
    implements java.lang.Cloneable
    implements java.io.Serializable
    extends java.util.AbstractMap
        implements java.util.Map
        extends java.lang.Object
```

After the `main` method is the declaration of the output stream to use, by default `System.out`. The `String` arrays are described shortly.

The `printType` method prints its own `type` parameter's description and then invokes itself recursively to print the description of `type`'s supertypes. The `depth` parameter keeps track of how far up the type hierarchy it has climbed, indenting each description line depending on its depth. The depth is incremented at each recursion level. The `labels` array specifies how to label the class—`labels[0]` is the label if the type is a class; `labels[1]` is for interfaces.

Three arrays are defined for these labels: `basic` is used at the top level, `supercl` is used for superclasses, and `iFace` is used for superinterfaces of interfaces, which extend, not implement, each other. After we print the right prefix, we use `getName` to print the name of the type. The `Class` class provides a `toString` method, but it already adds "class" or "interface" in front. We want to control the prefix, so we must create our own implementation.

After printing the type description, `printType` invokes itself recursively, first on all the interfaces that the original type implements and then on the superclass this type extends (if any), passing the appropriate label array to each. Eventually it reaches the `Class` object for `Object`, which implements no interfaces and whose `getSuperclass` method returns `null`, and the recursion ends.

There are some simple query methods to examine the kind of `Class` object that you are dealing with, one of which we used in the example:

public boolean **isInterface()**

> Returns `true` is this `Class` object represents an interface.

public boolean **isArray()**

> Returns `true` if this `Class` object represents an array.

public boolean **isPrimitive()**

> Returns `true` if this `Class` object is one of the `Class` objects representing the eight primitive types or `void`.

Other methods let you find out more specific information about the type and where it fits in the type hierarchy.

public Class[] **getInterfaces()**

> Returns an array of `Class` objects for each of the interfaces implemented by the type. If no interfaces are implemented, because, for example, a class type implements no interfaces or the current type is a primitive type, then an array of length zero is returned.

public Class **getSuperClass()**

> Returns the `Class` object for the superclass of the type. This returns `null` if this `Class` object represents the `Object` class, an interface, primitive type, or `void`, as there is no superclass. If this `Class` object represents an array

the `Class` object for `Object` is returned. By invoking this recursively you can determine all superclasses of a class.

public int getModifiers()

Returns the modifiers for the type, encoded as an integer. The value should be decoded using the constants and methods of class `Modifier`—see Section 11.2.4 on page 291. Type modifiers include the access modifiers (`public`, `protected`, `private`) as well as `abstract`, `final`, and `static`. For convenience, whether a type is an interface is also encoded as a modifier. Primitive types are always `public` and `final`. Array types are always `final` and have the same access modifier as their component type.

public Class getComponentType()

Returns the `Class` object representing the component type of the array represented by this `Class` object. If this `Class` object doesn't represent an array, `null` is returned. For example, given an array of `int`, the `getClass` method will return a `Class` object for which `isArray` returns `true` and whose `getComponentType` method returns the object `int.class`.

public Class getDeclaringClass()

Returns the `Class` object for the type in which this type was declared. If this type is not a nested type, `null` is returned.

Exercise 11.2: Modify `TypeDesc` to skip printing anything for the `Object` class. It is redundant because everything ultimately extends it. Use the reference for the `Class` object for the `Object` type.

11.2.2 Naming Classes

The `Class` objects in the `TypeDesc` program are obtained using the static method `Class.forName`, which takes a string argument and returns a `Class` object for the type with that name. The name must be a fully qualified name—that is, the name must include the full package name as well as the class name—such as `java.util.HashMap` or `java.lang.Object`. The fully qualified name for a class can be obtained by invoking `getName` on its `Class` object. For example, `Object.class.getName()` returns `"java.lang.Object"`.

Array types use a special notation to represent their names. This notation consists of a code representing the component type of the array, preceded by the character `[`. The component types are encoded as follows:

```
B               byte
C               char
```

```
D            double
F            float
I            int
J            long
Lclassname;  class or interface
S            short
Z            boolean
```

For example, an array of `int`s is named `[I`, while an array of `Object`s is named `[Ljava.lang.Object;` (note the trailing semicolon). A multi-dimensional array is just an array whose component type is an array, so, for example, a type declared as `int[][]` is named `[[I`—an array whose component type is named `[I`.

Nested types are also named using a special convention. Within a program a nested type is a member of its enclosing type and so is accessed via the dot operator, as in `Outer.Inner`. However, the external name of the class is actually `Outer$Inner`, using the dollar symbol `'$'` to separate the enclosing type name from the nested type name. Local and anonymous classes may be named using other conventions, but these cannot be instantiated using reflection.

For the primitive types, `Class` objects cannot be obtained using `forName`—you must use the class literals, such as `int.class`, or the TYPE field of the appropriate wrapper class, such as `Integer.TYPE`. If a name representing a primitive type is used with `forName`, it is assumed to be a user defined type and is unlikely to be found.

The `forName` method we have been using is a simpler form of the more general `forName` method:

public Class forName(String name, boolean initialize, ClassLoader loader) throws ClassNotFoundException

> Returns the `Class` object associated with the named class or interface, using the given class loader. Given the fully qualified name for a class or interface (in the same format returned by `getName`) this method attempts to locate, load, and link the class or interface. The specified class loader is used to load the class or interface. If `loader` is `null`, the class is loaded through the system class loader. The class is initialized only if `initialize` is `true` and it has not been initialized.

As this method description indicates, obtaining the `Class` object for a class can involve loading, linking and initializing the class—a fairly complex process which is described further in Section 11.3 on page 303. The simple `Class.forName` method uses the default class loader—the one returned by the expression `this.getClass().getClassLoader()`—and initializes the class if needed. If the class named cannot be found then the checked exception

ClassNotFoundException is thrown. The exception can contain a nested exception that describes what the problem was, which you can obtain by invoking the getException method on the exception object. This will be either the nested exception or null. Because of the complexities of loading, linking, and initializing a class, these methods can also throw the unchecked exceptions LinkageError and ExceptionInInitializerError.

11.2.3 Examining Class Members

The Class class contains a set of methods you can use to examine the components of the specified type. This includes fields, methods, nested types and constructors. Special types are defined to represent each of these, which you will learn about in detail in later sections: Field objects for fields, Method objects for methods, Constructor objects for constructors, and for nested types, the Class objects you have already seen.

These methods come in four variants depending on whether you want all members or a particular member, only public members or any members, only members declared in the current class or inherited members as well.

You can request all of the public members of a specific kind that are either declared in the class (interface) or inherited, by using one of the following:

```
public Constructor[] getConstructors()
public Field[] getFields()
public Method[] getMethods()
public Class[] getClasses()
```

Because constructors are not inherited, getConstructors returns Constructor objects only for public constructors declared in the current class.

You can also request the members of a specific kind that are actually declared in the current class (interface), not inherited, and which need not be public:

```
public Constructor[] getDeclaredConstructors()
public Field[] getDeclaredFields()
public Method[] getDeclaredMethods()
public Class[] getDeclaredClasses()
```

In each case, if there is no member of that kind, you will get an empty array. The getClasses methods return both nested classes and nested interfaces.

Requesting a particular member requires that further information be supplied. For nested types this is simply the name of the nested type and, in fact, there are no special methods to do this as `Class.forName` can be used for this purpose. Particular fields are requested using their name:

```
public Field getField(String name)
public Field getDeclaredField(String name)
```

The first form finds a public field that is either declared or inherited, while the second finds only a declared field that need not be public. If the named field does not exist, a NoSuchFieldException is thrown. Note that the implicit length field of an array is not returned when these methods are invoked on an array type.

Particular methods are identified by their signature—their name and an array of Class objects representing the number and type of their parameters.

```
public Method getMethod(String name, Class[] parameterTypes)
public Method getDeclaredMethod(String name,
                                Class[] parameterTypes)
```

Similarly, constructors are identified by their parameter number and type:

```
public Constructor getConstructor(Class[] parameterTypes)
public Constructor getDeclaredConstructor(
                                Class[] parameterTypes)
```

In both cases, if the specified method or constructor does not exist, you will get a NoSuchMethodException.

All the above methods require a security check before they can proceed and so will interact with any installed security manager—see "Security" on page 493. If there is no security manager installed then all of these methods will be allowed. Typically, security managers will allow any code to invoke methods that request information on the public members of a type—this enforces the normal language level access rules. However, access to non-public member information will usually be restricted to privileged code within the system. Note that the only distinction made is between public and non-public members—security managers do not have enough information to enforce protected or package-level access. If access is not allowed, a SecurityException is thrown.

The following program lists the public fields, methods, and constructors of a given class:

```
import java.lang.reflect.*;

public class ClassContents {
    public static void main(String[] args) {
        try {
            Class c = Class.forName(args[0]);
```

```
                System.out.println(c);
                printMembers(c.getFields());
                printMembers(c.getConstructors());
                printMembers(c.getMethods());
            } catch (ClassNotFoundException e) {
                System.out.println("unknown class: " + args[0]);
            }
        }

        private static void printMembers(Member[] mems) {
            for (int i = 0; i < mems.length; i++) {
                if (mems[i].getDeclaringClass() == Object.class)
                    continue;
                String decl = mems[i].toString();
                System.out.print("    ");
                System.out.println(strip(decl, "java.lang."));
            }
        }
    }
```

First we get the `Class` object for the named class. We then get the arrays of member objects that represent all of the public fields, constructors, and methods of the class and print them. The `printMembers` method uses the `Member` object's `toString` method to get a string that describes the member, skipping members that are inherited from `Object` since these are present in all classes and so not very useful to repeat each time (`strip` removes any leading `"java.lang."` from the name). Here is the output when run on the `Attr` class from page 66:

```
class Attr
    public Attr(String)
    public Attr(String, Object)
    public String Attr.toString()
    public String Attr.getName()
    public Object Attr.getValue()
    public Object Attr.setValue(Object)
```

The classes `Field`, `Constructor`, and `Method` all implement the interface `Member`, which has three methods for properties all members share:

`Class` **getDeclaringClass()**
    Returns the `Class` object for the class in which this member is declared.

`String` **getName()**
    Returns the name of this member.

int **getModifiers()**

Returns the language modifiers for the member encoded as an integer. This value should be decoded using the constants and methods of the Modifier class—see the next section.

Although a class or interface can be a member of another class, for historical reasons the class Class does not implement Member, although it supports methods of the same name and contract.

The toString method of all Member classes includes the complete declaration for the member, including modifiers and, for methods and constructors, signature information, not just the simple name returned by getName.

Exercise 11.3: Use reflection to write a program that will print a full declaration of a named class, including everything except the import statement, comments, and code for initializers, constructors, and methods.

11.2.4 The Modifier Class

The Modifier class encodes all of the modifiers for types and members as constants: ABSTRACT, FINAL, INTERFACE, NATIVE, PRIVATE, PROTECTED, PUBLIC, STATIC, STRICT, SYNCHRONIZED, TRANSIENT, and VOLATILE. For each of these constants, there is a corresponding query method is*Mod*(int modifiers) that returns true if modifier *mod* is present in the specified value. For example, if a field is declared

```
public static final int OAK = 0;
```

the value returned by its Field object's getModifiers method would be

```
Modifier.PUBLIC | Modifier.STATIC | Modifier.FINAL
```

The strictfp modifier is reflected via the constant STRICT. If code or a class is to be evaluated in strict floating point (see "Strict and non-Strict Floating-Point Arithmetic" on page 158), the modifiers for the method, class, or interface will include the STRICT flag.

The query methods can be used to ask questions in a more symbolic fashion. For example, the expression

```
Modifier.isPrivate(field.getModifiers())
```

is equivalent to the expression

```
(field.getModifiers() & Modifier.PRIVATE) != 0
```

11.2.5 The Field Class

The Field class defines methods for querying the type of a field and for setting and getting the value of the field. Combined with the inherited Member methods, this allows you to find out everything about the field declaration and to manipulate the field of a specific instance, or class.

The getType method returns the Class object for the type of the field. For example, if the field is a String field, the return value will be String.class. If the field is of a primitive type, such as long, the value returned will be that primitive type's class, such as long.class.

You can also get and set the value of a field using the get and set methods. There is a generic form of these methods that take Object arguments and return Object values, and more specific methods for dealing with primitive types directly. All of these methods take an argument specifying which object to operate on. For static fields the object is ignored and can be null. The following method prints the value of a short field of an object:

```
public static void printShortField(Object o, String name)
    throws NoSuchFieldException, IllegalAccessException
{
    Field field = o.getClass().getField(name);
    Short value = (Short) field.get(o);
    System.out.println(value);
}
```

The return value of get is whatever object the field references or, if the field is a primitive type, a wrapper object of the appropriate type. For our short field, value is a Short object that contains the value of the field.

The set method can be used in a similar way. A method to set a short field to a provided value might look like this:

```
public static void
    setShortField(Object o, String name, short nv)
        throws NoSuchFieldException, IllegalAccessException
{
    Field field = o.getClass().getField(name);
    field.set(o, new Short(nv));
}
```

We must create a Short wrapper to hold the value of nv because get and set work only on objects.

If the field of the specified object is not accessible and access control is being enforced, an IllegalAccessException is thrown. If the passed object does not have a type that declares the underlying field, an `IllegalArgumentException` is thrown. If the field is non-static and the passed object reference is `null`, a `NullPointerException` is thrown. Accessing a static field can require initializing a class, so it is also possible for an `ExceptionInInitializerError` to be thrown.

The `Field` class also has specific methods for getting and setting primitive types. You can invoke get*PrimitiveType* and set*PrimitiveType* on a `Field` object, where *PrimitiveType* is the primitive type name (with an initial upper-case letter). The get example just shown could have used the statement

```
short value = field.getShort(o);
```

The set example could have used the simpler

```
field.setShort(o, nv);
```

With some work you can use a `Field` object as a way to manipulate an arbitrary value, but you should avoid this when possible. The language is designed to catch as many programming errors as possible when the program is compiled. The less you write using indirections such as the `Field` object, the more your errors will be prevented before they are compiled into code. Also, as you can see, it takes more reading to see what is happening in the preceding code compared with what it would take if the name of the field were simply used in the normal syntax.

Exercise 11.4: Create an `Interpret` program that creates an object of a known type and allows the user to examine and modify fields of that object.

11.2.6 The `Method` Class

The `Method` class, together with its inherited `Member` methods allows you to obtain complete information about the declaration of a method, and allows you to invoke the method on a specified object.

`public Class` **getReturnType()**
> Returns the `Class` object for the type returned by this method. If the method is declared `void` the returned `Class` object is `void.class`.

`public Class[]` **getParameterTypes()**
> Returns an array of `Class` objects with the type of each parameter of this method, in the order in which the parameters are declared. If the method has no parameters an empty array is returned.

```
public Class[] getExceptionTypes()
```
Returns an array of Class objects for each of the exception types listed in the throws clause for this method, in the order they are declared. If there are no declared exceptions an empty array is returned.

```
public Object invoke(Object onThis, Object[] args) throws
    IllegalAccessException, IllegalArgumentException,
    InvocationTargetException
```
Invokes the method defined by this Method object on the object onThis, setting the parameters of the method from the values in args. For non-static methods the actual type of onThis determines the method implementation that is invoked. For static methods onThis is ignored and is traditionally null. The length of args must equal the number of parameters for the method, and types of parameters in args must all be assignable to those of the method. Otherwise you will get an IllegalArgumentException. If you attempt to invoke a method to which you do not have access, an IllegalAccessException is thrown. If onThis does not have a type that this method is a member of, an IllegalArgumentException is thrown. If onThis is null and the method is not static a NullPointerException is thrown. If the method is static, the class may need to be initialized and an ExceptionInInitializerError may be thrown. If the invoked method completes abruptly an InvocationTargetException is thrown—the getTargetException method of InvocationTargetException returns the exception that caused the abrupt completion.

When you use invoke, primitive types are passed in the argument array inside appropriate wrapper classes and automatically unwrapped. The type represented by a wrapper must be assignable to the unwrapped type. You can use a Long, Float, or Double to wrap a double argument, but you cannot use a Double to wrap a long or float argument because a double is not assignable to a long or a float. The Object returned by invoke is handled as with Field.get, returning primitive types as their wrapper classes. If the method is declared void, invoke returns null.

Simply put, you can use invoke only to invoke a method with the same types and values that would be legal in the language. The invocation

```
return str.indexOf(".", 8);
```

can be written using reflection in the following way:

```
Throwable failure;
try {
    Class StrClass = str.getClass();
    Method indexM = StrClass.getMethod("indexOf",
```

```
        new Class[] { String.class, int.class }
    );
    Object result = indexM.invoke(str, new Object[] {
        ".", new Integer(8) }
    );
    return ((Integer) result).intValue();
} catch (NoSuchMethodException e) {
    failure = e;
} catch (InvocationTargetException e) {
    failure = e.getTargetException();
} catch (IllegalAccessException e) {
    failure = e;
}
throw failure;
```

The reflection-based code has semantically equivalent safety checks, although the checks that are made by the compiler for direct invocation can be made only at run time when you use invoke. The access checking may be done in a somewhat different way—you might be denied access to a method in your package by the security manager, even if you could invoke that method directly.

These are good reasons to avoid using this kind of invocation when you can. It's reasonable to use invoke—or the get/set methods of Field—when you are writing a debugger or other generic applications that require interpreting user input as manipulations of objects. A Method object can be used somewhat like a method pointer in other languages, but there are better tools—notably interfaces, abstract classes, and nested classes—to address the problems typically solved by method pointers in those languages.

Exercise 11.5: Modify your Interpret program to invoke methods on the object. You should properly display any values returned or exceptions thrown.

11.2.7 Creating New Objects and the Constructor Class

You can use a Class object's newInstance method to create a new instance (object) of the type it represents. This method invokes the class's no-arg constructor and returns a reference to the newly created object. The reference is returned as type Object and so must be cast to the appropriate type.

Creating a new object in this way is useful when you want to write general code and let the user specify the class. For example, you could modify the generic sorting algorithm tester from "Designing a Class to Be Extended" on page 96 so that the user could type the name of the class to be tested and use that as a parameter to the forName lookup method. Assuming that the given class name was valid, newInstance could then be invoked to create an object of that type. Here is a new main method for a generic TestSort class:

```
static double[] testData = { 0.3, 1.3e-2, 7.9, 3.17, };

public static void main(String[] args) {
    try {
        for (int arg = 0; arg < args.length; arg++) {
            String name = args[arg];
            Class classFor = Class.forName(name);
            SortDouble sorter
                = (SortDouble) classFor.newInstance();
            SortMetrics metrics
                = sorter.sort(testData);
            System.out.println(name + ": " + metrics);
            for (int i = 0; i < testData.length; i++)
                System.out.println("\t" + testData[i]);
        }
    } catch (Exception e) {
        System.err.println(e);           // report the error
    }
}
```

This is almost exactly like TestSort.main (see page 100), but we have removed all type names. This main method can be used to test any subclass of SortDouble that provides a no-arg constructor. You don't have to write a main for each type of sorting algorithm—this generic main works for them all. All you need to do is execute

```
java TestSort TestClass ...
```

for any sorting class (such as SimpleSortDouble), and it will be loaded and run.

The newInstance method can throw a number of different exceptions if used inappropriately. If the class doesn't have a no-arg constructor, is an abstract class, is actually an interface, or if the creation fails for some other reason, an InstantiationException is thrown. If the class or the no-arg constructor is not accessible an IllegalAccessException is thrown. If the current security policy disallows the creation of a new object a SecurityException is thrown. Finally, creating a new object may require the class to be initialized so it is also possible for an ExceptionInInitializerError to be thrown.

The newInstance method of Class can invoke only a no-arg constructor. If you want to invoke any other constructor then you must use the Class object to get the relevant `Constructor` object and invoke `newInstance` on that `Constructor`, passing the appropriate parameters.

The `Constructor` class, together with its inherited `Member` methods allows you to obtain complete information about the declaration of a constructor, and allows you to invoke the constructor to obtain a new instance of that class.

`public Class[] getParameterTypes()`
> Returns an array of `Class` objects for each of the parameter types accepted by this constructor, in the order in which the parameters are declared. If the constructor has no parameters an empty array is returned.

`public Class[] getExceptionTypes()`
> Returns an array of `Class` objects for each of the exception types listed in the `throws` clause for this constructor, in the order they are declared. If there are no declared exceptions an empty array is returned.

To create a new instance of a class from a `Constructor` object, you invoke its `newInstance` method.

`public Object newInstance(Object[] args)`
> `throws InstantiationException, IllegalAccessException,`
> `IllegalArgumentException, InvocationTargetException`
> > Uses the constructor represented by this `Constructor` object to create and initialize a new instance of the constructor's declaring class, with the specified initialization parameters. A reference to the newly initialized object is returned. The length of `args` must equal the number of parameters for the constructor, and types of parameters in `args` must all be assignable to those of the constructor, or you will get an `IllegalArgumentException`. If the declaring class is abstract, and therefore cannot be instantiated, an `InstantiationException` is thrown. If you attempt to invoke a constructor to which you do not have access an `IllegalAccessException` is thrown. If the invoked constructor completes abruptly, you will get an `InvocationTargetException`.

Using `Constructor.newInstance` is very similar to using `Method.invoke`. Primitive arguments must be wrapped in the appropriate wrapper class and are automatically unwrapped.

An inner class never has a no-arg constructor, as the compiler transforms all inner class constructors to take a parameter that is a reference to the enclosing object. This means that `Class.newInstance` can never be used to create an inner class object so you must use `Constructor` objects. The `Constructor` objects for an inner class reflect the transformed code, not the code written by the programmer. For example, recall the `BankAccount` class and its associated inner `Action` class from page 124. The `Action` class had a single constructor that took a

`String` parameter, representing the action that had occurred (withdraw, deposit, and so on), and a `long` value, representing the amount involved. If you use reflection to obtain a `Constructor` object for that constructor and print its signature using `getName` and `getParameterTypes`, you will get the following:

```
BankAccount$Action(BankAccount, java.lang.String, long)
```

Here you can see both the use of the $ naming convention for inner classes, and the implicitly added constructor argument that refers to the enclosing object. If you want to construct an `Action` object you must supply an appropriate reference as in:

```
Action a = (Action) con.newInstance(
        new Object[] { acct, "Embezzle", new Long(10000) }
);
```

Exercise 11.6: Modify your `Interpret` program further to let users invoke constructors of an arbitrary class, display any exceptions, and, if a construction is successful, let them invoke methods on the returned object.

11.2.8 Access Checking and `AccessibleObject`

The classes `Field`, `Constructor`, and `Method` are all subclasses of the class `AccessibleObject`, which lets you enable or disable the checking of the language-level access modifiers, such as `public` and `private`. Normally, attempts to use reflection to access a member are subject to the same access checks that would be required for regular, explicit code—for example, if you cannot access a field directly in code, you cannot access it indirectly via reflection. You can disable this check by invoking `setAccessible` on the object with a value of `true`—the object is now accessible, regardless of language-level access control. This would be required, for example, if you were writing a debugger. The methods are:

public void **setAccessible(boolean flag)**
>   Sets the accessible flag for this object to the indicated boolean value. A value of `true` means that the object should suppress language-level access control (and so will always be accessible), while a value of `false` means the object should enforce language-level access control. If you are not allowed to change the accessibility of an object a `SecurityException` is thrown.

public static void **setAccessible(AccessibleObject[] array,**
  boolean flag)
>   A convenience method that sets the accessible flag for an array of objects. If setting the flag of an object throws a `SecurityException` only objects ear-

lier in the array have their flags set to the given value, all other objects are unchanged.

public boolean **isAccessible()**
> Returns the current value of the accessible flag for this object.

11.2.9 Arrays

An array is an object but has no members. Querying the Class object of an array for fields, methods or constructors will all yield empty arrays. To reflectively create arrays and to get and set the values of elements stored in an array, you can use the static methods of the Array class. You can create arrays with either of two newInstance methods.

public Object **newInstance(Class componentType, int length)**
> Returns a reference to a new array of the specified length and with component type componentType.

public Object **newInstance(Class componentType, int[] dimensions)**
> Returns a reference to a multi-dimensional array, with dimensions as specified by the elements of the dimensions array and with the component type componentType. If the dimensions array is empty, or has a length greater than the number of dimensions allowed by the implementation (typically 255), an IllegalArgumentException is thrown.

For primitive types, use the class literal to obtain the Class object—for example, use byte.class to create a byte array. The statement

```
byte[] ba = (byte[]) Array.newInstance(byte.class, 13);
```

is equivalent to

```
byte[] ba = new byte[13];
```

The second newInstance method takes an array of dimensions. The statement

```
int[] dims = { 4, 4 };
double[][] matrix =
    (double[][]) Array.newInstance(double.class, dims);
```

is equivalent to

```
double[][] matrix = new double[4][4];
```

Because the component type could itself be an array type, the actual dimensions of the created array can be greater than that implied by the arguments to newInstance. For example, if intArray is a Class object for the type int[],

then the invocation `Array.newInstance(intArray, 13)`, creates a two dimen-
sional array of type `int[][]`. When `componentType` is an array type, the component type of the created array is the component type of `componentType`. So, in the
previous example, the resulting component type is `int`.

The `Array` class has methods to `get` and `set` the individual elements of a
specified array, similar to the `get` and `set` methods of class `Field`. The generic
forms of the methods work with `Object`s only and so wrapping and casting must
be used. For example, given an `int` array, `xa`, the expression `xa[i]` can be more
laboriously and less clearly expressed as

```
Array.get(xa, i)
```

which returns an `Integer` object that must be unwrapped to extract the `int` value.
You can `set` a value in a similar way: `xa[i] = 23` is the same as the more awkward

```
Array.set(xa, i, new Integer(23));
```

If the object passed as the array is not actually an array, you will get an
`IllegalArgumentException`. If the value to be set is not assignable to the component type of the array (after unwrapping, if necessary), you will get an
`IllegalArgumentException`.

The `Array` class also supports a full set of get *Type* and set *Type* methods for
all the primitive types, as in:

```
Array.setInt(xa, i, 23);
```

The `getLength` method of `Array` returns the length of a given array.

Exercise 11.7: Modify `Interpret` further to allow users to specify a type and size
of array to create, set and get the elements of that array, and specify which element
of the array contains the object on which their expressions access fields and invoke
methods.

11.2.10 Packages

If you invoke the `getPackage` method on a `Class` object, you get a `Package`
object that describes the package in which the class lives (the `Package` class is
defined in `java.lang`). You can also get a `Package` object by invoking the static
method `getPackage` with the name of the package, or the static `getPackages`
method which returns an array of all known packages in the system.

The `getName` method returns the full name of that package.

Package objects are used differently to the other reflective types—you can't create or manipulate packages at run time. Package objects are used to obtain information about a package, such as its purpose, who created it, what version it is and so on. We defer a discussion on this until we look at packages in detail in Chapter 13.

11.2.11 The Proxy Class

The Proxy class lets you create classes at run time that implement one or more interfaces. This is an advanced, rarely needed feature, but when needed it is quite useful.

Suppose, for example, you want to log calls to an object so that when a failure happens you can print out the last several methods invoked on the object. You could write such code by hand for a particular class, with a way to turn it on for a particular object, but that requires custom coding work for each type of object you want to monitor, and also requires a check by each object on each method invocation to see if calls should be logged.

You could instead write a general utility that used a Proxy-created class to log a call history. Objects created by that class would implement the relevant interfaces, interposing code that you provide between the caller's invocation of a method and the object's execution of it.

The Proxy model is that you invoke Proxy.getProxyClass with a class loader and an array of interfaces to get a Class object for the proxy. Proxy objects have one constructor, to which you pass an InvocationHandler object. A Constructor object for this constructor can be obtained from the Class object and newInstance invoked on that constructor (passing in an invocation handler) to create a proxy object. The object created implements all the interfaces that were passed to getProxyClass, as well as the methods of Object. As a shortcut, you can invoke Proxy.newProxyInstance, which takes a class loader, an array of interfaces, and an invocation handler, and returns the appropriate proxy object directly. When methods are invoked on the proxy object, these method invocations are turned into calls to the invocation handler's invoke method.

Given all that, here is how a generic debug logging class might look:

```java
public class DebugProxy implements InvocationHandler {
    private final Object obj;              // underlying object
    private final List methods;            // methods invoked
    private final List history;            // viewable history

    private DebugProxy(Object obj) {
        this.obj = obj;
```

```
        methods = new ArrayList();
        history = Collections.unmodifiableList(methods);
    }

    public static synchronized Object proxyFor(Object obj) {
        Class objClass = obj.getClass();
        return Proxy.newProxyInstance(
            objClass.getClassLoader(),
            objClass.getInterfaces(),
            new DebugProxy(obj));
    }

    public Object
        invoke(Object proxy, Method method, Object[] args)
        throws Throwable
    {
        methods.add(method);
        return method.invoke(obj, args);
    }

    public List getHistory() {
        return history;
    }
}
```

If a programmer wants a debug proxy for a given object, they invoke proxyFor, as in:

```
Object proxyObj = DebugProxy.proxyFor(realObj);
```

The object proxyObj would implement all the interfaces that realObj implements, and the methods of Object. When a method is invoked on proxyObj, this would lead to an invocation of the invoke method on proxyObj. In our example invoke logs the invocation to its list of invoked methods and then invokes the method on the underlying realObj object, which was stored in the obj field—see "List" on page 433. The (read-only) history of method invocations on the object can be retrieved using the proxy's invocation handler:

```
DebugProxy h =
    (DebugProxy) Proxy.getInvocationHandler(proxyObj);
List history = h.getHistory();
```

If we hadn't used the `newProxyInstance` shortcut we would have needed to write the following:

```
Class proxyClass = Proxy.getProxyClass(
    objClass.getClassLoader(),
    objClass.getInterfaces());
Constructor ctor = proxyClass.getConstructor(
    new Class[] {InvocationHandler.class});
Object[] ctorArgs = new Object[] { new DebugProxy(obj) };
Object proxyObj = ctor.newInstance(ctorArgs);
```

The object passed to `invoke` is the proxy object. In our case we use that to get the invocation handler object, and from that we can get the underlying object. After logging the call, we then invoke the method on the underlying object.

The invocation handler's `invoke` method can throw `Throwable`. However, if `invoke` throws any exception that the original method could not throw, the invoker will get an `UndeclaredThrowableException` that contains the offending exception, available from its `getUndeclaredThrowable` method.

If you invoke `getProxyClass` twice with the same parameters (the same class loader and the same interfaces in the same order) you will get back the same `Class` object. If the interfaces are in another order, or if the class loader is different, you will get back different `Class` objects. The interface order matters because two interfaces in the list can potentially have methods with the same name and signature. If this happens, the `Method` object passed to invoke will have a declaring class of the first interface listed that declares that method (defined by a depth-first search of interfaces and superinterfaces).

The declaring class for the public non-final methods of `Object`—`equals`, `hashCode`, and `toString`—is always `Object.class`. The other methods of `Object` are not "proxied;" their methods are handled directly by the proxy object itself, not via a call to `invoke`. Most importantly, this means that a lock on a proxy object is just that—a lock on the proxy. Whatever object or objects the proxy uses to do its work (for example, in our case the underlying object whose methods are being traced) is not involved in the lock, including any uses of `wait`, `notifyAll`, or `notify`.

You can ask if an object is a proxy object using the static `Proxy.isProxy` method.

11.3 Loading Classes

The runtime system loads classes when they are needed. Details of loading classes vary between implementations, but most of them use a *class path* mechanism to search for a class referenced by your code but not yet loaded into the runtime system. The class path is a list of places in which the system looks for class files. This default mechanism works well in many cases, but much of the power of the Java virtual machine is the ability to load classes from places that make sense to your application. To write an application that loads classes in ways different from the default mechanism, you must provide a `ClassLoader` object that can get the bytecodes for class implementations and load them into the runtime system.

For example, you might set up a game so that players could write classes to play the game using whatever strategy the player chooses. The design would look something like this:

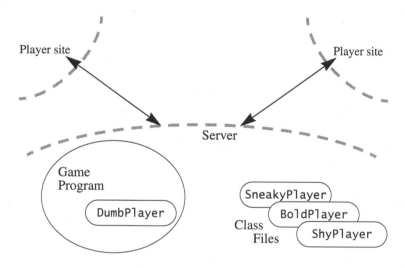

To make this work, you would provide a `Player` abstract class that players would extend to implement their strategy. When players were ready to try their strategy, they would send the compiled class's bytecodes to your system. The bytecodes would need to be loaded into the game, evaluated, and the score returned to the player.

At the server, the game program loads each waiting `Player` class, creates an object of the new type, and runs its strategy against the game algorithm. When the results are known, they are reported to the player who submitted the strategy.

The communication mechanism isn't specified here, but it could be as simple as electronic mail, with players mailing their classes and receiving the results by return mail.

The interesting part is how the game program loads the compiled class files into its runtime system. This is the province of a *class loader*, which must extend the abstract `ClassLoader` class and override its `findClass` method:

```
protected Class findClass(String name)
    throws ClassNotFoundException
```
Locates the bytecodes representing the class name and loads them into the virtual machine, returning the Class object created to represent that class.

In our example, we would provide a PlayerLoader class to read the bytecodes from the player classes and install each of them as a usable class. The basic loop would look like this:

```java
public class Game {
    public static void main(String[] args) {
        String name;    // the class name
        while ((name = getNextPlayer()) != null) {
            try {
                PlayerLoader loader = new PlayerLoader();
                Class classOf = loader.loadClass(name);
                Player
                    player = (Player) classOf.newInstance();
                Game game = new Game();
                player.play(game);
                game.reportScore(name);
            } catch (Exception e) {
                reportException(name, e);
            }
        }
    }
}
```

Each new game creates a new PlayerLoader object to load the class for that run of the game. The new loader loads the class, using loadClass, returning the Class object that represents it. That Class object is used to create a new object of the Player class. Then we create a new game and play it. When the game is finished, the score is reported. Without a new class loader for each run, attempting to load a class with the same name as one that had already been loaded, would return the original class. This would prevent players from submitting updated versions of their classes with the same name.

You can obtain the class loader for a given Class object from its getClassLoader method. System classes need not have a class loader, so the method may return null.

Class loaders define name spaces that separate the classes within an application. If two classes have different class loaders then they are distinct classes, even if the binary data for the class was read from the same class file. Each distinct class maintains its own set of static variables and modifications to the variables of one class have no affect on the other class.

Each thread has an associated `ClassLoader` that will be used by default to load classes. This *context class loader* can be specified at thread creation; if none is specified the parent thread's context class loader will be used. The context class loader of the first thread is typically the class loader used to load the application— the *system class loader*. The `Thread` methods `getContextClassLoader` and `setContextClassLoader` allow you to get and set the context class loader.

11.3.1 The `ClassLoader` Class

A class loader can delegate responsibility for loading a class to its *parent class loader*. The parent class loader can be specified as a constructor argument to `ClassLoader`:

protected **`ClassLoader()`**
   Creates a class loader with an implicit parent class loader of the system class loader, as returned by `getSystemClassLoader`.

protected **`ClassLoader(ClassLoader parent)`**
   Creates a class loader with the specified parent class loader.

A generic class loader, intended for use by others, should provide both forms of constructor to allow an explicit parent to be set.

The system class loader is typically the class loader used by the virtual machine to load the initial application class. A reference to it can be obtained using the static method `getSystemClassLoader`.

The parent class loader can be queried using the method `getParent`. If the class loader's parent is the system class loader, `getParent` may return `null`.

Class loaders are an integral part of the security architecture—see "Security" on page 493—so creating a class loader and querying the parent class loader are checked operations that may throw a `SecurityException`.

The primary method of `ClassLoader` is `loadClass`:

public Class **`loadClass(String name)`** throws ClassNotFoundException
   Returns the `Class` object for the class with the specified name, loading the class if necessary. If the class cannot be loaded you will get a `ClassNotFoundException`.

The default implementation of `loadClass`, which is not usually overridden, attempts to load a class as follows:

1. It checks to see if the class has already been loaded by invoking `findLoadedClass`. `ClassLoader` maintains a table of `Class` objects for

all the classes loaded by the current class loader. If a class has been previously loaded `findLoadedClass` will return the existing `Class` object.

2. If the class has not been loaded it invokes `loadClass` on the parent class loader. If the current class loader does not have a parent, the system class loader is used.

3. If the class still has not been loaded, `findClass` is invoked to locate and load the class.

The `PlayerLoader` class extends `ClassLoader` to override `findClass` as follows:

```
class PlayerLoader extends ClassLoader {
    public Class findClass(String name)
        throws ClassNotFoundException
    {
        try {
            byte[] buf = bytesForClass(name);
            return defineClass(name, buf, 0, buf.length);
        } catch (IOException e) {
            throw new ClassNotFoundException(e.toString());
        }
    }

    // ... bytesForClass, and any other methods ...
}
```

The `findClass` method generally has to perform two actions. First, it has to locate the bytecodes for the specified class and load them into a byte array—the job of `bytesForClass` in our example. Second, it uses the utility method `defineClass` to actually load the class defined by those bytes into the virtual machine and return a `Class` object for that class.

protected final Class **defineClass(String name, byte[] data, int offset, int length)** throws ClassFormatError

> Returns a `Class` object for the named class whose binary representation is held in data. Only the bytes in data from offset to offset+length are used to define the class. If the bytes in the sub-array do not conform to a valid class file format, a `ClassFormatError` is thrown. The `defineClass` method is responsible for storing the `Class` object into the table searched by `findLoadedClass`.

An overloaded form of `defineClass` takes an additional `ProtectionDomain` argument, while the previous form uses a default protection domain. Protection domains define the security permissions for objects in that domain—again see "Security" on page 493 for further details. Both forms of defineClass may throw SecurityException.

Before you can define a class you have to read the bytes for the class, and that is the purpose of bytesForClass:

```
protected byte[] bytesForClass(String name)
    throws IOException, ClassNotFoundException
{
    FileInputStream in = null;
    try {
        in = streamFor(name + ".class");
        int length = in.available(); // get byte count
        if (length == 0)
            throw new ClassNotFoundException(name);
        byte[] buf = new byte[length];
        in.read(buf);                           // read the bytes
        return buf;
    } finally {
        if (in != null)
            in.close();
    }
}
```

This method uses streamFor (not shown) to get a FileInputStream to the class's bytecodes, assuming that the bytecodes are in a file named by the class name with a ".class" appended. We then create a buffer for the bytes, read them all, and return the buffer.

When the class has been successfully loaded, findClass returns the new Class object returned by defineClass. There is no way to explicitly unload a class when it is no longer needed. You simply stop using it, allowing it to be garbage-collected when its ClassLoader is unreachable.

Exercise 11.8: Expand upon Game and Player to implement a simple game, such as tic-tac-toe. Score some Player implementations over several runs each.

11.3.2 Preparing a Class for use

The class loader assists in only the first stage of making a class available. There are three steps in all:

1. Loading: Getting the bytecodes that implement the class and creating a class object.

2. Linking: Verifying that the class's bytecodes conform to the language rules, preparing the virtual machine by allocating space for static fields and, optionally, resolving all references in the class by, if necessary, loading the classes referred to.

3. Initialization: Initializing the superclass (if necessary, including loading and linking it), then executing all the static initializers and static initialization blocks of the class.

The `Class` object returned by `defineClass` only represents a loaded class—it has not yet been linked. Linking can be performed explicitly by invoking the (mis-named) `resolveClass` method:

`protected final void` **`resolveClass(Class c)`**
> Links the specified class, if it has not already been linked.

The `loadClass` method we described does not resolve the class that is loaded. A protected, overloaded form of `loadClass` takes an additional `boolean` flag indicating whether or not to resolve the class before returning. The virtual machine will ensure that a class is resolved (linked) before it is initialized.

A class must be initialized before an instance of the class can be created, a static method of the class is invoked, or a non-final static field of the class is accessed. Exactly when this occurs depends on the implementation of the virtual machine.

11.3.3 Loading Related Resources

Classes are the primary resources a program needs, but some classes need other associated resources, such as text, images, or sounds. Class loaders have ways to find class resources, and they can use the same mechanisms to get arbitrary resources stored with the class. In our game example, a strategy might have an associated "book" that tells it how to respond to particular situations. The following code would get an `InputStream` for such a book:

```
String book = "BoldPlayer.book";
InputStream in;
ClassLoader loader = this.getClass().getClassLoader();
if (loader != null)
    in = loader.getResourceAsStream(book);
else
    in = ClassLoader.getSystemResourceAsStream(book);
```

System resources are associated with system classes, which are the classes that may have no class loader. The static method `getSystemResourceAsStream` returns an `InputStream` for a named resource. The preceding code checks to see whether it has a class loader. If it does not, it has been loaded by the system class loader; otherwise, it uses the class loader's `getResourceAsStream` method to turn its resource name into a byte input stream. The resource methods return `null` if the resource is not found.

The `Class` class provides a `getResourceAsStream` method to simplify getting resources from a class's class loader. The preceding code could be written more simply as:

```
String book = "BoldPlayer.book";
InputStream in = BoldPlayer.class.getResourceAsStream(book);
```

Resource names must be made up of one or more valid identifiers separated by / characters. This restriction helps class loaders use identical mappings for resources and class names.

The implementation of `getResourceAsStream` in `ClassLoader` just returns `null`. It is up to your specific class loader to override the method to use appropriate means to locate a resource. Usually this means that resources will be found in the same places and ways that classes are found. Here is an implementation of `getResourceAsStream` for `PlayerLoader`:

```
public InputStream getResourceAsStream(String name) {
    try {
        return streamFor(name);
    } catch (IOException e) {
        return null;
    }
}
```

This code uses the same `streamFor` method used by `loadClass` earlier, so the file `BoldPlayer.book` should live in the same place that `BoldPlayer.class` lives.

Two other resource methods—`getResource` and `getSystemResource`—return URL objects that name the resources. The class URL is covered briefly on page 537; it provides methods to use universal resource locators to access resources. You can invoke the `getContents` method on the URL objects returned by the class loader methods to get an object that represents the contents of that URL.

The `getResources` method returns an `Enumeration` object that steps through URL objects for all the resources stored under a given name. The static method `getSystemResources` does the same for system resources.

Just as `loadClass` is built on top of a `findClass` that you provide when you subclass `ClassLoader`, the resource methods are built on top of two methods that you can implement:

`public Enumeration` **`findResources(String name)`**
> Returns an `Enumeration` through all the resources of the given name. The default implementation in `ClassLoader` returns an enumeration through zero resources.

`public java.net.URL findResource` **`findResource(String name)`**
> Returns a `java.net.URL` for the resource of the given name, or `null` if none was found. If there are multiple resources of the same name the implementation determines which should be returned. The default implementation in `ClassLoader` always returns `null`.

The resource getting methods first query the parent class loader for the resource, or the system class loader if the class loader has no parent. If the resource cannot be found, then `findResources` or `findResource` is invoked. here is a `findResource` for `PlayerLoader`:

```
public java.net.URL findResource(String name) {
    File f = fileFor(name);
    if (!f.exists())
        return null;
    try {
        return f.toURL();
    } catch (java.net.MalformedURLException e) {
        return null;          // shouldn't happen
    }
}
```

The `fileFor` method is analogous to the `streamFor` method of `PlayerLoader`: it returns a `File` object that corresponds to the named resource in the file system. If the named file actually exists, then the URL for the resource is created from the path. (The `File` class represents a pathname in the file system; see "The `File` Class" on page 398.)

Exercise 11.9: Modify your results for Exercise 11.8 to allow player strategies to use attached resources by implementing `findResource` and `findResources`.

Be and not seem.
—Ralph Waldo Emerson

CHAPTER 12

Garbage Collection and Memory

Civilization is a limitless multiplication of unnecessary necessaries.
—Mark Twain

THE Java virtual machine uses a technique known as *garbage collection* to ensure that any referenced object will remain in memory, and to determine when an object is no longer referenced within a program, and so may be reclaimed to free up memory space. This chapter teaches the basic ideas behind garbage collection, how the programmer can be involved in the garbage collection process, and how special reference objects can be used to influence when an object may be considered garbage.

12.1 Garbage Collection

Objects are created using `new`, but there is no corresponding `delete` operation to reclaim the memory used by an object. When you are finished with an object, you simply stop referring to it—change your reference to refer to another object or to `null`, or return from a method so its local variables no longer exist and hence refer to nothing. Objects which are no longer referenced are termed *garbage*, and the process of finding and reclaiming these objects is known as *garbage collection*.

The Java virtual machine uses garbage collection to ensure that any referenced object will remain in memory, and to free up memory by deallocating objects that are no longer reachable from references in executing code. This is a strong guarantee—an object will not be collected if it can be reached by following a *chain* of references starting with a *root* reference, that is, a reference that is directly accessible from executing code.

In simple terms, when an object is no longer reachable from any executable code, the space it occupies can be reclaimed. We use the phrase "can be" because space is reclaimed at the garbage collector's discretion, usually only if more space is needed or if the collector wants to avoid running out of memory. A program may exit without running out of space or even coming close, and so may never need to perform garbage collection. An object is "no longer reachable" when no reference to the object exists in any variable of any currently executing method, nor can you find a reference to the object by starting from such variables and then following each field or array element, and so on.

Garbage collection means never having to worry about *dangling references*. In systems where you directly control when objects are deleted, you can delete an object to which some other object still has a reference. That other reference is now dangling, meaning it refers to space that the system considers free. Space that is thought to be free might be allocated to a new object, and the dangling reference would then reference something completely different from what the object thought it referenced. This situation could cause all manner of havoc when the program uses the values in that space as if they were part of something they are not. Garbage collection solves the dangling reference problem for you, because an object that's still referenced somewhere will never be garbage-collected and so will never be considered free. Garbage collection also solves the problem of accidently deleting an object multiple times—something that can also cause havoc.

Garbage is collected without your intervention, but collecting garbage still takes work. Creating and collecting large numbers of objects can interfere with time-critical applications, and you should design such systems to be judicious in the number of objects they create to reduce the amount of garbage to be collected.

Garbage collection is not a guarantee that memory will always be available for new objects. You could create objects indefinitely, place them in lists, and continue doing so until there is no more space and no unreferenced objects to reclaim. You could create a memory leak by, for example, allowing a list of objects to refer to objects you no longer need. Garbage collection solves many, but not all, memory allocation problems.

12.2 A Simple Model

Garbage collection is easier to understand with an explicit model, so we will describe a simple one—practical garbage collectors are far more sophisticated. Garbage collection is logically split into two phases: separating the *live* objects from the *dead* objects, and then reclaiming the storage of the dead ones. Live objects are those that are *reachable* from running code—the objects that some action of your code can still potentially use. Dead objects are the garbage that can be reclaimed.

One obvious model of garbage collection is reference counting: when object X references object Y, the system increments a counter on Y, and when X drops its reference to Y, the system decrements the counter. When the counter reaches zero, Y is no longer live, and can be collected, which will decrement the counts of any other objects to which Y refers.

Reference counting fails in the face of *cycles*, where loops are created in the references. If X and Y reference each other, neither object's counter will ever become zero, and so neither X nor Y will ever be collected, and neither will anything to which either object refers, directly or indirectly. Most garbage collectors do not use reference counting for this and other reasons.

The simplest model of garbage collection not subject to this problem is called *mark-and-sweep*. The name refers to the way the two phases of garbage collection are implemented. To find which objects are live, first a set of *roots* is determined which contains the set of directly reachable objects: references in local variables on the stack, for example, are reachable because you can use those variables to manipulate the object. Objects referred to by local variables are therefore clearly live.

Once a set of roots is determined, the collector will mark the objects referenced by those roots as reachable. It will then examine references in each of those objects. If an object referred to by such a reference is already marked reachable from the first step, it is ignored. Otherwise the object is marked reachable and *its* references are examined. This process is continued until no more reachable objects remain unmarked. After this marking process is complete, the dead objects (those which are not marked) can be reclaimed by sweeping them away.

Any change to the interconnection of objects during a run of mark-and-sweep will clearly interfere with the collection process. A marking run can miss an object that was unreachable at the beginning of the marking process, but which is assigned to a reachable reference in the middle. Running a basic mark-and-sweep pass requires freezing execution of the program, at least during the marking phase.

There are other problems with mark-and-sweep. Garbage collection is a complex area of research with no easy or universal answers. We present mark-and-sweep as a relatively simple mental model for you to use to understand garbage collection. Each virtual machine has its own collection strategy, and some let you choose among several. Use this mark-and-sweep model as a mental model only— do not assume that this is how any particular virtual machine actually works.

12.3 Finalization

You won't normally notice when an orphaned object's space is reclaimed—"it just works." But a class can implement a `finalize` method that is executed before an object's space is reclaimed. Such a `finalize` method gives you a chance to use the state contained in the object to reclaim other non-memory resources. The `finalize` method is declared in the `Object` class:

protected void **finalize()** throws Throwable

> Invoked by the garbage collector when it has been determined that this object is no longer reachable and its space is to be reclaimed. This method might clean up any non-memory resources used by this object. It is invoked at most once per object, even if execution of this method causes the object to become reachable again and later it becomes unreachable again. There is no guarantee, however, that `finalize` will be called in any specific time period; it may never be called at all. This method is declared to throw any exception but if an exception occurs it is ignored by the garbage collector. The virtual machine makes no guarantees about which thread will execute the `finalize` method of any given object, but it does guarantee that the thread will not hold any user-visible synchronization locks.

You should only rarely need to write a `finalize` method, and when you do so you should write it with great care. If your object has become garbage it is quite possible that other objects to which it refers are also garbage. As garbage, they may have been finalized before your `finalize` method is invoked, and may therefore be in an unexpected state.

Garbage collection collects only memory. When you are dealing with non-memory resources that are not reclaimed by garbage collection, finalizers look like a neat solution. For example, open files are usually a limited resource, so closing them when you can is good behavior. But this usually cannot wait until the `finalize` phase of garbage collection. The code that asks you to perform an operation that opens a file should tell you when it's done—there is no guarantee that your object holding the open file will be collected before all the open file resources are used up.

Still, your objects that allocate external resources could provide a `finalize` method that cleans them up so the class doesn't itself create a resource leak. For example, a class that opens a file to do its work should have some form of `close` method to close the file, enabling programmers using that class to manage the number-of-open-files resource explicitly. The `finalize` method can then invoke `close`. Just don't rely on this to prevent users of the class from having problems. They might get lucky and have the finalizer executed before they run out of open files, but that is risky—finalization is a safety-net to be used as a last resort, after the programmer has failed to release the resource manually. If you were to write such a method, it might look like this:

```
public class ProcessFile {
    private FileReader file;

    public ProcessFile(String path) throws
        FileNotFoundException
    {
        file = new FileReader(path);
    }

    // ...

    public synchronized void close() throws IOException {
        if (file != null) {
            file.close();
            file = null;
        }
    }

    protected void finalize() throws Throwable {
        try {
            close();
        } finally {
            super.finalize();
        }
    }
}
```

Note that `close` is carefully written to be correct if it is invoked more than once. Otherwise, if someone invoked `close`, finalizing the object would cause another close on the file, which might not be allowed.

Note also that, in this example, `finalize` invokes `super.finalize` in a `finally` clause. Train yourself so that you always do so in any `finalize` method you write. If you don't invoke `super.finalize`, you may correctly finalize your own part of the object, but the superclass's part will not get finalized. Invoking `super.finalize` is one of those good habits you should adopt even when your class doesn't extend any other class. In addition to being good training, invoking `super.finalize` in such a case means that you can always add a superclass to a class like `ProcessFile` without remembering to examine its `finalize` method for correctness. Invoking the superclass's `finalize` method in a `finally` clause ensures that the superclass's cleanup will happen even if your cleanup causes an exception.

The garbage collector may reclaim objects in any order or never reclaim them. Memory resources are reclaimed when the garbage collector thinks the time is appropriate. Not being bound to an ordering guarantee, the garbage collector can operate in whatever manner is most efficient, and that helps minimize the overhead of garbage collection. You can, if necessary, invoke the garbage collector to try to force earlier collection using `System.gc` or `Runtime.gc`, as you'll see in the next section, but there is no guarantee that garbage collection will actually occur.

When an application exits, no further garbage collection is performed, so any objects that have not yet been collected will not have their `finalize` methods invoked. In many cases this will not be a problem. For example, on most systems when the virtual machine exits, the underlying system automatically closes all open files and sockets. However, for non-system resources you will have to invent other solutions. (Temporary files can be marked as "delete on exit," which solves one of the more common issues—see "The `File` Class" on page 398.)

12.3.1 Resurrecting Objects during `finalize`

A `finalize` method can "resurrect" an object by making it referenced again—for example, by adding it to a static list of objects. Resurrection is discouraged, but there is nothing the system can do to stop you.

However, the virtual machine invokes `finalize` at most once on any object, even if that object is collected more than once because a previous `finalize` resurrected it. If resurrecting objects is important to your design, the object would be resurrected only once—probably not the behavior you wanted.

If you think you need to resurrect objects, you should review your design carefully—you may uncover a flaw. If your design review convinces you that you need something like resurrection, the best solution is to clone the object or create a new object, not to resurrect it. The `finalize` method can insert a reference to a new object that will continue the state of the dying object rather than a reference to the dying object itself. Being new, the cloned object's `finalize` method will be invoked in the future (if needed), enabling it to insert yet another copy of itself in yet another list, ensuring the survival, if not of itself, at least of its progeny.

12.4 Interacting with the Garbage Collector

Although the language has no explicit way to dispose of unwanted objects, you can directly invoke the garbage collector to look for unused objects. The `Runtime` class, together with some convenience methods in the System class, allows you to invoke the garbage collector, request that any pending finalizers be run and allows you to query the current memory state:

public void **gc()**
> Requests that the virtual machine expend effort towards recycling unused objects so that their memory can be reused.

public void **runFinalization()**
> Requests that the virtual machine expend effort running the finalizers of objects that are unreachable, but which have not yet had their finalizers run.

public long **freeMemory()**
> Returns an estimate of free bytes in system memory.

public long **totalMemory()**
> Returns the total bytes in system memory.

To invoke these methods you need to obtain a reference to the current Runtime object via the static method Runtime.getRuntime. The System class supports static gc and runFinalization methods that invoke the corresponding methods on the current Runtime—that is, System.gc() is equivalent to Runtime.getRuntime().gc().

The garbage collector may not be able to free any additional memory when Runtime.gc is invoked. There may be no garbage to collect, and not all garbage collectors can find collectable objects on demand. So invoking the garbage collector may have no effect whatsoever. However, before creating a large number of objects—especially in a time-critical application that might be affected by garbage-collection overhead—invoking gc may be advisable. Doing so has two potential benefits: you start with as much free memory as possible, and you reduce the likelihood of the garbage collector running during the task. Here is a method that aggressively frees everything it can at the moment:

```
public static void fullGC() {
    Runtime rt = Runtime.getRuntime();
    long isFree = rt.freeMemory();
    long wasFree;
    do {
        wasFree = isFree;
        rt.runFinalization();
        rt.gc();
        isFree = rt.freeMemory();
    } while (isFree > wasFree);
}
```

This method loops while the amount of freeMemory is being increased by successive calls to runFinalization and gc. When the amount of free memory doesn't increase, further calls will likely do nothing.

You will not usually need to invoke runFinalization, because finalize methods are called asynchronously by the garbage collector. Under some circumstances, such as running out of a resource that a finalize method reclaims, it is useful to force as much finalization as possible. But remember, there is no guarantee that any object actually awaiting finalization is using some of that resource, so runFinalization may be of no help.

The fullGC method is too aggressive for most purposes. In the unusual circumstance that you need to force garbage collection, a single invocation of the System.gc method will gather most if not all of the available garbage. Repeated invocations are progressively less productive—on many systems they will be completely unproductive.

12.5 Reachability States and Reference Objects

An object can be garbage collected only when there are no references to it, but sometimes you would like an object to be garbage collected even though you may have a specific reference to it. For example, suppose you are writing a web browser. There will be images that have been seen by the user, but that are not currently visible. If memory becomes tight, you can theoretically free up some memory by writing those images to disk, or even by forgetting about them since you can presumably re-fetch them later if needed. But since the objects representing the images are referenced from running code (and hence *reachable*) they will not be released. We would like to be able to have a reference to an object that doesn't force the object to remain reachable, if that is the only reference to the object. Such special references are provided by *reference objects*.

A reference object is an object whose sole purpose is to maintain a reference to another object, called the *referent*. Instead of maintaining direct references to objects, via fields or local variables, you maintain a direct reference to a reference object that wraps the actual object you are interested in. The garbage collector can determine that the only references to an object are through reference objects and so can decide whether to reclaim that object—if the object is reclaimed then, usually, the reference object is cleared so that it no longer refers to that object. The strength of a reference object determines how the garbage collector will behave—normal references are the strongest references.

12.5.1 The Reference Class

The classes for the reference object types are contained in the package `java.lang.ref`. The primary class is the abstract class `Reference`, which is the superclass of all the specific reference classes. `Reference` has four methods:

`public Object get()`
> Returns this reference object's referent object.

`public void clear()`
> Clears this reference object so it has no referent object.

`public boolean enqueue()`
> Adds this reference object to the reference queue with which it is registered, if any. Returns `true` if the reference object was enqueued and `false` if there is no registered queue, or this reference object was already enqueued.

`public boolean isEnqueued()`
> Returns `true` if this reference object has been enqueued (either by the programmer or the garbage collector), and `false` otherwise.

We defer a discussion of reference queues until Section 12.5.3 on page 324.

Subclasses of `Reference` must provide the means for binding the referent object to the reference object—the defined subclasses do this via a constructor argument. Once an object has been wrapped in a reference object you can retrieve the object via `get` (and thus have a normal strong reference to it), or you can `clear` the reference, perhaps making the referent unreachable. There is no means to change the object referred to by the reference object and you cannot subclass `Reference` directly.

12.5.2 Strengths of Reference and Reachability

In decreasing order of strength, the kinds of reference objects available to you are `SoftReference`, `WeakReference`, and `PhantomReference`. These correspond to the reachability stages an object can pass through:

- An object is *strongly reachable* if it can be reached through at least one chain of strong references (the normal kind of references).
- An object is *softly reachable* if it is not strongly reachable, but is reachable through at least one chain containing a soft reference.
- An object is *weakly reachable* if it is not softly reachable, but is reachable through at least one chain containing a weak reference.
- An object is *finalizer reachable* if it is not weakly reachable, but the object's `finalize` method has not yet been invoked. (If the object's class does not

override the finalize method defined in Object, this stage may be skipped.)

◆ An object is *phantom reachable* when it has been finalized, but is reachable through at least one chain containing a phantom reference.[1]

◆ Finally, an object is *unreachable* if it cannot be reached through references of any type.

Objects need not go through all these stages. For example, an object that is reachable only through strong references becomes finalizer reachable when it is no longer strongly reachable.

The reachability stages of an object trigger behavior in the garbage collector appropriate to the corresponding reference object types:

◆ A softly reachable object may be reclaimed at the discretion of the garbage collector. If memory is low the garbage collector may decide to clear a SoftReference object so its referent can be reclaimed. There are no specific rules for the order in which this is done (but a good implementation will bias against clearing recently used or created references—where "used" is defined as "invoked get"). You can be sure that all SoftReferences to softly reachable objects will be cleared before an OutOfMemoryError is thrown.

◆ A weakly reachable object will be reclaimed by the garbage collector. When the garbage collector determines that an object is weakly reachable, all WeakReference objects that refer to that object will be cleared. The object then becomes finalizer reachable and after finalization will be reclaimed (assuming it is not resurrected).

◆ A phantom reachable object isn't really reachable in the normal sense as the referent object cannot be accessed via a PhantomReference—get always returns null. Phantom references allow you to deal with objects whose finalize methods have been invoked and so can safely be considered "dead." Phantom references are used in conjunction with the reference queues we discuss in the next section.

Both SoftReference and WeakReference declare a constructor that takes a single referent object. All three classes declare a two argument constructor that takes referent object and a ReferenceQueue.

---

[1] Of course, if the object was resurrected during finalization its finalizer will have been invoked but it will be more than phantom reachable. This violation of the normal flow of reachability is one more reason to avoid resurrection.

Soft references provide you with a kind of caching behavior, clearing older references while trying not to clear new or used ones. Consider our web browser scenario. If we maintain our images via soft references, they will be reclaimed as memory runs low. Images are probably relatively unimportant to keep in memory should memory run low, and clearing the oldest or least used images would be a reasonable approach. In contrast, if we used weak references then all images would be reclaimed as soon as memory got low—this would probably induce a lot of overhead as we reload images that it may not have been necessary to get rid of in the first place.

Weak references are a way of holding a reference to an object but saying, "reclaim this object if this is the only type of reference to it."

Consider the following method which returns data read into memory from a file. The method has been optimized under the assumption that the same file is often named more than once in a row without reading from another file, and that reading the data is expensive:

```java
import java.lang.ref.*;
import java.io.File;

class DataHandler {
    private File lastFile;          // last file read
    private WeakReference lastData; // last data (maybe)

    byte[] readFile(File file) {
        byte[] data;

        // check to see if we remember the data
        if (file.equals(lastFile)) {
            data = (byte[]) lastData.get();
            if (data != null)
                return data;
        }

        // don't remember it, read it in
        data = readBytesFromFile(file);
        lastFile = file;
        lastData = new WeakReference(data);
        return data;
    }
}
```

When `readData` is called it first checks to see if the last file read was the same as the one being requested. If it is, it retrieves the reference stored in `lastData`, which is a weak reference to the last array of bytes returned. If the reference returned by `get` is `null`, the data has been garbage collected since it was last returned, and so it must be reread. The data is then wrapped in a new `WeakReference`. If `get` returns a non-`null` reference, the array has not been collected and can be returned.

If `lastData` were a direct, strong reference to the last data returned, that data would not be collected, even if the invoking program had long since dropped all references to the array. Such a strong reference would keep the object alive as long as the `DataHandler` object itself was reachable. This could be quite unfortunate. Using a `WeakReference` allows the space to be reclaimed, at the cost of occasionally rereading the data from disk.

Notice that invoking `get` on `lastData` makes the byte array strongly reachable once again because its value is bound to an active local variable—a strong reference. If `get` returns a non-`null` reference there is no possibility of the byte array being reclaimed as long as `readFile` is executing, or the block of code to which `readFile` returns the reference is executing. That invoking code can store the reference in a reachable place, or return it to another method, thus ensuring the data's reachability. An object can only be less than strongly reachable when none of its references are strong. Storing a non-`null` reference from a reference object's `get` method creates a strong reference which will be treated like any other strong reference.

Weak references are typically used to store annotations about an object that might be time-consuming to compute but which need not outlive the object itself. For example, if you had some complicated information built up from using reflection on an object, you might use the `WeakHashMap` class provided in `java.util`, which is a hashtable for mapping a weakly-held object to your annotation. If the object becomes unreachable the `WeakHashMap` will clean up the associated information, which presumably is no longer useful (since the object will not be used in any future computation due to its weak reachability). You will learn about `WeakHashMap` with the rest of the collection classes in Chapter 16, specifically in Section 16.7.3 on page 441.

Exercise 12.1: Modify `DataHandler` so that `lastFile` is also stored weakly.

12.5.3 Reference Queues

When an object changes reachability state, references to the object may be placed on a *reference queue*. These queues are used by the garbage collector to communicate with your code about reachability changes. They are usually the best way to detect such changes, although you can sometimes poll for changes as well.

For example, suppose you want a hash map that has weak references to its values instead of its keys, as `WeakHashMap` provides. With such a map, you can set up an association between a key, whose equivalent objects might come and go, and a value. For example, you might want to associate a class location with a class loader (see "Loading Classes" on page 303). Each time a new object arrives that should be loaded from the same location, you should use the same class loader. The class location would be a small object, such as a `String` or `File` object, that would be created anew for each incoming class. The class loader, on the other hand, is large, references numerous other objects, and should be collected whenever it is no longer referenced. Using a `WeakHashMap` to associate the code location key with the class loader value would be backwards: the key could get collected whenever loading was not in progress.

The following code creates such a "weak value" hash map, using a reference queue to notice when values have become weakly reachable. When the value of a key/value pair is only weakly reachable, the mapping is removed from the table. With the mapping removed, the key is no longer reachable from the map itself, and so may be reclaimed by the garbage collector (unless someone else is also holding a reference):

```java
import java.lang.ref.*;
import java.util.*;

public class WeakValueMap extends HashMap {
    private ReferenceQueue reaped = new ReferenceQueue();

    private static class ValueRef extends WeakReference {
        private final Object key;       // key for value

        ValueRef(Object val, Object key, ReferenceQueue q) {
            super(val, q);
            this.key = key;
        }
    }

    public Object put(Object key, Object value) {
        reap();
        ValueRef vr = new ValueRef(value, key, reaped);
        return super.put(key, vr);
    }
```

```java
    public Object get(Object key) {
        reap();
        ValueRef vr = (ValueRef)super.get(key);
        return vr.get();
    }

    public int size() {
        reap();
        return super.size();
    }

    // ... implement other Map methods similarly ...

    public void reap() {
        ValueRef ref;
        while ((ref = (ValueRef)reaped.poll()) != null)
            super.remove(ref.key);
    }
}
```

WeakValueMap is a HashMap that holds references to its values weakly, using its own ValueRef class, a subclass of WeakReference that remembers the key for efficient removal. When a value becomes weakly reachable, its ValueRef will be placed on the reaped queue. Each operation on the map first invokes the reap method, which removes from the map any entry whose reference is in the queue. Keys for mappings that are removed are no longer referenced by the map itself, so the garbage collector can reclaim them if no other reference exist from anywhere else. Note that there is little point using weak references for objects that are always strongly reachable, such as active Thread objects.

As noted in the comment, the full implementation of WeakValueMap overrides all the methods of HashMap that deal with keys to use code analogous to that shown in put and get.

The ReferenceQueue class provides three methods for removing references from the queue:

public Reference poll()
Removes and returns the next reference object from this queue, or null if the queue is empty.

public Reference remove() throws InterruptedException
Removes and returns the next reference object from this queue. This method blocks indefinitely until a reference object is available from the queue.

`public Reference` **`remove(long timeout)`** `throws InterruptedException`
> Removes and returns the next reference object from this queue. This method blocks until a reference object is available from the queue, or the specified time-out period elapses. If the time-out expires, `null` is returned. A time-out of zero means wait indefinitely.

Reference objects can be associated with a particular queue when they are constructed, as shown in the `WeakValueMap` example. Both weak and soft references are enqueued at some point after the garbage collector determines their reachability state, and in both cases the reference objects are cleared before being enqueued.

The `poll` method allows a thread to query the existence of a reference in a queue, taking action only if one is present, as in the example. The `remove` methods are intended for more complex (and rare) situations where a dedicated thread is responsible for removing references from the queue and taking the appropriate action—the blocking behavior of these methods is the same as that defined by `Object.wait` (as discussed from page 244). You can ask whether a particular reference is in a queue by invoking its `isEnqueued` method, though this doesn't remove the reference from the queue. You can force a reference into its queue by calling its `enqueue` method, but usually this is done by the garbage collector.

Reference queues are used with phantom references to determine when an object is about to be reclaimed. A phantom reference never lets you reach the object, even when it is otherwise reachable: its `get` method always returns `null`. In effect it is the safest way to find out about a collected object—a weak, or soft, reference will be enqueued after an object is finalizer reachable; a phantom reference is enqueued after the referent has been finalized and, therefore only after the last possible time that the object can do something. You should generally use a phantom reference if you can, because the other references still allow the possibility that a `finalize` method will use the object.

A phantom reference is not cleared when placed in the reference queue and so the referent object cannot be reclaimed until either the phantom reference is explicitly cleared, or the reference itself becomes unreachable.

Exercise 12.2: Complete the implementation of `WeakValueMap` so that all methods that deal with values are handled properly. Don't forget about the iterators, especially what happens if `hasNext` returns `true`.

Exercise 12.3: Rewrite `WeakValueMap` to be `PhantomValueMap`.

> *Don't ever take a fence down until you know the reason why it was put up.*
> —G.K. Chesterton

CHAPTER **13**

Packages

A library is an arsenal of liberty.
—Unknown

PACKAGES define units of software that can be distributed independently and combined with other packages to form applications. Packages have members that are related classes, interfaces, and subpackages, and may contain additional resource files (such as images) used by the classes in the package. Packages are useful for several reasons:

- Packages create groupings for related interfaces and classes. For example, a set of library classes for performing statistical analysis could be grouped together in a `stats` package. The package can be placed in an archive file, together with a manifest describing the package, and shipped to customers for use in their applications.

- Packages create namespaces that help avoid naming conflicts between types. Interfaces and classes in a package can use popular public names (such as `List` and `Constants`) that make sense in one context but might conflict with the same name in another package.

- Packages provide a protection domain for developing application frameworks. Code within a package can cooperate using access to identifiers that are unavailable to external code.

Let us look at a package for the attribute classes you saw in previous chapters. We will name the package `attr`. Each source file whose classes and interfaces belong in the `attr` package states its membership with its `package` declaration:

```
package attr;
```

This statement declares that all classes and interfaces defined in this source file are part of the `attr` package. A `package` declaration must appear first in your source file, before any class or interface declarations. Only one package declaration can appear in a source file. The package name is implicitly prefixed to each type name contained within the package.

If a type is not declared as being part of an explicit package, it is placed in an unnamed package. Every system must support at least one unnamed package, but they can support more—typically one per class loader. The existence of the unnamed package makes it simple to write small programs without being encumbered by the organizational requirements imposed on the members of named packages.

13.1 Package Naming

A package name should prevent collisions with other packages, so choosing a name that's both meaningful and unique is an important aspect of package design. But with programmers around the globe developing packages, there is no way to find out who is using what package names. Choosing unique package names is therefore a problem. If you are certain a package will be used only inside your organization, you can choose a name using an internal arbiter to ensure that no two projects pick clashing names.

But in the world at large, this approach is insufficient. Package identifiers are simple names. A good way to ensure unique package names is to use an Internet domain name. If you work at a company named Magic, Inc., that owns the domain name `magic.com`, the attribute package declaration should be

```
package com.magic.attr;
```

Notice that the components of the domain name are reversed from the normal domain name convention.

If you use this convention, your package names should not conflict with those of anyone else, except possibly within your organization. If such conflicts arise (likely in a large organization), you can further qualify using a more specific domain. Many large companies have internal subdomains with names such as `east` and `europe`. You could further qualify the package name using such a subdomain name:

```
package com.magic.japan.attr;
```

Package names can become quite long under this scheme, but it is relatively safe. No one else using this technique will choose the same package name, and programmers not using the technique are unlikely to pick your names.

13.2 Type Imports

The name of a type preceded by its package (and a dot) is known as the *fully qualified name* of the type. For example, the fully qualified name of the `String` class is `java.lang.String`. When you write code outside a package that needs types declared within that package you have two options. One is to use the fully qualified name of the type. This option is reasonable if you use only a few items from a package, but given the long names that packages tend to acquire (or even the shorter ones in the standard libraries) it can be quite tedious to use fully qualified names.

The other way to use types from a package is to *import* part or all of the package. A programmer who wants to use the `attr` package could put the following line near the top of a source file (after any `package` declaration but before anything else):

```
import attr.*;
```

Then the types in that package can be referred to simply by name, such as `Attributed`. An import that uses a * is called an *import on demand* declaration. You can also perform a *single type import:*

```
import attr.Attributed;
```

Code in a package imports the rest of its own package implicitly, so everything defined in a package is available to all types in the same package. The package `java.lang` is implicitly imported in all code.

The `import` mechanism is passive in that it does not cause information about the named packages and types to be read in at compile time—unless a type is used. The `import` statement simply tells the compiler how it can determine the fully qualified name for a type that is used in your program, if it can't find that type defined locally. For example, as described on page 155, if your class declares a reference of type `Attributed` the compiler will search for the type as follows:

1. The current type including inherited types.

2. A nested type of the current type.

3. Explicitly named imported types (single type import).

4. Other types declared in the same package.

5. Implicitly named imported types (import on demand).

If, after that, the type is still not found it is an error.

Type imports can also be used with nested class names. For example, in Chapter 5 we defined the BankAcount class and its nested Permissions class. If these classes were in the package bank and you imported bank.BankAccount, you would still need to use BankAccount.Permissions to name the Permissions class. However, you could instead import bank.BankAccount.Permissions and then use the simple name Permissions. You don't have to import BankAccount to import the class BankAccount.Permissions. Importing nested type names in this way loses the important information that the type is actually a nested type and should generally be avoided.

The package and import mechanisms give programmers control over potentially conflicting names. If a package used for another purpose, such as linguistics, has a class called Attributed for language attributes, programmers who want to use both types in the same source file have several options:

♦ Refer to all types by their fully qualified names, such as attr.Attributed and lingua.Attributed.

♦ Import only attr.Attributed or attr.*, use the simple name Attributed for attr.Attributed, and use the full name of lingua.Attributed.

♦ Do the converse: import lingua.Attributed or lingua.*, use the simple name Attributed for lingua.Attributed, and use the full name of attr.Attributed.

♦ Import all of both packages—attr.* and lingua.*—and use the fully qualified names attr.Attributed and lingua.Attributed in your code. (If a type with the same name exists in two packages imported on demand, you cannot use the simple name of either type.)

It is an error to import a specific type that exists as a top-level (that is non-nested) type within the current source file. For example, you can't declare your own Vector class and import java.util.Vector. Nor can you import the same type name from two different packages using two single type imports. As noted above, if two types of the same name are implicitly imported on demand, you cannot use the simple type name but must use the fully qualified name. Use of the simple name would be ambiguous and result in a compile-time error.

13.3 Package Access

You have two options when declaring accessibility of top-level classes and interfaces within a package: package and public. A public class or interface is accessible to code outside that package. Types that are not public have package scope:

they are available to all other code in the same package, but are hidden outside the package and even from code in subpackages. Declare as `public` only those types needed by programmers using your package, hiding types that are package implementation details. This technique gives you flexibility when you want to change the implementation—programmers cannot rely on implementation types they cannot access, and that leaves you free to change them.

A class member that is not declared `public`, `protected`, or `private` can be used by any code within the package, but is hidden outside the package. In other words, the default access for an identifier is "package" except for members of interfaces, which are public.

Fields or methods not declared `private` in a package are available to all other code in that package. Thus, classes within the same package are considered "friendly" or "trusted." This allows you to define application frameworks that are a combination of predefined code and placeholder code that is designed to be overridden by subclasses of the framework classes. The predefined code can use package access to invoke code intended for use by the cooperating package classes, while making that code inaccessible to any external users of the package. However, subpackages are not trusted in enclosing packages or vice versa. For example, package identifiers in package `dit` are not available to code in package `dit.dat`, or vice versa.

Every type has therefore three different contracts that it defines:

- The public contract, defining the primary functionality of the type.
- The protected contract, defining the functionality available to subtypes for specialization purposes.
- The package contract, defining the functionality available within the package to effect cooperation between package types.

All of these contracts require careful consideration and design.

13.3.1 Accessibility and Overriding Methods

A method can be overridden in a subclass only if the method is accessible in the superclass. If the method is not accessible in the superclass then the method in the subclass does *not* override the method in the superclass even if it has the same signature. When a method is invoked at run time the system has to consider the accessibility of the method when deciding which implementation of the method to invoke.

The following contrived example should make this clearer. Suppose we have a class `AbstractBase` declared in package P1 as follows:

```
package P1;

public abstract class AbstractBase {
    private   void pri() { print("AbstractBase.pri()"); }
              void pac() { print("AbstractBase.pac()"); }
    protected void pro() { print("AbstractBase.pro()"); }
    public    void pub() { print("AbstractBase.pub()"); }

    public final void show() {
        pri();
        pac();
        pro();
        pub();
    }
}
```

We have four methods, each with a different access modifier, each of which simply identifies itself. The method `show` invokes each of these methods on the current object. Because `show` is final it cannot be overridden and it will show which implementation of each method is invoked when applied to different subclass objects.

Now we define the class `Concrete1` which extends `AbstractBase`, but which resides in the package P2:

```
package P2;

import P1.AbstractBase;

public class Concrete1 extends AbstractBase {
    public void pri() { print("Concrete1.pri()"); }
    public void pac() { print("Concrete1.pac()"); }
    public void pro() { print("Concrete1.pro()"); }
    public void pub() { print("Concrete1.pub()"); }
}
```

This class redeclares each of the methods from the superclass and changes their implementation to report that they are in class `Concrete1`. It also changes their access to `public` so that they are accessible to all other code. Executing the code

```
new Concrete1().show();
```

produces the following output:

```
AbstractBase.pri()
AbstractBase.pac()
Concrete1.pro()
Concrete1.pub()
```

The private method `pri` is inaccessible to subclasses (or to any other class) and so the implementation from `AbstractBase` is always the one invoked from `show`. The package accessible `pac` method of `AbstractBase` is not accessible in `Concrete1` and so the implementation of `pac` in `Concrete1` does not override that in `AbstractBase`, so it is `AbstractBase.pac` that `show` invokes. Both the `pro` and `pub` methods are accessible in `Concrete1` and get overridden, so the implementation from `Concrete1` is used in `show`.

Next we define the class `Concrete2`, which extends `Concrete1`, but which is in the same package P1 as `AbstractBase`:[1]

```
package P1;

import P2.Concrete1;

public class Concrete2 extends Concrete1 {
    public void pri() { print("Concrete2.pri()"); }
    public void pac() { print("Concrete2.pac()"); }
    public void pro() { print("Concrete2.pro()"); }
    public void pub() { print("Concrete2.pub()"); }
}
```

Each method of `Concrete2` overrides the version from `Concrete1` because they are all public and therefore accessible. Also, because `Concrete2` is in the same package as `AbstractBase`, the method `AbstractBase.pac` is accessible in `Concrete2` and so is overridden by `Concrete2.pac`. Invoking `show` on a `Concrete2` object prints:

```
AbstractBase.pri()
Concrete2.pac()
Concrete2.pro()
Concrete2.pub()
```

---

[1] Having an inheritance hierarchy that weaves in and out of a package is generally a very bad idea. It is used here purely for illustration.

Finally, we define the class `Concrete3`, which extends `Concrete2`, but is in a different package P3:

```
package P3;

import P1.Concrete2;

public class Concrete3 extends Concrete2 {
    public void pri() { print("Concrete3.pri()"); }
    public void pac() { print("Concrete3.pac()"); }
    public void pro() { print("Concrete3.pro()"); }
    public void pub() { print("Concrete3.pub()"); }
}
```

Invoking show on a `Concrete3` object prints:

```
AbstractBase.pri()
Concrete3.pac()
Concrete3.pro()
Concrete3.pub()
```

Here the method `Concrete3.pac` appears to have overridden the inaccessible `AbstractBase.pac`. In fact, `Concrete3.pac` overrides `Concrete2.pac`, and `Concrete2.pac` overrides `AbstractBase.pac`—therefore `Concrete3.pac` transitively overrides `AbstractBase.pac`. By redeclaring pac as public, `Concrete2` made it accessible and overridable by any subclass.[2]

13.4 Package Contents

Packages should be designed carefully so they contain only functionally related classes and interfaces. Classes in a package can freely access each other's non-private members. Protecting class members is intended to prevent misuse by classes that have access to internal details of other classes. Anything not declared `private` is available to all types in the package, so unrelated classes could end up working more intimately than expected with other classes.

Packages should also provide logical groupings for programmers who are looking for useful interfaces and classes. A package of unrelated classes makes the programmer work harder to figure out what is available. Logical grouping of classes helps programmers reuse your code, because they can more easily find

---

[2] This illustrates why weaving in and out of a package can be confusing and should be avoided.

what they need. Including only related, coherent sets of types in a package also means that you can use obvious names for types, avoiding name conflicts.

Packages can be nested inside other packages. For example, `java.lang` is a nested package in which `lang` is nested inside the larger `java` package. The `java` package contains only other packages. Nesting allows a hierarchical naming system for related packages.

For example, to create a set of packages for adaptive systems such as neural networks and genetic algorithms, you could create nested packages by naming the packages with dot-separated names:

```
package adaptive.neuralNet;
```

A source file with this declaration lives in the `adaptive.neuralNet` package, which is itself a subpackage of the `adaptive` package. The `adaptive` package might contain classes related to general adaptive algorithms, such as generic problem statement classes or benchmarking. Each package deeper in the hierarchy—such as `adaptive.neuralNet` or `adaptive.genetic`—would contain classes specific to the particular kind of adaptive algorithm.

Package nesting is an organizational tool for related packages, but it provides no special access between packages. Class code in `adaptive.genetic` cannot access package-accessible identifiers of the `adaptive` or `adaptive.neuralNet` packages. Package scope applies only to a particular package. Nesting can group related packages and help programmers find classes in a logical hierarchy, but it confers no other benefits.

13.5 Package Objects and Specifications

Packages typically implement a specification, and are also typically from one organization. A `Package` object, unlike the other reflective types (see Chapter 11), is not used to create or manipulate packages, but acts as a repository for information about the specification implemented by a package (its title, vendor and version number) and also information about the implementation itself (its title, vendor and versions number). Although a package typically comes from a single organization, the specification for that package (such as a statistical analysis library) may have been defined by someone else. Programs using a package may need to be able to determine the version of the specification implemented by the package, so that they use only functionality defined in that version. Similarly, programs may need to know which version of the implementation is provided, primarily to deal with bugs that may exist in different versions. The main methods of `Package` allow access to this information:

`public String` **`getName()`**
> Returns the name of this package.

`public String` **`getSpecificationTitle()`**
> Returns the title of the specification this package implements, or `null` if the title is unknown.

`public String` **`getSpecificationVersion()`**
> Returns a string describing the version of the specification that this package implements, or `null` if the version is unknown.

`public String` **`getSpecificationVendor()`**
> Returns the name of the vendor that owns and maintains the specification that this package implements, or `null` if the vendor is unknown.

`public String` **`getImplementationTitle()`**
> Returns the title of the implementation provided by this package, or `null` if the title is unknown.

`public String` **`getImplementationVersion()`**
> Returns a string describing the version of the implementation provided by this package, or `null` if the version is unknown.

`public String` **`getImplementationVendor()`**
> Returns the name of the organization (vendor) that provided this implementation, or `null` if the organization is unknown.

For example, extracting this information for the `java.lang` package on our system yielded the following:

```
Specification Title:    Java Platform API Specification
Specification Version:  1.3
Specification Vendor:   Sun Microsystems, Inc.
Implementation Title:   Java Runtime Environment
Implementation Version: 1.3
Implementation Vendor:  Sun Microsystems, Inc.
```

Specification version numbers are non-negative numbers separated by periods, as in "2.0" or "11.0.12". This pattern allows you to invoke the `isCompatibleWith` method to compare a version following this pattern with the version of the package. The method returns `true` if the package's specification version number is greater than or equal to the one passed in. Comparison is done one dot-separated number at a time. If any such value in the package's number is greater than that from the passed in version, the versions are not compatible. If one of the version numbers has more components than the other, the missing components in the shorter version number are considered to be zero. For example, if the package's specification version is "1.2", and you compare it to "1.2",

"1.2.0", or "1.1.8", you will get `true`, but if you compare it to "1.2.2" or "1.3" you will get `false`. This comparison mechanism assumes backward compatibility between specification versions.

Implementation version numbers do not have a defined format as these will be defined by the different organizations providing the implementations. The only comparison you can perform between implementation versions is a test for equality—there is no assumption of backward compatibility.

Packages can be *sealed,* which means that no classes can be added to them. An unsealed package can have classes come from several different places in a class search path. A sealed package's contents must all come from one place—generally either a specific archive file, or a location specified by a URL. There are two methods that query if a package is sealed:

public boolean **isSealed()**
> Returns `true` if the package is sealed.

public boolean **isSealed(URL url)**
> Returns `true` if the package is sealed with respect to the given URL, that is, classes in the package can be loaded from the URL. Returns `false` if classes in the package cannot be loaded from the given URL or if the package is unsealed.

The specification and implementation information for a package is usually supplied as part of the manifest stored with the package—such as the manifest of a Java Archive (jar) file, as described in "Archive Files—`java.util.jar`" on page 544. This information is read when a class gets loaded from that package. A `ClassLoader` can define a `Package` object dynamically for the classes it loads:

protected Package **definePackage(String name, String specTitle,**
    String specVersion, String specVendor, String implTitle,
    String implVersion, String implVendor, URL sealBase)
> Returns a `Package` object with the given name, and with specification and implementation values set to the corresponding arguments. If `sealBase` is `null` the package is unsealed, otherwise it is sealed with respect to that URL. The `Package` object for a class must be defined before the class is defined and package names must be unique within a class loader. If the package name duplicates an existing name, an `IllegalArgumentException` is thrown.

You can get the `Package` object for a given class from the `getPackage` method of the `Class` object for that class. You can also get a `Package` object by invoking the static method `Package.getPackage` with the name of the package, or the static method `Package.getPackages` which returns an array of all known packages. Both of these methods work with respect to the class loader of the code making the call by invoking the `getPackage` or `getPackages` method of that class loader. These class loader methods search the specific class loader and all of its parents. If there is no current class loader then the system class loader is used.

Let me assure you that at First National, you're not just a number.
You're two numbers, a dash, three more numbers, another dash, and another number.
—James Estes

CHAPTER 14

Documentation Comments

Any member introducing a dog into the Society's premises shall be liable to a fine of £10.
Any animal leading a blind person shall be deemed to be a cat.
—Rule 46, Oxford Union Society

DOCUMENTATION comments, usually called *doc comments,* let you associate reference documentation for programmers directly with your code. The contents of the doc comment can be used to generate reference documentation, typically presented using HTML.

Doc comments are typically designed as fairly terse reference documentation. The reference documentation typically covers the contract of the documented interface, class, constructor, method, or field to the level of detail most programmers need. This approach is distinct from a full specification, which can be too long for reference documentation. A full specification might devote several pages of text to a single method, where the reference documentation might be one or two paragraphs, possibly even short ones. Specifications should be produced separately, although they can be cross-referenced by the doc comment, as you will soon see.

The procedure for generating documentation from the doc comments varies among development environments. One common procedure is to run the `javadoc` command on the packages or types; hence, the generated documentation is often called *javadoc.*

This chapter teaches what can go into documentation comments and how the contents are interpreted. You will also learn about features that are, strictly speaking, outside of the language but are conventions for creating the generated documentation, such as overall package documentation and the location for images and other resources. You development environment may not use these details in precisely the same way as `javadoc` but it is likely to, and if not it will usually have an analogous replacement. This are covered in the section "External Conventions" on page 352.

14.1   The Anatomy of a Doc Comment

Doc comments start with the three characters /** and continue until the next */.
Each doc comment describes the identifier whose declaration immediately follows. Leading * characters are ignored on doc comment lines, as are whitespace
characters preceding a leading *. The first sentence of the comment is the summary for the identifier; "sentence" means all text up to the first period with following white space. Consider the doc comment:

```
/**
 * Do what the invoker intends.  "Intention" is defined by
 * an analysis of past behavior as described in ISO 4074-6.
 */
public void dwim() throws IntentUnknownException;
```

The summary for the method dwim will be "Do what the invoker intends." Your
first sentence in a doc comment should be a good summary.

HTML tags are often embedded in doc comments as formatting directives or
cross-reference links to other documentation. You can use almost any standard
HTML tag except the header tags <h1>, <h2>, and so on, which are reserved for
use by the generated documentation. To insert the character <, >, or & you should
use <, >, or &, respectively. If you must have an @ at the beginning of
a line, use @—otherwise it is assumed to start a doc comment tag.

Only doc comments that immediately precede a class, interface, method, or
field are processed. If anything besides whitespace or comments are between a
doc comment and what it describes the doc comment will be ignored. For example, if you put a doc comment at the top of a file with a package or import statement between the doc comment and the class, the doc comment will not be used.
Doc comments apply to all fields declared in a single statement, so declaring multiple fields in a single statement is usually avoided where doc comments are used.

If no doc comment is given for an inherited method, the method "inherits" the
doc comment from the supertype. This is often quite enough, especially when a
class implements an interface—methods in the implementation often do nothing
more than what the interface specifies, or at least nothing that belongs in a doc
comment. You should put an explicit comment in when you are inheriting doc
comments so that someone doesn't think that you forgot to document the method,
for example:

```
// inherit doc comment
public void dwim() throws IntentUnknownException {
    // ...
}
```

If a method inherits doc comments from both a superclass and superinterface the interface comment is used.

14.2 Tags

Doc comments can contain *tags* that hold particular kinds of information. All these tags start with @, as in @see or @deprecated. These paragraphs are treated specially in the generated documentation, resulting in marked paragraphs, links to other documentation, and other special treatment. This section describes all tags except @serial, @serialData and @serialField which relate to object serialization and are described in "The Object Byte Streams" on page 405.

Except for tagged paragraphs, text in a doc comment is treated as input text for HTML. You can create paragraph breaks in the documentation using the standard <p> tag, blocks of example code using <pre>, and so on.

14.2.1 @see

The @see tag creates a cross-reference link to other javadoc documentation. You can name any identifier, although you must qualify it sufficiently. You can, for example, usually name a member of a class with its simple name. However, if the member is an overloaded method, you must specify which overload of the method you mean by listing the types of parameters. You can specify an interface or class that is in the current package by its unqualified name, but you must specify types from other packages with fully qualified names. You specify members of types using a # before the member name. The following are all potentially valid @see tags:

```
@see #getName
@see Attr
@see com.magic.attr.Attr
@see com.magic.attr.Deck#DECK_SIZE
@see com.magic.attr.Attr#getName
@see com.magic.attr.Attr#Attr(String)
@see com.magic.attr.Attr#Attr(String, Object)
@see com.magic.attr
@see <a href="spec.html#attr">Attribute Specification</a>
@see "The Java Developer's Almanac"
```

The first form refers to the method getName in the same class or interface as the doc comment itself, or in any enclosing class or interface; the same syntax can be used for fields. The second form refers to a class in the current package or an imported package. The third refers to a class by its fully qualified name.

The next four @see forms refer to members. The first two show forms for a field (DECK_SIZE) or method (getName). We can simply use the name of a method because there is exactly one getName method defined in the Attr class. The next two forms refer to constructors of the Attr class, one that takes a String argument and another that takes a String and an Object. When a constructor or method is overloaded you must specify the arguments of the one you mean.

The next @see form directs readers to a specific package: com.magic.attr.

The final two forms allow you to reference other documentation. The first defines a link using <a...>. The second defines normal text using "...". You might use these to direct readers to other documentation, such as the full specification.

The @see forms that name a language entity (any of the above forms except the last two) can have a *label* following the entity. This label name will be the one used in the generated documentation instead of the entity's name. For example,

```
@see #getName Attribute Names
```

will create a link to the documentation of getName but will display the text "Attribute Names" not "getName". Usually you should let the actual member name be used, but occasionally you may find this feature useful.

14.2.2 {@link}

The @see tag is useful for a "See also" section at the end of the documentation. You can embed an {@link} in-line tag in your text when the cross reference should belong in the text of your comment. The syntax for @link is

```
{@link package.class#member [label]}
```

The identifier specification is the same what you learned for @see, as is the optional label. The following sentence embeds a link to the getValue method:

```
Changes the value returned by calls to {@link #getValue}.
```

14.2.3 @param

The @param tag documents a single parameter to a method. If you use @param tags you should have one for each parameter of the method. The first word of the paragraph is taken as the parameter name, and the rest is its description:

```
@param max     The maximum number of words to read.
```

14.2.4 @return

The @return tag documents the return value of a method:

```
@return        The number of words actually read.
```

14.2.5 @throws and @exception

The @throws tag documents an exception thrown by the method. If you use @throws tags you should have one for each type of exception the method throws. This list often includes more than just the checked exceptions that must be declared in the throws clause—it is a good idea to declare all exceptions in the throws clause, whether or not they are required, and the same is true when you're using @throws tags. For example, suppose that your method checks its parameters to ensure that none is null, throwing NullPointerException if it finds a null argument. You should declare NullPointerException in your throws clause and your @throws tags.

```
@throws UnknownName    The name is unknown.
@throws java.io.IOException
           Reading the input stream failed; this exception
           is passed through from the input stream.
@throws NullPointerException
           The name is <code>null</code>.
```

The tag @exception is equivalent to @throws.

14.2.6 @deprecated

The @deprecated tag marks an identifier as being deprecated: unfit for continued use. Code using a deprecated type, constructor, method, or field may generate a warning when compiled. You should ensure that the deprecated entity continues working so that you don't break existing code that hasn't yet been updated. Deprecation helps you encourage users of your code to update to the latest version, but preserves the integrity of existing code. Users can shift to newer mechanisms when they choose to instead of being forced to shift as soon as you release a new version of your types. You should direct users to a replacement for deprecated entities:

```
/**
 * Do what the invoker intends.  "Intention" is defined by
 * an analysis of past behavior as described in ISO 4074-6.
 *
```

```
 * @deprecated   You should use dwishm instead
 * @see          #dwishm
 */
public void dwim() throws IntentUnknownException;
```

The @deprecated tag is noticed by the compiler if it is at the beginning of a line of the doc comment. The compiler marks the following identifier as being deprecated with the results described previously. This is the only time where the contents of a comment affect the behavior of the compiler.

14.2.7 @author

The @author tag specifies an author of the code.

```
@author Aristophanes
@author Ursula K. LeGuin
@author Ibid
```

You can specify as many @author paragraphs as you desire. You should use only one author per @author paragraph to get consistent output in all circumstances.

14.2.8 @version

The @version tag lets you specify an arbitrary version specification.

```
@version 1.1
```

14.2.9 @since

The @since tag lets you specify an arbitrary version specification that denotes when the tagged entity was added to your system.

```
@since 2.1
```

Tagging the "birth version" can help you track which entities are newer and therefore may need intensified documentation or testing. By convention an @since tag on a class or interface applies to all members of the class or interface that don't have their own @since tag. For example, if the above @since tag preceded a class, all constructors, fields, and methods of that class would be presumed to have been present in version 2.1 except any that had, for example, an @since 2.2 tag of its own.

14.2.10 {@docRoot}

The files generated by javadoc are put into a tree, with subdirectories that contain parts of the documentation. The exact placement of files in the tree is up to the javadoc implementation, and may change depending on your environment, user preferences, and the like. You may want to add things to the tree after it is built and then refer to those added pieces in your doc comments.

The in-line {@docRoot} tag lets you put into your doc comments a relative reference to other files in the documentation tree. The {@docRoot} tag will be replaced with a relative path to the top of the generated documentation tree. For example, the sentence

```
You should read <a href="{@docRoot}/license.html">our
license</a>.
```

would result in a sentence with a link to the file license.html in the root of the documentation tree. After generating the documentation from the doc comments, you could copy license.html into the top of the generated documentation tree, and the above link would always go from the generated output to your license.html file. For some applications you may find the mechanism described in Section 14.4.2 on page 353 more useful.

14.3 An Example

The following is a doc commented version of the Attr class from page 66:

```
/**
 * An <code>Attr</code> object defines an attribute as a
 * name/value pair, where the name is a <code>String</code>
 * and the value an arbitrary <code>Object</code>.
 *
 * @version 1.1
 * @author Plato
 * @since 1.0
 */
class Attr {
    /** The attribute name. */
    private final String name;
    /** The attribute value. */
    private Object value = null;

    /**
```

```java
 * Creates a new attribute with the given name and an
 * initial value of <code>null</code>.
 * @see Attr#Attr(String,Object)
 */
public Attr(String name) {
    this.name = name;
}

/**
 * Creates a new attribute with the given name and
 * initial value.
 * @see Attr#Attr(String)
 */
public Attr(String name, Object value) {
    this.name = name;
    this.value = value;
}

/** Returns this attribute's name. */
public String getName() {
    return name;
}

/** Returns this attribute's value. */
public Object getValue() {
    return value;
}

/**
 * Sets the value of this attribute.  Changes the
 * value returned by calls to {@link #getValue}.
 * @param newValue  The new value for the attribute.
 * @return  The original value.
 * @see #getValue()
 */
public Object setValue(Object newValue) {
    Object oldVal = value;
    value = newValue;
    return oldVal;
}
```

```
/**
 * Returns a string of the form <code>name=value</code>.
 */
public String toString() {
    return name + "='" + value + "'";
}
```

For simple methods like `getName`, whose whole description is what it returns, the `@return` tag is omitted as overkill. Similarly, the constructors do not use `@param` tags because the description is sufficiently complete. Different organizations will make different choices of when to use each tag. The following two pages show how the HTML javadoc output might look for this class.

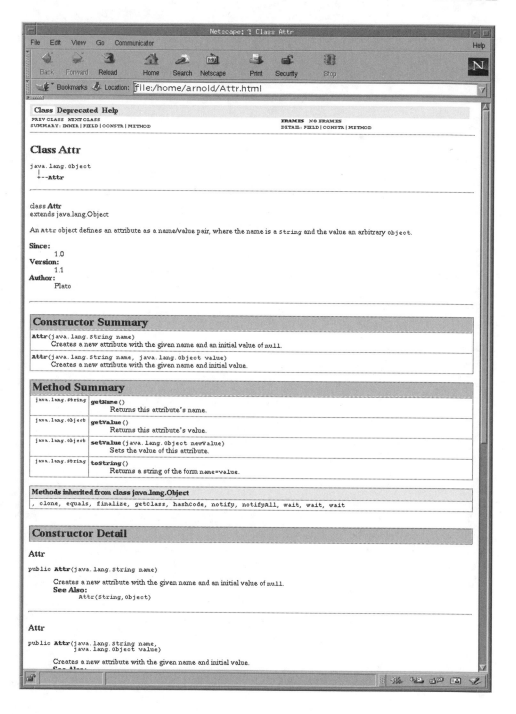

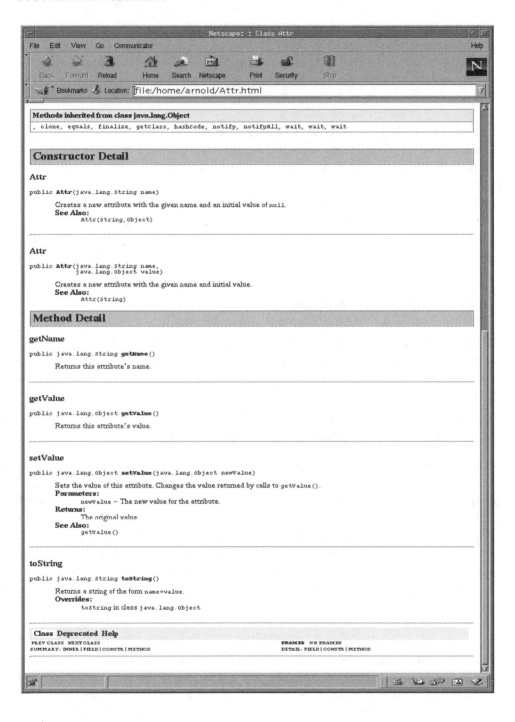

Methods inherited from class java.lang.Object

, clone, equals, finalize, getClass, hashCode, notify, notifyAll, wait, wait, wait

Constructor Detail

Attr

public **Attr**(java.lang.String name)

>   Creates a new attribute with the given name and an initial value of null.
>   **See Also:**
>>   Attr(String,Object)

Attr

public **Attr**(java.lang.String name,
          java.lang.Object value)

>   Creates a new attribute with the given name and initial value.
>   **See Also:**
>>   Attr(String)

Method Detail

getName

public java.lang.String **getName**()

>   Returns this attribute's name.

getValue

public java.lang.Object **getValue**()

>   Returns this attribute's value.

setValue

public java.lang.Object **setValue**(java.lang.Object newValue)

>   Sets the value of this attribute. Changes the value returned by calls to getValue().
>   **Parameters:**
>>   newValue – The new value for the attribute.
>   **Returns:**
>>   The original value.
>   **See Also:**
>>   getValue()

toString

public java.lang.String **toString**()

>   Returns a string of the form name=value.
>   **Overrides:**
>>   toString in class java.lang.Object

Class Deprecated Help

PREV CLASS NEXT CLASS   FRAMES   NO FRAMES
SUMMARY: INNER | FIELD | CONSTR | METHOD   DETAIL: FIELD | CONSTR | METHOD

You should use doc comments to document all members, including private and package-accessible ones. Documentation generators such as javadoc let you specify whether you want to generate documentation from these comments, and having organized, readable documentation of your class's internals is quite useful when someone else needs to learn about them.

Exercise 14.1: Add doc comments to your LinkedList class from Exercise 2.11. Generate the javadoc and ask someone else to write a simple program using your class. Repeat, improving your comments if necessary, until someone can do so.

Exercise 14.2: Expand on Exercise 14.1 by including the private members. Generate the full (private members included) javadoc and ask someone else to explain the class to you. Repeat, improving your comments if necessary, until someone can do so.

14.4 External Conventions

Not all of the documentation needed for a package can be ascribed to a specific source file, nor are source files the only types of files that need to be referred to in documentation. You can incorporate these external elements in your documentation.

14.4.1 Overview and Package Documentation

Doc comments associate documentation with elements in source files, but packages are not defined in source files. The javadoc command allows you to document the overall purpose of a package or set of packages using package.html and overview HTML files.

A package.html file is used in documentation generated for the particular package in which the file resides. When the package is processed for doc comments, the contents of the package.html between <body> and </body> will be read as if it were a doc comment (although it should not have the /**, */, or any leading *).

Not all tags will be processed: @deprecated, @author, and @version are not replaced in a package comment. As with other doc comments, the first sentence of the body of a package comment is used as a summary for the package. Any @see or {@link} tag that names a language element must use the fully qualified form of the entity's name, even for classes and interfaces within the package itself.

An overview HTML file is read in the same way as a package.html file. You specify the HTML file to use as an overview when generating the documentation.

14.4.2 The `doc-files` Directory

The `javadoc` program will copy the contents of a `doc-files` directory in a given package into the generated documentation for that package. You can use this feature to include images, HTML, class files, or any other component you want to reference in your doc comment. For example, you could include a set of formal rules in a large number of doc comments indirectly:

```
@see <a href="doc-files/semantics.html">Formal Semantics</a>
```

Or you could use the directory to store useful images:

```
Made by Magic, Inc.<img src="doc-files/magiclogo.gif">
```

14.5 Notes on Usage

Tightly coupling the reference documentation to the source code has many advantages, but it does not turn all programmers into good documentation writers. Programmers will continue to vary in their ability and interest in writing good reference documentation. Many organizations have technical writers to produce the reference documentation. Doc comments require write access to the source, and technical writers often do not have permission to modify source code. The use of doc comments will require a change in such organizations.

Another issue is *comment skew,* in which comments become out of date as the source code changes over time. You can reduce this problem by putting only contractual information in your doc comments, and not describing the implementation. When the implementation changes, the doc comment will still be correct as long as the contract remains unmodified. Changing the contract of an existing type, constructor, method, or field is a questionable practice in many cases, so such changes should be rare. Describing only the contract is generally a good practice in any case, because it frees you to change details of the implementation in the future. Implementation details of public methods need to be documented— use regular comments for this purpose.

You can further reduce the problem of comment skew by defining a standard marker for programmers to place in doc comments that need attention. For example, if you add a new method to a class, you could write the first draft of the doc comment, but flag the comment as one that might need review and rework by the documentation team:

```
/**
 * …initial draft…
 * @docissue Review -- programmer's first draft
 */
```

A script run over the source could find @docissue markers and show them to the documentation team, alerting them to work that remains to be done. Some documentation generators allow you to add your own doc comment paragraph tags, so using an @ tag—such as @docissue shown above—allows you to flag these or other issues directly in the generated documentation as well as in the source itself.

> *The universe is made of stories,*
> *not atoms.*
> —Muriel Rukeyser

CHAPTER 15

The I/O Package

*From a programmer's point of view,
the user is a peripheral that types when you issue a* read *request.*
—Peter Williams

T HE java.io package defines I/O (input/output) in terms of *streams*. Streams are ordered sequences of data that have a *source* (input streams) or *destination* (output streams). The I/O classes isolate programmers from the specific details of the underlying operating system, while enabling access to system resources through files and other means. Most stream types (such as those dealing with files) support the methods of some basic interfaces and abstract classes, with few (if any) additions. The best way to understand the I/O package is to start with the basic interfaces and abstract classes. You will also see examples of the abstractions in action with specific kinds of streams.

The package java.io has two major parts: *character streams* and *byte streams*. Characters are 16-bit Unicode characters, whereas bytes are (as always) eight bits. I/O is either text-based or data-based (binary). Text-based I/O works with streams of human-readable characters—such as the source code for a program—while data-based I/O works with streams of binary data—such as the bit pattern for an image. The character streams are used for text-based I/O while byte streams are used for data-based I/O. Streams that work with bytes cannot properly carry characters, and some character-related issues are not meaningful with byte streams—though the byte streams can also be used for older text-based protocols that use 7, or 8-bit characters. The byte streams are called *input streams* and *output streams,* and the character streams are called *readers* and *writers*. For nearly every input stream there is a corresponding output stream, and for most input or output streams there is a corresponding reader or writer character stream of similar functionality, and vice versa.

Because of these overlaps, this chapter describes the streams in fairly general terms. When we talk simply about streams, we mean any of the streams. When we talk about input streams or output streams, we mean the byte variety. The character streams are referred to as readers and writers. For example, when we talk about the `Buffered` streams we mean the entire family of `BufferedInputStream`, `BufferedOutputStream`, `BufferedReader`, and `BufferedWriter`. When we talk about `Buffered` byte streams we mean both `BufferedInputStream` and `BufferedOutputStream`. When we talk about `Buffered` character streams, we mean `BufferedReader` and `BufferedWriter`.

The classes and interfaces in `java.io` can be broadly divided into five groups:

♦ The general classes for building different types of byte and character streams—input and output streams, readers and writers and classes for converting between them—are discussed in Section 15.1 through to Section 15.3.

♦ A range of classes that define various types of streams—filtered streams, buffered streams, piped streams, and some specific instances of those streams, such as a line number reader and a stream tokenizer—are discussed in Section 15.4.

♦ The data stream classes and interfaces for reading and writing primitive values and strings are discussed in Section 15.5.

♦ Classes and interfaces for interacting with files in a system independent manner are discussed in Section 15.6.

♦ The classes and interfaces that form the *object serialization* mechanism—which transforms objects into byte streams and allows live objects to be reconstituted from the data read from a byte stream—are discussed in Section 15.7.

The `java.text` classes described in Chapter 19 can be used for some number-formatting purposes, and the integer wrapper classes provide some methods for decoding numbers from strings, but there is no general set of classes for formatted input and output.

The `IOException` class is used by many methods in `java.io` to signal exceptional conditions. Some extended classes of `IOException` signal specific problems, but most problems are signaled by an `IOException` object with a descriptive string. Details are provided in Section 15.8 on page 418. Any method that throws an `IOException` will do so when an error occurs that is directly related to the stream. In particular, invoking a method on a closed stream may result in an `IOException`. Unless there are particular circumstances under which the `IOException` will be thrown, this exception is not documented for each individual method of each class.

Similarly, `NullPointerException` and `IndexOutOfBoundsException` can be expected to be thrown whenever a `null` reference is passed to a method, or a supplied index accesses outside of an array. Only those situations where this does not occur will be explicitly documented.

All code presented in this chapter uses the types in `java.io`, and every example has imported `java.io.*` even when there is no explicit `import` statement in the code.

15.1 Byte Streams

The `java.io` package defines abstract classes for basic byte input and output streams. These abstract classes are then extended to provide several useful stream types. Stream types are almost always paired: for example, where there is a `FileInputStream` to read from a file, there is usually a `FileOutputStream` to write to a file.

Before you can learn about specific kinds of input and output byte streams, it is important to understand the basic `InputStream` and `OutputStream` abstract classes. The type tree for the byte streams of `java.io` in Figure 15–1 shows the type hierarchy of the byte streams.

There are some things that all byte streams have in common. For example, all streams support the notion of being open or closed. A stream is opened when you create it and can be read from or written to while it is open. A stream is closed by invoking its `close` method. Closing a stream is intended to release system resources (such as file descriptors) that may have been used by the stream and which should be reclaimed as soon as they are no longer needed. If a stream is not explicitly closed it will hold onto these resources. A stream class could define a `finalize` method to release these resources at garbage collection time but, as you learned on page 316, that could be too late. You should usually close streams when you have finished with them.

All byte streams also share common synchronization policies and concurrent behavior. These are discussed in Section 15.4.1 on page 370.

15.1.1 InputStream

The abstract class `InputStream` declares methods to read bytes from a particular source. `InputStream` is the superclass of most byte input streams in `java.io`, and has the following methods:

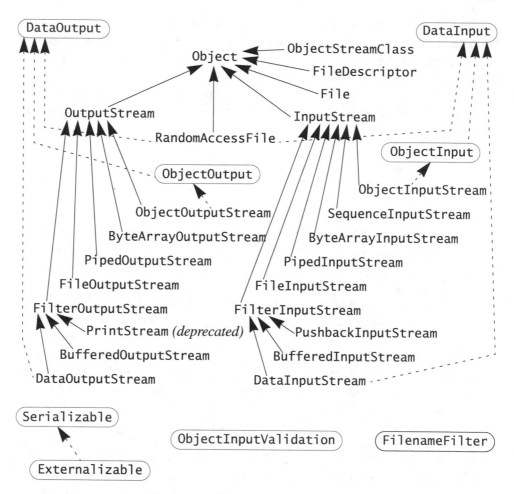

FIGURE 15–1: *Type Tree for Byte Streams in java.io*

```
public abstract int read() throws IOException
```
> Reads a single byte of data and returns the byte that was read, as an integer in the range 0 to 255, not –128 to 127; in other words, the byte value is treated as unsigned. If no byte is available because the end of the stream has been reached, the value –1 is returned. This method blocks until input is available, the end of stream is found, or an exception is thrown. The read method returns an int instead of an actual byte value because it needs to return all valid byte values plus a flag value to indicate the end of stream. This requires more values than can fit in a byte and so the larger int is used.

```
public int read(byte[] buf, int offset, int count)
   throws IOException
```
Reads into a part of a byte array. The maximum number of bytes read is count. The bytes are stored from buf[offset] up to a maximum of buf[offset+count-1]—all other values in buf are left unchanged. The number of bytes actually read is returned. If no bytes are read because the end of the stream was detected, the value –1 is returned. If count is zero then no bytes are read and zero is returned. This method blocks until input is available, the end of stream is found, or an exception is thrown. If the first byte cannot be read for any reason other than detecting the end of the stream—in particular, if the stream has already been closed—an IOException is thrown. Once a byte has been read, any failure that occurs trying to read subsequent bytes is not reported with an exception but is treated as encountering the end of the stream—the method completes normally and returns the number of bytes read before the failure occurred.

```
public int read(byte[] buf) throws IOException
```
Equivalent to read(buf, 0, buf.length).

```
public long skip(long count) throws IOException
```
Skips as many as count bytes of input or until the end of the stream is detected. Returns the actual number of bytes skipped. If count is negative, no bytes are skipped.

```
public int available() throws IOException
```
Returns the number of bytes that can be read (or skipped over) without blocking. The default implementation returns zero.

```
public void close() throws IOException
```
Closes the input stream. This method should be invoked to release any resources (such as file descriptors) associated with the stream. Once a stream has been closed, further operations on the stream will throw an IOException. Closing a previously closed stream has no effect. The default implementation of close does nothing.

The implementation of InputStream requires only that a subclass provide the single-byte variant of read, as the other read methods are defined in terms of this one. Most streams, however, can improve performance by overriding other methods as well. The default implementations of available and close will usually need to be overridden as appropriate for a particular stream.

The following program demonstrates the use of input streams to count the total number of bytes in a file, or from System.in if no file is specified:

```java
import java.io.*;

class CountBytes {
    public static void main(String[] args)
        throws IOException
    {
        InputStream in;
        if (args.length == 0)
            in = System.in;
        else
            in = new FileInputStream(args[0]);

        int total = 0;
        while (in.read() != -1)
            total++;

        System.out.println(total + " bytes");
    }
}
```

This program takes a filename from the command line. The variable in represents the input stream. If a file name is not provided, the standard input stream, System.in, is used; if one is provided, a FileInputStream object is created, which is a subclass of InputStream.

The while loop counts the total number of bytes in the file. At the end, the results are printed. Here is the output of the program when used on itself:

```
318 bytes
```

You might be tempted to set total using available, but it won't work on many kinds of streams. The available method returns the number of bytes that can be read *without blocking*. For a file, the number of bytes available is usually its entire contents. If System.in is a stream associated with a keyboard, the answer can be as low as zero: when there is no pending input, the next read will block.

15.1.2 OutputStream

The abstract class OutputStream is analogous to InputStream; it provides an abstraction for writing bytes to a destination. Its methods are:

`public abstract void` **`write(int b)`** `throws IOException`

> Writes b as a byte. The byte is passed as an `int` because it is often the result of an arithmetic operation on a byte. Expressions involving bytes are type `int`, so making the parameter an `int` means that the result can be passed without a cast to `byte`. Note, however, that only the lowest 8 bits of the integer are written. This method blocks until the byte is written.

`public void` **`write(byte[] buf, int offset, int count)`**
`  throws IOException`

> Writes part of an array of bytes, starting at `buf[offset]` and writing `count` bytes. This method blocks until the bytes have been written.

`public void` **`write(byte[] buf)`** `throws IOException`

> Equivalent to `write(buf, 0, buf.length)`.

`public void` **`flush()`** `throws IOException`

> Flushes the stream. If the stream has buffered any bytes from the various `write` methods, `flush` writes them immediately to their destination. Then, if that destination is another stream, it is also flushed. One `flush` invocation will flush all the buffers in a chain of streams. If the stream is not buffered, `flush` may do nothing—the default implementation.

`public void` **`close()`** `throws IOException`

> Closes the output stream. This method should be invoked to release any resources (such as file descriptors) associated with the stream. Once a stream has been closed, further operations on the stream will throw an `IOException`. Closing a previously closed stream has no effect. The default implementation of `close` does nothing.

The implementation of `OutputStream` requires only that a subclass provide the single-byte variant of `write`, as the other `write` methods are defined in terms of this one. Most streams, however, can improve performance by overriding other methods as well. The default implementations of `flush` and `close` will usually need to be overridden as appropriate for a particular stream—in particular, buffered streams may need to flush when closed.

Here is a program that copies its input to its output, translating one particular byte value to a different one along the way. The `TranslateByte` program takes two parameters: a `from` byte and a `to` byte. Bytes that match the value in the string `from` are translated into the value in the string `to`.

```
import java.io.*;

class TranslateByte {
    public static void main(String[] args) throws IOException
    {
```

```
            byte from = (byte)args[0].charAt(0);
            byte to   = (byte)args[1].charAt(0);
            int b;
            while ((b = System.in.read()) != -1)
                System.out.write(b == from ? to : b);
    }
}
```

For example, if we invoked the program as follows:

```
java TranslateByte b B
```

and entered the text `abracadabra!`, we would get the output

```
aBracadaBra!
```

Manipulating data from a stream after it has been read, or before it is written, is often achieved by writing `Filter` streams, rather than hardcoding the manipulation in a program. You'll learn about filters in Section 15.4.2 on page 371.

Exercise 15.1: Rewrite the `TranslateByte` program as a method that translates the contents of an `InputStream` onto an `OutputStream`, in which the mapping and the streams are parameters. For each type of `InputStream` and `OutputStream` you read about in this chapter, write a new `main` method that uses the translation method to operate on a stream of that type. If you have paired input and output streams, you can cover both in one `main` method.

15.2   Character Streams

The abstract classes for reading and writing streams of characters are `Reader` and `Writer`. Each supports similar methods to those of its byte stream counterpart—`InputStream` and `OutputStream`, respectively. For example, `InputStream` has a `read` method that returns a `byte` as the lowest eight bits of an `int`, and `Reader` has a `read` method that returns a `char` as the lowest 16 bits of an `int`. And where `OutputStream` has methods that write `byte` arrays, `Writer` has methods that write `char` arrays. The character streams were designed after the byte streams to provide full support for working with Unicode characters, and in the process the contracts of the classes were improved to make them easier to work with. The type tree for the character streams of `java.io` appears in Figure 15–2.

As with the byte streams, character streams should be explicitly closed to release resources associated with the stream. Character stream synchronization policies are discussed in Section 15.4.1 on page 370.

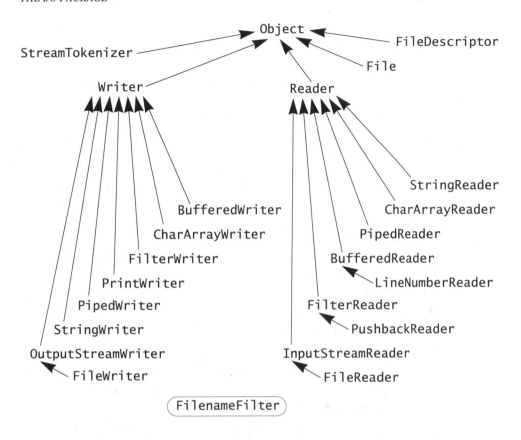

FIGURE 15–2: *Type Tree for Character Streams in `java.io`*

15.2.1 Reader

The abstract class `Reader` provides a character stream analogous to the byte stream `InputStream` and the methods of `Reader` essentially mirror those of `InputStream`:

`public int` **`read()`** `throws IOException`

> Reads a single character and returns it as an integer in the range 0 to 65535. If no character is available because the end of the stream has been reached, the value −1 is returned. This method blocks until input is available, the end of stream is found, or an exception is thrown.

```
public abstract int read(char[] buf, int offset, int count)
  throws IOException
```
Reads into a part of a char array. The maximum number of characters to read is count. The read characters are stored from buf[offset] up to a maximum of buf[offset+count-1]—all other values in buf are left unchanged. The number of characters actually read is returned. If no characters are read because the end of the stream was detected, the value –1 is returned. If count is zero then no characters are read and zero is returned. This method blocks until input is available, the end of stream is found, or an exception is thrown. If the first character cannot be read for any reason other than detecting the end of the stream—in particular, if the stream has already been closed—an IOException is thrown. Once a character has been read, any failure that occurs trying to read subsequent characters is not reported with an exception, but is treated as encountering the end of the stream—the method completes normally and returns the number of characters read before the failure occurred.

```
public int read(char[] buf) throws IOException
```
Equivalent to read(buf, 0, buf.length).

```
public long skip(long count) throws IOException
```
Skips as many as count characters of input or until the end of the stream is detected. Returns the actual number of characters skipped. The value of count must not be negative.

```
public boolean ready() throws IOException
```
Returns true if the stream is ready to read; that is, there is at least one character available to be read. Note that a return value of false does not guarantee that the next invocation of read will block, as data could have become available by the time the invocation occurs.

```
public abstract void close() throws IOException
```
Closes the stream. This method should be invoked to release any resources (such as file descriptors) associated with the stream. Once a stream has been closed, further operations on the stream will throw an IOException. Closing a previously closed stream has no effect.

The implementation of Reader requires that a subclass provide an implementation of the read method that reads into a char array, and the close method. Many subclasses will be able to provide better performance if they also override some of the other methods.

There are a number of differences between Reader and InputStream. With Reader the fundamental reading method reads into a char array and the other read methods are defined in terms of this method. In contrast the InputStream class uses the single-byte `read` method as its fundamental reading method. In the `Reader` class subclasses must implement the abstract `close` method in contrast to inheriting an empty implementation—many stream classes will at least need to track whether or not they have been closed and so `close` will usually need to be overridden. Finally, where `InputStream` had an `available` method to tell you how much data was available to read, `Reader` simply has a `ready` method that tells you if there is any data.

As an example, the following program counts the number of whitespace characters in a character stream:

```java
import java.io.*;

class CountSpace {
    public static void main(String[] args)
        throws IOException
    {
        Reader in;
        if (args.length == 0)
            in = new InputStreamReader(System.in);
        else
            in = new FileReader(args[0]);

        int ch;
        int total;
        int spaces = 0;
        for (total = 0; (ch = in.read()) != -1; total++) {
            if (Character.isWhitespace((char) ch))
                spaces++;
        }

        System.out.println(total + " chars, "
            + spaces + " spaces");
    }
}
```

This program takes a filename from the command line. The variable `in` represents the character stream. If a filename is not provided, the standard input stream, `System.in`, is used after wrapping it in an `InputStreamReader`, which converts an input byte stream into an input character stream; if a filename is provided, a `FileReader` object is created, which is a subclass of `Reader`.

The `for` loop counts the total number of characters in the file and the number of spaces, using the `Character` class's `isWhitespace` method to test whether a character is white space. At the end, the results are printed. Here is the output of the program when used on itself:

```
453 chars, 111 spaces
```

15.2.2 `Writer`

The abstract class `Writer` provides a stream analogous to `OutputStream` but designed for use with characters instead of bytes. The methods of `Writer` essentially mirror those of `OutputStream`, but add some other useful forms of `write`:

public void **write(int ch)** throws IOException
> Writes ch as a character. The character is passed as an `int` but only the lowest 16 bits of the integer are written. This method blocks until the character is written.

public abstract void **write(char[] buf, int offset, int count)**
throws IOException
> Writes part of an array of characters, starting at buf[offset] and writing count characters. This method blocks until the characters have been written.

public void **write(char[] buf)** throws IOException
> Equivalent to write(buf, 0, buf.length).

public void **write(String str, int offset, int count)**
throws IOException
> Writes count characters from the string str onto the stream, starting with str.charAt(offset).

public void **write(String str)** throws IOException
> Equivalent to write(str, 0, str.length()).

public abstract void **flush()** throws IOException
> Flushes the stream. If the stream has buffered any characters from the various `write` methods, `flush` writes them immediately to their destination. Then, if that destination is another stream, it is also flushed. One `flush` invocation will flush all the buffers in a chain of streams. If a stream is not buffered `flush` will do nothing.

public abstract void **close()** throws IOException
> Closes the stream, flushing if necessary. This method should be invoked to release any resources (such as file descriptors) associated with the stream. Once a stream has been closed, further operations on the stream will throw an `IOException`. Closing a previously closed stream has no effect.

Subclasses of `Writer` must implement the array writing variant of `write`, the `close` and the `flush` methods. All other `Writer` methods are implemented in terms of these three. This contrasts with OutputStream which uses the single-byte variant of write method as the fundamental writing method, and which provides default implementations of flush and close. As with Reader, many subclasses can provide better performance if they also override other methods.

15.2.3 Character Streams and the Standard Streams

The standard streams System.in, System.out, and System.err existed before the character streams were invented, so these streams are byte streams even though logically they should be character streams. This situation creates some anomalies. It is impossible, for example, to replace System.in with a LineNumberReader to keep track of the standard input stream's current line number. Using an InputStreamReader—an object that converts a byte input stream to a character input stream—attached to System.in, you can create a LineNumberReader object to keep track of the current line number (see "LineNumberReader" on page 381). But System.in is an InputStream, so you cannot replace it with a LineNumberReader, which is a type of Reader, not an InputStream.

The fields System.out and System.err are PrintStream objects. PrintStream has been replaced by its equivalent character based version PrintWriter. Generally you should avoid creating PrintStreams directly. You'll learn about the Print stream classes in Section 15.4.8 on page 380.

The types InputStreamReader and OutputStreamWriter convert to and from particular byte encodings of characters and Unicode char values

15.3 InputStreamReader and OutputStreamWriter

The conversion streams InputStreamReader and OutputStreamWriter translate between Unicode and byte streams using a specified encoding or the default encoding for the local system. An InputStreamReader object is given a byte input stream as its source and produces the corresponding Unicode characters. An OutputStreamWriter object is given a byte output stream as its destination and produces encoded byte forms of the Unicode characters written on it. For example, the following code would read bytes encoded under ISO 8859-6 for Arabic characters, translating them into the appropriate Unicode characters:

```
public Reader readArabic(String file) throws IOException {
    InputStream fileIn = new FileInputStream(file);
    return new InputStreamReader(fileIn, "iso-8859-6");
}
```

By default, these conversion streams will work in the platform's default encoding, but other encodings can be specified. These classes are the "glue" that lets you use existing 8-bit character encodings for local character sets in a consistent, platform-independent fashion. Encoding values are discussed in "Character Encodings" on page 221.

public **InputStreamReader(InputStream in)**
>   Creates an InputStreamReader to read from the given InputStream using the default character encoding.

public **InputStreamReader(InputStream in, String encoding)**
throws UnsupportedEncodingException
>   Creates an InputStreamReader to read from the given InputStream using the given character encoding. If the named encoding is not supported an UnsupportedEncodingException is thrown.

public **OutputStreamWriter(OutputStream out)**
>   Creates an OutputStreamWriter to write to the given OutputStream using the default character encoding.

public **OutputStreamWriter(OutputStream out, String encoding)**
throws UnsupportedEncodingException
>   Creates an OutputStreamWriter to write to the given OutputStream using the given character encoding. If the named encoding is not supported an UnsupportedEncodingException is thrown.

The *read* methods of InputStreamReader simply read bytes from their associated InputStream and convert them to characters using the appropriate encoding for that stream. Similarly, the *write* methods of OutputStreamWriter take the supplied characters, convert them to bytes using the appropriate encoding and write them to its associated OutputStream.

In both classes, closing the conversion stream also closes the associated byte stream. This may not always be desirable—such as when converting the standard streams—so consider carefully when closing conversion streams.

Both classes also support the method getEncoding, which returns a string representing the canonical name of the stream's character encoding, or null if the stream has been closed.

The FileReader and FileWriter classes are subclasses of these conversion streams. This helps you read and write local files correctly in a consistent, Unicode-savvy fashion using the local encoding. However, if the default local encoding isn't what you need, you must use an explicit InputStreamReader or OutputStreamWriter object. You will learn about the file related streams in more detail in Section 15.6 on page 394.

There are no `ReaderInputStream` and `WriterOutputStream` classes to translate character streams to byte streams. The data output stream you will learn about in Section 15.5.2 on page 393 can be used to write characters as bytes using a specific Unicode encoding.

15.4 A Quick Tour of The Stream Classes

The `java.io` package defines several types of streams. The stream types usually have input/output pairs, and most of them have both byte stream and character stream variants. Some of these streams define general behavioral properties. For example:

- ◆ `Filter` streams are abstract classes representing streams with some filtering operation applied as data is read or written using another stream. For example, a `FilterReader` object gets input from another `Reader` object, processes (filters) the characters in some manner, and returns the filtered result. You build sequences of filtered streams by chaining various filters into one large filter. Output can be filtered similarly (Section 15.4.2).

- ◆ `Buffered` streams add buffering so that `read` and `write` need not, for example, access the file system for every invocation. The character variants of these streams also add the notion of line-oriented text (Section 15.4.3).

- ◆ `Piped` streams are designed as pairs such that bytes written on, say, a `PipedOutputStream` can be read from a `PipedInputStream` (Section 15.4.4).

There are a group of streams, called in-memory streams, that allow you to use in-memory data structures as the source or destination for a stream:

- ◆ `ByteArray` streams use a `byte` array (Section 15.4.5).

- ◆ `CharArray` streams use a `char` array (Section 15.4.6).

- ◆ `String` streams use string types (Section 15.4.7).

The I/O package also has input and output streams that have no output or input counterpart:

- ◆ The `Print` streams provide `print` and `println` methods for formatting printed data in human-readable text form (Section 15.4.8).

◆ LineNumberReader is a buffered reader that tracks the line numbers of the input (characters only) (Section 15.4.9).

◆ SequenceInputStream converts a sequence of InputStream objects into a single InputStream so a list of concatenated input streams can be treated as a single input stream (bytes only) (Section 15.4.10).

There are also streams that are useful for building parsers:

◆ Pushback streams add a pushback buffer you can use to put back data when you have read too far (Section 15.4.11).

◆ The StreamTokenizer class breaks a Reader into a stream of tokens—recognizable "words"— that are often needed when parsing user input (characters only) (Section 15.4.12).

These classes can be extended to create new kinds of stream classes for specific applications.

Each of these stream types is described in the following sections. Before looking at these streams in detail, however, you need to learn something about the synchronization behavior of the different streams.

15.4.1 Synchronization and Concurrency

Both the byte streams and the characters streams define synchronization policies though they do this in different ways. The concurrent behavior of the stream classes is not fully specified but can be broadly described as follows.

Each byte stream class synchronizes on the current stream object when performing operations that must be free from interference. This allows multiple threads to use the same streams yet still get well-defined behavior when invoking individual stream methods. For example, if two threads each try to read data from a stream in chunks of n bytes, then the data returned by each read operation will contain up to n bytes that appeared consecutively in the stream. Similarly, if two threads are writing to the same stream then the bytes written in each write operation will be sent consecutively to the stream, not intermixed at random points.

The character streams use a different synchronization strategy to the byte streams. The character streams synchronize on a protected lock field which, by default, is a reference to the stream object itself. However, both Reader and Writer provide a protected constructor that takes an object for lock to refer to. Some subclasses set the lock field to refer to a different object. For example, the StringWriter class that writes its character into a StringBuffer object sets its lock object to be the StringBuffer object. If you are writing a reader or writer, you should set the `lock` field to an appropriate object if `this` is not appropriate. Conversely, if you are extending an existing reader or writer you should always synchronize on `lock` and not `this`.

In many cases, a particular stream object simply wraps another stream instance and delegates the main stream methods to that instance, forming a chain of connected streams, as is the case with `Filter` streams. In this case, the synchronization behavior of the method will depend on the ultimate stream object being wrapped. This will only become an issue if the wrapping class needs to perform some additional action that must occur atomically with respect to the main stream action. In most cases filter streams simply manipulate data before writing it to, or after reading it from, the wrapped stream, and synchronization is not an issue.

Most input operations will block until data is available, and it is also possible that output stream operations can block trying to write data—the ultimate source or destination could be a stream tied to a network socket. To make the threads performing this blocking I/O more responsive to cancellation requests an implementation may respond to `Thread` interrupt requests (see page 255) by unblocking the thread and throwing an `InterruptedIOException`. This exception can report the number of bytes transferred before the interruption occurred—if the code that throws it sets the value.

For single byte transfers, interrupting an I/O operation is quite straight-forward. In general, however, the state of a stream after a thread using it is interrupted is problematic. For example, suppose you use a particular stream to read HTTP requests across the network. If a thread reading the next request is interrupted after reading two bytes of the header field in the request packet, the next thread reading from that stream will get invalid data unless the stream takes steps to prevent this. Given the effort involved in writing classes that can deal effectively with these sorts of situations, most implementations *do not* allow a thread to be interrupted until the main I/O operation has completed and so you cannot rely on blocking I/O being interruptible.

Even when interruption cannot be responded to during an I/O operation many systems will check for interruption at the start and/or end of the operation and throw the `InterruptedIOException` then. Also, if a thread is blocked on a stream when the stream is closed by another thread, most implementations will unblock the blocked thread and throw an `IOException`.

15.4.2 `Filter` Streams

`Filter` streams—`FilterInputStream`, `FilterOutputStream`, `FilterReader` and `FilterWriter`—enable you to chain streams to produce composite streams of greater utility. Each filter stream is bound to another stream to which it delegates the actual input or output actions. `Filter` streams get their power from the ability to filter—that is process—the data that they read or write, transforming the data in some way.

Filter byte streams add new constructors that accept a stream of the appropriate type (input or output) to which to connect. `Filter` character streams similarly add a new constructor that accepts a character stream of the appropriate type (reader or writer). However, many character streams already have constructors that take another character stream, so those `Reader` and `Writer` classes can act as filters even if they do not extend `FilterReader` or `FilterWriter`.

The following example shows an input filter that converts characters to uppercase:

```java
public class UppercaseConvertor extends FilterReader {
    public UppercaseConvertor(Reader in) {
        super(in);
    }

    public int read() throws IOException {
        int c = super.read();
        return (c == -1 ? c : Character.toUpperCase((char)c));
    }

    public int read(char[] buf, int offset, int count)
        throws IOException
    {
        int nread = super.read(buf, offset, count);
        int last = offset + nread;
        for (int i = offset; i < last; i++)
            buf[i] = Character.toUpperCase(buf[i]);
        return nread;
    }
}
```

We override each of the `read` methods to perform the actual read and then convert the characters to upper case. The actual reading is performed by invoking an appropriate superclass method. Note that we don't invoke `read` on the stream in itself—this would bypass any filtering performed by our superclass. Also note that we have to watch for the end of the stream. In the case of the no-arg `read` this means an explicit test, but in the array version of `read`, a return value of −1 will prevent the `for` loop from executing. In the array version of `read` we also have to be careful to only convert to uppercase those characters that we stored in the supplied buffer.

We can use our uppercase convertor as follows:

```
public static void main(String[] args)
    throws IOException
{
    StringReader src = new StringReader(args[0]);
    FilterReader f = new UppercaseConvertor(src);
    int c;
    while ((c = f.read()) != -1)
        System.out.print((char)c);
    System.out.println();
}
```

We use a string as our data source by using a `StringReader` (see Section 15.4.7 on page 379). The `StringReader` is then wrapped by our `UppercaseConvertor`. Reading from the filtered stream converts all the characters from the string stream into uppercase. For the input `"no lowercase"` we get the output:

```
NO LOWERCASE
```

You can chain any number of `Filter` byte or character streams. The original source of input can be a stream that is not a `Filter` stream. You can use an `InputStreamReader` to convert a byte input stream to a character input stream.

`Filter` output streams can be chained similarly, so that data written to one stream will filter and write data to the next output stream. All the streams, from the first to the next-to-last, must be `Filter` output stream objects, but the last stream can be any kind of output stream. You can use an `OutputStreamWriter` to convert a byte output stream to a character output stream.

Not all classes that are `Filter` streams actually alter the data. Some classes are behavioral filters, such as the buffered streams you'll learn about next, while others provide a new interface for using the streams, such as the print streams. These classes are `Filter` streams because they can form part of a filter chain.

Exercise 15.2: Rewrite the `TranslateByte` class as a filter.

Exercise 15.3: Create a pair of `Filter` stream classes that encrypt bytes using any algorithm you choose—such as XORing the bytes with some value—with your `DecryptInputStream` able to decrypt the bytes that your `EncryptOutputStream` class creates.

Exercise 15.4: Create a subclass of `FilterReader` that will return one line of input at a time via a method that blocks until a full line of input is available.

15.4.3 Buffered Streams

The `Buffered` stream classes—`BufferedInputStream`, `BufferedOutputStream`, `BufferedReader` and `BufferedWriter`—buffer their data to avoid every `read` or `write` going directly to the next stream. These classes are often used in conjunction with `File` streams—accessing a disk file is much slower than using a memory buffer, and buffering helps reduce file accesses.

Each of the `Buffered` streams supports two constructors: one takes a reference to the wrapped stream and the size of the buffer to use, while the other only takes a reference to the wrapped stream and uses a default buffer size.

When `read` is invoked on an empty `Buffered` input stream, it invokes `read` on its source stream, fills the buffer with as much data as is available—only blocking if it needs the data being waited for—and returns the requested data from that buffer. Future `read` invocations return data from that buffer until its contents are exhausted, and that causes another `read` on the source stream. This process continues until the source stream is exhausted.

`Buffered` output streams behave similarly. When a `write` fills the buffer, the destination stream's `write` is invoked to empty the buffer. This buffering can turn many small `write` requests on the `Buffered` stream into a single `write` request on the underlying destination.

Here is how to create a buffered output stream to write bytes to a file:

```
new BufferedOutputStream(new FileOutputStream(path));
```

You create a `FileOutputStream` with the path, put a `BufferedOutputStream` in front of it, and use the buffered stream object. This scheme enables you to buffer output destined for the file.

You must retain a reference to the `FileOutputStream` object if you want to invoke methods on it later because there is no way to obtain the downstream object from a `Filter` stream. However, you should rarely need to work with the downstream object. If you do keep a reference to a downstream object, you must ensure that the first upstream object is flushed before operating on the downstream object because data written to upper streams may not have yet been written all the way downstream. Closing an upstream object also closes all downstream objects, so a retained reference may cease to be usable.

The `Buffered` character streams also understand lines of text. The `newLine` method of `BufferedWriter` writes a line separator to the stream. Each system defines what constitutes a line separator using the system `String` property `line.separator`, which need not be a single character. You should use `newLine` to end lines in text files that may be read by humans on the local system (see "System Properties" on page 481).

The method `readLine` in `BufferedReader` returns a line of text as a `String`. The method `readLine` accepts any of the standard set of line separators: line feed (\n), carriage return (\r), or carriage return followed by line feed (\r\n). This implies that you should never set `line.separator` to use any other sequence. Otherwise, lines terminated by `newLine` would not be recognized by `readLine`. The string returned by `readLine` does not include the line separator. If the end of stream is encountered before the end of a line `readLine` returns `null`.

15.4.4 Piped Streams

Piped streams—`PipedInputStream`, `PipedOutputStream`, `PipedReader` and `PipedWriter`—are used as input/output pairs; data written on the output stream of a pair is the data read on the input stream. The pipe maintains an internal buffer, with an implementation defined capacity that allows writing and reading to proceed at different rates—there is no way to control the size of the buffer.

Pipes provide an I/O based mechanism for communicating data between different threads. The only safe way to use `Piped` streams is with two threads: one for reading and one for writing. Writing on one end of the pipe blocks the thread when the pipe fills up. If the writer and reader are the same thread, that thread will block permanently. Reading from a pipe blocks the thread if there is no input available.

To avoid blocking a thread forever when its counterpart at the other end of the pipe terminates, each pipe keeps track of the identity of the most recent reader and writer threads. The pipe checks to see that the thread at the other end is alive before blocking the current thread. If the thread at the other end has terminated, the current thread will get an `IOException`.

The following example uses a pipe stream to connect a `TextGenerator` thread with a thread that wants to read the generated text. First, the text generator:

```
class TextGenerator extends Thread {
    private Writer out;

    public TextGenerator(Writer out) {
        this.out = out;
    }

    public void run() {
        try {
            try {
                for (char c = 'a'; c <= 'z'; c++)
                    out.write(c);
```

```
        } finally {
            out.close();
        }
    } catch (IOException e) {
        getThreadGroup().uncaughtException(this, e);
    }
    }
}
```

The TextGenerator simply writes to the output stream passed to its constructor. In the example that stream will actually be a piped stream to be read by the main thread:

```
class Pipe {
    public static void main(String[] args)
        throws IOException
    {
        PipedWriter out = new PipedWriter();
        PipedReader in = new PipedReader(out);

        TextGenerator data = new TextGenerator(out);
        data.start();

        int ch;
        while ((ch = in.read()) != -1)
            System.out.print((char) ch);
        System.out.println();
    }
}
```

We create the Piped streams, making the PipedWriter a parameter to the constructor for the PipedReader. The order is unimportant: the output pipe could be a parameter to the input pipe. What is important is that an input/output pair be attached to each other. We create the new TextGenerator object, with the PipedWriter as the output stream for the generated characters. Then we loop, reading characters from the text generator and writing them to the system output stream. At the end, we make sure that the last line of output is terminated.

Piped streams need not be connected when they are constructed—there is a no-arg constructor—but can be connected at a later stage by using the connect method. PipedReader.connect takes a PipedWriter parameter and vice-versa. As with the constructor, it does not matter whether you connect x to y, or y to x, the result is the same. Trying to use a Piped stream before it is connected, or trying to connect it when it is already connected, results in an IOException.

15.4.5 **ByteArray Byte Streams**

You can use arrays of bytes as the source or destination of byte streams by using ByteArray streams.

The ByteArrayInputStream class uses a byte array as its input source. It has two constructors:

public **ByteArrayInputStream(byte[] buf, int offset, int count)**
> Creates a ByteArrayInputStream from the specified array of bytes using only the part of buf from buf[offset] to buf[offset+count-1] or the end of the array, whichever is smaller. The input array is used directly, not copied, so you should take care not to modify it while it is being used as an input source.

public **ByteArrayInputStream(byte[] buf)**
> Equivalent to ByteArrayInputStream(buf, 0, buf.length).

Reading from a ByteArrayInputStream can never block.

The ByteArrayOutputStream class provides a dynamically growing byte array to hold output. It adds constructors and methods:

public **ByteArrayOutputStream()**
> Creates a new ByteArrayOutputStream with a default initial array size.

public **ByteArrayOutputStream(int size)**
> Creates a new ByteArrayOutputStream with the specified initial array size.

public byte[] **toByteArray()**
> Returns a copy of the bytes generated thus far by output operations on the stream.

public int **size()**
> Returns the number of bytes generated thus far by output operations on the stream.

public void **reset()**
> Resets the stream to reuse the current buffer, discarding its contents.

public String **toString()**
> Returns the current contents of the buffer as a String, translating bytes into characters according to the default character encoding.

`public String` **`toString(String enc)`**
    `throws UnsupportedEncodingException`
> Returns the current contents of the buffer as a `String`, translating bytes into characters according to the specified character encoding. If the encoding is not supported an `UnsupportedEncodingException` is thrown.

`public void` **`writeTo(OutputStream out)`** `throws IOException`
> Writes the current contents of the buffer to the stream `out`.

When you are finished writing into a `ByteArrayOutputStream` via upstream filter streams, you should flush the upstream objects before using `toByteArray`.

15.4.6 CharArray Character Streams

The `CharArray` character streams are analogous to the `ByteArray` byte streams—they let you use `char` arrays as a source or destination. You construct `CharArrayReader` objects with an array of `char`:

`public` **`CharArrayReader(char[] buf, int offset, int length)`**
> Creates a `CharArrayReader` from the specified array of characters using only the subarray of `buf` from `buf[offset]` to `buf[offset+length-1]` or the end of the array, whichever is smaller. The input array is used directly, not copied, so you should take care not to modify it while it is being used as an input source.

`public` **`CharArrayReader(char[] buf)`**
> Equivalent to `CharArrayReader(buf, 0, buf.length)`.

Reading from a `CharArrayReader` can never block.

The `CharArrayWriter` class provides a dynamically growing `char` array to hold output. It adds constructors and methods:

`public` **`CharArrayWriter()`**
> Creates a new `CharArrayWriter` with a default initial array size.

`public` **`CharArrayWriter(int size)`**
> Creates a new `CharArrayWriter` with the specified initial array size.

`public char[]` **`toCharArray()`**
> Returns a copy of the characters generated thus far by output operations on the stream.

`public int` **`size()`**
> Returns the number of characters generated thus far by output operations on the stream.

`public void` **`reset()`**
> Resets the stream to reuse the current buffer, discarding its contents.

public String toString()
    Returns the current contents of the buffer as a String.

public void writeTo(Writer out) throws IOException
    Writes the current contents of the buffer to the stream out.

When you are finished writing into a CharArrayWriter via upstream filter streams, you should flush the upstream objects before using toCharArray.

15.4.7 String Character Streams

The StringReader reads its characters from a String and will never block. It provides a single constructor that takes the string from which to read. For example, the following program factors numbers read either from the command line or System.in:

```
class Factor {
    public static void main(String[] args) {
        if (args.length == 0) {
            factorNumbers(new InputStreamReader(System.in));
        } else {
            for (int i = 0; i < args.length; i++) {
                StringReader in = new StringReader(args[i]);
                factorNumbers(in);
            }
        }
    }
    // ...
}
```

If the command is invoked without parameters, factorNumbers parses numbers from the standard input stream. When the command line contains some arguments, a StringReader is created for each parameter, and factorNumbers is invoked on each one. The parameter to factorNumbers is a stream of characters containing numbers to be parsed; it does not know whether they come from the command line or from standard input.

StringWriter lets you write results into a buffer that can be retrieved as a String or StringBuffer object. It adds the following constructors and methods:

public StringWriter()
    Creates a new StringWriter with a default initial buffer size.

public **StringWriter(int size)**

> Creates a new StringWriter with the specified initial buffer size. Providing a good initial size estimate for the buffer will improve performance in many cases.

public StringBuffer **getBuffer()**

> Returns the actual StringBuffer being used by this stream. Because the actual StringBuffer is returned, you should take care not to modify it while it is being used as an output destination.

public String **toString()**

> Returns the current contents of the buffer as a String.

The following code uses a StringWriter to create a string that contains the output of a series of println calls on the contents of an array:

```
public static String arrayToStr(Object[] objs) {
    StringWriter strOut = new StringWriter();
    PrintWriter out = new PrintWriter(strOut);
    for (int i = 0; i < objs.length; i++)
        out.println(i + ": " + objs[i]);
    return out.toString();
}
```

15.4.8 Print Streams

The Print streams—PrintStream and PrintWriter—provide methods that make it easy to write the values of primitive types and objects to a stream, in a human-readable text format—as you have seen in many examples. The Print streams provide print and println methods for the following types:

char	int	float	Object	boolean
char[]	long	double	String	

These methods are much more convenient to use than the raw stream write methods. For example, given a float variable f and a PrintStream out, out.print(f) is equivalent to:

```
out.write(String.valueOf(f).getBytes());
```

The println method appends a line separator after writing its argument to the stream—a simple println with no parameters ends the current line. The line separator string is defined by the system property line.separator, and is not necessarily a single newline character (\n).

Each of the `Print` streams acts as a `Filter` stream, so you can filter data on its way downstream.

The `PrintStream` class acts on byte streams while the `PrintWriter` class acts on character streams. Because printing is clearly character-related output, the `PrintWriter` class is the class you should use. However, for historical reasons `System.out` and `System.err` are `PrintStreams` that assume all bytes are Latin-1 characters—these are the only `PrintStream` objects you should use. We will only describe the `PrintWriter` class, though `PrintStream` provides essentially the same interface.

`PrintWriter` has four constructors.

public **PrintWriter(Writer out, boolean autoflush)**
> Creates a new `PrintWriter` that will write to the stream out. If `autoflush` is `true`, `println` invokes `flush`. Otherwise, `println` invocations are treated like any other method, and `flush` is not invoked. Autoflush behavior cannot be changed after the stream is constructed.

public **PrintWriter(Writer out)**
> Equivalent to `PrintWriter(out, false)`.

public **PrintWriter(OutputStream out, boolean autoflush)**
> Equivalent to
> `PrintWriter(new OutputStreamWriter(out), autoflush)`.

public **PrintWriter(OutputStream out)**
> Equivalent to `PrintWriter(new OutputStreamWriter(out), false)`.

One important characteristic of the `Print` streams is that none of the output methods throw `IOException`. If an error occurs while writing to the underlying stream the methods simply return normally. You should check if an error occurred by invoking the boolean method `checkError`—this flushes the stream and checks its error state. Once an error has occurred, there is no way to clear it. If any of the underlying stream operations result in an `InterruptedIOException`, the error state is not set, but instead the current thread is re-interrupted using `Thread.currentThread().interrupt()`.

15.4.9 LineNumberReader

The `LineNumberReader` stream keeps track of line numbers while reading text. As usual a line is considered to be terminated by any one of a line feed (\n), a carriage return (\r), or a carriage return followed immediately by a linefeed (\r\n).

The following program prints the line number where the first instance of a particular character is found in a file:

```java
import java.io.*;

class FindChar {
    public static void main(String[] args)
        throws IOException
    {
        if (args.length != 2)
            throw new IllegalArgumentException(
                                        "need char and file");

        int match = args[0].charAt(0);
        FileReader fileIn = new FileReader(args[1]);
        LineNumberReader in = new LineNumberReader(fileIn);
        int ch;
        while ((ch = in.read()) != -1) {
            if (ch == match) {
                System.out.println("'" + (char)ch +
                    "' at line " + in.getLineNumber());
                return;
            }
        }
        System.out.println((char)ch + " not found");
    }
}
```

This program creates a `FileReader` named `fileIn` to read from the named file and then inserts a `LineNumberReader`, named `in`, before it. `LineNumberReader` objects get their characters from the reader they are attached to, keeping track of line numbers as they read. The `getLineNumber` method returns the current line number; by default, lines are counted starting from zero. When this program is run on itself looking for the letter `'I'`, its output is

```
'I' at line 4
```

You can set the current line number using `setLineNumber`. This could be useful, for example, if you have a file that contains several sections of information. You could use `setLineNumber` to reset the line number to 1 at the start of each section so that problems would be reported to the user based on the line numbers within the section instead of within the file.

LineNumberReader is a BufferedReader that has two constructors: one takes a reference to the wrapped stream and the size of the buffer to use, while the other only takes a reference to the wrapped stream and uses a default buffer size.

Exercise 15.5: Write a program that reads a specified file and searches for a specified word, printing all the lines on which that word is found, preceded by the line's number.

15.4.10 SequenceInputStream

The SequenceInputStream class creates a single input stream from reading one or more byte input streams, reading the first stream until its end of input and then reading the next one, and so on through the last one. SequenceInputStream has two constructors: one for the common case of two input streams that are provided as the two parameters to the constructor, and the other for an arbitrary number of input streams using the Enumeration abstraction (described in "Enumeration" on page 456). Enumeration is an interface that provides an ordered iteration through a list of objects. For SequenceInputStream, the enumeration should contain only InputStream objects. If it contains anything else a ClassCastException is thrown when the SequenceInputStream tries to get that object from the list.

The following example program concatenates all its input to create a single output. This program is similar to a simple version of the UNIX utility cat—if no files are named, the input is simply forwarded to the output. Otherwise, it opens all the files and uses a SequenceInputStream to model them as a single stream. Then the program writes its input to its output:

```
import java.io.*;
import java.util.*;

class Concat {
    public static void main(String[] args)
        throws IOException
    {
        InputStream in; // stream to read numbers from
        if (args.length == 0) {
            in = System.in;
        } else {
            InputStream fileIn, bufIn;
            List inputs = new ArrayList(args.length);
            for (int i = 0; i < args.length; i++) {
                fileIn = new FileInputStream(args[i]);
```

```
            bufIn = new BufferedInputStream(fileIn);
            inputs.add(bufIn);
        }
        Enumeration files =
            Collections.enumeration(inputs);
        in = new SequenceInputStream(files);
    }

    int ch;
    while ((ch = in.read()) != -1)
        System.out.write(ch);
    }
    // ...
}
```

If there are no parameters, we use System.in for input. If there are parameters, we create an ArrayList large enough to hold as many BufferedInputStream objects as there are command-line arguments (see "ArrayList" on page 435). Then we create a stream for each named file and add the stream to the inputs list. When the loop is finished, we use the Collection class's enumeration method to get an Enumeration object for the list elements. We use this Enumeration in the constructor for SequenceInputStream to create a single stream that concatenates all the streams for the files into a single InputStream object. Then a simple loop reads all the bytes from that stream and writes them on System.out.

You could instead write your own implementation of Enumeration whose nextElement method creates a StringInputStream for each argument on demand, closing the previous stream, if any.

15.4.11 Pushback Streams

A Pushback stream lets you push back, or "unread," characters, or bytes, when you have read too far. Pushback is typically useful for breaking input into tokens. Lexical scanners, for example, often know that a token (such as an identifier) has ended only when they have read the first character that follows it. Having seen that character, the scanner must push it back onto the input stream so it is available as the start of the next token. The following example uses PushbackInputStream to report the longest consecutive sequence of any single byte in its input:

```
import java.io.*;

class SequenceCount {
    public static void main(String[] args)
```

```
            throws IOException
    {

        PushbackInputStream
            in = new PushbackInputStream(System.in);

        int max = 0;      // longest sequence found
        int maxB = -1;    // the byte in that sequence
        int b;            // current byte in input

        do {
            int cnt;
            int b1 = in.read(); // 1st byte in sequence
            for (cnt = 1; (b = in.read()) == b1; cnt++)
                continue;
            if (cnt > max) {
                max = cnt; // remember length
                maxB = b1; // remember which byte value
            }
            in.unread(b);   // pushback start of next seq
        } while (b != -1); // until we hit end of input

        System.out.println(max + " bytes of " + maxB);
    }
}
```

We know that we have reached the end of one sequence only when we read the first byte of the next sequence. We push this byte back using unread so that it is read again when we repeat the do loop for the next sequence.

Both PushbackInputStream and PushbackReader support two constructors: one takes a reference to the wrapped stream and the size of the pushback buffer to create, while the other only takes a reference to the wrapped stream and uses a pushback buffer with space for one piece of data (byte or char as appropriate). Attempting to push back more than the specified amount of data will cause an IOException.

Each Pushback stream has three variants of unread, matching the variants of read. We'll illustrate the character version of PushbackReader, but the byte equivalents for PushbackInputStream have the same behavior:

public void **unread(int c)** throws IOException

> Pushes back the single character c. If the pushback buffer is full an IOException is thrown.

```
public void unread(char[] buf, int offset, int count)
    throws IOException
```
Pushes back the characters in the specified subarray. The first character pushed back is buf[offset] and the last is buf[offset+count-1]. The subarray is prepended to the front of the pushback buffer, such that the next character to be read will be that at buf[offset], then buf[offset+1] and so on. If there is insufficient room in the pushback buffer an IOException is thrown.

```
public void unread(char[] buf) throws IOException
```
Equivalent to unread(buf, 0, buf.length).

For example, after two consecutive unread calls on a PushbackReader with the characters '1' and '2', the next two characters read will be '2' and '1', because '2' was pushed back second. Each unread sets its own list of characters by prepending to the buffer, so the code

```
pbr.unread(new char[] {'1', '2'});
pbr.unread(new char[] {'3', '4'});
for (int i = 0; i < 4; i++)
    System.out.println(i + ": " + (char)pbr.read());
```

produces the following lines of output:

```
0: 3
1: 4
2: 1
3: 2
```

Data from the last unread (the one with '3' and '4') is read back first, and within that unread the data comes from the beginning of the array through to the end. When that data is exhausted, the data from the first unread is returned in the same order. The unread method copies data into the pushback buffer, so changes made to an array after it is used with unread do not affect future calls to read.

15.4.12 StreamTokenizer

Tokenizing input text is a common application, and the java.io package provides a StreamTokenizer class for simple tokenization problems. A stream is tokenized by creating a StreamTokenizer with a Reader object as its source and then setting parameters for the scan. A scanner loop invokes nextToken, which returns the token type of the next token in the stream. Some token types have associated values that are found in fields in the StreamTokenizer object.

This class is designed primarily to parse programming language-style input; it is not a general tokenizer. However, many configuration files look similar enough to programming languages that they can be parsed by this tokenizer. When designing a new configuration file or other data, you can save work if you make it look enough like a language to be parsed with StreamTokenizer.

When nextToken recognizes a token, it returns the token type as its value and also sets the ttype field to the same value. There are four token types:

- ◆ TT_WORD: A word was scanned. The String field sval contains the word that was found.

- ◆ TT_NUMBER: A number was scanned. The double field nval contains the value of the number. Only decimal floating-point numbers (with or without a decimal point) are recognized. The tokenizer does not understand 3.4e79 as a floating-point number, nor 0xffff as a hexadecimal number.

- ◆ TT_EOL: An end-of-line was found.

- ◆ TT_EOF: The end-of-file was reached.

The input text is assumed to consist of bytes in the range \u0000 to \u00FF— Unicode characters outside this range are not handled correctly. Input is composed of *special* and *ordinary* characters. Special characters are those that the tokenizer treats specially—namely white space, characters that make up numbers, characters that make up words, and so on. Any other character is considered ordinary. When an ordinary character is the next character in the input, its token type is itself. For example, if the character '¿' is encountered in the input and is not special, the token return type (and the ttype field) is the int value of the character '¿'.

As one example, let's look at a method that sums the numeric values in a character stream it is given:

```java
static double sumStream(Reader in) throws IOException {
    StreamTokenizer nums = new StreamTokenizer(in);
    double result = 0.0;
    while (nums.nextToken() != StreamTokenizer.TT_EOF) {
        if (nums.ttype == StreamTokenizer.TT_NUMBER)
            result += nums.nval;
    }
    return result;
}
```

We create a `StreamTokenizer` object from the reader and then loop, reading tokens from the stream, adding all the numbers found into the burgeoning result. When we get to the end of the input, we return the final sum.

Here is another example that reads a file, looking for attributes of the form name=value, and stores them as attributes in `AttributedImpl` objects, described in "Implementing Interfaces" on page 114:

```java
public static Attributed readAttrs(String file)
    throws IOException
{
    FileReader fileIn = new FileReader(file);
    StreamTokenizer in = new StreamTokenizer(fileIn);
    AttributedImpl attrs = new AttributedImpl();
    Attr attr = null;

    in.commentChar('#');    // '#' is ignore-to-end comment
    in.ordinaryChar('/');   // was original comment char
    while (in.nextToken() != StreamTokenizer.TT_EOF) {
        if (in.ttype == StreamTokenizer.TT_WORD) {
            if (attr != null) {
                attr.setValue(in.sval);
                attr = null;         // used this one up
            } else {
                attr = new Attr(in.sval);
                attrs.add(attr);
            }
        } else if (in.ttype == '=') {
            if (attr == null)
                throw new IOException("misplaced '='");
        } else {
            if (attr == null)        // expected a word
                throw new IOException("bad Attr name");
            attr.setValue(new Double(in.nval));
            attr = null;
        }
    }
    return attrs;
}
```

The attribute file uses # to mark comments. Ignoring these comments, the stream is searched for a string token followed by an optional = followed by a word or number. Each such attribute is put into an `Attr` object, which is added to a set of attributes in an `AttributedImpl` object. When the file has been parsed, the set of attributes is returned.

Setting the comment character to # sets its character class. The tokenizer recognizes several character classes that are set by the following methods:

public void **wordChars(int low, int hi)**
> Characters in this range are word characters: they can be part of a TT_WORD token. You can invoke this several times with different ranges. A word consists of one or more characters inside any of the legal ranges.

public void **whitespaceChars(int low, int hi)**
> Characters in this range are white space. White space is ignored, except to separate tokens such as two consecutive words. As with the wordChars range, you can make several invocations, and the union of the invocations is the set of whitespace characters.

public void **ordinaryChars(int low, int hi)**
> Characters in this range are ordinary. An ordinary character is returned as itself, not as a token. This removes any special significance the characters may have had as comment characters, delimiters, word components, whitespace or number characters. In the preceding readAttrs example, we used ordinaryChar to remove the special comment significance of the '/' character.

public void **ordinaryChar(int ch)**
> Equivalent to ordinaryChar(ch, ch).

public void **commentChar(int ch)**
> The character ch starts a single-line comment—characters after ch up to the next end-of-line are treated as one run of white space.

public void **quoteChar(int ch)**
> Matching pairs of the character ch delimit String constants. When a String constant is recognized, the character ch is returned as the token, and the field sval contains the body of the string with surrounding ch characters removed. When reading string constants some of the standard \ processing is followed (for example, you can have \t in the string). The string processing in StreamTokenizer is a subset of the language's strings. In particular, you cannot use \u$xxxx$, \', \", or (unfortunately) \Q, where Q is the quote character ch. You can have more than one quote character at a time on a stream, but strings must start and end with the same quote character. In other words, a string that starts with one quote character ends when the next instance of that same quote character is found; if a different quote character is found in between, it is simply part of the string.

public void **parseNumbers()**

Specifies that numbers should be parsed as double-precision floating-point numbers. When a number is found, the stream returns a type of TT_NUMBER, leaving the value in nval. There is no way to turn off just this feature—to turn this off you must either invoke ordinaryChars for all the number-related characters (don't forget the decimal point and minus sign) or invoke resetSyntax.

public void **resetSyntax()**

Resets the syntax table so that all characters are ordinary. If you do this and then start reading the stream, nextToken always returns the next character in the stream, just as when you invoke InputStream.read.

There are no methods to query the character class of a given character or to add new classes of characters. Here are the default settings for a newly created StreamTokenizer object:

```
wordChars('a', 'z');        // lower case ASCII letters
wordChars('A', 'Z');        // upper case ASCII letters
wordChars(128 + 32, 255);   // "high" non-ASCII values
whitespaceChars(0, ' ');    // ASCII control codes
commentChar('/');
quoteChar('"');
quoteChar('\'');
parseNumbers();
```

This leaves the ordinary characters consisting of most of the punctuation and arithmetic characters (;, :, [, {, +, =, and so forth).

The changes made to the character classes are cumulative, so, for example, invoking wordChars with two different ranges of characters defines both ranges as word characters. To replace a range you must first mark the old range as ordinary and then add the new range. Resetting the syntax table clears all settings, so if you want to return to the default settings, for example, you must manually make the invocations listed above.

Other methods control the basic behavior of the tokenizer:

public void **eolIsSignificant(boolean flag)**

If flag is true, ends of lines are significant and TT_EOL may be returned by nextToken. If false, ends of lines are treated as white space and TT_EOL is never returned. The default is false.

public void **slashStarComments(boolean flag)**

If flag is true, the tokenizer recognizes /*...*/ comments. This occurs independently of the settings for any comment characters. The default is false.

public void **slashSlashComments(boolean flag)**

> If flag is true, the tokenizer recognizes // to end-of-line comments. This occurs independently of the settings for any comment characters. The default is false.

public void **lowerCaseMode(boolean flag)**

> If flag is true, all characters in TT_WORD tokens are converted to their lowercase equivalent if they have one (using String.toLowerCase). The default is false. Because of the case issues described in "Character" on page 275, you cannot reliably use this for Unicode string equivalence—two tokens might be equivalent but have different lowercase representations. Use the method String.equalsIgnoreCase for reliable case-insensitive comparison.

There are three miscellaneous methods:

public void **pushBack()**

> Pushes the previously returned token back into the stream. The next invocation of nextToken returns the same token again instead of proceeding to the next token. There is only a one-token pushback; multiple consecutive invocations to pushBack are equivalent to one invocation.

public int **lineno()**

> Returns the current line number. This is usually useful for reporting errors that you detect.

public String **toString()**

> Returns a String representation of the last returned stream token, including its line number.

Exercise 15.6: Write a program that takes input of the form *name op value*, where *name* is one of three words of your choosing, *op* is +, -, or =, and *value* is a number. Apply each operator to the named value. When input is exhausted, print the three values. For extra credit, use the HashMap class that was used for AttributedImpl so you can use an arbitrary number of named values.

15.5 The Data Byte Streams

Reading and writing text characters is useful, but you also frequently need to transmit the binary data of specific types across a stream. The DataInput and DataOutput interfaces define methods that transmit primitive types across a stream. The classes DataInputStream and DataOutputStream provide a default implementation for each interface. We cover the interfaces first, followed by their implementations.

15.5.1 `DataInput` and `DataOutput`

The interfaces for data input and output streams are almost mirror images. The parallel read and write methods for each type are:

Read	Write	Type
readBoolean	writeBoolean	boolean
readChar	writeChar	char
readByte	writeByte	byte
readShort	writeShort	short
readInt	writeInt	int
readLong	writeLong	long
readFloat	writeFloat	float
readDouble	writeDouble	double
readUTF	writeUTF	String (in UTF format)

UTF is Universal Transfer Format. Unicode characters are transmitted in Unicode-1-1-UTF-8, which is a usually compact binary form designed to encode 16-bit Unicode characters in 8-bit bytes. Encoding Unicode characters into bytes is necessary in many situations due to the continuing transition from 8-bit to 16-bit character sets.

In addition to these paired methods, `DataInput` has several methods of its own, some of which are similar to those of `InputStream`:

public abstract void `readFully(byte[] buf, int offset, int count)`
  throws IOException
> Reads into part of a byte array. The maximum number of bytes read is count. The bytes are stored from buf[offset] up to a maximum of buf[offset+count-1]. If count is zero then no bytes are read. This method blocks until input is available, the end of the file (that is, stream) is found—in which case an EOFException is thrown—or an exception is thrown due to an I/O error.

public abstract void `readFully(byte[] buf)` throws IOException
> Equivalent to readFully(buf, 0, buf.length).

public abstract int `skipBytes(int n)` throws IOException
> Attempts to skip over count bytes, discarding any bytes skipped over. Returns the actual number of bytes skipped. This method never throws an EOFException.

public abstract int **readUnsignedByte()** throws IOException

    Reads one input byte, zero-extends it to type int, and returns the result, which is therefore in the range 0 through 255. This method is suitable for reading the byte written by the writeByte method of DataOutput if the argument to writeByte was intended to be a value in the range 0 through 255.

public abstract int **readUnsignedShort()** throws IOException

    Reads two input bytes and returns an int value in the range 0 through 65535. The first byte read is made the high byte. This method is suitable for reading the bytes written by the writeShort method of DataOutput if the argument to writeShort was intended to be a value in the range 0 through 65535.

The DataInput interface methods usually handle end-of-file (stream) by throwing EOFException when it occurs. EOFException extends IOException.

The DataOutput interface supports signatures equivalent to the three forms of write in OutputStream and with the same specified behavior. Additionally it provides the following unmirrored methods:

public abstract void **writeBytes(String s)** throws IOException

    Writes a String as a sequence of bytes. The upper byte in each character is lost, so unless you are willing to lose data, this method should be used only for strings that contain characters between \u0000 and \u00ff.

public abstract void **writeChars(String s)** throws IOException

    Writes a String as a sequence of char. Each character is written as two bytes with the high byte written first.

There are no readBytes or readChars methods to read the same number of characters written using a writeBytes or writeChars invocation, therefore you must read strings written with these methods using a loop on readByte or readChar. To do that you need a way to determine the length of the string, perhaps by writing the length of the string first or using an end-of-sequence character to mark its end. You can use readFully to read a full array of bytes if you wrote the length first, but that won't work for writeChars because you want char values, not byte values.

15.5.2 The Data Stream Classes

For each Data interface there is a corresponding Data stream. In addition, the RandomAccessFile class implements both the input and output Data interfaces (see Section 15.6.2 on page 396). Each Data class is an extension of its corresponding Filter class, so Data streams can be used to filter other streams. Each

Data class has constructors that take another appropriate input or output stream. For example, the filtering can be used to write data to a file by putting a DataOutputStream in front of a FileOutputStream object. The data can then be read by putting a DataInputStream in front of a FileInputStream object:

```
public static void writeData(double[] data, String file)
    throws IOException
{
    OutputStream fout = new FileOutputStream(file);
    DataOutputStream out = new DataOutputStream(fout);
    out.writeInt(data.length);
    for (int i = 0; i < data.length; i++)
        out.writeDouble(data[i]);
    out.close();
}

public static double[] readData(String file)
    throws IOException
{
    InputStream fin = new FileInputStream(file);
    DataInputStream in = new DataInputStream(fin);
    double[] data = new double[in.readInt()];
    for (int i = 0; i < data.length; i++)
        data[i] = in.readDouble();
    in.close();
    return data;
}
```

The writeData method first opens the file and writes the array length. It then loops, writing the contents of the array. The file can be read into an array using readData. These methods can be rewritten more simply using the Object streams you will learn about in Section 15.7 on page 404.

Exercise 15.7: Add a method to the Body class of Chapter 2 that writes the contents of an object to a DataOutputStream and add a constructor that will read the state from a DataInputStream.

15.6 Working with Files

The java.io package provides a number of classes that help you work with files in the underlying system. The File stream classes allow you to read from and write to files and the `FileDescriptor` class allows the system to represent under-lying file system resources as objects. `RandomAccessFile` lets you deal with files as randomly accessed streams of bytes or characters. The actual interface to the local file system is the `File` class, which provides an abstraction of file path-names, including path component separators, and useful methods to manipulate file names.

15.6.1 File Streams and `FileDescriptor`

The `File` streams—`FileInputStream`, `FileOutputStream`, `FileReader` and `FileWriter`—allow you to treat a file as a stream for input or output. Each type is instantiated with one of three constructors:

- ◆ A constructor that takes a `String` that is the name of the file.
- ◆ A constructor that takes a `File` object that refers to the file (see Section 15.6.3 on page 398).
- ◆ A constructor that takes a `FileDescriptor` object (see below).

For the byte and character input streams, if a file does not exist, you will get a `FileNotFoundException`. In all cases, accessing a file requires a security check and a `SecurityException` is thrown if you do not have permission to access that file—see "Security" on page 493).

With a byte or character output stream, the first two constructor types create the file if it does not exist, or truncate it if it does exist. You can get control over truncation by using the additional output stream constructors that take two param-eters: a `String` that is the name of the file and a `boolean` that, if `true`, causes each individual write to append to the file. If this `boolean` is `false`, the file will be truncated and new data added. If the file does not exist, the file will be created and the `boolean` will be ignored.

A `FileDescriptor` object represents a system-dependent value that describes an open file. A file descriptor object can be obtained by invoking `getFD` on a `File` byte stream—you cannot obtain the file descriptor from `File` character streams. You can test the validity of a `FileDescriptor` by invoking its boolean `valid` method—file descriptors created directly using the no-arg constructor of `FileDescriptor` are not valid.

`FileDescriptor` objects are used to create a new `File` stream to the same file as another stream without needing to know the file's pathname. You must be careful to avoid unexpected interactions between two streams doing different things with the same file. You cannot predict what happens, for example, when two threads write to the same file using two different `FileOutputStream` objects at the same time.

The `flush` method of `FileOutputStream` and `FileWriter` guarantees that the buffer is flushed to the underlying file. It does not guarantee that the data is committed to disk—the underlying file system may do its own buffering. You can guarantee that the data is committed to disk by invoking the `sync` method on the file's `FileDescriptor` object, which will either force the data to disk or will throw a `SyncFailedException` if the underlying system cannot fulfill this contract.

15.6.2 RandomAccessFile

The `RandomAccessFile` class provides a more sophisticated file mechanism than the `File` streams. A random access file behaves like a large array of bytes stored in the file system. There is a kind of cursor, or index into the implied array, called the *file pointer*; input operations read bytes starting at the file pointer and advance the file pointer past the bytes read. If the random access file is created in read/write mode, then output operations are also available; output operations write bytes starting at the file pointer and advance the file pointer past the bytes written.

`RandomAccessFile` is not a subclass of `InputStream`, `OutputStream`, `Reader`, or `Writer` because it can do both input and output and can work with both characters and bytes. The constructor has a parameter that declares whether the stream is for input, output, or both.

`RandomAccessFile` supports methods of the same names and signatures as the `read` and `write` invocations of the byte streams; for example, `read` returns a single byte. `RandomAccessFile` also implements the `DataInput` and `DataOutput` interfaces (see page 392) and so can be used to read and write data types supported in those interfaces. Although you don't have to learn a new set of method names and semantics for the same kinds of tasks you do with the other streams, you cannot use a `RandomAccessFile` where any of the other input or output streams are required.

The constructors for `RandomAccessFile` are:

public **RandomAccessFile(String name, String mode)**
    throws FileNotFoundException
    Creates a random access file stream to read from, and optionally to write to, a file with the specified name. The mode can be either "r" or "rw" for read or read/write, respectively. Specifying any other mode will get you an `IllegalArgumentException`. If the mode is "rw" and the file does not exist, an attempt is made to create it, otherwise a `FileNotFoundException` is thrown.

public **RandomAccessFile(File file, String mode)**
  throws FileNotFoundException
> Creates a random access file stream to read from, and optionally to write to, the file specified by the File argument. Modes are the same as for the String-based constructor.

As accessing a file requires a security check, these constructors could throw a SecurityException if you do not have permission to access the file in that mode—see "Security" on page 493.

The "random access" in the name of the class refers to the ability to set the read/write file pointer to any position in the file and then perform your operations. The additional methods in RandomAccessFile to support this functionality are:

public long **getFilePointer()** throws IOException
> Returns the current location of the file pointer (in bytes) from the beginning of the file.

public void **seek(long pos)** throws IOException
> Sets the file pointer to the specified number of bytes from the beginning of the file. The next byte written or read will be the posth byte in the file, where the initial byte is the 0th. Positioning the file pointer beyond the end of the file will cause the file to grow if a write occurs with the file pointer in that position.

public int **skipBytes (int count)** throws IOException
> Attempts to advance the file pointer count bytes, discarding any bytes skipped over. Returns the actual number of bytes skipped. This method is guaranteed never to throw an EOFException. If count is negative, no bytes are skipped.

public long **length()** throws IOException
> Returns the file length.

public void **setLength(long newLength)** throws IOException
> Sets the length of the file to newLength. If the file is currently shorter, the file is grown to the given length, filled in with any byte values the implementation chooses. If the file is currently longer, the data beyond this position is discarded. If the current position (as returned by getFilePointer) is greater than newLength, the position is set to newLength.

You can access the FileDescriptor for a RandomAccessFile by invoking its getFD method.

Exercise 15.8: Write a program that reads a file with entries separated by lines starting with %%, and creates a table file with the starting position of each such entry.

Then write a program that prints a random entry using that table (see the Math.random method described in "Math and StrictMath" on page 477).

15.6.3   The File Class

The File class (not to be confused with the file streams) provides several common manipulations that are useful with file names. It provides methods to separate pathnames into subcomponents and for querying the file system about the file a pathname refers to.

A File object actually represents a path, not necessarily an underlying file. For example, to find out whether a pathname represents an existing file, you create a File object with the pathname and then invoke exists on that object.

A path is separated into directory and file parts by a char stored in the static field separatorChar and available as a String in the static field separator. The last occurrence of this character in the path separates the pathname into directory and file components. (*Directory* is the term used on most systems; some systems call such an entity a "folder" instead.)

File objects are created using one of three constructors:

public **File(String path)**

> Creates a File object to manipulate the specified path.

public **File(String dirName, String name)**

> Creates a File object for the file name in the directory named dirName. If dirName is null, only name. If dirName is an empty string, name is resolved against a system dependent default directory. Otherwise, this is equivalent to using File(dirName + File.separator + name).

public **File(File fileDir, String name)**

> Creates a File object for the file name in the directory named by the File object fileDir. Equivalent to using File(fileDir.getPath(), name).

Five "get" methods retrieve information about the components of a File object's pathname. The following code invokes each of them after creating a File object for the file "FileInfo.java" in the "ok" subdirectory of the parent of the current directory (specified by ".."):

```
File src = new File(".." + File.separator + "ok",
                    "FileInfo.java");
System.out.println("getName() = " + src.getName());
System.out.println("getPath() = " + src.getPath());
System.out.println("getAbsolutePath() = "
    + src.getAbsolutePath());
```

```
System.out.println("getCanonicalPath() = "
    + src.getCanonicalPath());
System.out.println("getParent() = " + src.getParent());
```

And here is the output:

```
getName() = FileInfo.java
getPath() = ../ok/FileInfo.java
getAbsolutePath() = /vob/java_prog/src/../ok/FileInfo.java
getCanonicalPath() = /vob/java_prog/ok/FileInfo.java
getParent() = ../ok
```

The canonical path is defined by each system. Usually, it is a form of the absolute path with relative components (such as ".." to refer to the parent directory) renamed and references to the current directory removed. Unlike the other "get" methods, `getCanonicalPath` can throw `IOException` because resolving path components can require calls to the underlying file system that may fail.

The methods `getParentFile`, `getAbsoluteFile`, and `getCanonicalFile` are analogous to `getParent`, `getAbsolutePath`, and `getCanonicalPath`, but return `File` objects instead of strings.

The overridden method `File.equals` deserves mention. Two `File` objects are considered equal if they have the same path, not if they refer to the same underlying file system object. You cannot use `File.equals` to test whether two `File` objects denote the same file. For example, two `File` objects may refer to the same file but use different relative paths to refer to it, in which case they do not compare equal. Relatedly, you can compare two files using the `compareTo` method, which returns a number less than, equal to, or greater than zero, if the current files pathname is lexicographically less than, equal to, or greater than the path name of the argument `File`. The `compareTo` method has two overloaded forms: one takes a `File` argument and the other takes an `Object` argument and so implements the `Comparable` interface.

Several boolean tests return information about the underlying file:

- `exists` returns `true` if the file exists in the file system.
- `canRead` returns `true` if a file exists and can be read.
- `canWrite` returns `true` if the file exists and can be written.
- `isFile` returns `true` if the file is not a directory or other special type of file.
- `isDirectory` returns `true` if the file is a directory.
- `isAbsolute` returns `true` if the path is an absolute pathname.

◆ isHidden returns true if the path is one normally hidden from users on the underlying system.

All of the methods that query or modify the actual file system are security checked and can throw SecurityException if you don't have permission to perform the operation. Methods that query the filename itself are not security checked.

File objects have many other methods for manipulating files and directories. There are methods to query and manipulate the current file:

public long **lastModified()**
> Returns a long value representing the time the file was last modified or zero if the file does not exist

public long **length()**
> Returns the file length in bytes, or zero if the file does not exist.

public boolean **renameTo(File newName)**
> Renames the file, returning true if the rename succeeded.

public boolean **delete()**
> Deletes the file or directory named in this File object, returning true if the deletion succeeded. Directories must be empty before they are deleted.

There are methods to create an underlying file or directory named by the current File:

public boolean **createNewFile()**
> Creates a new empty file, named by this File. Returns false if the file already exists, or the file cannot be created. The check for the existence of the file and its subsequent creation, is performed atomically with respect to other file system operations. This method, in combination with the method deleteOnExit, can therefore serve as the basis for a simple but reliable cooperative file-locking protocol.

public boolean **mkdir()**
> Creates a directory named by this File, returning true on success.

public boolean **mkdirs()**
> Creates all directories in the path named by this File, returning true if all were created. This is a way to ensure that a particular directory is created, even if it means creating other directories which don't currently exist above it in the directory hierarchy. Note that some of the directories may have been created even if false is returned.

However, files are usually created using FileOutputStream or FileWriter objects or RandomAccessFile objects, not using File objects.

Two methods let you change the state of the underlying file, assuming that one exists:

public boolean **setLastModified(long time)**
> Sets the "last modified" time for the file or returns `false` if it cannot do so.

public boolean **setReadOnly()**
> Makes the underlying file unmodifiable in the file system or returns `false` if it cannot do so. The file remains unmodifiable until it is deleted or externally marked as modifiable again—there is no method for making it modifiable again.

There are methods for listing the contents of directories and finding out about root directories:

public String[] **list()**
> Lists the files in this directory. If used on something that isn't a directory, it returns `null`. Otherwise, it returns an array of file names. This list includes all files in the directory except the equivalent of `"."` and `".."` (the current and parent directory, respectively).

public String[] **list(FilenameFilter filter)**
> Uses `filter` to selectively list files in this directory (see `FilenameFilter` described in the next section).

public static File[] **listRoots()**
> Returns the available filesystem roots, that is, roots of local hierarchical file systems. Windows platforms, for example, have a root directory for each active drive; UNIX platforms have a single / root directory. If none are available, the array has zero elements.

The methods `listFiles()` and `listFiles(FilenameFilter)` are analogous to `list()` and `list(FilenameFilter)`, but return arrays of `File` objects instead of arrays of strings. The method `listFiles(FileFilter)` is analogous to the `list` that uses a `FilenameFilter`.

Three methods relate primarily to temporary files (sometimes called "scratch files")—those files you need to create during a run of your program for storing data, or to pass between passes of your computation, but which are not needed after your program is finished.

public static File **createTempFile(String prefix, String suffix, File directory)** throws IOException
> Creates a new empty file in the specified directory, using the given prefix and suffix strings to generate its name. If this method returns successfully then it is guaranteed that the file denoted by the returned abstract pathname did not exist before this method was invoked, and neither this method nor any of its variants will return the same abstract pathname again in the current invoca-

tion of the virtual machine. The `prefix` argument must be at least three characters long, otherwise an `IllegalArgumentException` is thrown. It is recommended that the prefix be a short, meaningful string such as `"hjb"` or `"mail"`. The `suffix` argument may be `null`, in which case the suffix `".tmp"` will be used. Note that there is no predefined separator between the file name and the suffix, any separator, such as `'.'`, must be part of the suffix. If the `directory` argument is `null` then the system-dependent default temporary-file directory will be used. The default temporary-file directory is specified by the system property `java.io.tmpdir`.

`public static File` **`createTempFile(String prefix, String suffix)`**
   `throws IOException`
   Equivalent to `createTempFile(prefix, suffix, null)`.

`public void` **`deleteOnExit()`**
   Requests the system to remove the file when the virtual machine terminates—see "Shutdown" on page 488. This request only applies to a normal termination of the virtual machine and cannot be revoked once issued.

To create the temporary file, the prefix and the suffix may first be adjusted to fit the limitations of the underlying platform. If the prefix is too long then it will be truncated, but its first three characters will always be preserved. If the suffix is too long then it too will be truncated, but if it begins with a period (`.`) then the period and the first three characters following it will always be preserved. Once these adjustments have been made the name of the new file will be generated by concatenating the prefix, five or more internally-generated characters, and the suffix. Temporary files are not automatically deleted on exit, although you will often invoke `deleteOnExit` on `File` objects returned by `createTempFile`.

You can use `createNewFile` and `deleteOnExit` to create locks in the file system. For example:

```
public static void main(String[] args)
    throws DataBaseInaccessibleException, IOException
{
    File lockFile = new File("database.lck");
    boolean haveLock = lockFile.createNewFile();
    if (!haveLock)
        throw new DataBaseInaccessibleException();
    lockFile.deleteOnExit();
    try {
        useDataBase();
    } finally {
```

```
            lockFile.delete();
    }
}
```

This program uses a file as a lock to prevent multiple programs from accessing the same database. Each program that uses the database observes the same protocol. The lock file is created only if it doesn't exist—which is done atomically by the method `createNewFile`. If the file already existed then another program is using the database and this program terminates by throwing an exception. If the file was created then it is marked to be deleted upon exit. This ensures that during normal termination of the virtual machine the lock file is guaranteed to be deleted. As a matter of style the lock file is deleted once we have finished using the database. Note that we only mark the file for deletion if we created it—if we marked the file for deletion and it already existed then termination of this program would delete the lock file of another program. However, this means that we must ensure that no other part of our program can cause the virtual machine to exit before we mark the file for deletion. Only a normal termination of the virtual machine causes a marked file to be deleted on exit as it is reasonable to assume that if the virtual machine terminated abnormally (perhaps by a signal) the shared resource (in this case the database) may be left in an inconsistent state and should not be automatically made accessible to other programs.

Finally, the character `File.pathSeparatorChar` and its companion string `File.pathSeparator` represent the character that separates file or directory names in a search path. For example, UNIX separates components in the program search path using a colon, as in `".:/bin:/usr/bin"`, so `pathSeparatorChar` is a colon on UNIX systems.

Exercise 15.9: Write a method that, given one or more pathnames, will print all the information available about the file it represents (if any).

15.6.4 `FilenameFilter` and `FileFilter`

The `FilenameFilter` interface provides objects that filter unwanted files from a list. It supports a single method:

boolean **accept(File dir, String name)**
> Returns `true` if the file named `name` in the directory `dir` should be part of the filtered output.

Here is an example that uses a `FilenameFilter` object to list only directories:

```
import java.io.*;

class DirFilter implements FilenameFilter {
    public boolean accept(File dir, String name) {
        return new File(dir, name).isDirectory();
    }

    public static void main(String[] args) {
        File dir = new File(args[0]);
        String[] files = dir.list(new DirFilter());
        System.out.println(files.length + " dir(s):");
        for (int i = 0; i < files.length; i++)
            System.out.println("\t" + files[i]);
    }
}
```

First we create a `File` object to represent a directory specified on the command line. Then we create a `DirFilter` object and pass it to `list`. For each name in the directory, `list` invokes the `accept` method on the filtering object and includes the name in the list if the filtering object returns `true`. For our `accept` method, `true` means that the named file is a directory.

The `FileFilter` interface is analogous, but it works with a single `File` object:

boolean **accept(File pathname)**

> Returns `true` if the file represented by `pathname` should be part of the filtered output.

Exercise 15.10: Using `FilenameFilter` or `FileFilter`, write a program that takes a directory and a suffix as parameters and prints all files that have that suffix.

15.7 Object Serialization

The ability to save objects in a byte stream that can be transferred across the network (perhaps for use in remote method invocations), saved to disk in a file or database, and later reconstituted to form a live object, is an essential aspect of many real world applications.

The process of converting an object's representation into a stream of bytes is known as *serialization*, while reconstituting an object from a byte stream is *deser-*

ialization. When talking about the classes, interfaces and language features involved in this overall process, we generally just use the term serialization and understand that it includes deserialization as well.

There are a number of classes and interfaces involved with serialization. You have already learned about the basic mechanisms for reading and writing primitive types and strings—the Data stream classes (see page 391). In this section you will learn about the object byte streams—ObjectInputStream and ObjectOutputStream—that allow you to serialize and deserialize complete objects. Various other classes and interfaces provide specific support for the serialization process. Also, the field modifier transient, provides a language-level means of marking data that should not be serialized.

15.7.1 The Object Byte Streams

The Object streams—ObjectInputStream and ObjectOutputStream—allow you to read and write object graphs in addition to the well-known types (primitives, strings, and arrays). By "object graph" we mean that when you write an object to an ObjectOutputStream using writeObject, bytes representing the object—including all other objects that it references—are written to the stream. This process of transforming an object into a stream of bytes is called *serialization*. Because the serialized form is expressed in bytes, not characters, the Object streams have no Reader or Writer forms.

When bytes encoding a serialized graph of objects are read by the method readObject of ObjectInputStream—that is, *deserialized*—the result is a graph of objects equivalent to the input graph.

Suppose, for example, that you have a HashMap object that you wish to store into a file for future use. You could write the graph of objects that starts with the hash map this way:

```
FileOutputStream fileOut = new FileOutputStream("tab");
ObjectOutputStream out = new ObjectOutputStream(fileOut);
HashMap hash = getHashMap();
out.writeObject(hash);
```

As you can see, this approach is quite straightforward. The single writeObject on hash writes the entire contents of the hash map, including all entries, all the objects that the entries refer to, and so on, until the entire graph of interconnected objects has been visited. A new copy of the hash map could be reconstituted from the serialized bytes:

```
FileInputStream fileIn = new FileInputStream("tab");
ObjectInputStream in = new ObjectInputStream(fileIn);
HashMap newHash = (HashMap) in.readObject();
```

Serialization preserves the integrity of the graph itself. Suppose, for example, that in a serialized hash map, an object was stored in the table under two different keys:

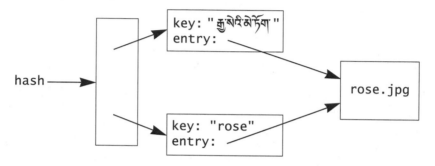

When the serialized hash map is deserialized, the two analogous entries in the new copy of the hash map will have references to a single copy of the `rose.jpg` object, not references to two separate copies of `rose.jpg`.[1]

15.7.2 Making Your Classes `Serializable`

When an `ObjectOutputStream` writes a serialized object, the object must implement the `Serializable` marker interface. This marker interface declares that the class is designed to have its objects serialized.

Being serializable can be quite simple. The default serialization process is to serialize each field of the object that is neither `transient` nor `static`. Primitive types and strings are written in the same encoding used by `DataOutputStream`; objects are serialized by calling `writeObject`. With default serialization, all serialized fields that are object references must refer to serializable object types. Default serialization also requires either that your superclass have a no-arg constructor (so that deserialization can invoke it), or that it also be `Serializable` (in which case declaring your class to implement `Serializable` is redundant but harmless). For most classes this default serialization is sufficient, and the entire

---

[1] The first key field is the word "rose" in Tibetan.

work necessary to make a class serializable is to mark it as such by declaring that it implements the Serializable interface:

```
public class Name implements java.io.Serializable {
    private String name;
    private long id;
    private transient boolean hashSet = false;
    private transient int hash;

    private static long nextID = 0;

    public Name(String name) {
        this.name = name;
        synchronized (Name.class) {
            id = nextID++;
        }
    }

    public int hashCode() {
        if (!hashSet) {
            hash = name.hashCode();
            hashSet = true;
        }
        return hash;
    }

    // ... override equals, provide other useful methods
}
```

The class Name can be written to an ObjectOutputStream either directly using writeObject, or indirectly if it is referenced by an object written to such a stream. The name and id fields will be written to the stream; the fields nextID, hashSet, and hash will not be written, nextID because it is static and the others because they are declared transient. Because hash is a cached value that can be easily recalculated from name, there is no reason to consume the time and space it takes to write it to the stream.

Default deserialization reads the values written during serialization. Static fields in the class are left untouched—if the class needs to be loaded then the normal initialization of the class takes place, giving the static fields an initial value. Each transient field in the reconstituted object is set to the default value for its type. When a Name object is deserialized, the newly created Name object will have name and id set to the same values as the original object's, the static field nextID will remain untouched, and the transient fields `hashSet` and `hash` will have their default values (`false` and `0`). These defaults work because when `hashSet` is `false` the value of `hash` will be recalculated.

Occasionally you will have a class that is generally serializable but has specific instances that are not serializable. For example, a container might itself be serializable, but contain references to objects that are not serializable. Any attempt to serialize a non-serializable object will throw a `NotSerializableException`.

15.7.3 Serialization and Deserialization Order

Each class is responsible for properly serializing its own state—that is, its fields. Objects are serialized and deserialized down the type tree—from the highest-level class that is `Serializable` to the most specific class. This order is rarely important when you're serializing, but it can be important when you're deserializing. Let us consider the following type tree for a `HTTPInput` class:

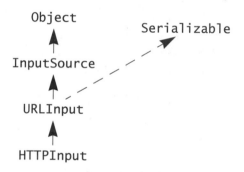

When deserializing a `HTTPInput` object, `ObjectInputStream` first allocates memory for the new object and then finds the first `Serializable` class in the object's type hierarchy—in this case `URLInput`. The stream invokes the no-arg constructor of that class's superclass (the object's last non-serializable class), which in this case is `InputSource`. If other state from the superclass must be preserved, `URLInput` is responsible for serializing that state and restoring it on deserialization. If your non-serializable superclass has state, you will almost certainly need to customize the first serializable class (see the next section). If the first serializable class directly extends `Object` (as the earlier `Name` class did), customizing is easy because `Object` has no state to preserve or restore.

Once the first serializable class has finished with its part of its superclass's state, it will set its own state from the stream. Then `ObjectInputStream` will walk down the type tree, deserializing the state for each class using `readObject`. When it reaches the bottom of the type tree, the object is completely deserialized.

As the stream is deserialized, other serialized objects will be found that were referenced from the object currently being deserialized. These other objects are deserialized as they are encountered. Thus, if `URLInput` had a reference to a `HashMap`, that hash map and its contents would be deserialized before the `HTTPInput` part of the object was deserialized.

Before any of this can happen, the relevant classes must first be loaded. This requires finding a class of the same name as the one written and checking to see that it is the same class. You'll learn about versioning issues shortly. Assuming it is the same class, the class must be loaded. If the class is not found or cannot be loaded for any reason, `readObject` will throw a `ClassNotFoundException`.

15.7.4 Customized Serialization

The default serialization methods work for many classes but not for all of them. For some classes default deserialization may be improper or inefficient. The `HashMap` class is an example of both problems. Default serialization would write all the data structures for the hash map, including the hash codes of the entries. This serialization is both wrong and inefficient.

It is wrong because hash codes may be different for deserialized entries. This will be true, for example, of entries using the default `hashCode` implementation.

It is inefficient because a hash map typically has a significant number of empty buckets. There is no point in serializing empty buckets. It would be more efficient to serialize the referenced keys and entries and rebuild a hash map from them than to serialize the entire data structure of the map.

For these reasons, `java.util.HashMap` provides private `writeObject` and `readObject` methods.[2] These methods are invoked by `ObjectOutputStream` and `ObjectInputStream`, respectively, when it is time to serialize or deserialize a `HashMap` object. These methods are invoked only on classes that provide them, and the methods are responsible only for the class's own state, including any state from non-serializable superclasses. A class's `writeObject` and `readObject` methods, if provided, should *not* invoke the superclass's `readObject` or `writeObject` method. Object serialization differs in this way from `clone` and `finalize`.

Let us suppose, for example, that you wanted to improve the `Name` class so that it didn't have to check whether the cached hash code was valid each time. You

---

[2] These methods are `private` because they should never be overridden and they should never be invoked by anyone using or subclassing your class. The serialization mechanism gains access to these private methods using reflection to disable the language level access control (see page 298). Of course this can only happen if the current security policy allows it—see "Security" on page 493.

could do this by setting hash in the constructor, instead of lazily when it is asked for. But this causes a problem with serialization—as hash is transient it does not get written as part of serialization (nor should it) and so, when deserializing you need to explicitly set it. This means that you have to implement readObject to deserialize the main fields and then set hash; which implies that you have to implement writeObject so you know how the main fields were serialized.

```java
public class BetterName implements Serializable {
    private String name;
    private long id;
    private transient int hash;

    private static long nextID = 0;

    public BetterName(String name) {
        this.name = name;
        synchronized (BetterName.class) {
            id = nextID++;
        }
        hash = name.hashCode();
    }

    private void writeObject(ObjectOutputStream out)
        throws IOException
    {
        out.writeUTF(name);
        out.writeLong(id);
    }

    private void readObject(ObjectInputStream in)
        throws IOException, ClassNotFoundException
    {
        name = in.readUTF();
        id = in.readLong();
        hash = name.hashCode();
    }

    public int hashCode() {
        return hash;
    }
```

```
    // ... override equals, provide other useful methods
}
```

We use `writeObject` to write out each of the non-static, non-transient fields. It declares that it can throw `IOException` because the write methods it invokes can do so, and, if one does throw an exception, the serialization must be halted. When `readObject` gets the values from the stream, it can then set `hash` properly. It, too, must declare that it throws `IOException` because the read methods it invokes can do so, and this should stop deserialization. The `readObject` method must declare that it throws `ClassNotFoundException` because, in the general case, deserializing fields of the current object could require other classes to be loaded—though not in the example.

There is one restriction when defining customized serialization: you cannot set a `final` field within `readObject` because `final` fields can only be set in initializers or constructors. For example, if `name` was declared `final` the class `BetterName` would not compile. You will need to design your classes with this restriction in mind when considering custom serialization. The default serialization mechanism can by-pass this restriction because it uses native code. This means that default serialization works fine with classes that have `final` fields.

The `readObject` and `writeObject` methods for `BetterName` show that you can use the methods of `DataInput` and `DataOutput` to transmit arbitrary data on the stream. However, the actual implementations replicate the default serialization and then add the necessary setup for `hash`. The read and write invocations of these methods could have been replaced with a simple invocation of methods that perform default serialization and deserialization:

```
private void writeObject(ObjectOutputStream out)
    throws IOException
{
    out.defaultWriteObject();
}

private void readObject(ObjectInputStream in)
    throws IOException, ClassNotFoundException
{
    in.defaultReadObject();
    hash = name.hashCode();
}
```

In fact, as you may have surmised, given that `writeObject` performs nothing but default serialization, we need not have implemented it at all.

A `writeObject` method can throw `NotSerializableException` if a particular object is not serializable. For example, objects of a class might be generally serializable, but a particular object might contain sensitive data. Such cases should be rare.

You will occasionally find that an object cannot be initialized properly until the graph of which it is a part has been completely deserialized. You can have the `ObjectInputStream` invoke a method of your own devising by calling the stream's `registerValidation` method with a reference to an object that implements the interface `ObjectInputValidation`. When deserialization of the top-level object at the head of the graph is complete, your object's `validateObject` method will be invoked to make any needed validation operation or check.

Normally an object is serialized as itself on the output stream, and a copy of the same type is reconstituted during deserialization. You will find a few classes for which this is not correct. For example, if you have an class that has objects that are supposed to be unique in each virtual machine for each unique value (so that `==` will return `true` if and only if `equals` also would return `true`), you would need to resolve an object being deserialized into an equivalent one in the local virtual machine. You can get control over these by providing `writeReplace` and `readResolve` methods of the following forms and with the appropriate access level:

<access> Object **writeReplace()** throws ObjectStreamException
> Returns an object that will replace the current object during serialization. Any object may be returned including the current one.

<access> Object **readResolve()** throws ObjectStreamException
> Returns an object that will replace the current object during deserialization. Any object may be returned including the current one.

In our example, `readResolve` would check to find the local object that was equivalent to the one just deserialized—if it exists it will be returned, otherwise we can register the current object (for use by `readResolve` in the future) and return `this`. These methods can be of any accessibility; they will be used if the are accessible to the object type being serialized. For example, if a class has a private `readResolve` method, it only affects serialization of objects that are exactly its type. A package-accessible `readResolve` affects only subclasses within the same package, while public and protected `readResolve` methods affect objects of all subclasses.

15.7.5 Object Versioning

Class implementations change over time. If a class's implementation changes between the time an object is serialized and the time it is deserialized, the

`ObjectInputStream` can detect this change. When the object is written, the *serial version UID* (unique identifier), a 64-bit `long` value, is written with it. By default, this identifier is a secure hash of the full class name, superinterfaces, and members—the facts about the class that, if they change, signal a possible class incompatibility. Such a hash is essentially a fingerprint—it is nearly impossible for two different classes to have the same UID.

When an object is read from an `ObjectInputStream`, the serial version UID is also read. Then an attempt is made to load the class. If no class with the same name is found or if the loaded class's UID does not match the UID in the stream, `readObject` throws an `InvalidClassException`. If the versions of all the classes in the object's type are found and all the UIDs match, the object can be deserialized.

This assumption is very conservative: any change in the class creates an incompatible version. Many class changes are less drastic than this. Adding a cache to a class can be made compatible with earlier versions of the serialized form, as can adding optional behavior or values. When you make a change to a class that can be compatible with the serialized forms of earlier versions of the class, you can explicitly declare the serial version UID for the class, for example:

```
private static final long
            serialVersionUID = -13077951722754062330L;
```

The value of `serialVersionUID` is provided by your development system. In many development systems, it is the output of a command called `serialver`. Other systems have different ways to provide you with this value, which is the serial version UID of the class before the first incompatible modification. (Nothing prevents you from using any number as this UID if you stamp it from the start, but it is usually a really bad idea. Your numbers will not be as carefully calculated to avoid conflict with other classes as the secure hash is.)

Now when the `ObjectInputStream` finds your class and compares the UID with that of the older version in the file, the UIDs will be the same even though the implementation has changed. If you invoke `defaultReadObject`, only those fields that were present in the original version will be set. Other fields will be left in their default state. If `writeObject` in the earlier version of the class wrote values on the field without using `defaultWriteObject`, you must continue to read those values. If you try to read more values than were written, you will get an `EOFException`, which can indicate that you are deserializing an older form that wrote less information. If possible, you should design your classes to read a class version number instead of relying on an exception to signal the version of the original data.

When an object is written to an `ObjectOutputStream`, the `Class` object for that object is also written. Because `Class` objects are specific to each virtual machine, serializing the actual `Class` object would not be helpful. So `Class` objects on a stream are replaced by `ObjectStreamClass` objects that contain the information necessary to find an equivalent class when the object is deserialized. This information includes the class's full name and its serial version UID. Unless you create one yourself, you will never directly see an `ObjectStreamClass` object.

15.7.6 Serialized Fields

The default serialization usually works well, but for more sophisticated classes and class evolution you may need to access the original fields. For example, suppose you were representing a rectangle in a geometric system using two opposite corner. You would have four fields: x1, y1, x2, and y2. If you later want to use a corner, plus width and height, you would have four different fields: x, y, width, and height. Assuming default serialization of the four original fields you would also have a compatibility problem: the rectangles that were already serialized would have the old fields instead of the new ones. To solve this problem you could maintain the serialized format of the original class and convert between the old and new fields as you encounter them in `readObject` or `writeObject`. To do this you use *serialized field* types to view the serialized form as an abstraction, and to access individual fields:

```
public class Rectangle implements Serializable {
    private static final long
                    serialVersionUID = -1307795172754062330L;

    transient private double x, y;
    transient private double width, height;

    private void readObject(ObjectInputStream in)
        throws IOException, ClassNotFoundException
    {
        ObjectInputStream.GetField fields;
        fields = in.readFields();
        x = fields.get("x1", 0.0);
        y = fields.get("y1", 0.0);
        double x2 = fields.get("x2", 0.0);
        double y2 = fields.get("y2", 0.0);
        width = (x2 - x);
        height = (y2 - y);
    }
```

```
        private void writeObject(ObjectOutputStream in)
            throws IOException
    {

        ObjectOutputStream.PutField fields = in.putFields();
        fields.put("x1", x);
        fields.put("y1", y);
        fields.put("x2", x + width);
        fields.put("y2", y + height);

    }
}
```

First notice that `Rectangle` defines the `serialVersionUID` of the original version to declare that the versions are compatible. Changing the fields that would be used by default serialization is considered (by default) to be an incompatible change, so we must declare the serialization UID.

The fields `x`, `y`, `width`, and `height` are marked `transient` because they are not serialized—during serialization these new fields must be converted into appropriate values of the original fields so that we preserve the serialized form. So `writeObject` uses an `ObjectOuputStream.PutField` object to write out the old form, using `x` and `y` as the old `x1` and `y1`, and calculating `x2` and `y2` from the rectangle's `width` and `height`. Each `put` method takes a field name as one argument and a value for that field as the other—the type of the value determines which overloaded form of `put` is invoked (one for each primitive type and `Object`). In this way the default serialization of the original class has been emulated and the serialized format preserved.

When deserializing a `Rectangle` object the opposite process occurs. Our `readObject` method gets an `ObjectInputStream.GetField` object from the object input stream. This object allows you to access fields from the serialized object by name. There is a `get` method for returning each primitive type, and for returning an `Object` reference. Each `get` method takes two parameters: the name of the field and a value to return if it is not defined for this version of the class. The type of the value to return chooses which overload of `get` will be invoked: a `short` return value will use the overload of `get` that returns a `short`, for example. In our `Rectangle` example, all the values are `double`: we get the old `x1` and `y1` fields to use for one corner of the rectangle, and get the old `x2` and `y2` fields to calculate the rectangle's `width` and `height`.

Using the above technique the new `Rectangle` class can deserialize old rectangle objects and a new serialized rectangle can be deserialized by the original `Rectangle` class, provided that both virtual machines are using compatible versions of the serialization stream protocol. The stream protocol defines the actual layout of serialized objects in the stream regardless of whether they use default serialization or the serialized field objects. This means that the serialized form of an object is not dependent on, for example, the order in which you invoke put, nor do you have to know the order in which to invoke get—you can use get or put to access fields in any order any number of times.

15.7.7 The `Externalizable` Interface

The `Externalizable` interface extends `Serializable`. A class that implements `Externalizable` takes complete control over its serialized state. An externalizable class assumes responsibility for all the data of its superclasses, any versioning issues, and so on. This capability is needed, for example, when the repository for serialized objects mandates restrictions on the form of those objects in ways that are incompatible with the provided serialization mechanism. The `Externalizable` interface has two methods:

```
public interface Externalizable extends Serializable {
    void writeExternal(ObjectOutput out)
        throws IOException;
    void readExternal(ObjectInput in)
        throws IOException, ClassNotFoundException;
}
```

These methods are invoked when the object is serialized and deserialized, respectively. They are normal public methods, so the exact type of the object determines which implementation will be used. Subclasses of an externalizable class will often need to invoke their superclass's implementation before serializing or deserializing their own state—in contrast to classes that use normal serialization.

You should note that the methods of the interface are public, and so can be invoked by anyone at anytime. In particular, a malicious program might invoke `readExternal` to make an object overwrite its state from some serialized stream, possibly with invented content. If you are designing classes where such security counts you have to take this into account either by not using `Externalizable`, or by writing your `readExternal` method to be only invoked once, and never at all if the object was created via one of your constructors.

15.7.8 Documentation Comment Tags

As you can see from the `Rectangle` code, the serialized form of an object can be an important thing, separate from its runtime form. This can happen over time due to evolution, or by initial design when the runtime form is not a good serialized form. When you write serializable classes that others will re-implement, you should document the persistent form so that other programmer's can properly re-implement the serialized form as well as the runtime behavior. You do this using the special javadoc tags `@serial`, `@serialField` and `@serialData`.

Use `@serial` tag to document fields serialized using default serialization. For example, the original `Rectangle` class could have looked like this:

```
/** X-coordinate of one corner.
 *  @serial */
private double x1;
/** Y-coordinate of one corner.
 *  @serial */
private double y1;
/** X-coordinate of opposite corner.
 *  @serial */
private double x2;
/** Y-coordinate of opposite corner.
 *  @serial */
private double y2;
```

The `@serial` tag can include a description of the meaning of the field. If none is given (as above), then the description of the runtime field will be used.

The `@serialField` tag documents fields that are created by `GetField` and `PutField` invocations, such as those in our `Rectangle` example. The tag takes first the field name, then its type, and then a description. The documentation for these could be:

```
/** @serialField x1 double X-coordinate of one corner. */
/** @serialField y1 double Y-coordinate of one corner. */
/** @serialField x2 double X-coordinate of other corner. */
/** @serialField y2 double Y-coordinate of other corner. */
transient private double x, y;
transient private double width, height;
```

You use the `@serialData` tag in the doc comment for a `writeObject` method to document any additional data written by the method. You can also use `@serialData` to document anything written by an `Externalizable` class's `writeExternal` method.

15.8 The `IOException` Classes

Every I/O-specific error detected by classes in `java.io` is signaled by an `IOException` or a subclass. Most I/O classes are designed to be general, so most of the exceptions cannot be listed specifically. For example, `InputStream` methods that throw `IOException` cannot detail which particular exceptions might be thrown, because any particular input stream class might throw a subclass of `IOException` for particular error conditions relevant to that stream. And the filter input and output streams pass through exceptions only from their downstream objects, which can also be of other stream types.

The specific subclasses of `IOException` used in the `java.io` package are:

CharConversionException extends `IOException`
> Thrown when a character conversion problem occurs during one of the character stream operations that must convert local character codes to Unicode or vice versa.

EOFException extends `IOException`
> Thrown when the end of the file (stream) is detected while reading from a stream.

FileNotFoundException extends `IOException`
> Thrown when the attempt to access the file specified by a given pathname fails—presumably because the file does not exist.

InterruptedIOException extends `IOException`
> Thrown when a blocking I/O operation detects that the current thread has been interrupted, prior to, or during, the operation. In principle, except for the `Print` stream methods, interrupting a thread should cause this exception if the thread is performing a blocking I/O operation. In practice most implementations only check for interruption before performing an operation and do not respond to interruption during the operation—see page 370—so you cannot rely on the ability to interrupt a blocked thread. This exception is also used to signify that a time-out occurred when performing network I/O.

InvalidClassException extends `ObjectStreamException`
> Thrown when the serialization mechanism detects a problem with a class: the serial version of the class does not match that read from the stream, the class contains unknown data types, or the class does not have an accessible no-arg constructor when needed.

InvalidObjectException extends `ObjectStreamException`
> Thrown when the `validateObject` method cannot make the object valid, thus aborting the deserialization.

NotActiveException extends `ObjectStreamException`
> Thrown when a serialization method, such as `defaultReadObject`, is invoked when serialization is not under way on the stream.

NotSerializableException extends `ObjectStreamException`
> Thrown either by the serialization mechanism or explicitly by a class when a class cannot be serialized.

ObjectStreamException extends `IOException`
> The superclass for all the `Object` stream related exceptions.

OptionalDataException extends `ObjectStreamException`
> Thrown when the optional data (that is, not part of default serialization) in the object input stream is corrupt or was not read by the reading method.

StreamCorruptedException extends `ObjectStreamException`
> Thrown when the internal object stream control information is missing or invalid.

SyncFailedException extends `IOException`
> Thrown by `FileDescriptor.sync` when the data cannot be guaranteed to have been written to the underlying media.

UnsupportedEncodingException extends `IOException`
> Thrown when an unknown character encoding is specified to a reader or writer.

UTFDataFormatException extends `IOException`
> Thrown by `DataInputStream.readUTF` when the string it is reading has malformed UTF syntax.

WriteAbortedException extends `ObjectStreamException`
> Thrown when an exception occurred during a serialization write operation.

In addition to these specific exceptions, other exceptional conditions in `java.io` are signaled with an `IOException` containing a string that describes the specific error encountered. For example, using a `Pipe` stream object that has never been connected throws an exception object with a detail string such as `"Pipe not connected"`, and trying to push more than the allowed number of characterscharacters onto a `PushbackReader` throws an exception with the string `"Pushback buffer overflow"`. Such exceptions are difficult to catch explicitly and so this style of exception reporting is not in favour; rather specific exception subtypes should be created for each category of exceptional circumstance.

Nothing has really happened until it has been recorded.
—Virginia Woolf

CHAPTER **16**

Collections

The problem with people who have no vices
is that generally you can be pretty sure they're going to have some pretty annoying virtues.
—Elizabeth Taylor

THE java.util package contains many useful interfaces and classes. They can be roughly divided into two categories: collections and everything else. This chapter describes the collection types. You will learn about the other general utilities in the next chapter.

16.1 Collections

Collections (sometimes called *containers*) are holders that let you store and organize objects in useful ways for efficient access. What will be efficient depends upon how you need to use the collection, so collections come in many flavors. Most programming environments provide some collection types, ranging from impoverished up through gargantuan.

In the package java.util you will find interfaces and classes that provide a general collection framework. This framework gives you a consistent and flexible set of collection interfaces and several useful implementations of these interfaces.

The collection framework is designed to be concise. The principle is to have a core set of valuable collection abstractions and implementations that are broadly useful, rather than an exhaustive set that is complete but conceptually complex and unwieldy.

One way to keep the size down is to represent broad abstractions in the interfaces instead of fine-grained differences. Notions such as immutability and resizability are not represented by different interface types. The core collection interfaces provide methods that allow all common operations, leaving it to specific

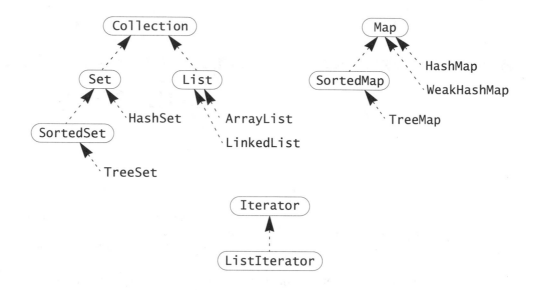

FIGURE 16–1: *Type Tree for Concrete Collections in* `java.util`

implementations to refuse to execute particular improper operations by throwing the unchecked `java.lang.UnsupportedOperationException`.

Figure 16–1 shows the collections interfaces and the concrete implementations provided in `java.util`.[1] The collections interfaces are:

- ◆ `Collection`—The root interface for collections. Provides such methods as `add`, `remove`, `size`, `toArray`, and (importantly) `iterator`.

- ◆ `Set`—A collection where no duplicate elements can be present, and whose elements are not necessarily stored in any particular order (extends `Collection`).

- ◆ `SortedSet`—A set whose elements are sorted (extends `Set`).

- ◆ `List`—A collection whose elements stay in a particular order unless the list is modified (extends `Collection`). This is a general use of the word "list," and does not mean "linked list," although that is one possible implementation.

---

[1]   The full list of collections includes abstract collections that help you write your own implementations. These are presented in Section 16.11 on page 450.

◆ Map—A map from keys to at most one value each. (Map does not extend Collection, although the concepts meaningful to both maps and collections are represented by methods of the same names, and maps can be viewed as collections.)

◆ SortedMap—A map whose keys are sorted (extends Map).

◆ Iterator—an interface for objects that return elements from a collection one at a time. This is the type of object returned by Collection.iterator.

◆ ListIterator—an iterator for List objects that adds useful List-related methods. This is the type of object returned by List.listIterator.

The interfaces SortedSet and SortedMap guarantee that iteration through the elements is done in sorted order. You will learn how to define an order for objects later in this chapter.

The java.util package also provides several useful concrete implementations of these interfaces that will suffice for most of your needs:

◆ HashSet—A Set implemented using a hashtable. A good, general purpose implementation for which searching, adding, and removing are mostly insensitive to the size of the contents.

◆ TreeSet—A SortedSet implemented using a balanced binary tree. Slower to search or modify than a HashSet, but keeps the elements sorted.

◆ ArrayList—A List implemented using a resizable array. It is expensive to add or delete an element near the beginning if the list is large, but relatively cheap to create and fast for random access.

◆ LinkedList—A doubly-linked List implementation. Modification is cheap at any size, but random access is slow. Useful for queues.

◆ HashMap—A hashtable implementation of Map. A very generally useful collection with relatively cheap lookup and insertion times.

◆ TreeMap—An implementation of SortedMap using a balanced binary tree that keeps its elements ordered by key. Useful for ordered data sets that require moderately quick lookup by key.

◆ WeakHashMap—An hashtable implementation of Map that references its keys via weak reference objects (see page 320). This is useful only in limited situations.

All these implementation classes are Cloneable and Serializable.

In this chapter you first learn about iteration, since it is useful with all the collection classes. We then cover ordering, since it is used by many of the collection types. We then present the details of the `Collection`-based types, followed by the `Map`-based types. After that we show you how to make unmodifiable and synchronized versions of your collections. Then you will learn how to write your own iteration and collection types in case you have a need that the provided classes do not fill. Finally, we cover the "legacy collections" in `java.util` that predate the overall collection system, but which you will find in much existing code. One of these legacy collection types—`Properties`—continues in common use.

16.1.1 Exception Conventions

There are a few conventions related to exceptions that are used through out the collections classes and interfaces, and which we do not want to document for every constructor and method where they may occur:

- ◆ Methods that are optional in an implementation of an interface throw `UnsupportedOperationException` when not implemented. We indicate which methods are optional as we go through.

- ◆ Methods or constructors that accept elements (either individually or as part of other collections) to be added to the current collection throw `ClassCastException` if the element is not of an appropriate type for the collection.

- ◆ Methods or constructors that accept elements (either individually or as part of other collections) to be added to the current collection throw `IllegalArgumentException` if the element's value is not appropriate for the collection—for example, some collections, such as subsets, define restricted ranges on the values of elements allowed in the collection.

- ◆ Methods that return individual elements of a collection will give you a `NoSuchElementException` if the collection is empty.

- ◆ Methods or constructors that take parameters of reference type usually throw `NullPointerException` if passed a `null` reference. The exception to this is when the reference is an object to be added, removed or looked for in the collection and the collection accepts `null` elements.

Other exceptions are documented on a case by case basis.

16.2 Iteration

The Collection interface defines an iterator method that returns an object implementing the Iterator interface.

public boolean **hasNext()**
> Returns true if the iteration has more elements.

public Object **next()**
> Returns the next element in the iteration. If there is no next element a NoSuchElementException is thrown.

public void **remove()**
> Removes from the underlying collection, the element last returned by the iteration. remove can be called only once per call of next. If next has not yet been called, or remove has already been called since the last call to next, an IllegalStateException is thrown. (Optional)

The following code uses all three methods of Iterator to remove all long strings from a collection:

```
public void removeLongStrings(Collection coll, int maxLen) {
    Iterator it = coll.iterator();
    while (it.hasNext()) {
        String str = (String)it.next();
        if (str.length() > maxLen)
            it.remove();
    }
}
```

First we use iterator to get an Iterator object that steps through the contents of the collection one element at a time. Then we loop as long as hasNext returns true to indicate that there is at least one more element left in the iteration. Each time through the loop we get the next element of the list using next. If any string is longer than the maximum allowed length, we use the iterator's remove method to remove the most recent element returned by next. When you use an iterator's remove method you modify the underlying collection safely for that iterator—the iterator will properly move through the subsequent elements of the collection. Removing elements from the collection any other way (using operations on the collection or through a different iterator on the same collection) is unsafe.

The ListIterator interface extends Iterator, adding methods you can use to manipulate an ordered List object during iteration. You can iterate forward using hasNext and next, or backwards using hasPrevious and previous, or back and forth by intermixing the calls as you please. The following code can be used to loop backward through a list:

```
ListIterator it = list.listIterator(list.size());
while (it.hasPrevious()) {
    Object obj = it.previous();
    System.out.println(obj);
    // ... use obj ...
}
```

This gets a `ListIterator` positioned one beyond the end of the list, and then backs up through the list one element at a time, printing each element out. List elements are indexed by position, just as array elements are, from 0 to `list.size()-1`. The methods `nextIndex` or `previousIndex` can be used to get the index of the element that a subsequent invocation of `next` or `previous` will return. The next index when the iterator is at the end of the list is returned as `list.size()`. The previous index when the iterator is at the first element in the list (index 0) is returned as −1.

The `remove` method on a `ListIterator` removes the last value returned by either `next` or `previous`. In addition to `remove`, you can use two additional methods to modify the list's contents:

public void **set(Object elem)**

> Replaces the last element returned by `next` or `previous` with `elem`. If you have called `remove` or `add` on the iterator since the last call to `next` or `previous`, calling `set` throws `IllegalStateException`. (Optional)

public void **add(Object elem)**

> Inserts the object `elem` into the list in front of the next element that would be returned, or at the end if `hasNext` returns `false`. The iterator is advanced—if you invoke `previous` after an `add` you will get the added element. (Optional)

The contract of `remove` is extended such that an `IllegalStateException` is thrown if `remove` is invoked and either `set` or `add` have been invoked since the last call to `next` or `previous`.

The contracts for `Iterator` and `ListIterator` do not include a *snapshot* guarantee. In other words, if the contents of the collection are changed while the iterator is in use, it can affect the values returned by the methods. For example, if the implementation of `next` uses the contents of the original collection for its list, it is dangerous to remove elements from the list as you step through it except via the iterator's own methods. A snapshot would return the elements as they were when the `Iterator` or `ListIterator` object was created, immune from future changes. You can rely on having a snapshot of the contents only if the method that returns an iterator object explicitly makes a snapshot guarantee. If you need a snapshot but don't have such a guarantee, you can create a snapshot by making a simple copy of the collection, such as via an `ArrayList`:

```java
public Iterator snapshotIterator(Collection coll) {
    return new ArrayList(coll).iterator();
}
```

Many of the iterators defined in the `java.util` package are what is known as *fail-fast* iterators. Such iterators detect when a collection has been modified other than through the iterator itself, and fail quickly and cleanly by throwing an exception—a `ConcurrentModificationException`—rather than risk performing an action whose behavior may be unsafe.

16.3 Ordering using `Comparable` and `Comparator`

The interface `java.lang.Comparable` can be implemented by any class whose objects can be sorted. The interface has a single method:

`public int compareTo(Object other)`
> Returns a value that is less than, equal to, or greater than zero as this object is less than, equal to, or greater than the `other` object. If this method returns zero, the `equals` method invoked with the two objects should return `true`; otherwise it should return `false`. If the objects are not mutually comparable (for example, an `Integer` is not comparable to a `String`), a `ClassCastException` is thrown.

The ordering defined by `compareTo` is a class's *natural ordering,* that is, the ordering that is most natural to objects of the class. Similarly, the `equals` method defines a *natural equivalence.*

Many existing classes are `Comparable`, including `String`, `java.io.File`, `java.util.Date`, and all the primitive wrapper class types. Most of these classes provide the general `compareTo` method, as well as a type-specific `compareTo` method. For example, the `Short` wrapper class has both `compareTo(Object)` and `compareTo(Short)` methods, the second to avoid the run time type checking that the first form requires to ensure that the incoming object is a `Short`. The compiler will use the second form if it can.

If a given class does not implement `Comparable`, or if its natural ordering is wrong for some purpose, you can often provide a `java.util.Comparator` object instead. The `Comparator` interface has one method:

```
public int compare(Object o1, Object o2)
```
Provides an ordering in the same manner as `Comparable.compareTo` for the two provided objects.

You can use `Comparable` and `Comparator` objects to sort and search `List` objects using the `Collections` class's static methods `sort` and `binarySearch`. The `Collections` class (see page 442) also provides static methods `min` and `max` to return the smallest and largest element in a `Collection`, respectively.

Comparing strings ignoring case is a common requirement, so the `String` class defines a `Comparator` for this purpose, available from the field `String.CASE_INSENSITIVE_ORDER`.

16.4   The `Collection` Interface

As you have seen, most collection types are subtypes of the `Collection` interface. The only exceptions are those that are subtypes of `Map`. In this section we cover the `Collection` interface. The following sections describe the interfaces that extend `Collection`, and the specific collection implementations provided in `java.util`. We leave `Map` and its related types for later. We also defer talking about implementing your own collection types.

The basis of much of the collection system is the `Collection` interface. As you saw in Figure 16–1, most of the actual collection types implement this interface, usually by implementing an extended interface such as `Set` or `List`. So `Collection` is a good place to start understanding collections. It has the following primary methods for working with an individual collection:

```
public int size()
```
Returns the size of this collection, that is, the number of elements it currently holds. The value returned is limited to `Integer.MAX_VALUE` even if the collection holds more elements.

```
public boolean isEmpty()
```
Returns `true` if this collection currently holds no elements.

```
public boolean contains(Object elem)
```
Returns `true` if the collection contains the object `elem`; that is, if this collection has an element on which invoking `equals` with `elem` returns `true`. If `elem` is `null`, returns `true` if there is a `null` element in the collection.

```
public Iterator iterator()
```
Returns an iterator that steps through the elements of this collection.

```
public Object[] toArray()
```
Returns a new array that contains references to all the elements of this collection.

```
public Object[] toArray(Object[] dest)
```
Returns an array that contains references to all the elements of this collection. If the elements will fit in dest, then they are placed in dest and it is dest that is returned. If dest has more elements than this collection, the first element in dest that follows the contents of the collection is set to null to mark the end of the collection. If the elements do not fit in dest a new array is created of the same type as dest, and the larger array is returned. If the type of dest is not compatible with the types of all elements in the collection an ArrayStoreException is thrown.

```
public boolean add(Object elem)
```
Makes sure that this collection contains the object elem, returning true if this required changing the collection. If this collection allows duplicates, add will always return true. If duplicates are not allowed and an equivalent element is in the collection already, add will return false. (Optional)

```
public boolean remove(Object elem)
```
Removes a single instance of elem from the collection, returning true if this required changing the collection (that is, if the element existed in this collection). If elem is null, returns true if there was a null element in the collection. (Optional)

All methods which need the notion of equivalence (such as contains and remove) use the equals method on the relevant objects.

The toArray method that has no parameters returns an array of Object. You can use toArray(Object[]) to create arrays of other types. For example, if your collection contains only String objects, you may want to create a String array. The following code will do so:

```
String[] strings = new String[collection.size()];
strings = (String[])collection.toArray(strings);
```

Notice that strings is assigned the return value of toArray. This is to be safe in case the size of the collection has increased since the array was allocated, in which case the returned array will not be the one originally allocated. You can also use an empty String array to pass in the desired type and let toArray allocate an array of exactly the right size:

```
String[] strings =
    (String[])collection.toArray(new String[0]);
```

Several methods of `Collection` operate in bulk from another collection. The methods are provided for convenience; also, a collection can often operate more efficiently in bulk.

public boolean **containsAll(Collection coll)**
>   Returns `true` if this collection contains each of the elements in `coll`.

public boolean **addAll(Collection coll)**
>   Adds each element of `coll` to this collection, returning `true` if any addition required changing the collection. (Optional)

public boolean **removeAll(Collection coll)**
>   Removes each element of `coll` from this collection, returning `true` if any removal required changing the collection. (Optional)

public boolean **retainAll(Collection coll)**
>   Removes from this collection all elements that are not elements of `coll`, returning `true` if any removal required changing the collection. (Optional)

public void **clear()**
>   Removes all elements from this collection. (Optional)

This `Collection` interface is purposefully very general. Each specific collection type can define restrictions on its parameters or other related behavior. A collection may or may not accept `null` elements, may be restricted to certain types of elements, may retain elements in a sorted order, and so on. Each collection that makes a restriction should state those restrictions in its documentation so that users can understand the contract for that collection.

16.5 Set and SortedSet

The `Set` interface extends `Collection`, providing a more specific contract for its methods, but adding no new methods of its own. A collection that is a `Set` contains no duplicate elements. If you add the same element twice to a set (in other words, if you add two objects that are `equal`), the first invocation will return `true`, while the second will return `false`. If after this, `remove` is similarly invoked twice, the first `remove` of the element will return `true`, since the set was changed by removing the element, while the second will return `false` since the element was no longer present. A set may also contain at most one `null` element.

The `SortedSet` interface extends `Set` to specify an additional contract—iterators on such a set will always return the elements in a specified order. By default this will be the elements natural order. In the implementations of `SortedSet` provided in `java.util` you can also specify a `Comparator` object that will be used to order the elements instead of the natural order.

The ordering places a requirement on the elements of the set—they must be ordered with respect to each other. Objects inserted into a sorted collection must be comparable to each other. Using an incompatible type (such as adding a Long object into a sorted set of String objects, or finding all String objects less than a Long object) will generate a ClassCastException.

SortedSet adds some methods that make sense in an ordered set:

public Comparator **comparator()**
> Returns the Comparator being used by this sorted set, or null if the elements' natural order is being used.

public Object **first()**
> Returns the first (lowest) object in this set.

public Object **last()**
> Returns the last (highest) object in this set.

public SortedSet **subSet(Object min, Object max)**
> Returns a view of the set that contains all the elements of this set whose values are greater than or equal to min, and less than max. The view is *backed by* the collection; that is, changes to the collection that fall within the range will be visible through the returned subset and vice versa. If min is greater than max, or this set is itself a view of another set and min or max fall outside the range of *that* view, an IllegalArgumentException is thrown. You will get an IllegalArgumentException if you attempt to modify the returned set to contain an element that is outside the specified range.

public SortedSet **headSet(Object max)**
> Returns a view of the set that contains all the elements of this set whose values are less than the value of max. This view is backed by the collection as with subSet. The exceptions thrown by this method, or by the returned set, are the same as those of subSet.

public SortedSet **tailSet(Object min)**
> Returns a view of the set that contains all the elements of this set whose values are greater than or equal to the value of min. This view is backed by the collection as with subSet. The exceptions thrown by this method, or by the returned set, are the same as those of subSet.

The notion of being *backed by* a collection is important in many methods. The sets returned by the subsetting methods are not snapshots of the matching contents, they are views onto the underlying collection that filter out certain elements, returning an empty collection if all elements are filtered out. Because the subsets are backed by the original collection, the views remain current, no matter which set you use—the subset or the original set. You can create snapshots by making copies of the view, as in:

```
public SortedSet copyHead(SortedSet set, Object max) {
    SortedSet head = set.headSet(max);
    return new TreeSet(head); // initial contents from head
}
```

This utilizes the copy-constructor provided by most of the concrete collection implementations to create a new collection whose initial members are the same as the collection passed to the constructor.

You can find one implementation of both `Set` and `SortedSet` ready to use in `java.util`: `HashSet` and `TreeSet`.

16.5.1 HashSet

`HashSet` is a `Set` implemented using a hashtable. Modifying the contents of a `HashSet` or testing for containment are constant-time operations: that is, they do not get larger as the size of the set increases (assuming that the `hashCode` methods of the contents are well written to distribute the hash codes widely across the full range of `int` values). `HashSet` has four constructors:

public **HashSet(int initialCapacity, float loadFactor)**
> Creates a new `HashSet` with `initialCapacity` hash buckets, and the given `loadFactor`, which must be a positive number. When the ratio of the number of elements in the set to the number of hash buckets is greater than or equal to the load factor, the number of buckets is increased.

public **HashSet(int initialCapacity)**
> Creates a new `HashSet` with `initialCapacity` and a default load factor.

public **HashSet()**
> Creates a new `HashSet` with a default initial capacity and load factor.

public **HashSet(Collection coll)**
> Creates a new `HashSet` whose initial contents are the elements in `coll`. The initial capacity is based on the size of `coll`; the default load factor is used.

16.5.2 TreeSet

If you need a `SortedSet`, you can use `TreeSet`, which stores its contents in a tree structure that is kept balanced. This means that the time required to modify or search the tree is $O(\log n)$, that is, the time increases with the log of the size of the set.[2] `TreeSet` has four constructors:

public **TreeSet()**
> Creates a new TreeSet that is sorted according to the natural order of the element types. All elements added to this set must implement the Comparable interface and be mutually comparable.

public **TreeSet(Collection coll)**
> Equivalent to using TreeSet() and then adding all the elements of coll to this set.

public **TreeSet(Comparator comp)**
> Creates a new TreeSet that is sorted according to the order imposed by comp.

public **TreeSet(SortedSet set)**
> Creates a new TreeSet whose initial contents will be the same as those in set, and that is sorted using the same order as set.

16.6 List

The List interface extends Collection to define a collection whose elements have a defined order—each element exists in a particular position in the collection, indexed from 0 to list.size(). This requires a refinement of the contracts of several methods inherited from Collection: when you add an element, it is placed at the end of the list; when you remove the nth element from the list, the element that was after it is shifted over, becoming the new n^{th} element; and the toArray methods fill in the array in the list's order. (The java.util.Vector class is a legacy collection that serves a similar purpose.)

List also adds several methods that make sense in an ordered collection:

---

[2]   The notation $O(f)$ is used in computer science to mean that the order of time for the execution of an algorithm increases in the manner of f. In this notation, n is traditionally the magnitude of the data under consideration. An algorithm that is $O(\log n)$ takes longer as a function of the log of n—the number of elements—multiplied by some constant C. Generally speaking, the constant is irrelevant when comparing algorithms, because as n gets large, the difference between an algorithm that is $O(\log n)$ compared to one that is, say, $O(n^2)$ is governed by n, not the constant—when n is 1,000, for example, $\log n$ is 6.9, whereas n^2 is 1,000,000. The multiplying constant for the $O(\log n)$ algorithm would have to be extremely large to make it worse than the $O(n^2)$ algorithm. Of course, when comparing two $O(\log n)$ algorithms the constant does matter, so in such a case it would be written. A similar argument means that for algorithms whose overhead has multiple terms, such as $O(C^2 + n)$, the smaller term is not relevant, and so would be typically described as $O(n)$. An algorithm that is not sensitive to the size of n is written as $O(1)$ or sometimes $O(C)$. You will see "big O" notation in this chapter because it is an effective way of comparing different collection implementations.

`public boolean` **`get(int index)`**
Returns the indexth entry in the list.

`public boolean` **`set(int index, Object elem)`**
Sets the indexth entry in the list to `elem`, replacing the previous element. (Optional)

`public boolean` **`add(int index, Object elem)`**
Adds the entry `elem` to the list at the indexth position, shifting every element farther in the list down one position. (Optional)

`public boolean` **`remove(int index)`**
Removes the indexth entry in the list, shifting every element farther in the list up one position. (Optional)

`public int` **`indexOf(Object elem)`**
Returns the index of the first object in the list that is `equal` to `elem`, or that is `null` if `elem` is `null`. Returns −1 if no match is found.

`public int` **`lastIndexOf(Object elem)`**
Returns the index of the last object in the list that is `equal` to `elem`, or that is `null` if `elem` is `null`. Returns −1 if no match is found.

`public List` **`subList(int min, int max)`**
Returns a `List` that is a view on this list over the range, starting with `min` up to, but not including, `max`. For example `subList(1, 5)` would return a list containing elements number 1, 2, 3, and 4 from this list. The returned list is backed by this list, so changes made to the returned list are reflected in this list. Changes made directly to the backing list are not guaranteed to be visible to a sublist, and can cause undefined results (so don't do it). Sublists allow you to do anything to part of a list that you could to do an entire list, and so can be a powerful tool—for example, you can clear part of a list using `list.subList(min, max).clear()`.

`public ListIterator` **`listIterator(int index)`**
Returns a `ListIterator` object that will iterate through the elements of the list starting at the indexth entry.

`public ListIterator` **`listIterator()`**
Returns a `ListIterator` object that will iterate through the elements of the list starting at the beginning.

All of the methods that take an `index` throw `IndexOutOfBoundsException` if `index` is less than zero, or greater than or equal to the list's size.

The `java.util` package provides two implementations of `List`—`ArrayList` and `LinkedList`.

16.6.1 ArrayList

ArrayList is a good basic list implementation that stores its elements in an underlying array. Adding and removing elements at the end is very simple—$O(1)$. Getting the element at a specific position is also $O(1)$. Adding and removing elements from the middle is more expensive—$O(n-i)$ where n is the size of the list and i is the position of the element being removed. Adding or removing the element requires copying the remainder of the array one position up or down.

An ArrayList has a *capacity,* which is the number of elements it can hold without allocating new memory for a larger array. As you add elements they are stored in the array, but when room runs out, a replacement array must be allocated. Setting your initial capacity correctly can improve performance. If the initial size of the data is significantly smaller than its final size, setting the initial capacity to a larger value reduces the number of times the underlying array must be replaced with a larger copy. Setting the size too large can waste space.

ArrayList has three constructors:

public **ArrayList()**
> Creates a new ArrayList with a default capacity.

public **ArrayList(int initialCapacity)**
> Creates a new ArrayList that initially can store initialCapacity elements without resizing.

public **ArrayList(Collection coll)**
> Creates a new ArrayList whose initial contents are the contents of coll. The capacity of the array is initially 110% of the size of coll to allow for some growth without resizing. The order is that returned by the collections iterator.

ArrayList also adds some methods to manage capacity:

public void **trimToSize()**
> Sets the capacity to be exactly the current size of the list. If the capacity is currently larger than the size, a new underlying array will be allocated that is smaller and the current values copied in. You can thus reduce the amount of memory necessary to hold the list, although at some cost.

public void **ensureCapacity(int minCapacity)**
> Sets the capacity to minCapacity if the capacity is currently smaller. You can use this if you are about to add a large number of elements to the list, which will ensure that the array will be reallocated at most once (when ensureCapacity is invoked) rather than possibly multiple times while the elements are added.

16.6.2 LinkedList

A LinkedList is a doubly-linked list whose performance characteristics are virtually the reverse of ArrayList: adding an element at the end is $O(1)$, but everything else is swapped—adding or removing an element in the middle is $O(1)$ because it requires no copying, while getting the element at a specific position i is $O(i)$ since it must start at one end and walk through the list to the ith element.

LinkedList provides two constructors, and adds methods that are useful and efficient for doubly linked lists:

public **LinkedList()**
> Creates a new empty LinkedList.

public **LinkedList(Collection coll)**
> Creates a new LinkedList whose initial contents are those of coll. The order is that returned by the collections iterator.

public Object **getFirst()**
> Returns the first object in this list.

public Object **getLast()**
> Returns the last object in this list.

public Object **removeFirst()**
> Removes the first object in this list.

public Object **removeLast()**
> Removes the last object in this list.

public Object **addFirst(Object elem)**
> Adds elem into this list as the first element.

public Object **addLast(Object elem)**
> Adds elem into this list as the last element.

A LinkedList is a good base for a queue or other list where most of the action is not at the end. For a stack, or building up a list of elements as you find them, an ArrayList is more efficient because it requires fewer objects: the one array instead of one object for each element in the list. Also, an ArrayList can be efficiently scanned without creating an Iterator object—you can use an int as an index. This can be a reason to use an ArrayList for a list that will be scanned frequently.

Here is a Polygon class that stores a list of Point objects that are the polygon's vertices:

```
import java.util.List;
import java.util.ArrayList;
```

```
public class Polygon {
    private List vertices = new ArrayList();

    public void add(Point p) {
        vertices.add(p);
    }

    public void remove(Point p) {
        vertices.remove(p);
    }

    public int numVertices() {
        return vertices.size();
    }

    // ... other methods ...
}
```

Notice that vertices is a List reference that is assigned an ArrayList object. You should declare a variable to be as abstract a type as possible, preferring the abstract List type to the implementation class ArrayList. As written, you could change Polygon to use a LinkedList if that would be more efficient by changing only one line of code—the line that creates the list. All the other code can remain unchanged.

Exercise 16.1: Write a program that opens a file and reads its lines one at a time, storing each line in a List sorted using String.compareTo. The line-reading class you created for Exercise 15.4 should prove helpful.

16.7 Map and SortedMap

The interface Map does not extend Collection because it has a contract that is different in important ways. The primary difference is that you do not add an element to a Map—you add a key/value pair. A Map allows you to lookup the value stored under a key. A given key (as defined by the equals method of the key) maps to one value or no values. A value can be mapped to by as many keys as you like. For example, you might use a map to store a mapping of a person's name to their address. If you have an address listed under a name, there will be exactly one in the map. If you have no mapping, there will be no address value for that name.

Multiple people might share a single address, so the map might return the same value for two or more names.

The basic methods of the Map interface are:

`public int `**`size()`**
> Returns the size of this map, that is, the number of key/value mappings it currently holds. The return value is limited to `Integer.MAX_VALUE` even if the map contains more elements.

`public boolean `**`isEmpty()`**
> Returns `true` if this collection currently holds no mappings.

`public boolean `**`containsKey(Object key)`**
> Returns `true` if the collection contains a mapping for the given key.

`public boolean `**`containsValue(Object value)`**
> Returns `true` if the collection contains at least one mapping to the given value.

`public Object `**`get(Object key)`**
> Returns the object to which key is mapped, or `null` if it is not mapped. Also returns `null` if key has been mapped to `null` in a map that allows `null` values. You can use `containsKey` to distinguish between the cases, although this adds overhead. It can be more efficient to put marker objects instead of `null` into the map to avoid the need for the second test.

`public Object `**`put(Object key, Object value)`**
> Associates key with the given value in the map. If a map already exists for key, its value is changed and the original value is returned. If no mapping exists, put returns `null`, which may also mean that key was originally mapped to `null`.

`public Object `**`remove(Object key)`**
> Removes any mapping for the key. The return value has the same semantics as that of put.

`public void `**`putAll(Map otherMap)`**
> Puts all the mappings in otherMap into this map.

`public void `**`clear()`**
> Removes all mappings.

Methods that take keys as parameters may throw `ClassCastException` if the key is not of the appropriate type for this map, or `NullPointerException` if the key is `null` and this map does not accept `null` keys.

You can see that, though Map is not an extended interface of `Collection`, methods with the same meaning have the same names, and analogous methods have analogous names. This helps you remember the methods and what they do.

Generally you can expect a Map to be optimized for finding values listed under keys. For example, the method containsKey will usually be much more efficient than containsValue on larger maps. In a HashMap for example, containsKey is $O(1)$, whereas containsValue is $O(n)$—the key is found by hashing, but the value must be found by searching through each element until a match is found.

Map is not a collection, but there are methods that let you view the map using collections:

`public Set keySet()`
> Returns a Set whose elements are the keys of this map.

`public Collection values()`
> Returns a Collection whose elements are the values of this map.

`public Set entrySet()`
> Returns a Set whose elements are Map.Entry objects that represent single mappings in the map. As you will see soon, Map.Entry is a nested interface with methods to manipulate the entry.

The collections returned by these methods are backed by the Map, so removing an element from one these collections removes the corresponding key/value pair from the map. You cannot add elements to these collections—they do not support the optional methods for adding to a collection. If you iterate through the key and value sets in parallel you cannot rely upon getting key/value pairs—they may return values from their respective sets in any order. If you need such pairing, you should use entrySet.

The interface Map.Entry defines methods for manipulating the entries in the map, as returned via the Map interface's entrySet method:

`public Object getKey()`
> Returns the key for this entry.

`public Object getValue()`
> Returns the value for this entry.

`public Object setValue()`
> Sets the value for this entry.

Note that there is no setKey method—changes to the key must be done by removing the existing mapping for the key and adding another.

The SortedMap interface extends Map refining the contract to require that the keys be sorted. This ordering requirement affects the collections returned by keySet, values, and entrySet. SortedMap also adds methods that make sense in an ordered map:

`public Comparator` **`comparator()`**
> Returns the comparator being used for sorting this map. Returns `null` if none is being used, which means that the map is sorted using the keys' natural order.

`public Object` **`firstKey()`**
> Returns the first (lowest value) key in this map.

`public Object` **`lastKey()`**
> Returns the last (highest value) key in this map.

`public SortedMap` **`subMap(Object minKey, Object maxKey)`**
> Returns a view of the portion of the map whose keys are greater than or equal to `minKey` and less than `maxKey`.

`public SortedMap` **`headMap(Object maxKey)`**
> Returns a view of the portion of the map whose values are less than `maxKey`.

`public SortedMap` **`tailMap(Object minKey)`**
> Returns a view of the portion of the map whose values are greater than or equal to `minKey`.

Any returned map is backed by the original map so changes made to either are visible to the other.

A `SortedMap` is to `Map` what `SortedSet` is to `Set` and provides almost identical functionality except `SortedMap` works with keys. The exceptions thrown by the `SortedMap` methods mirror those thrown by its `SortedSet` counterparts.

There are three map implementations in the `java.util` package: `HashMap`, `TreeMap`, and `WeakHashMap`.

16.7.1 HashMap

`HashMap` implements `Map` using a hashtable, where each key's `hashCode` method is used to pick a place in the table. With a well-written `hashCode` method, adding, removing, or finding a key/value pair is $O(1)$. This makes a `HashMap` a very efficient way to associate a key with a value—`HashMap` is one of the most commonly used collections. You already have seen a `HashMap` in "Implementing Interfaces" on page 114. The constructors for `HashMap` are:

`public` **`HashMap(int initialCapacity, float loadFactor)`**
> Creates a new `HashMap` with `initialCapacity` hash buckets, and the given `loadFactor`, which must be a positive number.

`public` **`HashMap(int initialCapacity)`**
> Creates a new `HashMap` with the given `initialCapacity` and a default load factor.

`public `**`HashMap()`**
> Creates a new `HashMap` with default initial capacity and load factor.

`public `**`HashMap(Map map)`**
> Creates a new `HashMap` whose initial mappings are copied from `map`. The initial capacity based on the size of `map`; the default load factor is used.

Load factor and size considerations are the same as those described for `HashSet` on page 432.

16.7.2 TreeMap

The `TreeMap` class implements `SortedMap`, keeping its keys sorted in the same way as `TreeSet`. This makes adding, removing, or finding a key/value pair $O(\log n)$. So you generally use a `TreeMap` only if you need the sorting, or if the hashCode method of your keys is poorly written, thereby destroying the $O(1)$ behavior of `HashMap`.

  TreeMap has the following constructors:

`public `**`TreeMap()`**
> Creates a new `TreeMap` that is sorted according to the natural order of the keys. All keys added to this map must implement the `Comparable` interface and be mutually comparable.

`public `**`TreeMap(Map map)`**
> Equivalent to using `TreeMap()` and then adding all the key/value pairs of map to this map.

`public `**`TreeMap(Comparator comp)`**
> Creates a new `TreeMap` that is sorted according to the order imposed by comp.

`public `**`TreeMap(SortedMap map)`**
> Creates a new `TreeMap` whose initial contents will be the same as those in map, and that is sorted using the same order as `map`.

16.7.3 WeakHashMap

The collection implementations all use strong references for elements, values, and keys. As with strong references elsewhere, this is usually what you want. Just as you occasionally need reference objects to provide weaker references, you also occasionally need a collection that holds the objects it contains less strongly. You can use the class `java.util.WeakHashMap` in such cases.

WeakHashMap behaves like HashMap with one difference—WeakHashMap refers to keys using WeakReference objects instead of strong references. As you learned in Section 12.5 on page 320, weak references let the objects be collected as garbage, so you can put an object in a WeakHashMap without the map's reference forcing the object to stay in memory. When a key is only weakly reachable, its mapping may be removed from the map, which drops the map's strong reference to the key's value object. If the value object is otherwise not strongly reachable, this could result in the value also being collected.

A WeakHashMap checks to find unreferenced keys when you invoke a method that can modify the list of contents (put, remove, or clear), but not before get. If you want to force removal you can invoke one of the modifying methods in a way that will have no effect, such as by removing a key for which there is no mapping (null, for example, if you do not use null as a key).

The WeakHashMap class exports the same constructors as HashMap: a no-arg constructor; a constructor that takes an initial capacity; a constructor that takes an initial capacity and a load factor; and a constructor that takes a Map whose contents will be the initial contents of the WeakHashMap.

Exercise 16.2: Rewrite the DataHandler class on page 323 to use a WeakHashMap to store the returned data instead of a single WeakReference.

16.8 Wrapped Collections and the Collections Class

The Collections class defines a range of static utility methods that operate on collections. The utility methods can be broadly classified into two groups: those that provide wrapped collections and those that don't. The wrapped collections allow you to present a different view of an underlying collection by synchronizing access to the collection, or by removing all methods that could modify the collection.

16.8.1 The Synchronization Wrappers

All the collection implementations provided in java.util are unsynchronized (except the legacy collections you will soon see). Your code must ensure any necessary synchronization for concurrent access from multiple threads. You can do this explicitly using synchronized methods or statements, or algorithmically by designing your code to use a given collection from only one thread. These techniques are how collections are often naturally used—as local variables in methods or as private fields of classes with synchronized code.

You can also use *synchronized wrappers* for your collections. A synchronized wrapper passes through all method calls to the wrapped collection after adding any necessary synchronization. You can get a synchronized wrapper by passing your collection to one of the following static methods of the `Collections` class: `synchronizedCollection`, `synchronizedSet`, `synchronizedSortedSet`, `synchronizedList`, `synchronizedMap`, or `synchronizedSortedMap`. These factory methods return wrappers whose methods are fully synchronized, and so are safe to use from multiple threads. For example, the following code creates a new `HashMap` that can be safely modified concurrently:

```
Map unsyncMap = new HashMap();
Map syncMap = Collections.synchronizedMap(unsyncMap);
```

The map referred to by `unsynchMap` is a full, but unsynchronized, implementation of the `Map` interface. The `Map` returned by `synchronizedMap` has all relevant methods synchronized, passing all calls through to the wrapped map (that is, to `unsyncMap`). Modifications made through either map are visible to the other—there is really only one map with two different views: the wrapped, unsynchronized view referenced by `unsyncMap`, and the wrapping, synchronized view referenced by `synchMap`:

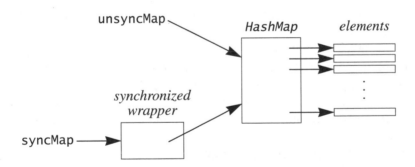

Because the underlying collection is unsynchronized, you must be very careful what you do with `unsyncMap`. The safest alternative is to drop the reference and do all work through `synchMap`. If you do not, you must be sure that you control concurrency carefully. The wrapper synchronizes on itself, so you could use `syncMap` to synchronize access, and then use `unsyncMap` safely inside such code:

```
// add a lot of elements but grab the lock only once
synchronized (syncMap) {
    for (int i = 0; i < keys.length; i++)
        unsyncMap.put(keys[i], values[i]);
}
```

Iterators returned by synchronized wrappers are not synchronized, but must be manually synchronized in a similar manner, when needed:

```
synchronized (syncMap) {
    System.out.println("--- map contents:");
    Iterator it = syncMap.keySet().iterator();
    while (it.hasNext()) {
        Object key = it.next();
        System.out.println(key + ": " + syncMap.get(key));
    }
}
```

If you use an unsynchronized collection concurrently the result is undefined— if you are lucky the error will be detected by the collection and you will get a ConcurrentModificationException. If you are unlucky the collection will quietly become corrupt.

16.8.2   The Unmodifiable Wrappers

The Collections class also has static methods that return *unmodifiable wrappers* for your collections: unmodifiableCollection, unmodifiableSet, unmodifiableSortedSet, unmodifiableList, unmodifiableMap, and unmodifiableSortedMap. The collections returned by these methods pass non-modifying methods through to the underlying collection. Modifying methods throw UnsupportedOperationException. As with a synchronized wrapper, an unmodifiable wrapper is backed by the original collection, so any changes you make to the collection will be visible through the wrapped collection. In other words, the contents of an unmodifiable wrapper can change, but not through the wrapper itself.

Unmodifiable wrappers are a reasonable way to represent unchanging sets of information. Consider the following dangerous example:

```
public final String suits[] = { // DANGEROUS
    "Hearts", "Clubs", "Diamonds", "Spades"
};
```

The suits array reference is not modifiable—it will always refer to the same array. But the array's contents can be changed by pranksters:

```
suits[3] = "Armani";
```

An unmodifiable wrapper would prevent this kind of mischief:

```
private final String suitNames[] = {
    "Hearts", "Clubs", "Diamonds", "Spades"
};
public final List suits =
    Collections.unmodifiableList(Arrays.asList(suitNames));
```

Now the array is private data, and so cannot be modified directly. It can only be accessed through the public `suits` list, and any attempt to use the modifying methods of `List` on this collection will throw an exception. (As you will see shortly, the `asList` method of the `Arrays` class creates a list backed by an array.)

16.8.3 The `Collections` Utilities

The `Collections` class defines many useful utility methods. You can find the minimum and maximum valued elements in a collection:

`public static Object` **`min(Collection coll)`**
  Returns the smallest valued element of the collection based on the elements' natural order.

`public static Object` **`min(Collection coll, Comparator comp)`**
  Returns the smallest valued element of the collection according to `comp`.

`public static Object` **`max(Collection coll)`**
  Returns the largest valued element of the collection based on the elements' natural order.

`public static Object` **`max(Collection coll, Comparator comp)`**
  Returns the largest valued element of the collection according to `comp`.

You can obtain a `Comparator` that will reverse the natural ordering of the objects it compares:

`public static Comparator` **`reverseOrder()`**
  Returns a `Comparator` that reverses the natural ordering of the objects it compares, so `Collections.reverseOrder().compare(o1, o2)` returns `-o1.compareTo(o2)`.

There are several methods for working with lists:

`public static void` **`reverse(List list)`**
  Reverses the order of the elements of the list.

`public static void` **`shuffle(List list)`**
  Randomly shuffles the list.

```
public static void shuffle(List list, Random randomSource)
```
Randomly shuffles the list using randomSource as the source of random numbers (see "Random" on page 470).

```
public static void fill(List list, Object elem)
```
Replaces each element of list with elem.

```
public static void copy(List dst, List src)
```
Copies each element to dst from src. If dst is too small to contain all the elements, throws IndexOutOfBoundsException. You can use a sublist for either dst or src to copy only to or from parts of a list.

```
public static List nCopies(int n, Object elem)
```
Returns an immutable list that contains n elements, each of which is elem. This only requires storing one reference to elem, so n can be 100 and the returned list will take the same amount of space it would if n were one.

There are also methods to create *singleton* collections—collections containing only a single element:

```
public static Set singleton(Object elem)
```
Returns an immutable set containing only elem.

```
public static List singletonList(Object elem)
```
Returns an immutable list containing only elem.

```
public static Map singletonMap(Object key, Object value)
```
Returns an immutable map containing only one a map from key to value.

There are methods for sorting:

```
public static void sort(List list)
```
Sorts list according its elements' natural ordering.

```
public static void sort(List list, Comparator comp)
```
Sorts list according to comp.

And methods for searching:

```
public static int binarySearch(List list, Object key)
```
Uses a binary search algorithm to find a key object in the list, returning its index. The list must be in its elements' natural order. If the object is not found, the index returned is a negative value encoding a safe insertion point.

```
public static int binarySearch(List list, Object key,
    Comparator comp)
```
Uses a binary search algorithm to find a key object in the list, returning its index. The list must be in the order defined by comp. If the object is not found, the index returned is a negative value encoding a safe insertion point.

The phrase "a negative value encoding a safe insertion point" requires some explanation. If you use a `binarySearch` method to search for a key, and the key is not found, you will always get a negative value. Specifically, if i is the index at which the key could be inserted and maintain the order, the value returned will be $-(i + 1)$. (The return value algorithm ensures the value will be negative when the key is not found, since zero is a valid index in a list.) So using the `binarySearch` methods you can maintain a list in sorted order: search the list to see if the key is already present. If not, insert it according to the return value of `binarySearch`:

```
public static void ensureKnown(List known, Object value) {
    int indexAt = Collections.binarySearch(known, value);
    if (indexAt < 0)          // not in the list -- insert it
        known.add(-(indexAt + 1), value);
}
```

If the list of `known` elements does not include the given `value`, this method will insert the value in its place in the list based on its natural ordering.

If you invoke one of the sorting, or searching methods that relies on ordering with a collection that contains objects that are not mutually comparable, or comparable by the given `Comparator`, you will get a `ClassCastException`.

You can get some powerful effects out of combining these operations with each other and with the operations of collections. For example, you can create a list with 100 elements initialized to an `Integer` value of –1 with the following:

```
Integer init = new Integer(-1);
List values = new ArrayList(Collections.nCopies(100, init));
```

Finally, `Collections` also has three final static fields: `EMPTY_LIST`, `EMPTY_SET`, and `EMPTY_MAP` so you do not need to create these useful objects when you need to pass an empty collection to a method.

16.9 The Arrays Utility Class

The class `Arrays` provides useful static methods for dealing with arrays. Most of these methods have a full complement of overloads: one for arrays of each primitive type (except `boolean` for searching and sorting) and one for `Object` arrays. There are also two variants of some methods: one acting on the whole array and one acting on the subarray specified by two supplied indices. The methods are:

◆ `sort`—Sort an array, using a technique that is not worse than $O(n \log n)$.

◆ `binarySearch`—Search a sorted array for a given key. Returns the key's index, or a negative value encoding a safe insertion point (as for the method `Collections.binarySearch` described previously). There are no subarray versions.

◆ `equals`—Returns true if the two arrays it is passed are the same object, are both `null`, or have the same size and equivalent contents. There are no subarray versions.

◆ `fill`—Fill in the array with a specified value.

The methods `sort` and `binarySearch` have two overloads for `Object` arrays. One assumes that its elements are comparable (implement the `Comparable` interface). The second uses a provided `Comparator` object instead, so you can manipulate arrays of objects that are not comparable, or for which you do not want to use the natural ordering. The `equals` method for `Object` arrays uses `equals` on each non-`null` element of the array; `null` elements in the first array must be matched by `null` elements of the second. `Arrays.equals` does not treat nested arrays specially, so it cannot generally be used to compare arrays of arrays.

You can view an array of objects as a `List` using the object returned by the `asList` method. The list is backed by the underlying store, so changes made to the array are visible to the list and vice versa. The returned list allows you to `set` elements, but not to `add` or `remove` them—it is a modifiable list, but not a resizable list. Using a `List` for access to an underlying array can give you useful features of list, such as using synchronized wrappers to synchronize access to the underlying array.

16.10 Writing Iterator Implementations

Iterators are generally useful, and you may want to write your own, even if you are not implementing a collection type. The following code demonstrates the basics of writing your own `Iterator` implementation, in this case for an iterator that will filter out strings longer than a given length:

```
public class ShortStrings implements Iterator {
    private Iterator strings;    // source for strings
    private String nextShort;    // null if next not known
    private final int maxLen;    // only return strings <=

    public ShortStrings(Iterator strings, int maxLen) {
        this.strings = strings;
        this.maxLen = maxLen;
```

```
                nextShort = null;
        }

        public boolean hasNext() {
            if (nextShort != null)   // found it already
                return true;
            while (strings.hasNext()) {
                nextShort = (String) strings.next();
                if (nextShort.length() <= maxLen)
                    return true;
            }
            nextShort = null;          // didn't find one
            return false;
        }

        public Object next() {
            if (nextShort == null && !hasNext())
                throw new NoSuchElementException();
            String n = nextShort;     // remember nextShort
            nextShort = null;          // consume nextShort
            return n;                  // return nextShort
        }

        public void remove() {
            throw new UnsupportedOperationException();
        }
    }
}
```

The class ShortStrings is a type of iterator that will read String objects from
another iterator, returning only those that are no longer than a specified length.
The constructor takes the iterator that will provide the strings and the maximum
length, storing those in the object's fields. The field nextShort will hold the next
short string, or null when there isn't one. If next is null, the hasNext method
searches for the next short string, remembering it in nextShort. If it reaches the
end of its source iteration without finding one, it returns false.

The method next checks to see if there is a next short string, either returning
it if there is one, or throwing NoSuchElementException if there aren't any to
return. Notice that hasNext does all the real work of finding the short strings, and
next just returns the results, setting nextShort to null to indicate that the next
short string, if any, is as yet undiscovered.

Finally, `remove` is not supported by this iterator implementation, so `remove` throws `UnsupportedOperationException`.

A few things to notice. First, `hasNext` is carefully written so that it will work if invoked multiple times before a `next`. This is required—the calling code may invoke `hasNext` as many times as it wants between invocations of `next`. Second, `next` is carefully written so that it works even if programmer using it has never invoked `hasNext`. Although it is generally a poor practice, it is completely legal to never invoke `hasNext` and simply loop invoking `next` until an exception is generated.

Third, `remove` is not allowed because it is not possible to do so correctly. Imagine, for example, if `remove` invoked `remove` on the underlying iterator. The following legal (although odd) code can cause incorrect behavior:

```
it.next();
it.hasNext();
it.remove();
```

Imagine that this were to happen when there was one more short string left in the iteration followed by some long ones. The invocation of `next` would return the last short string. Then `hasNext` would iterate through the list of strings, and finding no more short ones, return `false`. When `remove` was invoked, it would invoke `remove` on the underlying iterator, thereby removing the last (long) string that `hasNext` rejected. That would be incorrect. Since the above code is legal, you cannot fix this by forbidding the sequence of methods. You are effectively stuck. Because of this you cannot build a filtering iterator on top of another `Iterator` object. You can build one on top of a `ListIterator`, since it allows you to back up to the previously returned short string.

The methods of `ListIterator` have contracts similar to those of `Iterator`, as you have learned earlier in this chapter. You can provide `ListIterator` objects in some circumstances where you might otherwise write an `Iterator`. If you are writing a general utility class for others to use, you should implement `ListIterator` instead of `Iterator` if possible.

Exercise 16.3: Write a version of `ShortStrings` that implements `ListIterator` to filter a `ListIterator` object. Should your class extend `ShortStrings`?

16.11 Writing Collection Implementations

You will usually find that at least one of the collection implementations will satisfy your needs. If not, you can implement relevant collection interfaces yourself to provide collections that satisfy your particular needs. You will find skeletal

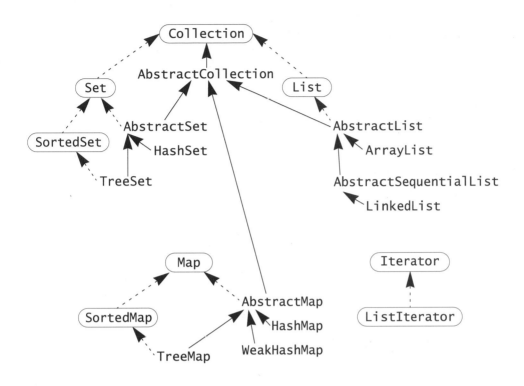

FIGURE 16–2: *Full Type Tree for Collections in `java.util`*

implementations in the abstract classes `AbstractCollection`, `AbstractSet`, `AbstractList`, `AbstractSequentialList`, and `AbstractMap`. You can extend these classes to create your own collections, often with less work than starting from the interfaces directly. The concrete collections shown in Figure 16–1 on page 422 each extend the appropriate abstract collection type, as shown in the full type tree in Figure 16–2.

These abstract collection classes are designed to be helpful superclasses for your own collection implementations. They are not required—in some cases you will find it easier or more efficient to directly implement the interfaces.

Each abstract collection class declares a few abstract methods, and uses these abstract methods in default implementations of other methods of the collection type. For example, `AbstractList` has two abstract methods: `size` and `get`. All other querying methods of `AbstractList` are implemented using these methods, including its iterators. You need only write your own implementation of the other methods if you want to, typically to either increase efficiency or to allow something disallowed by default. For example, if your list is modifiable, your subclass of `AbstractList` will have to provide an overriding implementation of the `set` method, which by default throws `UnsupportedOperationException`.

The root of the abstract collection types is `AbstractCollection`. If you need a collection that isn't a set, list, or map you can subclass this directly. Otherwise you will probably find it more useful to subclass one of the more specific abstract collections classes.

If the `Collection` class you are creating is unmodifiable (if the modification methods of your collection should throw `UnsupportedOperationException`), your subclass of `AbstractCollection` need only provide an implementation of the `size` and `iterator` methods. This means you must at least write an implementation of `Iterator` for your collection. If your collection is modifiable, you must also override the default implementation of the `add` method (which throws `UnsupportedOperationException`) and your iterator must support `remove`.

`AbstractSet` extends `AbstractCollection`, and the methods you must implement and can override are the same, with the additional constraint that a subclass of `AbstractSet` must conform to the contract of the `Set` interface.

`AbstractList` requires you to implement only `size` and `get(int)` to define an unmodifiable list class. If you also override `set(int,Object)` you will get a modifiable list, but one whose size cannot change. Your list can change size if you also override the methods `add(int,Object)` and `remove(int)`.

For example, suppose you need to view a bunch of arrays as a single list. You could use one of the existing `List` implementations, but at the cost of copying the information each time from the arrays into a new collection. You could instead subclass `AbstractList` to create an `ArrayBunchList` type that lets you do this without copying:

```
public class ArrayBunchList extends AbstractList {
    private Object[][] arrays;
    private int size;

    public ArrayBunchList(Object[][] arrays) {
        this.arrays = (Object[][])arrays.clone();
        int s = 0;
        for (int i = 0; i < arrays.length; i++)
            s += arrays[i].length;
        size = s;
    }

    public int size() {
        return size;
```

```
        }

        public Object get(int index) {
            int off = 0;      // offset from start of collection
            for (int i = 0; i < arrays.length; i++) {
                if (index < off + arrays[i].length)
                    return arrays[i][index - off];
                off += arrays[i].length;
            }
            throw new ArrayIndexOutOfBoundsException(index);
        }

        public Object set(int index, Object value) {
            int off = 0;      // offset from start of collection
            for (int i = 0; i < arrays.length; i++) {
                if (index < off + arrays[i].length) {
                    Object ret = arrays[i][index - off];
                    arrays[i][index - off] = value;
                    return ret;
                }
                off += arrays[i].length;
            }
            throw new ArrayIndexOutOfBoundsException(index);
        }
    }
}
```

When an ArrayBunchList is created, all the constituent arrays are remembered internally in the arrays field, and the total size of the collection in size. ArrayBunchList implements size, get, and set, but not add or remove. This means that the class provides a modifiable list, but one whose size cannot be changed. Any call that needs values from the underlying arrays will go through get. Any action that modifies the value of the ArrayBunchList will go through set, which modifies the appropriate underlying array.

AbstractList provides Iterator and ListIterator implementations for you on top of the other methods of the class. Because the iteration implementations use the methods of your underlying subclass of AbstractList, the modifying methods of the iteration will properly reflect the modifiability of your class.

The Iterator implementations of AbstractList use get to read values. As you will note, ArrayBunchList has a get that can do some significant work if the value is stored in one of the later arrays. We can make get smarter than shown here to help with this work, but we can be even more efficient for iteration because it accesses the data sequentially. Here is an optimized `Iterator`:

```
private class ABLIterator implements Iterator {
    private int off;        // offset from start of list
    private int array;      // array we are currently in
    private int pos;        // position in current array

    ABLIterator() {
        off = 0;
        array = 0;
        pos = 0;
        // skip any initial empty arrays (or to end)
        for (array = 0; array < arrays.length; array++)
            if (arrays[array].length > 0)
                break;
    }

    public boolean hasNext() {
        return off + pos < size();
    }

    public Object next() {
        if (!hasNext())
            throw new NoSuchElementException();
        Object ret = arrays[array][pos++];

        // advance to the next element (or to end)
        while (pos >= arrays[array].length) {
            off += arrays[array++].length;
            pos = 0;
            if (array >= arrays.length)
                break;
        }
        return ret;
    }

    public void remove() {
        throw new UnsupportedOperationException();
    }
}
```

This implementation uses our knowledge of the underlying data structures to know exactly where the next element is coming from. This is more efficient than invoking get to implement the iterator's next. (It is also written to handle empty arrays, or an empty ArrayBunchList.)

You can often substantially increase the performance of a resizable list by overriding the protected removeRange method, which takes two int parameters, min and max, and removes the elements starting at min, up to but not including max. The clear method uses removeRange to remove elements from lists and sublists. The default implementation is to invoke remove on each element one at a time. Many data structures can do bulk removes much more efficiently.

AbstractSequentialList extends AbstractList to make it easier to implement lists that are backed by a *sequential access* data store where moving from one element of the data to another requires examining each element of the data. In such a store, random access requires work, since you must traverse each element to get to the next. A linked list is a sequential access data store. By contrast, an array can be randomly accessed directly. This is why ArrayList extends AbstractList, while LinkedList extends AbstractSequentialList.

Where AbstractList implements its iterators via the random access method get, AbstractSequentialList implements the random access methods via an iterator you provide by implementing the listIterator method. You must also implement size. Your class will be modifiable in whatever ways your list iterator's methods allow. For example, if your iterator allows set but not add or remove, you will have a modifiable but non-resizable list.

To use the AbstractMap class you must implement the entries method to return an unmodifiable set of entries that contains the mappings of the set. This will implement an unmodifiable map. To make a modifiable map, you must override put, and the iterator your entries object returns must allow remove.

The abstract implementations provided in these classes are designed to be easy to extend, but efficiency is not always a consequence. You can often make your subclass of an abstract collection type much faster by judicious overriding of other methods, as shown for the ArrayBunchList iterator. As another example, the implementation of get in AbstractMap, having only a set of entries, must search through that set one at a time until it finds an appropriate entry. This is an $O(n)$ implementation. To get its $O(1)$ performance, HashMap overrides get and all other key-based methods to use its own hash buckets. However, HashMap does not override the implementation of equals because that requires iteration anyway and the implementation in AbstractMap is reasonably efficient.

Exercise 16.4: Implement a more efficient ListIterator for ArrayBunchList. Be careful of the specific contracts of ListIterator methods, such as set not being valid until either next or previous is invoked.

16.12 The Legacy Collection Types

The collection framework—the interfaces and classes described in this chapter, and shown in Figure 16–1 on page 422—are recent arrivals on the scene. The package `java.util` has always contained some other collections. Some are superseded by the new collection types. Even so, they are not deprecated because they are in wide use in existing code and will continue to be used until programmers shift over to the new types. You are therefore likely to encounter these *legacy collections* so you should learn about them, including their relationship to the newer collection types. The legacy collections consist of the following types:

- ◆ Enumeration—Analogous to Iterator.
- ◆ Vector—Analogous to ArrayList, maintains an ordered list of elements that are stored in an underlying array.
- ◆ Stack—A subclass of Vector that added methods to push and pop elements so you could treat the vector using the terms normal to a stack.
- ◆ Dictionary—Analogous to the Map interface, although Dictionary is an abstract class, not an interface.[3]
- ◆ Hashtable—Analogous to HashMap.
- ◆ Properties—A subclass of Hashtable, maintains a map of key/value pairs where the keys and values are strings. If a key is not found in a properties object a "default" properties object can be searched.

Of these types, only Properties is in active use—it is used to contain system properties, as described in "System Properties" on page 481 and by some applications to store configuration data. We describe the other legacy collections by contrasting them with their analogous types. We then describe Properties in more detail since you are more like to actually need to write code that uses it.

16.12.1 Enumeration

Enumeration is analogous to Iterator, but has just two methods: hasMoreElements which behaves like hasNext, and nextElement which behaves like next. You can get an Enumeration that iterates through a non-legacy collection using the static method Collections.enumeration.

---

[3] Dictionary is not an interface because it predates the addition of interfaces to the language, which gives you some idea of how old these legacy collections are.

Exercise 16.5: Rewrite the example program Concat on page 383 so that it uses an implementation of Enumeration that has only one FileInputStream object open at a time.

16.12.2 Vector

The Vector class is analogous to ArrayList. Although Vector is a legacy class, it has been made to implement List, and so it works as a Collection. All methods that access the contents of a Vector are synchronized. As a legacy collection, Vector contains many methods and constructors that are analogous to those of ArrayList, in addition to those it inherits from List. The legacy constructors and methods of Vector, and their analogs in ArrayList, are:

public **Vector(int initialCapacity, int capacityIncrement)**
    No analog. Creates a new Vector with the given initialCapacity that will grow by capacityIncrement elements at a time.

public **Vector(int initialCapacity)**
    Analogous to ArrayList(initialCacity).

public **Vector()**
    Analogous to ArrayList().

public **Vector(Collection coll)**
    Analogous to ArrayList(coll).

public final void **addElement(Object elem)**
    Analogous to add(elem).

public final void **insertElementAt(Object elem, int index)**
    Analogous to add(index, elem).

public final void **setElementAt(Object elem, int index)**
    Analogous to set(index, elem).

public final void **removeElementAt(int index)**
    Analogous to remove(index).

public final boolean **removeElement(Object elem)**
    Analogous to remove(elem).

public final void **removeAllElements()**
    Analogous to clear().

public final Object **elementAt(int index)**
    Analogous to get(index).

`public final void `**`copyInto(Object[] anArray)`**
>   No direct analog; the closest is `toArray(Object[])`, although `toArray` allocates a new array if the array is too small, where `copyInto` will throw an `IndexOutOfBoundsException`.

`public final int `**`indexOf(Object elem, int index)`**
>   Searches for the first occurrence of `elem`, beginning the search at `index`, and testing for equality using `equals`. The closest analog would be to create a sublist covering the range and use `indexOf` on the sublist.

`public final int `**`lastIndexOf(Object elem, int index)`**
>   Searches backwards for the last occurrence of `elem`, beginning the search at `index`, and testing for equality using `equals`. The closest analog would be to create a sublist covering the range and use `lastIndexOf` on the sublist.

`public final Enumeration `**`elements()`**
>   Analogous to `iterator()`. Equivalent to `Collections.enumeration`.

`public final Object `**`firstElement()`**
>   Analogous to `get(0)`.

`public final Object `**`lastElement()`**
>   Analogous to `get(size() - 1)`.

`public final void `**`setSize(int newSize)`**
>   No analogue. If `newSize` is less than the current size, any extra data is thrown away. If `newSize` is larger than the current size, the added elements are `null`.

`public final int `**`capacity()`**
>   No analogue. Returns the current capacity of the vector.

In addition to these public methods, protected fields are available to classes that subclass the `Vector` class. Be careful what you do (if anything) with these fields, because, for example, methods in `Vector` rely on `elementCount` being less than or equal to the length of the `elementData` array.

`protected Object `**`elementData[]`**
>   The buffer where elements are stored.

`protected int `**`elementCount`**
>   The number of elements currently used in the buffer.

`protected int `**`capacityIncrement`**
>   The number of elements to add to the capacity when `elementData` runs out of space. If zero, the size of the buffer is doubled every time it needs to grow.

16.12.3 Stack

The Stack class extends Vector to add methods for a simple last-in first-out stack of Objects. Use push to push an object onto the stack and use pop to remove the top element from the stack. The peek method returns the top item on the stack without removing it. The empty method returns true if the stack is empty. Trying to pop or peek in an empty Stack object will throw an EmptyStackException.

You can use search to find an object's distance from the top of the stack, with 1 being the top of the stack. If the object isn't found, –1 is returned. The search method uses Object.equals to test whether an object in the stack is the same as the one it is searching for.

These methods are trivial uses of the Vector methods, so using an ArrayList to implement a Stack would be simple: using add to implement push, and so on. There is no analogue to Stack in the collections.

Exercise 16.6: Implement a stack using ArrayList. Should your stack class be a subclass of ArrayList or use an ArrayList internally, providing different stack-specific methods?

16.12.4 Dictionary

The Dictionary abstract class is essentially an interface. It is analogous to the Map interface, but uses the terms "key" and "element" instead of "key" and "value." With two exceptions, each method in Dictionary has the same name as its analogous method in Map: get, put, remove, size, and isEmpty. The two exceptions are keys and elements. In Map, you get a Set of keys or values that you can iterate over or otherwise manipulate. In Dictionary, you can only get an Enumeration (iterator) for the keys and elements, using the keys and elements methods, respectively. The legacy collections did not contain a Set type, and so Dictionary could not be expressed in those terms.

16.12.5 Hashtable

The Hashtable class is similar to the HashMap class, implementing the methods of Dictionary. All methods of Hashtable are synchronized. Hashtable does not implement the Map interface since they are incompatible, although methods of the same name—containsKey, containsValue, putAll, keySet, entrySet, values, clear, equals, and hashCode—have analogous meanings. Beyond the methods inherited from Dictionary, Hashtable adds the following methods and constructors:

public **Hashtable()**
> Analogous to HashMap().

public **Hashtable(int initialCapacity)**
> Analogous to HashMap(initalCapacity).

public **Hashtable(int initialCapacity, float loadFactor)**
> Analogous to HashMap(initialCapacity, loadFactor).

public **Hashtable(Map map)**
> Analogous to HashMap(map).

public boolean **contains(Object elem)**
> Analogous to containsValue(elem).

16.13 Properties

A Properties object is used to store string keys and associated string elements. This kind of hashtable often has a default Properties object for properties not specified in the table. The Properties class extends Hashtable. Standard Hashtable methods are used for almost all manipulation of a Properties object, but to get and set properties, you can use string-based methods. In addition to inherited methods, the following methods and constructors are provided:

public **Properties()**
> Creates an empty property map.

public **Properties(Properties defaults)**
> Creates an empty property map with the specified default Properties object. If a property lookup fails, the default Properties object is queried. The default properties object can have its own default Properties object, and so on. The chain of default objects can be arbitrarily deep

public String **getProperty(String key)**
> Gets the property element for key. If the key is not found in this object, the default Properties object (if any) is searched. Returns null if the property is not found.

public String **getProperty(String key, String defaultElement)**
> Gets the property element for key. If the key is not found in this object, the default Properties object (if any) is searched. Returns defaultElement if the property is not found.

`public String `**`setProperty(String key, String value)`**

> Adds the property `key` to the map with the given `value`. This only affects the `Properties` object on which it is invoked—the default `Properties` object (if any) is unaffected.

`public void `**`store(OutputStream out, String header)`**
  `throws IOException`

> Saves properties to an `OutputStream`. This only works if this `Properties` object contains only string keys and values (as the specification says it must); otherwise you get a `ClassCastException`. If not `null`, the `header` string is written to the output stream as a single-line comment. Do not use a multiline header string, or else the saved properties will not be loadable. Only properties in this object are saved to the file; the default `Properties` object (if any) is not saved.

`public void `**`load(InputStream in)`**` throws IOException`

> Loads properties from an `InputStream`. The property list is presumed to have been created previously by `store`. This method puts values into this `Properties` object; it does not set values in the default `Properties` object.

`public Enumeration `**`propertyNames()`**

> Enumerates the keys, including those of any default `Properties` object. This method provides a snapshot, and hence can be expensive. The inherited keys method, by contrast, returns only those properties defined in this object itself.

`public void `**`list(PrintWriter out)`**

> Lists (prints) properties on the given `PrintWriter`. Useful for debugging.

`public void `**`list(PrintStream out)`**

> Lists (prints) properties on the given `PrintStream`. Also useful for debugging.

The default `Properties` object cannot be changed after the object is created. To change the default `Properties` object, you can subclass the `Properties` class and modify the protected field named `defaults` that contains the default `Properties` object.

> *Science is facts;*
> *just as houses are made of stones, so is science made of facts;*
> *but a pile of stones is not a house and a collection of facts is not necessarily science.*
> —Henri Poincaré

CHAPTER 17

Miscellaneous Utilities

Computers are useless—they can only give you answers.
—Pablo Picasso

YOU will find several standard utility interfaces and classes in the `java.util` package. You have seen the collection classes already in Chapter 16. This chapter covers the remainder of the classes, except those used for localization, which are in Chapter 19. The `java.util` classes covered in this chapter are:

- `BitSet`—A dynamically sized bit vector.
- `Observer/Observable`—This interface/class pair enables an object to be `Observable` by having one or more `Observer` objects that are notified when something interesting happens in the `Observable` object.
- `Random`—A class to generate sequences of pseudorandom numbers.
- `StringTokenizer`—A class that splits a string into tokens based on delimiters (by default, white space).
- `Timer/TimerTask`—A way to schedule tasks to be run in the future.

Finally, we look at two other useful utility classes, housed in the `java.lang` package:

- `Math`—A class for performing basic mathematical operations, such as trigonometric functions, exponentiation, logarithms and so on.
- `StrictMath`—A class that defines the same methods as `Math` but which guarantees the use of strict floating-point arithmetic, which ensures consistently reproducible results.

17.1 BitSet

The BitSet class provides a way to create a bit vector that grows dynamically. In effect, a bit set is a vector of 2^{31} true or false bits, all of them initially false. The bits are indexed from 0 to Integer.MAX_VALUE, and can be individually set, cleared, or retrieved. BitSet uses only sufficient storage to hold the highest index bit that has been set—any bits beyond that are deemed to be false.

There are two constructors for BitSet:

public **BitSet(int size)**

Creates a new bit set with enough initial storage to explicitly represent bits indexed from 0 to size-1. All bits are initially false.

public **BitSet()**

Creates a new bit set with a default amount of initial storage. All bits are initially false.

There are three methods for dealing with individual bits, each of which throws IndexOutOfBoundsException if the supplied index is negative.

public void **set(int index)**

Sets the bit specified by index to true.

public void **clear(int index)**

Sets the bit specified by index to false.

public boolean **get(int index)**

Returns the value of the bit specified by index.

Other methods modify the current bit set by applying bitwise logical operations using the bits from another bit set:

public void **and(BitSet other)**

Logically ANDs this bit set with other and changes the value of this set to the result. The resulting value of a bit in this bit set is true only if it is originally true and the corresponding bit in other is also true.

public void **andNot(BitSet other)**

Clears all bits in this bit set that are set in other. The resulting value of a bit in this bit set is true only if it is originally true and the corresponding bit in other is false.

public void **or(BitSet other)**

Logically ORs this bit set with other and changes the value of this set to the result. The resulting value of a bit in this bit set is true only if it is originally true or the corresponding bit in other is true.

`public void `**`xor(BitSet other)`**
>   Logically XORs this bit set with `other` and changes the value of this set to
>   the result. The resulting value of a bit in this bit set is `true` only if it has a
>   different value from the corresponding bit in `other`.

The remaining methods are:

`public int `**`size()`**
>   Returns the number of bits actually stored in this `BitSet`. Setting a bit index
>   greater than or equal to this value may increase the storage used by the set.

`public int `**`length()`**
>   Returns the index of the highest set bit in this `BitSet` plus one.

`public int `**`hashCode()`**
>   Returns a reasonable hash code for this set based on the values of its bits. Be
>   careful not to change the values of the bits while the `BitSet` is in the hash
>   map, or the set will be misplaced.

`public boolean `**`equals(Object other)`**
>   Returns `true` if all the bits in `other` are the same as those in this set.

Note that because of the way a `BitSet` conserves storage, there are no methods to complement each bit in the set. However, you can achieve the desired effect
by appropriate use of the other methods. For example, to complement the first n
bits in a bit set, `xor` it with a bit set of n `true` bits.

Here is a class that uses a `BitSet` to mark which characters occur in a string.
Each position in the bit set represents the numerical value of a character: the 0th
position represents the null character (\u0000), the 97th position represents the
character `'a'`, and so on. The bit set can be printed to show the characters that it
found:

```java
public class WhichChars {
    private BitSet used = new BitSet();

    public WhichChars(String str) {
        for (int i = 0; i < str.length(); i++)
            used.set(str.charAt(i));    // set bit for char
    }

    public String toString() {
        String desc = "[";
        int length = used.length();
        for (int i = 0; i < length; i++) {
            if (used.get(i))
```

```
                desc += (char) i;
        }
        return desc + "]";
    }
}
```

If we pass `WhichChars` the string `"Testing 1 2 3"` we get back:

`[ 123Teginst]`

which shows each of the characters (including the spaces) that were used in the input string, and which, incidentally, have now been sorted into numerical order.

Exercise 17.1: The `WhichChars` class has a problem marking characters near the top of the Unicode range because the high character values will leave many unused bits in the lower ranges. Use a `HashMap` to solve this problem by storing `Character` objects for each character seen. Remember to write an iterator class.

Exercise 17.2: Now use a `HashMap` to store a `BitSet` object for each different top byte (high 8 bits) encountered in the input string, with each `BitSet` storing the low bytes that have been seen with the particular high byte. Remember to write an iterator class.

17.2 Observer/Observable

The `Observer/Observable` types provide a protocol for an arbitrary number of `Observer` objects to watch for changes and events in any number of `Observable` objects. An `Observable` object subclasses the `Observable` class, which provides methods to maintain a list of `Observer` objects that want to know about changes in the `Observable` object. All objects in the "interested" list must implement the `Observer` interface. When an `Observable` object experiences a noteworthy change or event that `Observer` objects may care about, the `Observable` object invokes its `notifyObservers` method, which invokes each `Observer` object's `update` method.

The `Observer` interface consists of a single method:

public void **update(Observable obj, Object arg)**
> This method is invoked when the `Observable` object `obj` has a change or an event to report. The `arg` parameter is a way to pass an arbitrary object to describe the change or event to the observer.

The `Observer/Observable` mechanism is designed to be general. Each `Observable` class is left to define the circumstances under which an `Observer` object's update method will be invoked. The Observable object maintains a "changed" flag which is used by the subclass methods to indicate when something of interest has occurred.

protected void setChanged()
> Marks this object as having been changed—hasChanged will now return true—but does not notify observers.

protected void clearChanged()
> Indicates that this object is no longer changed, or has notified all observers of the last change—hasChanged will now return false.

public boolean hasChanged()
> Returns the current value of the "changed" flag.

When a change occurs, the Observable object should invoke its setChanged method and then notify its observers using one of the following:

public void notifyObservers(Object arg)
> Notifies all Observer objects in the list that something has happened, and then clears the "changed" flag. For each observer in the list, its update method is invoked with this Observable object as the first argument and arg as the second.

public void notifyObservers()
> Equivalent to notifyObservers(null). ·

The following Observable methods maintain the list of Observer objects:

public void addObserver(Observer o)
> Adds the observer o to the observer list, if it's not already there.

public void deleteObserver(Observer o)
> Deletes the observer o from the observer list.

public void deleteObservers()
> Deletes all Observer objects from the observer list.

public int countObservers()
> Returns the number of observers in the observer list.

The methods of Observable use synchronization to ensure consistency when concurrent access to the object occurs. For example, one thread can be trying to add an observer while another is trying to remove one and a third is effecting a change on the Observable object. While synchronization is necessary for maintaining the observer list and making changes to the "changed" flag, no synchronization lock should be held when invoking the update method of the observers, otherwise it would be very easy to create deadlocks. The default implementation of notifyObservers takes a synchronized snapshot of the current observer list before invoking update. This means that an observer that is removed while notifyObservers is still in progress will still be notified of the last change. Conversely, an observer that is added while notifyObservers is still in progress will not be notified of the current change. If the Observable object allows concurrent invocations of methods that generate notifications, it is possible for update to be called concurrently on each Observer object. Consequently, Observer objects must use appropriate synchronization within update to ensure proper operation.

The default implementation of notifyObservers uses the invoking thread to invoke update on each observer. The order in which observers are notified is not specified. A subclass could specialize notifyObservers to use a different threading model and/or provide ordering guarantees.

The following example illustrates how Observer/Observable might be used to monitor users of a system. First, we define a Users class that is an Observable type:

```
import java.util.*;

public class Users extends Observable {
    private Map loggedIn = new HashMap();

    public void login(String name, String password)
        throws BadUserException
    {
        if (!passwordValid(name, password))
            throw new BadUserException(name);

        UserState state = new UserState(name);
        loggedIn.put(name, state);
        setChanged();
        notifyObservers(state);
    }

    public void logout(UserState state) {
        loggedIn.remove(state.name());
        setChanged();
        notifyObservers(state);
    }

    // ...
}
```

A `Users` object stores a map of users who are logged in and maintains `UserState` objects for each login. When someone logs in or out, all `Observer` objects will be passed that user's `UserState` object. The `notifyObservers` method sends messages only if the state changes, so you must invoke `setChanged` on `Users`; otherwise `notifyObservers` would do nothing.

Here is how an `Observer` that maintains a constant display of logged-in users might implement `update` to watch a `Users` object:

```java
import java.util.*;

public class Eye implements Observer {
    Users watching;

    public Eye(Users user) {
        watching = user;
        watching.addObserver(this);
    }

    public void update(Observable user, Object whichState)
    {
        if (user != watching)
            throw new IllegalArgumentException();

        UserState state = (UserState)whichState;
        if (watching.loggedIn(state))    // user logged in
            addUser(state);              // add to my list
        else
            removeUser(state);           // remove from list
    }
}
```

Each `Eye` object watches a particular `Users` object. When a user logs in or out, `Eye` is notified because it invoked the `Users` object's `addObserver` method with itself as the interested object. When `update` is invoked, it checks the correctness of its parameters and then modifies its display depending on whether the user in question has logged in or out.

The check for what happened with the `UserState` object is simple here. You could avoid it by passing an object describing what happened and to whom instead of passing the `UserState` object itself. Such a design makes it easier to add new actions without breaking existing code.

The `Observer`/`Observable` mechanism is a looser, more flexible analog to the `wait`/`notify` mechanism for threads described in "wait, notifyAll, and notify" on page 244. The thread mechanism ensures that synchronized access protects you from undesired concurrency. The observation mechanism enables any relationship to be built between two participants, whatever the threading model. Both patterns have producers of information (`Observable` and the invoker of `notify`) and consumers of that information (`Observer` and the invoker of `wait`), but each one fills a different need. Use `wait`/`notify` when you design a thread-based mechanism, and use `Observer`/`Observable` when you need something more general.

Exercise 17.3: Provide an implementation of the `Attributed` interface that uses `Observer`/`Observable` to notify observers of changes.

17.3 Random

The `Random` class creates objects that manage independent sequences of pseudo-random numbers. If you don't care what the sequence is and want it as a sequence of `double` values, the method `java.lang.Math.random` creates a single `Random` object the first time it is invoked and returns pseudorandom numbers from that object—see Section 17.6 on page 477. You can gain more control over the sequence (for example, the ability to set the seed) by creating a `Random` object and getting values from it.

public **Random()**

> Creates a new random number generator. Its seed will be initialized to a value based on the current time.

public **Random(long seed)**

> Creates a new random number generator using the specified `seed`. Two `Random` objects created with the same initial `seed` will return the same sequence of pseudorandom numbers.

public void **setSeed(long seed)**

> Sets the seed of the random number generator to `seed`. This method can be invoked at any time and resets the sequence to start with the given seed.

public int **nextBoolean()**

> Returns a pseudorandom uniformly distributed `boolean` value.

public int **nextInt()**

> Returns a pseudorandom uniformly distributed `int` value between the two values `Integer.MIN_VALUE` and `Integer.MAX_VALUE`, inclusive.

`public int `**`nextInt(int ceiling)`**
> Like nextInt(), but returns a value that is at least zero and is less than the value ceiling. Use this instead of using nextInt() and % to get a range. If ceiling is negative, an IllegalArgumentException is thrown.

`public long `**`nextLong()`**
> Returns a pseudorandom uniformly distributed long value between Long.MIN_VALUE and Long.MAX_VALUE, inclusive.

`public void `**`nextBytes(byte[] buf)`**
> Fills the array buf with random bytes.

`public float `**`nextFloat()`**
> Returns a pseudorandom uniformly distributed float value between 0.0f (inclusive) and 1.0f (exclusive).

`public double `**`nextDouble()`**
> Returns a pseudorandom uniformly distributed double value between 0.0 (inclusive) and 1.0 (exclusive).

`public double `**`nextGaussian()`**
> Returns a pseudorandom Gaussian-distributed double value with mean of 0.0 and standard deviation of 1.0.

All the "next" methods are written using the protected synchronized method next, which returns an int of randomized bits. The setSeed method is also synchronized, so you can use Random from multiple threads safely.

The Random class specifies the algorithms to be used to generate the pseudorandom numbers but permits different algorithms to be used provided the general contract of each method is adhered to. The basic algorithm (a linear congruential generator) is defined in the next method and is used for all other methods except nextGaussian. You can create your own random number generator by overriding the next method to provide a different generating algorithm.

Exercise 17.4: Given a certain number of six-sided dice, you can calculate the theoretical probability of each possible total. For example, with two six-sided dice, the probability of a total of seven is one in six. Write a program that compares the theoretical distribution of sums for a particular number of six-sided dice with the actual results over a large number of "rolls" using Random to generate numbers between one and six. Does it matter which of the number-generating methods you use?

Exercise 17.5: Write a program that tests nextGaussian, displaying the results of a large number of runs as a graph (a bar chart of * characters will do).

17.4 StringTokenizer

The `StringTokenizer` class breaks a string into parts, using delimiters. A sequence of tokens broken out of a string is, in effect, an ordered enumeration of those tokens, so `StringTokenizer` implements the `Enumeration` interface (see page 456). `StringTokenizer` provides methods that are more specifically typed than `Enumeration`, which you can use if you know you are working on a `StringTokenizer` object. The `StringTokenizer` enumeration is effectively a snapshot because `String` objects are read-only. For example, the following loop breaks a string into tokens separated by spaces and commas:

```
String str = "Gone, and forgotten";
StringTokenizer tokens = new StringTokenizer(str, " ,");
while (tokens.hasMoreTokens())
    System.out.println(tokens.nextToken());
```

By including the comma in the list of separators in the `StringTokenizer` constructor, the tokenizer consumes commas along with spaces, leaving only the words of the string to be returned one at a time. The output of this example is

```
Gone
and
forgotten
```

The `StringTokenizer` class has several methods to control what is considered a word, whether it should understand numbers or strings specially, and so on:

public **StringTokenizer(String str, String delim,**
   boolean returnTokens)
   Constructs a `StringTokenizer` on the string `str`, using the characters in `delim` as the delimiter set. The `returnTokens` boolean determines whether delimiters are returned as tokens or skipped. If they are returned as tokens, each delimiter character is returned separately.

public **StringTokenizer(String str, String delim)**
   Equivalent to `StringTokenizer(str, delim, false)`, meaning that delimiters are skipped, not returned.

public **StringTokenizer(String str)**
   Equivalent to `StringTokenizer(str, " \t\n\r\f")`, meaning that the delimiters are the whitespace characters, and are skipped.

public boolean **hasMoreTokens()**
   Returns `true` if more tokens exist.

`public String` **`nextToken()`**

> Returns the next token of the string. If there are no more tokens, a `NoSuchElementException` is thrown.

`public String` **`nextToken(String delim)`**

> Switches the delimiter set to the characters in `delim` and returns the next token. There is no way to set a new delimiter set without getting the next token. If there are no more tokens, a `NoSuchElementException` is thrown.

`public int` **`countTokens()`**

> Returns the number of tokens remaining in the string using the current delimiter set. This is the number of times `nextToken` can return before it will generate an exception. When you need the number of tokens, this method is faster than repeatedly invoking `nextToken`, because the token strings are merely counted, not constructed and returned.

The methods `StringTokenizer` implements for the `Enumeration` interface—`hasMoreElements` and `nextElement`—are equivalent to `hasMoreTokens` and `nextToken`, respectively.

The section "`StreamTokenizer`" on page 386 described a class with greater control over how input can be tokenized. To use `StreamTokenizer` on a string, create a `StringReader` object for the string. For many cases, however, a simple `StringTokenizer` object is sufficient.

Exercise 17.6: Write a method that will take a string containing floating-point numbers, break it up using white space as the delimiter, and return the sum of the numbers.

Exercise 17.7: Write a program that uses a `StreamTokenizer` object to break an input file into words and counts the number of times each word occurs in the file, printing the result.

17.5 Timer and TimerTask

The `Timer` class helps you set up tasks that will happen at some future point, including repeating events. Each `Timer` object has an associated thread that wakes up when one of its `TimerTask` objects is destined to run. For example, the following code will set up a task that prints out the virtual machine's memory usage approximately once a second:

```
long start = System.currentTimeMillis();
Timer timer = new Timer(true);
timer.scheduleAtFixedRate(new MemoryWatchTask(), 0, 1000);
```

This code creates a new Timer object that will be responsible for scheduling and executing a MemoryWatchTask (which you will see shortly). The true passed to the Timer constructor tells Timer to use a daemon thread (see page 259), so the memory tracing activity will not keep the virtual machine alive when other threads are complete.

The schedule invocation shown tells timer to schedule the task starting with no delay (the 0 that is the second argument) and repeat it every thousand milliseconds (the 1000 that is the third argument). So starting immediately, timer will invoke the run method of a MemoryWatchTask:

```
import java.util.TimerTask;
import java.util.Date;

public class MemoryWatchTask extends TimerTask {
    public void run() {
        System.out.print(new Date() + ": " );
        Runtime rt = Runtime.getRuntime();
        System.out.print(rt.freeMemory() + " free, ");
        System.out.print(rt.totalMemory() + " total");
        System.out.println();
    }
}
```

MemoryWatchTask extends the abstract TimerTask to define a task that prints out the current free and total memory, prefixed by the current time. TimerTask implements the Runnable interface, and its run method is what is invoked by a Timer object when a task is to be run. Because the setup code told timer to execute once a second, the thread timer uses will wait one second between each task execution.

TimerTask has three methods:

public abstract void **run()**

Defines the action to be performed by this TimerTask.

public boolean **cancel()**

Cancels this TimerTask so that it will never run again (or at all if it hasn't run yet). Returns true if the task was scheduled for repeated execution, or was a once-only task that had not yet been run. Otherwise it returns `false`. Essentially this method returns `true` if it prevented the task from having a scheduled execution—the task need never have been scheduled, or may have been previously cancelled.

public long **scheduledExecutionTime()**

Returns the scheduled execution time of the most recent actual execution (possibly the in-progress execution) of this `TimerTask`. The returned value represents the time in milliseconds. This method is most often used inside `run` to see if the current execution of the task occurred soon enough to warrant execution; if the task was delayed too long `run` may decide not to do anything.

You can cancel either a single task or an entire timer by invoking its `cancel` method. Cancelling a task means it will not be scheduled in the future. Cancelling a `Timer` object prevents any future execution of any of its tasks.

Each `Timer` object uses a single thread to schedule its task executions. You can control whether this thread is a daemon thread by the boolean you specify to the `Timer` constructor.

public **Timer(boolean isDaemon)**

Creates a new `Timer` whose underlying thread has its daemon state set according to `isDaemon`.

public **Timer()**

Equivalent to `Timer(false)`.

If you use the no-arg constructor you will get a user (non-daemon) thread. When the timer is not reachable—which can only happen when all references to it are dropped and no tasks remain to be executed—the thread will be terminated. You should not strongly rely on this behavior because it relies upon the garbage collector discovering the unreachability of the timer object, and that can happen anytime or never.

There are three kinds of task scheduling. A *once-only* scheduling means that the task will be executed once. A *fixed-delay* scheduling lets you define the amount of time between the start of one execution and the next. The task essentially executes periodically, but any delay in the start of one execution (due to general thread scheduling considerations, garbage collection, or other background activity) causes the next execution to be similarly delayed, so that an execution starts relative to the start of the previous execution. In contrast, a *fixed-rate* scheduling starts each execution relative to the start of the initial execution. If one execution is delayed, there will be a shorter gap before the next execution—possibly no gap, depending on the extent of the delay. You use fixed-delay scheduling when the frequency of tasks is what matters, such as time delays between animation frames in some circumstances. You use fixed-rate scheduling when the absolute time matters, such as alarms or timers.

public void **schedule(TimerTask task, Date time)**
> Schedules the given task for a once-only execution at the specified time.

public void **schedule(TimerTask task, long delay)**
> Schedules the given task for a once-only execution after the specified delay (in milliseconds),

public void **schedule(TimerTask task, Date firstTime, long period)**
> Schedules the given task to execute on a fixed-delay schedule until cancelled, starting at firstTime, executing every period milliseconds.

public void **schedule(TimerTask task, long delay, long period)**
> Schedules the given task to execute on a fixed-delay schedule until cancelled, starting after the given delay, executing every period milliseconds.

public void **scheduleAtFixedRate(TimerTask task, Date firstTime, long period)**
> Schedules the given task to execute on a fixed-rate schedule until cancelled, starting at firstTime, executing every period milliseconds.

public void **scheduleAtFixedRate(TimerTask task, long delay, long period)**
> Schedules the given task to execute on a fixed-rate schedule until cancelled, starting after the given delay, executing every period milliseconds.

Any time you specify that is in the past schedules an immediate execution. All times are in milliseconds—the Date class's getTime method is used to convert a Date to milliseconds (see "Time, Dates, and Calendars" on page 510)—and are approximate because the timer uses Thread.wait(long) to schedule future executions, and wait, like sleep, does not guarantee precision. If a delay is so large that adding it to the current time would cause an overflow, you will get an IllegalArgumentException.

A TimerTask object can only be scheduled with one Timer, and a cancelled Timer cannot have any new tasks scheduled. If you attempt to schedule a task that violates either of these restrictions, or you cancel an already cancelled Timer or TimerTask, you will get an IllegalStateException.

A Timer's thread is subject to the usual thread scheduling of a system and takes no steps to influence its priority in any way—it is created with the priority of the thread that created the Timer. If you need to boost the priority of a given task when it is executing, set the thread priority within the run method. If you want to boost the priority of the Timer thread itself, you must create the Timer from a thread that already has the desired priority level.

There is no way to ask which tasks are being governed by a particular Timer.

17.6 Math and StrictMath

The Math class consists of static constants and methods for common mathematical manipulations that use normal floating point semantics. The StrictMath class defines the same constants and methods but always uses strict floating point semantics (see "Strict and non-Strict Floating-Point Arithmetic" on page 158)—in other words, StrictMath is always defined with the strictfp modifier, while Math need not be. Both classes have two useful double constants: E represents e (2.7182818284590452354), and PI represents π (3.14159265358979323846). In the following table of Math and StrictMath methods angles are in radians, and all parameters and return values are double, unless stated otherwise:

Function	Value
sin(a)	sine(a)
cos(a)	cosine(a)
tan(a)	tangent(a)
asin(v)	arcsine(v), with v in the range [−1.0, 1.0]
acos(v)	arccosine(v), with v in the range [−1.0, 1.0]
atan(v)	arctangent(v), returned in the range [−π/2,π/2]
atan2(x,y)	arctangent(x/y), returned in the range [−π,π]
toRadians(d)	given d in degrees, returns equivalent angle in radians
toDegrees(r)	given r in radians, returns equivalent angle in degrees
exp(x)	e^x
pow(y,x)	y^x
log(x)	ln x (natural log of x)
sqrt(x)	Square root of x
ceil(x)	Smallest whole number $\geq x$
floor(x)	Largest whole number $\leq x$
rint(x)	x rounded to the nearest integer; if neither integer is nearer, rounds to the even integer
round(x)	(int)floor(x + 0.5) for float x; (long)floor(x + 0.5) for double x
abs(x)	Absolute value of x for any numeric type (although the absolute value of the most negative value of an int or long is itself and therefore negative; that's how two's complement integers work).
max(x,y)	Larger of x and y for any numeric type
min(x,y)	Smaller of x and y for any numeric type

The static method `IEEEremainder` calculates remainder as defined by the IEEE-754 standard. The remainder operator %, as described in "Floating-Point Arithmetic" on page 156, obeys the rule

```
(x/y)*y + x%y == x
```

This preserves one kind of symmetry: if x%y is z, then changing the sign of either x or y will change only the sign of z, never its absolute value. For example, 7%2.5 is 2.0, and -7%2.5 is -2.0. The IEEE standard defines remainder for x and y differently, preserving symmetry of spacing along the number line—the result of `IEEEremainder(-7, 2.5)` is 0.5. The remainder operator makes values symmetric around zero on the number line, whereas the IEEE remainder mechanism keeps resulting values y units apart. The method is provided because both kinds of remainder are useful.

The static method `random` generates a pseudorandom number r in the range $0.0 \leq r < 1.0$. More control over pseudorandom number generation is provided by the Random class, as you learned on page 470.

See "`java.math`—Mathematics" on page 534 for brief coverage of some other math-related classes.

Exercise 17.8: Write a calculator that has all `Math` or `StrictMath` functions, as well as (at least) the basic operators +, -, *, /, and %. (The simplest form is probably a reverse Polish stack calculator because operator precedence is not an issue.)

> *Power is not revealed by striking hard or often, but by striking true.*
> —Honoré de Balzac

CHAPTER 18

System Programming

GLENDOWER: I can call spirits from the vasty deep.
HOTSPUR: Why, so can I, or so can any man;
But will they come when you do call for them?
—William Shakespeare, *King Henry IV, Part 1*

THIS chapter describes how your application can interact with the runtime system of the Java virtual machine and how the runtime system can be used to interact with the underlying operating system. Such interactions include reading and writing the system properties that allow communication between the operating system and the runtime system, executing other programs, and shutting down the runtime system. Three main classes in `java.lang` provide this access:

- The `System` class provides static methods to manipulate system state. It provides for the reading and writing of system properties, provides the standard input and output streams, and provides a number of miscellaneous utility functions. For convenience, several methods in `System` operate on the current `Runtime` object.

- The `Runtime` class provides an interface to the runtime system of the executing virtual machine. The current `Runtime` object provides access to functionality that is per-runtime, such as interacting with the garbage collector, executing other programs and shutting down the runtime system.

- The `Process` class represents a running process created using an invocation of `Runtime.exec` to execute another program.

We also look at security and how different security policies can be enforced in the runtime system. We start, though, by looking at the `System` class.

18.1 The System Class

The System class provides static methods to manipulate system state and acts as a repository for system-wide resources. System provides functionality in four general areas:

- ◆ The standard I/O streams,
- ◆ Manipulating system properties,
- ◆ Utilities and convenience methods for accessing the current Runtime, and
- ◆ Security

You'll learn about security in more detail in Section 18.5 on page 493.

18.1.1 Standard I/O Streams

The standard input, output, and error streams are available as static fields of the System class.

```
public static final InputStream in
```
Standard input stream for reading data.

```
public static final PrintStream out
```
Standard output stream for printing messages.

```
public static final PrintStream err
```
Standard error stream for printing error messages. The user can often redirect standard output to a file. But applications also need to print error messages that the user will see even if standard output is redirected. The err stream is specifically devoted to error messages that are not rerouted with the regular output.

For historical reasons, both out and err are PrintStream objects, not PrintWriter objects. See "Print Streams" on page 380 for a discussion about PrintStream and PrintWriter types.

Although each of the standard stream references is declared final, the methods setIn, setOut and setErr, allow you to redefine the actual streams to which these references are bound (by using native code to bypass the language level restriction of not assigning final variables). These methods are security checked and throw SecurityException if you do not have permission to change the standard streams.

18.1.2 System Properties

System properties define the system environment. They are stored by the System class in a Properties object (see page 460). Property names consist of multiple parts separated by periods. For example, here is a dump of the standard properties on one system:

```
#Standard System properties
#Mon Nov 29 17:30:23 EST 1999
java.version=1.3.0
java.vendor=Sun Microsystems Inc.
java.vendor.url=http://java.sun.com/
java.vm.specification.version=1.0
java.vm.specification.vendor=Sun Microsystems Inc.
java.vm.specification.name=Java Virtual Machine Specification
java.vm.version=1.3-0
java.vm.vendor=Sun Microsystems Inc.
java.vm.name=Java HotSpot(TM) Client VM
java.specification.version=1.3
java.specification.vendor=Sun Microsystems Inc.
java.specification.name=Java Platform API Specification
java.home=/disk/jdk1.3/jre
java.class.version=47.0
java.class.path=.:../classes:/vob/jive/jars/jini.jar:/vob/
    jive/jars/sun-util.jar:/vob/jive/jars/jini-core.jar
java.ext.dirs=/disk/jdk1.3/jre/lib/ext
os.name=SunOS
os.arch=sparc
os.version=5.6
file.separator=/
path.separator=:
line.separator=\n
user.name=arnold
user.home=/home/arnold
user.dir=/vob/java_prog/src
```

These properties are defined on all systems, although the values will certainly vary. On any given system there will be many more properties defined. Some of the standard properties are used by classes in the standard packages. The File class, for example, uses the file.separator property to build up and break down pathnames. You are also free to use properties. The following method looks for a personal configuration file in the user's home directory:

```
public static File personalConfig(String fileName) {
    String home = System.getProperty("user.home");
    if (home == null)
        return null;
    else
        return new File(home, fileName);
}
```

The methods of the System class that deal with the system properties are:

public static Properties getProperties()
    Gets the `Properties` object that defines all system properties.

public static String getProperty(String key)
    Returns the value of the system property named in key.

public static String getProperty(String key, String defaultValue)
    Returns the value of the system property named in key. If it has no definition, it returns `defaultValue`.

public static String setProperty(String key, String value)
    Sets the value of the system property named in `key` to the given `value`, returning the previous value or `null` if the property was not previously set.

public static void setProperties(Properties props)
    Sets the `Properties` object that defines all system properties to be `props`.

All these methods are security checked and may throw `SecurityException`. However, being denied access to the entire set of properties does not necessarily mean you will be denied access to individual properties.

Property values are stored as strings, but the strings can represent other types, such as integers or booleans. Methods are available to read properties and decode them into some of the primitive types. These decoding methods are static methods of the primitive type's class. Each method has a `String` parameter that names the property to retrieve. Some forms have a second parameter (shown as `def` later) that is the default value to return if no property is found with that name. Methods that lack a default value parameter return an object that contains the default value for the type. All these methods decode values in the standard formats for constants of the primitive type:

```
public static boolean Boolean.getBoolean(String name)
public static Integer Integer.getInteger(String name)
public static Integer
```

```
                    Integer.getInteger(String name, Integer def)
public static Integer
                    Integer.getInteger(String name, int def)
public static Long Long.getLong(String name)
public static Long Long.getLong(String name, Long def)
public static Long Long.getLong(String name, long def)
```

The getBoolean method is different from the others—it returns a boolean value instead of an object of class Boolean. If the property isn't present, getBoolean returns false; the other methods return null.

The classes Character, Byte, Short, Float, and Double do not have property fetching methods. You can get the value as a string and use the mechanisms described in "String Conversions" on page 217 to convert to the appropriate primitive type.

18.1.3 Utility Methods

The System class also contains a number of utility methods:

public static long **currentTimeMillis()**

> Returns the current time in milliseconds since the epoch (00:00:00 GMT, January 1, 1970). The time is returned in a long. Sophisticated applications may require more functionality: see "Time, Dates, and Calendars" on page 510.

public static void **arraycopy(Object src, int srcPos, Object dst, int dstPos, int count)**

> Copies the contents of the source array, starting at src[srcPos], to the destination array, starting at dst[dstPos]. Exactly count elements will be copied. If an attempt is made to access outside of either array an IndexOutOfBoundsException is thrown. If the values in the source array are not compatible with the destination array an ArrayStoreException is thrown. "Compatible" means that each object in the source array must be assignable to the component type of the destination array. For arrays of primitive types, the types must be the same, not just assignable; arraycopy cannot be used to copy an array of short to an array of int. The arraycopy method works correctly on overlapping arrays, so it can be used to copy one part of an array over another part. You can, for example, shift everything in an array one slot toward the beginning, as shown in the method squeezeOut on page 219.

```
public static int identityHashCode(Object obj)
```
Returns a hashcode for obj using the algorithm that Object.hashcode defines. This allows algorithms that rely on identity hashing to work, even if the class of obj overrides hashCode.

A number of other methods in System are convenience methods that operate on the current Runtime object—which can be obtained using the static method Runtime.getRuntime. For each method an invocation System.*method* is equivalent to the invocation Runtime.getRuntime().*method*; consequently these methods are described as we discuss the Runtime class. The methods are:

```
public static void exit(int status)
public static void gc()
public static void runFinalization()
public static void loadLibrary(String libname)
public static void load(String filename)
```

Exercise 18.1: Write the plugTogether method. You will need threads.

18.2 Creating Processes

As you have learned, a running system can have many threads of execution. Most systems that host a Java virtual machine also can run multiple programs. Applications can execute new programs using one of the Runtime.exec methods. Each successful invocation of exec creates a new Process object that represents the program running in its own *process*. You can use a Process object to query the process's state and invoke methods to control its progress. Process is an abstract class whose subclasses are defined on each system to work with that system's processes. The two basic forms of exec are:

```
public Process exec(String[] cmdArray) throws IOException
```
Runs the command in cmdArray on the current system. Returns a Process object (described below) to represent it. The string in cmdArray[0] is the name of the command, and any subsequent strings in the array are passed to the command as arguments.

```
public Process exec(String command) throws IOException
```
Equivalent to the array form of exec with the string command split into an array wherever white space occurs, using a default StringTokenizer (see page 472).

The newly created process is called a *child* process. By analogy, the creating process is a *parent* process.

Creating processes is a privileged operation and a `SecurityException` is thrown if you are not permitted to do it. If anything goes wrong trying to create the process an `IOException` is thrown.

18.2.1 The Process Class

The `exec` methods return a `Process` object for each child process created. This object represents the child process in two ways. First, it provides methods to get input, output, and error streams for the child process:[1]

`public abstract OutputStream` **`getOutputStream()`**

Returns an `OutputStream` connected to the standard input of the child process. Data written on this stream is read by the child process as its input.

`public abstract InputStream` **`getInputStream()`**

Returns an `InputStream` connected to the standard output of the child process. When the child writes data on its output, it can be read from this stream.

`public abstract InputStream` **`getErrorStream()`**

Returns an `InputStream` connected to the error output stream of the child process. When the child writes data on its error output, it can be read from this stream.

Here, for example, is a method that connects the standard streams of the parent process to the standard streams of the child process so that whatever the user types will go to the specified program and whatever the program produces will be seen by the user:

```
public static Process userProg(String cmd)
    throws IOException
{
    Process proc = Runtime.getRuntime().exec(cmd);
    plugTogether(System.in,  proc.getOutputStream());
    plugTogether(System.out, proc.getInputStream());
    plugTogether(System.err, proc.getErrorStream());
    return proc;
}
```

This code assumes that a method `plugTogether` exists to connect two streams by reading the bytes from one stream and writing them onto the other.

---

[1] For historical reasons these are byte stream objects instead of character streams. You can use `InputStreamReader` and `OutputStreamWriter` to convert the bytes to characters using the system default encoding.

The second way a `Process` object represents the child process is by providing methods to control the process and discover its termination status:

`public abstract int` **`waitFor()`** `throws InterruptedException`
> Waits indefinitely for the process to complete, returning the value it passed to either `System.exit` or its equivalent (zero means success, nonzero means failure). If the process has already completed, the value is simply returned.

`public abstract int` **`exitValue()`**
> Returns the exit value for the process. If the process has not completed, `exitValue` throws `IllegalThreadStateException`.

`public abstract void` **`destroy()`**
> Kills the process. Does nothing if the process has already completed. Garbage collection of a `Process` object does not mean that the process is destroyed; it will merely be unavailable for manipulation.

For example, the following method returns a `String` array that contains the output of the `ls` command with the specified command-line arguments. It throws a `LSFailedException` if the command completed unsuccessfully:

```java
// We have imported java.io.* and java.util.*
public String[] ls(String dir, String opts)
    throws LSFailedException
{
    try {
        // start up the command
        String[] cmdArray = { "/bin/ls", opts, dir };
        Process child = Runtime.getRuntime().exec(cmdArray);
        InputStream lsOut = child.getInputStream();
        InputStreamReader r = new InputStreamReader(lsOut);
        BufferedReader in = new BufferedReader(r);

        // read the command's output
        List lines = new ArrayList();
        String line;
        while ((line = in.readLine()) != null)
            lines.add(line);
        if (child.waitFor() != 0)   // if the ls failed
            throw new LSFailedException(child.exitValue());
        return (String[])lines.toArray(new String[] { });
    } catch (LSFailedException e) {
        throw e;
    } catch (Exception e) {
```

```
            throw new LSFailedException(e.toString());
    }
}
```

In the `ls` method we want to treat the output as character data, so we wrap the input stream that lets us read the child's output via an `InputStreamReader`. If we wanted to treat the child's output as a stream of bytes, we could easily do that instead. If the example were written to use the second form of `exec`, the code would look like this:

```
String cmd = "/bin/ls " + opts + " " + dir;
Process child = Runtime.getRuntime().exec(cmd);
```

`Process` is an abstract class. Each implementation of a Java virtual machine may provide one or more appropriate extended classes of `Process` that can interact with processes on the underlying system. Such classes might have extended functionality that would be useful for programming on the underlying system. The local documentation should contain information about this extended functionality.

Note that there is no requirement that the child process execute asynchronously or concurrently with respect to the parent process—in a particular system `exec` could appear to block until the child process terminates.

18.2.2 Process Environments

Two other forms of `Runtime.exec` enable you to specify a set of *environment variables*, which are system-dependent values that can be queried as desired by the new process. Environment variables are passed to `exec` as a `String` array; each element of the array specifies the name and value of an environment variable in the form *name=value*. The name cannot contain any spaces, although the value can be any string. The environment variables are passed as the second parameter:

```
public Process exec(String[] cmdArray, String[] env)
    throws IOException
```

```
public Process exec(String command, String[] env)
    throws IOException
```

The single argument forms of `exec` are equivalent to passing `null` for env, which means that the created process inherits the same environment variables as its parent.

Environment variables are interpreted in a system-dependent way by the child process's program. They can hold information such as the current user name, the current working directory, search paths or other useful information that may be needed by a running program. The environment variables mechanism is supported because existing programs on many different kinds of platforms understand them.

The environment variables of the current runtime process can be retrieved using the `System.getenv` method, which takes a string argument representing the name of the environment variable and returns a string representing its value. This method is deprecated because system properties (see page 481) are the preferred way to communicate between different virtual machine runtimes. However, this remains the only means of querying and subsequently modifying the environment when executing a non-Java program.

There remain two further forms of `exec` that allow the initial working directory of the child process to be specified:

```
public Process exec(String[] cmdArray, String[] env, File dir)
    throws IOException

public Process exec(String command, String[] env, File dir)
    throws IOException
```

The child process is given an initial working directory as specified by the path of `dir`. If `dir` is `null`, the child process inherits the current working directory of the parent—as specified by the system property `user.dir`. The one- and two-argument forms of `exec` are equivalent to passing `null` for `dir`.

18.2.3 Portability

Any program that uses `exec` is not portable across all systems. Not all environments have processes, and those that have them can have widely varying commands and syntax for invoking those commands. Also, because running arbitrary commands raises serious security issues, the system may not allow all programs to use `exec`. Be very cautious in choosing to use `exec` because it has a strong negative impact on your ability to run your program everywhere.

Exercise 18.2: Write a program that runs `exec` on its command-line arguments and prints the output from the command, preceding each line of output by its line number.

Exercise 18.3: Write a program that runs `exec` on command-line arguments and prints the output from the command, killing the command when a particular string appears in the output.

18.3 Shutdown

Normally an execution of a virtual machine terminates when the last user thread terminates. A `Runtime` can also be shut down explicitly by invoking its `exit` method, passing an integer status code that can be communicated to the environ-ment executing the virtual machine—zero to indicate successful completion of a task and non-zero to indicate failure. This method abruptly terminates all threads in the runtime system, no matter what their state. They are not interrupted, or even stopped, they simply cease to exist as the virtual machine itself stops running—no `finally` clauses are executed.

In either case, when `exit` is invoked, or the last user thread terminates, the shutdown sequence is initiated. The virtual machine can also be shut down exter-nally, such as by a user interrupting the virtual machine from a keyboard (on many systems by typing control-C) or when the user logs out or the computer is shut down.

All of the methods related to shutting down the runtime system are security checked and throw a `SecurityException` if you do not have permission to per-form them.

18.3.1 Shutdown Hooks

An application can register a *shutdown hook* with the runtime system. These are threads that represent actions that should be taken before the virtual machine exits. Hooks typically clean up external resources such as files and network con-nections.

`public void` **addShutdownHook(Thread hook)**
> Registers a new virtual machine shutdown hook. If hook has already been registered or has already been started an `IllegalArgumentException` is thrown.

`public boolean` **removeShutdownHook(Thread hook)**
> De-registers a previously registered virtual machine shutdown hook. Returns `true` if hook was registered and has been de-registered. Returns `false` if hook was not previously registered.

You cannot add or remove shutdown hooks after shutdown has commenced; you will get `IllegalStateException` if you try.

When shutdown is initiated, the virtual machine will invoke the `start` method on all shutdown hook `Thread` objects. You cannot rely on any ordering—shutdown hook threads may be executed before, after, or at the same time as any other shutdown hook thread depending on thread scheduling.

You must be careful about this lack of ordering. Suppose, for example, you were writing a class that stored state in a database. You might register a shutdown hook that closed the database. However a program using your class might want to register its own shutdown hook that writes some final state information through your class to the database. If your shutdown hook is run first (closing the database), the program's shutdown hook would fail in writing its final state. You can improve this situation by writing your class to reopen the database when needed, although this might add complexity to your class and possibly even some bad race conditions. Or you might design your class so that it doesn't need any shutdown hooks.

It is also important to realize that the shutdown hook threads will execute concurrently with other threads in the system. If shutdown was initiated due to the termination of the last user thread, then the shutdown hook threads will execute concurrently with any daemon threads in the system. If shutdown was initiated by a call to `exit`, then the shutdown hook threads will execute concurrently with both daemon and user threads. Your shutdown hook threads must be carefully written to ensure correct synchronization while avoiding potential deadlocks.

Your shutdown hooks should execute quickly. When users interrupt a program, for example, they expect the program to terminate quickly. And when a virtual machine is terminated because a user logs out or the computer is shut down, the virtual machine may be allowed only a small amount of time before it is killed forcibly. Interacting with a user should be done before shutdown, not during it.

18.3.2 The Shutdown Sequence

The shutdown sequence is initiated when the last user thread terminates, the `Runtime.exit` method is invoked, or the external environment signals the virtual machine to shutdown. When shutdown is initiated all the shutdown hook threads are started and allowed to run to completion. If any of these threads fails to terminate the shutdown sequence will not complete. If shutdown was initiated internally the virtual machine will not terminate. If shutdown was signalled from the external environment then failure to shutdown may result in a forced termination of the virtual machine.

If a shutdown hook thread incurs an uncaught exception, no special action is taken—the `uncaughtException` method of the thread's `ThreadGroup` is invoked as normal. In particular, it does not cause the shutdown process to abort.

When the last shutdown hook thread has terminated, the `halt` method will be invoked. It is `halt` that actually causes the virtual machine to cease running. The `halt` method also takes an integer status as an argument whose meaning is the same as that of `exit`: zero indicates successful execution of the entire virtual machine. A shutdown hook can invoke `halt` to end the shutdown phase. Invoking `halt` directly—either before or during the shutdown phase—is dangerous, since it prevents uncompleted hooks from doing their cleanup. You will probably never be in a situation where invoking `halt` is correct.

If `exit` is called while shutdown is in progress the call to `exit` will block indefinitely. The effect of this on the shutdown sequence is not specified, so don't so this.

There are some rare circumstances where the virtual machine will abort rather than perform an orderly shutdown. This can happen, for example, if an internal error is detected in the virtual machine that prevents an orderly shutdown—such as errant native code overwriting system data structures. However, the environment hosting the virtual machine can also force the virtual machine to abort—for example, under UNIX systems a SIGKILL signal will force the virtual machine to abort. When the virtual machine is forced to terminate in this way, no guarantees can be made about whether or not shutdown hooks will run.

18.3.3 Shutdown Strategies

Generally, you should let a program finish normally rather than forcibly shut it down via `exit`. This is particularly so with multithreaded programs, where the thread that decides it is time for the program to exit may have no idea what the other threads are doing.

Designing a multithreaded application in a way that makes it safe to exit at arbitrary points in the program is either trivial or extremely complex. It is trivial when none of the threads are performing actions that must be completed—for example, having a thousand threads all trying to solve a numerical problem. It is complex whenever any of the threads perform actions that must be completed.

You can communicate the fact that shutdown is required by writing your threads to respond to the `interrupt` method—as you learned on page 255. You can broadcast the shutdown request to all your threads by invoking the `interrupt` method of the parent `ThreadGroup` of your application. This is no guarantee that a program will terminate, however, as libraries that you have used may have created user threads that do not respond to interrupt requests—the AWT graphics library is one well known example.

There are two circumstances where you must invoke `exit`: when it is the only way to terminate some of the threads and hence your application; and when your application must return a status code. In both cases you need to delay the call to `exit` until all of your application threads have had a chance to terminate cleanly. One way is for the thread initiating the termination to `join` the other threads and so know when those threads have terminated. However, an application may have to maintain its own list of the threads it creates, as simply querying the `ThreadGroup` may return library threads that do not terminate and for which `join` will not return.

The decision to shutdown a program should be made at a high-level within the application—often within `main` or the `run` method of a thread in the top-level application ThreadGroup; or the code that responds to events in a graphical user interface. Methods that encounter errors should simply report those errors via exceptions that allow the high-level code to take appropriate action. Utility code should never terminate an application because it encounters an error—this code lacks knowledge of the application that allows an informed decision to be made; hence exceptions are used to communicate with higher-level code.

18.4   The Rest of the Runtime

The Runtime class provides functionality in five different areas:

- ◆ Interacting with the garbage collector,
- ◆ Executing external programs,
- ◆ Terminating the current Runtime,
- ◆ Loading native code libraries, and
- ◆ Debugging

The first three of these have been discussed previously (you learned about interacting with the garbage collector, using the gc and runFinalization methods, in Chapter 12, on page 318). Now is the time to cover the final two.

18.4.1   Loading Native Code

In Chapter 2, you learned about the native modifier (see page 63) that can be applied to methods and which signifies that the method's implementation is being provided by native code. At run time the native code for such methods must be loaded into the virtual machine so that the methods can be executed. The details of this process are system-dependent, but there are a two methods in Runtime that allow this activity to occur:

public void **loadLibrary(String libname)**
>   Loads the dynamic library with the specified library name. The library corresponds to a file in the local file system that is located in a place where the system knows to look for library files. The actual mapping from the library name to a file name is system-dependent.

public void **load(String filename)**
>   Loads the file specified by filename as a dynamic library. In contrast with loadLibrary, load allows the library file to be located anywhere in the file system.

Typically, classes that have native methods load the corresponding library as part of the initialization of the class, by placing the `load` invocation in a static initialization block. However, the library could be lazily loaded when an actual invocation of the method occurs.

Loading native code libraries is, naturally, a privileged operation and a `SecurityException` is thrown if you do not have permission to do it. If the library cannot be found, or an error occurs trying to load the library, an `UnsatisfiedLinkError` is thrown.

There is a related method in class `System`—`mapLibraryName`—that maps a library name into a system-dependent library name. For example, the library name `"awt"` might map to `"awt.dll"` under Windows, while under UNIX it might map to `"libawt.so"`.

18.4.2 Debugging

There are two methods in `Runtime` that are intended to support the debugging of applications:

public void **traceInstructions(boolean on)**
> Enables or disables the tracing of instructions depending on the value of on. If on is `true`, this method suggests that the virtual machine emit debugging information for each instruction as it is executed.

public void **traceMethodcalls(boolean on)**
> Enables or disables the tracing of method calls depending on the value of on. If on is `true`, this method suggests that the virtual machine emit debugging information for each method when it is called.

The format of this debugging information, and the file or other output stream to which it is emitted, depends on the host environment. Each virtual machine is free to do what it wants with these calls, including ignoring them if the local runtime system has nowhere to put the trace output, although they are likely to work in a development environment.

18.5 Security

Security is a very complex issue and a full discussion of it is well beyond the scope of this book—the interested reader is referred to *Inside Java 2 Platform Security: Architecture, API Design, and Implementation*, a companion book in this series, for all the details. What we can do, however, is provide an overview of the security architecture and some of its key components. Information on other aspects of security is given in "`java.security`— Security Tools" on page 543.

To perform a security checked operation you must have *permission* to perform that operation. All of the permissions in a system and the way they are assigned together define the *security policy* for that system. A *protection domain* encloses a set of class whose instances are granted the same set of permissions and which all come from the same *code source*. Protection domains are established using the class loading mechanism. To enable the security policy of a system and activate the protection domains, you need to install a *security manager*[2].

The classes and interfaces used for security are spread across a number of packages so we will use the fully qualified name the first time we introduce a specific class or interface.

18.5.1 The `SecurityManager` Class

The `java.lang.SecurityManager` class allows applications to implement a security policy by determining, before performing a possibly unsafe or sensitive operation, whether it is being attempted in a security context that allows the operation to be performed. The application can then allow or disallow the operation.

The `SecurityManager` class contains many methods with names that begin with the word "check." These methods are called by various methods in the standard libraries before those methods perform certain potentially sensitive operations, such as accessing files, creating and controlling threads, creating class loaders, performing some forms of reflection and controlling security itself. The invocation of such a check method typically looks like this:

```
SecurityManager security = System.getSecurityManager();
if (security != null) {
    security.checkXXX(argument, ...);
}
```

The security manager is given an opportunity to prevent completion of the operation by throwing an exception. A security manager routine simply returns if the operation is permitted but throws a `SecurityException` if the operation is not permitted.

The current security manager can be set and retrieved using methods of class `System`:

---

[2] Some virtual machines allow a startup argument that causes a default security manager to be created and installed. For example, using the Java 2 SDK you define the system property `java.security.manager` by passing the argument `-Djava.security.manager` to the `java` command.

`public static void `**`setSecurityManager(SecurityManager s)`**

> Sets the system security manager object. If there already exists a security manager this new manager will replace it provided the existing manager supports replacement and you have permission to replace it—otherwise a `SecurityException` is thrown.

`public static SecurityManager `**`getSecurityManager()`**

> Gets the system security manager. If none has been set `null` is returned, and you are assumed to have all permissions.

The security manager delegates the actual security check to an access control object. Each check method just invokes the security manager's `checkPermission` method, passing the appropriate `java.security.Permission` object for the action being requested. The default implementation of `checkPermission` then calls

```
java.security.AccessController.checkPermission(perm);
```

If a requested access is allowed, `checkPermission` returns quietly. If denied, a `java.security.AccessControlException` is thrown (which is a subclass of `SecurityException`).

This form of `checkPermission` always performs security checks within the context of the current thread—which is basically the set of protection domains of which it is a member. Given that a protection domain is a set of classes with the same permissions, a thread can be a member of multiple protection domains when the call stack contains active methods on objects of different classes.

The security manager's `getSecurityContext` method returns the security context for a thread as a `java.security.AccessControlContext` object. This class also defines a `checkPermission` method, but it evaluates that method in the context that it encapsulates, not the context of the calling thread. This feature is used when it is necessary for one context (such as a thread) to perform a security check for another context. For example, consider a worker thread that executes work requests from different sources. The worker thread has permission to perform a range of actions, but the submitters of work requests may not have those same permissions. When a work request is submitted, the security context for the submitter is stored along with the work request. When the worker thread performs the work, it uses the stored context to ensure that any security checks are performed with respect to the submitter of the request, not the worker thread itself. In simple cases, this might involve invoking the security manager's two-argument `checkPermission` method, which takes both a `Permission` object and an `AccessControlContext` object as arguments. In more general situations, the worker thread may utilize the `doPrivileged` methods of `AccessController`—which you will learn about shortly.

18.5.2 Permissions

Permissions fall into a number of categories, each managed by a particular class, for example:

- File—`java.io.FilePermission`
- Network—`java.net.NetPermission`
- Properties—`java.util.PropertyPermission`
- Reflection—`java.lang.reflect.ReflectPermission`
- Runtime—`java.lang.RuntimePermission`
- Security—`java.security.SecurityPermission`
- Serialization—`java.io.SerializablePermission`
- Sockets—`java.net.SocketPermission`

All but `FilePermission` and `SocketPermission` are subclasses of `java.security.BasicPermission`, which itself is an abstract subclass of the top-level class for permissions, which is `java.security.Permission`. `BasicPermission` defines a simple permission based around the name. For example, the `RuntimePermission` with name "exitVM" represents the permission to invoke `Runtime.exit` to shutdown the virtual machine. Here are some other basic `RuntimePermission` names and what they represent:

- "createClassLoader"—invoke the `ClassLoader` constructors.
- "setSecurityManager"—invoke `System.setSecurityManager`.
- "modifyThread"—invoke any of the `Thread` methods `interrupt`, `setPriority`, `setDaemon` or `setName`.

Basic permissions are something you either have or you don't. The names for basic permissions follow the hierarchical naming scheme used for system properties (see page 481). An asterisk may appear at the end of the name, following a ".", or by itself, to signify a wildcard match. For example: "java.*" or "*" are valid; "*java" or "x*y" are not valid.

`FilePermission` and `SocketPermission` are subclasses of `Permission`. These classes can have a more complicated name syntax than that used for basic permissions. For example, for a `FilePermission` object, the permission name is the pathname of a file (or directory) and can cover multiple files using "*" to mean all files in the specified directory, and "-" to mean all files in the specified directory and all files in all subdirectories.

All permissions can also have an *action list* associated with them that defines the different actions permitted by that object. For example, the action list for a `FilePermission` object can contain any combination of `"read"`, `"write"`, `"execute"`, or `"delete"`, specifying what actions can be performed on the named file (or directory). Many basic permissions do not use the action list, but some, such as `PropertyPermission` do: the name of a `PropertyPermission` is the name of the property it represents and the actions can be `"read"` or `"write"`, which let you invoke `System.getProperty` and `System.setProperty`, respectively, with that property name. For example, a `PropertyPermission` with the name `"java.*"` and action `"read"` allows you to retrieve the values of all system properties that start with `"java."`.

18.5.3 Security Policies

The security policy for a given execution of the runtime system is represented by a `java.security.Policy` object, or more specifically a concrete subclass of the abstract `Policy` class. The `Policy` object maintains the sets of permissions that have been assigned to the different protection domains, based on their code source. How the security policy is communicated to the `Policy` object is a function of the actual implementation of that Policy. The default implementation is to use policy files to list the different permissions that are granted to each code source.

For example, a sample policy file entry granting code from the /home/ sysadmin directory read access to the file /tmp/abc is

```
grant codeBase "file:/home/sysadmin/" {
    permission java.io.FilePermission "/tmp/abc", "read";
};
```

To find out how security policies are defined in your local system you will need to consult your local documentation.

18.5.4 Access Controllers and Privileged Execution

The `AccessController` class is used for three purposes:

◆ It provides the basic `checkPermission` method used by security managers to perform a security check.

◆ It provides the means for creating a "snapshot" of the current calling context, using `getContext` which returns an `AccessControlContext`.

◆ It provides a means to run code as *privileged*, thus changing the set of permissions that might otherwise be associated with the code.

We have discussed (to the extent we intend to) the first two of these. In this section we look at what it means to have privileged execution.

A *protection domain* (represented by `java.security.ProtectionDomain`) encompasses a *code source* (represented by `java.security.CodeSource`) and the permissions granted to code from that code source, as determined by the security policy currently in effect. A code source extends the notion of a code base (the location classes were loaded from) to include information about the digital certificates associated with those classes. Digital certificates can be used to verify the authenticity of a file and ensure that the file has not been tampered with in any way. Classes with the same certificates, and from the same location, are placed in the same domain, and a class belongs to one and only one protection domain. Classes that have the same permissions but are from different code sources belong to different domains.

Each applet or application runs in its appropriate domain, determined by its code source. In order for an applet (or an application running under a security manager) to be allowed to perform a secured action, the applet or application must be granted permission for that particular action. More specifically, whenever a secure action is attempted, all code traversed by the execution thread up to that point must have permission for that action, unless some code on the thread has been marked as *privileged*. For example, suppose that access control checking occurs in a thread of execution that has a chain of multiple callers—think of this as multiple method calls that potentially cross the protection domain boundaries. When the `AccessController checkPermission` method is invoked by the most recent caller, the basic algorithm for deciding whether to allow or deny the requested action is as follows:

> If the code for any caller in the call chain does not have the requested permission, an `AccessControlException` is thrown, unless a caller whose code is granted the said permission has been marked as *privileged* and all parties subsequently called by this caller (directly or indirectly) have the said permission.

Marking code as *privileged* enables a piece of trusted code to temporarily enable access to more actions than are available directly to the code that called it. This is necessary in some situations. For example, an application may not be allowed direct access to files that contain fonts, but the system utility to display a document must obtain those fonts, on behalf of the user. In order to do this, the system utility code becomes privileged while obtaining the fonts.

The doPrivileged method of AccessController take as an argument a java.security.PrivilegedAction object whose run method defines the code to be marked as privileged. For example, your call to doPrivileged can look like the following:

```
void someMethod() {
    // ...normal code here...
    AccessController.doPrivileged(new PrivilegedAction() {
        public Object run() {
            // privileged code goes here, for example:
            System.loadLibrary("awt");
            return null; // nothing to return
        }
    });
    // ...normal code here...
}
```

The doPrivileged method executes the run method in privileged mode. Privileged execution is a way for a class with a given permission to grant that permission, temporarily, to the thread that executes the privileged code. It will not let you gain permissions that you do not already have. The class defining someMethod must have the permission RuntimePermission("loadLibrary.awt") otherwise any thread that invokes someMethod will get a SecurityException. It is guaranteed that privileges will be revoked after the PrivilegedAction object's run method returns.

PrivilegedAction is an interface with a single method run that returns an Object. Another form of doPrivileged takes a PrivilegedExceptionAction, which has a run method that also returns an Object, but which can throw any checked exception. For both of these methods there is a second overloaded form of doPrivileged that takes an AccessControlContext as an argument and which uses that context to establish the permissions that the privileged code should run with.

You should use doPrivileged with extreme care and ensure that your privileged sections of code are no longer than necessary and only perform actions you fully control. For example, it would be an extreme security risk for a method with, say, all I/O permissions, to accept a Runnable argument and invoke its run method within a privileged section of code.

Power corrupts.
Absolute power is kind of neat.
—John Lehman, U.S. Secretary of the Navy

CHAPTER **19**

Internationalization and
Localization

Nobody can be exactly like me.
Sometimes even I have trouble doing it.
—Tallulah Bankhead

THE credo of "Write once, run anywhere" means that your code will run in many places where languages and customs are different from yours. With a little care you can write programs that can adapt to these variations gracefully. Keeping your programs supple in this fashion is called *internationalization.* You have several tools for internationalizing your code. Using internationalization tools to adapt your program to a specific locale—such as by translating messages into the local language—is called *localization.*

The first tool is inherent in the language: strings are in Unicode, which can express almost any written language on our planet. Someone must still translate the strings, and displaying the translated text to users requires fonts for those characters. Still, having Unicode is a big boost for localizing your code.

The nexus of internationalization and localization is the *locale,* which defines a "place." A place can be a language, culture, or country—anything with an associated set of customs that requires changes in program behavior. Each running program has a default locale that is the user's preferred place. It is up to each program to adapt to a locale's customs as best it can. The locale concept is represented by the `Locale` class, which is part of the `java.util` package.

Given a locale, several tools can help your program behave in a locally comprehensible fashion. A common pattern is for a class to define the methods for performing *locale-sensitive* operations. A generic "get instance" static method of this class returns an object (possibly of a subclass) suitable for the default locale. The class will also provide an overload of each "get instance" method that takes a locale argument and returns a suitable object for a particular locale. For example, you can get an appropriate `java.util.Calendar` object that works with the user's preferred dates and times by invoking the class's `getInstance` methods. The returned `Calendar` object will understand how to translate system time into dates using the customs of the default locale. If the user were Mexican, an object that was a `Calendar` adapted to Mexican customs could be returned. A Chinese user might get an object of a different subclass that worked under the Chinese calendar customs.

If your program displays information to the user, you will likely want to localize the output: saying "That's not right" to someone who doesn't understand English is probably pointless, so you would like to translate (localize) the message for speakers in other locales. The resource bundle mechanisms help you make this possible by mapping string keys to arbitrary resources. You use the values returned by a resource bundle to make your program speak in other tongues— instead of writing the literal message strings in your code, you look up the strings from a resource bundle by string keys. When the program is moved to another locale, someone can translate the messages in the resource bundle and your program will work for that new locale without changing a line of code.

The classes described in this chapter come mostly from the package `java.util`. There are occasional brief discussions of classes in the text internationalization and localization package `java.text`, with an overview of some of its capabilities in Section 19.5 on page 520, but a full discussion on this subject is outside the scope of this book.

19.1 Locale

A `java.util.Locale` object describes a specific place—cultural, political, or geographical. Using a locale, objects can *localize* their behavior to a user's expectations. An object that does so is called *locale-sensitive*. For example, date formatting can be localized using the locale-sensitive `DateFormat` class (described later in this chapter), so the date written in the United Kingdom as 26/11/72 would be written `26.11.72` in Iceland, `11/26/72` in the United States, or `72.26.11` in Latvia.

A single locale represents issues of language, country, and other traditions. There can be separate locales for U.S. English, U.K. English, Australian English, Pakistani English, and so forth. Although the language is arguably in common for these locales, the customs of date, currency, and numeric representation vary.

Your code will rarely get or create `Locale` objects directly but instead will use the default locale that reflects the user's preference. You typically use this locale implicitly by getting resources or resource bundles as shown with other locale-sensitive classes. For example, you get the default calendar object like this:

```
Calendar now = Calendar.getInstance();
```

The `Calendar` class's `getInstance` method looks up the default locale to configure the calendar object it returns. When you write your own locale-sensitive classes, you get the default locale from the static `getDefault` method of the `Locale` class.

If you write code that lets a user select a locale, you may need to create `Locale` objects. There are two constructors:

public **Locale(String language, String country, String variant)**
> Creates a `Locale` object that represents the given language and country, where `language` is the two-letter ISO 639 code for the language (such as "et" for Estonian) and `country` is the two-letter ISO 3166 code for the country (such as "KY" for Cayman Islands). "Further Reading" on page 563 lists references for these codes. The `variant` can specify anything, such as an operating environment (such as "POSIX" or "MAC") or company or era. If you specify more than one variant, separate the two with an underscore. To leave any part of the locale unspecified, use "", an empty string—not `null`.

public **Locale(String language, String country)**
> Equivalent to `Locale(language, country, "")`.

The language and country can be in any case, but they will always be translated to lowercase for the language and uppercase for the country to conform to the governing standards. The variant is translated into uppercase.

The `Locale` class defines static `Locale` objects for several well-known locales, such as `CANADA_FRENCH`, and `KOREA` for countries, and `KOREAN` and `TRADITIONAL_CHINESE` for languages. These objects are simply conveniences and have no special privileges compared to any `Locale` object you may create.

The static method `setDefault` changes the default locale. The default locale is shared state and should always reflect the user's preference. If you have code that must operate in a different locale, you can specify that locale to locale-sensitive classes either as an argument when you get resources or on specific operations. You should rarely need to change the default locale.

`Locale` provides methods for getting the parts of the locale description. The methods `getCountry`, `getLanguage`, and `getVariant` return the values defined during construction. These are terse codes that most users will not know. These methods have "display" variants—`getDisplayCountry`, `getDisplayLanguage`, and `getDisplayVariant`—that return human-readable versions of the values. The method `getDisplayName` returns a human-readable summary of the entire locale description, and `toString` returns the terse equivalent, using underscores to separate the parts. These "display" methods return values that are localized according to the default locale.

You can optionally provide a `Locale` argument to any of the "display" methods to get a description of the given locale under the provided locale. For example, if we print the value of:

```
Locale.ITALY.getDisplayCountry(Locale.FRANCE)
```

we get

```
Italie
```

the French name for Italy.

The methods `getISO3Country` and `getISO3Language` return three-character ISO codes for the country and language of the locale, respectively.

19.2 Resource Bundles

When you internationalize code, you commonly have units of meaning—such as text or sounds—that must be translated or otherwise made appropriate for each locale. If you put English text directly into your program, localizing that code is difficult—it requires finding all the strings in your program, identifying which ones are shown to users, and translating them in the code, thereby creating a second version of your program for, say, Swahili users. When you repeat this process for a large number of locales the task becomes a nightmare.

The resource bundle classes in `java.util` help you address this problem in a cleaner and more flexible fashion. The abstract class `ResourceBundle` defines methods to look up resources in a bundle by string key and to provide a parent bundle that will be searched if a bundle doesn't have a key. This inheritance feature allows one bundle to be just like another bundle except that a few resource values are modified or added. For example, a U.S. English bundle might use a U.K. English bundle for a parent, providing replacements for resources that have different spelling. `ResourceBundle` provides the following public methods:

`public final String getString(String key)`
   `throws MissingResourceException`
      Returns the string stored in the bundle under the given key.

`public final String[] getStringArray(String key)`
   `throws MissingResourceException`
      Returns the string array stored in the bundle under the given key.

```
public final Object getObject(String key)
    throws MissingResourceException
        Returns the object stored in the bundle under the given key.
```

```
public abstract Enumeration getKeys()
```
Returns an Enumeration of the keys understood by this bundle, including all those of the parent.

Each resource bundle defines a set of string keys that map to locale-sensitive resources. These strings can be anything you like, although it is best to make them mnemonic. When you want to use the resource you look it up by name. If the resource is not found a MissingResourceException is thrown. The resources themselves can be of any type, but are commonly strings—so the *getString* methods are provided for convenience.

The following example shows an internationalized way to rewrite the "Hello, world" example. The following internationalized version requires a program called GlobalHello and a resource bundle for the program's strings called GlobalRes, which will define a set of constants for the localizable strings. First, the program:

```
import java.util.*;

public class GlobalHello {
    public static void main(String[] args) {
        ResourceBundle res =
            ResourceBundle.getBundle("GlobalRes");
        String msg;
        if (args.length > 0)
            msg = res.getString(GlobalRes.GOODBYE);
        else
            msg = res.getString(GlobalRes.HELLO);
        System.out.println(msg);
    }
}
```

The program first gets its resource bundle. Then it checks whether any arguments are provided on the command line. If some are, it says good-bye; otherwise it says hello. The program logic determines which message to display, but the actual string to print is looked up by key (GlobalRes.HELLO or GlobalRes.GOODBYE).

Each resource bundle is a set of associated classes and property files. In our example, GlobalRes is the name of a class that extends ResourceBundle, implementing the methods necessary to map a message key to a localized translation of that message. You define classes for the various locales for which you want to localize the messages, naming the classes to reflect the locale. For example, the bundle class that manages `GlobalRes` messages for the Lingala language would be `GlobalRes_ln` because `"ln"` is the two-letter code for Lingala. French would be mapped in `GlobalRes_fr`, and Canadian French would be `GlobalRes_fr_CA`, which might have a parent bundle of `GlobalRes_fr`.

We have chosen to make the key strings constants in the `GlobalRes` class. Using constants prevents errors of misspelling. If you pass literal strings such as `"hello"` to `getString`, a misspelling will show up only when the erroneous `getString` is executed, and that might not happen during testing. If you use constants, a misspelling will be caught by the compiler (unless you are unlucky enough to accidentally spell the name of another constant).

You find resources by calling one of two static `getBundle` methods in `ResourceBundle`: the one we used, which searches the current locale for the best available version of the bundle you name; and the other method, which lets you specify both bundle name and desired locale. A fully qualified bundle name has the form *package.Bundle_la_CO_va*, where *package.Bundle* is the general fully qualified name for the bundle class (such as `GlobalRes`), *la* is the two-letter language code (lowercase), *CO* is the two-letter country code (uppercase), and *va* is the list of variants separated by underscores. If a bundle with the full name cannot be found, the last component is dropped and the search repeated with this shorter name. This process is repeated until only the last locale modifier is left. If even this search fails and if you invoked `getBundle` with a specified locale, the search is restarted using the full name of the bundle for the default locale. If this second search ends with no bundle found or if you were searching in the default locale, `getBundle` checks using just the bundle name. If even that bundle does not exist, `getBundle` throws a `MissingBundleException`.

For example, suppose you ask for the bundle `GlobalRes`, specifying a locale for an Esperanto speaker living in Kiribati who is left-handed, and the default locale of the user is for a Nepali speaker in Bhutan who works for Acme, Inc. The longest possible search would be:

```
GlobalRes_eo_KI_left
GlobalRes_eo_KI
GlobalRes_eo
GlobalRes_ne_BT_Acme
GlobalRes_ne_BT
GlobalRes_ne
GlobalRes
```

The first resource bundle that is found ends the search, being considered the best available match.

The examples you have seen use resource bundles to fetch strings, but remember that you can use `getObject` to get any type of object. Bundles are used to store images, URLs, audio sources, graphics components, and any other kind of locale-sensitive resource that can be represented by an object.

Mapping string keys to localized resource objects is usually straightforward—simply use one of the provided subclasses of `ResourceBundle` that implement the lookup for you: `ListResourceBundle` and `PropertyResourceBundle`.

19.2.1 `ListResourceBundle`

`ListResourceBundle` maps a simple list of keys to their localized objects. It is an abstract subclass of `ResourceBundle` for which you provide a `getContents` method that returns an array of key/resource pairs as an array of arrays of `Object`. The keys must be strings, but the resources can be any kind of object. The `ListResourceBundle` takes this array and builds the maps for the various "get" methods. The following classes use `ListResourceBundle` to define a few locales for `GlobalRes`. First, the base bundle:

```
public class GlobalRes extends ListResourceBundle {
    public static final String HELLO = "hello";
    public static final String GOODBYE = "goodbye";

    public Object[][] getContents() {
        return contents;
    }

    private static final Object[][] contents = {
        { GlobalRes.HELLO,      "Ciao" },
        { GlobalRes.GOODBYE,    "Ciao" },
    };
}
```

This is the top-level bundle—when no other bundle is found, this will be used. We have chosen Italian for the default. Before any "get" method is executed, `GlobalRes.getContents` will be invoked and the `contents` array's values will seed the data structures used by the "get" methods. `ListResourceBundle` uses an internal lookup table for efficient access; it does not search through your array of keys. The GlobalRes class also defines the constants that name known resources in the bundle. Here is another bundle for a more specific locale:

```
public class GlobalRes_en extends ListResourceBundle {
    public Object[][] getContents() {
        return contents;
    }
    private static final Object[][] contents = {
        { GlobalRes.HELLO,      "Hello" },
        { GlobalRes.GOODBYE,    "Goodbye" },
    };
}
```

This bundle covers the English-language locale en. It provides specific values for each localizable string. The next bundle uses the inheritance feature:

```
public class GlobalRes_en_AU extends ListResourceBundle {
    // mostly like the basic English locale
    public GlobalRes_en_AU() {
        parent = new GlobalRes_en();
    }

    public Object[][] getContents() { return contents; }

    private static final Object[][] contents = {
        { GlobalRes.HELLO,      "G'day" },
    };
}
```

This bundle is for English speakers from Australia (AU). It provides a more colloquial version of the HELLO string and inherits all other strings from the general English locale GlobalRes_en by setting its parent field to be a bundle for English in its constructor.

Given these classes, someone with an English-language locale (en) would get the values returned by GlobalRes_en unless the locale also specified the country Australia (AU), in which case values from GlobalRes_en_AU would be used. Everyone else would see those in GlobalRes.

19.2.2 `PropertyResourceBundle`

`PropertyResourceBundle` is a subclass of `ResourceBundle` that reads its list of resources from a text property description. Instead of using an array of key/ resource pairs, the text contains key/resource pairs as lines of the form

> *key=value*

Both keys and values must be strings. A `PropertyResourceBundle` object reads the text from an `InputStream` passed to the `PropertyResourceBundle` constructor and uses the read information to build a lookup table for efficient access.

The bundle search process that we described earlier actually has an additional step that looks for a file `resName.properties` after it looks for a class `resName`. For example, if the search process doesn't find the class `GlobalRes_eo_KI_left` it will then look for the file `GlobalRes_eo_KI_left.properties`. If that file exists, an input stream is created for it and that is used to construct a `PropertyResourceBundle` that will read the properties from the file.

Property files are easier to use than creating subclasses of `ListResourceBundle` but they have two limitations. First, they can only define string resources whereas `ListResourceBundle` can define arbitrary objects. Second, the only legal character encoding for property files is the byte format of ISO 8859-1. This means that other Unicode characters must be encoded using \u*xxxx* escape sequences.

19.2.3 Subclassing `ResourceBundle`

`ListResourceBundle`, `PropertyResourceBundle`, and `.properties` files will be sufficient for most of your bundles, but you can create your own subclass of `ResourceBundle` if they are not. You must implement two methods:

`protected abstract Object` **`handleGetObject(String key)`**
`throws MissingResourceException`
> Returns the object associated with the given key. If the key is not defined in this bundle, it returns `null`, and that causes the `ResourceBundle` to check in the parent (if any). Do not throw `MissingResourceException` unless you check the parent instead of letting the bundle do it. All the "get" methods are written in terms of this one method.

`public abstract Enumeration` **`getKeys()`**
> Returns an `Enumeration` that iterates over the keys in this bundle.

Exercise 19.1: Get `GlobalHello` to work with the example locales. Add some more locales, using `ListResourceBundle`, `.properties` files, and your own specific subclass of `ResourceBundle`.

19.3   Time, Dates, and Calendars

Time is represented as a `long` integer measured in milliseconds since midnight Greenwich Mean Time (GMT) January 1, 1970. This starting point for time measurement is known as the *epoch*. This value is signed, so negative values signify time before the beginning of the epoch. The `System.currentTimeMillis` method returns the current time. This value will express dates into the year A.D. 292,280,995, which should suffice for most purposes.

You can use `java.util.Date` to hold a time and perform some simple time-related operations. When a new `Date` object is created, you can specify a `long` value for its time. If you use the no-arg constructor, the `Date` object will mark the time of its creation. A `Date` object can be used for simple operations. For example, the simplest program to print the current time (repeated from page 31) is

```
import java.util.Date;

class Date2 {
    public static void main(String[] args) {
        Date now = new Date();
        System.out.println(now);
    }
}
```

This program will produce output such as the following:

```
Mon Nov 29 17:27:10 EST 1999
```

Note that this is not localized output. No matter what the default locale, the date will be in this format, adjusted for the current time zone.

You can compare two dates using `before` and `after` methods, which return `true` if the object on which they are invoked is before or after the other date. Or you can compare the `long` values you get from invoking `getTime` on the two objects. The method `setTime` lets you change the time to a different `long`.

The `Date` class provides no support for localization and has effectively been replaced by the more sophisticated and locale-sensitive `Calendar` and `DateFormat` classes.

19.3.1 Calendars

Calendars mark the passage of time. Most of the world uses the same calendar, commonly called the Gregorian calendar after Pope Gregory XIII, under whose auspices it was first instituted. Many other calendars exist in the world, and the calendar abstractions are designed to express such variations. A given moment in time is expressed as a date according to a particular calendar, and the same moment can be expressed as different dates by different calendars. The calendar abstraction is couched in the following form:

- An abstract `Calendar` class that represents various ways of marking time.

- An abstract `TimeZone` class that represents time zone offsets and other adjustments, such as daylight saving time.

- An abstract `java.text.DateFormat` class that defines how one can format and parse date and time strings.

Because the Gregorian calendar is commonly used, you also have the following concrete implementations of the abstractions:

- A `GregorianCalendar` class

- A `SimpleTimeZone` class for use with `GregorianCalendar`

- A `java.text.SimpleDateFormat` class that formats and parses Gregorian dates and times

For example, the following code creates a `GregorianCalendar` object representing midnight (00:00:00), October 26, 1972, in the local time zone, then prints its value:

```
Calendar cal =
    new GregorianCalendar(1972, Calendar.OCTOBER, 26);
System.out.println(cal.getTime());
```

The method `getTime` returns a `Date` object for the calendar object's time, which was set by converting a year, month, and date into a millisecond-measured `long`. The output would be something like this (depending on your local time zone of course):

```
Thu Oct 26 00:00:00 GMT+10:00 1972
```

The abstract `Calendar` class provides a large set of constants that are useful in many calendars, such as `Calendar.AM` and `Calendar.PM` for calendars that use 12-hour clocks. Some constants are useful only for certain calendars, but no calendar class is required to use such constants. In particular, the month names in `Calendar` (such as `Calendar.JUNE`) are names for the various month numbers (such as 5—month numbers start at 0), with a special month UNDECIMBER for the thirteenth month that many calendars have. But no calendar is required to use these constants.

Each `Calendar` object represents a particular moment in time on that calendar. The `Calendar` class provides only constructors that create an object for the current time, either in the default locale and time zone or in specified ones.

Calendar objects represent a moment in time, but they are not responsible for displaying the date. That locale-sensitive procedure is the job of the `DateFormat` class, which will be described soon.

You can obtain a calendar object for a locale by invoking one of the static `Calendar.getInstance` methods. With no arguments, `getInstance` returns an object of the best available calendar type (currently only `GregorianCalendar`) for the default locale and time zone, representing the current time. The other overloads allow you to specify the locale, the time zone, or both. The static `getAvailableLocales` method returns an array of `Locale` objects for which calendars are installed on the system.

With a calendar object in hand, you can manipulate the date. The following example prints the next week of days for a given calendar object:

```
public static void oneWeek(PrintStream out, Calendar cal) {
    Calendar cur = (Calendar) cal.clone(); //modifiable copy
    int dow = cal.get(Calendar.DAY_OF_WEEK);
    do {
        out.println(cur.getTime());
        cur.add(Calendar.DAY_OF_WEEK, 1);
    } while (cur.get(Calendar.DAY_OF_WEEK) != dow);
}
```

First, we make a copy of the calendar argument so that we can make changes without affecting the calendar we were passed. Instead of assuming that there are seven days in a week (who knows what kind of calendar we were given?), we loop, printing the time and adding one day to that time, until we have printed a week's worth of days. We detect that a week has passed by looking for the next day whose "day of the week" is the same as that of the original.

The `Calendar` class defines many kinds of *calendar fields* for calendar objects, such as `DAY_OF_WEEK` in the preceding code. These calendar fields are constants used in the methods that manipulate parts of the time:

MILLISECOND	DAY_OF_WEEK_IN_MONTH	MONTH_OF_YEAR
SECOND	DAY_OF_MONTH	YEAR
MINUTE	DATE	ERA
HOUR	DAY_OF_YEAR	ZONE_OFFSET
HOUR_OF_DAY	WEEK_OF_MONTH	DST_OFFSET
AM_PM	WEEK_OF_YEAR	FIELD_COUNT
DAY_OF_WEEK	MONTH	

An `int` is used to store values for all these calendar field types. You use these constants—or any others defined by a particular calendar class—to specify a calendar field to the following methods (always as the first argument):

`get`	Returns the value of the field
`set`	Sets the value of the field to the provided `int`
`clear`	Clears the value of the field to "unspecified"
`isSet`	Returns a `true` if the field has been set
`add`	Adds an `int` amount to the specified field
`roll`	Rolls the field up to the next value if the second `boolean` argument is `true`, or down if it is `false`
`getMinimum`	Gets the minimum valid value for the field
`getMaximum`	Gets the maximum valid value for the field
`getGreatestMinimum`	Gets the highest minimum value for the field; if it varies, this can be different from `getMinimum`
`getLeastMaximum`	Gets the smallest maximum value for the field; if it varies, this can be different from `getMaximum`

The greatest minimum and least maximum describe cases in which a value can vary within the overall boundaries. For example, the least maximum value for `DAY_OF_MONTH` on the Gregorian calendar is 28 because February, the shortest month, can have as few as 28 days. The maximum value is 31 because no month has more than 31 days.

The `set`, `clear`, and `isSet` methods allow you to specify a date by certain calendar fields and then calculate the time associated with that date. For example, you can calculate on which day of the week a particular date falls:

```
public static int dotw(int year, int month, int date) {
    Calendar cal = new GregorianCalendar();
    cal.set(Calendar.YEAR, year);
```

```
        cal.set(Calendar.MONTH, month);
        cal.set(Calendar.DATE, date);
        return cal.get(Calendar.DAY_OF_WEEK);
    }
```

The method dotw calculates the day of the week on the Gregorian calendar for the given date. It creates a Gregorian calendar object, sets the date fields for year, month, and day, and returns the resulting day of the week. You can use clear with no parameters to clear all calendar fields.

Three variants of set change particular fields you commonly need to manipulate, leaving unspecified fields alone:

public void **set(int year, int month, int date)**

public void **set(int year, int month, int date, int hrs, int min)**

public void **set(int year, int month, int date, int hrs, int min, int sec)**

You can also use setTime to set the calendar's time from a Date object.

A calendar field that is out of range can be interpreted correctly. For example, January 32 can be equivalent to February 1. Whether it is treated as such or as an error depends on whether the calendar is considered to be *lenient*. A lenient calendar will do its best to interpret values as valid. A strict (non-lenient) calendar will not accept any values out of range, throwing IllegalArgumentException. The setLenient method takes a boolean that specifies whether parsing should be lenient; isLenient returns the current setting.

A week can start on any day, depending on the calendar. You can discover the first day of the week using the method getFirstDayOfWeek. In a Gregorian calendar for the United States this method would return SUNDAY, whereas Ireland uses MONDAY. You can change this by invoking setFirstDayOfWeek with a valid weekday index.

Some calendars require a minimum number of days in the first week of the year. The method getMinimalDaysInFirstWeek returns that number; the method setMinimalDaysInFirstWeek lets you change it. The minimum number of days in a week is important when you are trying to determine in which week a particular date falls—for example, in some calendars, if January 1 is a Friday it may be considered part of the last week of the preceding year.

You can compare two Calendar objects by comparing the Date objects returned by their respective getTime methods. If you prefer, you can use the before and after methods to compare the objects.

19.3.2 Time Zones

`TimeZone` is an abstract class that encapsulates not only offset from GMT but also other offset issues, such as daylight saving time. As with other locale-sensitive classes, you can get the default `TimeZone` by invoking the static method `getDefault`. You can change the default time zone by passing `setDefault` a new `TimeZone` object to use—or `null` to reset to the original default time zone. Time zones are understood by particular calendar types, so you should ensure that the default calendar and time zone are compatible.

Each time zone has a string identifier that is interpreted by the time zone object and can be displayed to the user. These identifiers use a long form consisting of a major and minor regional name, separated by '/'. For example, the following are all valid time zone identifiers: `America/New_York`, `Australia/Brisbane`, `Africa/Timbuktu`. Many time zones have a short form identifier—often just a three letter acronym—some of which are recognized by `TimeZone` for backward compatibility. You should endeavour to always use the long form—after all, while many people know that EST stands for "Eastern Standard Time," that doesn't tell you for which country. `TimeZone` also recognizes generic identifiers expressed as the difference in time from GMT. For example, GMT+10:00 and GMT-4:00, are both valid generic time zone identifiers. An array of all the identifiers available on your system can be obtained by invoking the static method `getAvailableIDs`. If you want only those for a given offset from GMT, you can invoke `getAvailableIDs` with that offset. An offset might, for example, have identifiers for both daylight saving and standard time zones.

The identifier of a given `TimeZone` object can be found by invoking `getID` and can be set by using `setID`. Setting the identifier changes only the identifier on the time zone—it does not change the offset or other values. You can get the time zone for a given identifier by passing it to the static method `getTimeZone`.

A time zone can be converted into a displayable form using one of the `getDisplayName` methods, similar to those of `Locale`. These methods allow you to specify either the default or a specified locale to be used, and whether a short or long format should be used. The string returned by the display methods is controlled by a `DateFormat` object (which you'll see a little later). These objects maintain their own tables of information on how to format different time zones and on a given system they may not maintain information for all the supported time zones; in which case the generic identifier form is used—as was the case with the example on page 511.

Each time zone has a *raw offset* from GMT. It can be either positive or negative, but is always in the range –24 through 24. You can get or set the raw offset using `getRawOffset` or `setRawOffset`, but you should rarely need to do this.

Daylight saving time supplements the raw offset with a seasonal time shift. You can ask whether a time zone ever uses daylight saving time during the year by invoking the method `useDaylightTime`, which returns a `boolean`. The method `inDaylightTime` returns `true` if the `Date` argument you pass would fall inside daylight saving time in the zone.

You can obtain the exact offset for a time zone on a given date by using calendar fields to specify the year and month and so on.

**public int getOffset(int era, int year, int month, int day,
  int dayOfWeek, int milliseconds)**

> Returns the offset from GMT for the given time in this time zone, taking any daylight saving time offset into account. All parameters are interpreted relative to the calendar for which the particular time zone implementation is designed. The `era` parameter represents calendar-specific eras, such as B.C. and A.D. in the Gregorian calendar.

19.3.3 GregorianCalendar and SimpleTimeZone

The `GregorianCalendar` class is a concrete subclass of `Calendar` that reflects UTC (Coordinated Universal Time), although it cannot always do so exactly. Imprecise behavior is inherited from the time mechanisms of the underlying system.[1] Parts of a date are specified in UTC standard units and ranges. Here are the ranges for `GregorianCalendar`:

YEAR	1–292278994
MONTH	0–11
DATE	Day of the month, 1–31
HOUR_OF_DAY	0–23
MINUTE	0–59
SECOND	0–59
MILLISECOND	0-999

The `GregorianCalendar` class supports several constructors:

---

[1]   Almost all modern systems assume that one day is 24*60*60 seconds. In UTC, about once a year an extra second, called a *leap second,* is added to a day to account for the wobble of the Earth. Most computer clocks are not accurate enough to reflect this distinction, so neither is the `Date` class. Some computer standards are defined in GMT, which is the "civil" name for the standard; UT is the scientific name for the same standard. The distinction between UTC and UT is that UT is based on an atomic clock and UTC is based on astronomical observations. For almost all practical purposes, this is an invisibly fine hair to split. See "Further Reading" on page 563 for references.

public **GregorianCalendar()**

> Creates a GregorianCalendar object that represents the current time in the default time zone with the default locale.

public **GregorianCalendar(int year, int month, int date, int hrs, int min, int sec)**

> Creates a GregorianCalendar object that represents the given date in the default time zone with the default locale.

public **GregorianCalendar(int year, int month, int date, int hrs, int min)**

> Equivalent to GregorianCalendar(year, month, date, hrs, min, 0)—that is, the beginning of the specified minute.

public **GregorianCalendar(int year, int month, int date)**

> Equivalent to GregorianCalendar(year, month, date, 0, 0, 0)—that is, midnight on the given date (which is considered to be the start of the day).

public **GregorianCalendar(Locale locale)**

> Creates a GregorianCalendar object that represents the current time in the default time zone with the given locale.

public **GregorianCalendar(TimeZone timeZone)**

> Creates a GregorianCalendar object that represents the current time in the given timeZone with the default locale.

public **GregorianCalendar(TimeZone zone, Locale locale)**

> Creates a GregorianCalendar object that represents the current time in the given timeZone with the given locale.

In addition to the methods it inherits from Calendar, GregorianCalendar provides an isLeapYear method that returns true if the calendar object represents a date that happens in a leap year.

The Gregorian calendar was preceded by the Julian calendar in many places. In a GregorianCalendar object, the default date at which this change happened is midnight local time on October 15, 1582. This is when the first countries switched, but others changed later. The getGregorianChange method returns the time the calendar is currently using for the change as a Date. You can set a calendar's change-over time by using setGregorianChange with a Date object.

The SimpleTimeZone class is a concrete subclass of TimeZone that is used to express values for Gregorian calendars. It does not handle historical complexities, but instead projects current practices onto all times. For historical dates that precede the use of daylight saving time, for example, you will want to use a calendar with a time zone you have selected that ignores daylight saving time. For future dates, SimpleTimeZone is probably as good a guess as any.

19.4 Formatting and Parsing Dates and Times

Date and time formatting is a separate issue from calendars, although they are closely related. Formatting is localized in a different way. Not only are the names of days and months different in different locales that share the same calendar, but also the order in which things are expressed changes. In the United States it is customary in short dates to put the month before the date: July 5 becomes 7/5. In many European countries the date comes first, so 5 July becomes 5/7 or 5.7 or ...

In the previous sections the term "date" meant a number of milliseconds since the epoch, which could be interpreted as year, month, day-of-month, hours, minutes and second information. When dealing with the formatting classes a distinction is made between *dates,* which deal with year, month and day-of-month information, and *times,* which deal with hours, minutes and seconds.

Date and time formatting issues are text issues, so the classes for formatting are in the `java.text` package. The `Date2` program on page 510 is simple because it does not localize its output. If you want localization, you need a `DateFormat` object.

`DateFormat` provides several ways to format and parse dates and times. It is a subclass of the general `Format` class, discussed in Section 19.5.2 on page 522. There are three kinds of formatters, each returned by different static methods: date formatters from `getDateInstance`, time formatters from `getTimeInstance`, and date/time formatters from `getDateTimeInstance`. Each of these formatters understands four formatting styles: SHORT, MEDIUM, LONG, and FULL. And for each of them you can either use the default locale or specify one. For example, to get a medium date formatter in the default locale, you would use

```
Format fmt = DateFormat.getDateInstance(DateFormat.MEDIUM);
```

To get a date and time formatter, with dates in short form and times in full form in a Japanese locale, you would use

```
Locale japan = new Locale("jp", "JP");
Format fmt = DateFormat.getDateTimeInstance(
            DateFormat.SHORT, DateFormat.FULL, japan
        );
```

For all the various "get instance" methods, if both format and locale are specified the locale is the last parameter. The date/time methods require two format styles: the first for the date part and the second for the time. The simplest `getInstance` method takes no arguments and returns a date/time formatter for short formats in the default locale. The `getAvailableLocales` method returns an array of all `Locale` objects for which date and time formatting is configured.

The following list shows how each formatting style is expressed for the same date. The output is from a date/time formatter for U.S. locales using the same formatting mode for both dates and times:

```
FULL:    Friday, August 29, 1986 5:00:00 PM EDT
LONG:    August 29, 1986 5:00:00 PM EDT
MEDIUM:  Aug 29, 1986 5:00:00 PM
SHORT:   8/29/86 5:00 PM
```

Each `DateFormat` object has an associated calendar and time zone set by the "get instance" method that created it. They are returned by `getCalendar` and `getTimeZone`, respectively. You can set these values using `setCalendar` and `setTimeZone`. Each `DateFormat` object has a reference to a `NumberFormat` object for formatting numbers. You can use the methods `getNumberFormat` and `setNumberFormat`. (Number formatting is covered briefly in Section 19.5.2 on page 522.)

You format dates using one of several `format` methods based on the formatting parameters described earlier:

`public final String` **format(Date date)**
   Returns a formatted string for `date`.

`public abstract StringBuffer` **format(Date date, StringBuffer appendTo, FieldPosition pos)**
   Adds the formatted string for `date` to the end of `appendTo`.

`public abstract StringBuffer` **format(Object obj, StringBuffer appendTo, FieldPosition pos)**
   Adds the formatted string for `obj` to the end of `appendTo`. The object can be either a `Date` or a `Number` whose `longValue` will be treated as a time in milliseconds.

The `pos` argument is a `FieldPosition` object which tracks the starting and ending index for a specific field within the formatted output. A `FieldPosition` object is created by passing an integer code that represents the field that the object should track. These codes are static fields in `DateFormat`, such as `MINUTE_FIELD` or `MONTH_FIELD`. Suppose you construct a `FieldPosition` object `pos` using `MINUTE_FIELD` and then pass it as an argument to a `format` method. When `format` returns, the `getBeginIndex` and `getEndIndex` methods of `pos` will return the start and end indices of the characters representing minutes within the formatted string. A specific formatter could also use the `FieldPosition` object to align the represented field within the formatted string. To do that you would first invoke the `setBeginIndex` and `setEndIndex` methods of `pos`, passing the indices where you would like that field to start and end in the formatted string. Exactly how the formatter aligns the formatted text depends on the formatter implementation.

A `DateFormat` object can also be used to parse dates. Date parsing can be lenient or not, depending on your preference. Lenient date parsing is as forgiving as it can be, whereas strict parsing requires the format and information to be proper and complete. The default is to be lenient. You can use `setLenient` to set leniency to be `true` or `false`. You can test leniency using `isLenient`.

The parsing methods are:

`public Date` **`parse(String text)`** `throws ParseException`
> Tries to parse `text` into a date and/or time. If successful, a `Date` object is returned; otherwise, a `ParseException` is thrown.

`public abstract Date` **`parse(String text, ParsePosition pos)`**
> Tries to parse `text` into a date and/or time. If successful, a `Date` object is returned; otherwise, returns a `null` reference. When the method is called, `pos` is the position at which to start parsing; at the end it will either be positioned after the parsed text or will remain unchanged if an error occurred.

`public Object` **`parseObject(String text, ParsePosition pos)`**
> Returns the result of `parse(text, pos)`. This method is provided to fulfill the generic contract of `Format`.

The class `java.text.SimpleDateFormat` is a concrete implementation of `DateFormat` that is used in many locales. If you are writing a `DateFormat` class, it may be useful to extend `SimpleDateFormat`. `SimpleDateFormat` uses methods in the `DateFormatSymbols` class to get localized strings and symbols for date representation. When formatting or parsing dates, you should usually not create `SimpleDateFormat` objects; you should use one of the "get instance" methods to return an appropriate formatter.

`DateFormat` has protected fields `calendar` and `numberFormat` that give direct access to the values publicly manipulated via the set and get methods.

Exercise 19.2: Write a program that takes a string argument that is parsed into the date to print, and print that date in all possible styles. How lenient will the date parsing be?

19.5 Internationalization and Localization for Text

The package `java.text` provides several types for localizing text behavior, such as collation (comparing strings), and formatting and parsing text, numbers and dates. You have already learned about dates in detail so in this section we look at general formatting and parsing, and collation.

19.5.1 Collation

Comparing strings in a locale-sensitive fashion is called *collation*. The central class for collation is `Collator`, which provides a `compare` method that takes two strings and returns an `int` less than, equal to, or greater than zero as the first string is less than, equal to, or greater than the second.

As with most locale-sensitive classes, you get the best available `Collator` object for a locale using a `getInstance` method, either passing a specific `Locale` object, or specifying no locale and so using the default locale. For example, you get the best available collator to sort a set of Russian-language strings like this:

```
Locale russian = new Locale("ru", "");
Collator coll = Collator.getInstance(russian);
```

Then you can use `coll.compare` to determine the order of strings. A `Collator` object takes locality—not Unicode equivalence—into account when comparing. For example, in a French-speaking locale, the characters ç and c are considered equivalent for sorting purposes. A naïve sort that used `String.compare` would put all strings starting with ç after all those starting with c (indeed, it would put them after z), but in a French locale this would be wrong. They should be sorted based on the characters that follow the initial c or ç characters in the strings.

Determining collation factors for a string can be expensive. A `CollationKey` object examines a string once, so you can compare pre-computed keys instead of comparing strings using a `Collator`. The method `Collator.getCollationKey` returns a key for a string. For example, because `Collator` implements the interface `Comparator`, you could use a `Collator` to maintain a sorted set of strings:

```
class CollatorSorting {
    private TreeSet sortedStrings;

    CollatorSorting(Collator collator) {
        sortedStrings = new TreeSet(collator);
    }

    void add(String str) {
        sortedStrings.add(str);
    }

    Iterator strings() {
        return sortedStrings.iterator();
    }
}
```

Each time a new string is inserted in sortedStrings, the Collator is used as a Comparator, with its compare method invoked on various elements of the set until the TreeSet finds the proper place to insert the string. This results in several comparisons. You can make this quicker at the cost of space by creating a TreeMap that uses a CollationKey to map to the original string. CollationKey implements the interface Comparable with a compareTo method that can be much more efficient than using Collator.compare.

```
class CollationKeySorting {
    private TreeMap sortedStrings;
    private Collator collator;

    CollationKeySorting(Collator collator) {
        this.collator = collator;
        sortedStrings = new TreeMap(collator);
    }

    void add(String str) {
        sortedStrings.put(
            collator.getCollationKey(str), str);
    }

    Iterator strings() {
        return sortedStrings.values().iterator();
    }
}
```

19.5.2 Formatting and Parsing

The abstract Format class provides methods to format and parse objects according to a locale. Format declares an abstract format method that takes an object and returns a formatted String, throwing IllegalArgumentException if the object is not of a type known to the formatting object. Format also declares an abstract parse method that takes a String and returns an object initialized from the parsed data, throwing ParseFormatException if the string is not understood. Each of these methods is implemented as appropriate for the particular kind of formatting. The package java.text provides three Format subclasses:

- ◆ DateFormat was discussed in the previous section.
- ◆ MessageFormat helps you localize output when printing messages that contain values from your program. Because word order varies among lan-

guages, you cannot simply use a localized string concatenated with your program's values. For example, the English phrase "a fantastic menu" would in French have the word order "un menu fantastique." A message that took adjectives and nouns from lists and displayed them in such a phrase could use a `MessageFormat` object to localize the order.

◆ `NumberFormat` is an abstract class that defines a general way to format and parse various kinds of numbers for different locales. It has two subclasses: `ChoiceFormat` is used to choose among alternatives based on number (such as picking between a singular or plural variant of a word); `DecimalFormat` is used to format and parse decimal numbers.

`NumberFormat` in turn has three different kinds of "get instance" methods. Each method uses either a provided `Locale` object or the default locale.

◆ `getNumberInstance` returns a general number formatter/parser. This is the kind of object returned by the generic `getInstance` method.

◆ `getCurrencyInstance` returns a formatter/parser for currency values.

◆ `getPercentInstance` returns a formatter/parser for percentages.

Here is a method that prints a number using the format for different locales:

```
public void reformat(double num, String[] locales){
    for (int i = 0; i < locales.length; i++) {
        Locale pl = parseLocale(locales[i]);
        NumberFormat fmt = NumberFormat.getInstance(pl);
        System.out.print(fmt.format(num));
        System.out.println("\t" + pl.getDisplayName());
    }
}

public static Locale parseLocale(String desc) {
    StringTokenizer st = new StringTokenizer(desc, "_");
    String lang = "", ctry = "", var = "";
    try {
        lang = st.nextToken();
        ctry = st.nextToken();
        var = st.nextToken();
    } catch (java.util.NoSuchElementException e) {
        ; // fine, let the others default
```

```
        }
        return new Locale(lang, ctry, var);
    }
```

The first argument to reformat is the number to format; the following arguments specify locales. We use a StringTokenizer to break locale argument strings into constituent components. For example, cy_GB will be broken into the language cy (Welsh), the country GB (United Kingdom), and the empty variant "". We create a Locale object from each result, get a number formatter for that locale, and then print the formatted number and the locale. When run with the number 5372.97 and the locale arguments en_US, lv, it_CH, and lt, reformat prints:

```
5,372.97        English (United States)
5 372,97        Latvian (Lettish)
5'372.97        Italian (Switzerland)
5.372,97        Lithuanian
```

A similar method can be written that takes a locale and a number formatted in that locale, uses the parse method to get a Number object, and prints the resulting value formatted according to a list of other locales:

```
public void parseAndReformat(String locale, String number,
                             String[] locales)
    throws ParseException
{
    Locale loc = LocalNumber.parseLocale(locale);
    NumberFormat parser = NumberFormat.getInstance(loc);
    Number num = parser.parse(number);
    for (int i = 0; i < locales.length; i++) {
        Locale pl = LocalNumber.parseLocale(locales[i]);
        NumberFormat fmt = NumberFormat.getInstance(pl);
        System.out.println(fmt.format(num));
    }
}
```

When run with the original locale it_CH, the number string "5'372.97" and the locale arguments en_US, lv and lt, parseAndReformat prints:

```
5,372.97
5 372,97
5.372,97
```

19.5.3 Text Boundaries

Parsing requires finding boundaries in text. The class `BreakIterator` provides a locale-sensitive tool for locating such break points. It has four kinds of "get instance" methods that return specific types of `BreakIterator` objects:

- `getCharacterInstance` returns an iterator that shows valid breaks in a string for individual characters (not necessarily a `char`).

- `getWordInstance` returns an iterator that shows word breaks in a string.

- `getLineInstance` returns an iterator that shows where it is proper to break a line in a string, for purposes such as wrapping text.

- `getSentenceInstance` returns an iterator that shows where sentence breaks occur in a string.

The following code prints each break shown by a given `BreakIterator`:

```
static void showBreaks(BreakIterator breaks, String str) {
    breaks.setText(str);
    int start = breaks.first();
    int end = breaks.next();
    while (end != BreakIterator.DONE) {
        System.out.println(str.substring(start, end));
        start = end;
        end = breaks.next();
    }
    System.out.println(str.substring(start)); // the last
}
```

A `BreakIterator` is a different style of iterator to the usual `java.util.Iterator` objects that you have seen. It provides a range of methods for iterating forward and backwards within a string, looking for different break positions.

You should always use these boundary classes when breaking up text because the issues involved are subtle and widely varying. For example, the logical characters used in these classes are not necessarily equivalent to a single `char`—Unicode characters can be combined, so that more than one 16-bit Unicode value can together constitute a logical character. And word breaks are not necessarily spaces—some languages do not even use spaces.

Love thy neighbor as yourself, but choose your neighborhood.
—Louise Beal

CHAPTER 20

Standard Packages

*No unmet needs exist,
and current unmet needs that are being met will continue to be met.*
—Transportation Commission on Unmet Needs, California

THE Java 2 Platform Standard Edition comes with many standard packages. These packages, all subpackages of the root `java` package, define the main classes and interfaces for the platform. Throughout this book we have taught you about many of these classes, particularly those relating to the core language, and those most commonly used in general programs. The packages that we have covered are:

- `java.lang`—The main language classes, such as `Object`, `String`, `Thread`, `Class`, and so on. The subpackage `java.lang.reflect` provides a way to examine types in detail, and was covered in Chapter 11. The subpackage `java.lang.ref` defines the weak reference types that allow you to influence garbage collection, and was covered in Chapter 12.

- `java.io`—Input and output and some file system manipulation. This package was covered extensively in Chapter 15.

- `java.util`—Classes of general utility. Defines the collection classes both new and legacy that were covered in Chapter 16, and the localization classes covered in Chapter 19. Miscellaneous utilities were covered in Chapter 17.

- `java.security`—Defines the platform security architecture, which was briefly described in Chapter 18. It contains a number of other classes for encryption, authentication, digital signatures, and other useful security-related code.

- `java.text`—Internationalization and localization for formatting and parsing numbers and dates, sorting strings, and message lookup by key. These were touched on briefly in Chapter 19.

In addition, there are main packages we haven't covered at all:

- ◆ `java.awt`—The Abstract Window Toolkit abstraction layer for writing platform-independent graphical user interfaces.

- ◆ `java.applet`—The `Applet` class and related types for writing sub-programs that can be hosted inside other applications, such as HTML browsers.

- ◆ `java.beans`—The JavaBeans components for user-composable code.

- ◆ `java.math`—Mathematical manipulations. Currently this package has only two classes, which handle some kinds of arbitrary-precision arithmetic.

- ◆ `java.net`—Networking classes for sockets, URLs, and so on.

- ◆ `java.rmi`—Remote Method Invocation, which lets you invoke methods on objects running in other virtual machines, typically on other computers.

- ◆ `java.sql`—The JDBC package for using relational databases.

- ◆ `java.util.jar`—Classes for reading and writing JAR (Java ARchive) files. These archive files can be used to distribute packages of related classes and resources—as we mentioned in "Package Objects and Specifications" on page 337.

- ◆ `java.util.zip`—Classes for reading and writing ZIP files.

Further, there are packages that exist outside the `java` package of the platform, in what are known as the standard extensions, for example:

- ◆ `javax.accessibility`—A framework for developing GUIs that are more accessible to people with disabilities.

- ◆ `javax.naming`—Provides classes and subpackages for working with directory and naming services.

- ◆ `javax.sound`—Defines subpackages for creating and manipulating digitized sounds.

- ◆ `javax.swing`—With its various subpackages, provides the Swing package of GUI components.

And there are packages that provide interaction between the platform and other environments:

- ◆ `org.omg.CORBA`—With its various subpackages, contains the classes for interacting with Common Object Request Broker Architecture (CORBA), object request brokers (ORB's).

◆ `org.omg.CosNaming` — The Common Object Service's naming classes.

Other versions of the platform, such as the Java 2 Platform Enterprise Edition, contain even more packages.

This book cannot be large enough to contain full coverage of every one of these packages—some of them require complete books of their own. This chapter discusses each `java` package not otherwise covered in this book, giving an overview of the purpose and contents, as well as a number of the other packages we have listed. All these packages are covered in detail in your local documentation and the `java` packages are covered in *The Java Class Libraries*. Most of the `java` packages, including the AWT and applet packages, and some extensions, such as Swing, are taught in the different volumes of *The Java Tutorial*. These books and all others cited in this chapter are part of this official series of documentation from the source—the people who invented the Java programming language, its virtual machine, and its packages.

20.1 `java.awt`—The Abstract Window Toolkit

The Abstract Window Toolkit allows you to write graphical user interfaces (GUIs) that will run on every system in a reasonable way. The AWT displays GUI components (such as buttons, labels, and text fields) using (by default) the local platform's look and feel, showing Macintosh buttons on a Mac, Motif buttons on X platforms, Windows buttons on Windows systems, and so on.

For this to work, you may need to change how you think about laying out your GUI. You may be used to interactive tools that let you place the various GUI components on the screen exactly where you want them to be. Such *absolute placement* will not work for a portable interface because, for example, the size of a button is different on different systems. When your interface is used on a different system than the one on which you designed it, some buttons will overlap and others will have ugly gaps between them.

Although you can use absolute placement in AWT, it is not recommended. When you place a component into an AWT display frame, the frame's *layout manager* decides where to put it. Almost all the layout managers provided with the AWT use *relative placement:* components are placed and sized relative to other components. All the provided layout managers implement either the interface `LayoutManager` or its extended interface `LayoutManager2`. Layout managers range from the simple (`FlowLayoutManager` adds components to a line until they don't fit and then starts a new line) to the sophisticated (`GridBagLayoutManager` has a great deal of flexibility). You can also write your own layout manager.

Instead of thinking about where a check box should go on the screen, you should think about how it should be placed relative to other components. Then choose a layout manager for the frame in which the check box will be placed and add the components so that they have the expected relationships. If you do this right, your interface will look clean on all platforms.

AWT has a set of standard GUI components: labels, buttons, check boxes, choice lists, scroll bars, text fields, text regions, and so on. Several top-level containers, such as dialog boxes and windows, let you place other components inside them (preferably using a relative-placement layout manager).

When you need to draw your own graphics on the screen, the simplest mechanism is to subclass `Component` or `Container`, overriding the `paint` method to draw what you need using the `Graphics` object passed to `paint`. `Component` is the basis for many customized user-interface components when no standard component does what is needed. You would subclass `Container` if your drawn component contained other components.

The AWT is an event based system. When the user performs an action, such as moving a mouse, clicking a mouse button or typing a key, an event is generated that identifies the underlying component as the source of that event and which encapsulates the nature of that event. The event is then placed in a central *event queue*, and will be serviced by a single *event thread*. The event thread takes events from the queue one at a time and dispatches them to their source components. You can also generate events programmatically—for example, invoking `repaint` on a component, places an UPDATE event into the event queue—or can create event objects and insert them in the event queue directly.

Components are notified of events (mouse up, mouse down, mouse drag, keyboard events, and the like) by having methods invoked on them by the event thread. You can also register *listener* objects that are notified when an event occurs within a component. For example, a button that lets the user exit the program might be set up like this:

```
Button b = new Button("Exit");
b.addActionListener(
    new ActionListener() {
        public void actionPerformed(ActionEvent e) {
            System.exit(0);
        }
    }
);
gui.add(b);
```

Action events come from the basic action on the component, such as pressing a button or selecting a check box. The `ActionEvent` class has details of an action event, such as the keyboard modifiers (such as the Alt or Control key) that were being pressed when the action occurred. To receive this event you must register interest in action events, either by adding an `ActionListener` to the component as shown here or by invoking `enableEvents` with an appropriate mask.

The `ActionListener` interface in the previous example is a *listener interface*. Listener interfaces extend `java.util.EventListener` and exist for many kinds of events: mouse, keyboard, window, item, text, container, and general component events. You use objects that implement listener interfaces to trigger method execution when events occur—all of which get executed by the event thread. When an event occurs, the component's `processEvent` method is called, which in turn calls `processXXXEvent` for the specific event, and that in turn will call the *XXX*`Occurred` method of all registered listeners for that event.

Other classes in `java.awt` allow you to set colors, fonts, and so on. All these properties are inherited by default from outer components—the default colors of a button are those of the frame in which it has been placed. You can override this setting at any level by explicitly specifying a color for a component. That component and all its contained components will turn the specified color unless a sub-component has its color specified.

Various subpackages of `java.awt` allow you to manipulate images, sounds, and other media:

- ◆ `java.awt.color`—Color manipulation tools
- ◆ `java.awt.datatransfer`—Moving data between applications, for example, using cut, copy, and paste
- ◆ `java.awt.dnd`—drag-and-drop functionality
- ◆ `java.awt.event`—various event listener and adapter classes for connecting events to your code
- ◆ `java.awt.font`—font manipulation APIs
- ◆ `java.awt.geom`—2D geometry
- ◆ `java.awt.im`—input method interfaces for working with localized input devices
- ◆ `java.awt.image`—several interfaces and classes for reading and manipulating images
- ◆ `java.awt.print`—printing APIs

20.2 `java.applet`—Applets

Applets are a way to run code inside another application—commonly a Web browser. Applets are the first exposure many people have to the Java virtual machine and its uses. An applet is defined primarily by the protocol that governs its lifetime and the methods by which it can query and manipulate its runtime environment. The types in `java.applet`—primarily the `Applet` superclass itself—define this environment.

When an APPLET tag is found in a Web page's HTML, the browser downloads the code for the named class from a URL, creates an object of that class, creates a region on the Web page for that object to control, and then invokes the object's `init` method—often creating a `ThreadGroup` and `Thread` just for this applet. As the applet runs, it can download other classes from the server as needed. Applets are usually run in a tightly secured "sandbox" in which potentially dangerous operations (such as file access, network access, and running local programs) are restricted by the security policy.

The method `init` is one of four lifecycle methods defined for the applet in the `Applet` class. After `init` is called, `start` is called, which tells the applet that it is active and should perform its function. If the browser decides that the applet is no longer of interest to the user, for example the user leaves the page the applet was on, the applet's `stop` method is invoked to tell it to stop what it was doing. If the user returns to the applet's page the browser may invoke `start` again to tell the applet to recommence—so the applet can cycle through a stop-start sequence as the user presses the "Back" and "Forward" buttons (or their equivalents) to visit and leave the page. When the browser decides that the applet has been finished with (perhaps because the user has moved a number of pages away) the applet's `destroy` method is invoked to free up any resources used by the applet. If the applet's page is now revisited the lifecycle will recommence with `init` being called again. The browser ultimately defines the lifecycle of an applet and may choose to invoke `destroy` immediately after `stop` when the user leaves the page. Whether or not an applet class is unloaded and reloaded between visits to the applet is again a feature of the browser.

These lifecycle methods are typically overridden by applet classes. For example, if an applet uses a thread to do its work, `init` would typically create the thread; `start` would invoke the thread's `start` method the first time and ask it to continue execution on subsequent invocations; `stop` could ask the thread to pause to prevent it from consuming resources while the page is not visible; and `destroy` could interrupt the thread because the thread would no longer be needed.

An applet can get parameters from the APPLET tag to customize its behavior. It might get colors, fonts, or the URL of an image to display.

Applets usually run in a highly constrained security environment to protect your computer and network from unwelcome inspection or invasion by a hostile applet. This means that certain conveniences, such as a local scratch disk, may not be available by default. Permission to perform particular actions can be granted to individual applets by specifying an appropriate security policy.

The applet model is a good example of how the Java platform provides power. The fact that the same code runs on all systems in the same way allows a single piece of code (an applet) to run in a variety of browsers on a variety of windowing systems running on a larger variety of operating systems. The portability of Java bytecodes allows you to execute part of your application on the server and another part on the client system via downloaded code, whichever is appropriate. It is the same platform on both sides: the Java virtual machine. The ability to move code from one place to another and execute it in a secure environment enables new ways of thinking about where to execute what part of your design.

20.3 `java.beans`—Components

JavaBeans™ is a component architecture that helps independent vendors write classes that can be treated as components of larger systems assembled by users. The `java.beans` package provides necessary and useful classes for writing such *beans*. A bean exports properties, generates events, and implements methods. By following certain design patterns or by implementing methods that provide a description of these facets of behavior, you can compose beans using interactive tools to build a system the user needs.

Much of a bean's behavior is simplified if you follow expected design patterns. For example, if your bean class is called `Ernest` and you provide a class named `ErnestBeanInfo` that implements the `BeanInfo` interface, the JavaBeans tools will use it as a source of information about the behavior of the bean: the events it supports, the icons it uses, and so on.

Providing a `BeanInfo` object is itself optional—the JavaBeans system will use reflection to infer events and properties. For example, if a class `Ernest` has methods named `getImportance` and `setImportance`, the JavaBeans system will assume that you have an `importance` property that can be set, either directly or via another bean. Builder tools are expected to present the properties and events to users, who can use them to connect beans as components to build custom applications.

AWT components are beans, and the event model described earlier for AWT components is also the JavaBeans event model.

JavaBeans is designed to interoperate with existing component architectures, extending the "Write Once, Run Anywhere" capability to create a homogenous component platform.

The subpackage `java.beans.beancontext` defines interfaces and classes that are used to talk about the context in which a bean, or set of beans, is executing. Bean contexts can be nested.

20.4 `java.math`—Mathematics

The package `java.math` is destined for classes that help with mathematical calculations. Currently it has two classes: `BigInteger` and `BigDecimal`. The class `BigInteger` provides arbitrary-precision integer arithmetic, providing analogous operations for all integer operations except >>>, which is equivalent to >> because there is no sign bit to copy in an arbitrary-precision integer. Neither will the provided single-bit operations (`clearBit` and `setBit`) change the sign of the number on which they operate. Binary bitwise operations start by extending the sign of the smaller number and then executing the operation. `BigInteger` objects are immutable, so all operations on them produce new `BigInteger` objects. The following simple method returns an iterator over the prime factors of a number:

```java
static final BigInteger ONE = BigInteger.valueOf(1);
static final BigInteger TWO = BigInteger.valueOf(2);
static final BigInteger THREE = BigInteger.valueOf(3);

public static Iterator factors(BigInteger num) {
    ArrayList factors = new ArrayList();

    if (num.compareTo(ONE) <= 0) { // num<=ONE means skip it
        factors.add(num);
        return factors.iterator();
    }

    BigInteger div = TWO;                         // divisor
    BigInteger divsq = BigInteger.valueOf(4); // div squared

    while (num.compareTo(divsq) >= 0) {
        BigInteger[] res = num.divideAndRemainder(div);
        if (res[1].signum() == 0) { // if remainder is zero
            factors.add(div);
            num = res[0];
```

```
        } else {                    // try next divisor
            if (div == TWO)
                div = THREE;
            else
                div = div.add(TWO);
            divsq = div.multiply(div);
        }
    }
    if (!num.equals(ONE))    // leftover must be a factor
        factors.add(num);
    return factors.iterator();
}
```

The constants ONE, TWO, and THREE are used often, so we create objects for them once. If the number we are factoring is less than or equal to one, we treat it as its own factor (BigInteger and BigDecimal implement the Comparable interface described on page 427). After this validity test we perform the real work of the method: testing potential divisors. If a divisor divides into the number evenly, it is a prime factor, and we proceed with the result of the division to find more factors. We first try two, and then all odd numbers, until we reach a divisor whose square is larger than the current number. You could optimize this method in any number of ways, but it shows how to use some BigInteger functionality.

BigDecimal provides an arbitrary-precision signed decimal number consisting of an arbitrary-precision integer and an int scale that says how many decimal places are to the right of the decimal point.

Decimal division and changing a number's scale require rounding, which you specify on each operation. You can require that rounding be up, down, toward or away from zero, or toward the nearest value. You can also assert that no rounding will be necessary, in which case ArithmeticException will be thrown if you are found to be wrong.

20.5 java.net—The Network

The java.net package provides classes for working with network infrastructure, such as sockets, network addresses, and Universal Resource Locators (URLs).

The java.net package is centered around the Socket class, which represents a connection to another socket—possibly on another machine—across which bytes can flow. You typically create a socket with a host name or InetAddress and a port number. You can also specify a local InetAddress and port to which the socket will be bound. A ServerSocket class lets you listen on a port for incoming connection requests, creating a socket for each request. For example, the following program accepts input on a socket:

```java
import java.net.*;
import java.io.*;

public class acceptInput {
    public static final int PORT = 0xCAFE;

    public static void main(String[] args)
        throws IOException
    {
        ServerSocket server = new ServerSocket(PORT);
        byte[] bytes = new byte[1024];
        for (;;) {
            try {
                System.out.println("---------------------");
                Socket sock = server.accept();
                InputStream in = sock.getInputStream();
                int len;
                while ((len = in.read(bytes)) > 0)
                    System.out.write(bytes, 0, len);
                in.close();
            } catch (IOException e) {
                e.printStackTrace(System.err);
            }
        }
    }
}
```

This program creates a `ServerSocket` and repeatedly accepts connections to it. The `Socket` obtained for each connection is queried for an input stream and the data from that socket is read from the stream and written to the standard output stream, printing whatever bytes it receives. A client that shipped its standard input to the server might look like this:

```java
import java.net.*;
import java.io.*;

public class writeOutput {
    public static void main(String[] args)
        throws IOException
```

```
        {
            String host = args[0];
            Socket sock = new Socket(host, acceptInput.PORT);
            OutputStream out = sock.getOutputStream();
            int ch;
            while ((ch = System.in.read()) != -1)
                out.write(ch);
            out.close();
        }
    }
```

Once we have the actual `Socket` connection I/O is performed as with all other I/O using an appropriate input or output stream.

A URL object stores a URL, providing methods to examine and set its various parts (protocol, host, port number, and file). A URL object simply names a resource—you invoke `openConnection` to connect to the named resource. The `openConnection` method returns a `URLConnection` object that lets you get the header fields and content of the resource as input and output streams. The following program reads the contents of a URL:

```
import java.net.*;
import java.io.*;

public class readURL {
    public static void main(String[] args) {
        for (int i = 0; i < args.length; i++) {
            try {
                readURL(args[i]);
            } catch (Exception e) {
                System.err.println(args[i] + ":");
                e.printStackTrace();
            }
        }
    }

    private static void readURL(String name)
        throws MalformedURLException, IOException
    {
        URL url = new URL(name);
        URLConnection connect = url.openConnection();
        InputStream in = connect.getInputStream();
        byte[] bytes = new byte[1024];
```

```
        int len;        // number of bytes actually read
        while ((len = in.read(bytes)) >= 0)
            System.out.write(bytes, 0, len);
    }
}
```

The URLEncoder class lets you turn an ISO Latin-1 string (such as a user-typed query) into a form that can be included as part of a URL. ASCII letters and digits remain unchanged, the space character is converted to a +, and all other characters are represented by their lower eight bits in hex preceded by a %.

The File.toURL method creates a file URL for the path specified by that File object.

You can create DatagramSocket objects for sockets that send and receive DatagramPacket objects, which contain an array of bytes. Datagrams are a connectionless packet delivery service, in which each packet is individually addressed and routed and the receiver can get packets in any order. The MulticastSocket subclass of DatagramSocket lets you set up a socket that can send and receive packets to and from multiple addresses.

20.6 java.rmi—Remote Method Invocation

When you can download and run code on other systems, the face of distributed computing changes. The Java programming language's remote method invocation (RMI) gives you a way to create objects whose methods can be invoked from other virtual machines, including those running on completely different hosts. Because RMI is designed for communicating between Java virtual machines it can take advantage of the architecture's features and can operate in a natural fashion for programmers. RMI is contained in the package java.rmi and its subpackages, most notably the package java.rmi.server for RMI server implementations.

To use RMI you must first design one or more *remote interfaces*—interfaces whose methods can be invoked remotely. A remote interface extends the Remote interface, and its methods throw RemoteException in addition to any other exceptions. Here, for example, is a simple definition of a compute server interface that will accept Task objects for execution, returning the resulting Object:

```
import java.rmi.*;

public interface ComputeServer extends Remote {
    Object compute(Task task) throws RemoteException;
}
```

The `Task` interface is generic, allowing a `ComputeServer` to do any computation requested of it:

```
public interface Task extends java.io.Serializable {
    Object run();
}
```

`Task` itself is not a remote interface. Each `ComputeServer` object will run on a host and will be asked to execute tasks locally on its own host and return any results. (Traditionally, the application invoking a remote method is called the *client* of the invocation, and the application executing the method is called the *server,* although a client of one invocation may be the server of another.) `Task` extends `Serializable` because all local types passed to, or returned from, a remote method must be serializable.

Each method of a remote interface is required to throw `RemoteException` because any invocation of a remote method can have failures that must be signaled. Recovery from these failures is unlike recovery in local computation, where methods always arrive at their intended objects, and either results are always returned or you clearly know that they were not returned.

When you invoke a remote method, network failures create new uncertainties—if the network fails after the request is transmitted from the client, the client doesn't know whether the request was received. The failure may have happened before the invocation reached the server, or it may have happened after it reached the server but before results could be returned. There is no way for the client to know which of these two cases actually happened. If the request is to withdraw money from your bank account, you would not want to simply retransmit the request—it might get there twice. Remote interfaces must be designed to allow clients to recover from such *partial failures*. Methods may be *idempotent*—meaning the method can safely be re-invoked—or some other recovery method may be provided for the interface, such as transactions that can be aborted when non-idempotent methods fail. The users of a remote object must recover from such failures, and the declared `RemoteException` helps them do so.

Here is a simple implementation of the `ComputeServer` interface:

```
import java.rmi.*;
import java.rmi.server.*;

public class ComputeServerImpl
    extends UnicastRemoteObject
    implements ComputeServer
{
    public ComputeServerImpl() throws RemoteException { }
```

```
        public Object compute(Task task) {
            return task.run();
        }

        public static void main(String[] args)
            throws java.io.IOException
        {
            // use the default, restrictive security manager
            System.setSecurityManager(new RMISecurityManager());

            ComputeServer server = new ComputeServerImpl();
            Naming.rebind("ComputeServer", server);
            System.out.println("Ready to receive tasks");
        }
    }
```

This code is also straightforward. When an execute invocation arrives from a client, ComputeServerImpl implements the ComputeServer interface by taking the Task object it is given and invoking its run method, returning the resulting Object. Each incoming request typically gets its own thread, so this compute server implementation could have many concurrently executing tasks for different clients. ComputeServerImpl extends UnicastRemoteObject, which provides references for single-server remote method invocation. UnicastRemoteObject, like most types needed only by servers, is defined in java.rmi.server. The ComputeServerImpl constructor declares that it throws RemoteException because it can be thrown by the (implicitly invoked) UnicastRemoteObject constructor when registering the object with the RMI system.

Now comes the fun part. Clients can ask the server to perform any computation at all. Suppose, for example, that you want to compute π to some number of decimal places. You can have the compute server do this for you:

```
import java.math.BigDecimal;

public class Pi implements Task {
    private int decimals;

    /** Calculate Pi to a given number of decimal places */
    public Pi(int decimals) {
        this.decimals = decimals;
    }
```

```
    public Object run() {
        BigDecimal res = computePi();
        return res;
    }

    BigDecimal computePi() {
        // ...
    }
}
```

The Pi class implements the Task interface with a run method that returns a java.math.BigDecimal object containing the computed result. You then put the compiled Pi class someplace where it can be downloaded from a URL, just as an applet class would be. The URL from which to download the code will be set as a property for your client.

When you invoke the compute server's execute request, passing a Pi object, the server will need the Pi class. It will look at the URL that has been implicitly passed with the request, download the class, and run it in a secure sandbox. It will then invoke the Pi object's run method and return the result.

This ComputeServer example leverages the Java virtual machine's homogeneous computing model, in which all code means the same thing on all platforms, and its security model, in which downloaded code can be run in a secure manner.

Many environments can use the basic infrastructure just described. A compute farm that uses a large number of computers to render animation can use such a system to feed those computers images to be rendered, sound computations, and other tasks. This simple example needs some hardening to be used in other situations, especially when Task objects could not be trusted to be friendly. All you need is a Java virtual machine at both ends of the network.

UnicastRemoteObject references are for remote services that are started by the user or system. You can use java.rmi.activation.Activatable for references to remote objects that will be started automatically when they are first needed.

Because of the dangers inherent in running downloaded code, RMI requires that a security manager be installed. The RMISecurityManager class is a very conservative security manager that you can install to prevent any sensitive access to your system, or you can provide your own security manager.

Your server class may not be able to extend an RMI server class because your class must extend a different class. For example, an applet class must extend Applet and so cannot extend UnicastRemoteObject. You can create servers that do not extend `UnicastRemoteObject` by having your class's constructor invoke a static method:

```
public class SnazzyApplet extends Applet
    implements SnazzyRemote
{
    public SnazzyApplet() throws RemoteException {
        UnicastRemoteObject.exportObject(this);
    }
    // ... implement SnazzyRemote and Applet methods ...
}
```

Classes are downloaded from client to server (or server to client) only if they are needed. Classes will often be known on both sides. For example, `BigDecimal` is part of the core, so both the client and the server already know about it and it will not be downloaded. User-defined classes are treated in the same way—if both the client and server have a class installed, it will not be downloaded across the network.

Arguments and return values of remote methods are handled somewhat differently from those of local methods. RMI passes arguments and return values using object serialization (see page 404). When a remote reference is passed as an argument or return value, the receiver will get a reference to the same remote object that was passed. This is how local references act in local methods—an object reference refers to the same object in both the invoking code and the invoked method. Primitive types, too, are passed in the same way locally and remotely; the receiver gets a copy of the value.

References to local objects must be passed differently. Local objects are not designed to deal with partial failures, so it is not possible to pass across the network a remote reference to a local object. Local objects are instead passed by a deep copy made using serialization. Any remote references contained within the object or in any part of the graph of objects it denotes will be passed as described earlier. All other parts of the graph will be serialized on the sender's system and deserialized on the receiver's. Changes made on one side will not be visible to the other side, because each side has its own local copy of the object.

The RMI registry provides a simple naming system to store remote references for bootstrapping your clients. This is not a full naming system, but it will let you store objects that can be used to register or find top-level services. The registry is accessed via the `Naming` class.

Server objects are governed by a "best effort" distributed garbage collector. When no outstanding references to a remote object exist, that object can be collected. This is similar in principle to garbage collection for local objects, but the failures of distributed computing make surety impossible. If a client hasn't been in contact for a long time, it is presumed to have gone away without notifying the server (possibly the system crashed). If a long-lived network failure is actually at fault, the client may find that the server has been garbage-collected when the network reconnects. Every reasonable effort is made to preclude this possibility. A server can ensure that it will never be garbage-collected by simply holding on to a remote reference to itself, thus ensuring that at least one remote reference will keep it alive. This reference can be dropped when the server decides that it no longer must be forced to be alive.

RMI is explicitly designed to take advantage of having both client and server in the Java programming language. This gives it a form that is simple and direct for people who know the language. You can, of course, implement any server methods you like as `native` methods. Native methods can help you use RMI as a bridge to existing native code, such as in two- and three-tier systems.

The subpackage `java.rmi.activation` provides for activatable servers, which will be started when they receive messages if they are not already running. Multiple servers can be put in the same activation group, and will then be run in the same virtual machine.

20.7 `java.security`—Security Tools

The package `java.security` contains several useful tools for security-related functions. The package currently has tools for digital signatures, message digests, key management, certificates, cryptographic keys, and access control lists.

Because there are many ways to approach cryptography and there will be many more in the future, the security package is designed to provide abstractions of security interactions. Implementations of the abstractions are supplied by *providers*. Each platform has one or more providers. You can invoke methods to find out which providers are available. Providers can interoperate through the provided abstractions.

Subpackages define abstractions for access control lists to define who has access to what (`java.security.acl`), certificates (`java.security.cert`), RSA keys (`java.security.interfaces`), and key and algorithm parameter specifications (`java.security.spec`). Much more information on these packages, and on security in general in the virtual machine, is in *Inside Java 2 Platform Security: Architecture, API Design, and Implementation.*

20.8 `java.sql` — Relational Database Access

The package `java.sql` provides the Java Database Connectivity (JDBC) package for using relational databases. These classes and methods can be implemented directly by your database vendor or via the industry-standard Open Database Connectivity (ODBC) interface. JDBC is, in effect, a mapping of ODBC. The JDBC package and other issues about relational databases are covered in *JDBC Database Access with Java*.

20.9 Utility Subpackages

Some of the utility classes in `java.util` are not independent classes but groups of related classes that together provide a particular functionality. These classes are themselves grouped into subpackages within `java.util`.[1]

20.9.1 Archive Files—`java.util.jar`

The `java.util.jar` package provides classes for reading and writing the JAR (Java ARchive) file format, which is based on the standard ZIP file format with an optional manifest file. JAR files can be used to distribute the classes and resources of a `Package` as a single unit. The manifest stores information about the JAR file contents and provides the specification information for the `Package` contained therein—as we discussed on page 337.

Archive files define a format for storing multiple files within a single file, and allow for the compression of those original file contents. A full description of archive files and in particular the JAR format, is beyond the scope of this book. For illustration we briefly describe each of the classes within the `java.util.jar` package:

♦ `Attributes`—maps `Manifest` attribute names to their associated string values.

♦ `Attributes.Name`—represents an `Attribute` name. The main function of this class is to define static `Attribute.Name` objects for each attribute that a manifest may have. For example, `Attribute.Name.MANIFEST_VERSION`, is an object corresponding to the "manifest-version" attribute of a manifest.

♦ `JarEntry`—represents a JAR file entry.

---

[1] For pragmatic reasons the collections classes had to be defined at the top-level of `java.util`, rather than in a subpackage, because of the existing legacy collections.

- `JarFile`—represents an actual JAR file and allows that JAR file to be read or written.

- `JarInputStream`—reads a JAR file. Read operations exist that read each entry of the JAR file into a new `JarEntry` object.

- `JarOutputStream`—writes a JAR file. Write operations take a `JarEntry` that is written to the JAR file.

- `Manifest`—used to maintain the manifest entry names and their associated attributes.

A `JarFile` represents an actual JAR file and allows its contents to be read or written using the appropriate streams. A JAR file consists of a manifest and a number of JAR entries that can be read of written individually. The manifest contains all the attributes of the JAR file and all the attributes of the entries in the JAR file. The manifest is decoded using the `Manifest` and `Attribute` classes. Each `JarEntry` contains the per-entry attributes extracted from the manifest.

Most user's never need to use the classes within `java.util.jar`. JAR files can be created via tools supplied as part of your development environment, and are read automatically by the class loader within the virtual machine when needed.

20.9.2 ZIP Files—`java.util.zip`

The `java.util.zip` package provides classes for reading and writing standard ZIP and GZIP file formats. We mention it only for completeness as it predates, and forms the basis for, the newer JAR file format.

- `ZipFile`—represents a ZIP or GZIP format file.

- `ZipEntry`—represents an entry in a ZIP or GZIP format file.

- `ZipInputStream`—reads ZIP file format.

- `ZipOutputStream`—writes ZIP file format.

- `GZipInputStream`—reads GZIP file format.

- `GZipOutputStream`—writes GZIP file format.

- `Deflater`—provides general support for using ZLIB compression.

- `DeflaterOutputStream`—writes using ZLIB compression

- `Inflater`—provides general support for using ZLIB decompression.

- `InflaterInputStream`—reads ZLIB compressed data.

- `CheckedInputStream`—reads a stream, creating a checksum of the data.

- ◆ CheckedOutputStream—writes a stream, creating a checksum of the data.
- ◆ CRC32—computes a checksum using the CRC-32 algorithm.
- ◆ Adler32—computes a checksum using the Adler-32 algorithm.

20.10 javax.*—Standard Extensions

Standard extensions are packages or collections of packages that can be downloaded to extend the capabilities of a particular virtual machine. They will usually have names starting with javax, although in the future exceptions may be made. Conversely, packages with javax in the name may become part of the main set of packages over time. For example, the javax.swing and javax.accessibility packages are part of the main set. The name indicates that they were at first not part of the main set, but integrated later.

Standard extensions are a mechanism that allows growth in the capabilities of the platform without further extensions to the core packages required of all virtual machines. New standard extensions can be defined and made available, but only installed where they are needed. There are several standard extensions defined, and more are on the way. Listing them all is far outside the scope of this book—you can find more information on the Web, especially at http://java.sun.com.

20.11 javax.accessibility—Accessibility for GUIs

Graphical user interfaces traditionally assume certain kinds of abilities on the part of the user, such as the ability to use a mouse or keyboard. These assumptions are a problem for some people. The javax.accessiblity interfaces and classes provide a way to write interfaces that can use assistive technologies for input and output, allowing people with different abilities to use the same interfaces. If an application fully supports the accessibility API, then it should be compatible with, and friendly toward, assistive technologies such as screen readers and screen magnifiers.

20.12 javax.naming—Directory and Naming Services

This package defines the naming operations of the Java Naming and Directory Interface (JNDI), with the subpackage java.naming.directory, defining the directory operations. JNDI provides naming and directory functionality to applications written in the Java programming language. It is designed to be independent of any specific naming or directory service implementation. Thus a variety of services—new, emerging, and already deployed ones—can be accessed in a common way.

A context, represented by the `Context` interface, consists of a set of name-to-object bindings. `Context` is the core interface for looking up, binding, unbinding, and renaming objects, and for creating and destroying subcontexts. `lookup` is the most commonly used operation. You supply `lookup` the name of the object you want to look up, and it returns the object bound to that name. For example, the following code fragment looks up a printer and sends a document to the printer object to be printed:

```
Printer printer = (Printer)ctx.lookup("Duplex");
printer.print(report);
```

Every naming method in the `Context` interface has two overloads: one that accepts a `Name` argument and one that accepts a string name. `Name` is an interface that represents a generic name—an ordered sequence of zero of more components. For these methods, `Name` can be used to represent a composite name (`CompositeName`) so that you can name an object using a name which spans multiple namespaces.

The overloads that accept `Name` arguments are useful for applications that need to manipulate names: composing them, comparing components, and so on. The overloads that accept string names are likely to be more useful for simple applications, such as those that simply read in a name and look up the corresponding object.

The `Binding` class represents a name-to-object binding. It is a tuple containing the name of the bound object, the name of the object's class, and the object itself. The `Binding` class is actually a subclass of `NameClassPair`, which consists simply of the object's name and the object's class name. The `NameClassPair` is useful when you only want information about the object's class and do not want to pay the extra cost of getting the object.

Objects are stored in naming and directory services in different ways. If an object store supports storing objects created using the Java programming language it might store that object in its serialized form. However, some naming and directory services do not support the storing of such objects. Furthermore, for some objects in the directory, Java programs are but one group of applications that access them. In this case, a serialized object might not be the most appropriate representation. JNDI defines a reference, represented by the `Reference` class, which contains information on how to construct a copy of the object. JNDI will attempt to turn references looked up from the directory into the objects they represent, so that JNDI clients have the illusion that what is stored in the directory are objects defined by the Java programming language.

In JNDI, all naming and directory operations are performed relative to a context—there are no absolute roots. Therefore, JNDI defines an initial context class `InitialContext`, which provides a starting point for naming and directory operations. Once you have an initial context, you can use it to look up other contexts and objects.

The `DirContext` interface represents a directory context. It defines methods for examining and updating attributes associated with a directory object, or directory entry as it is sometimes called. You use `getAttributes` to retrieve the attributes associated with a directory object (for which you supply the name). Attributes are modified using `modifyAttributes`. You can add, replace, or remove attributes and/or attribute values using this operation.

`DirContext` also behaves as a naming context by extending the `Context` interface. This means that any directory object can also provide a naming context. For example, the directory object for a person might contain the attributes of that person, and at the same time provide a context for naming objects relative to that person such as his printers and home directory.

`DirContext` contains methods for performing content-based searching of the directory. In the simplest and most common form of usage, the application specifies a set of attributes—possibly with specific values—to match, and submits this attribute set, to the `search` method. There are other overloaded forms of `search` that support more sophisticated search filters.

The subpackage `java.naming.event` provides support for event notification related to directory and naming services. These events include adding or removing objects to or from the directory as well as events signifying changes in the stored objects themselves.

The subpackage `java.naming.spi` defines the Service Provider Interface (SPI) which allows for dynamically plugging in support for using JNDI.

20.13 `javax.sound`—Sound Manipulation

The `javax.sound` package consists only of subpackages. `javax.sound.midi` provides interfaces for reading, writing, sequencing and synthesizing data that conforms to the Musical Instrument Digital Interface (MIDI) format. `javax.sound.sampled` provides classes and interfaces for the capturing, processing and playback of digital (sampled) audio data. Each of these have a SPI subpackage to allow for dynamically adding sound services.

20.14 `javax.swing` — Swing GUI Components

The Swing components are a rich set of graphical user interface controls. They are written to look and behave for the user identically on all systems as far as possible. This is in contrast to the AWT components which rely upon the native GUI components. An AWT button will look like a Windows button on a Windows machine, a Macintosh button on a Macintosh computer, and so forth—its interaction with the program is the same on all platforms, but the user will see the native look and feel. A Swing component can have the same look on all platforms—its code is written in the Java programming language. The look and feel is "pluggable"—you or the user can use one of the standard look-and-feels or invent one. Swing components are also give you more control over the look and behavior of the system. You only occasionally need such control, but it is nice to have it when you do need it.

The Swing components use the same event model as AWT and JavaBeans components, although the components do define some new events.

Several subpackages define interface objects, how to define a pluggable look-and-feel, support for HTML and text editing, and handling some of the more complex components, such as tree displays and tables.

20.15 `org.omg.CORBA` — CORBA APIs

The package `org.omg.CORBA`, its various subpackages and other `org.omg` subpackages (such as `CosNaming`) provide the mapping of the OMG CORBA APIs and services to the Java programming language. (The package names are different from the standard core package names because they are defined by the Object Management Group and incorporated into the core package set.) CORBA is a way to send messages between processes that are not necessarily written in the same programming language. This is distinct from RMI, which communicates between programs written, at least in part, in the Java programming language (we use the phrase "at least in part" because RMI programs can include native code).

Programming today is a race
between software engineers striving to build bigger and better idiot-proof programs,
and the universe trying to produce bigger and better idiots.
So far the universe is winning.
—Rich Cook

Runtime Exceptions

The computer can't tell you the emotional story.
It can give you the exact mathematical design, but what's missing is the eyebrows.
—Frank Zappa

THE runtime system throws two primary kinds of exceptions: runtime exceptions, which are extensions of the RuntimeException class, and errors, which are extensions of the Error class. Both are unchecked exceptions, as defined in Chapter 8. Here is the top of the exception type hierarchy:

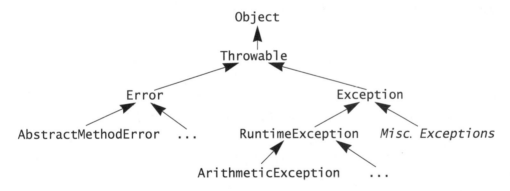

The Error exceptions indicate very serious problems that are usually unrecoverable and should never (well, hardly ever) be caught. Error exception classes are not extensions of RuntimeException, so people who write catch-all catch clauses for Exception or RuntimeException (often not a good idea anyway) won't catch Error exceptions. Of course, the finally clauses of try statements will always be executed as any exception—including Error exceptions—percolates up the call stack, so you can always clean up after any exception.

You can extend the RuntimeException and Error classes yourself to create your own unchecked exceptions—that is, exceptions that you can throw without declaring them in throws clauses. The only reason you should know this is so that you can be warned against doing it. The `throws` clause is there to make all the possible behaviors of a method clear to those who invoke it. By making exceptions extensions of `RuntimeException` or `Error`, you lie about the exception (that it is thrown by the runtime system). You also invalidate the assumptions of programmers using your method that they can understand the method's behavior by reading its `throws` clause.

Even if you are writing code only for yourself, you should not create unchecked exceptions, because programmers with only a partial understanding of your code would miss an important clue about how it works. And, after all, a few months after you write the code, *you* are one of the people who must maintain it with only a partial understanding. One way to keep your code clear is to pretend that the `RuntimeException` and `Error` classes can't be extended.

Most `RuntimeException` and `Error` classes support at least two constructors: a no-arg constructor and a constructor that accepts a descriptive `String` object. The descriptive string can be retrieved using `getMessage`, or in a localized form using `getLocalizedMessage`.

This appendix is in two parts—the `RuntimeException` classes and the `Error` classes. Each exception is named along with a description of when it is thrown, what it means, and any additional constructors it provides. If an exception is not part of `java.lang`, the package name follows the description in parentheses. Only exceptions in packages covered in this book are listed.

A.1   `RuntimeException` Classes

`ArithmeticException` extends `RuntimeException`
> An exceptional arithmetic condition arose, such as integer division by zero.

`ArrayIndexOutOfBoundsException` extends `IndexOutOfBoundsException`
> An array index was out of bounds. An additional constructor is provided that takes the errant index as a parameter and reports it in a descriptive message.

`ArrayStoreException` extends `RuntimeException`
> An attempt was made to store the wrong type of object in an array.

`ClassCastException` extends `RuntimeException`
> An invalid cast was attempted.

`ConcurrentModificationException` extends `RuntimeException`
> An object was modified concurrently in violation of contract (`java.util`).

EmptyStackException extends RuntimeException

A pop was attempted on an empty stack. This exception only has a no-arg constructor as the description is evident from the type of exception (java.util).

IllegalArgumentException extends RuntimeException

An invalid argument was passed to a method, such as passing a negative value to a method that requires positive arguments.

IllegalMonitorStateException extends RuntimeException

The wait, notifyAll or notify methods were invoked on an object for which the current thread does not hold the synchronization lock.

IllegalStateException extends RuntimeException

An object was not in the proper state for the requested operation. For example, attempting to add or remove a shutdown hook when the shutdown sequence has commenced.

IllegalThreadStateException extends IllegalArgumentException

A thread was not in the proper state for the requested operation. For example, start is invoked on a thread that has already been started.

IndexOutOfBoundsException extends RuntimeException

An array index or an index into a String object was out of bounds.

MissingResourceException extends RuntimeException

No matching resource bundle or resource was found. The only constructor for this exception takes three string arguments: a descriptive message, the name of the resource class, and the key for the missing resource. The class and key can be retrieved using getClassName and getKey, respectively (java.util).

NegativeArraySizeException extends RuntimeException

Someone tried to create an array with a negative size.

NoSuchElementException extends RuntimeException

An element lookup failed in one of the container class objects (java.util).

NullPointerException extends RuntimeException

A null reference was used to access a field or method. This exception also signals that a method received a null parameter when null was invalid for that method. In this usage it is like IllegalArgumentException.

NumberFormatException extends IllegalArgumentException

A string that was supposed to describe a number did not do so. This is thrown by such methods as Integer.parseInt.

SecurityException extends `RuntimeException`

An attempt to do something was vetoed by the security system, due to the currently enforced security policy.

StringIndexOutOfBoundsException extends
`IndexOutOfBoundsException`

An index into a `String` object was out of bounds. An additional constructor is provided that takes the errant index as a parameter and reports it in a descriptive message.

UndeclaredThrowableException extends `RuntimeException`

Thrown by a method invocation on a proxy instance if its invocation handler's `invoke` method throws a checked exception that is not assignable to any of the exception types declared in the throws clause of the method that was invoked on the proxy instance and dispatched to the invocation handler. This exception contains a reference to the undeclared checked exception that was thrown, which can be retrieved using the `getUndeclaredThrowable` methods. This exception supports two constructors: both take a reference to the undeclared throwable object; one also takes a descriptive string (`java.lang.reflect`).

UnsupportedOperationException extends `RuntimeException`

An operation was attempted on an object which did not support it, such as attempting to modify an object that was marked as "read only." This is used by the collection classes in `java.util` to signify that they don't support optional methods.

A.2   Error Classes

AbstractMethodError extends `IncompatibleClassChangeError`

An actual abstract method—one with no implementation—was invoked.

ClassCircularityError extends `LinkageError`

A circularity was detected when initializing a class.

ClassFormatError extends `LinkageError`

A class or interface that was being loaded was defined in an invalid format.

ExceptionInInitializerError extends `LinkageError`

An uncaught exception was thrown in an initializer. A third constructor takes the uncaught exception object as a parameter, storing it in this object. It can be accessed using `getException`.

IllegalAccessError extends `IncompatibleClassChangeError`
Access to a field or method was not permitted. Caused when the version of a class existing at runtime denies access to a member that was permitted when the original class was compiled.

IncompatibleClassChangeError extends `LinkageError`
When loading a class or interface, a change was detected that was incompatible with previous information about that class or interface. For example, a nonprivate method was deleted from a class between the time you compiled your code and the time your code was run and tried to use that class.

InstantiationError extends `IncompatibleClassChangeError`
Something tried to instantiate an abstract class or an interface.

InternalError extends `VirtualMachineError`
An internal runtime error occurred. This should "never happen."

LinkageError extends `Error`
`LinkageError` and its subclasses indicate that a class had some dependency on another class that could not then be satisfied.

NoClassDefFoundError extends `LinkageError`
A class could not be found when it was needed.

NoSuchFieldError extends `IncompatibleClassChangeError`
A particular field could not be found in a class or interface.

NoSuchMethodError extends `IncompatibleClassChangeError`
A particular method could not be found in a class or interface.

OutOfMemoryError extends `VirtualMachineError`
The virtual machine has no memory left to allocate.

StackOverflowError extends `VirtualMachineError`
An invocation stack overflow occurred. This may indicate infinite recursion.

ThreadDeath extends `Error`
A `ThreadDeath` object is thrown in the victim thread when `thread.stop` is called. If `ThreadDeath` is caught, it should be rethrown so that the thread will eventually die. An uncaught `ThreadDeath` is usually not reported. This error has only a no-arg constructor, but should never need to be instantiated.

UnknownError extends `VirtualMachineError`
An unknown but serious error occurred.

UnsatisfiedLinkError extends `LinkageError`
An unsatisfied linkage for a native method was encountered. This usually means that the library that implemented a native method was not found, or had undefined symbols that were not satisfied by any other loaded library.

UnsupportedClassVersionError extends `ClassFormatError`
A class being loaded has a version that is not supported by the virtual machine.

VerifyError extends `LinkageError`
When a class was being loaded it did not pass a verification test. Such tests are designed to ensure that loaded code does not violate safety features of the language.

VirtualMachineError extends `Error`
The virtual machine is broken or ran out of resources.

On the outskirts of every agony sits some observant fellow who points.
—Virginia Woolf

Useful Tables

All my life, as down an abyss without a bottom,
I have been pouring van-loads of information
into the vacancy of oblivion I call my mind.
—Logan Pearsall Smith

TABLE 1: **Keywords**

abstract	default	if	private	this
boolean	do	implements	protected	throw
break	double	import	public	throws
byte	else	instanceof	return	transient
case	extends	int	short	try
catch	final	interface	static	void
char	finally	long	strictfp	volatile
class	float	native	super	while
const[†]	for	new	switch	
continue	goto[†]	package	synchronized	

NOTE: Keywords marked with [†] are unused

TABLE 2: **Operator Precedence**

Operator Type	Operator
Postfix operators	`[] . (params) expr++ expr--`
Unary operators	`++expr --expr +expr -expr ~ !`
Creation or cast	`new (type)expr`
Multiplicative	`* / %`
Additive	`+ -`
Shift	`<< >> >>>`
Relational	`< > >= <= instanceof`
Equality	`== !=`
AND	`&`
Exclusive OR	`^`
Inclusive OR	`|`
Conditional AND	`&&`
Conditional OR	`||`
Conditional	`?:`
Assignment	`= += -= *= /= %= >>= <<= >>>= &= ^= |=`

TABLE 3: **Unicode Digits**

Unicode	Description
`\u0030-\u0039`	ISO Latin-1 (and ASCII) digits
`\u0660-\u0669`	Arabic–Indic digits
`\u06f0-\u06f9`	Extended Arabic–Indic digits
`\u0966-\u096f`	Devanagari digits
`\u09e6-\u09ef`	Bengali digits
`\u0a66-\u0a6f`	Gurmukhi digits
`\u0ae6-\u0aef`	Gujarati digits
`\u0b66-\u0b6f`	Oriya digits
`\u0be7-\u0bef`	Tamil digits (only nine—no zero digit)
`\u0c66-\u0c6f`	Telugu digits
`\u0ce6-\u0cef`	Kannada digits
`\u0d66-\u0d6f`	Malayalam digits
`\u0e50-\u0e59`	Thai digits
`\u0ed0-\u0ed9`	Lao digits
`\u0420-\u0f29`	Tibetan digits
`\uff10-\uff19`	Fullwidth digits

TABLE 4: **Unicode Letters and Digits**

Unicode	Description
\u0041-\u005A	ISO Latin-1 (and ASCII) uppercase Latin letters ('A'–'Z')
\u0061-\u007A	ISO Latin-1 (and ASCII) lowercase Latin letters ('a'–'z')
\u00C0-\u00D6	ISO Latin-1 supplementary letters
\u00D8-\u00F6	ISO Latin-1 supplementary letters
\u00F8-\u00FF	ISO Latin-1 supplementary letters
\u0100-\u1FFF	Latin extended-A, Latin extended-B, IPA extensions, spacing modifier letters, combining diacritical marks, basic Greek, Greek symbols and Coptic, Cyrillic, Armenian, Hebrew extended-A, Basic Hebrew, Hebrew extended-B, Basic Arabic, Arabic extended, Devanagari, Bengali, Gurmukhi, Gujarati, Oriya, Tamil, Telugu, Kannada, Malayalam, Thai, Lao, Tibetan, Basic Georgian, Georgian extended, Hangul Jamo, Latin extended additional, Greek extended
\u3040-\u9FFF	Hiragana, Katakana, Bopomofo, Hangul compatibility Jamo, CJK miscellaneous, enclosed CJK characters and months, CJK compatibility, Hangul, Hangul supplementary-A, Hangul supplementary-B, CJK unified ideographs
\uF900-\uFDFF	CJK compatibility ideographs, alphabetic presentation forms, Arabic presentation forms-A
\uFE70-\uFEFE	Arabic presentation forms-B
\uFF10-\uFF19	Fullwidth digits
\uFF21-\uFF3A	Fullwidth Latin uppercase
\uFF41-\uFF5A	Fullwidth Latin lowercase
\uFF66-\uFFDC	Halfwidth Katakana and Hangul

NOTE: A Unicode character is a letter or digit if it is in one of the above ranges and is also a defined Unicode character.

NOTE: A character is a letter if it is in Table 4, "Unicode Letters and Digits," and not in Table 3, "Unicode Digits."

Table 5: **Special Characters Using **

Sequence	Meaning
\n	Newline (\u000A)
\t	Tab (\u0009)
\b	Backspace (\u0008)
\r	Return (\u000D)
\f	Form feed (\u000C)
\\	Backslash itself (\u005C)
\'	Single quote (\u0027)
\"	Double quote (\u0022)
ddd	An octal char, with each *d* being an octal digit (0–7)
\u*xxxx*	A Unicode char, with each *x* being a hex digit (0–9, a–f, A–F)

Table 6: **Documentation Comment Tags**

Tag	Description
@see	Cross reference to another doc comment or URL
{@link}	In-line cross reference to another doc comment or URL
@param *p*	Description of the single parameter *p*
@return	Description of the return value of a method
@throws *E*	Description of the exception *E* that the method may throw
@exception *E*	Older form of @throws *E*
@deprecated	Marks a deprecated entity, with text directing user to a replacement, if any; the compiler will generate a warning if a deprecated entity is used
@author	An author of the code
@version	A version string for the entity
@since	The version string for when this entity first appeared
@serial	Identifies a field serialized using default serialization
@serialField	Documents fields created by GetField or PutField objects
@serialData	Documents additional data that is written during serialization
{@docroot}	Expands to a relative path to the root of the documentation tree; for use within links

TABLE 7: **Unicode Character Blocks**

BASIC_LATIN	NUMBER_FORMS
LATIN_1_SUPPLEMENT	ARROWS
LATIN_EXTENDED_A	MATHEMATICAL_OPERATORS
LATIN_EXTENDED_B	MISCELLANEOUS_TECHNICAL
IPA_EXTENSIONS	CONTROL_PICTURES
SPACING_MODIFIER_LETTERS	OPTICAL_CHARACTER_RECOGNITION
COMBINING_DIACRITICAL_MARKS	ENCLOSED_ALPHANUMERICS
GREEK	BOX_DRAWING
CYRILLIC	BLOCK_ELEMENTS
ARMENIAN	GEOMETRIC_SHAPES
HEBREW	MISCELLANEOUS_SYMBOLS
ARABIC	DINGBATS
DEVANAGARI	CJK_SYMBOLS_AND_PUNCTUATION
BENGALI	HIRAGANA
GURMUKHI	KATAKANA
GUJARATI	BOPOMOFO
ORIYA	HANGUL_COMPATIBILITY_JAMO
TAMIL	KANBUN
TELUGU	ENCLOSED_CJK_LETTERS_AND_MONTHS
KANNADA	CJK_COMPATIBILITY
MALAYALAM	CJK_UNIFIED_IDEOGRAPHS
THAI	HANGUL_SYLLABLES
LAO	SURROGATES_AREA
TIBETAN	PRIVATE_USE_AREA
GEORGIAN	CJK_COMPATIBILITY_IDEOGRAPHS
HANGUL_JAMO	ALPHABETIC_PRESENTATION_FORMS
LATIN_EXTENDED_ADDITIONAL	ARABIC_PRESENTATION_FORMS_A
GREEK_EXTENDED	COMBINING_HALF_MARKS
GENERAL_PUNCTUATION	CJK_COMPATIBILITY_FORMS
SUPERSCRIPTS_AND_SUBSCRIPTS	SMALL_FORM_VARIANTS
CURRENCY_SYMBOLS	ARABIC_PRESENTATION_FORMS_B
COMBINING_MARKS_FOR_SYMBOLS	HALFWIDTH_AND_FULLWIDTH_FORMS
LETTERLIKE_SYMBOLS	SPECIALS

TABLE 8: **Required Character Encodings**

Encoding Name	Description
US-ASCII	Seven-bit ASCII, also known as ISO646-US, and as the Basic Latin block of the Unicode character set
ISO-8859-1	ISO Latin Alphabet No. 1, also known as ISO-LATIN-1
UTF-8	Eight-bit Unicode Transformation Format
UTF-16BE	Sixteen-bit Unicode Transformation Format, big-endian byte order
UTF-16LE	Sixteen-bit Unicode Transformation Format, little-endian byte order
UTF-16	Sixteen-bit Unicode Transformation Format, byte order specified by a mandatory initial byte-order mark (either order accepted on input, big-endian used on output)

Comparing information and knowledge
is like asking whether the fatness of a pig
is more or less green than the designated hitter rule.
—David Guaspari

Further Reading

The best book on programming for the layman is Alice in Wonderland, *but that's because it's the best book on anything for the layman.*
—Alan J. Perlis

W<small>E</small> offer this list of works for further reading on related topics. The list is necessarily duosyncratic—other excellent works exist on many of these topics. Of course, all the books in this series are recommended for their respective topics.

J<small>AVA</small> P<small>LATFORM</small> T<small>OPICS</small>

- `http://java.sun.com/`, Sun Microsystems, Inc.
  Current information on the Java programming language and related topics, including releases, security issues, and online documentation.

- `http://java.sun.com/Series/`, Sun Microsystems, Inc.
  Current information about books in this series, including errata and updates. Of special interest will be those errata and updates for this book.

- *The Unicode Standard: Second Edition*, Version 2.0, Addison-Wesley, 1996, ISBN 0-201-48345-9.
  More data on Unicode, including data on Unicode 2.1, is available at `http://www.unicode.org`.

- *IEEE/ANSI Standard for Binary Floating-Point Arithmetic*. Institute of Electrical and Electronics Engineers, 1985, IEEE Std 754-1985.

- `http://www.unicode.org/unicode/onlinedat/languages.html`
  One site where you can find two-letter ISO 639 codes for languages.

- `http://www.unicode.org/unicode/onlinedat/countries.html`
  One site where you can find two-letter ISO 3166 codes for countries.

- "Uniprocessor Garbage Collection Techniques," by Paul R. Wilson, University of Texas, in revision for *ACM Computing Surveys*—also available from `http://www.cs.utexas.edu/users/oops/`

    A good survey of garbage collection techniques that may or may not be used by your particular virtual machine implementations.

- `http://www.w3.org/`

    Main site for the World Wide Web Consortium, where you can find documentation for HTML tags, which are usable in doc comments.

- `http://tycho.usno.navy.mil`

    U.S. Naval Observatory data on time paradigms used in the `Date` class. See `http://tycho.usno.navy.mil/systime.html`

OBJECT-ORIENTED DESIGN

- *An Introduction to Object-Oriented Programming*, by Timothy Budd. Addison-Wesley, 1991, ISBN 0-201-54709-0

    An introduction to object-oriented programming as well as a comparison of C++, Objective C, Smalltalk, and Object Pascal.

- *Pitfalls of Object-Oriented Development*, by Bruce F. Webster. M&T Books, 1995, ISBN 1-55851-397-3.

    A collection of traps to avoid in object technology. Alerts you to problems you're likely to encounter and presents some solutions for them.

- *Design Patterns,* by Erich Gamma, Richard Helm, Ralph Johnson, and John Vlissides. Addison-Wesley, 1995, ISBN 0-201-63361-2.

- *Object-Oriented Analysis and Design with Applications, Second Edition*, by Grady Booch. Benjamin/Cummings, 1994, ISBN 0-8053-5340-2.

- *Structured Programming*, by Ole-Johan Dahl, Edsger Wybe Dijkstra, and C. A. R. Hoare. Academic Press, 1972, ISBN 0-12-200550-3.

- *Object-Oriented Programming: An Evolutionary Approach, Second Edition*, by Brad J. Cox and Andrew Novobilski. Addison-Wesley, 1991, ISBN 0-201-54834-8.

MULTITHREADED PROGRAMMING

- *Concurrent Programming in Java: Design Principles and Patterns, Second Edition,* by Doug Lea. Addison-Wesley, 1999, ISBN 0-201-31009-0.

- *Programming with Threads*, by Steve Kleiman, Devang Shah, and Bart Smaalders. Prentice Hall, 1996, ISBN 0-13-172389-8.

- *Programming with POSIX Threads*, by David R. Butenhof. Addison-Wesley, 1997, ISBN 0-201-63392-2.

- *The Architecture of Concurrent Programs,* by Per Brinch Hansen. Prentice Hall, 1977, ISBN 0-13-044628-9.

- "Monitors: An Operating System Structuring Concept," by C. A. R. Hoare. *Communications of the ACM,* Volume 17, number 10, 1974, pp. 549–557. The seminal paper on using monitors to synchronize concurrent tasks.

RELATED LANGUAGES

- *The C Programming Language, Second Edition*, by Brian W. Kernighan and Dennis M. Ritchie. Prentice Hall, 1988, ISBN 0-13-110362-8 and ISBN 0-13-110370-9 (hardcover).

- *The C++ Programming Language, Third Edition,* by Bjarne Stroustrup. Addison-Wesley, 1997, ISBN 0-201-88954-4.

- *The Evolution of C++*, edited by Jim Waldo. A USENIX Association book from MIT Press, ISBN 0-262-73107-X. A history of C++ as told by many of the people who contributed.

- *Eiffel: The Language*, by Bertrand Meyer. Prentice Hall, 1992, ISBN 0-13-247925-7.

- "A Structural View of the Cedar Programming Environment," by Daniel Swinehart, Polle Zellweger, Richard Beach, and Robert Hagmann. *ACM Transactions on Programming Languages and Systems,* Volume 8, no. 4, Oct. 1986.

- *Mesa Language Manual,* version 5.0, by James G. Mitchell, William Maybury, and Richard Sweet. Xerox Palo Alto Research Center Report CSL-79-3, April 1979.

- *Systems Programming with Modula-3*, edited by Greg Nelson. Prentice Hall, 1991, ISBN-0-13-590464-1. Introduces Modula-3. Chapter 4 is an excellent discussion of thread programming. Chapter 8 is a fascinating case history of language design.

- *Programming in Oberon—Steps Beyond Pascal and Modula*, by Martin Reiser and Niklaus Wirth. Addison-Wesley, 1992, ISBN 0-201-56543-9.

- *Objective C: Object-Oriented Programming Techniques,* by Lewis J. Pinson and Richard S. Wiener. Addison-Wesley, 1991, ISBN 0-201-50828-1.

- "Self: The Power of Simplicity," by David Ungar and Randall B. Smith. Sun Microsystems Laboratories Technical Report SMLI-TR-94-30, 1994.

- *Data Processing—Programming Languages—SIMULA*. Swedish standard SS 636114, SIS, 1987, ISBN 91-7162-234-9.

- *Smalltalk-80: The Language,* by Adele Goldberg and Dave Robson. Addison-Wesley, 1989, ISBN 0-201-13688-0.

SOFTWARE ENGINEERING

- *The Decline and Fall of the American Programmer*, by Ed Yourdon. Yourdon Press, 1993, ISBN 0-13-203670-3.

  Analysis of the revolution taking place in programming. Several chapters discuss object-oriented design. Two chapters of particular interest are "The Lure of the Silver Bullet" and "Programming Methodologies."

- *The Mythical Man-Month, Anniversary Edition*, by Frederick P. Brooks, Jr. Addison-Wesley, 1995, ISBN 0-201-83595-9.

  Essays describing how software projects are really managed and how they should be managed. Especially read Chapter 16, "No Silver Bullet: Essence and Accidents of Software Engineering." You cannot design good classes without understanding how they will be used and changed over time.

- *Peopleware*, by Tom DeMarco and Timothy Lister. Dorset House, 1987, ISBN 0-932633-05-6.

VISUAL DESIGN & GUI DESIGN

- *Designing Visual Interfaces,* by Kevin Mullet and Darrel Sano. Prentice Hall, 1995, ISBN 0-13-303389-9.

  This book describes fundamental techniques that can be used to enhance the visual quality of graphical user interfaces.

- *About Face,* by Allen Cooper. Prentice Hall, 1995, ISBN 0-13-303389-9.

  Basics of good GUI design in a straightforward presentation.

- *Usability Engineering*, by Jakob Nielsen. Academic Press, 1993, ISBN 0-12-518405-0.

  A direct how-to guide on testing your interfaces to make sure they are usable by actual human beings.

◆ *The Visual Display of Quantitative Information,* by Edward R. Tufte. Graphics Press, 1983.

  You shouldn't communicate using graphical media without reading this.

◆ *The Non-Designer's Design Book,* by Robin Williams. Peachpit Press, 1994, ISBN 1-56609-159-4.

  How to use type, space, alignment, and other basic techniques to make your designs visually appealing and user-friendly. Applicable to paper documents, HTML documents, displaying data, and user interfaces.

◆ *The Design of Everyday Things,* by Donald A. Norman. Doubleday/Currency, 1988, ISBN 0-385-26774-6.

  Discusses usability design for everyday items (doors, typewriters, and so on) with lessons applicable to any design that humans are meant to use.

> *The cure for boredom is curiosity.*
> *There is no cure for curiosity.*
> —Dorothy Parker

Index

It's a d–mn poor mind that can only think of one way to spell a word!
—Andrew Jackson

A

Q

R

S

Then the bowsprit got mixed with the rudder sometimes...
—Lewis Carroll, *The Hunting of the Snark (an Agony in Eight Fits)*

Colophon

When confronted by a difficult problem,
you can solve it more easily be reducing it to the question:
"How would the Lone Ranger have handled this?"
—Brady's First Law of Problem Solving

THIS book is printed primarily in 11-point Times. Code text is in `Lucida Sans Typewriter` at 85% of the size of the surrounding text. A few decorations are in Zapf Dingbats.

The text was written in FrameMaker on several Sun Solaris systems, several Macintosh computers, including laptops, and several Intel systems running various versions of Windows, including, for a mercifully brief while, a 486i laptop computer running Windows 3.1.

The non-ISO Latin-1 text on pages 138, 140, and 406 were created on Macintosh computers using Adobe Illustrator to make PostScript drawings of the letters included as pictures in the text. The fonts used are Kourier for Cyrillic, ParsZiba for Persian, Palladam for Tamil, Sambhota for Tibetan, and Ryumin for Kanji.

Code examples were written and compiled on the Sparc systems and then broken into fragments by a Perl script looking for specially formatted comments. Source fragments and generated output were inserted in the book by another Perl script.

NOTE TO TRANSLATORS

The fonts in this book have been chosen carefully. The font for code, when mixed with body text, has the same "x" height and roughly the same weight and "color." `Code in text` looks even—if you read quickly it can seem like body text, but it is nonetheless easy to tell that `code` text *is* different. Please use the fonts that we have used (we would be happy to help you locate any that you do not have) or choose other code and body fonts that are balanced in the same way.

I love deadlines.
I like the whooshing sound they make as they fly by.
—Douglas Adams

Register
Your Book

at www.aw.com/cseng/register

You may be eligible to receive:

- Advance notice of forthcoming editions of the book
- Related book recommendations
- Chapter excerpts and supplements of forthcoming titles
- Information about special contests and promotions throughout the year
- Notices and reminders about author appearances, tradeshows, and online chats with special guests

Contact us

If you are interested in writing a book or reviewing manuscripts prior to publication, please write to us at:

Editorial Department
Addison-Wesley Professional
75 Arlington Street, Suite 300
Boston, MA 02116 USA
Email: AWPro@aw.com

Addison-Wesley

Visit us on the Web: http://www.aw.com/cseng

The Java™ Series

ISBN 0-201-70433-1

ISBN 0-201-70323-8

ISBN 0-201-70393-9

ISBN 0-201-48558-3

ISBN 0-201-43299-4

ISBN 0-201-43297-8

ISBN 0-201-31002-3

ISBN 0-201-31003-1

ISBN 0-201-48552-4

ISBN 0-201-70329-7

ISBN 0-201-31000-7

ISBN 0-201-31008-2

ISBN 0-201-63453-8

ISBN 0-201-63459-7

ISBN 0-201-63456-2

ISBN 0-201-70277-0

ISBN 0-201-31009-0

ISBN 0-201-70502-8

ISBN 0-201-32577-2

ISBN 0-201-43294-3

ISBN 0-201-70456-0

ISBN 0-201-71041-2

ISBN 0-201-43321-4

ISBN 0-201-43328-1

ISBN 0-201-70969-4

Please see our web site (http://www.awl.com/cseng/javaseries)
for more information on these titles.